Matthew Boulton: ORMOLU

Matthew Boulton:

ORMOLU

Nicholas Goodison

CHRISTIE'S

First published in Great Britain by
Phaidon Press Ltd in 1974
Amended extensively in 2002 and
published by
Christie's
8 King Street, St James's
London SW1Y 6QT

ISBN: 0-903432-70-6

This book was produced by
Checkmate at Art Books International
Unit 007, The Chandlery
50 Westminster Bridge Road
London SE1 7QY

Design: Ray Carpenter
Typesetting: Tom Knott
Project and editorial management:
Mandi Gomez for Checkmate at
Art Books International
Picture research: Nicholas Goodison
Index: Hilary Bird
Repro, printing and binding:
Singapore, under the supervision of
MRM Graphics.

A CIP catalogue record for this book is available from the British Library.
British Library Cataloguing-in-Publication Data.

Contents

Introduction

Josiah Wedgwood described Matthew Boulton in 1767 as 'the most complete manufacturer in England in metal'. This book is about the ormolu ornaments produced by Boulton and Fothergill at their Soho Manufactory, near Birmingham, between 1768 and 1782. In France these ornaments were called '*bronzes d'ameublement d'or moulu*', a term which included not only furniture mounts but also other objects made of gilt metal such as door and shutter knobs and escutcheons, candelabra, chimneypiece mounts, sconces, ink stands, clock cases and, above all, ornamental vases.

The French term '*or moulu*' means literally 'ground gold', that is to say gold reduced (but not literally ground, which is virtually impossible) to a powder so that it can be easily amalgamated with mercury for use in the gilding process. The contributor to Diderot's *Encyclopédie* defined it as '*l'or qui a été amalgamé avec du mercure, pour appliquer sur des pièces d'argent ou de cuivre que l'on veut dorer solidement*'. Matthew Boulton was aware of the correct meaning, as several of the contemporary documents quoted in this book show. He was probably aware of the definition in the *Encyclopédie*, parts of which he owned, and he would have come across the phrase *d'or moulu* when he was looking into the work of his French competitors. In England the word 'ormolu' has come to be used both as an adjective, meaning 'made of gilt brass (or bronze etc.)', and as a noun denoting brass, but also sometimes bronze or copper, which has been gilt by the process of fire gilding or mercurial gilding. Boulton seems to have been one of the first to use the word in these senses.

Very little has been written about ornamental ormolu in England in the eighteenth century or about the craftsmen who produced it. It has seldom been adequately discussed or explained, and ornaments have very seldom been confidently attributed to identifiable workshops. The omission has been largely due to the lack of evidence. Records of metalworking workshops and invoices for their work are rare.

Fortunately, and partly because Matthew Boulton took a keen interest in his firm's production of ormolu ornaments, a great number of relevant documents has survived among the records of his businesses. I describe these archives, now in the City Archives in the Central Library in Birmingham, in the introduction to the Bibliography (see pp. 477–8). They have formed the basis of my work, although I have relied to a certain extent on secondary sources in the first chapter. They are a prolific source of information: and one of my initial problems was to decide how to present the evidence in such a way as to cater for readers with differing interests. I hope the arrangement on which I have decided has solved this problem.

I have started in Chapter 1 with an account of Boulton and Fothergill's button and 'toy' manufacturing business at their Soho Manufactory in order to give an idea of the industrial and financial context in which they produced their ormolu ornaments. Soho was one of the largest manufactories of its day, one of the wonders of the age. Ornamental ormolu was only one of its many products and I have dwelt at some length on the range of wares produced there, the industrial methods of production, the firm's markets and the reasons for its financial failure. In the earlier part of the chapter I have given a brief account of the growth of the metalworking and 'toy' trades in Birmingham in order to place Soho itself in context. This is followed in Chapter 2 with a narrative account of the rise and decline of the ormolu business. I have discussed in this chapter the influences which inspired and helped Boulton in the early stages of his interest in ormolu, including the work of some of his predecessors and contemporaries: and I have tried to give an idea both of the extent of Boulton and Fothergill's production during the years 1768–82 and of the types of ornament that they were producing during these years. I have kept this account as short as possible by excluding from it most of the evidence concerning individual ornaments and by deferring detailed discussion of the firm's methods of design, manufacture and marketing.

These three facets of the business are the subjects of the next three chapters. Each was a natural choice for individual and detailed study because together they are the three processes necessary in the production of any object. Chapter 3 is about Boulton's methods of design and shows how, like many of the manufacturers of his day, he hoped to take advantage of the fashion for the antique taste, and of the attendant craze for vases; and how suitably eclectic his search for models was. I have studiously avoided using the term 'neo-classical' in the text of the book because Boulton himself was not aware of it. To Boulton the revival of classical forms in art and decoration was a revival of the 'antique taste'. The chapter about manufacturing (Chapter 4) shows how industrial methods were applied to the production of works of art and gives an account of the manufacturing processes, notably gilding and colouring, and of the sources of some of the materials. The chapter about marketing (Chapter 5) is perhaps of greater interest to students of economic history, showing how Boulton and Fothergill set about the marketing of what would today be called a 'luxury product'. The outlets through which they sold their more basic products, such as buttons, buckles and 'toys', were not suitable for expensive ornaments. The Survey of ornaments consists of a detailed account of the various ornaments produced at Soho. It is planned as a work of reference and not as a narrative and it inevitably repeats some of the evidence on which the earlier chapters are based. I have, however, avoided repetition of detailed aspects of design by referring the reader to Chapter 3 for the origins of the designs of several of the objects. The Appendices are self-explanatory.

The book reveals the extraordinary degree of Boulton's personal involvement in the ormolu business. He later became, through his promotion of James Watt's steam engine, one of the most notable figures in the so-called Industrial Revolution. It is chiefly for this achievement, and for his establishment of the Soho mint, that his name is famous. But he began his commercial life as a button manufacturer and he would not have succeeded as a promoter of steam engines, or a major producer of medals and coins, if he had not learnt several expensive lessons in his earlier business ventures. A study of the ormolu business can be criticised on the grounds that it was only a modest part of the business at the Soho Manufactory. But, with the possible exception of silverware, the ormolu trade is the most interesting part of the factory's output. It provides an opportunity of studying a business, which was curiously modern in many of its aspects, and, at the same time, works of art that were produced in a factory environment at the height of the 'neo-classical' period. To Boulton, it seemed in 1770, to borrow a phrase from a recent author, that elegance was good business. He did not then foresee the failure of his plans or his later involvement in steam engines or coins. He wanted to make money by applying advanced business techniques to the production of works of art and, incidentally, to rise in the world by exploiting a fashionable market. Elegance and business are the themes of this book.

Many people helped me in the preparation of the first edition, and many more in the writing of this revised edition. My initial research on the Boulton archives was much helped, when they were in the library of the Assay Office, Birmingham, by the Assay Master, A. H. Westwood, and by Michael Roberts who gave signal help during my work in Birmingham and illuminating advice on the interpretation of the gilding and colouring recipes which I have discussed in Chapter 4. Latterly Adam Green and his colleagues working on the Soho Archives Project in the Birmingham Central Library have been equally helpful, as have Rita McLean of the Birmingham Museum and Art Gallery and Val Loggie at Soho House, Matthew Boulton's home and now marvellously a museum illustrating his work and achievement. My old friends Geoffrey de Bellaigue, Geoffrey Beard, Timothy Clifford, Christopher Gilbert, John Hardy, James and Ana Johnston, and Hugh Roberts have helped in countless ways: and John Harris's work and advice on William Chambers have always been a great inspiration. Others who aided me with their help and advice at various times with relevant references, access to objects, photography, and by many other means include Andrew Barber, Sue Baumbach, Clare Baxter, Charmian Baynham, Elizabeth Bellord, Michael Brook, Christopher Brown, Lucy Campbell, Christopher Claxton Stevens, Nicholas Day, George Demidowicz, Melanie Doderer Winkler, Kjeld von Folsach, Jeremy Garfield-Davies, Philippa Glanville, Janet Green, Caroline de Guitaut, Natalia Guseva, George and Patricia Harewood, Eileen Harris, Alexander von Hessen, John and Michael Hill, Paula Hunt, Tania Illingworth, Simon Jervis, Brian and Robin Kern, Philip King, Martin Levy, James Lomax, Danuta Luniewicz-Koper, Lynda McLeod, John Mallet, George Mallinckrodt, Natalia Mavrodina, Leela Meinertas, John Milburn, Markus Miller, Nick Molyneux, Jennifer Montagu, John Murdoch, Tessa Murdoch, Peter Northover, Sam Oakley, Richard Pailthorpe, Dan Parkes, Lucy Peltz, Richard Perillo, Catherine Phillips, Kenneth Quickenden, Rosemary Ransome-Wallis, Bill Rieder, Eustace Robb, Gaye Blake Roberts and her colleagues at the Wedgwood Museum, Matthew Ridley, Duncan Robinson, Alan Rubin, Nick Savage, Gertrud Seidmann, Ann Smith, David Smith, Michael Snodin, Timothy Stevens, Dorothy Stroud, Terry Suthers, Charles Thomas, Simon Thurley, Keith Verrall, Clare Vincent, Claudia Wagner, Helen Walsh, Joanna Whalley, Keith Whiteman, Jane Willoughby de Eresby, John Wingfield Digby, James Yorke, and Yuna Zek. I am indebted to them all, as I am to the many librarians, archivists and museum curators both in this country and overseas who have helped me both in person and by correspondence.

I owe a special debt to Charles Cator of Christie's for his keen interest in persuading his colleagues to publish the book, and I am grateful to all those at Christie's, to Ray Carpenter, the designer, Mandi Gomez, the editor, Tom Knott, Judith Gray and Hilary Bird, for the efficient way in which the book has been produced. Special thanks are also due to the Paul Mellon Centre for Studies in British Art for their grant towards the high cost of new photography, and to the Director Brian Allen for his encouragement. Finally I am indebted to the owners, private and corporate, of many of the ornaments illustrated, and to the owners of the many documents that I have consulted. I have not acknowledged their help or their permission individually in the notes, but do so here with gratitude.

N.P.G. 2002

Note on the illustrations

I have kept the captions brief because the illustrations are covered in detail in the text. In the Survey of ornaments all the objects illustrated are by Boulton and Fothergill and all the sketches accompanying them are from the firm's Pattern Books. I have, therefore, not repeated their names in the captions from plate 122 onwards, unless the attribution is uncertain. The reproductions of the Pattern Book sketches are not to scale.

The majority of the photographs were taken specially for this book. Most of the colour photographs of ornaments are the work of Philip Brakefield of Christie's, for whose care and imagination I am extremely grateful. It was great fun working with him. The remaining photographs illustrate ornaments which are not readily accessible or for which adequate photographs already existed. I am very grateful to all those owners who have allowed me to commission photographs of their possessions.

Plates 5, 36, 70, 160–1, 231, 246, 260, 331, 339–40 and 355–7 are reproduced by gracious permission of Her Majesty The Queen (The Royal Collection © 2001, Her Majesty Queen Elizabeth II).

Plates 13–14, 50, 135, 138 and 241–2 are reproduced by kind permission of His Grace the Duke of Marlborough; Plates 11, 12, 62, 229–30 and 258 by kind permission of His Grace the Duke of Northumberland; and Plate 269 by kind permission of the Earl and Countess of Harewood. The many reproductions of drawings in Boulton and Fothergill's pattern books and of other Boulton archives are reproduced by permission of the Central Reference Library, Birmingham.

I am grateful to the following for their permission to reproduce photographs and, in certain cases, for supplying me with transparencies or prints:

ADC Heritage – Plate 16; Norman Adams – Plates 288–9, 334; Ashmolean Museum, Oxford – Plate 224; Assay Office, Birmingham – Plates 90–3, 95; Beazley Archive, Ashmolean Museum, Oxford – Plates 69, 74, 78; City of Birmingham Museum and Art Gallery – Plates 2–4, 118–21, 130–1, 173, 176–82, 186–7, 196–7, 208–9, 253, 281, 362; H. Blairman and Sons – Plates 73, 220–1; Trustees of the British Museum – Plates 54–5, 59; Christie's – Plates 18, 64, 140, 144, 152, 166–8, 185, 199, 247–8, 251, 261–2, 265–6, 268, 270, 273, 277, 300, 305, 317–18, 329, 336, 347, 358, 363, 364, 372; A. Cook – Plate 298; Courtauld Institute Gallery – Plates 8–10, 162–4; The David Collection, Copenhagen – Plate 243; Svend Eriksen – Plate 19; Syndics of the Fitzwilliam Museum, Cambridge – Plate 6; Rupert Gentle – Plate 184; Hessische Hausstiftung, Schloss Fasanerie – Plates 153–4; Hotspur Ltd – Plates 46, 57, 129, 256, 291, 319–20, 323, 373; Jeremy Ltd – Plates 141, 293, 295; Leeds City Art Gallery, Temple Newsam – Plates 94, 175, 240, 263–4, 304; Mallett – Plates 169–72, 189–91, 216–17, 285–6; National Trust – Plates 7, 15, 25, 26–7, 68, 109, 115, 193–4, 337–8, 342–5, 365–9; Partridge Fine Arts – Plate 259; Sherborne Castle Estates – Plates 113, 238–9, 296; Trustees of Sir John Soane's Museum – Plates 23–4, 201–2; Society of Antiquaries – Plates 56, 58, 60–1, 63, 65, 83, 84; Sotheby's – Plate 47; State Hermitage Museum, St Petersburg – Plates 349–50; M. Turpin – Plate 280; University of Edinburgh – Plates 86–8: Vatican Museum – Plate 67; Victoria and Albert Museum – Plates 22, 28–9, 32–5, 37–44, 49, 51, 53–5, 66, 89, 107, 200, 203–7, 212–13, 351–4; Royal Castle, Warsaw – Plate 17; Trustees of the Wedgwood Museum, Barlaston, Staffordshire – Plates 45, 75, 79, 82, 85, 222; Weston Park Foundation – Plates 77, 110, 301; Michael Winner – Plates 71, 327.

CHAPTER 1

Birmingham and Soho

The partnership between Matthew Boulton (Plate 1) and John Fothergill began in 1762. The firm produced nearly all the ormolu ornaments described in this book at their manufactory at Soho, near Birmingham, between the years 1768 and 1780, and a high proportion of them between 1770 and 1772. During their twenty years of partnership Boulton and Fothergill won the reputation of being the largest producers of decorative metalware, including ormolu ornaments, of their day. Their manufactory (Plates 2 and 3) was one of the wonders of the age. They were widely patronised by the aristocracies of both England and Europe. A portrait of Boulton, dressed for the part, painted by J. S. C. Schaak in 1770, survives at Soho House, Birmingham.[1]

Much of the historical narrative in this and the following four chapters will be concerned with the means by which Matthew Boulton himself consciously caused this blossoming of his firm's reputation for ormolu ornaments. It could be argued that it flourished solely because he seized the opportunity created by the craze for the 'antique taste'. But this would be facile. He would not have succeeded in exploiting the craze unless he had been able to command the necessary sources of design and the appropriate manufacturing techniques. Nor would his ambitious plans have had much hope of success unless he had organised effective means of marketing his products.

1. Tilly Kettle, Matthew Boulton, *c.*1762–4, Private Collection.

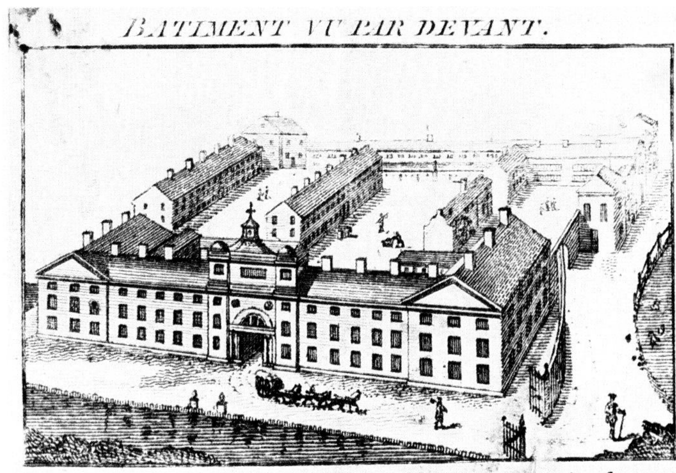

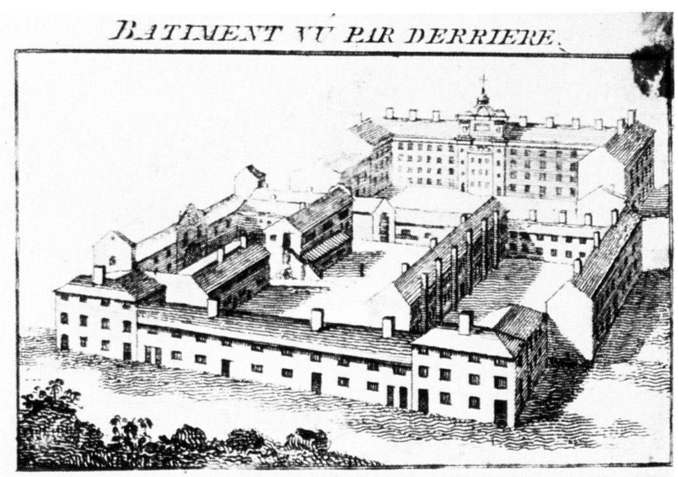

2–3. Boulton and Fothergill's manufactory, Soho, *c.*1769.

In order to show how and to what extent Boulton was in a position to exploit the craze it is necessary to give a brief account of the firm of Boulton and Fothergill and to place it in the context of Birmingham in the eighteenth century. I hope by this means to explain why, at a time when most of the artists and craftsmen concerned with the decorative arts worked in London, Boulton was able to build such a reputation for objects of fashion in a provincial town and to export a large part, probably the greater part, of his production. I hope also to show how ormolu ornaments, although they could not be mass produced in quite the same way as buttons and buckles and were financially a failure, fitted naturally into the range of Boulton and Fothergill's products.

Birmingham

In the middle of the seventeenth century Birmingham was little more than a village. William Hutton, whose history of Birmingham was first published in 1781 and went through many later editions, stated that in 1650 the population was 5,472. By 1741 it had expanded to 24,660 and by 1781 to 50,295.[2] This sharp increase coincided with, and was caused by, the growth of the metalworking trades. By 1750 Birmingham was the largest centre in England for the production of fashioned steel, iron, brass and copper goods. Its buttons, buckles and 'toys', a word which was used for a great variety of objects, were sold throughout England and exported to most of the countries on the continent and further afield. Edmund Burke called the town the 'toy-shop of Europe'.[3]

Most historians agree that there were two basic reasons for the flowering of the town's metalworking trades between 1650 and 1750. Its location was not one of them. Birmingham was inconveniently situated and anyone planning a major metalworking centre from scratch in the eighteenth century would not have chosen to establish it there. Raw materials had to be transported to it over some distance from the iron and coalfields of Staffordshire and the copper and brass mills at Cheadle and Bristol. It was not on the main road from London to the north of England, which passed through Coventry, nor could it be reached by water until the first canals were constructed. It did not have more than a few local streams to provide the power needed for the factories' mills.

Nevertheless there were many smiths in the village in the sixteenth century, a historical accident that owed its origins perhaps to the proximity of an ample supply of wood. In 1538 John Leland wrote that he –

> came through a pretty street[4] or ever I entered Bermingham towne ... In it dwell smithes and cutlers ... There be many smithes in the towne that use to make knives and all mannour of cutting tooles, and many lorimers that make bittes, and a great many naylors, soe that a great part of the towne is maintained by smithes who have theire iron and seacole out of Staffordshire.[5]

In 1586 William Camden found Birmingham 'echoing with the noise of the anvils, for here are great numbers of smiths, and of other artificers in iron and steel, whose performances in that way are greatly admired both at home and abroad'.[6]

This iron working tradition was fundamental to Birmingham's later rise to pre-eminence. When brass was introduced in the second half of the seventeenth century, it was simple for the metalworkers of Birmingham to adapt themselves to it because it did not require working skills which were radically different from those used in the working of iron.[7]

But Birmingham's metalworking tradition is not enough to account alone for the expansion of the town's trade. Historians from William Hutton onwards have attributed Birmingham's success to the liveliness and inventiveness of its inhabitants. Hutton compared the elegance of the buildings in Birmingham in 1741 with the wretched dwellings of other towns and commented that he 'was surprised at the place, but more so at the people ... they possessed a vivacity I had never beheld ... their very step along the street shewed alacrity'.[8] Maybe his pride in the town's achievements prejudiced him in favour of his subject, but there seems to be general consent that the men of Birmingham in the eighteenth century were unusually able, energetic and industrious.

There was a reason for this. Birmingham attracted artisans and entrepreneurs from elsewhere in the seventeenth and eighteenth centuries because it placed few restrictions on trade and eschewed religious persecution. It was a small but growing town which had neither charter nor craft guilds, and where the apprenticeship system was only partially practised. And, perhaps because of its keen support of the Parliamentarian cause in the civil war, it particularly welcomed the dissenters who came to the town after the Restoration. Men who had rejected the Church following the Act of Uniformity in 1662 and who felt intolerably restricted by the Five Mile Act in 1665[9] naturally fled to towns like Birmingham which, because they had no corporate status and sent no one to Parliament, were largely unaffected by the new laws: and their followers came too. Birmingham became known as a place where people could settle without interference[10] and take advantage of the absence of craft restrictions.[11]

Thus men were encouraged to set up their workshops and businesses: and, perhaps because non-conformists who had altered the pattern of their lives tended to be strong-minded men, Birmingham became a lively and inventive business community. The successful merchants and manufacturers of the eighteenth century were typically liberal in their social views, courageous and outward looking in their ventures and, above all, inquisitive. They had an eager interest in science and technology and in the practical application of new ideas. Some were born and bred in the town but many others were attracted to it by the ferment of activity and the hope of success. The resultant concentration of talent could be proved, if the historians did not already agree, by the extraordinary number of patents that were granted to Birmingham men during the eighteenth century.[12] Most of these inventions were concerned with methods of working metals, such as casting, rolling and stamping, or with metal products such as buttons, buckles, silver plate, nails, guns, or simply with alloys; but others, for example patents concerned with japanning and papier mâché, demonstrate the variety of trades carried on in the town. At Birmingham, as Hutton said, invention was 'ever at work'.[13]

The introduction of brass in the second half of the seventeenth century greatly extended the scope of the Birmingham metalworking trades. It coincided approximately with the Restoration, which created a demand for what today would be called fashion goods: and the demand was all the greater for having been suppressed during the Protectorate. There was a boom in novelties and trinkets, in jewellery, in buttons and buckles, and all sorts of filigree work. The metalworkers of Birmingham were peculiarly suited to make what was wanted. They were already expert in such techniques as cutting steel for sword hilts and jewellery. The fashioning of brass trinkets and toys added a new dimension to their existing trades. The rapid growth of the town's production of hardware dates from the introduction of brass. It was helped on its way by legislation in 1662 that banned the importation of foreign buttons, and by the prohibition in 1688 of trade with France, which was the chief producer of luxury goods in the seventeenth century. Thus while many workshops continued to produce heavy iron products, and especially guns for the French wars, the makers of the lighter metal goods fashioned from brass, copper, steel and precious metals prospered from a fast growing and protected market. They were enabled, moreover, by their manufacturing skills and low production costs to surmount the difficulties caused by the town's distance both from its raw materials and from its main markets, which was not so easy for the makers of heavy iron castings. The town quickly became the chief customer of the leading brass manufactories in the country, which were established at Bristol and Cheadle in 1702 and 1719 respectively and which largely replaced the previous imports from Sweden and the continent.

Brass was converted by the workshops of Birmingham into a vast assortment of light goods. Probably the most important in quantity were the products of the brassfounders. In 1770 thirty-three brassfounders were listed in Sketchley and Adams's directory for Birmingham and Wolverhampton and their products were described as 'sconces, cabinet handles, escutcheons, hinges, cloak pins etc., etc. ...'.[14] This list omits many products, such as castors, door handles, curtain rings, tapestry hooks, fireplace fittings, cooking utensils and candlesticks, which were clearly produced in great quantities, some by the brassfounders and others by more specialised workshops.[15] There were for example four brass candlestick makers listed in Sketchley and Adams's directory, two of whom are also listed among the brassfounders. There were also two cabinet brassfounders in Wolverhampton, five cockfounders in Birmingham, and numerous makers of brass nails, compasses, corkscrews, frying pans, harness fittings, hinges, locks, surgical instruments, thimbles, and other objects.

The makers of buttons, buckles, jewellery and 'toys' also used a lot of brass: but they used a wide variety of other materials as well. Buckles were made not only for belts and straps but also for shoes, for which fashion demanded a changing variety.[16] 'An infinite variety' of buckles was made, according to Sketchley and Adams, 'both in white, yellow, Bath metal, pinchbeck,[17] silver, tuetinage,[18] and soft white, also of copper and steel.'[19] There were forty-four buckle makers in the town. The list of button makers included eighty-three names:

> This branch is very extensive, and is distinguished under the following heads, viz. gilt, plated, silvered, lacquered, and pinchbeck, the beautiful new platina, inlaid, glass, horn, ivory, and pearl: metal buttons, such as Bath, hard and soft white, etc. There is likewise made link buttons in most of the above metals, as well as of paste, stones, etc. In short the vast variety of sorts in both branches is really amazing, and we may with truth aver that this is the cheapest market in the world for these articles.[20]

The directory lists forty-eight toy makers:

> An infinite variety of articles that come under this denomination are made here, and it would be endless to attempt to give an account of the whole ... these artists are divided into several branches, as the gold and silver toy makers, who make trinkets, seals, tweezers, toothpick cases, smelling bottles, snuff boxes and philligree work, such as toilets, tea chests, inkstands etc. etc. The tortoise toy maker makes a beautiful variety of the above and other articles: as does also the steel, who make cork screws, buckles, draw and other boxes, snuffers, watch-chains, stay hooks, sugar nippers etc., and almost all these are likewise made in various metals ...[21]

It is almost impossible, as the author of this section of the directory admits, to define the products of the Birmingham toy maker in the eighteenth century. There was scarcely a metal trinket or small article of daily utility which was neglected. Brooches, bracelets and rings, watch chains and châtelaines, snuff boxes and spectacle frames, sword hilts and mounts for guns and pistols, were made after all sorts of designs and sold in prodigious quantities all over England and the continent.

The brassfounders and the button makers and toy makers could not have produced this variety or this quantity of wares without using machinery or practising some division of labour. This does not imply any great advance in technical competence. The metalworking workshops of Birmingham were not, perhaps surprisingly, in the forefront of the Industrial Revolution. Stamping and pressing, made possible by the introduction of brass alloys, were important advances for the manufacture of a wide variety of buttons, buckles, toys and hardware. But for these processes the workshops relied heavily on hand operated methods and refinements to them.[22] Water power did however enable manufacturers to install simple machinery for the more or less continuous functions such as rolling, lathe turning and polishing. The efficient use of hand technology and water power, and the productive division of labour, helped to put Birmingham manufacturers ahead of their competitors and to contribute to the town's unusual growth in the eighteenth century.[23]

In the larger workshops the division of labour was carried to logical extremes. It was such an obvious economy to set a craftsman onto one task in the process of production rather than employ him to fashion the entire object that it is odd to find that the division of labour seems to have been a source of wonder, almost surprise, to contemporary writers. Hutton commented on it during his account of the brassfoundry trade as if it were a remarkable feature of the Birmingham workshops,[24] and Lord Shelburne thought it sufficiently unusual to be worthy of comment when he wrote an account of the hardware and button trades for his wife in 1766.[25]

The skills of its craftsmen and the energy of its entrepreneurs took Birmingham into export markets at an early date. There is evidence that the hardware and gun manufacturers increased their foreign sales dramatically when the African trade was opened to all in 1698. Within little more than a decade English brassware had achieved a wide reputation on the European continent. This was especially true in France, where English watches, clocks, locks, buckles, buttons and all sorts of brass toys were popular.[26] According to Daniel Defoe, large quantities of English brassware were sent 'into Holland, France, Italy, Venice and to all parts of Germany, Poland and Muscovy'.[27] Toys were sent to the Court of France, and Birmingham was one of the chief sources. Many of these export sales were generated by foreign merchants who toured the country in search of suitable goods. As the eighteenth century wore on, however, merchanting or factoring firms grew up which bought goods from the small manufacturers and distributed them at their own risk: and the larger manufacturers, such as John Taylor, Samuel Garbett[28] and Matthew Boulton, developed their own merchanting contacts in towns all over Europe and sometimes went in for factoring themselves.[29] John Taylor's success illustrates the power and wealth which the making of trinkets for the markets of Europe could bring. He was one of the largest, and was financially the most successful, of the button and toy manufacturers in Birmingham. Born in 1711, he specialised in gilt, plated and enamel buttons and snuff boxes, and in 1755, according to a contemporary account, was employing five hundred people. It was said that in his factory the making of buttons was split into seventy separate processes. Lady Shelburne called him the 'principal' manufacturer in Birmingham in 1766[30] and Lord Palmerston thought his factory 'an amazing branch of business'.[31] When he died in 1775 his estate was valued at £200,000.[32]

Thus by the middle of the eighteenth century the Birmingham button and toy manufacturers had achieved a position of ascendancy both in England and in Europe, and had made fruitful trading contacts further afield. According to Garbett and Taylor the total annual production of toys in Birmingham and the neighbouring towns by 1759 amounted in value to £600,000, of which five-sixths were exported.[33] At least 20,000 people worked in the trade. It was a remarkable achievement, although not entirely without dross. For the metalworkers of Birmingham also achieved a reputation for making goods which were cheap and somehow deceitful. Rolling metals, many of them alloys, and stamping them into shapes and patterns, seemed to many, and especially to the traditional craftsmen, to be a poor substitute for the worthy and laborious arts of casting and chasing. But it was the cheapness of the Birmingham products, resulting from the use of new alloys susceptible to labour saving processes such as stamping, which won the business.[34]

By the 1770s the town was known far and wide as the chief metal-working centre in England. One of Boulton's visitors in 1775 recorded in a letter that 'Birmingham is a very large and thickly populated town, where almost everybody is busy hammering, pounding, rubbing and chiseling'.[35]

Matthew Boulton and Soho

This was the Birmingham in which Matthew Boulton grew up and developed his business. It was a society well accustomed to the techniques, opportunities and problems of the metalworking trades. It was an environment in which scientific enquiry was encouraged and inventiveness prospered. It was a competitive commercial centre where the ambitious manufacturer had to be on his mettle.

Boulton is so well known in his role as the promoter of James Watt's steam engine that historians tend to relegate his earlier business ventures to the background, if they mention them at all.[36] The promotion and successful development of the steam engine was Boulton's most significant achievement. But it is misleading to isolate his partnership with Watt from his earlier partnership with John Fothergill, because it was from this that he gained much of his commercial experience and acquired many of the contacts necessary for the marketing of Boulton and Watt's engines. Indeed, as one historian has observed, it is being wise after the event to assess Boulton's achievement chiefly in terms of his success with steam engines.[37] The later partnership could not have prospered without the commercial experience derived from the earlier one, and it was very much in Boulton's mind as late as 1778 that it might be prudent to stick to making buttons, which he described as 'a sheet anchor', rather than risk the further development of the engine trade.[38] To allow Boulton's engine trade to overshadow his production of ornamental metalwork also neglects his very important place in the history of the decorative arts in England.

Boulton was born in 1728.[39] He was named after his father, who owned a buckle and toy making business with a workshop in Steelhouse Lane from which he moved in 1731 to Snow Hill. At the age of fourteen he left his local school and started work in his father's business. It is clear from his later notebooks, diaries and letters, many of which will be quoted in this book, that he had a quick and enquiring mind, which he seems to have turned towards fostering the family business at an early age: by the time he was seventeen he is said to have invented a way of inlaying steel buckles with enamel.[40] According to James Watt, he was 'the first inventor of inlaid buttons'.[41] It is not known how large the business was at the time, but it has been shown that the firm exported toys to the continent before 1750 and that by 1760 the younger Boulton seems to have had some experience of trade with the Low Countries, Spain and Portugal.[42] It is also known that the elder Boulton owned a water-powered rolling mill at Sparkbrook in 1756.[43] His workshop was probably one of the more important metal-working workshops in Birmingham at the time.

In 1759 the elder Boulton died. His son had been his partner for nine years and for many of them had been effectively running the business. He had furthermore strengthened his hand considerably by marrying, in 1749, Mary Robinson, the daughter of a rich mercer in Lichfield. She also died in 1759.

From this time and throughout his life Boulton was very much the master of his business. As will be seen in later chapters he took a close interest in its affairs. He clearly believed that personal attention to detail pays dividends.[44] He was constantly looking for profitable ways of increasing the range of his products, and for means of improving his designs and manufacturing techniques. He schemed continuously to promote the sales of his products to all corners of the civilised world. His friend and partner James Watt described his industrial and commercial skills:

> Mr Boulton was not only an ingenious mechanick, well skilled in all the practices of the Birmingham manufactures, but possessed in a high degree the faculty of rendering any new invention of his own or others useful to the publick, by organising and arranging the processes by which it could be carried on as well as by promoting the sale by his own exertions and by his numerous friends and correspondents. His conception of the nature of any invention was quick and he was not less quick in perceiving the uses to which it might be applied and the profits which might accrue from it.[45]

He was, in the words of a recent author, a 'born promoter'.[46] The steam engine was only one of a succession of expensive but potentially lucrative projects on which he embarked at one time or another during his life. Apart from his original business in toys, the range of which he greatly extended, he was probably the first manufacturer in Birmingham to make silver plate[47] and he tied up capital and labour at one time or another in the production of japanned goods, clocks, silver and plate, ormolu, mechanical paintings, lamps, copying machines, coins and medals. Many of these ventures were financial failures, but it never seems to have occurred to him to limit his ambitions and so restrict his business. His friend James Keir[48] said that 'to understand perfectly the character of Mr Boulton's mind, it is necessary to recollect that whatever he did or attempted, his successes or his failures were all on a large scale'.[49]

Keir also drew attention to two further facets of Boulton's character that it is important to recall when looking into his business activities. These were his natural affability and his keen interest in the natural sciences. Josiah Wedgwood was particularly struck by these qualities when he first met Boulton in 1767. He described him as 'very ingenious, philosophical and agreeable'.[50] So, when visitors came to Soho to look at the elegant works of art and the factory where they were made, Boulton entertained them at his own expense and spent valuable hours with them so that 'however agreeably their curiosity was gratified, they were still more pleased with the proprietor'.[51] As Keir observed, Boulton's willingness to oblige wasted many valuable hours but it was not without its subsequent reward: for he 'thus gained the acquaintance of most men distinguished for rank, influence and knowledge in the kingdom', which helped him later when he had to defend his steam engine patent in several applications to Parliament.[52] It also ensured the spread of his fame and was an essential part of his marketing campaign.

Boulton's interest in the natural sciences also served to spread his fame and brought him into contact with some of the liveliest minds of the age. He had no formal training. Keir commented:

> Mr Boulton is a proof how much scientific knowledge may be acquired without much regular study, by means of a quick and just apprehension, much practical application, and nice mechanical feelings. He had very correct notions of the several branches of natural philosophy, and was master of every metallic art, and possessed all the chemistry that had any relation to the objects of his various manufactures. Electricity and astronomy were at one time among his favourite amusements.[53]

Much of Boulton's interest in the natural sciences, and especially his interest in chemistry, was generated by his drive to improve his manufactures. His earliest notebook contains recipes for many compositions such as waxes, ink, varnish, enamels, solders, japan and imitation tortoiseshell,[54] all of which had practical applications in his business. A later notebook contains many recipes for gilding and colouring solutions.[55] But he was equally interested, as were many of his lively contemporaries, in enquiries that had no immediate relevance to his trade. His earliest notebook, for example, contains notes about the thermometer, steam, a compensated pendulum, the planets and observations of the barometer.[56]

James Keir said that Boulton owed much of his knowledge 'to the best preceptor, the conversation of eminent men',[57] and he listed among the celebrated men who dined at Boulton's table Erasmus Darwin, William Small, James Ferguson, John Whitehurst, William Withering, Joseph Black, Joseph Priestley, Thomas Day and Benjamin Franklin. I do not propose to discuss here the important place that these well known scientists held in Boulton's world or the colossal influence that they exercised on his affairs. Nor is this the place to describe the evolution of the Lunar Society, which grew from the informal circle of natural philosophers and manufacturers who used to meet at Boulton's house from about 1765. They included Keir, Watt and Wedgwood, and, from the men mentioned above, Darwin, Small, Whitehurst, Withering and Priestley.[58] It is enough to say that the Lunar Society was indirectly responsible, through the regular conversations and correspondence between its members, for the application of many scientific ideas to the processes of industry, and thus exercised a potent influence on the progress of what is called the Industrial Revolution. Matthew Boulton was its most active member. The Society grew from his friendship and common interests with Darwin and Whitehurst and would probably not have flourished had it not been for his abundant energy and enthusiasm. Some of his commercial contacts with three of its members, James Keir, John Whitehurst[59] and Josiah Wedgwood, will be mentioned later, as will occasions when he took advice from others, notably James Ferguson[60] and William Small,[61] on details of design and marketing. It is in fact impossible to understand either Boulton or his business activities without seeing him in the society of these distinguished men.

By 1760 Boulton's activities and ambitions had outgrown his workshop on Snow Hill. There is little doubt that the decision to enlarge his manufacturing capacity was considerably eased by the inheritance of his father's estate, but it was typical of the man that he should seek to extend his trade in competition with powerful rivals such as Garbett and Taylor rather than

4. Tilly Kettle, Anne Boulton, *c.*1762–4, Private Collection.

sitting back and living off his capital. It was, as events turned out, a decision fraught with financial risks. Boulton would probably not have survived financially had it not been for his second marriage in 1760 to Anne Robinson, his late wife's younger sister, who became a few years later the sole heiress to a fortune of £28,000 (Plate 4).[62]

Boulton's plan was to enlarge the range of his manufactures, his father's business having concentrated on buckles, buttons and toys, and to improve and cheapen the processes of production. He considered a water mill essential.[63] In 1761 he bought, for £1,000, the lease of some land at Handsworth, about two miles from the centre of Birmingham, and with it Soho House and Soho Mill, which the previous leaseholder had recently built, having made a canal half a mile long to convey the water from a nearby brook. Boulton was pleased with his purchase and with the scope it gave him for enlarging and cheapening his products. He wrote to one of the London merchants to whom he was sending some buttons and buckles:

> I have lately purchased the most convenient water mill in England for my business, which I shall not work before Lady Day, by the conveniency of which and other alterations I shall make at that time I hope then to send you some patterns upon such terms as I presume will greatly increase our dealings.[64]

While wanting to produce more cheaply, Boulton had no wish to reduce the quality of his products. He understood that in order to compete effectively with his powerful rivals he had to maintain or improve the quality of his wares. His letters contain frequent complaints about the quality of the products of Soho: in 1772 he reminded his partner, in a letter complaining about the chasing of some buttons, of the keen competition from Taylor.[65] Many years earlier he had said that to reduce the quality would ruin the trade.[66] Rather than reduce the quality he had to rely on keen prices and the only means to this end was manufacturing efficiency.

In the summer of 1761 Boulton built a warehouse and several workshops at Soho and then, dissatisfied with the capabilities of the mill, demolished and rebuilt it.[67] He did not abandon the workshop on Snow Hill but tried to carry on his trade in both places at once. It was not a satisfactory arrangement and the control and improvement of the workshops must have absorbed a great deal of his time and energy. In addition to this he had to find new customers, and foster old ones, among the merchants and retailers both in England and overseas. Thus, when John Fothergill approached him early in 1762 with proposals for a partnership, Boulton, who at first declined the offer, was probably persuaded eventually more by Fothergill's marketing experience and connections than by his need for more capital. The partnership would mean that he could devote more of his time to improving the manufactory and extending the range of products, while Fothergill would bring in the orders. The partnership came into being on Midsummer Day 1762. The partners signed no agreement but the chief provisions of the arrangement were that they should divide the profits equally after receiving interest on their capital, which in Boulton's case included the value of the fixed assets and stock at the time.[68]

John Fothergill had inherited neither Boulton's capital nor his entrepreneurial daring. He has always come out badly from any comparison with his partner. Having no property to fall back on he was constantly worried, as his surviving letters show, about the firm's financial troubles, while Boulton, who was admittedly conscious of the risks, seemed to take them in his stride rather than letting them interfere with his determination to expand. Fothergill was financially more prudent than Boulton. But because he was more timid, because most of the surviving documents concerning their later dispute were written by Boulton, and because Boulton's subsequent success through the engine trade has overshadowed his earlier business ventures, Fothergill's skills have been underrated. Little is known of his earlier career, but he had considerable experience of the hardware trade on the continent, where he had probably acted as a travelling salesman for Joseph Duncumb, a Birmingham hardware merchant.[69] He also had connections with bankers and financiers, which stood to bolster the partnership's trade and credit.[70] One of Fothergill's first tasks in 1762 was to visit the London shopkeepers in an attempt to boost the sales of cut steel buttons.[71]

In 1763 Boulton listed the firm's products as including:

> chapes, inlaid buckles and buttons platina, coat, breast and sleeve buttons platina, watch chains, bell locks, watch keys, watch hooks, tapestry hooks, com[mon] met[al] buttons, steel watch chains, platina buckles, steel and en[amelle]d butt[on]s.[72]

The list suggests that the range of materials used in the production of buttons, buckles and toys was expanding.

In 1765 the partners decided to build a new warehouse and workshops at Soho and to concentrate manufacture there. It was proving impossible to keep track of materials and patterns or to supervise the workmen in the two separate workshops, and the business was unprofitable.[73] The new buildings at Soho[74] became one of the wonders of the industrial world almost immediately after their completion and a constant stream of visitors came to see them. One of the first visitors was Lady Shelburne, who came in 1766 and also visited the workshops of Boulton's rivals, Garbett and Taylor. She found Boulton's products very similar and bought some watch chains and trinkets at an 'amazing cheap price'.[75] It is unlikely that Boulton was enabled to keep his prices down by the renewal of his workshops, the erection of which proved disastrously expensive. More probably he was forced to do so by the competition. Fothergill reported to Boulton on 7th May 1762 that one of the London jewellers told him that other Birmingham toy makers, including John Taylor, had been to him 'like so many wolves for orders' and that Taylor had 'offered him any encouragement he would accept of for the sake of a little business'.[76]

Boulton's determination to compete effectively is clear from his constant interest in expanding the range of his wares. In 1765 he was planning to add several varieties to the range of buttons and buckles including gilt, lacquered and plated buttons and pinchbeck buckles, as well as steel candle snuffers, earrings, silvered candlesticks and corkscrews.[77] Silver plate, of which the firm became one of the largest manufacturers,[78] was already among the products[79] and, although the workshops did not produce brass-foundry on any scale,[80] they may have made brass candlesticks[81] and could make such things as candle branches, door knobs and escutcheons to order. Other products at this date included such diverse objects as decorative japanned wares and tapestry hooks,[82] of which there appear to have been several patterns.[83]

James Watt recalled that when he first visited Soho in 1767:

> the goods then manufactured there were steel, gilt and fancy buttons, steel watch chains and sword hilts, plated wares, ornamental works in or moulu, tortoise shell snuff boxes, Bath metal buttons inlaid with steel and various other articles which I have now forgot.[84]

He was probably wrong about the 'or moulu' (see Chapter 2, p. 44), but his account gives some idea of the range of products. Boulton himself said in 1767 that he had lately begun to make 'snuff boxes, instrument cases, tooth picks, etc. in metal gilt, and in tortoiseshell inlaid, likewise gilt and pinchbeck watch chains ...'.[85] Count von Zinzendorf, an Austrian who visited the Soho manufactory in September 1768, recorded that he saw 'a prodigious number of watch chains, tortoiseshell boxes, gilt and mother-of-pearl chains, plated ware, and belt clasps in the Turkish fashion'. He called the building 'extremely handsome'.[86] A month or so later Boulton's list of articles manufactured at Soho, which included a record of pattern numbers and prices, noted the products under the following headings:

Buttons	Belt locks
Chains	Cane heads
Buckles	Trinkets
Boxes	Tapestry hooks
Instrument cases	Chapes
Links and sleeve buttons	Watch hooks
Candlesticks	Watch keys[87]
Plated wares and braziery	

The list gives no idea of the variety of materials and types of object catalogued under each heading. It was an impressive range of wares for an eighteenth-century workshop and it enabled Boulton to boast in 1768 that he ran 'the largest hardware manufactory in the world'.[88] It was small wonder that Josiah Wedgwood, after his visit to the new factory at Soho in 1767, commented that he believed Boulton to be 'the most complete manufacturer in England in metal'.[89] The business was all absorbing, as growing businesses short of working capital tend to be, and Boulton told Wedgwood on one occasion in 1767 that he was 'a little run aground in it'.[90] Two years later he wrote to Richard Tonson in the same vein that 'the business I planted within these few years hath so much taken root and extended its branches that I am entirely enveloped with it'.[91]

This remark was written as an excuse for not having repaid a loan, and was probably designed to reassure Tonson that the business was so prosperous that he would certainly get his money back. Boulton's preoccupations did not prevent him from adding still further to his range of products during the remaining years of his partnership with Fothergill. First came silverware, a natural extension of the plate business, then ormolu and the mounting of vases, the origins and development of which will be discussed in the next chapter. By 1772 the firm was listing as its main manufactures (the writer of the letter finding it difficult to remember them all):

> Men's and women's steel, pinchbeck and gilt watch chains; steel, pinchbeck, gilt, teutenague and silver buckles; platina, sterling gilt and plated, steel, steel inlaid, Bath metal, and filligree plated buttons on box and on bone moulds; gilt, silver, plated, shagreen, tortoise, plain and inlaid with silver and gold in 4 colours snuff boxes; instrument cases; toothpick cases; gilt, glass and steel trinkets; silver filligree boxes; needle books etc., etc.; all manner of plated goods, as tea kitchins, tankards, cups, coffee Potts, cream juggs, candlesticks, sauceboats, terrines etc., etc.; bronzed tea kitchin and tea kettles as well plated as tinned inside, saucepans, cheese-toasters etc., etc., etc.; buckle chapes of all qualitys; platina, inlaid and steel links; candle vases with 2 to 6 branches, girandolles, sugar basons, essence-pots, clock cases etc., etc., and all manner of chimney piece ornaments, intirely gilt in or moulu, or of radix amethysti mounted in or moulu, such as we sell annually great quantities to the Nobility and tradesmen; plated bottle stands, cruet frames, inkstands, pencil cases, teutenague candlesticks and a number of other articles.[92]

Among the objects not mentioned in this list were stone vases and obelisks, which, from the evidence of the pattern books, Boulton and Fothergill must have sold in their showroom as part of their merchanting business.[93]

The full range of ormolu products is discussed later in this book. An idea of Soho's enormous production of silverware, which received a great stimulus from the establishment of an Assay Office at Birmingham in 1773, can be gained from the first selection of goods which the firm sent to be hallmarked in that year:

Buckles, spoons, spurs, ladles, knife handles, candlesticks, branches, salts, gun furniture, tea tongs, instrument cases, bottle stands, snuffers, snuffer pans, labels for bottles, sword hilts, buttons, punch ladles, wine strainers, shoe clasps, whip handles, epergnes, terrines, tea vases, coffee pots and lamps, tea pots, canisters, bread baskets, sugar dishes, castors, ice pails, cream jugs, two-handled cups, waiters, salvers, table crosses, sauce boats, sacramental plates, argyles, tankards, pint and half-pint cups, dishes, plates, tumblers, cheese toasters, fanes, skewers, ink-stands, cassolets, toilet plate, fish and pudding trowels, bells, monteiths, and mazareens.[94]

Later in the 1770s the firm increased its range of silverware and flirted with the production of clocks and of mechanical pictures for the decoration of door and ceiling panels and furniture. None of its products, according to James Keir, 'showed more the extent and versatility of the mechanical and scientific talents employed at Soho, than the manufacture of clocks ... No article was better suited to the display of invention ...'.[95] But in the event neither clocks nor mechanical pictures[96] paid their way and both faded from the range of products after brief periods. The firm bought the movements which were needed for its ormolu clock cases from other clockmakers.

It would not have been possible to produce the range or quantity of wares which these sources reveal without advanced methods of manufacture. Boulton paid particular attention both to labour-saving machinery and to the division of labour. As James Keir said,

it was always in Mr Boulton's mind to convert such trades as were usually carried on by individuals into great manufactures by the help of machinery, which might enable the articles to be made with greater precision and cheaper than those commonly sold.[97]

These words were written with Boulton's foray into clockmaking in mind but they might have been applied to any of his ventures. I have already mentioned that Boulton's stated reason for moving his workshop to Soho was to gain the convenient use of an efficient water mill. This gave him the power needed to operate the rolling mill,[98] the lathes and the polishing machines which were essential for the mass production of buttons and other toys. James Watt recalled the scene at Soho when he first visited the factory in 1767:

A mill with a water wheel was employed in laminating metal for the buttons, plated goods etc., and to turn laps for grinding and polishing steel work and I was informed that Mr Boulton was the ... first who had applied a mill to turn the laps. Mr Boulton at that [time] also carried on a very considerable trade in the manufacture of buckle chapes, in the making of which he had made several very ingenious improvements besides the laps in the mill. I saw an ingenious lap turned by a hand wheel for cutting and polishing the steel studs for ornamenting buttons, chains, sword hilts etc., and a shaking box put in motion by the mill for scowering button blanks and other small pieces of metal which was also a thought of Mr Boulton's. There was also a steelhouse for converting iron into steel, which was frequently employed to convert the cuttings and scraps of the chapes and other small ironwares into steel, which was afterwards melted and made into cast steel for various uses.[99]

In a letter to the architect James Adam in 1770, Boulton claimed that he had at Soho almost every machine that was needed in the working of metals, semi-metals, tortoiseshell, stones, glass, enamel, and other materials. 'I have two water mills', he observed, 'employed in rolling, pollishing, grinding and turning various sorts of laths.'[100]

It would be wrong to conclude from these references that the factory was geared to mass production as we know it today. It was not. It was still heavily reliant on handcraft rather than continuous processes.[101] Pressing and stamping were carried out on hand-operated machines and much of the making and finishing of the ornaments illustrated in this book should be described as skilled craftwork. The machinery employed, however, was more advanced than in most workshops and one of Boulton's constant preoccupations was the improvement to processes and machinery in order to achieve more efficient production.

A fascinating picture of a large part of the factory has survived in the account of Dorothy Richardson, who visited it in May 1770, when ormolu production was well established but was still only a small part of the total production:[102]

About a mile and half beyond Birmingham upon the side of a wild heath, stands Soho; where a very great manufactory in all kinds of hardware etc. is carried on by Messrs Bolton and Fothergill. Mr Bolton's house (a brick building) stands upon a hill, from whence plantations of trees and shrubs, and winding walks go down to an immense brick building round a court; in the center of one of the fronts in a turret is a bell for calling the people to work, this place is as large as a town, besides a great number of work shops thirty families live under the roof; many more hands besides them both men, women and children are employed. In the middle of the court stands a large mill, turned by a water wheel, which keeps in motion several of the machines and there is also another mill in this court, which is a large wheel laid flat and answers the same purpose as the first being turned by a horse when they are scarce of water; which probably may often happen; as the brook is very small.
Mr Fothergill shewed us all the rooms. In the 1st people were gilding watch chains with a preparation of gold and mercury, they look a dirty yellow till they are put into a charcoal fire, and then a blast, gives them polish.
2d room: They were stamping plates, silver on one sides, and copper on the other, into rounds for button tops; the metal is heated before it is put into the frame which is struck by a very heavy iron weight, falling upon the mould.
3d room: enamelling glass lockets; they are put into a charcoal fire, and dotted with different colour'd liquid glass, in such a manner as to form sprigs of roses etc. when they come out of the fire they look brown, and the colours which are very beautiful do not appear till they are cold.
4th room: men were casting buttons in loam, which is a very fine kind of black sand; they first put the patterns of all the buttons into it, pressing them down as hard as possible; when they are taken out, liquid metal is immediately poured in which receives a very sharp impression.
5th room: they were stamping an impression upon the plain round pieces cut for button tops; the die lies under, and a heavy piece of iron falls upon the button, in the same manner as in the second room only that there is a hole in the top, to form the shank.
6th room: people were stamping buttons enlaid with steel; the bits of steel are first put into the die, in what form they chuse, after which the buttons are struck in the same manner as in the last room. Some women were also shaving off the edges; they stand upon their right foot, with their left they press a treddle, the left hand is used for putting the buttons into an engine, the right for turning the engine, and with their right elbow upon an iron, they make them drop out. They were also boring holes in the shanks with the same kind of engine.
7th room: stamping bits of steel to enlay buttons.
8th room: men casting ornaments and figures in loam in the same manner as the buttons, only a reverse is join'd to the underpart and there are holes thro the frame where the liquid metal is poured in.
9th room: they were stamping the tops of steel watch chains, in the same manners as the buttons; and by an engine giving them the diamond cut.
10th room: they were stamping pieces of very thin metal silvered and gilt in all kinds of figures for button tops.
11th room: men were incorporating copper plates with silver; after they are heated, they are beat very thin upon an anvil by three men with very heavy hammers.

12th room: they were polishing button tops, by rubbing them with wet sands.
13th room: polishing enlaid buttons.
14th room: polishing steel buckles etc. by files.
15th room: they were stamping the links of watch chains in the same manner as the buttons in the 5th room; only that the impression is on the upper side instead of the lower and cutting out the flourishes in the chains, which are put into an engine; there is a different tool used for every division.
16th room: making small steel studs for the chains in an engine. Screwing them into the holes and cutting them diamond cut. These look like marquisette.
17th room: polishing them, and making holes in the chain to receive them.
18th room: people drawing silver, brass silvered over, and copper wire. It is wrapt round one sheet, and drawn thro a small hole as tight as possible upon another. If it is to be very fine, this is several times repeated thro smaller, and smaller holes.
19th room: they were putting brass plates upon the tops of inkstands etc. Making steel screw plates by an engine, and lacquering snuff boxes for gilding.
20th room: women polishing steel watch chains, by rubbing them with sand and water.
21st room: polishing them higher, and wire, with oil and putty.
22d room: women polishing steel chains with their hands and putty and polishing the holes in the chains by rubbing a piece of leather thro them.
23d room: women cutting iron wire into lengths by an engine; and drawing it thro a hole so as to make it round and hollow for fastening the anchor and tongue to the buckle.
24th room: polishing anchors and tongues, with a file.
25th room: dipping copper buttons first into a very hot spirit, and then into cold water out of which they come a gold colour.
26th room: a great number of women piercing holes in steel buttons by an engine, and cutting the ragged edges off. A different tool is fixed in the engine for every division.
27th room: cutting bits of steel for enlaying.
28th room: polishing steel ornaments by a file.
29th room: polishing Chinese plate, a new composition, which looks exactly like silver, and never changes colour.
30th room: men hammering out plated waiters.
31st room: finishing and polishing them, and also some real silver candlesticks.
32d room: cutting exceeding thin, plates of metal; for the undersides of open buttons, and gilding them, a different colour from the buttons.
33d room: inlaying tortoise shell snuff boxes etc. with gold, silver, and ivory. The bites are first stuck upon paper in a pattern with gum; after which the tortoise shell being softened by boiling; the paper is laid upon it, and the work stuck in by a weight; the paper is last rubbed off.
34th room: plating several things, and among the rest a copper fish kettle with silver.
35th room: women fastening pieces of horn under the tops of buttons with resin.
36th room: turning the Derbyshire congeald water into vases etc.[103]
37th room: polishing tortoise shell boxes after they are enlaid.
38th room: stamping steel watch chains etc.
39th room: women enlaying upon paper for tortoise shell snuff boxes.
I believe we did not see half the rooms but as the people were going to their dinner, we could not wait till they returned.
We last saw the two warehouses, and the counting house.
In the large warehouse, were vast quantities of all the manufactories; particularly real plate, Chinese plate, and plated candlesticks, of different kinds, Corinthian and Ionic pillars — bottle stands, waiters etc. a very handsome plated kitchen, and a bread basket — great variety of gilt snuff boxes, enlaid tortoise shell snuff boxes, gilt tooth pick cases, steel and gilt men and womens watch chains; all kind of buttons, and buckles; trinkets; tortoise shell combs etc. — Also several tooth pick cases of the finest silver filigree I ever saw.
In the counting house stood a very elegant silver gilt tea kitchen made for Sir

do with the less valuable articles. It consists of more costly and highly finished commodities. The making of buttons of various kinds, plated, lacquerd, gilt employs a little army of all ages. The great contrivance and ingenuity of the people here have taught them to produce some articles for sale at about half the price they could a few years ago be sold for. Tis wonderful, astonishing, amazing.

Before we leave this pile of buildings we take a view of the warehouses, where the goods are for sale. This is a cabinet of curiosities, splendid, magnificent and gaudy; more like the costly pageantry of some Eastern court than the toys of a Birmingham shop. The goods here are all covered with glass cases so that they are exposed to the greatest advantage.[115]

As if the manufactory and its warehouses at Soho were not enough, Boulton and Fothergill also maintained a warehouse in Birmingham, where buyers could see the range of manufactures and where from about 1766 the firm also sold the products of other workshops on commission. Of the turnover in 1767, £22,000 represented goods manufactured at Soho and £8,000 sales on commission.[116] This commission business, which Boulton and Fothergill felt obliged to continue partly because it was profitable and partly because their foreign agents preferred to deal with one supplier in order to reduce the costs of freight, caused frequent embarrassments with other factors who bought the products of Soho for transmission abroad.[117] The goods included ironware, brassware, cutlery, ceramics, toys and buttons.

The firm's direct export business was large. The export of toys was a competitive business but Boulton's prices were keen. It was the cheapness of his products which enabled him to send them –

to every corner of Europe although in many places they have as good and as cheap materials as we have, and have labour cent per cent cheaper, yet nevertheless by the superactivity of our people, and by the many mechanical contrivances and extensive apparatus which we are possessed of, our men are enabled to do from twice to ten times the work that can be done without the help of such contrivances ...[118]

Boulton and Fothergill both had considerable experience of continental markets before 1762. Their exporting methods and achievements have been summarised elsewhere,[119] and I shall discuss them in relation to the ormolu business in Chapter 5. It is enough to say here that dealing with overseas agents added greatly to the complexity of the business. Foreign restrictions on trade, the competition from manufacturers both in England and on the continent, the need to ensure that foreign agents were provided with exclusive patterns,[120] the difficulties of both employing and being factors, the problems of foreign exchange, the costs of freight and insurance, the credit worthiness of new agents, and the agreement of terms of credit, let alone the constant bookkeeping and correspondence, all absorbed time and money.

The range and quantity of the partnership's products might suggest at first sight that it was a successful and profitable business. Unfortunately it was not. The ormolu trade contributed to the partnership's difficulties, as I shall show in the next chapter, but it only aggravated a basically weak financial position, which derived from the expansion of the Soho manufactory in 1765–7.[121] The original agreement between Boulton and Fothergill laid down that the partners should share the profits equally after crediting themselves with interest on the capital that they had in the business. Boulton's initial capital was £6,206 17s. 9d., which included the buildings, tools and materials at Soho, and Fothergill's was £5,394 16s. 0d.[122] No profit and loss account was drawn up until the end of 1764 when there was a recorded loss of £3,829 10s. 0d. The cause of this loss is uncertain but the firm was probably suffering from the usual losses which must be expected of a new venture during the initial phase of expansion before enough orders have been generated. There is little doubt that both pricing policy and stock control were lax.[123] The loss was followed in the three succeeding years by profits of £402 18s. 2d., £1,905 17s. 4d. and £2,175 18s. 6d., figures which looked more satisfactory but which cannot be trusted because no provision was made for doubtful debts, which later proved to be very large.[124] By 1767, when the new buildings at Soho were completed, Boulton's capital had increased to £14,789 5s. 11d., and Fothergill's to £6,868 10s. 5d., both partners having made up the initial loss and contributed to the finance for the expansion by putting in more money. The partners were credited with interest in 1767 amounting to £933 10s. 7d., which is an indication of the business's chief problem: the fixed assets had cost too much.

The business had been short of liquid capital before the rebuilding of Soho. The new workshops at Soho, which were started in 1765, nearly ruined it. The cost turned out to be about £10,000 against the original estimate of £2,000. The consequent shortage of capital made itself felt to no uncertain effect. The partners' correspondence, especially Fothergill's, is full of worries about it. Boulton himself knew that the new buildings at Soho were far bigger than was necessary to sustain the current level of production[125] and later attributed the creation of the firm's debt, or 'Bill Account', to the investment in buildings.[126] In 1771 he described the fixed assets at Soho, or the 'dead stock' as he called them, as 'monstrously large'.[127]

The issuing of bills was a common method of finance in the eighteenth century. Merchants and bankers would accept bills on behalf of clients from which they would deduct a commission. When the bills fell due the client was expected to finance them by cash or alternative bills. As time went by Boulton and Fothergill found it increasingly difficult to service their Bill Account. Many of Fothergill's letters reveal his worries on this score. He wrote to Boulton for example in May 1772: 'I could not exert myself much towards procuring any further assistance to B/A [i.e. the Bill Account]; indeed Mr Walker gives me hardly any hopes from any quarter'.[128] The shortage of liquid capital, which made it difficult to pay either the workmen or the suppliers of raw materials,[129] led Boulton and Fothergill to look for other partners as well as for men who would be willing to advance money on loan. After some extensive correspondence, a merchant of Iserlohn named J. H. Ebbinghaus became a partner in 1766 and contributed £2,000 to the capital of the firm.[130] H. F. Bargum, the Danish financier, advanced £500 in 1767,[131] and Boulton received loans from Jacob Tonson the publisher in 1764,[132] and from the London factor John Motteux in 1766.[133]

The partnership never recovered from the shortage of capital caused by the investment in fixed assets in 1765–7, in spite of the steady expansion of turnover. It was a miracle that it survived as long as it did, considering its financial troubles from 1767 onwards. In that year Tonson's executor asked for the repayment of his loan. This was followed by the refusal of Ebbinghaus, who was becoming disillusioned by Boulton's requests for further capital, to put any more money into the business.[134] In 1772, after sustaining losses for four years amounting to £6,946 7s. 7d., the partners were faced with repaying a loan of £8,000, which had been raised in Holland in 1769,[135] and had still to repay Tonson's executor. In the same year Boulton resolved, with a typical lack of financial caution, to back James Watt's scheme for a steam engine. He decided to buttress the partnership and to find the money for the venture with Watt from the sale of a property. But 1772 brought a further storm in the shape of the bankruptcy of the London banking house Neale, James, Fordyce and Down, which created a serious financial crisis and led to the failure of several other bankers. Boulton and Fothergill did not lose a great deal as a result of this crisis in spite of having deposited money with the defaulters shortly before their bankruptcy, but the crisis had a serious effect on trade[136] and made it more difficult than ever to lay hands on ready money. And in the same year Ebbinghaus, impatient at Boulton's reluctance to send proper accounts, gave notice of withdrawing his capital.[137]

In spite of these appalling difficulties the partnership lasted for another ten years. There is not much evidence available for the years following 1772, but it is clear that Boulton and Fothergill continued to lose money[138] and by 1777 the Bill Account had risen to nearly £25,000.[139] Some improvement took place thereafter but it is clear that Boulton's engine business, which occupied more and more of his time, was bolstering the fortunes of the ailing hardware partnership in its last years.[140] James Keir summarised the situation in a note that he wrote in about 1775, analysing the prospects of the partnership which Boulton and Fothergill had offered him and setting out his reasons for refusing:

> 1. The proposal before made … is impracticable, because the expences attending a large paper debt is included in the general accounts, and this debt having been contracted in former years, ought not to make a part of the present trade. This circumstance renders it impossible for a new partner to enter into a general connection.
> 2. The whole business consists of three branches. First, that as merchants at Newhall. Secondly that as manufacturers at Soho. Thirdly the fire engine. The above objection is inseparable from the first branch, and it does not affect the third. If the second branch was separated from the first, it [i.e. the mercantile business] might also be cleared of the objection …
> 3. The manufacture has evidently been carried on for many years past with great loss. Witness the Bill Account. For the mercantile business is said to have gained. Therefore there must be some great abuses, many of which will be difficult to remove soon. The building, stock of tools, etc., are much too great for the quantity of business that is carried on …[141]

Fortunately for Boulton the engine trade was beginning to be profitable.[142] In 1781, after a dispute with Fothergill about profits from the engine company (on which Fothergill had no claim), which was settled in Boulton's favour, plans for a new partnership were discussed. This was to include Zacchaeus Walker, the firm's accountant, and James Cabrit, another clerk at Soho, whose signature appears under many of the firm's letters. The plans came to nothing owing to a further dispute with Fothergill. Fothergill died in June 1782, before any further attempt could be made to reconstruct the partnership. His estate was insolvent because of debts to a widow from whose husband's estate he had borrowed money for the partnership.

There were other reasons for the constant difficulties of the toy manufacturing business in addition to the shortage of working capital. The most serious was inadequate management. Boulton has to bear part of the blame. He was frequently absent from Soho after 1772 owing to his increasing interest in other matters – first in the establishment of the Assay Office at Birmingham, which kept him in London during most of 1773, and later in the development of the engine trade. He was doing too much and did not keep an adequate eye on the firm's core business. In the words of Jabez Maud Fisher in 1776, Boulton was a

> sensible, ingenious and enterprising man, who plans and executes with equal expedition, but like many other great men he has his hobby horse. He is scheming and changeable, ever some new matter on the anvil to divert his attention from a steady pursuit of some grand object. He is always inventing, and by the time he has brought his scheme to perfection, some new affair offers itself. He deserts the old, follows the new, of which he is weary by the time he has arrived at it. This volatility prevents him from becoming very rich.[143]

It sounds as if the writer had listened to Fothergill's views during his visit, but there is substance in his account. Fothergill on the other hand, as Boulton bitterly recorded on one occasion, was not up to managing the manufactory – a criticism that was not entirely fair because Boulton had always taken the prime interest in the factory himself. The partners were clearly at loggerheads on the supervision of the factory when Boulton was away: and John Scale, the manager, was overworked.[144] The result was confusion.

There was no consistent policy, for example, on the order in which commissions were to be executed: this caused misunderstandings in the factory and delays that annoyed customers. There was also no adequate pricing policy: the idea seems to have been to guess the price of an object rather than to relate it to its precise cost. These problems were among the reasons for the partnership's difficulties that John Scale listed in a document that he drew up in 1773.[145] He also mentioned the continual increase in the amount of 'dead stock', i.e. tools and materials, and the abuses which arose from the system of paying workmen by the day. He wanted to institute piecework, a system under which the workmen would be expected to provide their own tools and materials, and to charge them rent for their workshops. It was a classic recipe for releasing capital by regaining control of the stock, which had clearly got out of hand.

The failure to assess accurately the costs of production and to price individual products accordingly is a common enough fault in manufacturing businesses today. It would be unduly critical to take Boulton and Fothergill to task for failing to apply the detailed costing techniques which are practised by efficient modern manufacturers. They seem however to have neglected, or at any rate underestimated, the primary costs of both labour and capital. Scale saw that it would be easier to assess the cost of labour if the workmen were converted to piecework and that the failure to control the level of stock-in-trade made it impossible to control the costs of production. Keir pointed out that the annual cost of excessive fixed assets increased real production costs to the point where they exceeded income. These criticisms were a serious indictment of Boulton and Fothergill's managerial talents. It is perhaps symptomatic of their faults that they frequently allowed their customers six months' credit while they had to pay their own suppliers within six weeks, a situation which could only lead to a further squeeze on their liquidity and raise the real cost of their products. Such lax control made nonsense of any attempt to produce at a profit, especially when many customers, in accordance with aristocratic custom in the eighteenth century, delayed paying their bills anyway.[146] Ebbinghaus saw the problem clearly. When he wrote to request the withdrawal of his capital in 1772 he observed that orders were all very well, but only if they produced a profit.[147] Boulton was guilty of a fault which has ruined many a business, the pursuit of turnover without sufficiently counting the cost. It was remarkable that his hardware business survived into the 1780s.

It would not have survived but for two things. The first was Boulton's personal wealth, or rather the wealth of his wives. The second was the success of the engine trade. Both enabled him to support the expenses of the ailing hardware trade. And if the business was poorly conducted, there is little doubt that Boulton learned valuable lessons from it. His later partnerships were run on more businesslike lines and, perhaps as a result of Scale's agitation, benefited from the maintenance of more accurate accounts. These however are another story, and I must now turn to the part of Boulton and Fothergill's hardware trade that is the subject of this book.

CHAPTER 2

The ormolu trade at Soho

In the 1770s Boulton and Fothergill's reputation for 'ornamental pieces in or moulu' was second to none. Their ornaments were, in the words of a contemporary directory, 'admired by the nobility and gentry, not only of this kingdom, but of all Europe; and are allowed to surpass anything of the kind made abroad'.[1] This last claim was an exaggeration. Boulton and Fothergill's keenest competitors were on the continent, especially in Paris, and the design and workmanship of the ornaments produced at Soho never surpassed the work of the best French craftsmen such as Philippe Caffieri and Pierre Gouthière.[2] There is, however, no denying the firm's pre-eminence in England. For a brief time they were the largest producers of ormolu ornaments in the country: and, thanks largely to Boulton's energetic practise of the arts of puffery, they were certainly the best known.

Besides boasting about the quality of the ormolu ornaments produced at Soho, Boulton claimed that he had been the first to introduce their manufacture into England.[3] If we define ormolu, in its widest sense, as gilt brass or bronze ornament for almost any application, this claim cannot be justified. There was a long tradition of ornamental mount making in England before Boulton arrived on the scene. There were, for example, the many makers of mounts for clock cases, furniture and chimneypieces, and of knobs, escutcheons and finger plates for doors and shutters. A high proportion of these ornamental mounts were made of gilt bronze or brass and were, therefore, just as entitled to the description 'made in or moulu' as anything produced at Soho.

Unfortunately very little is known of the craftsmen who fashioned or gilded such decorative mounts in England in the seventeenth and eighteenth centuries. There was no guild of casters or gilders. Consequently the metal-workers did not achieve the powerful position occupied by their opposite numbers in France, where an *ébéniste* was not allowed to make his own mounts,[4] and there are few separate references to them in surviving accounts or inventories. There is nothing to compare, for example, with the archives of the royal furniture in France, in which the names of mount makers occur often.[5] The English patron generally looked to one or two chief contractors for the furnishing of his house – the cabinet maker or upholsterer – and seldom received bills from the subcontractors who supplied many of the individual pieces or parts of them. Mount makers moreover probably sold a lot of their wares to cabinet makers and case makers without keeping written records: or, if they kept records, they have disappeared. Knowledge of their activities relies on the survival of their work and on a few scattered references in archives.

The anonymity of the English metalworkers in the seventeenth and eighteenth centuries is regrettable. The quality of the best surviving work shows that some of them practised the arts of chasing and gilding to a fine degree. Some of the earliest and finest work can be seen in the mounts on clock cases supplied towards the end of the seventeenth century to such leading clockmakers as Thomas Tompion and Joseph Knibb. The decoration of furniture with gilt brass mounts was not common in England until the 1760s, but some splendid examples of craftsmanship survive from the middle decades. Certain cabinets and other pieces of furniture which have been attributed to the workshop of John Channon, for example, are ornamented with gilt mounts which prove that there were skilled metal-workers in London at this time.[6] The tradition is demonstrated by the fine gilt mounts and handles which were fitted to many of the most elaborate pieces of furniture of the rococo period: and the tradition continued as the antique taste supplanted the rococo. At present we do not know who was responsible for the mounts and handles supplied to John Channon, William Vile, Thomas Chippendale, John Linnell or practically any of the leading cabinet makers. Nor do we know who made the mounts for such remarkable

5. Christopher Pinchbeck, table clock, the case designed by William Chambers, 1768, Royal Collection.

clock cases as those supplied to George III by Alexander Cumming in 1765[7] and Christopher Pinchbeck in 1768 (Plate 5).[8] It is clear, from the appearance of mounts of identical pattern on different clock cases and on different pieces of furniture, that mount making was a distinct craft from an early stage. But whether the craftsmen were generally brassfounders by trade, or silversmiths, or general metalworkers, is not at present known. We do not know whether they carried out all the processes of manufacture – modelling, casting, chasing and gilding – or some of them, or only one of them; nor to what extent they imported or were influenced by techniques practised on the continent.

Some of them worked in Birmingham. There were at least thirty-three general brassfounders in the town in 1770 and, as I have remarked earlier, their products included sconces, cabinet handles and escutcheons. The compiler of the 1770 directory reckoned that Birmingham was 'the only place for merchants and others to be provided' with these things on the best terms,[9] which even after allowing for his prejudice, is evidence for Birmingham's strong hold on the production of furniture mounts.[10] A lot of these mounts would not have been gilt. There was a great demand from furniture makers for plain brassfoundry – castors, handles, key plates, candlesticks, sconces, etc. – which the workshops of Birmingham were well suited to meet. Such objects were probably a substantial part of their trade. It is arguable that the finest gilt mounts were probably made in London, because it was the centre of the fashionable furniture trade. The distance from Birmingham must have made it difficult to control work commissioned for a particular purpose. But the Birmingham metalworkers were capable of carrying out the various gilding processes,[11] and the lack of documented cases of London cabinet makers or architects ordering their gilt mounts in Birmingham does not prove that they never did so. Casting models could be sent from one town to the other, and distance was no obstacle to the determined Birmingham manufacturer. Boulton himself received commissions for furniture mounts and door furniture which are described later (see Survey of ornaments, pp. 246–56, 240–3). And a Birmingham brassfounder named William Tovey, who was listed in the directory in 1770,[12] may have supplied mounts to the leading London cabinet maker, Samuel Norman, in the 1760s.[13]

A notable metalworker in Birmingham in the 1760s was Thomas Blockley (1708–88), who was particularly known for his locks and door furniture. He supplied locks, bolts, hinges, window bars, grates, fenders and other metal goods. He worked in iron, brass and gilt metal. His work included commissions, some of them substantial, for several country and town houses and for public buildings.[14] Many references to gilt objects appear among his bills. He supplied gilt door furniture to the Earl of Coventry at Croome Court in 1759–60. His son, another Thomas Blockley, supplied gilt door furniture and shutter ornaments, including escutcheons, knobs and handles, to Edwin Lascelles at Harewood in 1773–4.[15] It is possible that Blockley was the otherwise untraced 'Mr Bermingham' or 'Mr Brimingham' who appears in the accounts for the furnishing of Syon for the Duke of Northumberland in 1766–7 as supplying gilt ornaments for doors and shutters in the drawing room.[16]

Information about metalworkers in London in the eighteenth century is almost more sparse than the evidence concerning the Birmingham brassfounders. But some at least of the London craftsmen who supplied gilt metal ornaments to cabinet makers and others are beginning to emerge from obscurity. Boulton's notes record a Charles Magniac, who carried out work for James Cox, the jeweller.[17] Cox was well known for his flamboyant watch stands and automata, some of which were exported to the Far East in the late 1760s. He mounted an exhibition of some of his larger and more extravagant pieces in 1772,[18] many of which incorporated finely worked ormolu ornaments, as did his smaller watch stands and caskets.[19] There were also some pieces of ormolu-mounted porcelain among the 'large and valuable stock in trade' which he sold at James Christie's saleroom in 1772.[20] Cox subcontracted much of his work[21] and Boulton, who was trying at the time to discover something about gilding, noted in his diary in 1769 that 'Mr Charles Magniac, No 1 in Crown Court, Old Change, near St Pauls, is a fine designer modeller and chaser: he designs all for Cox in Shoe Lane'.[22] Very little is known about Magniac but he was described as a chaser in the records of apprenticeship in 1754[23] and Boulton's note suggests that he was responsible for most if not all of Cox's ormolu ornaments.[24]

In the same diary Boulton made notes of two other craftsmen who were likely to know something about gilding. The first of these was a German sword-hilt maker and chaser named Keisel, who had worked in Paris. He was probably a silversmith – Boulton thought he might find him 'at the Kings in Clerkenwell Green where all the chasers and silversmiths go to' – and may therefore be less relevant to this study than the second craftsman whom he noted, Dominique Jean. Evidence of Jean's work is accumulating steadily and it is becoming clear that he was an important supplier of fine mounts to the fashionable furniture makers. Boulton noted in his diary that he had 'married the daughter of Monsieur Langlois[25] who sells inlaid wood cabinets on the same side as Piercy Street, Tottenham Court. You see a sign of commode tables etc. Mr Dominique[26] is a French gilder. He gets up work himself'. Dominique Jean was apparently a brass-founder and gilder. It is tempting, on the strength of Boulton's description of his work, to attribute to him the gilt mounts which are fitted to the splendid inlaid commodes which were supplied from the workshop of his father-in-law, Pierre Langlois.[27] Daniel Langlois, who was probably Pierre's son, was formally apprenticed to him in 1771[28] and probably carried on the Langlois workshop, which seems to have concentrated in later years on silver and metalwork. There is an inlaid commode in the Fitzwilliam Museum, Cambridge, on the carcase of which the signature of Daniel Langlois has been found (Plate 6).[29] If, as seems very likely, the finely chased and gilt mounts on this commode are the work of Dominique Jean, then it follows that he was probably responsible for the mounts on several other pieces of case furniture which came from the Langlois workshop and from other furniture makers. It is seldom possible to be certain about attributing work to a craftsman on the grounds of its similarity to his other known work. This is especially true of metalwork, because two or more craftsmen could have worked, and often did, from the same models. But the close similarity of the patterns and of the chasing and gilding suggests that Dominique Jean was responsible for the mounts on a similar pair of commodes at Woburn Abbey, which have been attributed to Pierre Langlois,[30] on a drop-front secretaire desk, which has been attributed to the Swedish craftsman Christopher Fürloh,[31] and perhaps also for the mounts on the library desk at Osterley Park which is customarily attributed to John Linnell.[32] There is no other proof available at present of an association between Jean and Linnell, but that he worked on occasions for Fürloh is proved by a bill that he submitted to the Prince of Wales in 1783, which included charges for gilding the ornaments of some commodes and tables and delivering them

6. Commode, attributed to Pierre Langlois, the mounts probably by Dominique Jean, *c.*1767, Fitwilliam Museum, Cambridge.

OVERLEAF:
7. Diederich Nicolaus Anderson, plate warmer, 1760, National Trust, Kedleston Hall.

8. Lord Charlemont's medal cabinet, designed by William Chambers, 1767–8, Courtauld Institute Gallery, London.

9–10. Diederich Nicolaus Anderson and workshop, mounts for Lord Charlemont's medal cabinet, 1767–8, Courtauld Institute Gallery, London.

to Fürloh[33] and by an account which he submitted for work at Audley End.[34] He was also known by Robert and James Adam[35] and was responsible for work at various houses.[36] He remained active as a gilder and founder until at least 1807.[37]

Another bronze worker in London who appears to have had something of a reputation was Diederich Nicolaus Anderson, who was of Danish origin. Anderson's full name appears on a plate warmer at Kedleston Hall, Derbyshire (Plate 7), which was made in 1760 to a design which has survived at Kedleston.[38] The record of his death in 1767[39] made it possible to identify him with a significant series of contemporary references in archives, which do not give his full names. It is clear for example that he was the Anderson whom the architect William Chambers employed to make objects in bronze and ormolu for Lord Charlemont in 1767,[40] and whose death Chambers reported to his patron in the same year.[41] He had commissioned Anderson to make the ormolu ornaments for a medal cabinet, some 'triton' candlesticks and girandoles.[42] The medal cabinet has survived (Plate 8) and is now in the galleries of the Courtauld Institute of Art in London.[43] The ormolu ornaments, which are of very fine quality, are set behind the doors on each side and frame the titles to each of the Greek and Roman collections (Plates 9, 10). Chambers's drawings for the cabinet have also survived and include a design for the mounts for the Greek side.

Another patron who commissioned work from Anderson was the Duke of Northumberland, for whom he made the gilt brass borders for some mosaic tables and the medals for the drawing room doors at Syon House in 1767 (Plates 11, 12).[44] It is also clear that the Mrs Anderson, from whom Boulton bought some candlesticks and vases during a visit to London in 1768,[45] was Diederich Nicolaus Anderson's widow, and that it was the sale of his 'last things' which Boulton attended in February 1770.[46] Anderson was thus a well-known craftsman. In my opinion it was in his workshop that the first tripods of the type illustrated in Plate 28, examples of which survive at Althorp (from Spencer House), Kedleston and the Victoria and Albert Museum (from Wentworth Woodhouse), were made (see Chapter 3, pp. 72–5):[47] and he can safely be identified with the Anderson who exhibited a tripod made from an original design of Mr Stuart's at the Free Society of Artists in 1761 (see Chapter 3, p. 75). His association with Stuart also suggests that he was probably the author of the finely chased and gilt candle vases, with their admirable contrasts between matt and polished surfaces, an example of which is illustrated in Plate 33 (see Chapter 3, p. 76). Anderson's association with William Chambers makes it likely that he also made the griffin candlesticks designed by Chambers, several examples of which survive in varying states of preservation. The fine pair at Blenheim is illustrated in Plate 13 (see also Chapter 3, pp. 85–6).

Another craftsman in London who appears to have known about the art of gilding metals was 'Mr Pyke the proprietor of the Temple of Calliope', to whom Fothergill advised his partner to apply when he was looking into gilding methods in 1765.[48] A few weeks later Fothergill wrote again to Boulton advising him to apply to 'Pyne the organ builder'.[49] It is clear from Fothergill's phraseology that the two men were the same. There is little doubt that he was referring to George Pyke of Bloomsbury, who made chamber organs, barrel organs[50] and musical clocks in the middle of the eighteenth century.[51] There is a complicated musical clock with gilt mounts at Temple Newsam House, Leeds,[52] and a barrel organ set in a mahogany case with gilt brass mounts at Burton Constable, Yorkshire,[53] both of which are signed by George Pyke. In both cases the chasing and gilding of the ornaments show that Fothergill had some justification in recommending a visit to his workshop.

Two further London craftsmen or retailers who are known to have

OPPOSITE:
11–12. Diederich Nicolaus Anderson, door frame medallions, 1767, Syon House.

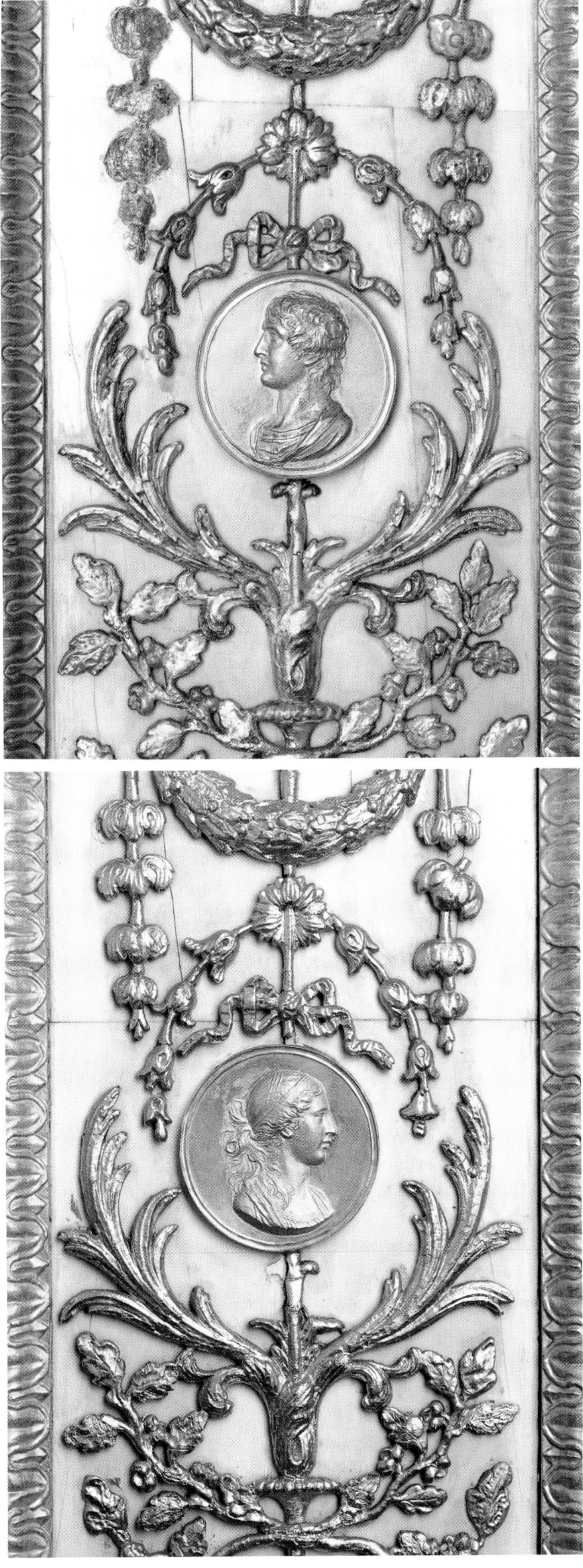

made or supplied gilt brass ornaments in the 1760s were William Bent, who supplied the door furniture for the library doors at Nostell Priory in 1767,[54] and Thomas Harrache, a jeweller and dealer in toys, china and ornaments, who had a shop in Pall Mall where Boulton bought some vases in 1768[55] and who appears to have visited Soho in June 1769.[56] Harrache stocked ormolu ornaments such as vases, perfume burners, candlesticks and watch stands among his wares[57] and in 1771 he supplied Paul Methuen of Corsham with a 'pair of statuary marble vauses mounted in or moulu' at a cost of £18 18s. 0d.[58] Harrache probably retailed some of Boulton's products, but there is no evidence.

Boulton visited London frequently. He was very interested, as his diaries and notebooks show, in the designs and the techniques of rival metal-

13. Griffin candlesticks, possibly by Diederich Nicolaus Anderson, *c.*1760–5, Blenheim Palace.

14. Griffin candlestick, detail of medallion of Diana, Blenheim Palace.

workers, which he often appropriated to his own use. He knew very well that many other workshops were making mounts and complete objects in 'or moulu' before he set his own craftsmen on to it. What then was the justification, if any, for his claim that he had been the first to introduce the manufacture of ormolu ornaments into England?

Strictly speaking, as I have shown, there was no justification at all. The techniques of casting, chasing and gilding were well established long before Boulton started production. But there were differences between Boulton's ambitions and achievements and those of other workshops that entitled him to make some such boast. First, he was the first English manufacturer to venture into the speculative production of ormolu ornaments on a large scale. The making of models was expensive. So were the materials. Blue john, the veined spar from Derbyshire that he used a great deal for vases, was both costly and fragile, and the gilding process was tricky and liable to expensive errors. It was a financial risk for the partnership to carry so much stock in the early 1770s, and Boulton and Fothergill were the first to offer such a rich choice of ornaments. Second, Boulton was the first important manufacturer to plan a conscious attack on the French metalworkers' domination of the market. It was probably Boulton's eagerness to compete with the French that led him to use the description 'or moulu' for his gilt mounts. Ormolu ornament in itself was nothing new, but the term does not appear to have been generally used by other English manufacturers or retailers before the 1770s. Third, Boulton was one of the first manufacturers to seize on the commercial opportunities created by the craze for the 'antique taste', and especially for ornamental vases, which flourished in the 1760s.

The use of ornamental vases as a form of decoration had been fashionable in aristocratic English houses for a long time.[59] Until early in the eighteenth century they were ranged on the tops of cabinets and were placed on the stretchers beneath cabinets and pier tables. They nestled in profusion on chimneypieces, so that the potters made a practice from early in the century of producing sets of five or seven vases designed as '*garnitures de cheminée*'. They remained popular throughout the classical revival of the 1730s and during the rococo period, when chimneypieces, mirrors and side tables were often made with perches for vases skilfully incorporated into their extravagant designs. But a veritable mania for vases developed in the 1760s. This coincided in England with the craze for the 'antique taste', which was being encouraged in various forms by architects such as James Stuart, William Chambers, and the brothers Robert and James Adam. Books illustrating classical vases sold readily, culminating in d'Hancarville's splendid coloured prints of the Etruscan, Greek and Roman vases in the collection of William Hamilton, the English envoy at Naples. The first volume of these appeared in 1766–7, the second in 1770. They had a discernible influence on the designers and manufacturers of the day and must have done a lot to encourage the fashionable world in its pursuit of vases based on classical models and motifs. Commercially minded manufacturers such as Boulton, Wedgwood and William Duesbury could scarcely neglect the opportunities created by the craze for such vases. Wedgwood said in 1769 that 'an epidemical madness reigns for vases, which must be gratified'.[60] Later in the same year he was told by an eyewitness that at their showroom in Newport Street in London 'vases ... vases was all the cry':[61] and in 1770 he said that 'vase madness' was like a disorder which should be 'cherished in some way or other'.[62]

15. Sèvres, green ewer, probably 1767, National Trust, Waddesdon Manor.

Boulton's way of cherishing it was to imitate what the French metalworkers had been doing for some time, namely the mounting of vases with ormolu, which in England was something new. In France the opulent taste of the period of Louis XV had brought with it a fashion for decorating vases with rococo pedestals and rims: the fashion persisted when classical designs began to come into favour in the 1760s. A Chinese vase, however beautiful in itself, must have seemed too restrained to a French patron who was accustomed to furniture lavishly decorated with gilt bronze mounts and borders. Thus vases, which to modern eyes might have been better if left untouched, were dressed in gilt finery that was sometimes so elaborate that the eye scarcely saw the vase at all. Not every mount maker, however, offended against the canons of taste. Many vases were heightened both in stature and in elegance, and some were transformed from mediocrity by the addition of ormolu mounts. Wedgwood had seen 'two or three old China bowles, for want of better things, stuck rim to rim, which have had no bad effect, but look whimsical and droll enough'.[63] The Royal porcelain factory at Sèvres was producing vases specifically for mounting in the late 1760s, the first recorded sale of vases for this purpose being in July 1767 when two plain green '*vases à monter*' were sold to a dealer.[64] These were probably the two ewers that are now at Waddesdon Manor (Plate 15), the vases for which were based on a simple Chinese shape and were possibly intended to pass as genuine Chinese porcelain.[65]

Apart from being used as ornaments, vases were often turned into objects of utility. A dull vase, or a fine one, became an elegant ewer. By inserting a pierced metal rim beneath the lid, or by fashioning a new pierced metal lid, the metalworker turned the vase into a pot-pourri jar[66] or a perfume burner. Perfume burners, which were often called cassolettes or essence pots, were popular in France, where they seem to have been known from early in the sixteenth century,[67] and many were imported into England in the eighteenth century. Although the habit of burning perfumes in cassolettes was known in England from an early date, they were probably not used as much as might be supposed from the number that have survived. Creating fragrant aromas must have been very acceptable in an age when few people bothered about taking baths and sanitary standards were low. There is however remarkably little literary or pictorial evidence for the custom in the eighteenth century. Many perfume burners were probably bought simply as ornaments, owing their popularity to the craze for all things classical and to a vague idea that the Romans spent a lot of time burning incense. They were a fancy of the fashionable world. This does not mean that they were not used at all. Mrs Montagu, for example, when she had lent one of her silver perfume burners to Boulton so that he could study it and perhaps even copy it,[68] asked for its return, 'for my friends reproach me that I do not regale their noses with fine odours after entertaining their plates with soup and ragouts. The cassolettes used to make their entry with the dessert and chase away the smell of dinner.'[69]

Vases were also converted, more usefully, into candelabra and time-pieces. The combination of ornament and utility was calculated to appeal and caught on well in France: there are examples of vases from the Sèvres factory with ormolu mounts and branches dating from the 1760s.[70] Boulton seized on the idea and produced candle vases of many designs, some to hold a single candle and others with ormolu branches for two, four or six candles, and clock cases of several patterns, some of which were fitted with horizontal watch movements in imitation of the French. Many of these vase candelabra and timepieces could serve also as perfume burners, as will be seen from the descriptions and illustrations later in this book. But although the candle vases, perfume burners and vase timepieces produced by Boulton and Fothergill and by their French rivals had their uses, their designs were emphatically biased towards ornament. Boulton's letters and advertisements dwelt on the ornamental aspects of his vases as their chief attraction. His small candle vases were made so that the candle holder could be inverted when not in use and the vases could revert to being ornaments.

So it was Boulton's production of vases, on a large scale and in competition with the French that justified his boast that he had been the first to introduce the manufacture of ormolu ornaments into England. Vases were by far the most numerous of his products, whether they were made purely for ornament or for burning perfume, holding candles or housing watch movements. His other ormolu products, such as candlesticks, ice pails, girandoles, knife urns, tripods and the more elaborate clock cases, which were also made with a keen competitive eye on his French rivals, were not made in anything like the same numbers.

It has been commonly supposed that Boulton and Fothergill began producing ormolu ornaments in 1762:[71] but production does not seem to have started at Soho until 1768. Previous authors seem to have been misled by a conviction that Boulton was the only manufacturer in England capable of producing ormolu of any quality[72] and have fixed on 1762 for no better reason than that it was the date of his partnership with Fothergill. But in its early years the partnership concentrated on the button and hardware trades.

There is no hint in the surviving archives of any interest in vases before 1767 and no mention of any plan actually to produce ormolu-mounted vases before 1768.[73] It might be argued that because the firm's records in the 1760s are incomplete the production of ormolu might well have begun in the early years of the decade. But the evidence is against this. Most of the factory's products are mentioned at one time or another in the surviving documents. Ormolu ornaments were a significant addition to the range because they were something of a new departure. Their appeal was entirely to the fashionable world. They were luxuries, and expensive to make. It would be very odd if production had started and yet been totally ignored by Boulton when he was making notes in his diaries and notebooks or writing letters to his partners, agents and patrons. There is, for example, no mention of ormolu or vases in the long and detailed series of letters between Boulton and J. H. Ebbinghaus[74] and no hint of either in Boulton's notebook of 1765, in which he jotted down a list of metal wares which he wanted to make[75] and another list of wares which he thought he might take with him to Paris.[76] Had there been any plan to produce ornamental ormolu at the time he would surely have mentioned it.

Just as significant is Boulton's statement in October 1771 that 'between two and three years ago, at the request of some of our nobility, we began to manufacture a great variety of ornamental furniture in metals and other material capable of receiving decorations from sculpture and form and from that art of gilding called or moulu'.[77] This rather pompous description of the firm's vases and clock cases makes it clear that production began in about 1768–9. James Watt stated that ormolu was among the factory's products when he first went there in 1767,[78] but he was writing in 1809 and was probably referring to what he saw during his visits a year or two later.

The evidence suggests that the Soho workshops had some experience of making – or at least knew where to buy – minor pieces of gilt brass hardware as early as 1765. During his visit to Birmingham in April 1765 the Earl of Shelburne gave Boulton a letter of introduction to Robert Adam, which requested the architect 'to bespeak for him of Mr Boulton some girandoles for holding two and three candles at Bowood, or branches for the same purpose, or tripods'.[79] None of these objects survives at Bowood. There is no evidence that Boulton even delivered the note. Nor is there anything in it to suggest that the objects were to be gilt. The door knobs and escutcheons which Boulton and Fothergill made in 1765–6 for the dining room at Kedleston Hall were gilt (Plate 193). They are the only surviving examples of gilt brasswork dating from before 1768 which can be attributed beyond doubt to the firm. But while these shreds of evidence suggest that in 1765–6 the firm could supply pieces of brassfoundry to order, they do not prove either that brassfoundry, such as door furniture, furniture mounts and sconces, were a regular part of the firm's stock or that the firm could do its own gilding. Indeed there are references which suggest the opposite in both cases. Boulton made a note in 1765 that the firm ought to buy 'Tovy's brass foundry',[80] which suggests that it did not make much of its own. And in the same notebook he recorded that the firm should make gilt buttons,[81] which suggests that it did not already do so. Boulton was trying at the time to learn about gilding processes and especially about what his partner called the 'fine gold colour' that the French applied to their gilt work.[82] There is no proof that his workshops were capable of gilding ornamental metalwork at this time and it is possible that the firm subcontracted the gilding to other metalworkers such as Thomas Blockley. It is, however, equally possible that there were craftsmen at Soho in the mid-1760s who knew how to gild. Boulton's enquiries into the gilding processes may have been an attempt to improve his craftsmen's techniques rather than to discover a new one. And certainly the techniques of gilding were practised at Soho by 1767, when the firm began to manufacture gilt snuff boxes, instrument cases, toothpicks and watch chains.[83]

It was probably in 1767 that Boulton's interest in vases began to crystallise. During the summer an agent in Italy subscribed on his behalf for the four volumes of d'Hancarville's coloured prints of William Hamilton's collection of vases.[84] Boulton was very pleased with this purchase, immediately recognising how useful the prints would be as a source of classical designs[85] (see Chapter 3, p. 89). He may have had in mind the application of the various classical motifs to work, such as silver plate and snuff boxes, but there is little doubt that the idea of producing vases had by then occurred to him. He was well aware of the craze for vases, which his friend Wedgwood and several other manufacturers were busily encouraging. He told Wedgwood, who sent him some of his vases in 1767, how much he and his wife admired Wedgwood's vases.[86] He had probably seen examples of the work of the French metalworkers, whom he considered rivalled 'all the world in elegance and cheapness',[87] during his visit to Paris in 1765, and he must have seen some of their finest work in the houses of his patrons during the next few years. After the end of the Seven Years' War in 1763 the English aristocracy again began to purchase French furniture in some quantity,[88] and during the second half of the decade an increasing number of objects, including ormolu-mounted vases and other ormolu ornaments, flowed into England. Harrache was probably only one of many merchants and retailers who imported ornaments from Paris,[89] and Boulton was incensed that the French metalworkers could buy cheap vases in London, ornament them, and sell them again even in London. According to Wedgwood, Boulton told him early in 1768 that he would be surprised to learn the extent of the trade that had

> lately been made out of vases at Paris. The artists have even come over to London, picked up all the old whimsical ugly things they could meet with, carried them to Paris, where they have mounted and ornamented them with metal, and sold them to the virtuosi of every nation, and particularly to Millords d'Anglise, for the greatest raritys.[90]

By the end of 1767 he had decided that the mounting of vases was a practical proposition. He began looking round both for vases and for materials which could be used for vase bodies. He seems to have taken a close personal interest in the development of the vase trade from the beginning. He sent an order to Wedgwood for 'some bodys of vases for mounting'. He was not after anything ambitious. Wedgwood, who both admired Boulton and, as a competitor, grudged his success, thought that he must either comply with the order or 'affront him, and set him a-trying to get them elsewhere, and they are so simple, the drawings he has sent me, that he may get them done'.[91] He would not have forgotten that in the summer of 1767 Boulton had half-jestingly remarked that he so much admired Wedgwood's vases that he almost wished to be a potter himself.[92] By 1768 Boulton was buying pieces of marble and fashioned stone ornaments, including vases, candlesticks and obelisks, from the quarries in Derbyshire where there was already a flourishing trade in cut and polished marble and spar ornaments. He probably bought some of these ornaments with the intention of re-selling them through the firm's warehouse in Birmingham[93] but there seems little doubt that he was also collecting materials that he could mount, and shapes and designs which he could copy. The same is probably true of the purchases that he made during his journey to London in October 1768. 'Mr Boulton is picking up vases', wrote Wedgwood, who went with him to Harrache's shop, 'and [is] going to make them in bronze'.[94]

There is no evidence that vases were produced at Soho in any quantity in 1768. Neither Zinzendorf, recording his visit in September 1768, nor Boulton, compiling a list of products in his notebook a month later, mentions ormolu ornaments. They cannot have yet been an established line. But at least two new chasers were taken on in the autumn of 1768,[95] which suggests that the work on decorative metalwork was increasing, and by the late autumn Boulton was suggesting a joint venture with Wedgwood. He had hinted at this earlier in the year[96] but it had now become a firm proposition. As usual it brought out Wedgwood's fear of his friend's competitive zeal and he wrote to Bentley:

Mr Boulton proposes an alliance betwixt the pottery and metal branches, viz. that we shall make such things as will be suitable for mounting, and not have a pott look, and he will finish them with the mounts. What do you think of it? Perhaps you would rather he would let them alone. Very true, but he will be doing, so that the question is whether we shall refuse having anything to do with him, and thereby affront him and set him of doing them himself, or employing his friend Garbett.[97]

Whatever Wedgwood and Bentley decided, they received some orders from Boulton before the end of the year. Boulton wrote to Wedgwood:

Please to send me one, two or three dozen pair of the vessell part of some good formed vases for the small candlestick I have done a little since my return towards making proper patterns to cast from as those I bought would not do for that purpose. I have also just received a French vase from London with an order for a few pairs. The vessel part of it is made of china quite plain and is all green exactly of the colour of the blood stone, I mean the green blood stone that hath a few red specks in it. The form I know you will say is hugly [sic] but nevertheless when mounted it is a handsome vase. However be that as it will I must adhere to my order. Therefore pray tell me per return if you can and will make the china part. I suppose if the body of the china is not so perfect, yet if the surface is as good a coulor [sic] and has as good face, it will do, but yet 'tis much better for the mounting if the vase is made of a strong material not easy to be broke by fixing on the metal parts. I would have some of the little ones to be of the black Etruscan clay, some green, some blew or any other simple coulor you think proper.[98]

Another order for china vases followed a month later when Boulton made it clear that he was producing mounts in quantity from standard patterns.[99] By the beginning of 1769 he was planning to apply some of the principles of mass production to the manufacture of vases, although he realised that it would be some time before he could make them in any quantity. He was pleased with the quality of his mounts, reckoning, somewhat optimistically, that it already exceeded that achieved by his French rivals,[100] and he considered the mounting of vases to be 'a large field for fancy'.[101] He was particularly taken by the idea of converting 'a very ugly vessell into a beautiful vase',[102] anticipating no doubt a fat profit from the transformation.

It seems that Boulton and Fothergill produced very few mounted vases with china bodies. Boulton's ideas of co-operating regularly with Wedgwood came under some strain in 1769. Wedgwood reckoned – indeed he was told – that Boulton and Fothergill were affronted because he had not complied with their orders for vases. His informant even reported that the partners had been offered vases by several other potters but that they were in fact set on producing black earthenware vases themselves and were building works for the purpose. They had also hinted at an association with James Cox[103] who had just bought the Chelsea porcelain factory.[104] Wedgwood was patently worried about the possible competition from Boulton but he admired Boulton's spirit and was determined to fight hard. He wrote to his partner:

If we must fall, if Etruria cannot stand its ground, but must give way to Soho, and fall before her, let us not sell the victorie too cheap, but maintain our ground like men, and endeavour even in our defeat to share the laurels with our conquerors. It doubles my courage to have the first manufacturer in England to encounter with.[105]

A few days later he commented:

I have no fear at all even from the combination of Chelsea and Soho. If that should ever happen we have got and shall keep the lead so long as our lives and healths are continued to us. I am persuaded they are thoroughly in earnest at Soho.[106]

Wedgwood need not have whistled for courage. Although they were mounting vases with china bodies in 1769, there is no evidence that Boulton and Fothergill seriously intended to produce their own china or earthenware vases or to buy vases from the Chelsea factory. Whatever they threatened in the autumn of 1769 they seem to have decided at an early stage to concentrate on materials other than china for their vase bodies. They had probably discovered that it was rather difficult to fit mounts to china vases satisfactorily. They were not trying merely to ornament the vases, but to turn them into candle vases and perfume burners. This meant that the china had to bear the weight of candle branches or to be pierced so that handles or decorative swags could be pinned in position. China was fragile and not suited to these uses. It was also expensive to buy from manufacturers such as Wedgwood, who was not a producer of 'old whimsical ugly things'. Boulton was still proposing co-operation with Wedgwood in 1770, but it led to no more than occasional orders for china bodies and requests for models.[107] Later, Boulton sold Wedgwood's cameos and intaglios and probably copied some of them (see Chapter 3, pp. 103 ff.) He also received clay-casting models from him for silverware.[108] The friendship between the two men was important to both of them. They inspired each other in design, manufacturing and marketing both in England and overseas, and worked together on broader business matters such as canals and tariffs. But there was no deep co-operation between their two manufacturing businesses of the sort suggested by their early correspondence. Clay and ormolu did not meet the fashionable success that they had achieved in France. China vases did not become part of Boulton and Fothergill's regular production.

The materials that most attracted Boulton were the fluorspars and marbles of Derbyshire, and especially the fluorspar known as blue john. This colourful and decorative stone was mined near Castleton in Derbyshire.[109] It was probably known from outcrops as early as 1700 and the local lapidaries probably began to make ornaments from it, such as obelisks and vases, when mining started in about 1760.[110] Boulton may have seen vases or ornaments made out of this stone in the houses of local patrons or in shops or workshops. It is even possible, if there is any truth in the theory that French metalworkers used the stone before Boulton, that he had seen examples of their work: but no evidence has yet come to light to suggest that the French metalworkers imported blue john in the 1760s or that Boulton knew about such a trade.[111]

Whatever the source of Boulton's idea, he had arrived at it by the end of 1768. He had come to the view that stone was a far more appropriate material than china for vase bodies. In December he wrote to his friend John Whitehurst, who was well known for his interest in local geology:

The principle intention of this letter is to tell you that I have found a use for Blew John which will consume some quantity of it. I mean that sort which is proper for turning into vases. I therefore should esteem it a singular favour if you would enquire wether the mine of it has lately been let or when it is to be let again, for I wish to take for a year and if you find that it is not possible to come at it then please to learn how I can come at any of the best and largest sort of the produce of it. But above all I beg you will be quite secret as to my intentions, and never let M. Boulton and John Blue be named in the same sentence ...[112]

Boulton does not appear to have acquired a lease of the blue john mines, although he later boasted to a gullible shopkeeper in Bath that he had an exclusive right to their production.[113] He went to Derbyshire in the spring of 1769 and made contact with the lessees of the mines and the mineral agents. He noted the names of several suppliers in his diary and recorded a few of the places where various stones were mined. He bought some blue john and some vase bodies from the 'widow Hall'[114] (and paid her too much) and paid small sums of money to Robert Howe[115] and Robert Bradbury[116] both of Castleton. He also bought some 'tyger stone' from John Noel, a stonemason at Bradwall.[117] But his biggest purchase was more than fourteen tons of blue john which he bought from John Platt.[118] This was a great quantity of stone. There is no other order for materials suitable for vase bodies of anything like this size in the surviving archives. It was followed, furthermore, by the purchase of two casks nine months later from Robert Howe, who promised to do his best to purchase any 'very large, very good, or very beautifull' pieces which might be found.[119] Boulton obviously meant business.

Although blue john loomed large in Boulton's plans in 1769, it was only one of several materials that he considered suitable for vases. He made a list of suitable vase bodies in the same year:

Gilt metal	China
Plated ditto[120]	Etruscan ware[121]
Laquered ditto	Japaned and varnished
Boyled or sauced ditto[122]	Glass blew and other colours
Aleblaster white and vained	Enameled
Blew john	Black Darbyshire marble
Marble[123]	

Some of these materials were never used in any quantity, and some, for example plated metal, lacquered, boiled and 'sauced' metal, japan and black marble, were probably considered for use on their own without ormolu mounts. As for the others, I have already shown how Boulton was actively interested in the Derbyshire stones other than blue john in 1768, and how in the early stages of production he considered china. Coloured glass was used occasionally and gilt or enamelled copper frequently (Plates 249, 334 etc.), because the copper rolling was carried out at Soho.

At the same time as planning the most likely materials from which to fashion vases and thinking about the forms in which the vases should be made, for example standing on steps, plinths, pedestals or tripod feet,[124] Boulton was still actively learning about the gilding processes, and especially about the methods of imparting colour to gilt work. He wanted to learn about gilding for his trade in buttons, snuff boxes and other toys, but there is little doubt that in 1768–9 his researches into gilding were directed also, and perhaps primarily, towards the production of mounts which could rival the best work of the French. He thought of visiting Dominique Jean, Keisel and Magniac in London in order to pick their brains, and he tried his hand at some industrial espionage in Paris through his agent there, Solomon Hyman. He asked Hyman to obtain some recipes for him even if they cost 'a few guineas'.[125]

It was an active programme. Boulton's enthusiasm for his vases was growing. He was beginning to broadcast his new line, and to claim that it was already worthy of the attention of the most sophisticated patrons. 'I am now busy', he wrote to Hyman with characteristic self-confidence, 'in makeing such sorts of vases as I am sure you will be able to find a sale for at Paris, they being such as cannot be made there'.[126] Few specific orders are recorded in the archives in 1769 or 1770 but the number of designs was increasing. The few recorded orders include gilt vases 'with heads', large green vases,[127] vases 'Kentish pattern with a gilt body',[128] goat's head vases with blue (china or enamelled), green[129] and blue john bodies,[130] candlestick urns, an essence pot,[131] Cleopatra vases,[132] green and blue china essence pots,[133] 'Wedgwood' vases,[134] lacquered and japanned vases,[135] and other vases described more briefly or only by order numbers. Only the Cleopatra and goat's head vases can be matched with known patterns (Plates 327–9, 331–4): the others are not described in sufficient detail. But these scattered references show that, besides extending the number of designs, Boulton was using a variety of materials for his vase bodies. Bodies of stone, glass, gilt metal, china, lacquer and japan are all mentioned. He was also considering what other objects besides vases might be fashioned in ormolu. In the autumn of 1769 he discussed the idea of making a dessert service in metal with the Member of Parliament Thomas Pownall[136] who, after enquiring 'amongst those who have nothing to do but to copy or invent new modes of luxury and magnificence and who have lived amongst the French, who understand these things best of any nation', advised against the plan. 'But', continued Pownall, 'it was agreed that very elegant vases etc. might be made for ice potts', and he recommended two further products as particularly suitable – 'clock-cases, of which there are a thousand fancies, for chimney-pieces etc., and just now these fancied clock-cases of the ormullie, inlaied and enamelled etc. are all the mode-Francaise which they sett on tables, bracketts, toiletts, chimneypieces' and 'inkstands for ladies' toiletts and escritoires in every mode of elegance and fancy of the same work', which were also 'much in vogue'. [137]

Whether or not this letter gave Boulton the idea of making clock cases and ice pails in ormolu is not clear, but it is the first occasion in the surviving manuscripts in which they are mentioned. Clocks entered the repertoire in 1770, when Boulton received an order from the King, although none were offered for sale publicly until 1771. The first reference to an order for ice pails does not occur in the archives until 1772. There are no references to orders for ink stands.

In 1769–70 Boulton was beginning to have some success with aristocratic patrons, a class of customer that he correctly considered vital if the vase business was to flourish. Vases were ordered for or supplied to Sir William Guise, Sir Harbord Harbord, Lord Willoughby de Broke, Lord Scarsdale, Thomas Anson, the Earl of Shelburne, Henry Hoare, the Marquess of Rockingham,[138] and probably many others whose commissions are not recorded. James Stuart ordered a tea kitchen for Mrs Montagu which was to have a body made of Etruscan ware by Wedgwood,[139] and in March 1770 the Dowager Princess of Wales, who had asked Boulton to show her his 'things',[140] ordered two pairs of candle vases. 'One of them', wrote Boulton to his partner,

> must be natural blew john and the other of transparent honeycomb stones with red, and silvered within side. If I had also pairs of goats head with blew john and some with the leopard or tyger stone[141] or a Cleopatra she would probably take a pair of each.[142]

In the same month Boulton achieved the summit of his ambition when he visited the Royal Family and received an order for several vases from the Queen.[143] 'Some of 'em,' said Boulton, should be 'about as large as the 4-branched vase and the smallest not larger that Kentish's vase or about the size of Wedgwood's in Eginton's shop: the largest of all may be feneered with blew john and like the new tea kitchen'.[144] The vases included the King's vases (Plates 339–40) and almost certainly the sphinx vases of Plate 355. The patronage of the Royal Family gave great support to Boulton's marketing plans and he used the connection to good effect.

Encouraged thus by the patronage of the fashionable world, the partners built up the production of ormolu, or at any rate of vases, at Soho. Dorothy Richardson reported seeing, during her visit to Soho in May 1770, 'the greatest variety' of blue john (she used the vulgar term 'congealed water' to describe the blue john) vases 'embelished with gilt, and silvered, ornaments, many of the tops take off and form candlesticks'. She also saw a tea kitchen which from her description sounds like the tea urns of Plates 229 and 231, blue john obelisks and candlesticks, and a tripod perfume burner which was probably of the type illustrated in Plate 25 (see Chapter 1, p. 25). Fothergill was reported to have said in 1769 that 'the vase trade would be inexhaustable, it would be impossible to supply the demand for good things in that way',[145] and in 1770 Boulton reckoned that they would need twenty more good chasers to cope with the demand that they expected.[146]

To encourage the demand an exhibition and sale of vases was held at James Christie's saleroom in Pall Mall in April 1770. No catalogue for this sale has yet been found and there are very few references to it in the archives.[147] The advertisements for it, however, list 'vause candlesticks, branches, arms, tea and other vauses, perfume and essence pots', all 'of exquisite workmanship, and finished in the antique taste'.[148] The sale seems to have achieved its purpose. Like similar exhibitions mounted in London by Wedgwood and others it attracted the attention of the nobility and gentry, who were fortunately still ailing from 'vase madness'. Horace Walpole reported that a 'tea-kettle' sold for an extravagant price (see Chapter 5, p. 168). The sale illustrates Boulton's aim of selling ornaments direct to his customers rather than relying on merchants and retailers. It also indicates that vases were now being made at Soho in some quantity. Lord Shelburne thought that the production of ormolu at Soho was progressing so well that he made a point of mentioning it to James Adam and said that it 'only wanted a variety of elegant designs to make it one of the most magnificent manufactures in Europe'.[149] For a while, as a result of Lord Shelburne's suggestion, the Adam brothers and Boulton flirted with the idea of a joint venture, but nothing came of the negotiations. The Adams took the plan seriously, recognising that Boulton had become an important manufacturer of ormolu ornaments and that he, if any one, was the one manufacturer in England capable of producing the 'useful and ornamental' metal furniture for which they foresaw a large market. The suggestion must have pleased and interested Boulton. The recognition of the most fashionable architects was a tribute to his achievement, and since (whatever he said to his patrons) he was still dissatisfied with the limited range of his designs, the prospect of co-operation with such leaders of fashion promised well.

Besides being dissatisfied with his designs, in 1770 Boulton was unhappy about the quality of the workmanship. He wrote to his partner from London complaining that the gilt work was tarnishing for want of better drying after burnishing,[150] and at the beginning of March he wrote again that he had

> one very serious remark to make which if not attended to there will soon be an end of the sale of all vases both great and small and that is, our vases are so nastily turned out of hand, they are so carelessly got up in every particular, that I fear I shall have great difficulty to sell those I have here,[151] and great difficulty to retrieve my character as to clean good work. For all of them are now tarnished and spotted to such a degree as to render them unsaleable – I have sent a pair for you to see – whereas if our manager was a man of care, industry and judgment, the work might be turned out of hand 50 per cent better without more expence, but I am fearfull I shall never be able to succeed with Bentley's management. His mind is not right

turned for business, nor any man whose affairs are lying in such confusion as I too often find his warehouse, whilst he is reading newspapers and magazines, or perhaps writeing out a love song, and yet I perceive his opinion of his own abilitys is different from mine, I'll venter a wager if you examine his bed chamber you'l find a looking glass, I wish he had one that would not deceive him. The business in his department is now becoming an object of too much consequence to be trifled with and if he don't remeady these complaints and pay more attention and take more delight in that which he is to get his living by and I may loose a living by I say if he don't remeady these complaints I must.[152]

Such attention to the details of production and the quality of his products was typical of Boulton. He could not hope to fulfil his boast of competing effectively with the French makers of decorative ormolu unless he could offer his aristocratic patrons objects that approached the quality of French chasing and gilding. New designs, even if they appealed to the more sober English taste, were not enough.

In his desire to produce the best at this time Boulton paid little regard to costs. It seems that he was keener to establish a name for excellence. It must have been an exciting prospect to become known for producing artistic ornaments of superior quality when his accustomed trade had consisted largely of practical hardware, to provide objects that decorate famous men's saloons and dining rooms rather than merely fasten their shoes, uniforms and waistcoats. It is easy to see how the encouragement of Lord Shelburne and James Adam might have gone to his head. And so he rushed headlong in 1769–70 into improving the production of ormolu ornaments, pricing his vases by rule of thumb and reckoning that somehow some of the money received from sales would be profit.

It is not easy to give an adequate account of the types of vase from which a purchaser could choose in 1769–70. One difficulty is that patterns were continued for some years without much alteration. Another is that not enough manuscripts survive from before 1771. I have attempted later in this book, however, during my survey of the various ormolu ornaments produced at Soho, to give an idea of the approximate dates when certain types of vase were first made. It is clear from the archives that goat's head and Cleopatra vases were among the earlier products (Plates 327–9, 331–4). Both answer well to the description 'vause candlesticks'. Other early products include lion-faced candlesticks (Plate 135), vases of the types illustrated in Plates 241, 244, 247 and 248 and the tea urns of Plates 229–31. The mounts on some (but not all) of these earlier vases are relatively poorly modelled, chased and gilded, suggesting that there was some substance in Boulton's criticisms of Bentley.

Boulton's agitation in 1770 led to the solution of the two chief impediments to progress, as he saw them. By the end of the year the number of vase designs had increased, some of them devised by the simple expedient of arranging the same components in different combinations. And the quality of the chasing and gilding was improved. He was able to plan another exhibition and sale of ormolu ornaments at James Christie's saleroom in London in the spring of 1771 with some confidence. He told the Earl of Warwick that he hoped to show 'specimens of many new things in our or moulu'[153] and convinced Wedgwood that he would have 'a superb shew of vases for the spring'.[154] He wrote to his noble patrons that 'the variety and taste of the models, the neatness of the workmanship, the richness and durability of the guilding, exceeds my first essay very much',[155] a claim repeated and expanded in the preface to the catalogue:

Induced by the encouragement with which we were favoured last year from the nobility and gentry, we have extended and improved the manufacture of bronze ornamental furniture in the antique taste, finished in or moulu, and we now offer

to sale another assortment of these articles, which we hope will be thought not unworthy of further encouragement.
We have availed ourselves of the remarks and criticisms which were made upon our last year's productions. The color of the gilding is considerably improved since that time. It is now intermediate betwixt the color of the French gilding, which was observed to be too near that of brass, and the color of our own former gilding, which was very justly censured for being too red; the gilding of the present assortment is at least equal to any that we have ever seen of the manufacture of any other country, either in richness of appearance, or in durability.
The articles now exhibited, will be found greatly to exceed those of the last year, in design, sculpture, and execution in general.
With much pleasure and sincere gratitude, we acknowledge the patronage of certain personages of the highest rank, and the zeal shewn by them and by many of the nobility and gentry to promote the establishment of this new branch of our manufacture, by giving us access to every thing curious in their possession that hath a tendency to improve or correct our taste.
We hope by a continuance of the same liberal encouragement, and of the assistance of persons of taste, that we may be enabled to make further advances in elegance, correctness and execution: and to establish and extend this new manufactory, by which not only large sums may be prevented from being sent abroad for the purchase of a foreign commodity, but also a considerable branch of commerce may (as we have great occasion to believe from our last year's exports) be established.[156]

The sale, which was held at Christie's saleroom on 11th–13th April, was, like the sale in 1770, a reflection of Boulton's policy of selling ormolu direct to his customers rather than relying on merchants and retailers. Preparations were thorough. Boulton advertised the sale widely, arranging for announcements in the London newspapers and writing flattering letters to the nobility and gentry inviting them to a private view.[157] The advertisements for the sale repeat much of the wording of the title page of the catalogue, mentioning 'clock cases, candle branches, perfume and essence pots, and many other ornaments, replete with elegance and true taste, and most elaborately furnished'.[158] As in 1770 the advertisement talked of the produce of 'Mr Boulton's Or Moulu Manufactory at Soho in Staffordshire', omitting his partner's name and demonstrating his dominant handling of the ormolu business.*

The exhibition was a display of which Boulton could justly be proud. It contained 265 lots, but many of these were pairs of vases and the total number of objects in the sale was nearly four hundred.[159] Of these only eight (four lots) – a pair of blue john obelisks, two blue john vases and four silver candlesticks – were not ormolu. It was a massive display. It is not surprising that the workshops in which the ormolu ornaments were made at Soho had little time for anything else in the early months of the year[160] or that certain customers' orders could not be completed until the sale was over.[161] Sir John Griffin Griffin, who had complained at the delay in the delivery of his order, was told that the delay was deliberate so that he could have an 'opportunity of chusing from among our collection such as might perhaps please better than those you ordered': his vases, which were completed, were on the way to London with the other goods for the sale.[162] It sounds as if the firm was deliberately delaying the delivery of completed commissions in order to swell the show.

Most of the ornaments in the sale were vases. There were more candle vases than perfume burners but many of the candle vases combined both functions. The perfume burners ranged from the simple 'essence pot lined with silver' with a blue john, enamel or china body, of which there were forty-one in the sale,[163] to the highly finished and ornamented griffin and sphinx blue john vases which are described and illustrated later (see Survey of ornaments, Plates 336, 356). The reserve prices for these three vases were £3 10s. 0d., £10 10s. 0d., and £12 12s. 0d.[164] The two most numerous candle vases were described respectively as 'candle vases radix amethysti [i.e. blue john] and or moulu', of which there were forty-seven pairs,[165] and '[radix amethysti and or moulu] candle vases with laurel festoons', of which there were twenty-eight pairs.[166] The reserve price for most of the former was £4 4s. 0d.,[167] and of the latter £3 13s. 6d.[168] Several other types of candle vase at the cheaper end of the range were offered in some numbers. Among the more expensive vases were six two-branched blue john vases reserved at £10 10s. 0d.,[169] four three-branched vases, each on a 'richly embellished' altar, at £16 16s. 0d.,[170] three 'large marbled' vases at £21,[171] and twenty-four candle vases which were also lined and pierced for use as perfume burners. Among these were some of the vases that are described in detail later in the Survey of ornaments, including six vases with branches supported by caryatids reserved at prices from £25 to £31 10s. 0d. (Plate 317), two vases with branches supported by 'demy satyrs ... after a model that hath been executed for his majesty', reserved at £42 (Plate 339), and, grandest of all, 'a magnificent Persian candelabra for 7 lights' which was reserved at £200 and was the last lot in the sale (Plate 351). There were also five allegorical pieces representing Venus weeping at the tomb of Adonis, which consisted of a vase on a pedestal, two of them made as perfume burners (Plate 359) and three of them fitted with horizontal timepieces (Plate 191). The reserve prices were £15 15s. 0d. and £25. In addition to all these lots there were several vases which were not described specifically as either candle vases or perfume burners, but which might have been either, and a 'tea vase or moulu decorated with festoons of flowers and lined with silver'.[172]

Apart from vases there were two further allegorical clock cases, one representing a boy studying astronomy (reserve price £42, Plate 152) and the other Minerva unveiling a votive vase (Plate 166), which was reserved at £150, several table candlesticks, most of them made entirely of ormolu but one pair made of alabaster with ormolu ornaments,[173] four tripod perfume burners with candle branches 'after a design of Mr Stuart's', most of them reserved at £50 (Plate 233), six blue john sugar dishes reserved at £5 5s. 0d., a triton candlestick reserved at £15 15s. 0d. (Plate 139), and two 'most beautiful pieces' of blue john mounted in ormolu.[174] Two large vases 'with medalians and other ornaments' did not arrive in time (Plate 349).

The complete catalogue is reproduced in Appendix III. As this brief summary has shown, the sale was dominated by vases and the material most frequently used for the bodies of the vases was blue john. Other bodies were made of gilt or enamelled copper, china or marble. The vases comprised over thirty different designs. Some of them represented a substantial investment in models, materials and working time. Others were practically mass-produced. There were only five clock cases and three of them, the Venus clock cases, were of the same design. The other products – tripods, candlesticks, sugar basins, etc. – were also comparatively few in numbers.

Many of the vases in the sale in 1771 cannot be identified with vases that have survived because the descriptions in the catalogue are inadequate. But it is clear from those that can be identified that the firm's technical competence had advanced considerably. The exhibition thus succeeded in strengthening Boulton's reputation for quality among the fashionable classes, even if they did not all like his prices. One of the visitors, Mrs Delaney, commented:

> I have seen the fine show at Christie's and am much pleased with the neatness and elegance of the work, but it bears a price only for those who have superfluous money, though I had rather game there than at Almacks, and it would be more rational ...[175]

The exhibition and sale in 1771 was a considerable achievement, and Boulton was pleased with his progress. Encouraged by the reception, he planned a further sale a year later. The arrangements were similar but were conceived on a grander scale.[176] He asked Christie to make more rooms available than in the previous year[177] and confidently expected the exhibition to cause a considerable stir in fashionable circles. His confidence was inspired by further advances in technical proficiency and grandeur of design. In 1771 some private rooms had to be available at the exhibition for repairing and 'recommoding' the objects, but on this occasion Boulton reckoned that everything was perfect.[178] The preparation of the vases was more advanced than it had been in 1771,[179] in spite of some valuable but time-consuming orders that were being executed for the Earl of Kerry.[180] As in the previous two years the sale was advertised. The advertisement read:

> An elegant assortment of vases and candlesticks, with and without branches, girandoles, cassoletts, pots pourris, tripods, watch stands, obelisks, dressing boxes, clocks astronomical and geographical, also clock cases of various designs, with rich decorations. The whole furnished in or moulu, excepting some few pieces, which are antique bronz. NB Most of the designs are entirely different from those exhibited at the two former sales, and it is hoped will be found to be still nearer approaches to the models of Grecian antiquity, which have been the patterns for their formation.[181]

Because the catalogue of the sale in 1772 has not survived it is not possible to say how many new items were included. Despite the claim that most of the designs were entirely different from those in the 1770 and 1771 sales, it is clear from the correspondence that many of the old designs were continued. There were for example several goat's head vases, a sphinx vase, a Persian vase candelabrum,[182] and a griffin vase,[183] all of which had been offered for sale a year earlier. There were also some sugar dishes,[184] as in 1771, and a large number of the cheaper and less easily identified vases which formed the major part of the firm's production. But Boulton was looking forward particularly to the nobility's appreciation of the 'quite new and very elegant things' in which he had every confidence.[185] He was especially pleased with his two remarkable 'philosophical' clocks. One of these was an astronomical or sidereal clock (Plate 177), which gave a quantity of astronomical information in addition to the time and date, and the other, which Boulton named the geographical clock, was surmounted by a revolving terrestrial globe and showed the position of the sun at any date in the year (Plate 155). Both clocks were fitted in sumptuous allegorical cases, which fully reflected Boulton's eclectic methods of design. He had taken a keen personal interest in their design and manufacture and had kept in close touch with John Whitehurst, in whose workshop the two movements were made, throughout the months of creation. He had high hopes of achieving a success fully in accordance with the extravagance of their design and the cost of their manufacture. They were the centrepieces of the exhibition.

Other new designs included an allegorical clock case representing the emperor Titus (Plates 183, 185), which in the event was not ready in time for the exhibition, a clock case similar to the one made for the King in 1770–1 (Plate 160) and some wing-figured perfume burners and candle vases (Plates 362, 367). There were no ewers in the sale although these, too, were first produced at this time (Plate 196). These objects, which are all described later in the Survey of ornaments, show that by 1771–2 Boulton and Fothergill had considerably improved the quality of their chasing and gilding. The exhibition in April 1772 must have been a glittering sight, despite Wedgwood's comment that James Cox so far outshone Boulton that the latter would be 'under some little bit of an eclipse'.[186] Wedgwood was referring to Cox's exhibition at the Spring-Gardens, which achieved great publicity and notoriety.[187] The clockmaker Christopher Pinchbeck called Cox's show 'the most amazing mechanical exhibition' and added that 'there never was, or ever will be, anything equal to it for magnificence, ingenuity, and execution'.[188] Sheridan assumed that his fashionable theatre audience would be familiar with Cox's automata and would know what Sir Anthony Absolute was referring to when he said in *The Rivals* that 'her one eye shall roll like the bull's in Cox's Museum'.[189]

The arrangements for the sales in 1771 and 1772 dominate the surviving records of Boulton and Fothergill's business in those years. They were not, however, the only means of furthering the ormolu business. Other plans were being laid and other orders were regularly being taken and carried out. A warehouse in which the vases could be properly displayed for the convenience of visitors was opened at Soho, attempts were made to encourage an export business, and vases were supplied to retailers on sale or return in spite of Boulton's dislike of this method of sale. The firm received substantial orders from customers whose patronage must have delighted Boulton. Vases and dressing boxes were made for the Countess of Craven[190] and candle vases for the Duchess of Montagu.[191] A candle vase was delivered to Lord Grantham, who gave an order for a 'friend' for four 'Persian slave' candelabra at a cost of £500,[192] and Lord Kerry bought several things including a pair of five-branched marble vases, some wall lights, four tripod candelabra and ormolu ornaments for a chimneypiece. His invoice amounted to nearly £300.[193] Sir Lawrence Dundas bought a Persian candelabrum at a cost of £150 6s. 0d. (Plate 351)[194] and the Duke of Northumberland a tripod, probably the tripod tea urn illustrated in Plate 229, and an essence pot.[195] The Earl of Stamford bought a 'wing-figured' vase and two smaller vases when he visited Soho in January 1772,[196] and among many other patrons who bought vases were Sir John Griffin Griffin and Lord Mountstuart, the son of the Earl of Bute.[197] Such orders must have encouraged Boulton to think of his manufacture of ormolu as well established. He would have agreed with his clerk's letter to a prospective agent, if indeed he did not draft it himself, in which, after listing the firm's ormolu products – candle vases with two to six branches, girandoles, sugar basins, essence pots, clock cases, chimneypiece ornaments, all entirely gilt or of blue john mounted with ormolu – he claimed that the firm sold annually great quantities of ormolu to the nobility and tradesmen.[198] Maybe it was not quite true when it was written, maybe it inflated one or two individual orders to the level of regular stock, but its boasts were to some extent justified by the growing demand for the firm's vases among the nobility. No advertiser ever minded stretching a point for a promising cause.

The two sales in 1771 and 1772 were intended both to impress the firm's noble patrons and to bring in some cash. There is little doubt that they helped towards achieving the first objective. The nobility and gentry can scarcely have failed to notice the publicity that Boulton organised, even if he was outshone by Cox. If they did not receive the individual letters that Boulton sent to prospective patrons, they probably saw one of the advertisements in the newspapers. A visit to the saleroom was a fashionable excursion in the spring and Christie's rooms were a popular place to parade and to view. Wedgwood was afraid that the nobility and gentry would be dazzled by all the exhibitions in the spring of 1772, 'for what with the fine things in gold, silver and steel from Soho, the almost miraculous magnificence of Mr Coxes exhibition, and the glare of the Derby and other china shews' they would need some relaxation and repose.[199] But many came to Boulton's shows at Christie's in both years and several gave testimony of their approval by making purchases. In 1771 the purchasers included the Earl of Exeter, the Earls of Bessborough, Fitzwilliam and Kerry, Lords Arundell, Melbourne and Orwell, Lady Elliott, Lady Godolphin and Sir Watkin Williams Wynn. In 1772, purchases were made by the Prince of Wales, the Duke of Northumberland, the Duke of Manchester, the Earl of Sefton, Lady St John and the banker Robert Child. Thus Boulton and Fothergill's clients during these years included several of the political and social leaders of the day. Not all the nobility and gentry would have subscribed to Mrs Montagu's description of Soho as 'that great temple of *les beaux arts*',[200] but Soho's reputation had certainly risen high among them and the sales in London helped.

Financially they were a failure. A large number of lots in 1771 remained unsold and it seems that the sale brought in only about half of the amount which Boulton hoped for.[201] 'I hope it will not be known', he wrote to his manager John Scale, 'by J. T. Esquire [Boulton's rival, John Taylor] or any body else wither we have won or lost by our auction game'.[202] It would not do to admit failure. In May the firm duly, and untruthfully, stated to a shopkeeper that it had sold all its 'vases etc. in or moulu about 6 weeks ago' and was thus unable to send more than three vases, which was not 'such an assortment of them as we could wish'.[203]

The sale in 1772 appears to have been an even greater failure. It is impossible to say how much Boulton was hoping to raise because the catalogue has not survived. But the sale was planned on a grander scale than its predecessor and the proceeds of £834 15s. 4d. must have been very disappointing.[204] Several of the larger pieces remained unsold and the prices were well below what Boulton had hoped for. He was obliged, so he said, 'to knock down many things much under their value' owing to lack of support, in order to ensure the employment of 'the artists he hath been at so much expense in the training up'.[205]

Among the unsold items were the geographical and sidereal clocks, which were expected to fetch about £180 and £275, respectively. The failure to sell these clocks, which Boulton rightly regarded as two of the finest of his productions, was a bitter blow to him, but his disappointment took the form more of disillusion with the frivolity of his English patrons than of thoughts about the financial consequences. There was perhaps a veiled reference to Cox's show of automata in Boulton's cynical remark that his clocks would have had better bidders 'if I had made them play jiggs upon bells and a dancing bear keeping time, or if I had made a horse race upon the faces'.[206] His partner seems to have been much more aware of the financial risks: while Boulton could recover his self-esteem with sales to the King of 'a pair of cassoletts, a Titus, a Venus clock and some other things',[207] Fothergill was reckoning that the vase business would be 'very detrimental to the proffits of this year and consume all our labours'.[208] Worse still, the gentry who bought ornaments at the sale were only too slow at paying.[209]

Thus 1771 seems to mark the peak period of demand for the firm's ormolu goods. The sale in the spring was a financial disappointment but it was not a disaster. A substantial number of ornaments were sold and many of those that remained unsold were shipped to Holland or sold to agents or patrons later in the year. Subsequent to the sale there were several princely orders. Most of the larger orders were, however, special commissions. The attempts to encourage shopkeepers to develop business on sale or return suggest that the firm was not finding it easy to move its stock.[210] Much of the effort in the latter half of 1771 was directed towards the planned sale in 1772. The failure of this sale heralded the decline of the business. The surviving evidence suggests that there were fewer orders for ormolu ornaments in 1772 than in the previous year, and the vases delivered to shopkeepers often did not sell easily.[211] This decline cannot have been anything to do with the quality of the firm's ormolu, which had very greatly improved. It must have been due to the price. The fashion for vases persisted but there were cheaper ways of indulging it. The ormolu products of Soho were expensive luxuries because the raw materials were expensive. And in June 1772 came the financial crisis caused by the bankruptcy of the bankers Neale, James, Fordyce and Down.[212] It was a hard time for business and especially for businesses concerned with the manufacture of luxuries. Never again was Soho to produce ormolu ornaments in such quantity as in these two years.

There was no sale in 1773. There seems no doubt that Boulton's decision not to try another sale was due to the failure in 1772. But this was not the reason he gave. He wrote to the Earl of Warwick in November 1772:

> I have improved my or moulu manufacture since I had the honor of shewing your Lordship my specimens of it, yet I think I shall not be able to make any publick exhibition in the approaching spring as all my hands are fully employed in various things that are already ordered, both in silver plate and or moulu, some specimens of which I will endeavour to shew your Lordship during the course of this winter.[213]

Boulton did not admit publicly that the ormolu trade was disappointing. The picture that he painted for his patrons was one of large and diverse orders and of a factory stretched to capacity. Writing to Sir John Dalrymple in the summer of 1772 one of his clerks described the ormolu business as follows:

> All sorts of chimney ornaments in or moulu are made at our manufactory and form even a considerable branch thereof, such as vases with proper socketts to serve as candlesticks – we make them of any size and suitable to any base with 1, 2, 3, 4, 5, 6 branches – and more cassolettes or insence pots, large tripod with branches, all manner of girandoles in or moulu, candlesticks with and without branches, clocks astronomical and geographical upon constructions entirely new, clock cases and many more articles of which we have sold a great many to the nobility and gentry of this kingdom and have even now pretty large orders under hands ...[214]

The claims in this letter are exaggerated. Some of the objects listed were never made in large numbers at Soho: and the 'astronomical and geographical' clocks were made only once. Such boasting was in the best traditions of advertising, but it scarcely accorded with Boulton's statement at the end of the year, in the wake of the troubles caused by Fordyce's bankruptcy, that

> the trade of Birmingham and of this place is rather dead at this juncture, even so much that our London waggons have lately been obliged to make up their loading with coals, for want of merchandise.[215]

The aristocracy was suffering from the doubts spread abroad by the commercial slump. The firm's letters record several orders in May and June 1772[216] (the month of the Fordyce failure), but not so many thereafter until trade generally picked up in the following year.[217] Efforts were therefore made to enlarge the export trade, probably in an attempt to clear the manufactured stock, which was building up. This had been Boulton's first thought after the sale in 1771, when many of the unsold pieces were sent to Amsterdam,[218] and it had been in his mind in April 1772 when he thought of sending his two precious clocks to the Empress of Russia, who he imagined would appreciate them.[219] He made positive efforts to sell ormolu ornaments in Sweden and some of the other European courts,[220] sending samples or offering to do so, and he must have been pleased when a 'Spanish gent' bought some vases and ordered a Titus clock case which he intended for the King of Spain.[221]

It is difficult to tell, in the absence of sales ledgers, whether the attempts to sell accumulated stock abroad met with much success. From the correspondence it seems unlikely. In March 1773 Fothergill, who was becoming desperate for means of raising cash in order to keep the manufactory going, wrote to his partner, who was in London, that everything at Soho had 'the most gloomy aspect, except being full of button orders. Is it not possible to dispose of some of our vases which are in hand at London'.[222] He too thought that hope might lie in encouraging the Russian market and, at a loss to know how to dispose of the sidereal clock, which the 'gambling nobility' had spurned at the sale, suggested that Boulton should present it to the Empress of Russia in an attempt to stimulate demand. It was in fact no time for confidence. Sales were slow and stock was accumulating. Boulton, however, seems to have been unwilling to consider reducing the ormolu trade. Attempts were made to encourage customers but not to cut production to the size of the market.

The reasons for this lack of control in 1772–3 are not hard to find. First, it is not always easy to take commercial decisions when trade is slack and the market is nervous: there is always hope of a revival. It is especially hard to accept that the market for products, for which the manufacturer has a high reputation, is falling away. Second, Boulton was becoming preoccupied with other things and was unable to devote as much of his time as before to persuading the leaders of fashion to buy his ormolu ornaments.

The most absorbing of these other interests was the silver trade. Boulton and Fothergill had been making objects of silver plate for some time but their production of silver articles was growing steadily. Like the ormolu business, the production of silver objects had begun in 1768–9 and by 1772 had built up substantially. Silver and silver plate was capable of substantial growth because so many of the objects were almost necessities and the range of prices could be kept sufficiently wide to attract a large clientele. They were not so susceptible as ormolu to the vagaries of fashion. Wedgwood visited Soho in July 1772 and commented favourably on the silverware, adding that the plated pieces that he had observed in Boulton's showroom were 'of the best forms' he had seen.[223] It was probably the basic button business and orders for silver and plate rather than ormolu that were keeping the workshops busy at the end of the year, whatever the impression that Boulton wanted to give. The increasing demand for silverware gave Boulton, who by now was the largest manufacturer of silver and silver plate in Birmingham, a close personal interest in the establishment of an assay office in the town. It had long been his ambition to become a major manufacturer of silver. His workshops possessed all the necessary skills and his methods of manufacture allowed him to undercut the prices charged in London. But sending all silverware to be hallmarked at London or Chester added greatly both to the time and to the cost of manufacture. It also led to greater risk of damage to the objects during their journey. It thus limited the trade.

Boulton spent a lot of time in London in 1773 campaigning for the establishment of the Birmingham Assay Office. He made a point of lobbying those of his noble patrons who were in Parliament or who were members of the administration – the Dukes of Portland and Richmond, the Earl of Bute, the Earl of Shelburne, the Earl of Dartmouth and others – and was largely responsible for the success of the Bill when it came before Parliament, in spite of strong opposition from the silversmiths of London.[224] I have quoted in Chapter 1 the long list of silver objects with which Boulton and Fothergill celebrated the opening of the office (see p. 22).

Boulton's energies were also becoming absorbed by the engine trade. He had kept in touch with James Watt since Watt's first visit to Soho in 1767 and his own first meeting with him a year later.[225] In 1769, after protracted negotiations, Boulton and William Small had agreed to purchase a one-third interest in Watt's patent from John Roebuck, the industrialist, who initially financed the development of Watt's engine. During the next four years Watt worked in Scotland on perfecting his engine while Boulton and Small experimented in Birmingham and tried to help him solve some of his problems. In 1773 Roebuck's business collapsed owing to lack of finance and the patent became Boulton's property. Watt moved to Soho in 1774, and in 1775 entered into partnership with Boulton, the patent having been extended for twenty-five years by a special Act of Parliament. Although a few years passed before Boulton finally made up his mind to build up the engine trade, it commanded a lot of his time and energy from the middle years of the decade. His efforts were, in due course, amply justified.

Thus from 1773 onwards the ormolu business took a back seat. Production of silver rose until the late 1770s, the general button and toy business continued steadily (and for many years accounted for the major part of the manufactory at Soho) and Boulton began to build up the engine trade. Even so, there were several good orders for ormolu pieces from people of rank once trade generally picked up again in the years 1774–7.[226] Perhaps the most remarkable commission during these years was for the mounts for the Duchess of Manchester's cabinet (Plate 200). The firm claimed to have 'several large orders' in hand in March 1775[227] and was still ordering blue john bodies in some quantity in the same month.[228] The boast was still that the quality of gilding and chasing was superior to comparable work carried out in France:[229] although this claim was unsupportable, exports to the continent of Europe continued. Further samples were sent to the Empress Catherine of Russia in 1774,[230] which appear to have led to a 'very large order',[231] and several pieces were delivered to agents on the continent in 1776.[232] Wedgwood thought that Boulton and Fothergill hoped to supplant their French rivals in the Russian market and remarked that most of the surprisingly large quantity of ormolu pieces which they made was sold abroad. According to him, they sold as many tripods, vases and groups of figures as they could make and even managed to sell two hundred Venus watch stands (Plates 191, 359), at twenty-five guineas each including the watch, in spite of the poor modelling of the figure.[233]

Ormolu wares, clocks and cases, were high among the list of products which Boulton planned to sell in the showroom which he thought of establishing in London in 1776. But they ranked below 'wrought silver plate of all kinds' and 'plated wares of all kinds'. It is very clear both from the firm's letters and from its earliest surviving ledger that ormolu accounted for a far smaller proportion of the firm's sales than did silver and plate.[234] When the firm wrote that 'our hands in the or moulu and silver branch have been by far inadequate to the number of orders we have had to execute during this year'[235] it was misleading the recipient in giving ormolu precedence.

In 1778 the production of ormolu ornaments was palpably outstripping demand. John Hodges mentioned to Boulton in January that he had 'about seven hundred pounds worth of vases finished ready for sale, among which are above 1 dozen with figures, part with time pieces'.[236] When, a week later, Hodges completed a catalogue of the pieces, this amount proved to be a serious underestimate. At retail prices the finished vases were worth £1,300 and there were several more pieces in hand which had not been gilt.[237] Neither Hodges nor Francis Eginton had any idea that the amount was so much,[238] which is further evidence of the lax control of stocks which bedevilled the business at Soho, but it is clear from the tone of Hodges's letters that he was at least concerned at the amount. So was Fothergill. 'We have a prodigious stock of or moulu', he wrote to Boulton in London, and he suggested selling some of it at Christie's when Lord Kerry's things came up for sale.[239] As before, he seems to have been more keenly aware than his partner of the folly of having too much capital tied up in stocks. Boulton agreed with the suggestion of a sale and pressed the apparently unwilling

Christie into holding one in April.[240] Alarmed perhaps by the extent to which the unsold ormolu had mounted up, he took the view that even if only a third of the pieces were sold, it would be better than having them all returned from London whither they had already been sent.[241]

As before, the sale was advertised in advance, but not much in advance. The sale was billed as 'an elegant assortment of the much admired or moulu' brought from Soho and 'consisting of a great variety of most beautiful vases, clock-cases, candle branches, essence pots, and many other tasteful ornaments'.[242] Later versions of the advertisement listed 'vases, clocks, altars, tripods, candelabrums, essence pots, in statuary marble, radix amethysti, etc. The ornaments and figures in bronze and or moulu, elegant in design, and accurately finished after the most approved antique'.[243] An editorial comment in the same newspaper stated that the ornaments to be sold 'are a convincing proof of the improvement that has been made within these few years, in correctness of taste, and elegance in execution'.[244]

Despite the build-up, the sale was a failure, raising only about £200.[245] To some extent this might have been due to the haste of the preparations and to the fact that this time Boulton took little personal interest in them.[246] It might also have been partly due to the fact that the sale was postponed until May for fear of a clash with the sales of the effects of Lord Kerry and of the French ambassador, the Marquis de Noailles, both of which included several ormolu pieces.[247] May was not a good month because many of the people of fashion had departed to the country for the summer, although in 1778 Parliament sat into June.[248] Boulton refused to take Christie's advice to postpone the sale until after the holidays.

The sale was not as large as the sales in 1771 and 1772. The catalogue is reproduced in Appendix III. The sale lasted for only one day and there were only 127 lots. Nineteen of these were objects made of silver, many of them filigree, plate and enamel,[249] and three others were not ormolu.[250] The total number of ormolu pieces was one hundred and sixty-six. There were fourteen pairs of candle vases with bodies of either marble or blue john[251] and fifteen pairs of candle vases with branches for two or three lights, some of them designed to be fitted only when needed.[252] Three of these were mounted on square pedestals[253] and may well have been vases of the type illustrated in Plate 301: two were mounted on round pedestals.[254] There were several other vases, fitted up as candle vases or essence pots or both, which cannot be identified because the descriptions in the catalogue are too scanty. There were also some ormolu candlesticks, girandoles, tripods with branches and ice pails, and three blue john sugar basins mounted with ormolu. An unusual lot was a japanned vase on a mahogany pedestal with ormolu mounts, which was fitted to contain knives, forks and spoons,[255] which sounds similar to the urns illustrated in Plates 216–19. There were several allegorical vases and clock cases, which confirm the impression, gained from the letters, that the range and quantity of allegorical pieces increased in the later years of the decade. Some of them were based on designs that the firm had been making in 1771–2. There were for example two Titus clock cases and a Minerva clock case, a Persian candelabrum and five pieces representing Venus and Cupid at the tomb of Adonis, all of which were probably fitted as perfume burners. There was also a clock executed 'from a design of Sir William Chambers' which can be identified with the King's clock case. Some of these pieces may well have been old stock. The new allegorical designs included figures of Apollo and Diana holding candle branches (Plates 130–1), and eleven timepieces adorned severally with Cleopatra at the tomb of Mark Antony, an offering to Diana (Plate 153), Narcissus admiring himself in a fountain (Plate 173), Penelope petitioning Minerva, Urania (Plate 189), and a group of boys. There were also two vase perfume burners each decorated with a bas-relief depicting

Mercury giving the infant Bacchus to Ino (Plates 313–14). All of these designs are discussed later in the Survey of ornaments.

The pieces in this sale show that the firm was making increased use of white marble for vase bodies and plinths. This confirms an impression given by the archives and by Wedgwood's correspondence. The identifiable pieces also show that the quality of the ormolu had improved still further. The candle vases of Plates 301–2, which were probably made in about 1776–7, are highly finished productions. The Bacchanalian vases of Plates 313–14 are among the best things made at Soho. The quality was not, however, enough to appeal to an unwilling public. Most of the ornaments returned to Soho.[256]

The failure of this sale undermined any hopes that the partners still had that the ormolu business would pay. But there is really no evidence that they had any such hopes. Fothergill had for a long time regarded the ormolu business as an expensive luxury, and Boulton was becoming deeply absorbed in developing the steam engine business and was flirting with a new fancy, the production of mechanical pictures, to which he devoted his usual energetic enthusiasm for a fresh project.[257]

The occasional orders for ormolu pieces at the end of the decade were far outnumbered, indeed almost eclipsed, by orders for buttons, toys and plate. There were some valuable individual orders for certain patrons – Robert Child, Mrs Montagu, the Earl of Chesterfield and others – and for agents overseas,[258] but these were rare orders, and it is clear from the surviving documents that the trade was dying. Some of Hodges's lists of sales from Soho even in 1778 contain no mention of ormolu pieces in spite of the frequent visitors who still came to Soho and who saw presumably the 'shewy things' with which the showroom was stocked once the vases had returned from London.[259] In February 1779 the very words 'or moulu' were dropped from the description of the business, which was now entitled 'Silver Plated etc. goods' in the firm's ledgers.[260] By 1781 there was scarcely any demand for vases with blue john bodies,[261] and at one time during the same year the chasers had not enough to do.[262]

The shrinking of the ormolu trade is best illustrated by the sparse references to ormolu ornaments in the ledgers and journals and by the inventory of stock occasioned by Fothergill's death in 1782 (see Appendix IV). The quantity of ormolu pieces in Richard Bentley's workshop, which presumably represented most if not all of the work-in-progress, was very small.[263] In the Toy Room there were a mere fourteen ornaments, including Belisarius, Narcissus and Venus clock cases, and griffin, saddle and Venus vases, presumably all in a saleable condition.[264] Several of the pieces in the warehouses were damaged and many of the entries refer only to parts or to partially completed objects. The completed pieces that were stored in 'Warehouse No. 17' were, as a note explains, most of them 'very old and mostly damaged'[265] and their values were heavily written down. Some of the pieces among the old stock – for example Narcissus and Venus vases, a dancing boy vase and a King's clock case – can be recognised as having remained unsold in the sale of 1778, having even then perhaps been made for many years. The stock of stones[266] and the pieces in Bentley's workshop, some completed and others almost completed, show that occasional orders were still expected. But it is not a picture of a thriving trade.

After 1782 there are few references to orders for ormolu in the archives.[267] The turnover of the manufactory consisted mostly of buttons, toys and silver.[268] Even repairs of stone bodies had to be subcontracted.[269] Sales took place, some of them no doubt helping to clear the ornaments in stock, for example a Bacchanalian vase sold to Lord Stormont in 1783.[270] Occasional orders for ormolu ornaments were still sought[271] but they were few and far between. Apart from the manufacture of gilt frames for cameos, which were linked to the button trade, and pictures, the ormolu business was dormant by the middle of the decade.[272] Even so it was not until 1799 that Boulton admitted in writing that he no longer carried on the trade. In his notebook he recorded, probably as notes for the evidence which he was to give to a committee of the House of Commons,[273] that he had lately given up the manufacture of gilt, plated pearl and metal buttons, inlaid steel buttons, steel watch chains, hilts, buttons and other steel toys, tortoiseshell pieces, gilt watch chains, toys and trinkets, japanned wares and ormolu clocks, vases and ornaments.[274]

The ormolu business failed for two reasons. First, despite the attractiveness of many of the ornaments, the beauty of some of the stones and the richness of the gilding, the overall quality of the workmanship was not up to the best work produced by the finest French chasers and gilders. A French diplomat, visiting Soho in the 1780s, commented that 'Mr Boulton has also undertaken working in ormolu but although some very fine examples come from his workshops, they remain very inferior to those that are made in Paris'.[275] Perhaps his remark showed some Gallic bias, but there was truth in it. Second, it was impossible to attract a large number of buyers because the costs of production were high. In Keir's words it was 'too expensive for general demand, and therefore not a proper object of wholesale manufacture'.[276] It was thus a commercial error, and was in direct contradiction of Boulton's usual policy, which was to aim at making a great quantity of any object by streamlined methods of production and to work for a small profit margin. That it was Boulton's error is indubitable. It was his idea to develop the business and his personal interest in it was out of all proportion to its commercial importance. His partner even reproved him for dissipating the firm's finances by trading in such products rather than prosecuting sales of the commoner articles such as buttons.[277]

Although the ormolu business was itself a failure it helped Boulton to success in other ways. First, there is little doubt that the firm's reputation for quality helped to stimulate sales of silver and plate. Second, some of the designs and techniques were useful in other departments, such as those that manufactured silverware and gilt toys. Third, the contacts that Boulton made through the ormolu trade in the fashionable world of London and elsewhere proved extremely useful. Many of his patrons were for example Members of Parliament, and their help during the establishment of the Assay Office and the application to extend the steam engine patent, both of which required Acts of Parliament, was invaluable. Fourth, the ormolu trade enhanced Boulton's personal reputation. As James Keir said in his memoir of his friend, it may not have been profitable but it 'greatly tended to his celebrity and admiration of his various talents, taste and enterprise'.[278] Thus when in 1795 the Parliamentary Commission wanted someone to adjudicate on the claims against the Prince of Wales by the suppliers to Carlton House of the various 'articles in or moulu', Boulton was their choice.[279] Finally, and above all, the ormolu trade taught him some commercial lessons that must have stood him in good stead in later years. It taught him the financial disadvantages of the failure to cost his products effectively and of trying to produce a large and diverse range of manufactures. It also gave him considerable experience of the three stages necessary to the successful production of any item: design, manufacture and marketing. The close attention that Boulton paid to detail, as he set about each of these stages, will become apparent during the next three chapters.

CHAPTER 3

Design

The aim of this chapter is to show how Boulton set about creating the designs of the ormolu ornaments that were produced at Soho. Few of his sources will surprise those readers who are familiar with the methods of his contemporaries and rivals. Wedgwood's methods of design, for example, provide a close parallel, and it is obvious from the work of contemporary silversmiths that their repertoire of sources was very similar. Boulton himself was a silversmith on a large scale and it will sometimes be difficult in this account to distinguish between his plans for ormolu and those for silver or plate. The same motifs were often used for both and in his search for ideas he often had both in mind.

The fact that I have started this chapter talking about Boulton without any mention of his partner is indicative of the personal interest that he took in the firm's designs. By modern standards it would be considered a waste of resources for the owner of a large business to spend so much of his time and effort on detailed development. But the ormolu trade was very much one of Boulton's favourite projects, and his personal involvement in it, at any rate until the middle 1770s, is a recurring theme of this book. It provided him, as I have shown in the previous chapter, with a means of entry into the fashionable world, which he was eager to achieve.

Quite apart from this ambition he was keenly interested in design and recognised its importance. His youthful foray into designing a new button, the fine new buildings at Soho, and his later patronage of artists both privately and in the furtherance of his business would prove the point, even if none of the letters or notes on which this chapter is based had survived. He also took a lively entrepreneurial interest in creating the markets for his products, and one of his more impressive talents as a businessman was his determination to relate design to marketing prospects. Even today many manufacturers and providers of services pay scant attention to what their potential customers really want. Boulton, like his friend Wedgwood, intended to make no such mistake. He visited the houses of the aristocracy in order to assimilate their tastes and asked his travelling agent in Italy to observe what taste and fashion prevailed in the various parts of Europe.[1] He understood the importance of keeping abreast with fashion[2] and took immense trouble over individual orders. 'I only wish to excell in the execution of that taste which my employers most approve' he assured one of his patrons.[3] He said at one moment of disappointment that a particular failure was due to the frivolity of fashion,[4] but the success of his silver business proves this momentary diagnosis to have been wrong. It was the cost and not the design of his vases and clock cases which led to the financial failure of the ormolu trade. They could not be produced cheaply enough. From most quarters his designs received high praise.

The overriding influence on Boulton's designs for ormolu was the fashion for the 'antique taste', as the revival of the classical idiom in architecture and design was called. Writing in 1777, the French architect Pierre Patte observed that:

> at last the return of the Antique taste having extended its influence over all our decorative arts, especially during the last fifteen years or so, it can be said that the interior decoration of suites of rooms and the style of their furnishings have become in some sense a new art.

Following the excesses of the rococo, which he described as 'tormenting interior decorations in every possible manner' and as a 'torrent of fashion', he welcomed the return to 'sager, less eccentric forms', and observed that

> to the correct style of the last century's decorations has been added less severity, more delicacy, more variety in the forms ... the ornaments that are most admired in the best works of antiquity, like acanthus and laurel leaves, festoons, ovate

ornaments, ogees, shells, flutes, guilloche work, Vitruvian scrolls, medallions etc., have been applied to interior decorations ...[5]

Interestingly Boulton and Fothergill continued to produce a few rococo designs in silver and plate, and in some other products, into the 1770s, reflecting perhaps the lingering demand for the previous fashion.[6] But Boulton took to the new fashion for the antique taste like the entrepreneur that he was. His ormolu ornaments and his silverware from the late 1760s are replete with the 'ornaments that are most admired in the best works of antiquity'. The guilloche, Vitruvian scroll, Greek fret and anthemion friezes, the gadrooned rims, the fluted feet, borders, stems and nozzles, the medallions and paterae, the acanthus and 'egg and tongue' borders, the laurel borders with crossed ribbons, the laurel, oak and floral festoons, the acanthus leaves applied to the cradles of vase bodies and to candle branches, the rams' heads and many other ornaments show how fully Boulton adopted the new fashionable style.

His methods were entirely eclectic. Writing of design to his friend and patroness Mrs Montagu in 1772 he said:

> Fashion hath much to do in these things, and as that of the present age distinguishes itself by adopting the most elegant ornaments of the most refined Grecian artists, I am satisfyed in conforming thereto, and humbly copying their style, and makeing new combinations of old ornaments without presuming to invent new ones.[7]

This eclecticism was fully in keeping with the methods of other designers and manufacturers who were adopting the taste for the antique. Quotation from the most admired sources was highly esteemed, and the elegant combination of ornaments from antique models was regarded as the acme of artistic achievement. Imitation was not despised but admired. Sir Joshua Reynolds said in a lecture delivered at the Royal Academy in 1774 that not only variety but even 'originality of invention' was produced by imitation:

> Even genius, at least what generally is so called, is the child of imitation ... A mind enriched by an assemblage of all the treasures of ancient and modern art, will be more elevated and fruitful in resources, in proportion to the number of ideas which have been carefully collected and thoroughly digested. There can be no doubt that he who has the most materials has the greatest means of invention ...[8]

Boulton, like his contemporaries, was an inventor in the eighteenth-century sense, and his ormolu work must be seen in this context. His commercial sense probably told him that originality, at the height of the fashion for the antique taste, would not attract his intended customers.

Much has been written about the flowering of the 'antique taste' in France and England in the 1760s and about its origins. One view is that its adoption by craftsmen in England owed most to the influence of French architects and designers. Also familiar to English craftsmen were folios of engravings and designs published in France, such as the Comte de Caylus's *Recueil d'Antiquités Égyptiennes, Étrusques, Grecques et Romaines* (1752–67), J. F. de Neufforge's *Recueil Élémentaire d'Architecture* (1757–68)[9] and J.-C. Delafosse's *Nouvelle Iconologie Historique* (1768), which contained a large collection of designs for frames, medallions, trophies, vases, friezes, pedestals and brackets. The importation of works of art both during the Seven Years' War and, in increasing quantities, after its ending in 1763 must also have had an effect on English design. But it is probably wrong to attribute too much to such influences. To do so disregards the work of the English architects, who were themselves influenced by their contacts with Italy and France, and other English interpreters of classical architecture and artefacts. The antique taste had a firm foothold in the work of English designers from the middle 1750s. James Stuart's patently classical design for a wall of the proposed hall at Kedleston,[10] which contains a classically rectilinear table, was contemporary with some of the earliest furniture designed in the '*style antique*' in France.[11] The development of the style in France and England appears to have taken place in parallel.

France

Manufacturers had plenty of opportunities both to buy source books such as those by Neufforge and Delafosse and to study the work of their Parisian rivals in the houses of their English patrons. Boulton especially, because he made a practice of visiting his patrons' houses and the showrooms of shopkeepers who imported works of art from Paris, such as Thomas Harrache, would have been well aware of the classical designs of his French competitors. He must also have seen work executed in the antique taste when he visited Paris in 1765: for, as Baron Grimm said two years earlier, '*la décoration extérieure et intérieure des batimens, les meubles, les étoffes, les bijoux de toute espèce, tout est à Paris à la grecque* ...'[12] It was his observation of French work that gave Boulton the idea of mounting vases to serve as candelabra, perfume burners and clock cases in the first place. It may also have influenced him in his eager adoption of the antique taste as his dictionary of motifs.

He was not a slavish imitator of French designs. Little of his ormolu or silver work is wholly French in feeling. The highly ornamented work of his contemporaries in France, which was holding sway in Paris and as far afield as St Petersburg in the 1760s, was too extravagant for his English taste. He hankered after emulating the quality of the French work but simplifying the ornament. Whatever the approved taste of his employers, he said on one occasion,

> whether it be French, Roman, Athenian, Egyptian, Arabesk, Etruscan or any other ... I would have elegant simplicity the leading principal, whereas in my opinion such of the *orfèvre* of the French as I have generally seen is *trop chargé*.[13]

Such was his policy with ormolu, and he must have been pleased both by the considerable encouragement with which he met among his English patrons and by the opinion of the Empress Catherine of Russia, who in 1772 was reported to have said that his ormolu vases were 'superiour in every respect to the French'.[14]

Among Boulton's early designs was the lion-faced candlestick (Plate 135). This candlestick appears in the pattern books both without branches (Plate 133) and with curling branches typical of some of Boulton's silverwork (Plate 134). Boulton and Fothergill made it principally in silver but also in ormolu, the latter invariably with the addition of candle branches. Other English silversmiths copied the design, including notably Thomas Heming, but Boulton and Fothergill appear to have made the earliest silver versions in England. A set of four of their candlesticks, hallmarked 1768–9, is illustrated in Plate 16.

Boulton appears to have derived this design from France. Its origin there is uncertain. It is usually attributed to the well-known *doreur-ciseleur* Pierre Gouthière (1732–1813), and ormolu versions without candle branches attributed to him are thought to date from the mid-1760s or earlier.[15] Boulton's candlesticks are closer to Gouthière's model than those of other English silversmiths, which strengthens his claim to have been the first silversmith to make these candlesticks in England.[16] How he acquired the design is not known. He may have secured it during his visit to Paris in 1765, or copied it from a Gouthière candlestick in the collection of an English patron or shopkeeper.

16. Boulton and Fothergill, lion-faced candlesticks, silver, 1768–9, ADC Heritage.

Much the same is probably true also of the squared candle branches which Boulton and Fothergill mounted on ormolu versions of these candlesticks (Plate 135). They appear on other ormolu ornaments (Plates 262, 263–4) and there are sketches of the design, probably for silver or plate, in the pattern book (Plates 136–7). These branches are French in feeling and clearly owe more to the style of Boulton's French rivals than to the work of his predecessors in England. Again, Boulton and Fothergill appear to have been the earliest users of the design in England – I have not yet seen an earlier lion-faced candlestick fitted with these branches by another English silversmith[17] – and again their exact source is uncertain. Several *bronziers* in Paris used similar branches with a squared bend and acanthus decoration, not least the *fondeur* and furniture designer Jean-Louis Prieur (*c.*1725–*c.*1785). His designs for candelabra for the Polish Court in Warsaw in *c.*1765–6 (Plate 17) suggest that he could have been the origin of Boulton's design, although his branches are by no means the exact model.[18] The similarities are striking, including the use of acanthus leaves to enfold the branches and the indented decoration on the sides of the branches (an unusual feature of Boulton's mounts): but Boulton's branches are different in proportion and have a leaf ornament on top of the squared part of the branch which is lacking in Prieur's candelabrum. This distinctive mount appears elsewhere on French mounts.[19] Prieur may not have been the origin, but it is surely likely that Boulton was working from a French design or using as a model a branch fitted to an imported ornament.

17. Candelabrum, attributed to Jean-Louis Prieur, *c.*1765–6, Royal Castle, Warsaw.

The lions' masks and feet reappear on the vases illustrated in Plate 244, which I have described in the Survey of ornaments as the most French in feeling of all Boulton's vases, echoing as they do the somewhat archaic style of early French designs in the antique taste. This vase, sometimes sold without branches, was clearly one of the earliest of his ormolu ornaments. I have not found a French prototype, and assume that the lions' masks and feet were repeated from the lion-faced candlestick.

The inspiration of French models is apparent in several other ornaments and decorative motifs. This is not to say that Boulton copied motifs directly. There were many sources from which he could cull models and designs inspired by French originals, and his most likely sources were architects, books, engravings, sculptors, plaster shops, and other manufacturers in England, all of whom absorbed French taste either directly or indirectly. I shall come to these sources later in this chapter. It is however clear that he was greatly influenced by French ideas and models, whatever the actual sources of the models he used. Thus the inspiration of Boulton's rather poor figure of Venus (Plates 191, 359) may well have been François Vion's figure of '*La Douleur*' (Plate 18), or a clock case based on it,[20] although it seems to me more likely that it was derived from a print of a French painting published in England (see p. 96 and Plate 65). But whatever the actual source, the inspiration was French. The idea of fitting a horizontal movement to a vase clock, as Boulton did with his Venus clocks, also came from France. Similarly the inspiration of the Minerva clock case (Plates 166, 169), and especially of the boy representing the genius of Time,[21] probably came from France: and Urania, the Muse of Astronomy (Plate 179), reclines on many French clock cases. The use of figures of Apollo and Diana, representing night and day, to hold candelabra (Plates 130–1) was a conceit employed by French *bronziers*. The use of figures, many of them to convey an allegory, to decorate clock cases was a common theme of French clockmakers, and French *bronziers* frequently mounted ewers and obelisks as well as vases.

18. François Vion, design for clock case, *La Douleur*, *c.*1765, Bibliothèque Doucet, Paris.

The parallels with individual mounts are legion – the use of satyr masks on ewers and vases (Plates 196, 293), goats' heads (Plate 331), the fitting of coiled snakes to tripods, symbolising healing (Plate 238), the urn on the top of the King's clock case which looks like so many urns surmounting French candelabra (Plate 164), were all familiar motifs to French designers, quite apart from the whole repertoire of classically inspired mounts. The clock case illustrated in Plate 19, which has been attributed to Philippe Caffieri and was probably made in about 1757,[22] is unlikely to have been a direct model for Boulton, but it illustrates how leading French designers led the way in incorporating motifs which became part of Boulton's stock-in-trade – for example the ringed lion masks (cf. Plate 345), the stem with its spiral flutes (cf. Plates 262, 331), the circular moulding at the base which is chased with a design of laurel leaves and crossed ribbons (cf. Plate 346 and the bezel in Plate 155), and the square stepped base.

Architects

The principal English architects under whose guidance the taste for the antique flowered in England were promoting the style for several years before the production of ormolu began at Soho. They exerted a considerable influence on manufacturers, partly through direct contacts and partly through the concept of uniting the style of furniture and decoration with that of rooms and buildings. Architects had concerned themselves before with interior decoration, with furniture and with ornament, but never to such an extent. The name of Robert Adam is particularly associated with the change. The traditional view, until fairly recent years, has been that his influence was pervasive, a view that was well expressed and probably originated in Sir John Soane's well-known lecture in 1812, in which he said:

> It is to the activity of the Messrs Adam that we are more particularly indebted for breaking the talismanic charm, which the fashion of the day had imposed, and for the introduction from ancient works of a light and fanciful style of decoration ... This taste soon became general; everything was Adamitic: buildings and furniture of every description ... To Mr. Adam's taste in the ornaments of his buildings, and

19. Julien le Roy, table clock, the case attributed to Philippe Caffieri, *c.*1757, Musée Condé, Chantilly.

furniture, we stand indebted, in-as-much as manufacturers of every kind felt, as it were, the electric power of this revolution in art.[23]

Taken at its face value Soane's summary is an exaggeration. Adam was the most fashionable, successful and influential architect of his day, but tradition, aided and abetted by Soane's glorification of him, sets him almost alone on a pinnacle and disregards the work of his predecessors and contemporaries. The tradition has been so powerful that it used to be commonly assumed that Boulton and Fothergill worked frequently for the Adam brothers, that the ormolu work in houses designed or decorated by them must have been made at Soho, and that Adam was, in short, the major influence on Boulton's designs. It is clear from the archives that all three assumptions were wrong. Boulton received very few direct commissions from the Adam brothers, and even on those occasions when he worked to their designs they do not appear to have given him the orders. The order for the door furniture at Kedleston (Plate 193), which was made at Soho in 1765–6 and was modelled on one of Adam's favourite designs (Plate 20), was

20. Robert and James Adam, *Works in Architecture*, Vol. II, no. IV, Plate VIII, door furniture.

sent to Boulton with a wooden pattern by Samuel Wyatt, who was acting as clerk of the works at the house:[24] it is reasonable to assume that it was Wyatt, with whose family Boulton was well acquainted, and not Adam, who chose Boulton and Fothergill as the manufacturers. Similarly the direction of the order for some girandoles or tripods which Lord Shelburne wanted in 1765 for the rooms which Adam was building for him at Bowood originated with Lord Shelburne and not with his architect.[25] Adam had nothing to do with the commission for the four candle vases which Mrs John Parker wanted for the new saloon at Saltram in 1771, although he probably designed the stands on which they were to be placed (Plate 342, see Survey of ornaments, p. 339). Although Boulton occasionally worked on commissions with which Adam was connected, there is not a single instance recorded in the archives either of the Adam brothers asking Boulton to carry out an order for ormolu work or of their corresponding with him about the details of any design. Lord Shelburne, who was a particular patron of Boulton and whose attempt to have some light fittings made at Soho has already been mentioned, tried in 1770 to get Boulton and the Adams to co-operate in a joint venture. The Adams were to provide the designs and Boulton the manufacturing capacity, a plan which, if it had come to anything, would no doubt have altered the style of many objects produced at Soho quite dramatically. After a lengthy correspondence, however, the plan fell through in its early stages.

It would be wrong to say that Adam had no influence at all on Boulton's designs. Boulton could hardly have avoided assimilating some of Adam's ideas when he saw his decorative designs in houses such as Kedleston, which he visited before 1766, or Shelburne House (later Lansdowne House) in London, which he visited on several occasions in the late 1760s. He was constantly on the look-out for patterns which he could copy, making drawings and even borrowing objects, and a perusal of the ornaments illustrated in this book and of his silverware reveals a minor host of motifs which appeared repeatedly in the decorative work which Boulton must have seen in Adam's interior designs. At the very least Adam's work must have had some effect in training his eye in the classical repertory.

Another way in which Boulton assimilated Adam's classical style was through his *Ruins of the Palace of the Emperor Diocletian at Spalatro in Dalmatia*, a copy of which he bought in 1765 on the advice of Lord Shelburne, soon after it was published.[26] According to Lord Shelburne Boulton wanted to adopt Adam's taste 'in his things', which was the motive

21. Robert Adam, *Ruins of the Palace of the Emperor Diocletian*, Plate XLIX, a capital in the peristyle of the Temple of Aesculapius.

for buying the book. It would be far-fetched to suggest that this book was the source of many of Boulton's motifs: it served more, like Adam's executed works, as a general influence on his taste. It does, however, contain one drawing – of a capital from the peristyle of the Temple of Aesculapius at Spalatro (Plate 21) – which was clearly the model for the capitals at the top of the cabinet made for the Duchess of Manchester in 1774 (Plate 22). Even so, this mount cannot be taken as evidence of a direct design relationship with the architect. It seems likely that Boulton and Fothergill received the design not from Adam directly, but from the cabinet makers Mayhew and Ince, who commissioned the ornaments for the cabinet (see Survey of ornaments, pp. 249 ff.).

A more likely source of designs was James Stuart, whom Boulton had come across as early as 1758.[27] Any discussion of Stuart's influence on Boulton has to start with tripods, and particularly the type of tripod illustrated in Plates 25 and 28. The tripod became a favourite theme of designers and architects both in England and in France at an early stage in the revival of the taste for the antique. It found its way frequently into the decorative designs of architects such as James Stuart and Robert Adam in two and three dimensions. A design-conscious manufacturer such as Boulton was unlikely to neglect it. Apart from knowing that tripods were a familiar part of the architects' repertoire in their published works, he probably saw candelabra and perfume burners made in the form of tripods in the houses

22. The Duchess of Manchester's cabinet, detail, Victoria and Albert Museum.

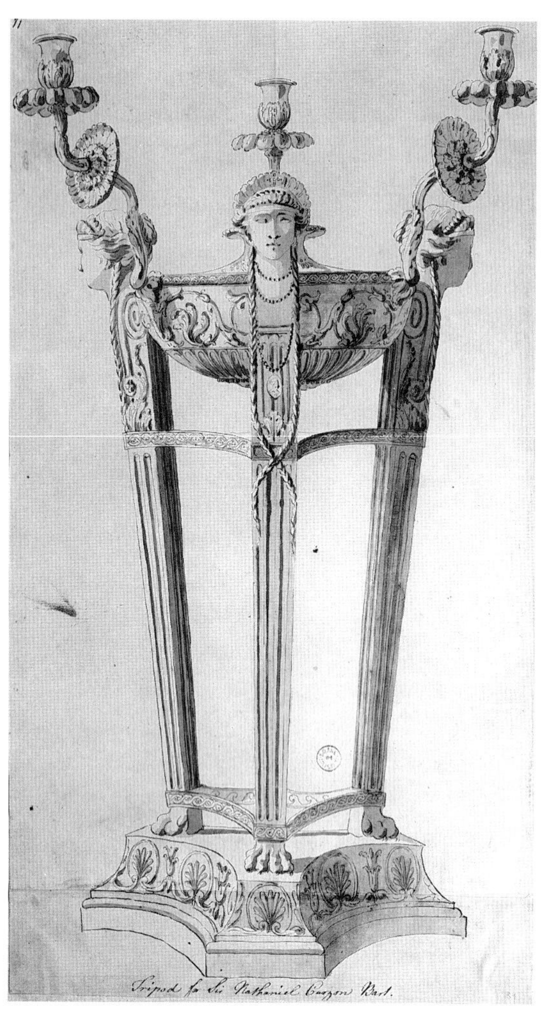

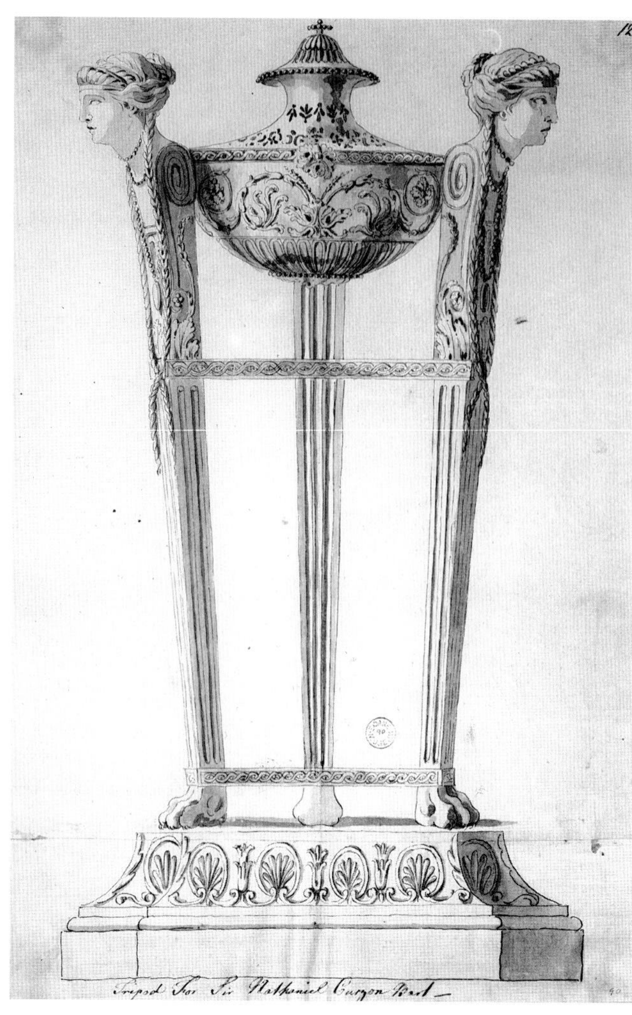

23. Soane Manuscripts, Vol. 25, no. 89, 'Tripod for Sir Nathaniel Curzon Bart.', Sir John Soane's Museum.

24. Soane Manuscripts, Vol. 25, no. 90, 'Tripod for Sir Nathaniel Curzon Bart.', Sir John Soane's Museum.

of his aristocratic friends and patrons.[28] The archives show that he was aware of the possibilities. I have mentioned above that the Earl of Shelburne asked Adam in 1765 to order some girandoles from Boulton 'or branches for the same purpose or tripods'. In 1768 Boulton bought a pattern of a tripod from a Mr Ryder, probably the engraver Thomas Ryder, at Lord Shelburne's house, which may well have been a pattern of Stuart's.[29] In 1769 he was commissioned by Stuart to make the great tripod that was to stand on top of the 'Lanthorn of Demosthenes' which Stuart had designed for Shugborough:[30] the making of this tripod, the legs of which weighed five hundredweight, could scarcely be described as practice for the manufacture of more humble ornaments, but it brought Boulton into contact with Stuart at a time when he was actively seeking ideas and designs.

Boulton put four tripods 'after a design of Mr Stuart's' into the sale at Christie's in 1771 (see Survey of ornaments, p. 276). They were probably similar to the tripod perfume burners which have survived at Kedleston Hall (Plate 25), Althorp, Northamptonshire, and elsewhere, the original design of which should be attributed to James Stuart.[31] It is likely that the two tripods made by Boulton and Fothergill for the Earl of Shelburne in 1771 were the same model.[32] Boulton supplied four tripods based closely on the pattern to Lord Gower in 1774 (Plate 233, see Survey of ornaments, p. 276).

The design of these tripods has been attributed to the Adam brothers, among whose manuscripts there are three drawings of two such tripods, one with and the other without candle branches, for Sir Nathaniel Curzon, the owner of Kedleston Hall (Plates 23 and 24).[33] But it looks as if these

25–7. Tripod perfume burner, designed by James Stuart, probably made by Diederich Nicolaus Anderson, *c.*1760, National Trust, Kedleston Hall.

drawings were either the work of Stuart, or copies of his work, or were drawings of the finished tripod made by one of the Adams' draughtsmen.[34] Two of Stuart's sketches for the interior decoration of Kedleston, tentatively dated 1757–8, contain tripods of this pattern, in one case with candle branches. Two others portray tripods as plaster decoration over doors.[35] His design for the entrance wall of the painted room at Spencer House, London, which dates from 1759,[36] includes a tripod of the same pattern with three candle branches, which is suggestive of the two tripods now at Althorp. Stuart's claim to be the originator of the design is also supported by an entry in the diary of the Duchess of Northumberland, who visited Kedleston in the mid-1760s and noted that on the sideboard in the alcove of the dining room stood 'Mr Stewart's tripod'.[37]

In addition to the tripod at Kedleston and the pair at Althorp (from Spencer House) there is a fourth from Wentworth Woodhouse, now in the Victoria and Albert Museum (Plate 28).[38] Each of these tripods is made of ormolu and stands on a triangular marble base carved with a formal anthemion frieze. The female heads are adorned with stylised plaits of hair, which fall down the tripod's legs. They wear triple-bead necklaces from which hang medallions portraying male heads in profile. These portray the three ages of man – a youth, a hero crowned with a wreath, and a distinctly Socratic old man. The shoulders of each of the female figures are decorated with a spiral scroll, acanthus foliage, a single flower, and an acanthus flower stem or ear of wheat (Plate 29). The legs are fluted on all four sides and the connecting stretchers are decorated with a chased guilloche pattern on the outside surfaces and a Vitruvian scroll motif on the inside. The feet are fashioned in the form of lions' paws which are bolted to the marble base. The bowl, which rests in notches in the backs of the figures (Plate 29), is decorated with a scrolling arabesque motif incorporating honeysuckle and other flowers (Plate 27), and a satyr's mask set in a circle of gadrooned rays (Plate 26). The bowl is fitted with a copper lining, which in some cases is tinned, and covering the bowl is a lid which is pierced with a symmetric scrolling pattern. Candle branches, with one nozzle (Kedleston) or three nozzles (Althorp) are fitted but are detachable. The tripod from Wentworth Woodhouse (Plate 28) was probably fitted originally with branches. The screw holes for them can be seen on the rim of the bowl.

The design and workmanship of these three tripods are so similar, as are the details of the construction and assembly, that it is difficult to escape the conclusion that they were made in the same workshop and that the craftsman was working from a common design and re-using the same casting moulds.

The origins of Stuart's design probably go back to his travels in Greece with Nicholas Revett. He and Revett were in Athens from March 1751 to the end of 1753 when, following a proposal which they had made jointly in 1748, they surveyed and made measured drawings of many of the classical buildings in the city. They were fortunate in being delayed on their way to Athens in Venice,[39] where James Gray was the English Resident. Gray was enthusiastic about the project and set in hand the first subscription for financing it through the Society of Dilettanti, of which his brother was then secretary. Stuart and Revett arrived back in London in 1755, after visiting Salonica, Smyrna and the Aegean Islands, and the first volume of their *Antiquities of Athens* was published in 1762. Among the subscribers were the Marquess of Rockingham, Lord Scarsdale and Lord Spencer, the owners of Wentworth Woodhouse, Kedleston and Spencer House.[40]

In Chapter IV of this first volume the authors discussed and illustrated a building of the late fourth century BC, the Monument of Lysicrates, which was then embedded in the walls of a Capuchin monastery (Plate 30). The building was vulgarly known as the 'Lanthorn of Demosthenes', the popular

28–9. Tripod perfume burner, designed by James Stuart, probably made by Diederich Nicolaus Anderson, *c.*1760, Victoria and Albert Museum.

30. James Stuart and Nicholas Revett, *Antiquities of Athens*, Vol. I, Plate III, the Choragic Monument of Lysicrates, or 'Lanthorn of Demosthenes'.

ABOVE RIGHT:
31. James Stuart and Nicholas Revett, *Antiquities of Athens*, Vol. I, p. 36, suggested reconstruction of tripod on the Choragic Monument of Lysicrates.

story, current at the time, being that it had been built by the great orator as a place of retirement and study. Stuart correctly observed that it had been erected, as the inscriptions on it say, by Lysicrates of Kikyna as a memorial to the victory of the boys of the tribe of Akamantis in the dramatic contest. He deduced, from the holes in the upper surface of the 'flower'[41] at the top of the building and from the evidence of classical literature and tradition, that the ornament which surmounted the flower had been a brazen tripod.[42] His conjectural reconstruction of the tripod (Plate 31) owes something to the tripods carved in relief between the capitals of the monument. The design of the tripods of Plates 25 and 28 suggests that Stuart's drawing for the Choragic Monument's tripod was the origin of his later design. The shape of the legs, the lion's paw feet, the two concave stretchers, the gadrooning on the underside of the bowl, and the triangular plinth with its concave sides, all herald the later design.

The tripods made to Stuart's design in the early 1760s for Rockingham, Scarsdale and Spencer have often been attributed to Boulton, but such an attribution is very unlikely. Boulton and Fothergill were not capable of producing gilt ornaments of such size and quality in the early 1760s. It is also of some significance that the brass alloy used for the manufacture of the tripod of Plate 28 is quite different from Boulton's usual alloy, having a much higher zinc content.[43] I have suggested elsewhere[44] that these tripods were made by Diederich Nicolaus Anderson, who exhibited 'a tripod, from an original design of Mr Stuart' in 1761.[45]

However, it looks as if Boulton indulged his habit of copying other people's designs. The tripods which he sold at Christie's in 1771 were modelled 'after a design of Mr Stuart's', and from the description and the price there seems little doubt that they were copies of Anderson's tripods.

Boulton's source is uncertain. He may have borrowed a tripod from Stuart or Anderson and copied it. Alternatively he may have bought one from Anderson's widow (see p. 100): or he may have received the models from William Chambers, who recorded one of the tripods in a slight sketch which survives in his Franco-Italian Album (Plate 32).[46]

The attribution of all the tripods of this design is extraordinarily difficult. There seems little doubt about the tripods made for Rockingham, Scarsdale and Spencer, but others survive, the chasing and gilding of which are not easily distinguishable. Minor differences such as the chasing of the eyes of the satyr mask, the lack of medallions, or the carving of the marble plinth, may justify an attribution either to Anderson or to Boulton and Fothergill, but so far a reliable pattern of differences has not emerged. In some cases, such as the two tripods once owned by the Earl of Ashburnham, later modifications and re-gilding by Vulliamy have made attribution even more hazardous.[47] Metallurgical tests may help, but have not been methodically carried out.

Boulton was not the only manufacturer to copy this design of tripod. Wedgwood later used the design of the legs, rather inappropriately, on a *rosso antico* perfume burner with Egyptian decoration and on a candelabrum.[48] He also used the decoration on the bowl – the scrolling frieze, the gadrooned rays and the satyr's mask – on some of his black basalt 'Michelangelo' lamps.[49] The coincidence is another example of the common sources of designs tapped by different artists.[50]

The tripod was not Stuart's only contribution to Boulton's designs. In 1769 he made some drawings of a border for a tea table and a 'tripodic' tea kitchen,[51] and later he was concerned, like James Wyatt, with designs for silverware.[52] The tea kitchen was almost certainly the tea urn made by Boulton and Fothergill in 1770, examples of which survive in the Royal Collection (Plate 231) and at Syon (Plate 229). Several features of the design of these tea urns reflect the design of the tripod, not least the legs with their fluted sides and paw feet, the two triangular guilloche stretchers with their Vitruvian scroll decoration on the inner side, and their manner of attachment, and the base of the tea urn in Plate 231. These coincidences open up the possibility that the candle branches on these tea urns also derive from Stuart. Since they occur on other vases (Plates 241, 244, 265), they would, if designed by Stuart, represent an important contribution to the style of Boulton's early ornaments. Unfortunately there is no proof, but they do reflect, with their circular loop, the more refined branches on the candle vases of the type illustrated in Plate 33, which I have tentatively attributed to Anderson and which were probably also designed by Stuart.

The case for attributing these candle vases to Stuart rests on not just stylistic grounds, but also on the survival of pairs of them from Spencer House and Hagley, two houses at which Stuart designed interiors.[53] If they were designed by Stuart, they represent a further influence on Boulton's designs, since the spiral stem with its floral collar appears on early vases made by Boulton and Fothergill (Plates 241, 243), and the stem and the tripod support and triangular base (Plate 34) were copied on the caryatic vases of Plates 324–6. The case for attributing their manufacture to Anderson rests on no more than his association with Stuart, the fine quality chasing and gilding, and the lack of other known fine metalworkers of the period.[54] One day, I hope, more positive proof will appear to back, or undermine, both attributions. Where Boulton got his models from – from Stuart perhaps, or from Anderson, or even from the vases at Hagley, the home of the Lyttelton family with whom Boulton had contacts from at least 1767 – is not known.

It was an architect of a very different stamp, William Chambers,

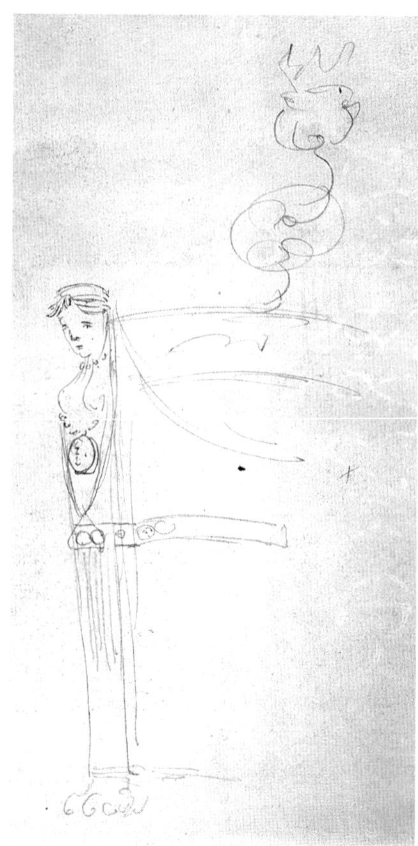

32. William Chambers, 'Franco-Italian Album', facing p. 2, sketch of tripod perfume burner, Victoria and Albert Museum.

OPPOSITE:
33–4. Vase candelabrum, probably designed by James Stuart, possibly made by Diederich Nicolaus Anderson, *c.*1765, Victoria and Albert Museum.

who was probably the greatest influence on Boulton's style. Chambers was one of the first architects to react against the taste for the rococo and to encourage the revival of the classical idiom.[55] While attending Jacques-François Blondel's *École des Arts* in Paris in 1749–50 he met, as fellow students, such revolutionary French architects as Charles de Wailly and Marie-Joseph Peyre, both of whom remained friends for the rest of his life.[56] They were together again in Rome, where Chambers spent four years between 1751 and 1755 surveying the ancient and modern cities. His studies in Paris and Rome, and especially his contact with the artists and architects who had come under the influence of Laurent le Geay while studying at the French Academy in Rome,[57] gave him a solid grounding in the early forms of the '*style antique*'. His preoccupation with Roman, or rather Italian,[58] models set him apart from the architects such as James Stuart and, later, Robert Adam, whose styles were based more on Greek models. He became architect and tutor to the future George III, probably through the influence of the Earl of Bute, and remained the King's preferred architect after his accession to the throne in 1760.[59] He was appointed joint architect with Robert Adam to the Office of Works in 1761 and Comptroller of the Works in 1769. He was effectively the Royal architect during the later years of the eighteenth century, while Adam built a substantial private practice for the aristocracy.

Boulton does not appear to have met Chambers until the spring of 1770; but having met him he discovered in him a fruitful source of designs. It may be that the friendship between the two men was responsible in some way for the failure of Boulton's attempts to co-operate with the Adam brothers. Robert Adam's relationship with Chambers was always strained, being compounded of a mixture of honest professional rivalry, envy of Chambers's success[60] and disdain for his rather archaic style. Boulton's meeting with Chambers in 1770 and his eager use of his models and designs might well have discouraged Adam from pursuing an association. Alternatively Boulton might have considered that in Chambers he had found what he wanted, namely an influential architect who could supply him with designs which were acceptable in the highest social circles and who could drop a word in his favour where it most mattered. I have no doubt at all that Boulton was attracted by Chambers's links with the King and Queen. A link with Adam was no longer necessary and a business link was likely to need too much capital.

It was probably from Chambers that Boulton derived many of the French motifs which I have discussed above. The architect had made a considerable study of French designs. He would have seen and studied the unpublished designs of the French artists and architects whom he knew from his time in Paris and Rome. He corresponded with several of them, including de Wailly,[61] and was considerably more familiar than Boulton both with the trends in French ornamental design and with the published works of the French designers. These included folios of vases, which were often published in series and later assembled into book form, compiled by J.-F. Saly (1746),[62] J. Beauvais,[63] C. de Wailly (1760),[64] J.-M. Vien (1760)[65] and E.-A. Petitot (1764),[66] and Jean Laurent le Geay's etchings of vases, tombs, ruins, etc., which were published separately from 1767 and assembled in one book in 1770.[67] Boulton's earlier flirtations with French models such as the lion-faced candlestick may have biased him in favour of Chambers's Franco-Italian style.

Chambers drew many of the architectural decorative details, statues, busts, friezes, vases, furniture and other ornaments that interested him during his travels in Italy and France in 1749–55. Over five hundred of these drawings are pasted into his so-called 'Franco-Italian Album', now in the Victoria and Albert Museum.[68] This album is one of the most important

35. William Chambers, 'Franco-Italian Album', p. 25 *verso*, sketch of throne for Sheldonian Theatre, Oxford, Victoria and Albert Museum.

documents for the study of the revival of the 'antique taste' in Europe and, in the words of the recent editors of the museum's collection of Chambers's drawings, 'the key resource for the study of the origins of Chambers's decorative style'.[69] His later work shows that he often referred back to these drawings,[70] and the inspiration for some of the mounts used on Boulton and Fothergill's ornaments can be traced to them.

Boulton's first meeting with Chambers seems to have gone well. They had breakfast together. Boulton described the meeting to his wife:

I breakfasted with the King's architect who shewed me some civility and made me a present of some valuable, usefull and acceptable modells. He is makeing me a drawing from a sketch of the King's for a better foot to our 4-branched vase ...[71]

The 'better foot' was, without much doubt, the foot decorated with twisted flutes that was fitted to the large vase candelabra supplied to the King (Plate 339), and later to Mrs John Parker (Plate 343) and other patrons. It replaced the inelegant ball foot that Boulton and Fothergill had fitted to their caryatic vase (Plate 317), which was probably the type of vase described in Boulton's letter as 'our 4-branched vase'. The same improved foot appears on other objects, notably on the Titus clock case supplied to the King in 1772 (Plate 183), and, in an elongated form, on different versions of the King's clock case (Plates 160, 162). The decoration of this foot is reminiscent of Chambers's design in 1759 for the President's chair for the Royal Society of Arts, which has been described as 'the first strictly neoclassic piece of furniture in England',[72] and of his design for the Vice Chancellor's throne in the Sheldonian Theatre, Oxford (Plate 35).[73] His Franco-Italian Album contains several other drawings of objects decorated with these spiral flutes on curved surfaces.[74] The new foot also has an affinity to the design of the foot on the commode whose mounts I have attributed earlier to Dominique Jean (Plate 6), a parallel which opens up an interesting avenue of speculation.[75]

Boulton's reference to Chambers's gift of 'valuable, usefull and acceptable modells' is tantalising. Although few of his realised designs have survived, Chambers specialised to some extent in designing ormolu ornaments, notably the griffin candlesticks (Plate 13), the ormolu mounts which he commissioned from Anderson for Lord Charlemont's medal cabinet (Plates 9, 10) and the ormolu-mounted case for Pinchbeck's astronomical clock for the King (Plate 5).[76] It is conceivable that, having lost the services of Anderson at the end of 1767, he looked upon Boulton as a possible successor for the manufacture of ormolu work to his designs. The models that he gave to Boulton were perhaps designs that he had prepared for ormolu work on earlier occasions: but what exactly they were remains a matter for conjecture. Boulton did not describe them.

It is possible that the models were for the mounts of the King's clock case (Plate 160), which Chambers designed and which was completed a year later. It may be that the meeting was arranged specially so that Chambers could give Boulton this design. This possibility is suggested by a letter from Boulton to his partner the day before, telling him about the coming meeting with Chambers: 'I shall breakfast with him in the morning and receive the King's design which I will send down'[77] – but this passage may refer only to the drawing from the King's sketch of a 'better foot' which I have already discussed. If the models were for the mounts of the King's clock case Boulton certainly found them 'valuable, usefull and acceptable', using them with characteristic plagiarism not only on other versions of the King's clock case but also on other clock cases (Plates 155, 177).

36. William Chambers, sketch for clock case, Royal Collection.

There is a pencil drawing of a clock case among the royal archives (Plate 36)[78] which has been identified as Chambers's work.[79] There are material differences between this sketch and the final design of the King's clock case made by Boulton and Fothergill, but they share the plan of a square clock case with rams' heads and swags and an urn on the top. It is likely that this was an early sketch by Chambers for a clock case that was not made, but it may have been a preliminary sketch for the King's clock case that was superseded by the drawing given to Boulton. It draws quite heavily on Chambers's unpublished drawings. The supporting sphinxes, for example, are inspired by a sphinx with raised wings and a fish's tail that Chambers sketched at the Tuileries.[80] The rams' heads and swags owe a lot to drawings that he made in Italy (Plates 37–8).[81] The urn on the top, a characteristically French use of a decorative urn, also reflects Chambers's familiarity with French models and designs.[82]

37. William Chambers, 'Franco-Italian Album', p. 42, Victoria and Albert Museum.

The final design of the King's clock case, with its rams' heads and swags and urn clearly owes a debt to the same sources, and the ewers, with handles fashioned in the form of fishes or dolphins, appear in a drawing in Chambers's *Treatise on Civil Architecture* (Plate 39). These fishes or dolphins, rising to bite the rim of the ewer, appear in several of Chambers's drawings and designs[83] and on a design for a ewer by Chambers's assistant John Yenn, dating from about 1770 (Plate 40).[84] Yenn was presumably drawing a fair copy of Chambers's design, as he did on other occasions. Wedgwood used the motif on a black basalt 'dolphin' ewer.[85] The engraved design on the back door of the King's clock case (Plate 161) is also likely to have come from Chambers. The griffins, with raised wings and looped tails, echo a drawing of a winged horse with a looped tail in a sketch by Chambers,[86] although the griffins' tails are somewhat truncated.

38. William Chambers, 'Franco-Italian Album', p. 25, Victoria and Albert Museum.

Models for any or all of these mounts may have been among the models given to Boulton by Chambers at breakfast that day. But so many of Boulton's component motifs can be found in Chambers's work that the possibilities are legion. For example, Chambers is the likely source of the model for the three figures which support the Persian vase (Plates 351–2), despite Boulton's acquisition of the similar but smaller figure for the geographical clock (Plate 155) from a quite different source. I shall discuss the origin of this figure later in this chapter (see pp. 97–8). Chambers had illustrated it under the heading of 'Persians and Caryatides' in his *Treatise on Civil Architecture* in 1759 (Plate 41, Fig. 3). The term 'Persian' was an accepted architectural term applied to any male figure that was used for the support of an entablature in place of a column: the female equivalent was the caryatid. Chambers devoted a chapter of the first edition of his *Treatise on Civil Architecture* to 'Persians and Caryatides', in which he commented that the

> male figures may be introduced with great propriety in arsenals, or galleries of armour, in guard rooms, and other military places; where they may be represented under the figures either of captives, or of martial virtues; such as strength, valour, etc.[87]

It is likely that Boulton was quoting Chambers when he described his figures as 'Persian slaves' and the military trophies on the plinth as 'proper for the subject'. It is also likely that when Boulton described the three figures on the Persian vase in the sale at Christie and Ansell's in 1778 as 'finely modelled in bronze after M. Angelo',[88] he was also quoting Chambers, who described the figures illustrated in his *Treatise* as 'cast from models of Michael Angelo Buonaroti, and repaired either by himself, or under his direction'.[89]

Chambers designed vases for the King and Queen, and exhibited 'various vases, etc., to be executed in or moulu, by Mr Bolton for their Majesties' at the Royal Academy in 1770.[90] It seems highly likely that the models for these vases were not available in March 1770 in time to give them to Boulton. The Queen only asked Boulton in the same month about

39. William Chambers, *Treatise on Civil Architecture*, un-numbered plate, detail, a temple for Sir Thomas Worsley, Victoria and Albert Museum.

40. John Yenn, design for an ewer, Victoria and Albert Museum.

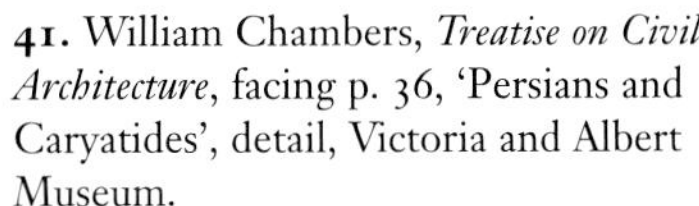

41. William Chambers, *Treatise on Civil Architecture*, facing p. 36, 'Persians and Caryatides', detail, Victoria and Albert Museum.

the possibility of making some new vases, and it seems more likely that Chambers set to designing them after Boulton had received the order. They were almost certainly the King's vases and the sphinx vases which survive in the Royal Collection at Windsor Castle (Plates 339, 355). Perhaps the 'etc.' in Chambers's exhibit at the Royal Academy was the clock case, in which case the models for this would not have been available in March either, but a clock case hardly seems to justify the description 'etc.'.

A drawing of the King's vase by Chambers's assistant John Yenn (Plate 42) may give an idea of Chambers's design.[91] It shows a slenderer vase than Boulton's executed version, with much less elaborate and less satisfactory oak leaf mounts on the body, no vine leaves on the heads of the satyrs, clusters of grapes and vine at the satyrs' waists, and a Vitruvian scroll band round the upper rim of the vase instead of the pierced guilloche and quatrefoil rim of the executed version. The branches in the drawing are similar to the executed version, but the drip rings and nozzles are more decorated and there is a bolder acanthus leaf decoration on the branches. Another drawing by Yenn of a double branch for a silver candlestick also has some similarity to the branch of the King's vase (Plate 43).[92] There seems no doubt from the existence of these drawings that Chambers was responsible for the design of the King's vase: it also seems likely that he supplied Boulton with the designs or the models for many if not all of the mounts. The finished King's vases (Plates 339–40) echo many of the features of Chambers's archaic classical taste.

There also seems little reason to doubt that Chambers was responsible for the design of the sphinx vases (Plate 355), despite the lack of any evidence other than their association with the King's vases and the use of

43. John Yenn, design for candle branches, Victoria and Albert Museum.

42. John Yenn, design for King's vase, Victoria and Albert Museum.

the plural 'vases' in the catalogue entry of the Royal Academy exhibition in 1770.

Was Chambers responsible for the model for Boulton's triton candlestick (Plate 139)? The evidence suggests that he was one of the two likely sources, and that even if Boulton received the model from the other source, namely Wedgwood, Chambers was still the origin of the design.

In 1767 Chambers wrote to Lord Charlemont, saying that Anderson, whom he had commissioned to make the gilt ornaments for Charlemont's medal cabinet (Plates 8–10) and other ornaments, was on the point of death, and that 'as soon as I can get the models I must employ some other person to do the work, both for the medal cases and the tritons'.[93] That these tritons were the same design as the triton in Boulton and Fothergill's sketch is suggested by a drawing by Chambers for Lord Charlemont of the Eating Room at Charlemont House (Plate 44).[94] The pencil sketch of the candelabra on the chimneypiece is slight, but there seems little doubt that they are tritons, probably holding the two inked candle branches (the three above being either a first sketch or representing a sconce attached to the mirror frame). Chambers stopped the work when one of the tritons had been cast because they were proving expensive, and recommended making them of wood 'well bronzed': in the event they were made in bronze and finished by Anderson's man, 'all but the bronzing', by March 1768. 'They are so finely executed,' wrote Chambers, 'that it would be a pity not to have them quite complete. I have therefore ordered them to be entirely gilded, for I feared that bronzing would make them appear dull, and partly gilding upon the bronze would look tawdry.'[95] He was not going to have his design, which probably originated during his time in Rome and appears to be indebted to the fountains by Bernini in Rome or to an earlier model,[96] spoiled by inferior finish.

44. William Chambers, design of chimneypiece for 'Lord Charlemont's Eating Room', detail, Victoria and Albert Museum.

45. Wedgwood and Bentley, London Pattern Book, sketch of triton candlestick, Wedgwood Museum, Barlaston.

46. Triton candlestick, Hotspur Ltd.

47. Triton candlesticks, Sotheby's.

It would not be surprising if the triton was among the models that Chambers gave to Boulton in 1770. He seems to have treated him as Anderson's successor as a maker of ormolu ornaments. Alternatively the figure may have been one of the two tritons that Chambers lent to Boulton in order to have copies made. He asked Boulton in 1773 to return models of two tritons and a griffin, because they did not belong to him and he had to return them to the owner.[97] Might the owner have been Lord Charlemont? And is it possible that Chambers lent the figures as early as 1770? Even if the answer to these two questions is no, it is still entirely possible that Boulton acquired a model from Chambers in 1770 or that he bought it from Anderson's stock after his death (see p. 100).

The same model was produced by Wedgwood in black basalt,[98] and later in blue and white jasper, and a drawing of a triton candlestick survives in Wedgwood's London pattern book, which consists of drawings probably used in Wedgwood's London showroom (Plate 45).[99] It is thus also possible that Boulton received the model for his triton from Wedgwood rather than from Chambers. I summarise the evidence in favour of Wedgwood later (see p. 102). The actual source may be academic because Wedgwood's model, too, is likely to have derived from Chambers (see p. 102).

Plates 46 and 47 illustrate triton figures that correspond to Chambers's design and to Wedgwood's and Boulton's sketches. I have discussed them briefly in the Survey of ornaments (see pp. 189–90). None of them can be firmly attributed to Boulton and Fothergill. Any of them may well have originated with Chambers, but none of them has any sign of candle branches. The gilt tritons of Plate 47 are intriguing. Were the figures once bronzed? Might there be some connection with Chambers's instruction to gild entirely the figures which Anderson's workshop was making for Lord Charlemont in 1768? The answers have to wait for the discovery and study of other triton figures.

The griffin that Chambers lent to Boulton may have served as Boulton's model for one of his griffin vases (Plates 336–7), although again the loan may have been too late to influence objects made in 1770–1. It is perhaps more likely that Boulton was influenced by an ormolu griffin made to Chambers's design. A griffin candlestick was among Chambers's designs for 'ornamental utensils' which were published in the third edition of his *Treatise on Civil Architecture* in 1791 (Plate 48), and a finished drawing by John Yenn, presumably after a sketch by Chambers, survives in the Victoria and Albert Museum (Plate 49).[100] Candlesticks modelled on this design have survived, which I have attributed to Anderson (Plate 50, see Chapter 2, p. 38).[101] Wedgwood copied the design in black basalt.[102] Boulton's griffins are not identical, but the similarities between Chambers's design and Boulton's less finely modelled beasts, especially in the treatment of the tail and the curious necklace and medallion, are striking.[103]

Chambers may also have given Boulton models for some of the less obvious decorative motifs that appear on Boulton's vases. The four sphinxes on the sidereal clock (Plate 182) do not have the same tails as the sphinxes on Chambers's sketch of a clock case (Plate 36), but he is very likely to have been the source of the model for them. He could also have been responsible for the dolphins' heads on the handles of the vases of Plate 258, which echo a sketch in his Franco-Italian Album.[104] The Greek key-pattern frieze, the use of which was typical of Chambers's leanings towards the archaic, appears for example on other objects besides the King's clock case (Plates 183, 244), and other decorative motifs, including arabesque and other decorative friezes and borders, flutes decorated with husks (Plates 211, 349), festoons and swags, lyres, masks, bucrania, perched eagles and ringed lions' masks all appear in Chambers's drawings or executed works. He might have had models of any of these available in 1770.

48. William Chambers, *Treatise on Civil Architecture* (1791), griffin candlestick.

ABOVE RIGHT:
49. John Yenn, griffin candlestick, Victoria and Albert Museum.

50. Griffin candlestick, possibly made by Diederich Nicolaus Anderson, *c.*1760–5, Blenheim Palace.

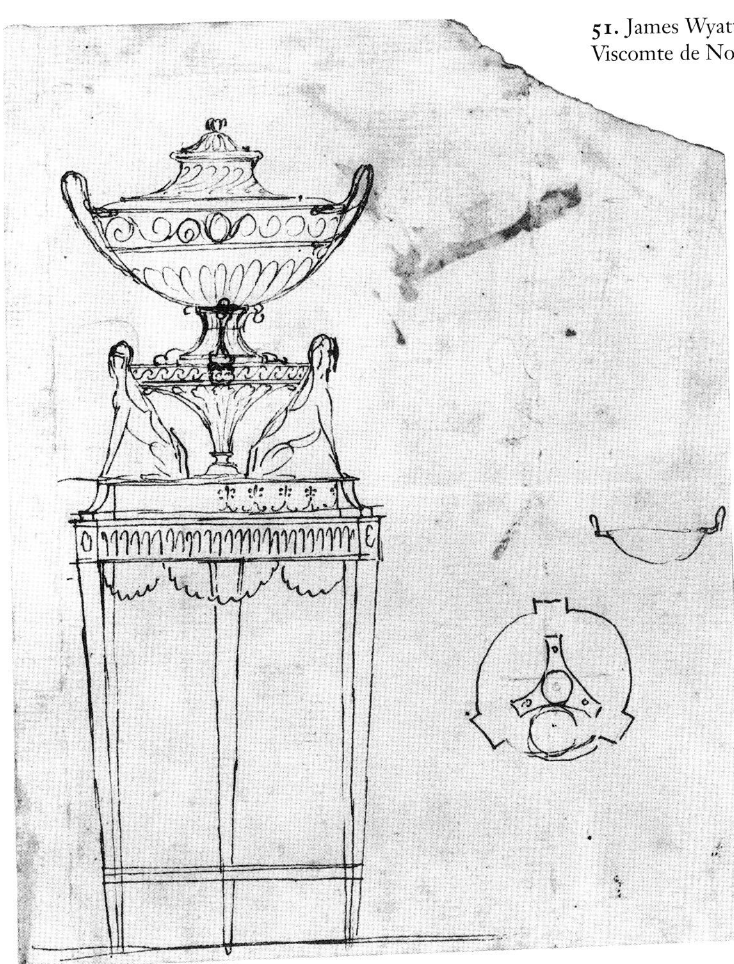

51. James Wyatt, design for tureen, Viscomte de Noailles Album, Paris.

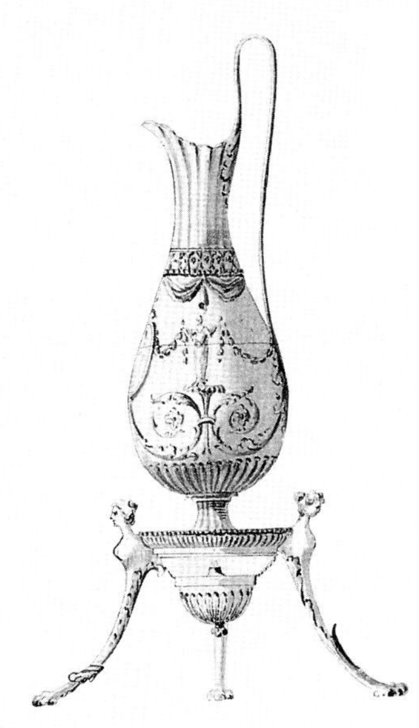

52. Boulton and Fothergill, Pattern Book 1, p. 83.

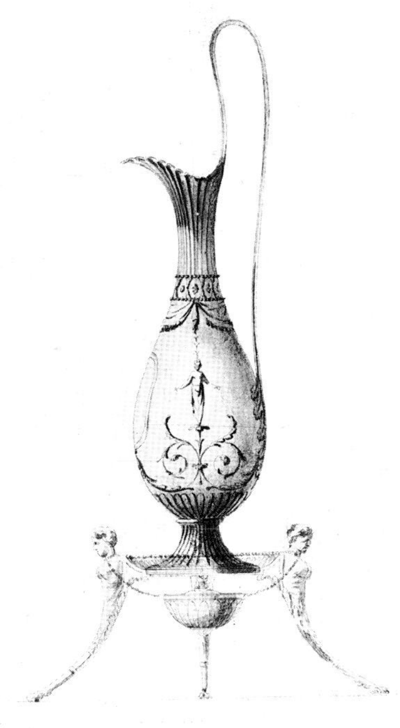

53. James Wyatt, design for ewer, Viscomte de Noailles Album, Paris.

Quite apart from Boulton's direct contacts with the architect, he was probably influenced in his ideas of design, both in general and in particular, by Chambers's published works, which he bought in 1770.[105] The *Treatise on Civil Architecture* in particular was an influential book, and must have done much to form Boulton's taste. It may even have given him ideas for particular forms of ornamentation.

Among other architects on whom Boulton may have drawn for his pool of designs were James and Samuel Wyatt, and Robert Mylne. Boulton was on friendly terms with Samuel Wyatt and was corresponding with him from 1765. He was also friendly with both Mylne and James Wyatt and on occasions supplied them with products of manufacture.[106] Both provided designs for silverware in the 1770s.[107] James Wyatt was a particularly helpful source of designs for silverware and some of his drawings appear in Boulton and Fothergill's pattern books.[108] Not surprisingly his designs had some influence on some of Boulton's ormolu ornaments. The triangular perfume burners supported by three crouching sphinxes (Plate 251), for example, reflect a drawing by Wyatt of a tureen and stand in an album of designs by Wyatt in the collection of the Vicomte de Noailles (Plate 51).[109] The sphinxes reappear on the silver coffee pot made by Boulton and Fothergill and hallmarked 1769–70 (Plate 95), the design of which can be attributed to Wyatt on the same grounds.[110] The female supporters of the triangular perfume burners in Plate 304 reflect a design in the pattern books for a ewer on a stand (Plate 52), which in turn is based on another drawing in the de Noailles album (Plate 53). The winged figures of the perfume burners in Plate 362 are related to figures on an epergne designed by Wyatt.[111]

Books and prints

Boulton also culled ideas from books and prints. He was familiar with the three important books by the leading English architects, namely the first volume of Stuart and Revett's *Antiquities of Athens* (1762), Chambers's *Treatise on Civil Architecture* (1759) and Adam's *Ruins of the Palace of the Emperor Diocletian* (1764). He was also a subscriber to Martyn and Lettice's *Antiquities of Herculaneum* (1773), as were Wedgwood and Duesbury, and by 1771 he owned the first five volumes of *Le Antichità di Ercolano*.[112] This was an account, published in Naples in nine volumes, of the discoveries made during the excavation of Herculaneum. These discoveries were nothing short of astounding, because the solidified lava had protected the buildings and their contents from natural deterioration and, more important, from pilfering. The publication of the findings provided a major stimulus to the designers of buildings and ornaments.

Boulton's eagerness to consult such works was typical of his eclectic methods. He was not content to rely solely on his visits to London or on his occasional if stimulating meetings with the arbiters of the antique taste. He valued highly the many archaeological books that stimulated the rising tide of the classical revival. He was not unusual in this. Such books were used practically as pattern books by many craftsmen and designers of the time, all over Europe. They were a prolific source of 'invention'. They contain many details that may have led Boulton and his modellers to create particular mounts, borders or friezes, although without documentary evidence it is impossible to be certain about this. There were many alternative sources for any one ornament. What is certain is that these books generally influenced Boulton's repertoire of classical ornament and they put a stamp of authority on his work.

Some of the books that Boulton bought or consulted cannot, unfortunately, be identified. In 1768, for example, he paid a subscription for a book of vases[113] and in 1773 he apparently borrowed another book of vases from 'Mr Hoare'.[114] The first of these might have been E.-A. Petitot's collection of vases which was published in 1767, but there is no evidence.

Equally there are several books which a manufacturer of Boulton's standing and experience would almost certainly have studied or owned, but there is no evidence in the archives that he did. Such books include the celebrated surveys of classical sites by Robert Wood[115] and Thomas Major.[116] They also include the classical miscellanies which I have mentioned earlier, such as those by J. F. de Neufforge and J.-C. Delafosse. He is also likely to have seen at least some of G. B. Piranesi's engravings, the first series of which appeared in 1756. Some of the mounts on Boulton's ornaments reflect drawings in Piranesi's works – for example the winged figure with claw feet (Plate 362), the perching eagles (Plate 184), the swags of husks with bowed ribbons (Plate 253), the sphinx's wings (Plate 182), the knotted-drapery festoon (Plate 263), and the handle with two masks (Plate 213) – all appear in Piranesi's engravings, most of them on a single page of ornament which Piranesi wrongly attributed to the Etruscans.[117] Whether the designs were adapted direct from Piranesi's prints, or came from William Chambers who knew Piranesi in Rome and was familiar with his works, or have no connection with Piranesi at all, cannot at present be known. All that can be said about these various authors of works in the classical taste is that Boulton's compelling interest in the antique taste and his familiarity with it, suggest that he must have seen many of their books.

Fortunately some of the books that he owned or consulted can be identified. His library included furniture designs by J.-C. Delafosse and designs of vases by Delafosse, Saly and others.[118] In 1771 he asked William Matthews to procure a new book of vases that was being published from the bookseller Darly in the Strand.[119] This was presumably Matthew Darly, who produced engraved plates of vases and exhibited 'sketches of vases, and other antique ornaments' at the Society of Artists' exhibition in 1769 and 'eight sketches of vases, in imitation of the antique, for the different manufactures of Great Britain' in 1771.[120] In 1772 he published a book of ornaments in the antique taste, which was probably the book that Boulton hoped to acquire.[121]

Another publication which Boulton was pleased to acquire was the set of coloured prints of the ancient vases in the collection of the British ambassador at Naples, William Hamilton, produced by 'Baron d'Hancarville'. I have mentioned in Chapter 2 that P. J. Wendler, who was travelling in Italy on Boulton's behalf, subscribed for these prints in Boulton's name in 1767.[122] The edition consisted of more than four hundred and fifty beautifully produced prints collected into four volumes, but only the first volume was published in 1767. One of the purposes of the edition was to encourage manufacturers in the use of correct classical models:

> We think also that we make an agreeable present to our manufacturers of earthen ware and china, and to those who make vases in silver, copper, glass, marble etc. Having employed much more time in working than in reflexion, and being besides in great want of models, they will be very glad to find here more than two hundred forms, the greatest part of which are absolutely new to them; there, as in a plentiful stream, they may draw ideas which their ability and taste will know how to improve to their advantage, and to that of the public.[123]

Wendler thought the edition a very suitable work from which to choose 'handsome designs and patterns for the Birmingham manufactorys' and reckoned that Boulton 'could not do wrong to subscribe for the same'.[124] He even suggested that John Taylor and the other leading manufacturers in Birmingham, including John Baskerville, the japanner and printer, would be glad to have them, and suggested to Boulton that they should write for them. Boulton was delighted with the purchase:

> I thank you kindly for the things you have purchased for me which are all very agreeable to me, but none more so than the 456 prints of ornaments and vases which will be very usefull in my manufactory.[125]

Whether Boulton received the first volume in 1767 or had copies of the proof sheets, which were circulating in England, is uncertain. But he had the book by 1768, and the Austrian visitor Count von Zinzendorf saw and admired it when he visited Soho in September.[126] The second volume was published in 1770.[127]

The influence of the engravings on Boulton's ornaments is not as obvious as their influence on Wedgwood, whose 'Etruscan' ware owed a great deal to them.[128] This may seem surprising at first sight, bearing in mind the importance ascribed to d'Hancarville's engravings both at the time by designers and subsequently by art historians. But it is not so surprising. In 1767 Boulton was fascinated by the vase craze and saw a big manufacturing opportunity in it (see Chapter 2, pp. 42–3). He had not at that stage decided on how he might fulfil the ambition. He was certainly interested in ceramic vases, and in the summer of 1767 expressed half an inclination, in a letter to Wedgwood, to try his hand at pottery (see Chapter 2, p. 45). In the event his interest turned to gilt bodies and to the stones of Derbyshire. Ceramic bodies took a lesser role, and painted ceramic bodies no role at all. Boulton's chief practical interest in d'Hancarville's prints probably centred on the decorative borders and on the use of the book as a means of instruction to the young draughtsmen whom he employed in the factory. A comparison of some of the plates with Boulton and Fothergill's work, and especially with their silverware,[129] suggests that the borders of the prints may have been a source of inspiration (Plate 54).[130] Their ormolu-mounted

54. d'Hancarville, *Collection of Etruscan, Greek and Roman Antiquities*, Vol. II, Plate 106.

55. d'Hancarville, *Collection of Etruscan, Greek and Roman Antiquities*, Vol. II, Plate 23.

56.1. Montfauçon, *Antiquité Expliquée*, Vol. III, Part 1, Plate XXIV, Julia, daughter of the Emperor Titus, Society of Antiquaries.

56.2. Montfauçon, *Antiquité Expliquée*, Vol. II, Part 1, Plate XCII, sacrifice group, Society of Antiquaries.

56.3. Montfauçon, *Antiquité Expliquée*, Vol. I, Part 2, Plate CCXI, Clementia, Society of Antiquaries.

LEFT:
57. Boulton and Fothergill, Clementia, medallion from a Titus clock case, Hotspur Ltd.

ABOVE:
58. Montfauçon, *Antiquité Expliquée*, Vol. IV, Part 1, Plate XCIX, Triumph of the Emperor Titus, Society of Antiquaries.

ewers (Plate 196) may also owe something to d'Hancarville. They echo not only the shape of an ewer illustrated in d'Hancarville's second volume but also the decoration of the neck and the application of a mask at the base of the handle (Plate 55).[131] Boulton's eagerness to acquire the prints anyway demonstrates his keen interest in design and in the development of a vase trade.

Boulton bought a copy of another great classical miscellany, Bernard de Montfauçon's *Antiquité Expliquée*, in 1764.[132] This celebrated account of ancient buildings, objects and customs, which had originally been published in 1719,[133] contained a wealth of classical, Egyptian and 'barbaric' designs. There are several images in Montfauçon's work which could have inspired Boulton or even have been the origins of his designs, although it is extremely difficult without documentary proof to say whether his models were copied from one source or another, or whether he bought a model, coincidentally based on an engraving, from elsewhere. Plate 56.1 for example shows the representation of Julia, the daughter of the Emperor Titus, from the gem in the Treasury of St Denis, Paris.[134] Julia's renowned coiffure, quite apart from her unfortunate treatment at the hands of her uncle the Emperor Domitian, appears to have caught the fancy of engravers, and gems with her image were widely illustrated. Montfauçon called her hairstyle the '*chef d'œuvre de l'art*'.[135] Boulton used the image on a gilt medallion (Plate 73) and it appears on the knife urn in Plate 220. It may also be the medallion sketched on the obelisk in the pattern book drawing in Plate 223, which depicts a female bust with necklace and earrings but a less distinct coiffure. I shall summarise later the medallions used by Boulton on a number of ornaments, including this gem of Julia, when I discuss the copies made by James Tassie and the ceramic versions made by Wedgwood. Meanwhile, this image of Julia published by Montfauçon seems the most likely, of the many reproductions of it, to have been Boulton's source. Plate 56.2 shows another reproduction of a gem, depicting a sacrifice group that may have been the basis of Boulton's version (Plate 76.4),[136] although I argue later in this chapter for a different source. At least Boulton would have been aware of the image in Montfauçon when choosing which medallions to apply to his vases. Montfauçon is also a possible source of the medallion of Clementia, which appears on the urns of two recorded Titus clock cases (Plate 57, see Survey of ornaments, p. 234). Montfauçon's version (Plate 56.3)[137] shows her with fewer clothes, a different coiffure, and holding a staff in her left hand, and Boulton's version shows more of the chair and puts it into the perspective of the floor, but there are also similarities. Another possibility is that Boulton's modeller used an image of Concordia, several images of whom appear in an adjacent engraving,[138] but used the name Clementia as being more appropriate to Titus's regret that he had lost a day ('*Diem Perdidi*') without doing good to anyone.

The only explicit reference to the use of Montfauçon's book in the archives occurs in connection with the first design of the Titus clock case in 1771. One of Boulton and Fothergill's designs for this clock case showed the emperor wearing 'the long toga such as he [is] represented in his triumphal arch (viz. Montfacon) …'[139] and it was this design that their patron chose. The actual figure was not, however, modelled on the representation of Titus in Montfauçon's work, which is a drawing of the relief of his triumphal progress after the taking of Jerusalem, taken from the triumphal arch in Rome (Plate 58).[140] Boulton and Fothergill's reference was only to the type of dress and was made perhaps with the intention of impressing the patron with the learning on which their work was founded. The model for the figure came from A. F. Gori's *Museum Florentinum*.

Wendler asked Boulton in 1767 if he would like 'the prints of all the curiositys and antiquitys of Florence'.[141] This probably refers to Gori's massive work, which appeared in twelve volumes under the title *Museum Florentinum* between 1731 and 1766. Gori's work was an illustrated and annotated survey of gems, statues, coins and paintings in the most important collections in Florence. Boulton did not apparently buy it in 1767 and he seems never to have bought all twelve volumes. One of his clerks asked Mayhew and Ince in 1771 if they could send their copy to Soho on loan: alternatively he asked them to order from the bookseller Peter Elmsley, with whom Boulton and Fothergill had an account, 'such of the volumes ... as he thinks will be usefull to us, there being so many volumes in that work that will be of little use and we know not the particulars of it'.[142] A month later Boulton ordered the first three volumes from Elmsley himself.[143] They did not arrive until towards the end of the year.[144] They therefore had no perceptible influence on the firm's ormolu designs during 1770–1, which were the years of the greatest speculative output. They were, however, a rich mine of possible designs. The first two volumes, which were published in 1731 and 1732, were devoted to engravings of carved classical gems, many of them drawn from the collection of the Medicis. The engravings consisted of portraits of gods and eminent men and of various classical figures and mythological scenes. The third volume, published in 1734, depicted statues in the same collection.

59. Gori, *Museum Florentinum*, Vol. III, *Statuae Antiquae*, Plate LXXXV, *Vir Consularis*.

Boulton and Fothergill's letter to Pechell makes it clear that the figure of Titus would be copied from a 'delineation of a gem in the Mideum collection', a misprint presumably for 'Medici' by the clerk who wrote the letter. The figure of the emperor on the clock case (Plate 183) bears a close resemblance to one of Gori's engravings entitled '*Vir Consularis*' (Plate 59) in the third volume of his *Museum Florentinum*, not an impression of a gem as suggested in the letter to Pechell, but of a statue.[145] The modelling of the drapery is particularly close to the engraving and the only substantive differences are the addition of a laurel crown, the treatment of the left hand and the change of sandals. Boulton clearly had this image in mind from the start. Either he or Eginton must have been struck by the imposing '*Vir Consularis*' in their newly acquired copy of Gori's book and seen in the figure the potential for a clock case design. It would be interesting to know who had the idea of converting him into the Roman Emperor with his famous motto.

There are other engravings in Gori's book which may have been sources of Boulton's inspiration. One possibility is that the design of the clock case showing an offering to Diana (Plate 153) owes something to one of the gems engraved in Gori's book showing women bringing offerings to celebrate the success of athletes. Plate 60 shows one of these.[146]

60. Gori, *Museum Florentinum*, Vol. II, *Gemmae Antiquae*, Plate LXXV, Society of Antiquaries.

With the gems engraved in Plate 61 we are on surer ground.[147] All four of these gems were reproduced in Gori's second volume, and all four appear as gilt medallions (Plate 62) on the vases illustrated in Plate 258, which I have attributed to Boulton and Fothergill (see Survey of ornaments, pp. 295–7). Gori describes the images as (1) *Thalia, Musa Comoediae* (Plate 61.1), (2) *Victoria Hygaea Salutaris, potius vero Nemesis* (Plate 61.2), (3) *Sacerdos Femina ad aram stans* (Plate 61.3), and (4) *Femina ad tumulum immolanda, forte Polyxena* (Plate 61.4).[148] Later in this chapter I shall summarise the likely origins of Boulton's various medallions in the context of James Tassie's extensive collection of paste gems and Wedgwood's use of many of them. All four of these gems appear in Tassie's collection (see p. 103), but none of them were used by Wedgwood, and there seems little doubt that Gori was Boulton's ultimate source for the four images. I have, however, dated the vases on which they are mounted a year or more earlier than Boulton's purchase of Gori's book, which may mean that he copied the images from someone else's copy of the book or bought plaster casts of the images. The images on the medallions, while very close to the originals,

OPPOSITE:
62. Boulton and Fothergill, medallions from one of the vases in Plate 258, Syon House.

61.1–4. Gori, *Museum Florentinum*, Vol. II, *Gemmae Antiquae*, Plates XVI (Thalia), LXIX (Victory Salutaris), LXXIII (Woman at altar), LXXVII (Polyxena), Society of Antiquaries.

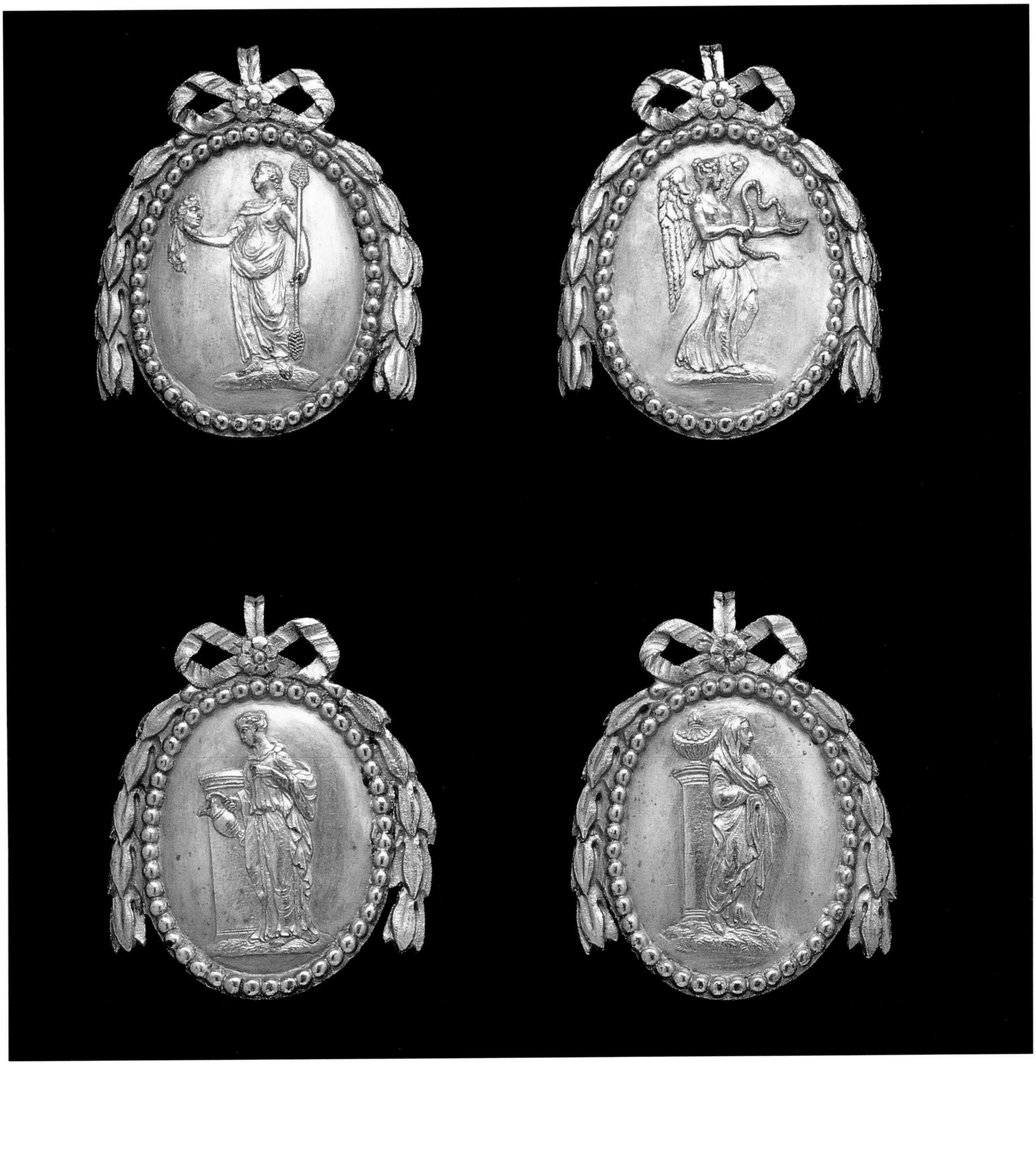

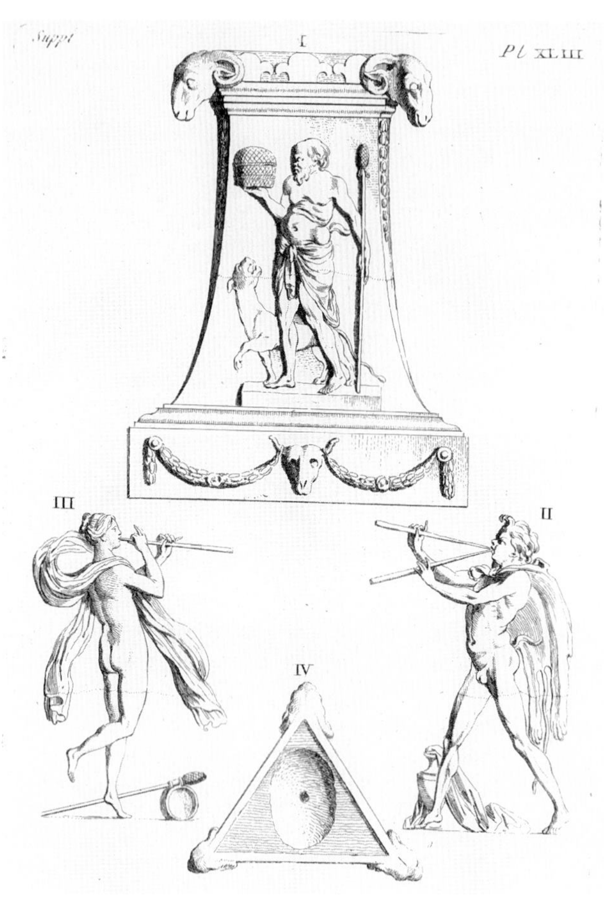

63. De Caylus, *Recueil d'Antiquités*, Vol. VII, Plate XLIII, Society of Antiquaries.

are not exact copies, which might argue for an intervening source. As with most of Boulton's medallions there is no obvious connection between the chosen images. They were chosen because they convey a general picture of classicism and, perhaps, because they were available.

Boulton appears to have owned the seven volumes of the Comte de Caylus's *Recueil d'Antiquités Égyptiennes, Étrusques, Grecques et Romains*, which was published in Paris in 1761–7 and was another of the miscellanies of classical objects and ornaments which acted as a source book for artists and designers.[149] The pedestals of the wing-figured perfume burners illustrated in Plate 363, with their rams' heads and pendants of husks at the corners and the bucrania and swags on the triangular base, are directly modelled on an engraving of a triangular altar in de Caylus's collection (Plate 63).[150] There are only minor differences in the treatment of the body of the pedestal, notably the guilloche frieze between the rams' heads instead of the more interesting motif in the engraving.

The differences in the treatment of the three panels (Plate 64), which depict Bacchic revellers, are also minor, and tempt the playing of one of those 'spot the difference' pictorial games. The three figures are a Silenus-like faun carrying the winnowing-basket and a thyrsus and accompanied by a leopard (Plate 64.1), a faun blowing a double pipe with a vase and drapery at his feet (Plate 64.2), and a maenad blowing a single pipe with a thyrsus and a tambourine at her feet (Plate 64.3). De Caylus was not entirely complimentary about these representations of Bacchic revels. After describing the three figures – the first not Bacchus himself but a faun, identified by his tail, holding the '*van*' or '*corbeille*', the second a faun with two '*flutes*', the third a '*danseuse*' with the '*thyrse et l'instrument circulaire*' – he criticised the artist's addition of the attributes of the younger faun and the maenad. The placing of these objects at their feet did not accord with their celebratory poses, and the choice of a vase and drapery for the male reveller was more appropriate to women who go to the baths. The ancient artists would never have committed such follies – '*ils etoient trop sages dans la partie des Arts pour admettre rien de pastiche et d'affecte.*'[151] De Caylus's criticisms had substance, but I doubt if Boulton or his customers noticed.

Whether Boulton's modeller used de Caylus's engraving as the pattern or Boulton bought plaster casts of the whole altar cannot be known without further evidence, but the origin of the design is beyond doubt.

The books that I have discussed do not exhaust the titles that Boulton is known to have owned. He probably owned, for example, Antoine Desgodetz's influential account of the ancient monuments of Rome, *Les Édifices Antiques de Rome*, which was first published in Paris in 1682.[152] Boulton noted the title in his diary in 1767, perhaps as a reminder to buy a copy.[153] The book contained measured drawings of the principal monuments of Rome and thus provided yet another possible dictionary of classical motifs. There is little evidence that Boulton derived particular ideas for ornaments from Desgodetz, but his book was another source of classical inspiration. He also had a copy of Gabriel Huquier's collection of thirteen works on architectural detail and ornament, mostly engraved by Huquier and including designs of vases, trophies, fountains and other ornaments by Boucher, Bouchardon, Charpentier, le Geay, Richardson, Watteau and others.[154] He subscribed to George Richardson's *Iconology*, published in London in 1778, a collection of the 'most approved emblematical representations of the ancient Egyptians, Greeks and Romans and from the compositions of Cavaliere Cesare Ripa ...'. Ripa's *Iconologia* had first been published in Rome in 1593, and was reprinted in many editions in the next two centuries. Richardson's colour illustrations were a useful source of design to the many artists and craftsmen who, like Boulton, subscribed to the volumes. This volume was published too late to have any effect on

OPPOSITE:
64.1–3. Boulton and Fothergill, panels from the pedestal of one of the wing-figured vases in Plate 363, Christie's.

65. Ravenet (attrib.), Venus and Adonis, from Sayer's *Compleat Drawing Book*, Society of Antiquaries.

66. Enamel plaque, Battersea, Schreiber Collection, Victoria and Albert Museum.

designs for ormolu, but Boulton may have been aware from its predecessors of some of the iconography associated with classical figures, for example the winged head of Science who is seen teaching the laws of Nature on the sidereal clock (Plate 181, see Survey of ornaments, p. 227).

The design of the Venus vase seems to owe its origin to an engraving attributed to Simon François Ravenet of Venus mourning for Adonis (Plate 65), published by Robert Sayer in one of the editions of his *Compleat Drawing Book*.[155] Plate 66 shows an enamel plaque, probably from the Battersea Enamel Works, based on Ravenet's engraving.[156] Boulton's source could have been either the engraving or copies of it, such as this plaque, but there is no evidence of how his modellers might have acquired the print or models based on it.[157] I have not so far been able to identify the artist, presumably French, of the picture that Ravenet engraved, nor has the picture itself been traced. Ravenet's engraving shows Venus, mostly naked but with an ample robe and accompanied by a fellow mourner, leaning in a posture of grief on a pedestal. There is an urn on the pedestal, and a square plaque on the pedestal depicts the death of Adonis while fighting the wild boar. Cupid, with his bow, nestles under Venus's robe and wipes a tear from his eye. The ensemble is shown in a landscape of trees. There are many differences between this engraving and Boulton and Fothergill's version – indeed there are few details that are exactly reproduced – but the coincidences of theme and overall design are striking.

Sculptors, plaster shops and other sources

Boulton also gathered models and designs from sculptors, from friends and rivals among the shopkeepers and manufacturers, from correspondents and travelling agents, and from his patrons. The possibility of finding a fresh idea, a fresh motif or a new material was constantly in his mind.

Sculptors were a prolific source of models for the manufacturers of the time. The close link after 1775 between Wedgwood and the younger John Flaxman (1755–1826) is well known. Flaxman also supplied Boulton with figures and medal designs during the last thirty years of the century.[158] It was from his father, however, that Boulton bought models for his ormolu. John Flaxman senior made and sold plaster casts and, as a modeller, numbered sculptors such as Louis François Roubiliac and Peter Scheemakers among his employers.[159] He also supplied Wedgwood with models. Boulton presumably went to see him during one of his visits to London in 1770. He immediately saw that Flaxman's casts could be very useful to him and bought several of them. The following invoices give an idea of his purchases:

16th November 1770	£	s	d
To 2 cwt of fine plaister	1	4	0
To 1 lion		12	0
To a base releif of ditto		4	0
To a ram's head		8	0
To a deer's head		6	0
To a packing box		2	0
	2	16	0

26th November 1770	£	s	d
A sleeping Bacchus	1	1	0
11 boys at 3s each	1	13	0
2 groups of ditto		10	0
A packing box		3	0
	3	7	0

5th December 1770	£	s	d
Group of Hercules and Atlas	2	2	0
Figure of Michel Angelo's Anatomy		14	0
Packing Box		5	0
	3	1	0[160]

Several of these casts were probably used as models for ormolu ornaments. Rams' heads and lion masks appear on several designs, and figures of boys were used not only for the Boy and Minerva clock cases (Plates 152, 166) but also for other watch stands.[161]

The 'group of Hercules and Atlas' was the group of three figures which Boulton used for the case of the geographical clock (Plates 157–8, see Survey of ornaments, p. 203). Boulton used the names 'Hercules and Atlas' to describe the figures in the description of the geographical clock when he wrote to Lord Cathcart in 1771 (see p. 203), which neatly identifies them with the figures in Flaxman's invoice. Boulton must have known the origin of the three figures because Chambers illustrated two of them in his *Treatise on Civil Architecture* (Plate 41, Figs. 1, 3) and gave their origin in the accompanying text. They were copies of three of the four figures on a silver-gilt crucifix made by Antonio Gentile da Faenza in about 1582, which is now in the Treasury of St Peter's, Rome (Plate 67). Gentile may have copied the figures from Michelangelo,[162] and Chambers was under the impression that Michelangelo was the originator – they were, he said, 'copied from

67. Gentile da Faenza, silver crucifix, Vatican Museum, Treasury of St Peter's, Rome.

candelabres, in St Peter's of the Vatican. They are cast from models of Michael Angelo Buonaroti, and repaired either by himself, or doubtless under his direction: for the workmanship is very perfect.'[163] Boulton had already used one of the figures, in a larger version, for the Persian vase (Plates 352–4, see Survey of ornaments, pp. 346–50): I have suggested earlier in this chapter that the name of the vase and the martial theme of the trophies on the pedestal both derive from Chambers's description. I have also suggested that Boulton received the model of the figure for the Persian vase from Chambers (see p. 80). It is not clear why Chambers recorded only two of the four figures on the crucifix in his *Treatise*.

For the figures for the geographical clock it is clear that Flaxman was the supplier, not the architect. He presumably modelled the figures in plaster, and it is interesting that he added a headband and a belt across the body of the figure corresponding to the Persian vase figure. Assuming that Boulton knew well the origin of these three figures, it is perhaps surprising that he went along with Flaxman's description of them as 'Hercules and Atlas', but the names of Hercules, and especially Atlas, once Flaxman had used them, were appropriate for the supporters of the terrestrial globe on the top of the clock.

The somewhat startling combination, in the geographical clock case, of ornament in the 'antique taste' and Italian *cinquecento* sculptural figures betrays Boulton's true nature as a producer of decorative ornament. He was not a totally consistent follower of the new style. He was happy to borrow designs and models from anywhere if the resulting ornament might appeal to the buyer. I suspect that he liked the look of the figures, recognised one of them from Chambers's Persian model (or maybe two of them from his copy of Chambers's *Treatise*), and thought that he had a good use for them. He probably thought that, blessed by such exponents of the new style as Chambers and Flaxman, the figures were somehow part of the accepted classical canon. The clock case is a prime example of his wish to make 'new combinations of old ornaments without presuming to invent new ones'. It is also a rare example of an object whose ornaments and figures derived directly from two known sources – William Chambers's models for the King's clock case and John Flaxman's plaster casts.

Wedgwood used the same three figures as decorative supports for his black basalt 'Michelangelo' lamps, two examples of which are at Saltram (Plate 68).[164] He too probably bought his models from Flaxman. Why Flaxman modelled only three of the four figures on Gentile's crucifix is as unclear as why Chambers illustrated only two of them. Perhaps the model of one of the four was broken on the way from Rome.[165]

Another sculptor who supplied both Boulton and Wedgwood with models was John Bacon (1740–99). Boulton paid him five and a half guineas in 1773 for 'a model and mould of a figure of Urania'.[166] This was too late for it to have been the model for the figure of Urania which surmounted the sidereal clock (Plate 179), but it could have been the pattern for the 'elegant figure of Urania in bronze, holding a time piece against an obelisk of statutory marble ...' (Plates 189–90, see Survey of ornaments, p. 236), two versions of which were included in the sale in 1778. The modelling of this figure of Urania is a cut above the quality of the modelling of several other figures modelled at Soho, and an attribution to Bacon is entirely credible. Bacon may have modelled other mounts for Boulton, but so far no other documentary evidence has come to light.[167]

Boulton derived models, patterns and ideas from many others, including artists, manufacturers and shopkeepers. He bought a pattern of a tripod in 1768 from a 'Mr Ryder', probably the engraver Thomas Ryder, which I have mentioned in the context of James Stuart (see p. 72). Daniel Pincot (d.1797) sent details of his manufacture of copies of the Borghese vase in

68. Wedgwood and Bentley, black basalt 'Michelangelo' lamps, National Trust, Saltram House.

1771, and supplied another vase, which one of the Wyatts had ordered, from the artificial stone manufactory in Lambeth.[168] Boulton was given some models by a 'Mr Wright' in 1770[169] and in 1768 bought stone ornaments in Derbyshire, including obelisks,[170] which may have given him some of his ideas for clock cases and other ornaments (Plates 192, 223).

Flaxman's invoices are rarities in the Boulton archives. It is surprising that there are no other mentions of plaster shops, many of which flourished in London in the eighteenth century by supplying models to architects and to the manufacturers of ornament. It somehow passes belief that Boulton did not buy models from some of them. Their role in supplying manufacturers has been generally understated.[171] Wedgwood bought models from some of them,[172] and it may be that Boulton did too and that invoices and correspondence have either not survived or have yet to come to light. It certainly seems likely, given Boulton's insatiable curiosity, that he visited such shops during his visits to London, and it may be that he did so when he was in London in 1768 and went 'a-curiosity hunting' with Wedgwood and bought several objects of direct relevance to the ormolu and vase business.

It is clear from Wedgwood's comments on this visit that Boulton was eagerly collecting designs, as well as buying vases with the intention of copying or using them. He wrote to his partner:

Mr Boulton is still in town and has not done half his business nor shall have time, he says, if he stays a month longer. He has seen so many pretty things that he has sent for his artist to come up to him, and we have been alltogether, the ladys and all, at Harraches this afternoon, where we have amongst us spent near twenty pounds ...[173]

According to Wedgwood, Harrache had just been to Paris and had 'brought a great many fine things with him'. These probably included vases mounted in ormolu and Boulton probably bought some of them, besides picking up some plain vases, which he intended to decorate with metal mounts. Although Harrache later bought goods from Boulton and Fothergill,[174] there seems little doubt that in the early years the trade was the other way and that Boulton found his visits to Pall Mall a useful means of collecting designs. In the autumn of 1768 Boulton bought from Harrache:

	£	s	d
A transparent tortoiseshell box inlaid with stripes of gold	7	7	0
A pair of vases for candles	5	15	6
A red varnished box with gilt pierced outside	1	16	0[175]

It is clearly more than coincidence that three of the vases in Boulton and Fothergill's sale at Christie's in 1771 were called, in the correspondence, 'Harrach pattern 2 branched vases' (see Survey of ornaments, p. 283).

Boulton made other purchases during this visit to London, and noted in his diary:

	£	s	d
Bought of Mrs Anderson a Persian candlestick	15	15	0
A vase and branches	6	6	0
A plainer vase and horse [?] candlestick	4	4	0
Paid by a bill on Motteux[176]			
	26	5	0[177]

The purpose of these purchases was almost undoubtedly to cull ideas. On the strength of Anderson's association with William Chambers it is tempting to suppose that the Persian candlestick was so called because it incorporated one or more supporting male figures based on Chambers's 'Persian' figures, but there is no proof. Two years later, in February 1770, Boulton attended an auction 'where was sold the remains of Anderson's last things ...'.[178] He bought two 'little bronzed figures' which he sent to Soho for use as models.[179] Also in London, Boulton received an offer of permission to take drawings of the antique vases in the British Museum (the offer resulted from Wedgwood's application to do likewise),[180] and visited exhibitions that he thought would produce suitable ideas.[181]

He kept a sharp eye open when he visited the houses of his patrons. Their collections were an important source of ideas. In the preface to the catalogue of the sale at Christie's in 1771, Boulton and Fothergill acknowledged the patronage and zeal of the nobility and gentry, who had not only promoted the establishment of the ormolu business but had also allowed 'access to every thing curious in their possession that hath a tendency to improve or correct our taste'. Boulton made a habit of visiting his patrons' collections when he could. Thus when Wedgwood and Boulton went 'a-curiosity hunting' in London in 1768 they started with a visit to the Earl of Shelburne,[182] and in 1769 Boulton made special notes to inspect the Earl of Coventry's two houses and Sir Andrew Fountaine's house in Norfolk, where there was 'a fine room furnished with vases of all kinds and ages'.[183] In 1770 a copy was made of a lamp in the Earl of Shelburne's collection.[184] In the same year the Duke of Richmond arranged for Boulton to see Horace Walpole's vases at Strawberry Hill, which he considered to be 'better worth your seeing than any thing in England'. The Duke's introduction was not entirely unselfish – 'I wish you would have an exact drawing of them taken,' he said, 'as I may very possibly like to have them copied by you'.[185] The Earl of Dartmouth lent him a vase and offered the loan of anything in his possession that might be of use,[186] and I have mentioned earlier that Boulton may have copied the stems of the vases in Plates 241 and 243, and the legs and bases of the vases in Plates 324–5 from vases at Hagley, a house owned by another member of the local nobility (see p. 76). In 1771 Mrs Montagu sent a silver perfume burner in the same spirit of encouragement.[187]

Boulton also asked his friends and correspondents to send him patterns and examples of objects or materials which he might turn to advantage. Most of the surviving evidence for this is more relevant to the toy trade than to ormolu, but it underlines his methods. Wendler for example collected pieces of variegated marble, seals and cameos in Italy in 1767[188] and Hyman sent impressions of some gold boxes from Paris in 1769.[189] There is unfortunately no evidence of Hyman sending patterns of ormolu work although he was well placed to do so. The most curious of all the letters which Boulton received from those who provided him with models was a macabre and laboured note from the surgeon John Hunter, who wrote in 1772:

> Dear Boulton, I have sent you inclosed in a packing box *Death*. I hope it will have a good effect upon the living, and make them represent things to the life; and in the sculpure [*sic*] place [?] death itself done to the life. Let it animate gold and silver, let even brass be enlivened by its influence, may the rude block of marble rise and freese the soul to death by the living representation. I am dear Boulton yours till death ...[190]

Wedgwood and Tassie

Wedgwood was more than just a fellow curiosity hunter. Boulton regarded his friend as a source of ideas and as a potential collaborator in the development of the vase trade. There is evidence that Wedgwood was the source of some of the components, notably some of the medallions, incorporated into Boulton's ornaments.

The relationship between the two men was warm but delicate. They were close friends and shared many common interests, both through their membership of the Lunar Society and, as two of the leading manufacturers of their day, in the development of trade and transport. Boulton first approached Wedgwood for vase bodies in 1768, but Wedgwood declined to supply him. This led to Wedgwood fearing that Boulton might set himself up as a competitor in the production of ceramic vases, but in the event he need not have worried (see Chapter 2, pp. 46–7). He saw advantage in limited co-operation rather than in large-scale joint operation. Thus, in December 1770, when he heard from James Stuart that Boulton was making the bronze tripod to top the new 'Lanthorn of Demosthenes' at Shugborough, he visited the site and suggested that the bowl should be made of black basalt rather than bronze, which would be much heavier and more unwieldy. He got the job. 'Mr Stewart,' he wrote, 'said he knew Mr Anson would glory in having the arts of Soho, and Etruria united in his tripod.'[191] Neither the tripod nor the bowl has survived, and there is some uncertainty whether the bowl was ever installed, but the project showed that the two manufacturers could usefully work together. At the same time Wedgwood was making some 'tea kitchen' bodies and necks in 'Etruscan painted ware', one of which 'Mr Stewart has bespoke for Mrs Montagu'.[192] The components of a tea vase were sent to Soho in February 1771.[193]

There is thus a case for thinking that Boulton may have copied designs from Wedgwood's repertoire of ornament – and there are many parallels between the models used by the two manufacturers. There are the copious satyrs' heads, rams' heads, winged figures and other decorative motifs and borders that appear on ornaments from the two factories. But there are few ornaments that are so exactly alike that they would lead to a presumption of direct borrowing or even a common source. For those ornaments that are very similar, the two men seem to have generally tapped common sources rather than exchanged models. Boulton was keen in 1770 to share models, and wrote to Wedgwood that if he remembered correctly:

> there is another partnership model bought at Pinchbecks. There are many other things of a similar nature that he [i.e. Boulton] would be glad to go partners in: when any occurs to him he will let Mr Wedgwood in, and he hopes Mr W will do the same by him.[194]

The suggestion was typical of Boulton's eager search for models from all sources.

The 'partnership model' bought from Pinchbeck suggests that he and Wedgwood occasionally shared models, but there is little evidence that they regularly did so. The sense of rivalry persisted.

One shared model may have been the triton figure for the candlestick that they both made (Plates 45, 139), although I have suggested earlier that Chambers could equally have been their common source (see pp. 83–5). Wedgwood had the design from Chambers in 1769. 'Mr Chambers lent me the model of the triton candlestick,' he wrote to his partner, 'and was to have the first pair as a present.'[195] But this was not the only triton that Wedgwood acquired. In the same letter in which he suggested sharing models in 1770, Boulton wrote:

> Mr Boulton approves of Mr Wedgwood's purchasing the Triton, wishes he would take as many casts from it as he thinks proper, and then send it to Soho – after the same operation is performed there then begs to toss up or play any other game for the fee simple of the bronze or put it up to auction.

Wedgwood had bought the models of this triton in the previous month from the London plaster moulders Hoskins and Oliver. Their invoice listed:

	£	s	d
To a mold of a triton from the bronze	3	8	0
To a cast from ditto for a patern	1	1	0
To a mold of ditto for pressing	4	0	0[196]

Whether Wedgwood ever sent or took this triton to Soho is not known, but it is clearly a candidate for Boulton's model.

The story is further confused by the fact that this was not the only triton that Boulton was interested in. Later in the same letter in June 1770 he said:

> He [i.e. Boulton] likewise would be glad to have a pair of the small Trytons in earthen bronze or any other things that Mr Wedgwood wishes to have mounting for. The branches mentioned in Mr W's last letter can not be sent until more particular descriptions are sent to Soho as neither size, tast [?] or fittings are described. Mr Boulton therefore begs that the necessary description with a sketch or drawing may be sent to him.

Wedgwood took a triton to Soho later in 1770, probably in order to commission some branches for it.[197] His triton candlesticks, of which Wedgwood and Bentley made many, were almost invariably made with ceramic nozzles, and no example with ormolu branches has yet come to light.[198]

Chambers was probably the common source of the fish or dolphin handles used by Boulton on the King's clock case (see p. 80) and by

69.1–4. James Tassie, gems of Thalia, Victory Salutaris, Woman at altar ('Religious Ceremonies') and Polyxena, Beazley Archive, Ashmolean Museum, Oxford.

Wedgwood on ceramic ewers. I have also suggested that Boulton and Wedgwood bought the figures for their geographical clock case and 'Michelangelo lamps' from Flaxman rather than one borrowing from the other (see pp. 97–8). Later in this chapter I shall suggest that although both men used the same frieze of the 'Birth of Bacchus' they also derived it from independent sources (see p. 118).

The medallions used by the two men may be a more clear-cut story. Wedgwood's cameos and intaglios, and Boulton's medallions, were clearly derived from classical and Renaissance gems. There were several notable collections of gems in Europe, and they were well publicised in published books – I have already cited Gori's *Museum Florentinum* in which the gems in the Medici collection were engraved. Gems were objects of high fashion among the rich – Catherine II of Russia was a voracious collector – and not surprisingly they attracted imitators, the most notable of whom were James Tassie (1735–99) and Wedgwood, whose cameos and intaglios were sold both direct to collectors and to manufacturers and retailers. Wedgwood, the less prolific of the two, produced ceramic versions with bodies of black basalt, terracotta and, later, jasper.[199] Tassie came from Pollackshaws, near Glasgow, and according to his biographer[200] learnt his technique of reproduction in glass-based paste in Dublin. By 1766 he was in London and he exhibited paste and wax portrait medallions annually at the Royal Academy from 1767.[201] In 1775 he issued *A Catalogue of Impressions in Sulphur of Antique and Modern Gems, from which Pastes are Made and Sold by J. Tassie, Compton Street, Soho, London*. The definitive record of Tassie's collection of paste copies of cameos and intaglios was published by R. E. Raspe in 1791, by which time there were some 15,800 impressions, under the title *A Descriptive Catalogue of a General Collection of Ancient and Modern Engraved Gems, Cameos as well as Intaglios, taken from the most celebrated Cabinets in Europe, and cast in Coloured Pastes, White Enamel, and Sulphur, by James Tassie, Modeller ...*[202] Tassie would be described today perhaps as a populariser of gems previously confined to rich collectors' cabinets, and his impressions were much in demand. Both Wedgwood and Boulton used versions of many of the gems reproduced by Tassie, and Wedgwood bought gems from Tassie.[203] Did Tassie supply Boulton with impressions? Or did Boulton acquire his models from some other source – patrons, correspondents, plaster shops, manufacturers, or from Wedgwood?

I do not think there can be any doubt about the four medallions on the vases of Plate 258, which I have earlier shown came from engravings in Gori's *Museum Florentinum* (Plate 61) and not from either Tassie or Wedgwood. Tassie reproduced gems with all four images. Thalia (Plate 69.1), the Muse of the Theatre, is shown 'holding a mask in the right hand, and a thyrsus in the left' and the gem is engraved, as shown also in Gori's engraving, with the name *Kallimorphos* in Greek script, presumably the name of the artist.[204] 'Victory Salutaris' (Plate 69.2) is shown 'feeding a serpent, and holding a branch in the left hand'.[205] Gori's gem of the woman at an altar is reproduced under the heading of 'Religious Ceremonies', and shows 'a woman pouring water on the sepulchre of her parents' (Plate 69.3).[206] Polyxena is shown mostly naked, without a knife, and there is no urn on the pillar (Plate 69.4).[207] Tassie's reproductions of these four images are not as close to Boulton's medallions in their detail as Gori's engravings are. Wedgwood does not appear to have used any of the images.

In the earlier years of ormolu production Boulton also used medallions depicting Alexander the Great, Cleopatra, Ceres, and Julia, the daughter of the Emperor Titus. It is worth comparing these with both Tassie's and Wedgwood's versions:

70. Boulton and Fothergill, medallion of Alexander from one of the goat's head vases in Plate 331, Royal Collection.

71. Boulton and Fothergill, image of Cleopatra from one of the Cleopatra vases in Plate 327, Michael Winner.

72. Boulton and Fothergill, medallion of Ceres from one of the Cleopatra vases in Plate 328.

73. Boulton and Fothergill, medallion of Julia, the daughter of the Emperor Titus, from the knife urn in Plate 220, H. Blairman and Sons.

74.1–4. James Tassie, gems of Alexander, Cleopatra, Ceres and Julia, Beazley Archive, Ashmolean Museum, Oxford.

Alexander the Great *(Plate 70)*

75. Wedgwood and Bentley, cameo mould, Alexander, Wedgwood Museum, Barlaston.

Boulton used this image on goat's head vases (Plate 331, see Survey of ornaments, pp. 331–3). Raspe reproduced several images of Alexander in Tassie's collection, none of them precisely corresponding with Boulton's medallion but some of them not too distant (Plate 74.1).[208] Images of Alexander with rams' horns identify him with Ammon, or Amun, the Egyptian deity whose shrine he visited in 331 BC, identified by the Greeks with Zeus.[209] Raspe identified his images with Alexander on the grounds that the heads 'resemble those heads of Alexander which many of the Roman emperors caused to be put on their medals to preserve the remembrance of that extraordinary robber'. Wedgwood and Bentley listed a cameo of a head of 'Alexander the Great' in their 1773 catalogue of cameos and intaglios, and an intaglio in 1774.[210] Their mould for an intaglio is illustrated in Plate 75.[211]

Cleopatra *(Plate 71)*

Boulton's Cleopatra vase (see Survey of ornaments, pp. 328–30) was named after the image of Cleopatra which decorated the pedestal on the earliest models of the vase, of which so far only two are recorded (Plate 327). Boulton's medallion shows her with a diadem and a veil, with an asp at her breast. There are ten gems in Tassie's collection depicting Cleopatra, 'the last Queen of Egypt, daughter of Ptolemy Auletes'.[212] Raspe described the image as a 'head and bust of Cleopatra dying, ornamented with a diadem and veil, without the aspic'. She is shown with the diadem and veil in all the images (Plate 74.2),[213] but there are significant differences from Boulton's version. Nine of them face to the right. None includes an asp. In every case except one, which has no veil, the veil covers half the diadem. None has a diadem of the type depicted in Boulton's image or the same coiffure. Wedgwood and Bentley listed a portrait cameo of Cleopatra in their 1773 catalogue under the heading 'Illustrious Romans', which Cleopatra would not have been pleased at.[214] Wedgwood's image of Cleopatra shows her face in three-quarters profile and with no asp.[215] The image is closer to some of Tassie's versions than to Boulton's.

Ceres *(Plate 72)*

Ceres, the goddess of plenty, appears on many of Boulton's Cleopatra vases (Plate 328, see Survey of ornaments, pp. 328–30), perhaps in the mistaken belief that the image represented Cleopatra. Ceres also appears, more appropriately, on the knife urns of which one is illustrated in Plate 216. She is shown with a veil and a crown of ears of corn. On the vases, but not on the knife urns, the name Aspasiou, presumably the name of the artist, appears under the bust of Ceres in Greek script. Raspe listed several profile heads of Ceres in Tassie's collection, including one which is clearly the same gem as Boulton's model (Plate 74.3) with the name Aspasiou in the same position.[216] Raspe described this image as a 'bust of Ceres veiled, and crowned with ears of corn', and added that it was 'a resemblance of Agrippina; and, what seems accidental, of the Duchess of Gloucester'. The gem was from the Duke of Marlborough's collection. Wedgwood and Bentley listed a cameo of a head of Ceres in their 1773 catalogue, and two intaglios in 1774.[217] Their image of Ceres omitted the name Aspasiou.[218]

Julia, daughter of Titus *(Plate 73)*

A medallion of Julia, with her elaborate coiffure, and with necklace and earrings, is mounted on the knife urns of which one is illustrated in Plate 220 (see Survey of ornaments, p. 265). She may also be the image on the medallion on the obelisk in the sketch from the pattern book in Plate 223.4 (see Survey of ornaments, p. 266). I have illustrated Montfauçon's reproduction of this famous gem in Plate 56.1. Tassie's collection included several versions, including the same gem illustrated by Montfauçon (Plate 74.4).[219] Boulton's treatment of the hair in front of the diadem is closer to Montfauçon's engraving than to Tassie's gem, and is very close to Wedgwood's version. Wedgwood and Bentley listed a cameo of 'Julia, daughter of Titus', under the heading 'Illustrious Romans', in their 1773 catalogue.[220]

Later in the 1770s, nine further images, all of them recorded by Raspe in his catalogue of Tassie's collection, and all of them known to have been used by Wedgwood, appeared as medallions on Boulton's vases and clock cases, and particularly on the pedestals of the candle vases of the type illustrated in Plates 301 and 302 (see Survey of ornaments, pp. 314–15) but also on other ornaments (e.g. Plates 153, 304, see Survey of ornaments, p. 200 and pp. 315–16). Examples of Boulton's nine medallions are illustrated in Plates 76 and 77. These images were:

Pomona *(Plate 76.1)*

Raspe described Tassie's gem of Pomona, a Roman goddess of fruits, especially of those fruits that grow on trees such as apples, as 'carrying a basket on her head overloaded with fruit, which are falling to the ground' (Plate 78.1).[221] Wedgwood and Bentley listed two cameos of 'The Goddess Pomona' and an intaglio in their 1774 catalogue,[222] and a cameo mould is illustrated in Plate 79.1.[223]

Neptune *(Plate 76.2)*

Tassie's gem is illustrated in Plate 78.2. Neptune, the god of the sea, is shown, in Raspe's words, 'drawn in a car by four sea-horses'.[224] Wedgwood and Bentley listed a cameo of 'Neptune upon his chariot drawn by four sea horses' in their 1773 catalogue, citing the same gem as the origin of the design,[225] and an intaglio in 1774.[226] Wedgwood produced the cameo both as an upright oval and as a lateral one. In the lateral versions the tail of the hippocamp on the left was extended and a rock formation was added on the right. Wedgwood's cameo mould for an upright oval version is illustrated in Plate 79.2.[227]

Venus Victorious *(Plate 76.3)*

Raspe described Tassie's image as 'Venus Victorious, seen behind. Callipyga[228] examining the sword of Mars, Cupid presents her his helmet'.[229] The reference is to Venus's amatory conquest of Mars. The gem shows Venus naked, with a drape over her left arm (Plate 78.3). In Boulton's version Venus is clothed, and the shield is decorated with studs round the rim. Wedgwood and Bentley listed a cameo of 'Venus Victrix' in their 1774 catalogue, and an intaglio in the same year.[230] One of their cameo moulds is illustrated in Plate 79.3. It shows Venus clothed and the rim of the shield studded, as in Boulton's version.[231]

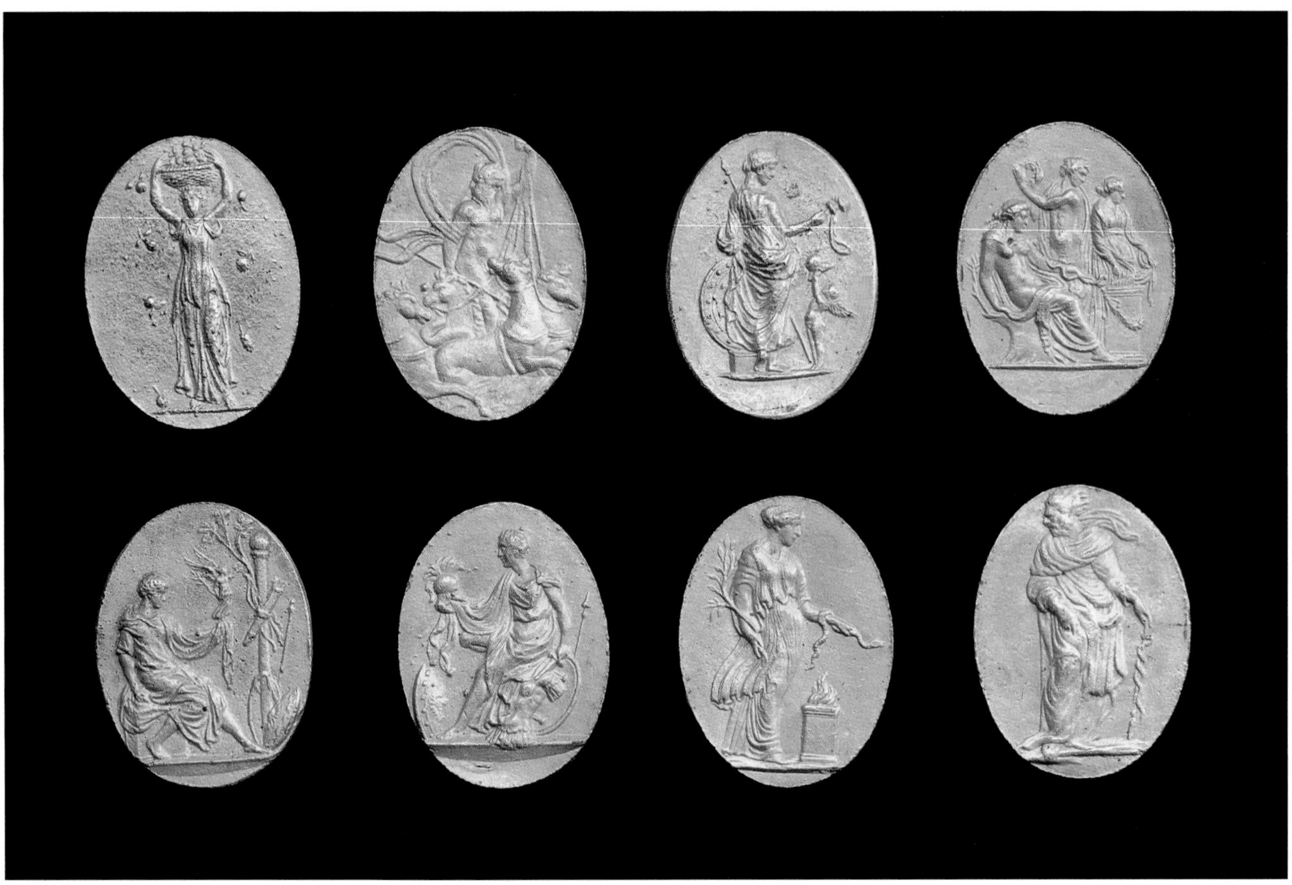

76.1–8. Boulton and Fothergill, medallions from the vases in Plate 302, Private Collection.

77. Boulton and Fothergill, medallion of Filial Piety from one of the vases in Plate 301, Weston Park Foundation.

OPPOSITE:
78.1–9. James Tassie, gems, Beazley Archive, Ashmolean Museum, Oxford.

Sacrifice Group *(Plate 76.4)*

This gem was published by Montfauçon (Plate 56.2) as a modern image of a 'sacrifice group'. Raspe described Tassie's reproduction (Plate 78.4) as 'a woman gracefully sitting, and crowned by a young hero, places a serpent upon an altar decorated with garlands, in presence of a woman who brings something in her bosom'.[232] Raspe listed the gem under the heading of 'Health, Prosperity, Salus'. It is a rock crystal intaglio by Valerio Belli, the leading gem engraver of his day.[233] Wedgwood and Bentley's 1773, 1774 and 1777 catalogues included a number of sacrifice groups,[234] but they could have been different images, including possibly the medallion illustrated in Plate 82, and a number of cameo and intaglio moulds survive at the Wedgwood Museum. One of these is illustrated in Plate 79.4.[235]

Achilles Victorious *(Plate 76.5)*

The image appears not only on the vases of Plates 302 and 304, but also on the clock case illustrating an offering to Diana (Plate 154). Raspe described Tassie's gem (Plate 78.5) as 'a young hero, sitting without arms, with the statue of Victory in his left hand, before a cippus on which his arms are suspended. It may be called Achilles victorious, in his retirement'.[236] Wedgwood and Bentley called the gem an 'Offering to Victory' or an 'Offering of Victory to a Trophy', and it appears in their 1773 catalogue under the latter name.[237] There are several cameo and intaglio moulds in the Wedgwood Museum. The cameo mould illustrated in Plate 79.5[238] shows the hero clothed, as does Boulton's version. There are other differences from Tassie's gem – the decorated shield, the spear behind the shield, the more pronounced garland in the hand of Victory, the arrows in the quiver – in both Wedgwood's and Boulton's versions.

OPPOSITE:
79.1–9. Wedgwood and Bentley, cameo moulds, Wedgwood Museum, Barlaston.

Heroic Figure *(Plate 76.6)*

There are two gems in Tassie's collection that are close to this medallion (Plate 78.6–7).[239] Raspe listed the first under the heading 'Mars' as 'an heroic figure in a paludamentum having his helmet in his right hand'. The second shows a mostly naked figure and is listed under the heading 'Heroic or Fabulous Age'. Raspe described this second gem as 'Achilles, or some other warrior, sitting unarmed'. Wedgwood and Bentley called the gem 'A Conquering Hero, probably Perseus' or 'Diomedes or Perseus', and listed a cameo under the former title in their 1773 catalogue.[240] Their mould of the cameo listed in the 1773 catalogue is illustrated in Plate 79.6, and is very close to Boulton's version.[241]

Aesculapius, or Moses *(Plate 76.8)* and Hygieia, or Peace *(Plate 76.7)*

Raspe lists Tassie's gem, which shows both figures (Plate 76.8), under the heading of 'The Old Testament'.[242] He described the gem as 'Moses, with a rod, speaking to Peace, holding a branch of olive in the right hand'. He criticised the engraver, Valerio Belli, for being like many *cinquecento* artists in confusing the sacred and the profane and neglecting 'the good allegory and costume of the ancients … If he wanted to represent Esculapius in this piece, he has failed in the air of the head and the drapery, which covers the two shoulders with a large magnificent cloak of a Platonic Philosopher, and which modern artists have very properly given to the Apostles and Evangelists. One of his shoulders should be naked, if he intended to represent Moses, to whom the modern artists give the rod with a serpent, the

same as is given to Esculapius.'[243] Collectors and manufacturers seem to have decided from an early date that the figures represented Aesculapius, the god of healing, rather than Moses, and his daughter Hygieia, the personification of health. Wedgwood and Bentley made a cameo of the two figures,[244] and they appear also in friezes with an altar between them, either alone[245] or accompanied by other figures, representing a sacrifice to Aesculapius, on Wedgwood and Bentley vases.[246] They were, however, usually reproduced as separate figures and I shall treat them separately in the order illustrated in Plate 76:

Hygieia *(Plate 76.7)*

Plate 76.7 shows Hygieia with the olive branch in her right hand, as in Tassie's reproduction of Belli's gem, and holding a snake in her left hand over an altar, which is entirely missing from Belli's original gem. Wedgwood and Bentley produced the same image both as a cameo and as an intaglio. They listed a cameo of 'Hygia, etc.' in the 1773 catalogue and a cameo of 'Hygiea, standing with the serpent' in the 1774 catalogue, and three intaglios in the same year.[247] One of their cameo moulds is illustrated in Plate 79.7.[248] It bears a close correlation to Boulton's version. Boulton used a modified version of the figure, with no altar, in the larger medallion mounted on the obelisk of the Narcissus clock case (Plate 173). There are differences in the dress and the figure holds what may be a branch or a firebrand but looks like a modification of the snake in her left hand.

Aesculapius *(Plate 76.8)*

Wedgwood and Bentley listed a cameo of Aesculapius 'standing with the serpent' in their 1773 catalogue, and two further cameos and an intaglio in 1774.[249] A cameo mould in the Wedgwood Museum is illustrated in Plate 79.8.[250]

Filial Piety *(Plate 77)*

Raspe listed Tassie's gem (Plate 78.9) under the heading 'Allegories'. He described the gem as 'Filial Piety leaning her right elbow upon a cippus with a tripod. At her feet, a stork.'[251] The stork often represents filial piety in Renaissance art, classical and later writers having recorded the belief that it fed its parents when they were no longer able to feed themselves. Wedgwood and Bentley did not use the name 'Filial Piety'. The cameo mould illustrated in Plate 79.9 is described as 'Diana' in the Wedgwood Museum's Accession Register. [252] The mould is incised with the catalogue number '94', and in the 1774 catalogue number 94 was listed as Juno. The cataloguer, or even Wedgwood or his partner, must have confused the stork with a peacock. The mould, like Boulton's version of the gem, omits the tripod on top of the *cippus*.

The fact that all Boulton's medallions have their parallels in Tassie's well-known collection suggests that Boulton may have bought impressions from him in order to model them for his ornaments. But the evidence is thin. There is no correspondence between the two men in the archives in the 1760s and 1770s, and there are no bills: nor is there any mention, in either Boulton's or the partnership's correspondence, of any contact with Tassie during this period.[253] The only documentary evidence of dealings with Tassie is the record in the 1782 inventory of:

	s	d
2 Tasseys seals 3/–	6	0
8 ditto ditto 2/–	16	0
41 glass Tassie's seal impressions, sorted sizes 4/– doz.	13	0[254]

These were in the toy room and the warehouse, and were clearly in stock for resale. It is a possibility that Boulton and Fothergill took impressions from some of these intaglios ('seals'). There are however two technical objections to this possibility. First, Boulton's modellers would have had to reduce the sizes of some impressions and enlarge others, since Tassie's gems varied in size and did not conform to Boulton's cast metal versions. Second, most of Boulton's medallions differ in detail from Tassie's impressions, close as they are. Did Boulton's modellers make the changes? Or were there other sources than Tassie?

There clearly were. Boulton acquired models, as I have shown earlier in this chapter, from many sources – patrons, travelling agents, shops, other metalworkers and architects – and some or all of the medallions may well have come from any of these sources. Wendler for example sent cameos and seals from Italy in 1767.[255]

But the most likely source of Boulton's medallions, at least of the nine medallions listed above as being used on the later vases, is Wedgwood. The evidence is strong. First, there is a close correspondence between Boulton's and Wedgwood's versions of these nine medallions, as a comparison of Plates 76, 77 and 79 readily shows. Many of the details that vary from Tassie's gems are precisely the same in the two manufacturers' versions. Second, the archival evidence is supportive.

Wedgwood wrote to his partner in September 1769 that 'gems are the fountain head of fine and beautiful composition, and we cannot you know employ ourselves too near the fountain head of taste'.[256] His remarks were in the context of rising production of black basalt or Etruscan ware. It is clear from the letter that Wedgwood's sources included collectors of gems.[257] He also observed that although some gems ('the gems from Italy') may be too small to apply to vases, 'they will make very good studys and we can have larger modelled by them much better than from prints'.[258] Their production of cameos and intaglios was in full swing by 1771, and in 1773 they produced their first catalogue of cameos, intaglios and other ornaments, which were offered for sale at their London showroom in Great Newport Street. The introduction to the catalogue emphasised how cameos and intaglios could be used to enrich not just rings and bracelets, but also furniture, 'at a moderate expence'.[259]

In May 1773 Wedgwood and Bentley sent 'about 50 dozen of seals to Birmingham'.[260] In June Wedgwood heard from Soho 'desiring me to send by first conveyance a small assortment of cameos suitable for setting in boxes, lockets, bracelets, etc., etc., as Mr Boulton thinks he may have opportunities for disposing of some this year'.[261] In November he reported that cameos were selling well at Soho, presumably from the toy room, but that Boulton and Fothergill were buying his intaglios from Boden and Smith,[262] and that they were doing their own colouring. Wedgwood suggested that in addition to the use of cameos in the decoration of boxes and other trinkets, they could be set in vase pedestals or candlesticks. Boulton and Fothergill, in the making of their tortoiseshell boxes, set the cameos 'under chrystals' and would therefore 'be content with them of a white bisket, without polish or color'd grounds, as they would do the latter themselves in water colour'.[263] Wedgwood enthused about the sale of cameos, and Fothergill thought they would 'sell in quantitys abroad'.[264] By 1782, there were quantities of Wedgwood seals and impressions for seals in the Soho toy room and warehouse, presumably for resale.[265]

Wedgwood and Bentley were uncertain about encouraging Boulton and Fothergill to colour their cameos. 'I will attempt,' wrote Wedgwood in December 1773, 'to confine the water colouring to cameo buttons but if he will order plain white cameos it will be dangerous to refuse him.'[266] At the end of December he had still 'settled nothing with Mr Boulton about the white cameos,' but some large ones were sent from Etruria without Wedgwood's knowledge or authority, and he did not know how to countermand the delivery without appearing foolish.[267]

When he visited Soho in 1776, Wedgwood noted that most of Boulton's 'time pieces and groups of figures have pyramids or alters of white marble to lean upon', and he suggested, to Boulton's apparent pleasure, that these should be inlaid 'with our statues with blue grounds', in other words jasperware. Wedgwood told his partner that he would send Boulton a few of these when he got home. He reckoned that appropriate subjects could be modelled for Russia or 'any other place whither his time pieces are to be sent'.[268]

In the event, very few, if any, of the medallions used by Boulton seem to have been chosen for an intended market, although there is an intriguing sketch in the pattern book that suggests that the medallion on an obelisk is of the Empress of Russia (Plate 223.1).

The case for believing that Wedgwood was the source of the later medallions is strengthened by the vases illustrated in Plate 80. Two of the medallions on these vases are biscuit cameos, coloured by hand, of the seated heroic figure discussed on p. 110 (Plates 76.6, 79.6). These are, I suggest, confirmation that Boulton used Wedgwood cameos, as Wedgwood himself had suggested. They would have been bought as plain white biscuit cameos and coloured at Soho. These cameos also prompt the conclusion that Boulton copied them, and the other images, to produce the metal versions.

Tassie is not entirely out of the frame. It is quite likely that Wedgwood was not the source of the earlier medallions. I have suggested other sources for some of these. Ceres (Plate 72) is a close copy of Tassie's gem (Plate 74.3). Alexander and Julia are not too distant (Plates 70, 74.1, 73, 74.4). Cleopatra is unlikely (Plates 71, 74.2), and the source of Boulton's image has yet to be traced. Tassie was one of Wedgwood's suppliers, and may well have been one of the sources used by Wedgwood's modellers, who refined the detail in many cases and in others clothed the figures.

Wedgwood was probably also the source of the round sacrifice medallion which Boulton used on the vases of Plates 321, 323 and 349. Wedgwood used this medallion on black basalt ware and, later, on jasperware.[269] A large, white terracotta version of it survives in the Wedgwood Museum (Plate 82). Both it, and a smaller experimental version, also in the Wedgwood Museum, are marked beneath the figures with a Greek *phi* and the date 1502. These marks do not appear on the medallions on Wedgwood and Bentley's vases, nor on Boulton's versions of the medallion (Plate 81). The image does not appear to derive from Tassie, although Tassie reproduced gems with the same seated figure on the left and the same altar, but with a standing figure in the centre and no bee.[270] The curious modelling of the image, with the torso of the figure in the rear not reappearing between the nearer figure's arm and leg, and the apparent absence of the rear figure's right leg, might suggest that the image is a somewhat amateur adaptation of one of Tassie's gems, but this is speculation. It is one of many images on gems depicting a sacrifice group with an altar and a snake, probably signifying a sacrifice to Aesculapius, the god of healing. So far the original source for this medallion, if there is one beyond Tassie, has eluded me. It clearly derives from a Renaissance gem or engraving, but how it reached Wedgwood is unclear.

80. Boulton and Fothergill, pair of vases with ceramic medallions, *c.*1775, 11.4 in., Private Collection.

81. Boulton and Fothergill, sacrifice medallion from the vase of Plate 321, Private Collection.

82. Wedgwood and Bentley, sacrifice medallion, white terracotta, Wedgwood Museum, Barlaston.

There is usually no detectable theme in Boulton and Fothergill's choice of decorative medallions for a particular ornament. Venus is quite properly accompanied by the portrayal of the death of Adonis (Plate 359), and Minerva unveils an offering to Time (Plate 172). But why Alexander the Great should grace the goat's head vase (Plate 331), or why Julia, the daughter of Titus, should adorn a knife urn (Plate 220) is not clear. Ceres is appropriate to the knife urn of Plate 216 but must find herself surprised to be mounted on vases named after Cleopatra (Plate 328) or accompanying Narcissus falling in love with his reflection in a pool (Plate 175). Echo would have been more appropriate. The medallions on the vases of Plates 301, 302 and 304 bear no thematic relationship to each other, except that they all illustrate classical subjects and all derive from gems. Perhaps this was the point. Perhaps the vases were to be seen as miniature collections of classical gems, although this explanation is stretched a bit when an ornament is mounted with more than one copy of a particular gem (Plates 153, 301). In truth, the medallions were treated generally at Soho as just another form of ornament appropriate to the antique taste. It is likely that the assemblers of the vases fitted medallions that were available in stock.[271]

Bacchanalian Vase

The Bacchanalian vase (Plates 313–14) is an object-lesson both on the classical origins of Boulton's designs and on the difficulty of being sure, in the absence of archival evidence, of precisely where each design, or even the idea for a design, came from. It provides a fitting conclusion to this survey of his eclectic methods. The vase is clearly based on the shape of a classical urn. It has mounted on it a frieze depicting Hermes (Mercury) delivering the infant Dionysus (Bacchus) to the care of Semele's sister Ino, after his birth from Zeus's thigh. The premature baby had been stitched into his father's thigh following Semele's unfortunate incineration when she insisted on seeing her lover in his visible form. Mercury is accompanied by a number of Bacchic figures, all framed in a trellis of vines. The story was well known when educated people were familiar with classical myth, and was highly appropriate to a vase shaped like a wine vessel or, as in Boulton's version, to a perfume burner intended probably for a dining room. Boulton obviously borrowed the design from a classical model somewhere 'without presuming to invent' anything new, and the question is where?

The answer lies indirectly in the so-called 'Gaeta' vase by the Athenian sculptor Salpion, which has survived in the National Museum in Naples.[272] Until 1805 this vase was used as a font in the cathedral at Gaeta, an appropriate use perhaps for a vase depicting the 'Birth of Bacchus'. Although Salpion's vase is clearly the original source of Boulton's design, it is equally clearly not the actual source. Boulton's frieze is not a precise copy of Salpion's. Boulton's modeller has inserted a youth blowing a horn between Ino and the maenad with the thyrsus who stands behind her, and, on the other side of the vase, has replaced Salpion's figures of a dancing and tambourine-playing maenad and a youth with a more statuesque figure reaching out with her right arm and a youth carrying an ewer. He has also inserted two vine stems, from which the overhead vine branches and grapes, which also appear in Salpion's frieze, grow. Boulton's vase is less thickly set, its lip is more pronounced, the lower part of the body is less bulbous, and a slender stem and base have been added.

It is unlikely, therefore, that Boulton's direct source was the Gaeta vase. It was, however, a well-known classical vase and perhaps Boulton borrowed its frieze from one of the books of antiquities in which it was illustrated. There is an illustration of it in Montfauçon's *L'Antiquité Expliquée* (Plate

83. Montfauçon, *Antiquité Expliquée*, Vol. I, Part 2, Plate CXLII, 'Bacchus' vase by Salpion, Society of Antiquaries.

84. Montfauçon, *Antiquité Expliquée*, Vol. I, Part 2, Plate CLIII, 'Bacchanales' vase, Society of Antiquaries.

85. Wedgwood and Bentley, plaque of 'Birth of Bacchus', jasperware, Wedgwood Museum, Barlaston.

83).[273] Montfauçon's version was not as squat as Salpion's original vase, and he illustrated six Bacchic figures in addition to Mercury, Ino and the child. Boulton owned a copy of Montfauçon's book, and it is conceivable that one of his modellers created a new frieze using Montfauçon's illustration as a guide. More compelling perhaps, Montfauçon illustrated another Bacchic vase a few pages later (Plate 84)[274] which might have been a model for Boulton's design. Both of Montfauçon's vases have vines running round the rim. But Boulton's vase has fewer figures than are shown in Montfauçon's engraving of Salpion's vase, and two of them are entirely new. Montfauçon, therefore, may have given Boulton the idea of the vase, but is unlikely to have been the direct source of the executed design.

Wedgwood used a Bacchic frieze very close to Boulton's. He used a broken version of it on black basalt vases,[275] and produced a plaque of 'The Birth of Bacchus' in jasperware (Plate 85) that was modelled by William Hackwood in 1776.[276] The plaque has the same six figures as Boulton's frieze, although there are differences in their treatment, quite apart from Hackwood's neater modelling. The horn-player's horn is sadly truncated in Boulton's version, and the maenad in Boulton's version with outstretched arm has no cup. Most significantly there are no vines in Wedgwood's version, and the ground is modelled in more detail. It therefore seems unlikely that Wedgwood was the direct source.

The likelihood is that either Boulton and Wedgwood tapped a common source, such as one of the London plaster shops, or that Boulton bought or borrowed a model separately. Whatever model he acquired may well have been derived from the frieze of the original vase or from one of the reproductions such as Montfauçon's. The most likely link with Salpion is probably through Zoffoli, a name that unfortunately does not appear in Boulton's notes or letters. Giacomo and Giovanni Zoffoli produced, in their studio in Rome, many bronze statuettes and vases based on antique marbles for the benefit of tourists and collectors. Giacomo, who was born in about 1731 and died in 1785, appears to have been active as a silversmith and bronze worker from the late 1750s. Giovanni, who was about fourteen years younger and was probably his brother or nephew, took over his studio in 1787 and died in 1805.[277] The vase illustrated in Plates 86–8[278] is signed 'G. Zoffoli F.' and is strikingly similar to Boulton's version of Salpion's vase. It has a similar shape, pronounced lip, cradle, and slender support and base. It uses in the frieze the same substitute figures and the same upright vine stems. The female figure with outstretched arm has no cup. The only substantial differences are the decorative treatments of the lip and stem and the addition in Zoffoli's version of the scrolling handles.[279]

The similarities between the two designs are so close that it seems likely that Boulton either copied his vase from a vase of Zoffoli's or used a common source. Unfortunately no record of Zoffoli's products from the 1770s appears to survive. The only reference so far discovered to a copy of Salpion's vase is in a catalogue of the works offered for sale by Giovanni Zoffoli in about 1795. In this catalogue the vase is listed as '*Vaso di Gaeta*'. The catalogue was sent to the architect Henry Holland by Charles Heathcote Tatham,[280] who shortly afterwards sent a drawing of a *garniture de cheminée* of five vases, of which Zoffoli's was the centrepiece (Plate 89). Tatham described it as 'a very beautiful bronze vase, copied from the best antique and of the best workmanship'.[281] It is probable that the Gaeta vase had been in Zoffoli's range of products for some time. None of this is proof of Boulton's source, but it does seem likely that he somehow derived his design from Giacomo Zoffoli, either from a correspondent in Italy such as P. J. Wendler, who sent him many objects and designs in 1767 and was still corresponding with him in 1776 (see pp. 89 and 378, note 127), or from one of the London modellers or plaster shops, or from a patron's collection, and

86–8. Zoffoli, Bacchus vase, bronze, Torrie Collection, University of Edinburgh.

89. C. H. Tatham, sketch of Bacchus vase by Zoffoli, Victoria and Albert Museum.

it seems probable that his first sight of the theme, which maybe gave him the idea of using it, was either in the pages of Montfauçon or the vases or plaques of Wedgwood.

Modelling

There is regrettably very little in the surviving manuscripts to show how the patterns, drawings and models were assimilated into Boulton and Fothergill's designs at Soho. It is clear that on occasions casts were taken from objects that had been lent or bought. Francis Eginton[282] in particular was responsible on many occasions for carrying out the work or for having it done.[283] Some of the modelling leaves much to be desired, for example the figures of Venus (Plate 191) and Minerva (Plate 166). A comparison of the medallions taken from Wedgwood's models (Plates 76–7) with others modelled probably at Soho (Plates 57, 62) also suggests that the modellers at Soho had something to learn. But their models were not sculptures, and not all French ormolu ornaments are well modelled. The relative lack of modelling skill was made up for by the richness of the gilding and the overall effect of the ornaments.

It is also clear that Boulton and Fothergill employed draughtsmen to draw objects and to sketch designs. I have already quoted Wedgwood's remark that Boulton had brought an artist to make sketches in London in 1768. Artists of the calibre of Francis Eginton and his brother John[284] would have been of the greatest assistance in this. Boulton tried also to train any young men who revealed any aptitude for drawing.[285] I doubt, however, that Boulton was developing a 'school of industrial design' at Soho, as one modern author has suggested,[286] or that he ever achieved anything like a sophisticated design office. Indeed there is evidence to the contrary. The drawings of ormolu ornaments that have survived in the pattern books, for example, are not in any sense working drawings. They are a record of ornaments made or examples of the sketches which were sent to patrons and agents to enable them to choose the objects which they wanted, and many of them are only rough guides as to the ornaments which they depict. The letters suggest that, far from there being a sophisticated design office, there was a shortage of competent draughtsmen at Soho. In 1771 Mayhew and Ince were asked if they could find someone who could 'draw neatly to copy three books of ornaments'[287] and later in the same year there were 'no loose drawings of vases' available.[288] In 1777 Lord Arundell had to be satisfied with drawings which were 'but slightly executed, by reason them being done by a young hand'.[289] The evidence suggests that there was no organised method of producing working drawings, and no such drawings have survived. Boulton's modellers probably worked either from objects that had been bought or borrowed or from their own interpretations of sketches or engravings.

I hope I have said enough to demonstrate Boulton's eclectic approach to the design of his ormolu ornaments. He could justifiably claim that in the early years he and his partner had 'spared neither money nor industry in procuring and inventing designs in the Grecian taste',[290] although the word 'Grecian' hardly suits the sources of some of his designs, especially those from France and from the Franco-Italian architect William Chambers. He carried the 'combination of old ornaments' to great lengths, in the best eighteenth-century traditions of 'invention'.

The illustrations in this book show too that, in the same spirit of 'invention', identical ornaments were used on many different objects. Because so many of the ornaments were interchangeable, designs could be

90. Boulton and Fothergill, cup and cover, silver, 1777, Assay Office, Birmingham.

91. Boulton and Fothergill, candlestick, silver, 1774, Assay Office, Birmingham.

92. Boulton and Fothergill, tureen, silver, 1773, Assay Office, Birmingham.

93. Boulton and Fothergill, bowl, silver, 1780, Assay Office, Birmingham.

altered to suit the whim of the customer.[291] Perfume burners could become candelabra and *vice versa*. The same interchangeability of ornament was true of Boulton and Fothergill's silverware and it is important to remember, as I mentioned at the beginning of this chapter, that Boulton often had both ormolu and silver in mind when he was seeking designs. Parallels consequently abound. The snake-handled vase of Plate 90, for example, which was made in 1777, is ornamented with a band of Vitruvian scrolling similar to the chased ornament on certain ormolu vases (Plates 271, 298), and its plinth also has its counterparts (Plate 298). The plinths and fluted stems of the candlestick illustrated in Plate 91 provide equally obvious parallels (Plates 268–9). The frieze of the silver tureen illustrated in Plate 92 reappears on the vases of Plates 304–5, and the guilloche band and beaded ring of the bowl illustrated in Plate 93 appears frequently in gilt copper (Plates 186, 253, 268). The winged female figures of the perfume burner of Plate 94, which is also ornamented with guilloche and Vitruvian scroll friezes, are similar to the figures which decorate the vases of Plates 304–5. The sphinxes on the perfume burner in Plate 251 reappear on the coffee pot in Plate 95. The page of drawings of tureens from the pattern book illustrated in Plate 96 shows other parallels – with for example the pierced friezes of Plates 264 and 355, the feet of Plate 355, and the ribbons and swags of Plate 253. These are but a few of the large number of motifs which

94. Boulton and Fothergill, perfume burner, silver, 1779, Leeds City Art Gallery, Temple Newsam.

95. Boulton and Fothergill, candlestick, 1774, coffee pot, 1769–70, ewer, 1775, silver, Assay Office, Birmingham.

96. Boulton and Fothergill, Pattern Book 1, p. 111.

appear on pieces of both ormolu and silver. Others are mentioned later during my discussion of particular ornaments. It is clear that ornaments of different metals were frequently cast from the same models or stamped with the same dies. Such methods were typical of Boulton's industrial techniques. These will be examined in the next chapter.

Whether or not Boulton's methods of design were successful is for each eye to judge. Mrs Montagu praised his 'taste and elegance'.[292] Wedgwood, on the other hand, on at least one occasion, was not so flattering.[293] The consensus of opinion, both in Boulton's day and subsequently, has on the whole favoured Mrs Montagu's judgement.

CHAPTER 4

Manufacture

Many people still imagine that the manufacturers and suppliers of works of decorative art in the eighteenth century were themselves active craftsmen. The idea is dying, as scholars discover and publish more about the organisation of eighteenth-century workshops, but it is dying hard. Those who have studied the evidence no longer seriously believe that Thomas Tompion fashioned all the wheels of his clocks and assembled them, that Thomas Chippendale and William Vile carved every decorative detail of their fine mahogany furniture, or that Paul de Lamerie did all the chasing on his silver. The leading suppliers had workshops, some large, some small, in which they employed craftsmen and apprentices. They subcontracted specialist work to other workshops. They bought goods from others for onward sale under their own names. The belief that the more renowned suppliers fashioned each outstanding object is kept alive by the facile use of their names in the antique trade and in the work of certain writers. Many buyers of works of art do not have the eye or the experience to distinguish quality, but they know enough to recognise a famous name. Juliet may have been right when she said that the rose would smell as sweet, were it not called a rose, but when it comes to antiques there is value in a name.

Matthew Boulton has been less subjected to this misunderstanding than others. His place in industrial history is well documented. It is inconceivable to think of an industrialist of his stature standing at the workbench. He may have learnt at the bench in his early youth, and he certainly maintained a keen interest in materials and techniques, but once he owned the business his chief tasks were to manage it, to employ the right people as managers and workers, to produce ideas, to initiate production, to pursue efficiency, to worry about quality, to create markets, to lead the sales effort, to ensure adequate finance. These are the predominant themes of his correspondence and notes. His methods were industrial. The phrase 'by Matthew Boulton' is a misleading description of any object produced in his workshops.

Equally the theory that everything at Soho was made by advanced industrial methods should not be carried too far. There was nothing at Soho to compare with a modern production line. There was a division of labour and, as is obvious from a study of the extant ornaments, the same components were used repeatedly in different products. There was even a reluctance to carry out individual orders unless they could afterwards become part of the firm's range. But although Soho was the *locus classicus* of the development of the metalworking trades towards modern industrial methods, its organisation had not reached the point of excluding the craftsman. The techniques of mass production were more advanced in the textile industry than in the production of toys, silver, plate and ormolu, which required a high degree of handcraft. Water power was only used for the rolling and polishing shops. Lathes and stamping machines were operated by traditional methods. The contents of the workshops of the metalworking craftsmen, as recorded in the inventory taken in 1782, were not the equipment of high-technology workshops.

A complete study of the methods employed in the manufacture of ormolu ornaments at Soho is almost impossible. There is not enough evidence in the surviving documents for the crucial period from 1768 to the middle 1770s. Boulton's designing and marketing methods are easier to study because there is a great deal of evidence in the letters between him and his customers and in other documents. His manufacturing techniques were not their concern, nor were the sources of the necessary materials. A close study of surviving ornaments affords certain clues about the methods of rolling, forming, casting, chasing, gilding and assembly, but these clues are not enough. Evidence about the identity of all the craftsmen, their individual terms of employment, and the organisation of production is all too scant. There are no lists of craftsmen, no detailed description, plan or layout of the manufactory, no detailed accounts of the costing or processing of individual orders. Only one detailed inventory of stock-in-trade has survived and this, the inventory which was compiled on the termination of the partnership after Fothergill's death in June 1782, was compiled when the ormolu business was no longer an important activity. Another difficulty is that it is not always easy to discern whether a particular reference in the archives pertains to the production of ormolu, or to other parts of the hardware trade, or to both. The same chasers worked on both silver and ormolu, just as the casting shop seems to have worked in several metals.[1] Boulton and Fothergill reserved the right to direct workmen to any task, and there is enough evidence to show that several workmen worked in more than one metal.[2] When Boulton compiled his notes on gilding he probably had buttons chiefly in mind, although his notes had an obvious application to the production of ormolu.

I have made no attempt in this chapter to give a comprehensive account of the Soho manufactory. I have tried instead to extract from the records a series of notes about the materials used in the manufacture of ormolu ornaments, about the processes by which the ornaments were made, and about some of the craftsmen and suppliers concerned. A feature of this account will again be the remarkable personal interest which Boulton took in every step in the process of production – in the research into gilding recipes and suitable materials for vase bodies, in the quality of the work, and in the workshops' ability, or rather inability, to complete commissions on time.

Metals and processes

I have defined ormolu in the preface to this book as metal, normally brass but sometimes bronze or copper, which has been gilt by the process of mercurial gilding. Brass is an alloy of copper and zinc, the exact composition varying greatly. Strictly the word means an alloy made exclusively of these metals, containing more copper than zinc, but most eighteenth-century brasses contain traces of other metals which probably entered the alloy as impurities at the time of the melt. The colour of brass with a high content of copper is a warm reddish hue, but as the copper content is reduced the colour is gradually changed. Brasses containing 95 to 80 per cent copper have a range of golden hues, tending to yellow as the copper content falls, and are commonly called 'gilding' metals. 'Bath metal', for example, was made of about 83 per cent copper and 17 per cent zinc. 'Pinchbeck', which was named after its inventor, the clockmaker Christopher Pinchbeck, was likewise made up of about five parts of copper and one part of zinc and was used widely to simulate gold. Common brass, which was known as 'yellow metal' in the eighteenth century, contains about 30 per cent zinc. When the copper content of brass is reduced to about 70 per cent, the yellow hue becomes paler, with a greenish tinge, but it becomes warmer again at 60 per cent. A golden hue reappears when the copper content is reduced to 55 per cent, and when the proportion of zinc is further increased the colour becomes silver-white and finally grey. Other metals such as tin, lead and iron can be added to give the alloy certain qualities. Lead, for example, helps the casting process, but interferes with the process of mercury gilding. In the eighteenth century recipes for different alloys such as common brass, pinchbeck, Bath metal and white metal were by no means precise. The composition of eighteenth-century furniture mounts varies considerably.

Most of the ornaments illustrated in this book are made of brass. Boulton took trouble to differentiate between the many brass alloys in his production of buttons and toys. A metallurgical analysis of the brass from eight ornaments, chosen to represent different dates during the decade of ormolu production, shows that the cast and rolled mounts are made of brass with a zinc content of between about 8 per cent and 10 per cent, rising occasionally to 11 per cent or sinking to below 7 per cent. Broadly speaking, therefore, Boulton and Fothergill consistently used a brass alloy, allowing for the impurities, with about 88 to 92 per cent copper. The impurities are also remarkably consistent. Arsenic and lead show the greatest variation, but this is not surprising because they are the elements most likely to be unevenly distributed in the metal. Lead and tin are both below 0.5 per cent. The lead is kept low, no doubt because of its potential interference with the gilding process. The alloy has a reddish colour, which needs a rich gilding to appear golden. The consistency of the alloy suggests that Boulton's foundry was well equipped to meet the requirement of consistency when, in later years, he founded the mint.[3]

In addition to brass, copper was also used in the production of ornaments, especially for the internal linings of perfume burners (Plate 97) and for some of the mounts which could be made from thin strips such as decorative bands (Plate 269). The use of copper for these applications reflected the workshops' skills in the production of silver plate and the application of the same skills and tools to the production of components for both products. Indeed some of the linings and a few of the vase bodies were made of silver plate. None of the mounts were made of bronze, which is strictly an alloy of copper and tin, and Boulton was perhaps less than honest when he described them as 'bronze ornamental furniture'. 'Bronze' had less of a connotation of cheapness than 'brass'. But, to do him justice, the terms were frequently confused in the eighteenth century.[4] French metalworkers used the term '*bronze doré*' to describe furniture mounts made of gilt brass, although the terms '*laiton doré*' and '*cuivre doré*' also occur in contemporary references. It was the finish that mattered to the cabinet maker and to his customer rather than the composition of the alloy. The distinction of having gilt mounts was in marked contrast to the commoner furniture mounts, which were simply '*mis en couleur d'or*'. This usually meant that they were dipped in nitric acid, washed, dried and lacquered, a process that had to be repeated when the condition of the lacquer deteriorated.

It is not clear where Boulton and Fothergill bought their metals. The consistency of their brass does not necessarily imply that the raw materials came from the same source. I have mentioned in Chapter 1 that the Birmingham brassfounders bought metals from the important brass manufacturers at Bristol and Cheadle. No doubt they also patronised Turner's brass works, established in Coleshill Street, Birmingham, in 1740. This enterprise tried to compete with the larger companies but was forced by them into a pricing agreement. The powerful combination established a warehouse in Birmingham for the sale of brass in the town and its monopolistic power enabled it to raise prices when it wanted to.[5] Boulton and Fothergill bought brass from Turner and Palmer[6] and probably also from the combination's warehouse. These were probably the sources of most of their brass and copper, although there is evidence that Boulton turned his hand, secretly, to the manufacture of his own brass in 1769.[7] This attempt to bypass the monopoly of the combination is particularly interesting in view of Boulton's rather cool support of the plans of other Birmingham manufacturers in 1780 to set up their own metal company in protest against the raising of prices.[8]

The metal would have arrived at Soho mostly in the form of ingots or sheets. The copper or brass which was needed in sheet form or in the form of long straight mouldings – the copper pieces for example for decorative bands (Plates 253, 267, 268, 367) and the inner bowls of candle vases, ice pails and perfume burners (Plates 97, 106, 109–11), the brass pieces for the

97. Boulton and Fothergill, inner linings of vases in Plates 313, 346, 274.

flat and curved panels of clock cases and long continuous mouldings (Plate 177) – were rolled mechanically.[9] It is possible that some of the decorative bands were made by sinking the pattern into the steel rollers, but it is hard to tell in most cases whether they were produced by rolling or stamping. There was a limit to the size of the pieces that could be fashioned by rolling, and there are plenty of ornaments whose larger components are created by soldering rolled components such as panels or mouldings together, for example the base mouldings and panels of the sidereal clock case (Plates 118–19). The solder is usually a silver-based solder, a recipe for which was recorded by Boulton in an early notebook.[10] Orders for steel rolls appear in the archives, notably an order for rolls 7¼ inches wide in 1764.[11] In 1769 Boulton was considering '2 feet rolls which may be dressed truer than any body's' for similar work on silverware.[12] The rolling mill would have been used not only for brass and copper but also for silver plate and silver.

The sheet metal which was used for vase bodies or linings, decorative bands or paterae, was cut after rolling and sent to be shaped or (if the ornament had not already been applied by rolling) to have its ornament applied. This was done with the use of hammers and dies and in presses or stamping machines. Obvious examples of pieces shaped by hammering over moulds (a process seen at Soho in the preparation of plate by Dorothy Richardson in 1770 – see Chapter 1, p. 24, '30th room') are the thin bases of the pedestals of the vases in Plate 328, the vase bodies in Plates 249 and 334, and the many inner copper linings of perfume burners and ice pails, some of them gilt, some silvered or tinned, and some uncoated (Plates 108, 110). The smaller linings, such as the gilt lining of the Venus vase in Plate 359, were formed out of sheet copper by first beating them into a shallow bowl and then using raising hammers to deepen them and planishing hammers to give them a smooth finish. The larger linings were finished in the same way, but were formed by bending the sheet copper into a cylinder and soldering the join with a silver-based solder, with a second piece of sheet copper soldered onto it to create the bottom of the bowl. Plate 97 shows the linings of three vases, the largest and smallest clearly made in this way, the lining for the lyre vase being made of thicker metal and probably pressed, although it is difficult to be certain because the metal has been liberally filed and hammered.

Likely examples of pressed or stamped ornaments are the paterae and the copper bands decorated with a guilloche frieze in Plate 268. This decoration was applied by hammering the metal over steel dies, or by screwing it onto the dies in a press. These techniques were widely practised in the production of silver plate, because they saved on materials and enabled long production runs of identical ornaments.[13] Ornaments produced in this way did not require further chasing. Pressing and stamping were also applied, once more powerful presses and mechanical hammers had been evolved, to fashioning articles of brassfoundry, and a London toy maker named John Pickering obtained a patent in 1769 for the application of the process to ornaments for coffins, furniture and coaches. He was quickly followed by others.[14] Boulton listed the process among a number of 'mechanical improvements' which he thought might be made to the manufacture of silver wares at Soho in 1769, and noted that 'all our ornaments may be stamped or may be press in the fly press or may be formed in the Leviathan',[15] which was a form of press. By 1773 at the latest Boulton and Fothergill were able to produce complete candlesticks in silver by the use of stamps and dies.[16] They seem to have used the same process for some of their brass ornaments and in the same year they had 'several ... dies for ormoulu or silver borders or ornaments'.[17] Apart from borders, many of the brass ornaments such as the swags on the clock case in Plate 183 and the medallions on the pedestal of the candelabra in Plate 301 may have been produced by this process. Most ornaments, however, are more likely to have been cast because the stamping process, owing to the cost of dies, was more applicable to components that were needed in large quantities. Small runs of silver buttons were better cast than made with expensive dies[18] and it is likely that the same principle applied to ormolu ornaments. The fly press was also used for piercing metal sheet.[19] This was a particularly useful process in the production of silver pieces. It is unlikely that it was used for ormolu and more likely that pierced panels, such as the side of the clock case in Plate 163 and the pierced lids of the many perfume burners (Plates 268, 315), were made with the use of piercing saws.

It appears that the bulk of the ormolu ornaments were fashioned by casting. The traditional method of casting, with moulds of clay or sand, has been used since the earliest times but does not seem to have been applied to the manufacture of brass objects until early in the eighteenth century. This may have been because the brass works, other than those which were concerned with making heavy castings such as cannons and bells, were chiefly concerned with making things which could be fashioned by other methods – for example cooking pans and kettles, which were made by battery, and wire.[20] Other possible reasons may have been the difficulty of obtaining the special casting sand and the shortage of skilled mould makers.[21] As the Birmingham brass workers turned to making a wider variety of wares during the eighteenth century, casting came into its own, and the necessary materials and skills were acquired. The process was the accepted method of manufacture by the time Boulton came onto the scene and was used, for example, both in common brassfoundry and for decorative silver and plate.

For the common casting process a model of the object was made, usually of a fine-grained wood such as boxwood or pearwood. The pattern of the model was impressed in a mould, which usually consisted of a rectangular metal or wooden case made in two halves in which casting sand was packed closely round the model. The two halves, or sides, of the case were then split and the model removed. After further preparation, which included the insertion of casting jets, the two sides were firmly joined again and the metal poured into the mould. If necessary several castings of the same pattern could be made at once by this process, either in the same casting box or in a series of boxes clamped together. The illustrations to the account of this method of casting in Diderot's *Encyclopédie* (Plates 98–103) show the process in graphic detail. Plate 99 shows a trough over which the casting sand was worked into the proper consistency ('tewed') by rolling and chopping. Plates 100–3 show various moulds and casts and a clamped

OPPOSITE:
98–9. Diderot, *Encyclopédie*, *Fondeur en sable*.

Fig. 1e
Fig. 2
Fig. 3
Fig. 4
Fig. 5

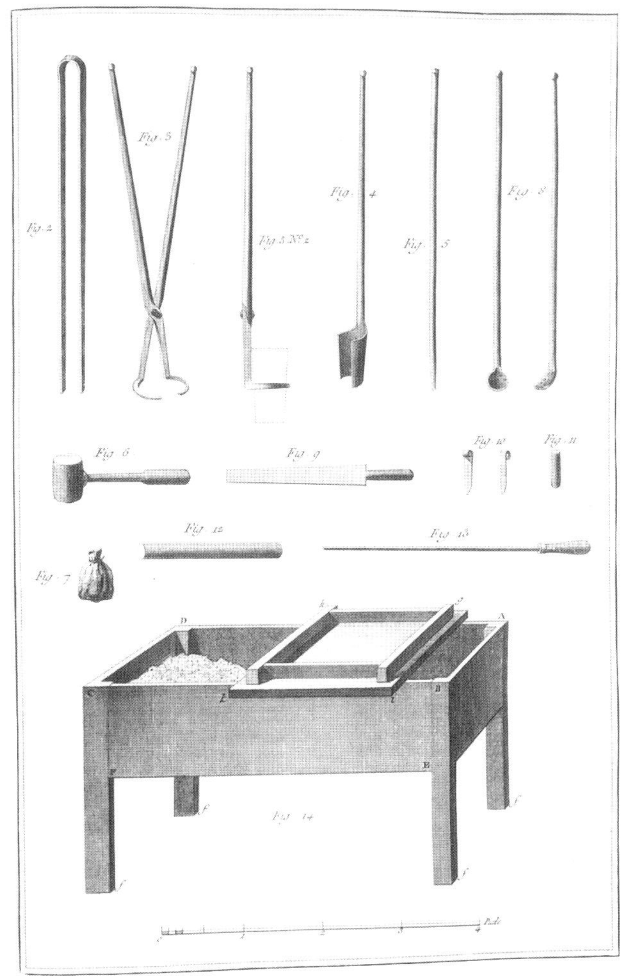

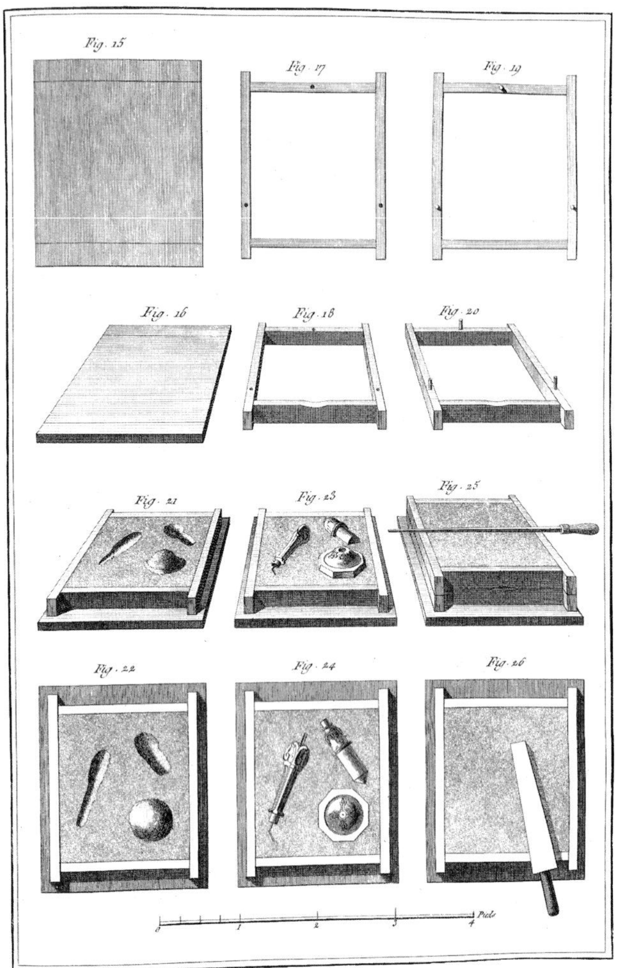

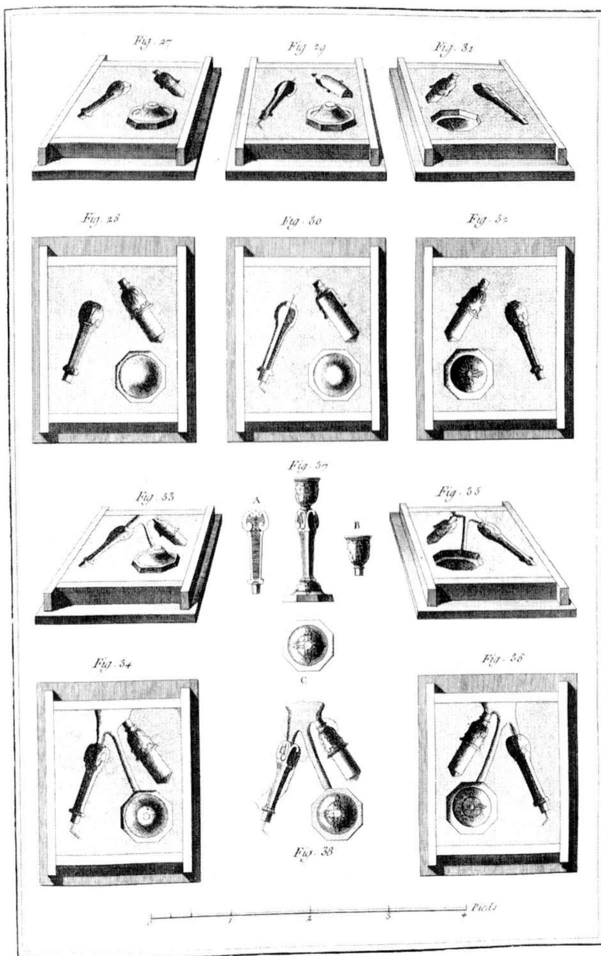

100–1. Diderot, *Encyclopédie*, *Fondeur en sable.*

stack of casting boxes (Plate 103). Plate 98 shows a workman pouring the molten metal into the stack of moulds. If a casting was only one-sided, as in the case of the door furniture of Plate 193 and the swags and eagle of Plate 184, the casting could be carried out in sand in open wooden trays. In either case the original wooden model could be re-used for taking further impressions, or copies could be made of previous castings.

The other chief method of casting was by the process known in France as *cire perdue*. In its simplest form this process began with a rough core of clay, often mixed with ashes, on which the modeller fashioned his model of wax. The model was encased in a mould of casting sand or clay and then baked, which melted the wax: metal was then poured into the cavities left by the wax. When the metal had solidified the outer mould was broken away and the core broken and extracted, leaving a hollow casting. This method resulted in a more exact reproduction of the model than the traditional method of sand-casting, and it used less metal. It was however more complicated, and it was not easy to ensure that the molten metal had completely filled the cavities left by the melted wax. It was used chiefly for larger castings such as figures (and especially for large-scale statues)[22] and was used at Soho for the figures of Diana, Minerva, Titus, Urania, Venus, the figures supporting the Persian vase and the globe of the geographical clock, and the other figures which adorned the various allegorical ornaments (Plates 153, 166, 183, 189, 191, 351, 157–8). Plates 118–19 show the hollow interior of the figures of Urania and a sphinx from the sidereal clock made by this process. Because the original models of most of these figures were needed for further castings a preliminary step in the process was necessary. The

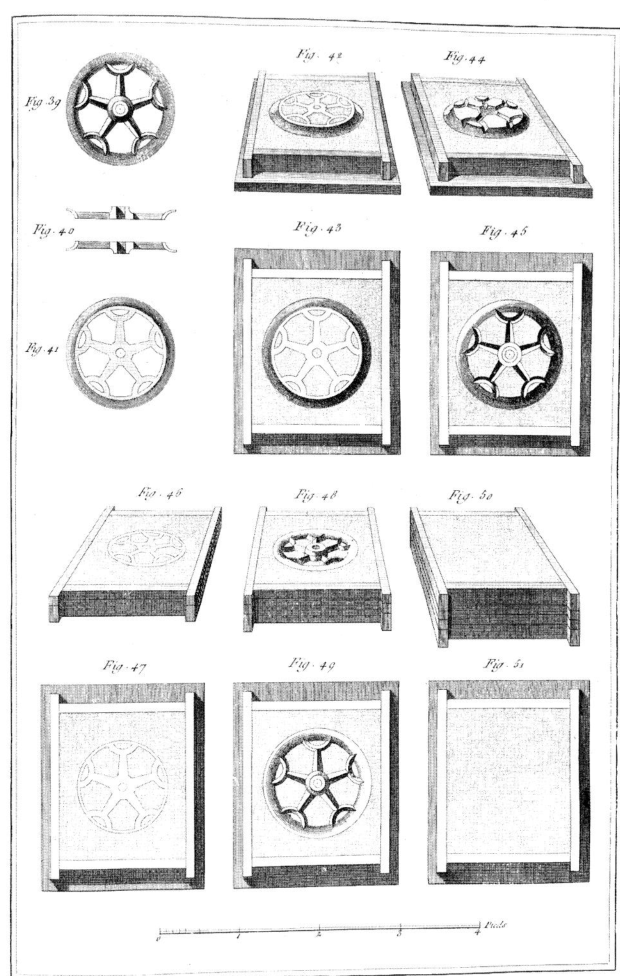

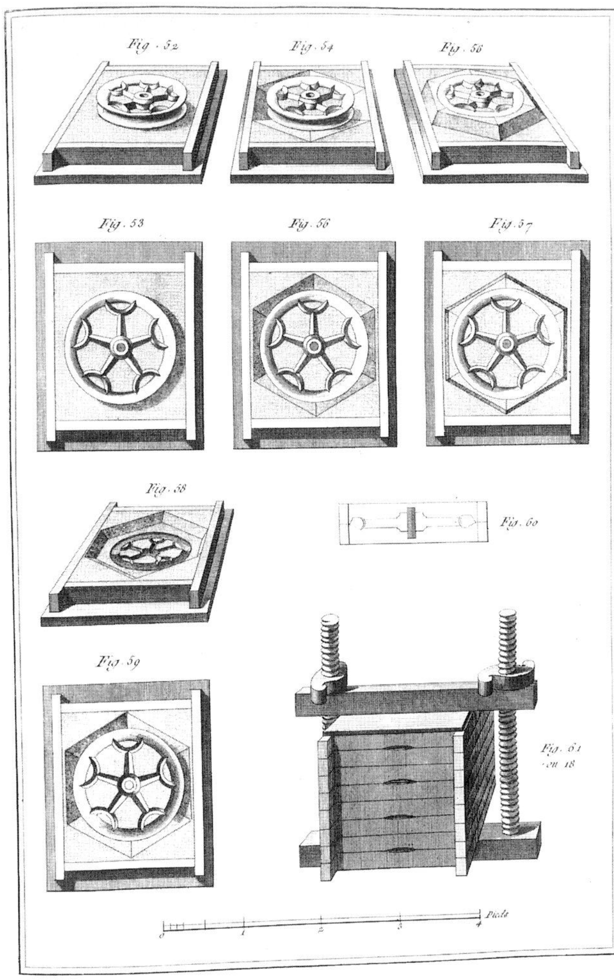

102–3. Diderot, *Encyclopédie*, *Fondeur en sable.*

model was used initially to make a mould, probably of plaster, which was then used to produce the subsequent wax model used in the casting. In the case of the Titus figure of Plate 183 there is a hole in the toga beneath his left arm, which exemplifies the difficulty of ensuring that the molten metal reaches every part of the mould during this process of casting. The Titus clock in Plate 186 has similar casting blemishes in the right foot and right sleeve.

The available evidence, sparse as it is, suggests that the models at Soho were usually made of wood, frequently boxwood,[23] and that casts were taken on occasions from wooden models supplied by designers such as architects if the work was for a special commission.[24] Wooden models were the accepted means of making the necessary moulds and a complete workshop was devoted to the fashioning of 'box-moulds' for buttons etc.[25] Boulton even considered buying ready-made moulds on occasion, although when he did they were not always suitable.[26] Casts were also taken from plaster models, especially those which were bought from artists such as John Flaxman, for example the models for the figures on the geographical clock (Plates 157–8), or those which were made for the purpose by Francis Eginton. Orders for plaster survive in the archives[27] but it is not always clear whether the plaster was wanted as a material for modelling or for use in the process of casting either with or instead of sand. Casts were also taken on occasion direct from objects fashioned in metal and from previous casts.[28] Early in 1770 Boulton wanted Eginton to take casts of existing figures and said that 'we should omitt no opportunity of taking good casts'.[29]

Most of the ormolu ornaments produced at Soho were cast by the traditional method of sand-casting. Dorothy Richardson saw the process in operation during her visit in 1770 and noted the casting of 'ornaments and figures ... in the same manner as the buttons, only a reverse is join'd to the underpart and there are holes thro the frame where the liquid metal is poured in' (see Chapter 1, p. 23, '8th room'). The list of materials and utensils in the casting shop in 1782 included loam and sand, along with the binding agent potassium sulphate ('sal enixen'), many 'sides' of brass and wooden moulds, and fifteen wooden boxes.[30] The casting method is evident from the roughened surfaces of unfinished parts (Plate 106) and in some cases from the lines left by the joint of the two halves of the mould. It should not be assumed, however, that all the ornaments were cast in this way. It is possible that besides the hollow figures mentioned earlier some of the flatter mounts were cast by the *cire perdue* process, as they sometimes are today.

Several illustrations (Plates 106–15, 118–21) show how ornaments were assembled from separately cast pieces. Cast vase bodies, such as the ice pail of Plate 212, were made in segments, in the case of the ice pail, in quarters, and in at least two layers, and then soldered together.

The standardisation of cast ornaments, which made it necessary for the vase bodies to be made in standard sizes from an early date,[31] ended once the rough casts had emerged from the casting shop and proceeded to other workshops to be finished and to receive their decoration. There was a 'chasing shop' recorded in the 1782 Inventory, and specialist workshops probably existed in the early 1770s. There is, however, some evidence that workmen specialising in ormolu carried out more than one process. Whichever was true, it is clear that different workmen applied their skills to the casts of identical ornaments. The turning of circular casts, such as the ornaments of the vase in Plate 110, and the polishing of the smooth surfaces were probably done on lathes and polishing machines which were driven by water power, but there was plenty of room for variable work between the different workmen. The outside measurements of 'identical' mounts are seldom exact. Far greater and more easily detectable differences can be seen in the quality and style of the chasing. The cheaper vases were poorly worked in comparison with the finer things (Plates 249 and 262). Differences in style can be readily seen by comparing the chiselling of the mounts on similar vases or even sometimes of similar mounts on the same vase. This variation is illustrated graphically by the treatment of the feathers and the drapery of the two winged figures shown in Plate 115, which are taken from the same vase, by the different treatment of the acanthus mount cradling the two Cleopatra vases of Plate 327, and by the variations in the quality of the chasing on the vases of Plate 241, on which the working of the Vitruvian scroll decoration round the rim does not match the quality of the pierced decoration on the body of the vase. Another example is the different dimensions of the lined decoration on the squared mounts of the lion masks on the vases of Plate 246. There were thirty-five chasers at Soho in 1770, according to Wedgwood,[32] and their individual techniques obviously differed. Mounts were made in quantity, but the mounts for particular vases were usually chosen to match each other in style: Plate 115 shows that this was not an invariable rule.

So much of the work on the mounts, once they had emerged from the casting shop, was done by hand that each vase eventually became an individual work of art in spite of sharing common origins. The mounts of each vase, and most of its components, were therefore often marked with a distinctive number so that when they had been machined, chased and fitted to the vase body they would not be muddled with others during the subsequent process of gilding. These marks sometimes took the form of punched dots: the components of the branch illustrated in Plate 107, for example, are punched with three each, and the pieces of the goat's head vase illustrated in Plate 106 are each punched with no less than nine. Other vases are marked with Roman numerals or with notches.

In some cases marks were also used to indicate the correct positioning of mounts, so that they fit together. An example is the notching on the marble pedestal of the vase in Plate 114 to match the notching of the rams' heads, so that they can be fixed on the right corners. Cast mounts are often similarly marked. The same system of identification was often used to ensure the correct assembly of candle branches. The branches of the first four King's vases supplied to Mrs John Parker (Plate 343) were all marked with numbers corresponding to numbers on the mounts into which the branches were to be slotted, and a similar system of identification was used for the wing-figured vases sent to Robert Child in 1772.[33]

These identification marks do not occur invariably but when they do they are a distinctive means of recognising the work of the craftsmen at Soho. Another typical feature of the best ormolu work produced at Soho is the mode of construction, which is well illustrated by Plates 106–15. These demonstrate clearly the carefully fitted components, which are machined to lock into each other exactly, sometimes with the help of pins and holes, and which are assembled rather in the manner of a child's set of grooved building barrels. They also show the typical long-threaded rods, often fitted to an iron or brass base plate, the slotted or holed nuts which hold the vases together, and the characteristic pins and nuts which were used to fasten mounts to the vase bodies and pedestals.

It is obvious that at no time did even the finest of Boulton and Fothergill's craftsmen match the most highly finished and delicate chased work of their rivals in France, in spite of Boulton's boasts. It is difficult to attribute this to any deficiency of equipment, there being no records of the factory in the years of 1768–72. We cannot know whether Boulton's chasers were as well equipped as their French rivals. The list of tools in the chasing shop in 1782 shows that there were plenty of them, but it does not detail them beyond calling them chasing punches, cutting tools, riflers, chasing hammers, scalpers, etc.[34] Some idea of the variety of tools in chasing workshops of the time can be gained from the tools listed and illustrated in Diderot's *Encyclopédie* (Plates 104–5).[35] But although the chiselling did not compare with the standards of the finest French work, the contrast between matted and burnished surfaces and between profusely chiselled and plain ornament were modes of decoration in which Boulton and Fothergill matched the practice of the ablest French craftsmen. The geographical and sidereal clock cases (Plates 155–8, 177–81) demonstrate these contrasts. As Boulton was well aware, they gave the ornaments depth and vitality. He considered it 'almost impossible' to make certain silverware 'very elegant' without a contrast between brightly burnished and 'beautiful white dead matt' parts,[36] and he followed the same principle with ormolu. He was particularly anxious on one occasion that the gilders of an ormolu figure of Titus should not undo the work of the chasers and scratch off the matt surface.[37]

Gilding, colouring and burnishing

Much as the 'sculpture and form' of the ornaments mattered, it was the mastery at Soho of 'that art of gilding called or moulu' which gave Boulton and Fothergill a special claim to pre-eminence.[38] The technique is known in England as fire gilding or mercurial gilding. Gold is reduced either to fine leaf or powder and amalgamated with mercury at a considerable heat. The usual solution consists of about six parts of mercury to one of gold. When the gold has been absorbed by the mercury the solution is cooled and the

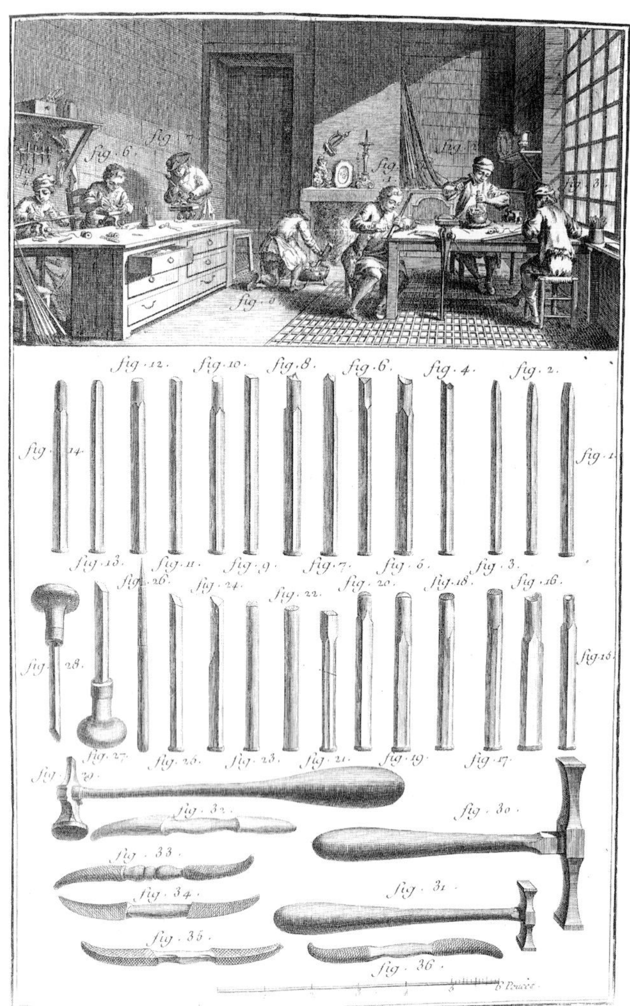

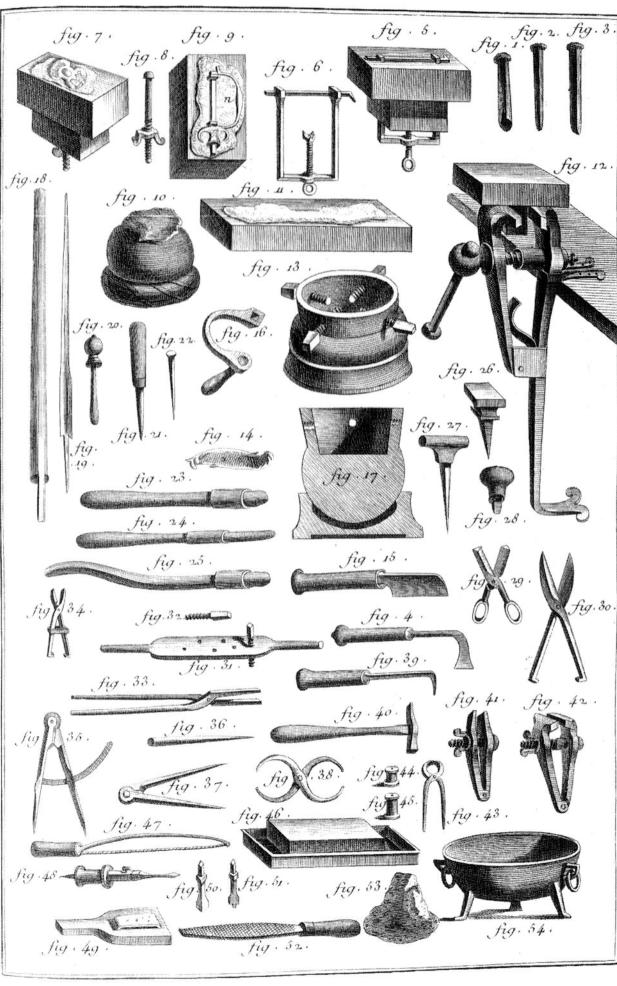

104–5. Diderot, *Encyclopédie, Ciseleur et Damasquineur.*

cold amalgam is squeezed through chamois leather in order to separate the superfluous mercury. This leaves a substance of the consistency of butter, consisting of about two parts of mercury to one of gold. The object that is to be gilt is carefully cleaned, usually with a wire brush and nitric acid ('aqua fortis')[39] and smeared with nitrate of mercury. This preliminary smearing forms a superficial amalgam and facilitates the application of the gilding amalgam when it is spread over it. The amalgam of gold and mercury is applied with a special brass wire brush or a gilding knife, and the object is then heated sufficiently so that the mercury evaporates, leaving the gold alloyed to the surface. The heat has to be carefully judged in order to prevent the gold amalgam from running and leaving parts of the object ungilt, but more of the amalgam can be applied, if it is needed, during the heating process. Furthermore, if thicker gilding is required, the whole process can be repeated many times.

Because mercury fumes are toxic the process of fire gilding is forbidden today except under carefully controlled conditions. Gilding is usually carried out by the process of electrolysis. An object which has been gilt by the mercurial process is however easily recognisable, firstly by its colour and patination and secondly by an examination of the parts which needed no gilding. An object which has been gilt electrolytically will be gilt all over, back and front. There was no need for the mercurial gilder to gild the parts of an object that would not be seen. To do so would be a senseless waste. The amalgam was not applied to such surfaces. This is well illustrated in the treatment of the panels of the sidereal clock shown in Plate 119, on

106. Boulton and Fothergill, goat's head vase of Plate 332, Private Collection.

which the extravagance of the gilding is in rich contrast to the ungilt brass. An examination of other mounts will often, indeed usually, reveal that the amalgam has spread to the edges of the ungilt surfaces, either when the gilder was brushing the amalgam onto the piece or during the heating process. Examples of such gilding 'spills' are illustrated in Plates 112 and 118.

Mercurial gilding is extremely durable, because it creates an alloy on the surface of the metal. It was by far the most suitable gilding process for household ornaments. For this reason it was well known in England, as I have said in Chapter 2, long before Boulton adopted it. Accounts of it, some very brief and others quite detailed, had been published in reference books such as Diderot's *Encyclopédie*, Chambers's *Cyclopaedia*, and the works of John Stalker and George Parker,[40] Herman Boerhaave,[41] Peter Shaw,[42] G. Smith,[43] and Pierre-Joseph Macquer,[44] some of which Boulton owned.[45] Boulton took the process so much for granted that his normally detailed notes contain no precise account of it. Such notes as he made were concerned only with certain aspects of the process such as the composition of the amalgam or the most suitable type of brass for gilding work. In 1768 for example he noted that a gilder named Leech was using an amalgam of one part of gold to 1.63 parts of mercury, and commented that it 'would have done very well' if the proportion had been 1:1.5. This probably referred to the mixture after it had been squeezed through a chamois leather: it would have been an impractical and inefficient recipe for the initial amalgam. At the same time Boulton was wondering whether 'fine brass is not better to gild upon than pinchbeck or copper as the gold sinks into the latter more than the former'.

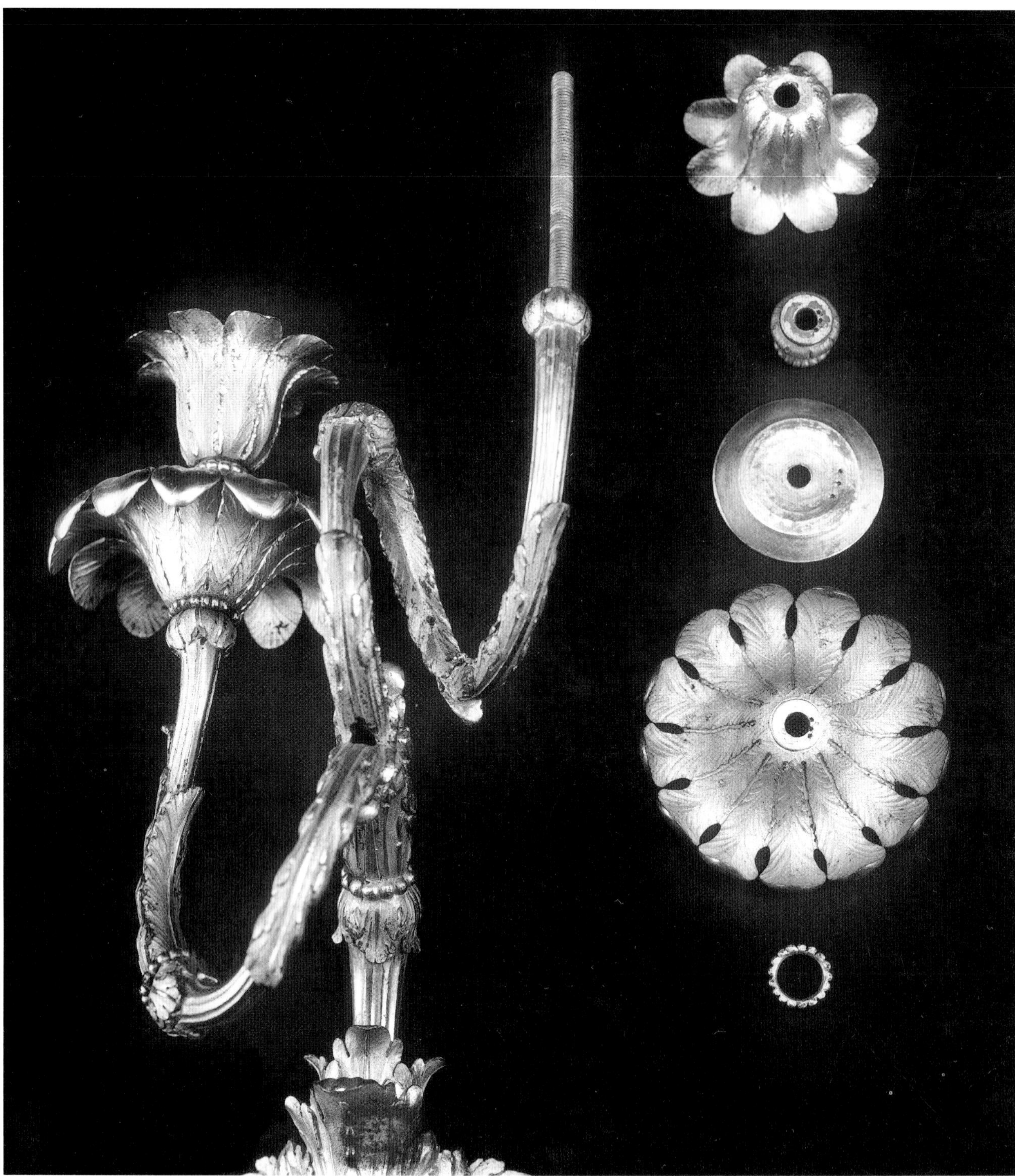

107. Boulton and Fothergill, branch of Persian vase of Plate 351, Victoria and Albert Museum.

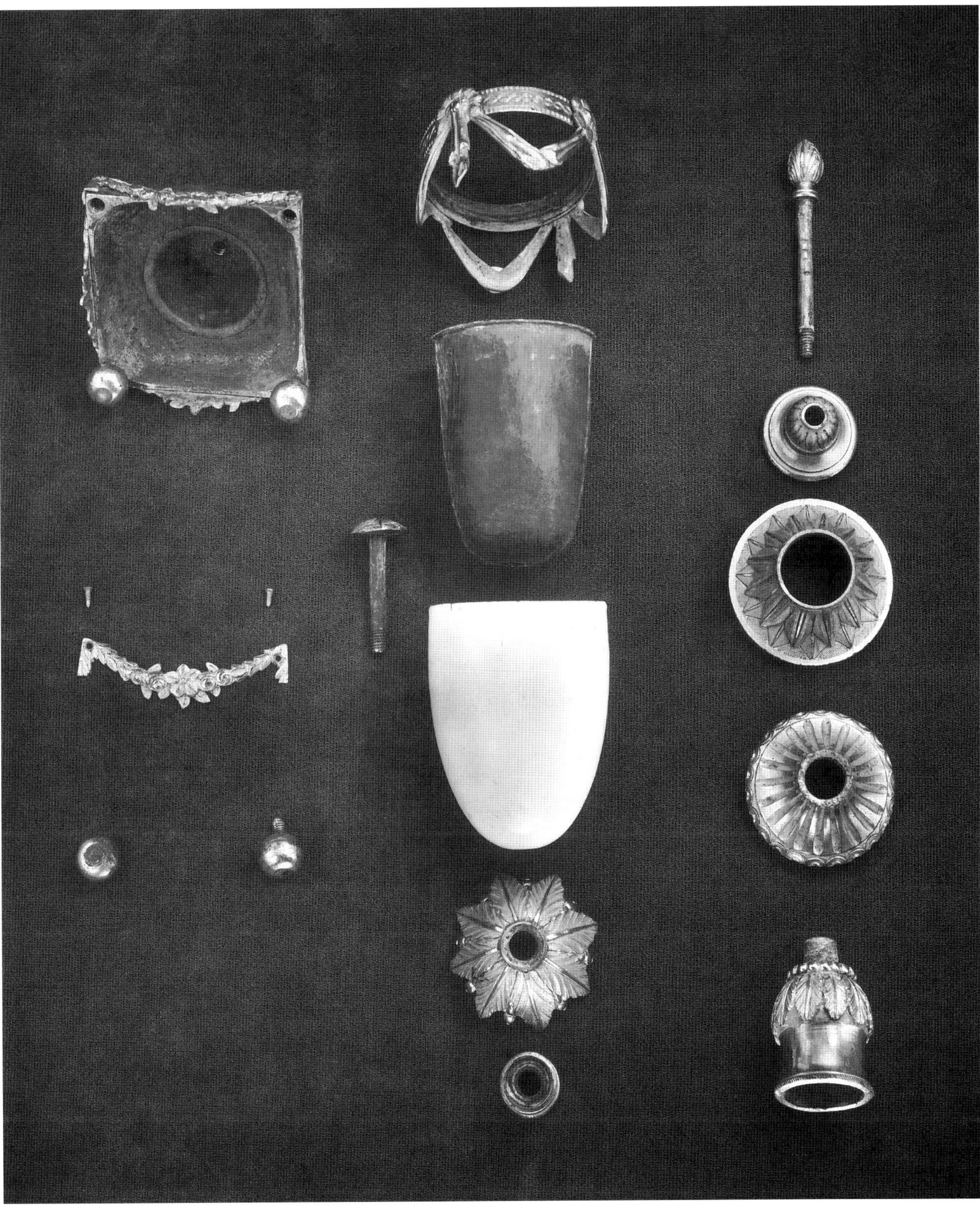

108. Boulton and Fothergill, one of the candle vases of Plate 249, Howard Antiques Ltd.

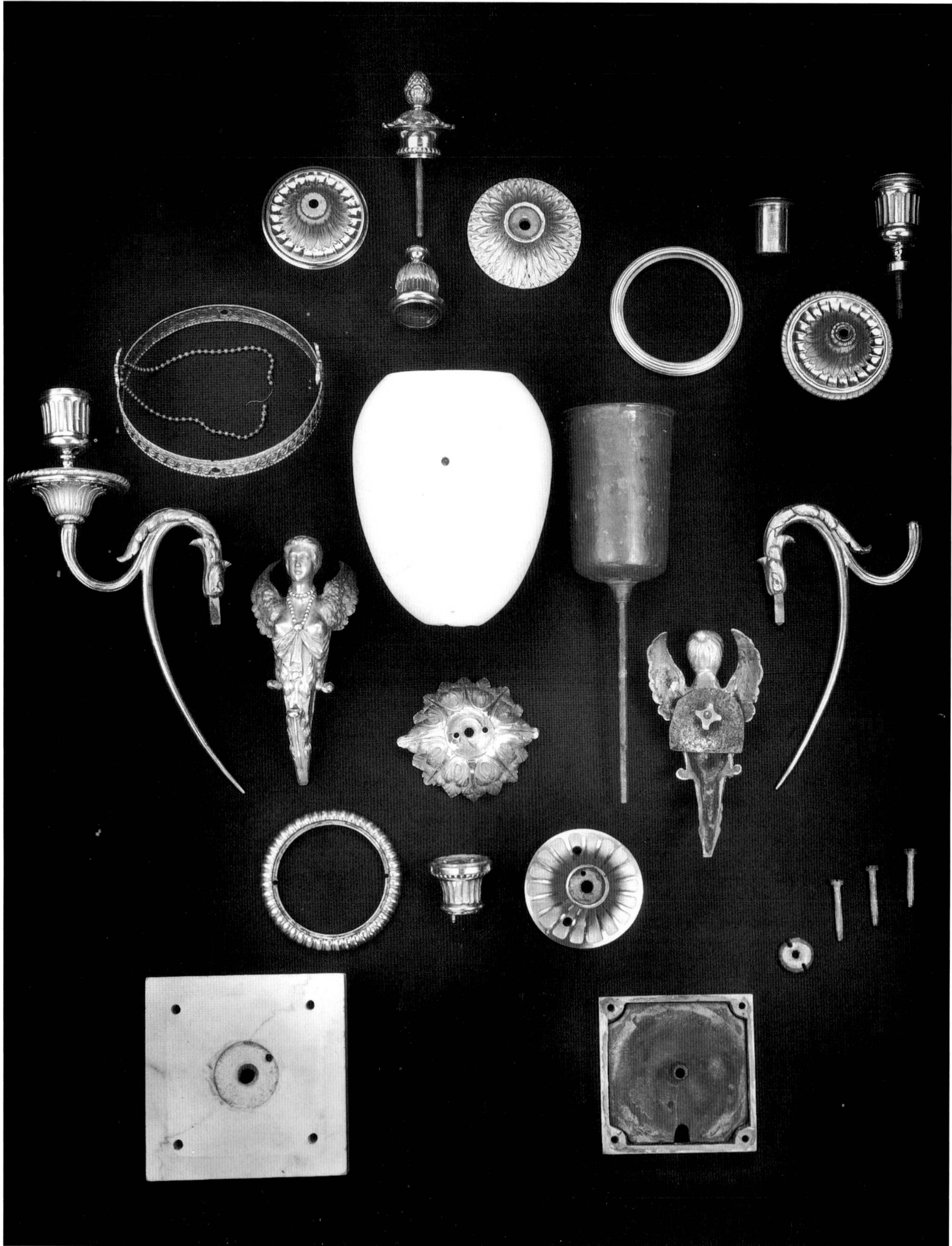

109. Boulton and Fothergill, wing-figured vase of Plate 367, National Trust, Osterley Park.

OPPOSITE:
110. Boulton and Fothergill, vase perfume burner similar to Plate 268, Weston Park Foundation.

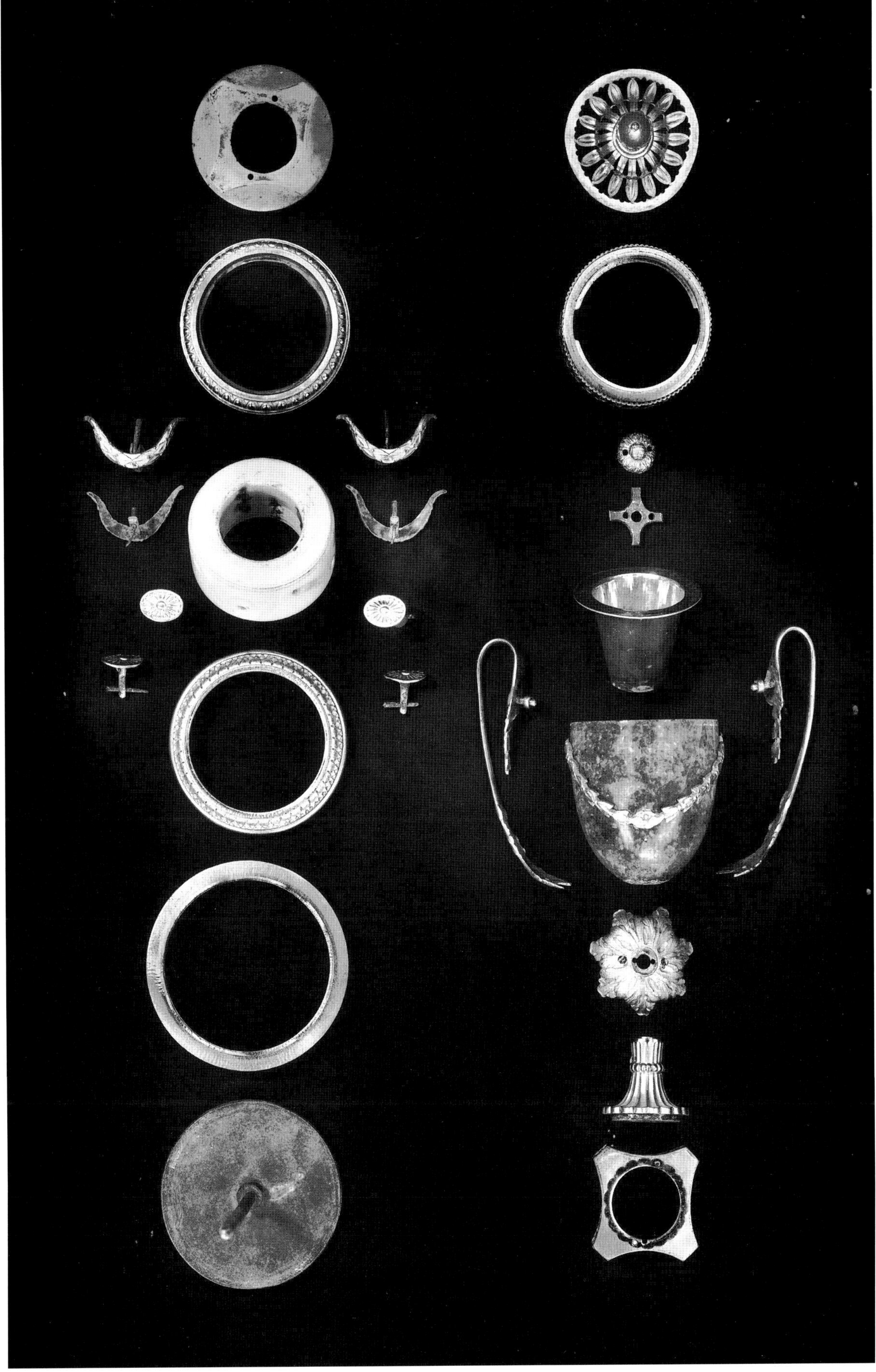

111. Boulton and Fothergill, one of the candle vases of Plate 274, Private Collection.

A brass with high zinc content would absorb gold more readily than one with low zinc content.[46]

The paucity of Boulton's notes on the gilding process is, however, of no importance. The gilding process itself was not what mattered most. The technique that he was most anxious to learn was the art of applying colour to the gilt work after the initial gilding. It was in this art that the secret of successful competition with his French rivals lay. After the initial gilding process the object has a lustreless yellow surface that is very durable but unattractive. It is therefore subjected to further processes that heighten its colour and give it lustre. The first and essential part of all colouring processes is the cleansing of the object with a fine brass wire brush, which is known as a scratch-brush. If the gilder then wishes to achieve a reddish colour the simplest method is to heat the metal again, which absorbs the gold further into the surface and produces an alloy coating of copper and gold: this surface can then be brushed with nitric acid or heated again with a coating of beeswax in order to remove the copper oxide. The wax has the additional effect of producing a patina on the surface. Some gilders would have done no more than this. Others would either omit this process altogether or proceed to some form of chemical colouring process, the recipes for which were numerous and varied.[47]

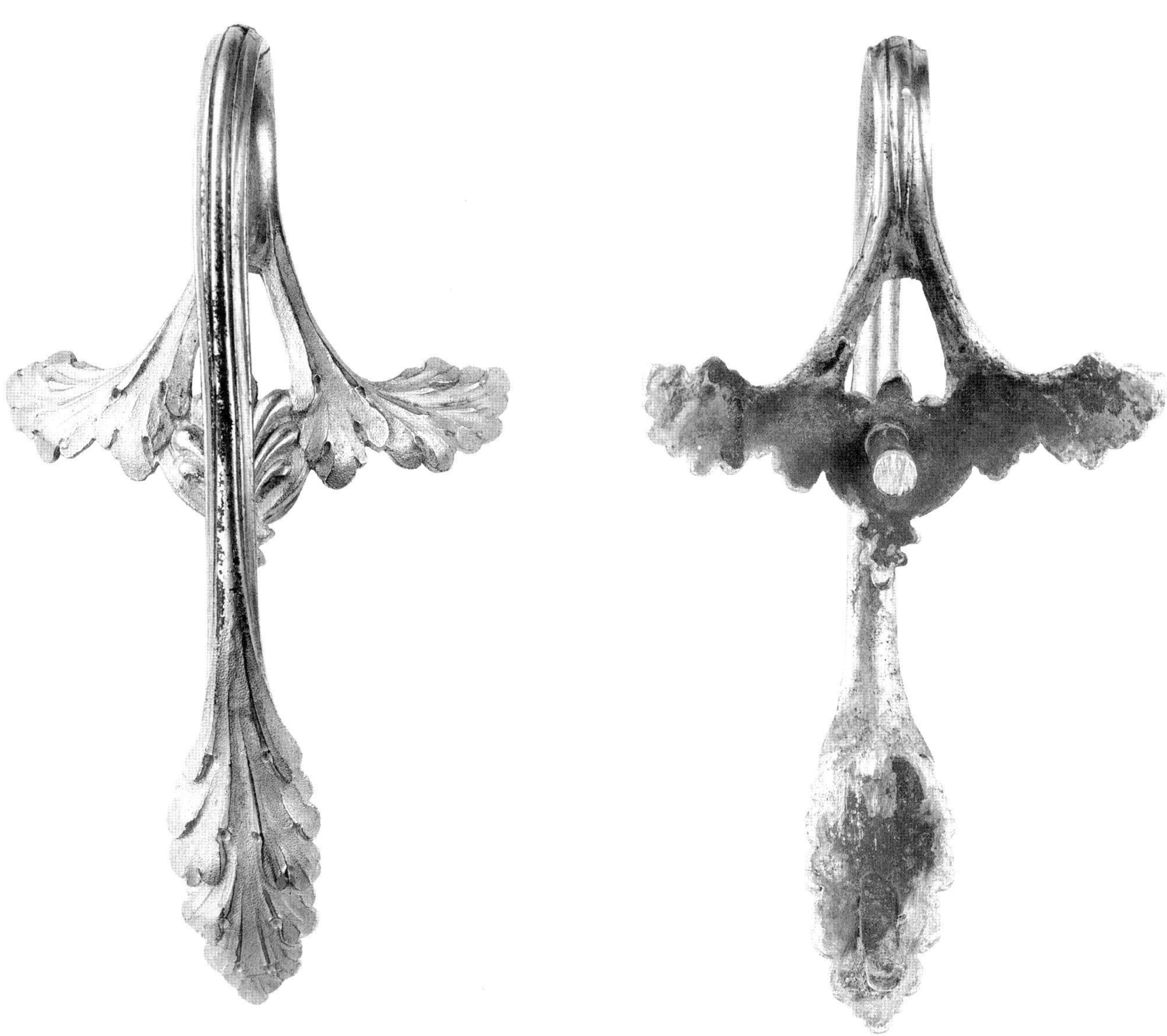

112. Boulton and Fothergill, handles of one of the candle vases of Plate 274, Private Collection.

It is not clear whether Boulton's gilders omitted the simple process of reheating or not, but a note which he made in one of his notebooks suggests that he placed some importance on it: 'After having scratch-brushed the piece you must bring it back to the fire as much as possible, throw it in water, then withdraw it. Put it to dry in a cloth'. The note then proceeds to describe the further process of chemical colouring:

> Afterwards grind the colour with the finest possible vinegar, so that one can no longer see the grains of the colour. The brighter you want it [the colour] the thicker you put it on. Once it is daubed you put it on the hottest fire possible. Let the colour boil on the piece, then turn it upside down and leave it a small instant, for too long will burn it. Throw it into the water where it should be left half a quarter of an hour – [?]. After, if there is any place which has taken a bit too much colour, remove it with a little brush.[48]

The exact composition of Boulton's colouring solutions is unknown. The precise nature of the substances which were bought for the use of the gilders was seldom specified in the ledgers.[49] Several notes and recipes that Boulton compiled himself have, however, survived. He probably took these notes either from books[50] or from conversations with craftsmen whom he visited with the express purpose of learning about the gilding colours. They

OVERLEAF:
113. Boulton and Fothergill, one of the candle vases of Plate 296, Sherborne Castle.

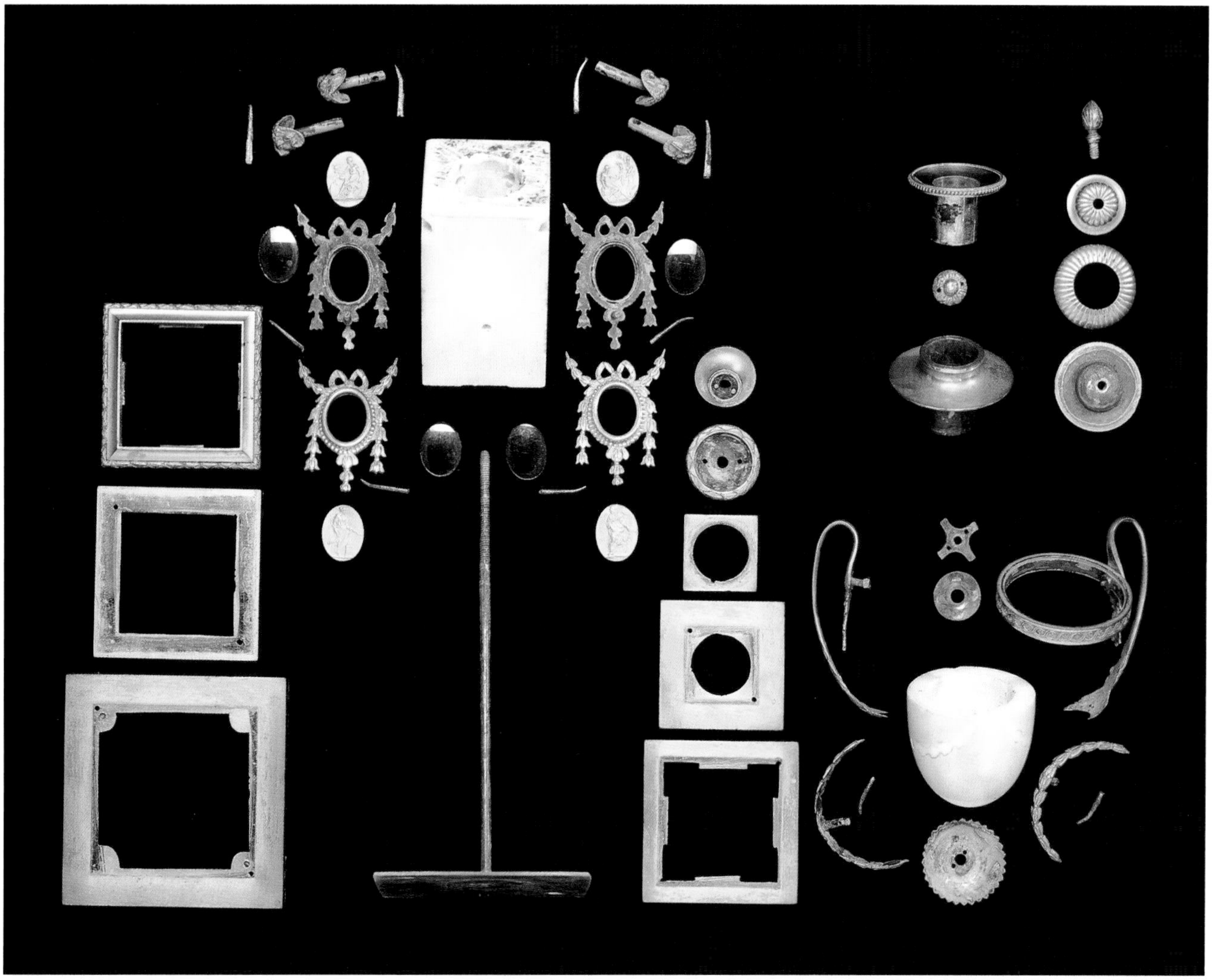

114. Boulton and Fothergill, one of the candle vases of Plate 302, Private Collection.

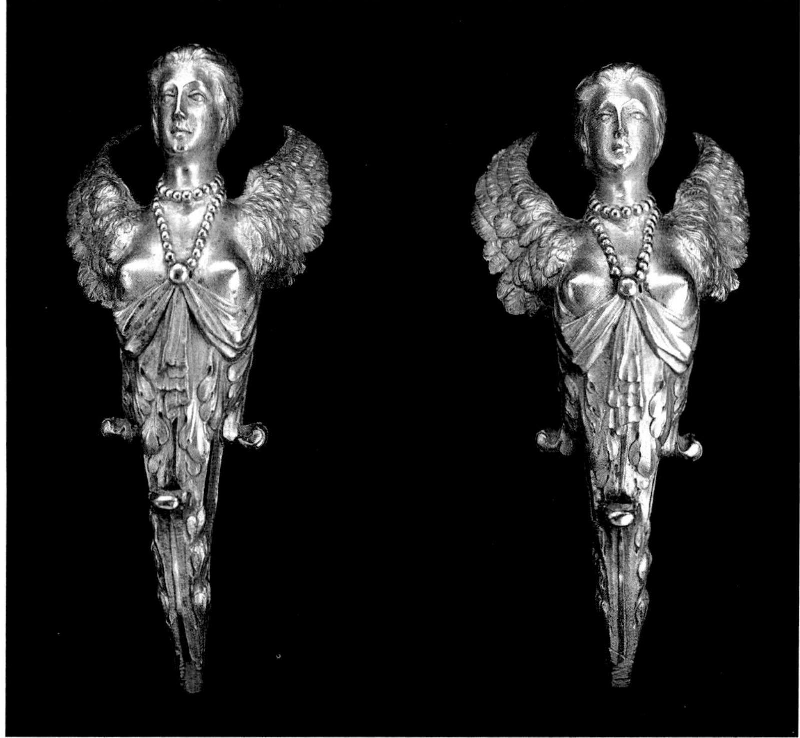

115. Boulton and Fothergill, winged figures from the vase of Plate 367, National Trust, Osterley Park.

coincided with his awakening interest in the making of ornamental ormolu and some of them specifically refer to this new branch of manufacture. It is, therefore, likely that his notes give some idea of the colouring processes used on ormolu ornaments at Soho.

Two methods of colouring gilt work by chemical means were employed in the eighteenth century. One of these consisted of dipping the gilt object in a boiled solution that contained some yellow substances such as turmeric, sulphur or yellow arsenic. The colours were thus absorbed onto the surface of the gilding. The colour of turmeric was usually fixed by boiling in common salt or ammonium chloride, but urine was also used and Boulton noted a recipe which used it.[51] Dipping recipes of this sort are mentioned in several contemporary books and the chief advantage claimed for them was that some of the yellow colouring matter remained in the hollows of deeply chased work, where the original gilding was apt to be imperfect.

The other common process, which was the process used at Soho, consisted of covering the gilt object with a composition called gilding wax and then applying heat. The wax contained various substances, which could tint or heighten the colour of the gold. The precise effect of this process, which was probably not perfectly understood in the eighteenth century, was to dissolve the gold again and to redeposit it on the surface. The simplest example of a recipe of this sort in Boulton's notes is one for a plain matt finish, which he called 'the dead colour':

	oz	pwt
Sal petre	2	
Allum	1	
Salt		5[52]

(i.e. potassium nitrate 61.5 per cent, potassium aluminum sulphate 30.8, sodium chloride 7.7). In this recipe the sodium chloride and potassium nitrate would dissolve the gold and the potassium aluminum sulphate re-deposit it. Ammonium chloride ('sal ammoniac'), or any chloride in the form of an impurity, might be substituted for sodium chloride and are recorded elsewhere in Boulton's notes in this role. The matt finish is caused by chlorine, which etches the surface of the gold. If a smooth surface is wanted the ingredients must be rid beforehand of hydrochloric acid and other soluble chlorides, which Boulton classed under the name of 'marine acid': 'For all coulers (except the dead couler) it is absolutely necessary that every ingredient should before 'tis compounded be quite freed from the marine acid …'.[53]

To achieve a heightened colour other compounds were added to the solving and precipitating agents. Thus in order to create what Boulton called a 'pale, middle or clearing[54] colour' copper was introduced into the solution in the form of cupric acetate ('verdigris') or cupric sulphate ('Roman vitriol' or 'blue vitriol') and was induced to precipitate with the gold by the use of iron or zinc in the form of ferrous sulphate ('copperas'), finely divided iron ('ethiops martial')[55] or zinc sulphate ('white vitriol'). Boulton noted the following recipes:

	oz	pwt
Sal ammoniack	1	10
Green copperas	1	10
Salt	1	
Verdegrees	0	15
Salt petre	0	15[56]

(i.e. ammonium chloride 27.3 per cent, ferrous sulphate 27.3, sodium chloride 18.2, cupric acetate 13.6, potassium nitrate 13.6); and:

	oz
Salt petre	7½
Sal ammoniack	10
Verdigrese	7½
Roman vitriol	7½
Green copperas	7½
Allum	7½
Sal prunell a little[57]	

(i.e. potassium nitrate 15.8 per cent, ammonium chloride 21, cupric acetate 15.8, cupric sulphate 15.8, ferrous sulphate 15.8, potassium aluminum sulphate 15.8, and a little calcined potassium nitrate) which, by precipitating the gold back to the surface with the finely divided copper, would give the gilding a reddish tinge.

The colour could be enhanced further by introducing into these recipes colouring matters such as sulphur, red or yellow ochre, red chalk, turmeric or saffron. As Boulton noted, these colouring matters had to be finely ground,[58] in order to ensure that they would be carried to the surface of the object with the precipitate and absorbed: 'The materials of the yellow coulor must be all pounded together in a mortar, then boyl it with water till all is disolved and becomes thickish, then pour it out on a stove and grind it fine and put it into cakes for use.' As with the earlier recipes the use of wax ensured the binding of the surface and gave it a patina. There are several colouring recipes of this sort among Boulton's notes. The 'red middle yellow coulor' for example is achieved by a recipe of:

	oz	pwt
Salt	1	
Sal petre	0	15
Verdegrees	0	15
Green copperas	0	15
Red chaulk	0	15
Sal ammoniack	1	10[59]

(i.e. sodium chloride 18.3 per cent, potassium nitrate 13.6, cupric acetate 13.6, ferrous sulphate 13.6, red chalk 13.6, ammonium chloride 27.3). 'Crocket's gilding coulers' are given as:

Wax	lb	oz	pwt
Bees-wax	2	8	
Verdegrees	1		
Red chaulk	2		
Allum	0	2	
Borax	0	2	
Sal ammoniack burnt	0	0	3[60]

(i.e. wax 44.4 per cent, cupric acetate 16.6, red chalk 33.2, potassium aluminum sulphate 2.8, borax 2.8, ammonium chloride 0.2: borax was probably used because it helped the wax to burn off clearer); and:

Red couler	oz	pwt
Red argil	4	
Cream tarter	4	
Verdegrees	1	
Red chaulk	0	10[61]

(i.e. potassium hydrogen tartrate 42.1 per cent, probably coloured with iron oxides, potassium hydrogen tartrate 42.1, cupric acetate 10.5, red chalk 5.3).[62] These are all recipes for imparting a reddish tinge to the gilding. Boulton noted and received other recipes which gave a yellow or golden tinge,[63] including one which, being mostly in French, he probably acquired from a French immigrant.[64]

These notes reveal some of the care which Boulton took to discover the secrets of good colouring. He had been concerned with the problem of improving the quality of the gilding at Soho since 1765, and Fothergill advised him at the end of that year to apply to Pyke, who was probably George Pyke the organ builder, so that he could learn 'the secret whereby the French give that fine gold colour to their sconces':[65] he thought it would be useful for the manufacture of buttons. By 1769 Boulton's researches into gilding processes were motivated more by his interest in the developing ormolu trade. He was particularly anxious to discover the secrets of the colours created by craftsmen in France. Perhaps Keisel, he noted in his diary in 1769, could tell him something about the French colour, or perhaps he could learn it from Dominique Jean.[66] In the same year he asked Solomon Hyman in Paris –

> how and with what ingredients the French gilders colour their fine gilt sconces after they are gilt, for I observe that most of them gild upon brass instead of pinchbeck which gilding upon brass always will be paler than that upon pinchbeck, yet nevertheless their sconces when finished appear of deep golden orange red and therefore I presume they are boyled in some sauce or other after they are gilt.[67]

He was dissatisfied with the colour of the gilding at Soho in 1770 because it was too red,[68] one cause of which could have been the reddish colour of the brass alloy, and he was still trying to learn the French gilders' techniques several years later.[69] The recipes and notes which I have quoted in this chapter were the results of his own energetic research, and their application enabled him to boast in the mid-1770s, with some truth, that his gilding was richer and more durable than that of his French competitors.[70] The richness of the gilding on some of his finest ornaments is one of their greatest attractions (Plates 155, 160, 177).

There are no estimates in the records of the 1770s of the cost of gilding, which was obviously an important component of the total cost of each object. There is, however, an intriguing note from John Hodges in 1785, giving the results of an examination of 'old calculations' and estimating the gilding costs as:

> Plain plinths or necks common yellow or red 2d per inch workmanship included
> Frames including dead mouldings or such as ice pails 4d per inch ditto
> Figures such as Titus etc. 8d per inch ditto.

A Titus figure needed about 10 pennyweight of gold to cover a surface of about 120 square inches.[71]

Having been gilt and suitably coloured the ornaments were taken to the burnishing shop. Here, with the usual burnishing tools, which traditionally included hard substances such as agate or the tooth of a dog or wolf, the gilt surface was polished. Sometimes it was only partly polished, if a contrast between matt and polished surfaces was required, as on the swags which decorate the Titus clock case illustrated in Plate 184. This was the last process to be carried out before the ornaments were ready for assembly. Even at this stage, in spite of the durability of the gilding, the work could be spoiled, and sometimes was, by carelessness.[72]

The tools and materials which were listed in the gilding, colouring and burnishing shops at Soho in 1782 give an idea of the sort of equipment which was used for the gilding of ornaments, although by then the workshops were mostly concerned with buttons, toys and silver. They include furnaces, mercury, ladles, gilding brushes, waxing pans, burnishers and blocks to burnish on.[73] A more graphic illustration of a gilding shop is provided by the plates in Diderot's *Encyclopédie* (Plates 116–17) which,

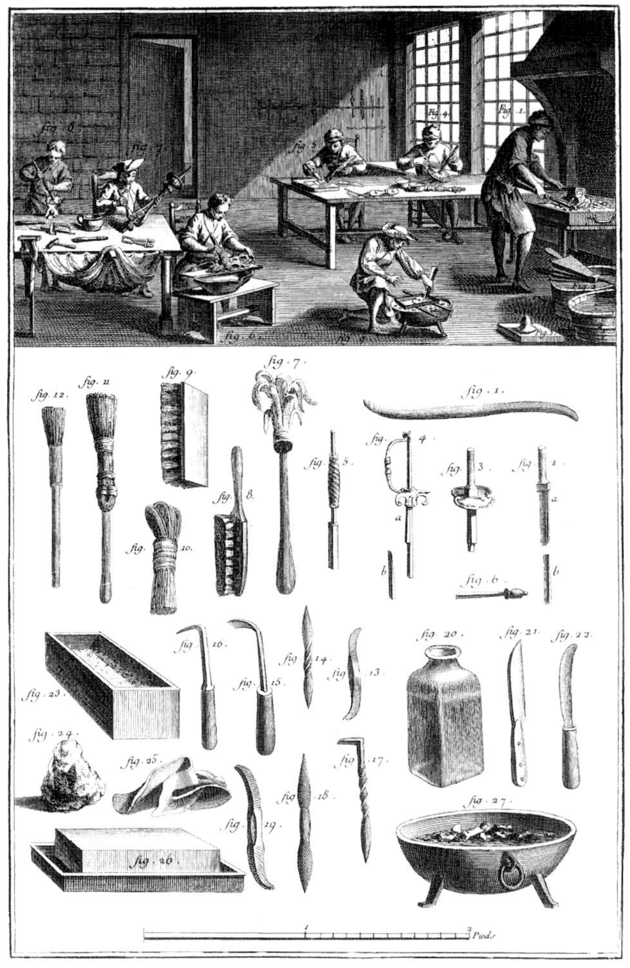

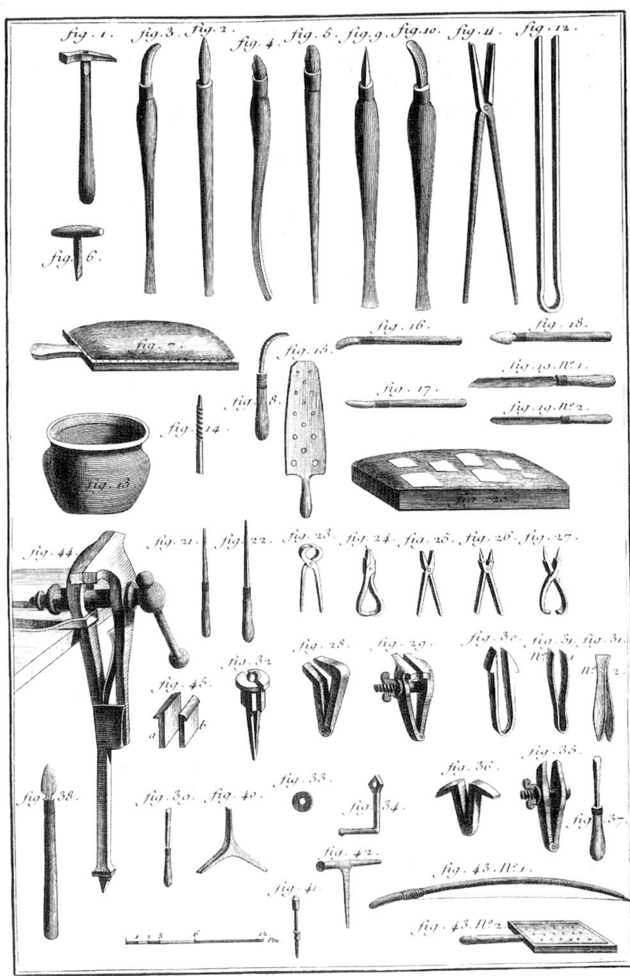

116–17. Diderot, *Encyclopédie, Doreur sur Metaux.*

besides showing workmen engaged in the various processes such as cleaning (Plate 116, Fig. 4), applying the amalgam (Fig. 5), cleaning with a scratch-brush (Fig. 6), applying the colouring solution (Fig. 7), heating the object (Fig. 1) and burnishing it (Fig. 8), also illustrates with meticulous detail the tools which were used. Many of the tools would have been recognised by Boulton's workmen, for example the gilding knives (Plate 117, Fig. 19, nos. 1, 2) the scratch-brushes (Plate 116, Figs. 10–12), the various scrapers (Plate 116, Figs. 13–17, Plate 117, Figs. 9–10), the burnishers (Plate 117, Figs. 2–5, 16–18, 38), one of which is described as *dent de loup* (Fig. 16), and even the bottle for the nitric acid (Plate 116, Fig. 20) and the jar for the amalgam (Plate 117, Fig. 13).

Craftsmen

It is not easy to identify the craftsmen engaged on the manufacture of ormolu ornaments. Francis Eginton, originally a chaser and engraver, played a key role, as he did in the silver business.[74] He modelled figures and mounts,[75] was described as the firm's chief designer,[76] and was in charge of the chasing and of expensive metalwork generally. He supervised the best work of the early 1770s, and was involved in its design and its costing. Casting was probably carried out by John Allen, who was working at Soho by 1763,[77] and Isaac Ryley,[78] who worked at Soho from 1771 or earlier.[79] Among several workmen involved in stamping, pressing and die sinking were Thomas Moore and Joseph Sanders, who were working at Soho by

1762,[80] and whose workshops were recorded in the 1782 Inventory.[81] Francis Eginton's brother John, who was at Soho by 1768 and was dismissed in 1777, was involved with the making of dies[82] and was certainly involved in the ormolu business.[83] He taught apprentices to engrave and draw, and may have been responsible for the engraving of the rare engraved panels on certain ornaments (Plates 161, 180). He may also have been responsible for some of the finer chasing work. He was certainly capable of the techniques, although it is likely that most of his work was concerned with gilt boxes, instrument cases and similar toys. Perhaps the otherwise unknown chasers Edward Pardoe and Joseph Burton, whose indentures in 1768 have survived,[84] or a chaser named William Wilson, whom John Eginton wanted to supplant in 1780,[85] worked on ormolu mounts. But it is impossible to know in most cases whether chasers and the other craftsmen engaged on finishing objects were working exclusively on silver, plate and other wares or also worked on ormolu.

Besides the Eginton brothers, the archives record the names of some of the workmen who were definitely involved with ormolu. John Duval, who was at Soho by 1770, worked on the King's clock case (Plate 160) under the supervision of Francis Eginton in 1772, and on Samuel Pechell's Titus clock case in the same year.[86] It can safely be assumed that he worked on other ormolu ornaments until he left Soho, probably in 1777.[87] Two further workmen, William Chamberlain and William Hancock, are mentioned in the 1782 Inventory as having made ornaments. Little is known of Chamberlain. Hancock was at Soho by 1763[88] and was chiefly concerned with silver and plate. Both names were recorded in a list of objects and equipment in the workshop of 'Bentley', probably Richard Bentley, who in 1782 was clearly the chief craftsman concerned with the ormolu business, such as it was by then.[89] It was probably Richard Bentley whom Boulton described as having the 'management' of the department in 1770. Boulton criticised him severely. In 1772 he was responsible for finishing the goods for the sale at Christie's.[90] A list of the stock in his workshop was drawn up for the 1782 Inventory and, apart from listing three pairs of vases with mounts made partly by Chamberlain and a 'circophicus ... made by W. R. Hancock' it valued certain pieces of chasing work which were probably done by Bentley himself.

It is likely that William Bingley, who was at Soho by 1762 and became a partner in the silver, ormolu and plate business in 1779,[91] was also involved in the ormolu business at an early date. The Bingley's vase was probably named after him (see Survey of ornaments, pp. 287–92).

The identity of most of the gilders is unknown. The only named craftsman is Thomas Bradbury, who was at Soho at least by 1768[92] and supplied work between 1776 and 1782.[93] He can presumably be identified with the Bradbury whose recipe for 'yellow couler' Boulton noted in 1770[94] and who in April 1771, having regaled himself in the company of several others from Soho, was so drunk that he had to be helped home, after which he was 'determined on a week's play' and thus delayed the completion of a pair of vases.[95] He left Soho in 1782.

Vase bodies and other materials

I have already said a little, during my account of the early development of the ormolu business in Chapter 2, about the sources of the materials which were used for the bodies of vases. Some of the vase bodies, such as the gilt copper vases of Plates 248, 334, 349 and 359, were entirely made at Soho. The enamelling of the copper vases of Plates 249 and 258 may also have been done at Soho, but it is more likely that the enamelling was subcontracted to one of the many specialist craftsmen in Birmingham.[96] Wedgwood reported at the beginning of 1769 that Boulton was making enamelled vases,[97] and Boulton himself claimed that enamelling was one of the many skills practised at Soho in 1770,[98] but neither of these references provides conclusive evidence that the enamelling of vases was actually carried out at Soho. There are other references that contradict them. ''Tis true we do sometimes enamel', a customer was told in 1772, but the ability did not extend to even quite a small dial plate.[99]

Several of the other vase bodies were bought from specialist producers. Boulton ordered earthenware vases from Wedgwood in 1768–9,[100] and Etruscan ware bodies and necks for tea urns in 1770.[101] He sent vases (possibly the vases of Plate 258) to Baskerville in 1770 'to be japanned of the opaque blew',[102] asked his partner to order some green china vases for perfume burners from Worcester in the same month,[103] and ordered twenty-four glass vases from James Keir in 1772, twelve in each of two moulds.[104] Some of these white glass bodies were probably for the wing-figured vases illustrated in Plates 365 and 367, and others like them that have survived. Others could have been for the glass versions of the vases with satyr masks on their handles (Plate 293). Also in 1772 some vase bodies were ordered from William Duesbury's porcelain factory at Derby,[105] and a year later Keir's firm was asked to supply three pairs of white opaque glass bodies to the dimensions of a drawing appended to the letter, and another three to the dimensions of a drawing sent two months earlier. Boulton and Fothergill were anxious that these should be round, 'for if they have any flat places in them they will be of no use because we turn the surface of in a lathe besides the work will not fit nor do they look so well'.[106] This letter adds to the evidence in the archives that vases had to be made to fit the pre-designed mounts and that some re-working of vase bodies was carried out at Soho.

Most of the vases were made with stone bodies. The proximity of the mines and quarries of Derbyshire, where there was a flourishing lapidary and marble working trade by the middle of the eighteenth century, made natural stones an obvious answer to Boulton's needs. In Chapter 2, I have mentioned how in 1768 he was buying pieces of marble, as well as marble ornaments such as obelisks and vases, from craftsmen in Derbyshire. In January 1768 he bought:

	£	s	d
23 pieces of Darbyshire marble	1	3	0
12 ditto polished on both sides		12	0
One obelisque	1	5	0
One vase	2	12	6
	5	18	6
Bought one ditto at Ashford	1	11	6
	7	10	0[107]

Later in the same year he bought from Hall:

	£	s	d
Obelisques	5	0	0
1 pair vases	8	0	0
1 pair ditto	4	0	0
	17	0	0[108]

Boulton was considering at this time several other stones including blue john, which rapidly became his most favoured material for vase bodies, alabaster, which was mined in southern Derbyshire, black marble, which was mined at Ashford, and ordinary marble (presumably white). I have yet to find mounted ornaments using alabaster or black marble, but unmounted stone ornaments with black marble components feature in the pattern

118. Boulton and Fothergill, sidereal clock case, Birmingham Museum and Art Gallery, Soho House.

books. He used white marble for the bases of vases and clock cases in the earlier years (Plates 351, 359) and used it frequently for the pedestals for vases and other ornaments and for the bodies of the vases made later (Plates 153, 173, 186, 301, 304, 313). In 1774 he toyed with the idea of 'all the Derbyshire stones' of which vases were customarily made,[109] and on occasions used certain fluorspars related to blue john, such as the yellow fluorite mined at Crich and named after the place, and a combination of barytes and fluorite known as 'hatterel', which has been identified with the description 'tiger stone' used by contemporary writers.[110] Boulton was

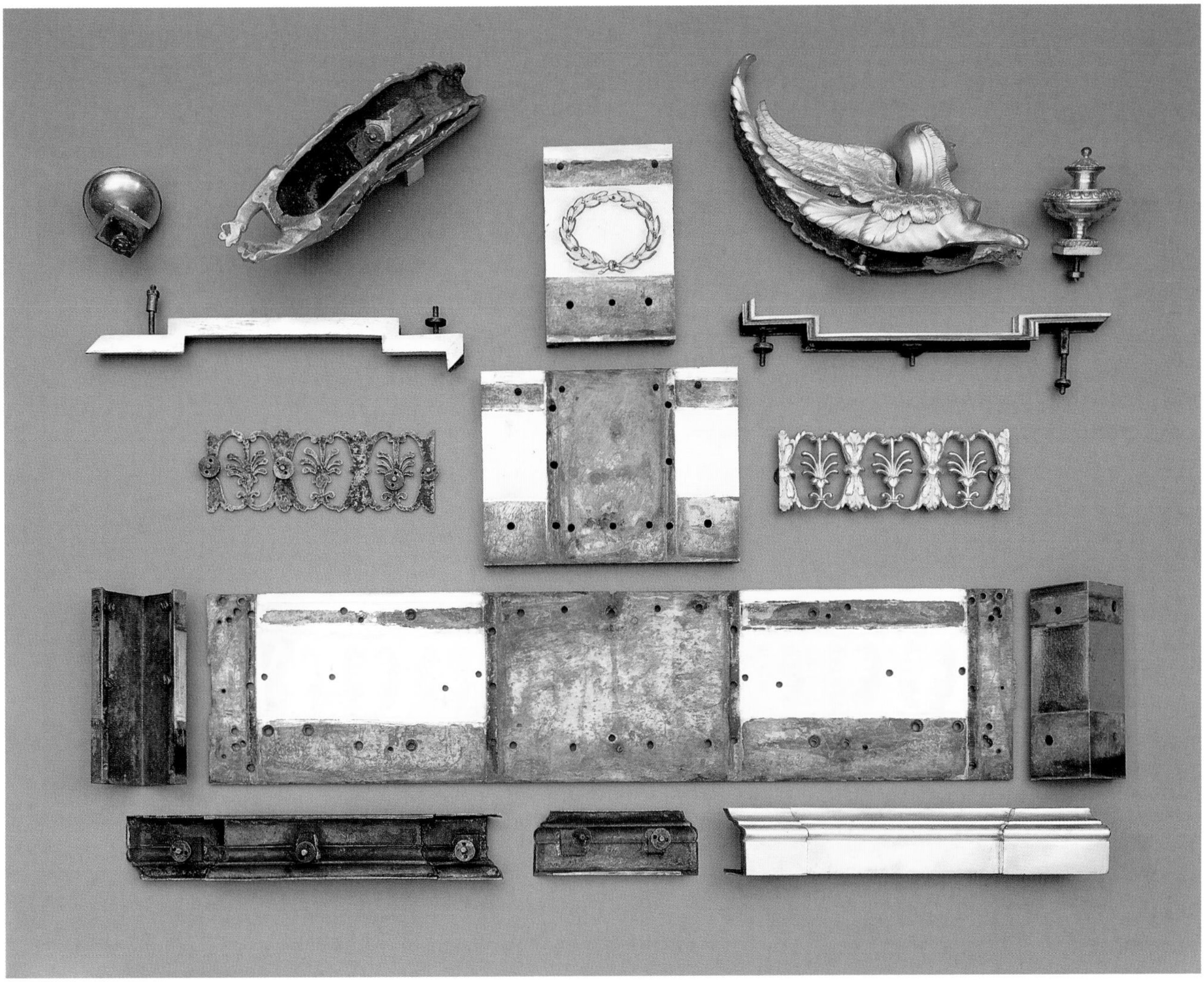

119–20. Boulton and Fothergill, sidereal clock case, Birmingham Museum and Art Gallery, Soho House.

probably aware of the geological differences between the various types of fluorspar but seems to have been content to name them all 'blue john' or 'radix amethysti' in correspondence, invoices and catalogues.

Blue john is, as I have mentioned in Chapter 2, a type of fluorspar.[111] Its name was originally derived in some way from its dominant colour, just as black jack was the name given by miners to the zinc mineral sphalerite.[112] Boulton's name for the stone in the sale catalogues, 'radix amethysti', was in accordance with eighteenth-century practice but is geologically confusing: it is not the same stone as amethystine quartz.[113] It has a radiating crystalline structure, with cubic crystals, and contains bands of blue and purple, intersected with other bands, which vary in colour from white or yellow to lighter blue. Occasionally it has patches of red or brown. Its colour can be lightened by the application of heat, and it can be turned and polished until its crystals are shown off to the best effect. The stone is found only at Treak Cliff, near Castleton in Derbyshire. The many different veins of the stone are usually classified into fourteen main varieties, each distinguishable by its colour and pattern. These fourteen varieties were given names in the late eighteenth century so that buyers could order the colour of stone which they required, but some of the veins contain stone of a colour and pattern associated with another vein. An experienced man can tell the difference between each vein – for example the reddish stone of the vases shown in Plates 276 probably came from the Bull Beef vein in the Blue John Caverns – but it is unlikely that Boulton tried to distinguish between the different veins, or even that they were named by their distinctive titles in his day. The orders which were sent by his clerks to the lapidaries and stone merchants often specified the colour of stone which was required but never named the veins.

OPPOSITE:
121. Boulton and Fothergill, Narcissus clock case, Birmingham Museum and Art Gallery, Soho House.

The working of blue john demands a great deal of skill because it is soft and brittle, and its colour can be easily spoiled by excessive heat. The stone must first be carefully dried and sawn into rough shapes. It can then be subjected to gentle heat if the craftsman wants to lighten the colour. Because it has many flaws it is then usually bound with resin or shellac, either by immersion in the molten binder or by the application of small pieces of resin when the stone has been heated. The pieces of stone are then ground to a more accurate shape, turned on a lathe, smoothed and polished.[114]

It is unlikely that all, or even most of the stone used for vases at Soho, were fashioned on the spot. But some certainly were. Boulton's first substantial purchases of blue john in 1769, nearly fifteen tons from John Platt and two casks from Robert Howe,[115] seem to have consisted of unworked stone, and he made notes in his diary about suitable cements for sticking pieces of stone together.[116] Workmen at Soho had the necessary skills of turning and polishing stones and other materials,[117] and Dorothy Richardson recorded a workshop during her visit in 1770 in which the workmen were turning blue john 'into vases' (see Chapter 1, p. 24, '36th room'). In some cases the stone beneath the pre-designed mounts has been left rough and unpolished, which suggests that it was processed at Soho. Plate 106 shows an example of this. In other cases, particularly on some of the earlier vases, the stones are crudely shaped or are of a relatively unattractive dark colour. On yet other examples there are flaws concealed by mounts. Plate 247 shows another stone body probably fashioned at Soho: it is not vase-shaped at all but economises on stone by extending only down to the ormolu cradle. It may even be that some of the many vases made up of two or more pieces of stone cemented together (Plates 241, 332) were also fashioned at Soho, although this work was also done by lapidaries to meet Boulton's specified dimensions.[118]

The weight of evidence suggests that many of the stone bodies were

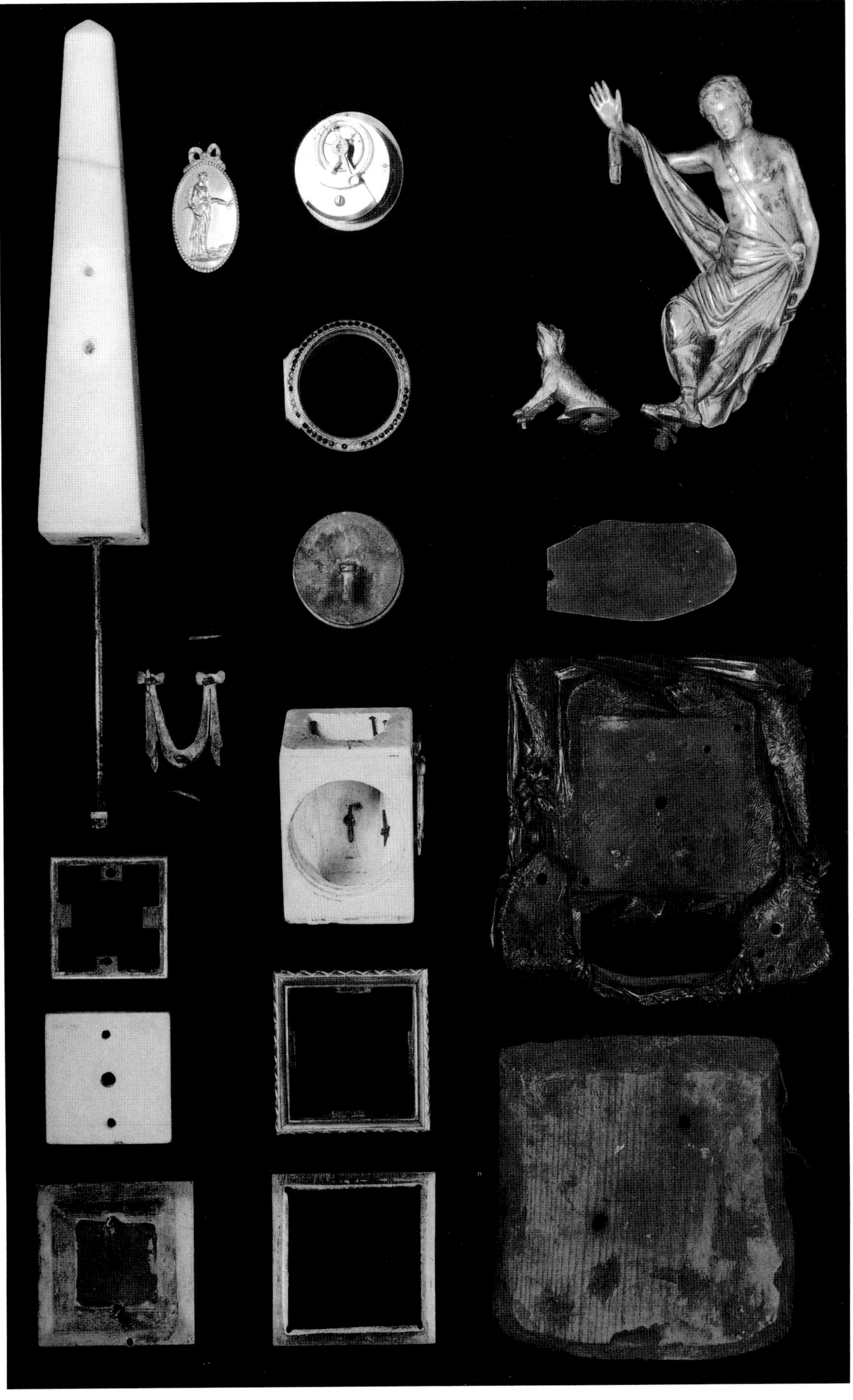

fashioned and polished by the stone workers before they were delivered to Soho. From 1771 the most regular supplier of blue john was Robert Bradbury of Castleton and the orders sent to him or to his son were nearly always for stones of specified shapes, sizes and colours.[119] Thus the first recorded order to Bradbury in February 1771 was for the largest piece of blue john that he could find, of an oval shape and polished 'on both sides',[120] and a month later he was asked for:

6 sphinx compt
4 Eginton 4 branch compt
4 Jess [?] 2 branchd
2 Lord Shelburns great vase[121]

which suggests that he had been given the precise measurements required to fit the mounts of these standard vases. On many later occasions the need for vases made exactly to pattern was impressed upon him, and besides measurements he was frequently sent drawings of the required vases,[122] which he was asked to keep for reference in case of subsequent orders.[123] In 1774 the elder Bradbury was asked for vase stones designed for the 'ram's head pattern'.[124] Several of the requests emphasise that the stone must be very good, and on one occasion Boulton and Fothergill wanted the 'most butiful stones or otherwise none at all'.[125] The requirement that vases should be made to exact measurements was due to the quantity production of the mounts. The vase had to fit the mounts because they were already made.[126] Wedgwood, Keir and Duesbury all received similar instructions,[127] which were not always faithfully carried out.

Besides vase bodies and the stone pieces used in the pedestals of vases, several other components had to be bought from subcontractors, such as clock and watch movements, dials and glasses,[128] because such things could not be produced at Soho. Many of the decorative materials such as the tortoiseshell veneers (Plates 155, 231) and the glass panels which are lacquered to simulate polished stones (Plates 328–9, 355–8), were possibly made at Soho, where the techniques were already practised for the toy trade, but the lacquering may have been done, and was on occasion, by John Baskerville.

The account in this chapter of the processes in the production of ormolu ornaments has shown how difficult it is to separate the ormolu trade from the other trades at Soho. Thus the production processes such as casting, stamping, chasing, gilding and burnishing were the same processes as those used in the production of buttons, toys, plate and silverware, and many of the different products were processed in the same workshops. Similarly Francis Eginton had more on his plate than the ormolu business, and other managers, such as John Scale and John Hodges, and the clerks, such as Charles Wyatt[129] and Andrew Cabrit,[130] and the accountant, Zacchaeus Walker, were concerned with far more than ormolu even if, as demonstrated by their signatures beneath so many of the letters which I have cited in this book, they were at times concerned minutely with it. Occasionally the complexities and problems of production at Soho are well demonstrated by documents concerned with the ormolu business. Such problems as the delays of subcontractors in completing their orders, the disruption to production caused by holidays, the annual inventories of stock,[131] the behaviour of certain workmen, the seasonal nature of demand and the risks of breakage during transport, occur frequently in the letters. But these references give only a small part of the total picture of Soho. A fuller account of the factory, its workmen (and women and children), its managers and its organisation and problems would have to cover the complete range of products and needs a book on its own.

CHAPTER 5

Marketing

I have shown in the second chapter that ormolu ornaments were only a part of Boulton and Fothergill's extensive toy business and that production did not begin until several years after the toy business was well established. It is not surprising that the partners made attempts to sell their ormolu ornaments by the same methods and through the same channels that they used for their buttons, buckles, toys, plate and silver.[1] This account of their marketing methods will touch on their relationships with the retailers, merchants and agents, both in England and overseas, who bought or who handled the sales of their toys and other products. But ormolu ornaments were luxury products and needed a different approach. Boulton understood that he needed to sell his up-market goods directly to the affluent, and this chapter will show how much the sales of ormolu depended on direct sales to customers. It will also throw some light on the personal effort, which Boulton found it necessary to make in the 1770s in order to keep his business going. After the expensive construction and equipment of the new factory at Soho he would have liked to double production and sales, which, given the necessary finance, he reckoned he could do without increasing manufacturing capacity any further.[2] The need for increased sales, and for a wider geographical spread of sales, would be understood by the manager of any modern business that has progressed beyond the initial stages of its growth. Higher annual costs and the expense of financing the growth of fixed assets and stock make the organisation seem suddenly vulnerable, just when it has become an established force in its industry.

Boulton did not have the aids of fast transport or the popular means of communication such as widely circulated newspapers, television and the internet. Nor did he have the analysis of postcodes that a modern business can use in the direct marketing of up-market services and goods. But neither the travelling salesman nor advertising was omitted from his plans. His marketing techniques, many of which were also practised by his contemporaries, such as John Taylor, Samuel Garbett, Josiah Wedgwood and William Duesbury, illustrate the development of consumer-oriented business in the eighteenth century.

Retailers

In the early stages in 1768–70 Boulton and Fothergill hoped to encourage sales of ormolu ornaments through retailers. But they soon ran up against a problem. Buttons, buckles, watch chains, toothpicks, snuff boxes and many other toys and trinkets were inexpensive to produce and to a large extent were in everyday demand. The toy shops, when they took in a stock of buttons, were running the risk of a change in fashion which might cut demand for a particular type of button, but on the whole they could expect steady sales and could afford to carry a certain amount of stock. They could even succeed sometimes in selling most of their stock before the expiry of the period of credit which the manufacturer usually gave them: or, if they preferred to pay immediately for their stock, they could expect a discount from the manufacturer, who in the eighteenth century was usually much in need of ready cash. In either event they could reckon on a reasonably quick turnover and steady revenue. Ormolu-mounted vases were different. They were expensive luxuries. Sales of expensive vase candelabra, without prior orders, were unpredictable and, at worst, infrequent. The shopkeepers were not eager to carry stock in any quantity. Nor were Boulton and Fothergill willing to finance an excessive amount of stock in retailers' hands on a sale or return basis. It threatened to add to their financial problems, which were acute enough. They wrote to William Evill at Bath, when he had ordered some vases in 1771:

As to our sending you goods upon sale or return, it is a method of dealing by which we have sustained many very considerable losses and very great inconveniences, and hath almost obliged us to make a rule never to deal so in future. It must be obvious to every person who will reflect a little, that the fortune of a Prince would scarce be able to support such a manufactory as ours, were we to stock every shop in England (with whom we have connections) on this footing ...[3]

Writing to Henry Morris, a London goldsmith, in the same year they said:

Every shilling worth of goods we send to your new shop upon the terms proposed by you is so much addition to our dead stock. As that is already monstrously large, even to a greater extent than any other silversmith's shop in London (when we include our tools) we therefore are thinking of the means to lessen it instead of increasing it ...

To Morris they added a second reason, which was perhaps more an excuse than a genuine fear, but which had some substance:

We are likewise apprehensive that if we were to furnish the shops with all those articles we do or can make in or moulu it would hurt the fashion and sale of them.[4]

There had to be some rarity value to justify the price. A new owner who had just bought a fine ornament would not be pleased to see several identical objects in the shops.

By 1771 the partners were convinced that they could never achieve much by encouraging sales through the shops. They claimed to have been very disappointed when, after having exerted their 'utmost efforts, and bestowed much time, assedious attention and heavy expence in establishing' the manufacture of ormolu, they did not meet 'with that probable prospect of obtaining an extensive sale thereof among the toy shops notwithstanding we made a particular application to all the most emminent'.[5] Boulton told James Adam that the London shopkeepers were 'the bane of all improvements'[6] – eliciting the reply from the architect that in his view common shopkeepers everywhere were 'without spirit honor or integrity'.[7] Like so many of the furniture retailers today they were indifferent to, or afraid of, innovation.

These opinions did not deter Boulton and Fothergill from selling their ormolu ornaments to shopkeepers whenever they could, nor from encouraging sales by methods which they disliked, such as sale or return, if success was at all likely. Several sales to retailers are recorded. Among the more interesting transactions in the early years were sales of vases in 1769 to John Kentish,[8] a goldsmith in Cornhill, who appears to have given his name to a particular design of vase in Boulton and Fothergill's internal records,[9] and in 1771 to Christopher Pinchbeck the clockmaker,[10] who appears to have carried on a considerable trade in toys and whom I have mentioned earlier in connection with the clock which William Chambers designed for the King (Plate 5). Also in 1771 they sent some vases on sale or return to William Evill in spite of the pithy arguments put forward in their letter to him for not doing so, because they thought that his 'mode of sale' was likely to be successful and the Bath season was attended by the fashionable world.[11] In the same year vases were sent to many other retailers, including James Todd of York,[12] John le Coq and Thomas Wilkinson of London,[13] and Patrick Robertson of Edinburgh.[14] On the whole the partners' prejudices proved correct and the retailers met with little success. Boulton and Fothergill wrote to Robertson in November:

We are sorry to observe that the disposal of the vases did not turn out so well as you and we expected but acknowledge with sincere thanks the kindness you are pleased to shew us in returning none of them and in keeping them for your own account.[15]

Le Coq returned two vases[16] and after five months Wilkinson had not sold all of his consignment.[17] Fothergill commented early in 1772 that they were unlikely to achieve much by this method of sale.[18] Bent,[19] Todd and many others had all proved to be disappointing.

Shopkeepers were encouraged in other ways. Several of them visited Soho to look at both the manufactory and its products.[20] More practically, they were offered both discounts and credit. Boulton and Fothergill grudged both of these concessions but were obliged to grant them. It was their normal practice to allow dealers a fifteen per cent discount on buttons and other toys and to grant a period of credit, usually six months, or to allow a further discount of five per cent for immediate payment.[21] They did not as a rule apply these terms to their ormolu ornaments. They claimed that, because the shopkeepers proved unable to stimulate a satisfactory trade in vases, they were forced to sell direct to the nobility and gentry in order to move their large and expensive stock. Vases were therefore invoiced at the full price and shopkeepers were expected to add their usual margin of profit. Some of them, as might be expected, complained at this arrangement because it meant that Boulton and Fothergill were selling their vases direct to customers at prices that were cheaper than the shopkeepers could manage. On the whole the partners disregarded such complaints. But in 1771 they gave Patrick Robertson a discount of ten per cent, having invoiced him originally at 'the same as we charge them to gentlemen', claiming that they had never previously made such an allowance to any toy shop in England but that they were anxious to encourage the sale of vases in the north: having made this concession they proceeded to offer him terms on future sales which conformed to their regular practice on sales of toys, namely a discount of fifteen per cent and six months' credit or a further five per cent discount for ready money.[22] In subsequent years a discount of ten per cent was more normal on their sales of ormolu.[23] But in addition to this discount, which often represented only part of the retailer's profit because he often added a further ten or fifteen per cent margin to Boulton and Fothergill's price,[24] the retailer customarily received six months' credit as with Boulton and Fothergill's other goods, or a further five per cent discount for immediate payment.[25] On one occasion Boulton and Fothergill said firmly that six months was the 'utmost period of credit that we are enabled to allow any of our friends'[26] but in letters to others they made it clear that their intention was only to draw on their debtors at the expiry of the six months for payment two months later, thus extending the effective term of credit to eight months.[27]

These were generous terms. In 1782 John Scale's inventory recorded a notional profit margin on many of the firm's goods of ten per cent.[28] In the earlier years the partners probably had no idea what profit they were trying to make on each line or what it cost them to give credit: if Scale's estimate had been true of the years of maximum output, the financial inducement offered to shopkeepers would have eaten heavily into the firm's profit margins. They show how anxious the partners were to move their stock, an anxiety that is confirmed by the regular contacts, which were maintained with many of the London retailers such as William Bent and James Cox and by some of the extravagant claims with which Boulton dressed his sales talk. Wedgwood wrote from Bath to his partner Thomas Bentley:

> We met with a large assortment of Mr Boulton's vases in a very rich shop in the market place. The gentleman[29] told me a long tale of Mr Boulton's having ingaged at several £1000 expence the only mine in the world of the radix amethyst, and that nobody else could have any of that material. I heard him patiently, but afterwards took an opportunity of advising him when we were alone in a corner of his shop not to tell that story too often, as many gentlemen who came to Bath had been in Derbyshire, seen the mine, and knew it to be free and open to all the world, on

paying a certain known mine rent to the land owner. The gentleman stared, and assured me upon his honor that he had not said a word more than Mr Boulton had assured him was true. Well done Boulton, says I *inwardly*. I told the gentleman Mr Boulton might possibly have ingaged them lately as I had not been in that country since the last summer. Nay, says he, 'tis three years since he told me this story. I was glad to change the subject, and inquired how they sold – but so, says he. I am afraid they will never answer Mr Boulton's end as a manufacture.[30]

Wedgwood wrote this comment in 1772, the year in which some of the finest and grandest ormolu pieces came from Soho. The shopkeeper's lack of confidence is obvious. Sales were clearly infrequent. The shrug of his shoulders can almost be seen as he says 'but so' to Wedgwood's question about how the vases were selling. It illustrates the usual fate of vases from Soho in the hands of the toy shops.

Direct sales to patrons

Because the shopkeepers were the 'bane of all improvements' Boulton and Fothergill determined early to sell as many of their ormolu ornaments as they could direct to their customers, being resolved that the shopkeepers would never buy many of the 'capital things' and that they could sell them better themselves.[31] They must have found support for this policy in the argument that it pays the manufacturer of a fashionable object to convert the leaders of fashion first. Other customers would follow. This was very much the policy of Boulton's friend Wedgwood, who well understood that to sell his wares to the leaders of society was the best form of advertisement.[32] Besides, leaders of fashion would seldom buy an object which had become common currency in the shops.

One way of converting the fashionable patron was to gain the favour of the leading architects. It was especially important to do so in the 1770s, when so many rich patrons were indulging themselves in the new fashion for the antique and extending and refurnishing their houses, and in some cases building new ones. The architects were the arbiters of taste. Wedgwood wrote to Bentley in 1779:

Fashion is infinitely superior to merit in many respects; and it is plain from a thousand instances that if you have a favorite child you wish the public to fondle and take notice of, you have only to make choice of proper sponcers. If you are lucky in them no matter what the brat is, black, brown, or fair, its fortune is made. We were really unfortunate in the introduction of our jasper into public notice, that we could not prevail upon the architects to be godfathers to our child.[33]

There is not a great deal of documentary evidence to prove that architects introduced Boulton to many patrons. But he knew several of them well, pursued his connections, and undoubtedly enhanced his reputation through them.

Boulton's earliest links were with the Wyatts. The Wyatt family building business in Staffordshire was founded by Benjamin Wyatt (1709–72).[34] Among his seven sons were William (1734–80), who was probably in charge of the design and construction of the Soho Manufactory, and Samuel (1737–1807), who was Robert and James Adam's clerk of works at Kedleston. Samuel Wyatt was established on his own in London by 1774, where he carried on a successful business as architect, builder and timber merchant.[35] He sent Boulton his first recorded commission for door furniture when he was working at Kedleston in 1765 (Plate 193, see Survey of ornaments, pp. 240–1). Also on Lord Scarsdale's behalf he ordered some sconces, which were probably candle branches for some mirror frames, in the following year,[36] and a blue john cup in 1769.[37] In spite of Boulton's delays in delivering these pieces Wyatt spoke very highly of his work to Lord Scarsdale[38] and it can be assumed that he was a useful ally in the fashionable world of London.[39]

Benjamin Wyatt's sixth son James was better known and more precocious, finding himself established in 1772, at the age of only twenty-six, as a fashionable London architect.[40] He carried out work for several of Boulton's patrons, including Mrs Montagu, and, as I have said in the discussion of Boulton's designs in Chapter 3, he was responsible for several designs of silver objects commissioned from Soho and had some influence on certain designs for ormolu (see p. 87). There is no evidence of any orders for ormolu initiated by him but it is unlikely that he failed to mention it to his patrons when occasion demanded.

The Earl of Shelburne introduced Boulton to Robert Adam in 1765 when, in a letter of introduction, the architect was asked to commission from Boulton some pieces for Bowood.[41] The letter was written at Birmingham and was to be handed to Adam personally by Boulton: the wording suggests almost that it was written at Boulton's request. There can be no doubt that Boulton saw the potential of making a favourable impression on the architect, which he in turn could impress on his patrons. The only recorded order from the Adam brothers is a request for some lamp chains, again for Lord Shelburne, in 1770. There is thus no proof that Boulton received many orders as a result of their commendation, but they thought highly of his work and he carried out commissions for several of their patrons, possibly with their approval.

Four other fashionable architects appear from the archives to have commissioned ornaments from Soho, or at least to have helped to do so. James Paine, most of whose work was carried out before Boulton and Fothergill were producing ormolu at all, ordered two samples of door furniture for Lord Arundell at Wardour Castle,[42] which he built in 1770–6. Robert Mylne ordered some silver mounts for a chimneypiece for one of his clients in 1775[43] and bought some candlesticks and an ormolu frame in 1777.[44] William Chambers was responsible for the design of the King's clock case and, judging from his influence on Boulton's designs after 1770, may have recommended his work widely. James Stuart was in touch with Boulton from 1769. Boulton's likely debt to him for certain designs for ormolu, including the tea urns of Plates 229 and 231, is discussed in Chapter 3 (see pp. 71–6 and Survey of ornaments, pp. 271–5). There were several occasions when he was in touch with Boulton and Fothergill over some of their silver products and he was the architect of Mrs Montagu's new house in Portman Square, for which Boulton and Fothergill made the ormolu decorations for the doors.[45] Like James Wyatt and the Adam brothers, he carried out work for several of Boulton's patrons during the years in which the ormolu trade reached its peak. Boulton no doubt saw him, as he saw all the fashionable architects, as a useful means of approach to his noble customers.

The ease with which Boulton and Fothergill had been able to make contacts with potential patrons even before 1770 must have encouraged their policy of selling direct to their clients. As Boulton's stature among the manufacturers of Birmingham increased he inevitably met men with lands in the vicinity, such as the Earls of Aylesford, Craven, Dartmouth, Harrowby, Hertford and Warwick, the Earl Gower, and Lord Lyttelton. Most of the local landowners visited the manufactory, often with their wives and their children, and sometimes with friends.[46] But quite apart from these local contacts, some of which were particularly useful to Boulton in the advancement of projects such as the Assay Office, the steam engine patent and canal building, the aristocracy were attracted from further afield to look at the wonderful new factory at Soho from the time of its completion in 1766. Like Wedgwood's new 'ornamental' works at Etruria, which was opened in 1769, Soho was a must for aristocratic sightseers. They came to marvel at the size of it and to see the modern methods of machine production and the division of labour in operation. They admired the toys and trinkets that they were shown, and bought them.

The number of visitors was substantial as early as 1767, but appears to have increased sharply from 1770. They came from far and wide. They included many titled men, often with their ladies, and people from a wide range of occupations.[47] To the shopkeeper who complained that Boulton and Fothergill were acting as retailers themselves and, worse still, were maintaining a price advantage, the partners described their visitors as 'troublesome' and affected to be almost forced into selling them their wares.[48] But this was misleading. Boulton always welcomed his visitors warmly and encouraged the idea that a visit to Soho was a fashionable and instructive pastime. By 1767 he was able to say that during the summer scarcely a day passed 'without haveing one, two or 3 companys of foreigners or strangers to wait upon, as well as many of our nobility'.[49] A visit to Soho became a 'fashion among the higher and opulent ranks ...'[50] The fashion hindered the work of the factory but increased the number of the firm's correspondents and established its reputation where it most mattered.[51] Boulton would not have put an end to it for anything, and his energies and charm were directed into encouraging it and profiting from it. His personal acquaintance with an ever-increasing number of rich, noble and influential men was the foremost of the several means by which he aimed to sell his ornaments.

Soho showroom

In order that the visitors to Soho could see the vases properly displayed the partners opened a showroom in one of the warehouses. The idea does not seem to have occurred to them until early in 1771. 'We have some thoughts', they wrote to Matthews, 'of fitting up one of our warehouses at Soho for the conveniency of keeping our or moulu goods and showing them off to the best advantage'.[52] They ordered display cabinets from Mayhew and Ince,[53] the only firm of leading London cabinet makers with whom they seem to have had any regular dealings. They also had the warehouse replastered 'as a good room should be, viz. flat and square with a plain moulding round the beams', so that the nobility who were expected to come to Soho in some numbers during the summer could see the assortment of vases 'in a genteel room'.[54] The showroom was nearly finished by June 1771, but Mayhew and Ince had failed to send the display cabinets, and it was probably not ready for the visitors who were 'crowding continually' to Soho until later in the summer.[55] It was fully in use by the end of the year and Wedgwood, who visited Soho in July 1772, described it as a 'superb gallery': he saw 'a great many good things ... besides the vases' and mentioned a silver coffee pot and some 'silver plated ware of the best forms I have seen'.[56] It is clear from this letter and from other references that vases formed a prominent part of the showroom's display. Fothergill called it the 'vase room'.[57]

From 1775 the partners delegated the management of the 'toy room', as it came to be known, to managers who took a commission on sales, which may have been an attempt to convince retailers that Boulton and Fothergill were not in the business of retailing,[58] or an attempt to raise the level of sales. In 1778 John Hodges was in charge. Although by then the production of ormolu had declined and the vases on show were displayed rather as patterns than with the intention of being immediately available, Hodges thought it a pity if he could not show a good assortment of vases to the frequent visitors. He was pleased when some vases arrived and the toy room could be 'not a little garnished with shewy things'.[59] The showroom at Soho was a useful part of Boulton's marketing effort.[60]

Unfortunately no complete or even adequate record of the orders taken from visitors to Soho has survived, but it can be assumed that the better display of the vases served to stimulate sales. Several visitors, shortly after the opening of the new showroom, either ordered vases during their visits to Soho or received ornaments shortly after their visits, which probably means the same thing. They include Colonel (later General) Burgoyne (girandoles), the Earl of Catherlough (Cleopatra vases), Sir James Cockburn (vases), Charles Dunbar (vases and a Venus perfume burner), William Gale (a vase) and Lord Mountstuart (vases) (see Appendix I). In later years visitors who appear to have ordered ornaments during their visits to the showroom include the Earl of Chesterfield, Sir Henry Hunloke, Lord Algernon Percy and the Earl of Plymouth (see Appendix I). Visitors were impressed, generally, by the goods on show. An American Quaker, following a visit in 1776, described the warehouse as

> a cabinet of curiosities, splendid, magnificent and gaudy; more like the costly pageantry of some Eastern Court than the toys of a Birmingham shop. The goods here are all covered with glass cases so that they are exposed to the greatest advantage.[61]

Boulton's London visits

In addition to welcoming visitors to Soho Boulton kept in touch with his patrons during his frequent visits to London. Initially, as I have shown in Chapter 3, he was eager to cull ideas from their collections for his designs. But there is little doubt that he took every opportunity to recommend his vases, and several of the patrons from whom he derived designs and ideas, including the Dukes of Northumberland and Richmond, the Earls of Coventry and Shelburne, and Mrs Montagu, bought ormolu ornaments from him (see Appendix I). No single document gives a better picture of his sociable and yet businesslike life in London, or of his obvious enjoyment of it, than his letter to his wife on Tuesday 6th March 1770. On the Sunday he had visited the Earl of Shelburne, and

> after siting an hour with him in his liberary Lady Shelburne sent a message desiring that she might come down but as she was ill of a putrid soar throat my Lord desired she would not and therefore wished she could have a few of my pretty things in her room to amuse her. I therefore took coach and fetched a load for her and sat with her Ladyship two hours explaining and hearing her criticisms.

The rest of the day he passed in a 'philosophical society'. On Monday he breakfasted with William Chambers, the King's architect, after which

> at about 12 o'clock I waited upon the Duke and Dutchess of Northumberland, by their appointment. I was very politely received and drank chocolate with them. The Duke himself shewed me his great picture gallery and many of his curiositys. He made me sit down with him till 3 o'clock and talked about various arts ...

This visit was followed by dinner with Thomas Wright, the King's clock-maker, three of the Wyatts and 'some ingenious artists'. On Tuesday the Earl of Dartmouth visited him and on the following day he was due to show some of his things to the Dowager Princess of Wales.[62]

It was during this visit to London that Boulton went to the palace.

He met four of the young princes and formed a very favourable impression of the Queen's character and skills.

> The Queen I think is much improvd in her person and she now speaks English like an English lady, she draws very fine, she is a great musician ... She is extremely sensible, very affable, and is a patroness of English manufactorys, of which she gave me a particular instance, for after the King and she had talked to me near 3 hours, they withdrew but the Queen sent for me into her bed chamber, shewed me her chyney [*sic*] piece and asked my opinion how many vases it would take to furnish it, for says she all that china shall be taken away ...[63]

It was a 'passing agreeable' visit. More, it was a triumph. It was only little more than a year since, in Wedgwood's phrase, Boulton had been 'scheming to be sent for by his Majesty'[64] and now, on his first visit to the palace, he had achieved the custom of the first family in the land for his vases. He was moreover to call again in order to show them a 'tripod tea kitchen'. Meanwhile he asked his wife to get John Scale to send him seven or eight good blue john vases for the Queen within a fortnight.

The patronage of the King and Queen was important to Boulton because it set an example for the fashionable world to follow. He did not, like Wedgwood, seek to achieve any sort of Royal appointment but he understood the publicity value of supplying goods to the palace. He was not slow, when on a later occasion he was commissioned to make a clock case for the King (Plate 160), to seize the opportunities that the commission offered. He not only used parts of the design for other pieces (Plates 155, 177), he made clocks of the same pattern in the hope that some of the King's loyal subjects would buy them (Plate 162).

The two letters to his wife reveal the personal effort which Boulton put into marketing his vases. There were many other occasions when either by letter or by a personal approach he sold vases and ornaments to the nobility and gentry in the years 1770–2. In his earlier letter to his wife he asked her to:

> desire Mr Scale to inform me how many of the blew john and other vases could be got by this day fortnight and how many by this day month for all the push I can make must be before the parliment breaks up ...[65]

Boulton was his own best salesman. By the early 1770s the circle of his acquaintance among the aristocracy was as wide as any manufacturer could hope for. His methodical approach to the problem of capturing their patronage is apparent from his letters. It is perhaps most graphically illustrated by the letters, which he wrote before his sales in 1771 and 1772, which will be mentioned later and by a memorandum in his notebook before or during a visit to London in 1773, in which he listed the 'Lords and Dukes which I should wait on':

> Duke of Ancaster, Lord Archer, Lord Ashburnham, Lord Aylesford, Lord Besborough, Bishop of Bristol, Duke of Bucclough, Archbishop of Canterbury, Lord Cathcart, Bishop of Chester, Lord Coventry, Lord Craven, Lord Dartmouth, Lord Denbeigh, Lord Gower, Duke of Grafton, Lord Grosvenor, Lord Hertford, Lord Hilsborough, Lord Holderness, Lord Dispenser, Bishop of Litchfield, Lord Littleton, Duke of Manchester, Lord March, Lord Marchmont, Duke of Malborough, Duke of Montague, Duke of Northumberland, Lord Paget, Bishop of Peterborough, Duke of Richmond, Marquess of Rockingham, Bishop of St Asaph, Lord Sandwich, Lord Scarsdale, Lord Shelburne, Lord Stamford, Lord Warwick, Lord Willoughby de Brook, Lord Waldegrave.[66]

Boulton was probably planning these visits not in order to sell vases but to promote the passing of the Assay Office Bill. But that he could contemplate such a programme illustrates the contacts that he had made in earlier years, and many of the men whom he listed bought vases or other ormolu ornaments at one time or another (see Appendix I).

London agents

It was not enough, however, to rely on Boulton's personal contacts with his aristocratic patrons and their architects, or on the unpredictable visits of the fashionable world to Soho. Other means of promoting sales were necessary.

One answer to the problem was the employment of an agent in London. From 1767 Boulton and Fothergill's chief agent in London was William Matthews, whose letters show him to have been regularly involved in every aspect of their business in London. He was more than an agent. He was a personal friend and adviser, and Boulton stayed at his house during his visits to London.[67] In 1781 he was considered by Fothergill to be the most suitable arbitrator in his dispute with Boulton over the profits of the engine trade. Early in 1768 Boulton appointed him 'to receive orders from merchants on the same terms as if I were present' and provided him with a 'set of patterns' for buyers to consult and order from.[68] Much of Matthews's work consisted of seeking orders from potential customers, including the toy shops and jewellers,[69] showing drawings and samples, delivering the goods and collecting payment. The task of delivery was especially important in the case of vases, many of which were sent to London in pieces and had to be correctly assembled. Matthews also dealt with some of the craftsmen in London who were making parts, such as enamelled dials, for Boulton and with the never-ending variety of tasks which had to be done in the capital, including the arrangements for the sales at Christie's, the ordering of gold, silver and other raw materials, and so on. These activities are best illustrated by the countless letters to him, many of which are quoted in this book. He also acted as one of the firm's bankers, a function which arose from his position as agent. This was because Boulton and Fothergill customarily drew bills in favour of Matthews on customers in and about London who had bought their goods.[70] If the customer was a shopkeeper or merchant they usually allowed him six months' credit before drawing on him. They drew on other customers on delivery or, if Matthews was responsible for the sale, debited him. When Matthews received payment from a customer he credited Boulton and Fothergill's Bill Account with it after deducting his commission and any other charges. The existence of this credit in the Bill Account enabled the partners to draw cash against Matthews in Birmingham in order to pay their expenses. Their drawings inevitably exceeded the amount of their credit in his books.

In 1776 Boulton and Fothergill sent one of their clerks, John Wyatt, a cousin of the architects Samuel and James, to London to act as an agent for the toy business. Matthews remained the firm's main agent and banker in London but was by then becoming more deeply involved in the affairs of the engine trade. Wyatt arrived in London in February 1776, with 'patterns of different branches of the manufacture' and drawings of all the firm's ormolu and plated ware.[71] He visited and received potential customers,[72] and generally looked after the affairs of the hardware trade, but he and another clerk, John Stuart, who was acting as London agent from 1778,[73] were no more than salesmen. Whereas Matthews probably made his profit on the financial transactions, Wyatt and Stuart appear, like Richard Chippindall who took on the job from 1782, to have worked on commission.[74] They relieved Matthews of his earlier tasks on behalf of the button, toy, silver and ormolu trades and performed a useful service in encouraging and completing sales to the firm's patrons. Many such sales are mentioned in the correspondence between these agents and Boulton and Fothergill at Soho.[75]

London exhibitions and sales

Another means of stimulating sales in London which occurred to Boulton before long was the staging of a public exhibition. It was a well-tried method of storming the fashionable world. Wedgwood, his friend and rival, had opened a showroom in London in 1765 or 1766,[76] which, besides increasing his sales, had become a fashionable place for the nobility and gentry to visit.[77] Boulton probably noticed and must have envied Wedgwood's instant success with this scheme. He conceived the plan of emulating it some time in 1769, when his production of vases was building up. Like Wedgwood he aimed to attract the aristocracy and to discourage others who might either lower the tone of the rooms or attempt to copy his manufacture. He was spurred by the ambition to compete as Wedgwood's production of vases increased, following the establishment of his new factory at Etruria in 1769. There was probably never much of a prospect that Boulton would, as Wedgwood feared, turn his skills to the making of earthenware vases himself (see Chapter 2, p. 47), but because they were both making ornamental vases they were competing to some extent for a share of the same business. Wedgwood was worried by Boulton's competition while being confident at the same time of his own superiority. He had the advantage, in that size for size his vases were considerably cheaper, but in 1769 this competitive advantage had not become apparent.

The first hint of Boulton's intention to display his vases in London occurs in a letter from Wedgwood to his partner in September 1769. According to Wedgwood, Boulton and Fothergill had taken a room in Pall Mall and were to hold an exhibition there during the winter.[78] There appears to be no further evidence for this exhibition and it seems safe to conclude that Wedgwood's information was wrong. Either his informant, his clerk William Cox, misunderstood Boulton's plans or Wedgwood himself misunderstood Cox's report. It is likely that Cox was referring to Boulton's projected exhibition and sale at James Christie's room in Pall Mall in the spring of 1770, which I shall describe later.

Boulton was certainly contemplating a showroom in London, however, at the beginning of 1770. He wanted a room, but could not find one to his liking.[79] He was greatly tempted later in 1770 by James Adam's suggestion that they should co-operate in the manufacture of ormolu and silver plate.[80] He was not interested in moving the manufacture to London, but he responded eagerly to the idea of a joint showroom. He liked the idea of 'a proper connection in London and a commodious situation for sale'.[81] James Adam had suggested that they should use a corner shop in Durham Yard which fronted partly onto the Strand. Boulton favoured the situation but differed from Adam in his ideas of the type of shop:

> I would rather choose a large elegant room upstairs, without any other window than a sky light. By this sort of concealment you excite curiosity. More, you preserve your improvements from street walking pirates. The nobility would like that less publick repository. The novelty would please more and last longer than the present mode of exhibition. The great customers for plate are such as are not to be caught by shew as they walk along the street and you know that un-private shops are only customary in London, for at Paris all their finest shops are upstairs. If a large room upon this plan could be had with proper apendages in the neighbourhood of Durham Yard I should be glad to become tenant of it (whether we can fix upon any joint plan or not). The lower parts might be appropriated to the sale of the grosser articles of our manufacture and for the reception of gentlemens' servants. The upper handsom room for plate d'or moulu and such other fine toys as we make. You cannot but be sensible that a vast variety of articles may be comprehended under these heads.[82]

Adam concurred with Boulton's suggestions but still wanted him to take the shop:

Your idea also of the warehouse in preference to the shop is what I have been turning much in my mind, since I received yours, and upon my word the longer I think of it, I like it the better. The novelty alone of such a thing would attract all ranks in this great capital, where novelty and fashion carry everything irresistably before them. Your idea therefore of such a warehouse lighted from the top by a sky light pleased me greatly and the more so, as I know from experience, that every object whatever shows to more advantage in that light than in any other. I have in Durham Yard a place exactly suited for such a purpose, and answerable in every respect to your idea. It was indeed planned originally for another purpose, but I have been rather trifled with by the society for whom it was designed and am under no engagements to them, so that if we can bring our joint scheme to any regular well digested plan, this building is still convertible to the use you propose ... With respect to the show shop in the Strand, I am not sure, but it might be found an useful appendix to the ware-house as it is certainly in the best part of the town, for chance custom and I find all the shopkeepers, especially those who deal in the silver and toy way, put great stress upon chance custom. In this way it might be useful for common things, and likewise for those of our own patterns that may after a time become common, or perhaps at first exposing some few things, in a new stile in the show shop, might serve as a decoy to lead people to the warehouse. However if you should still continue to think this useless or an unnecessary expence I shall be extremely ready to yeild my opinion to a person so much more capable of judging well upon this subject.[83]

The Adam brothers subsequently prepared a design for Boulton's show-room, the 'great room' of which James Adam described as 'a very fine room indeed'.[84] Nothing came of the negotiations. According to Wedgwood both he and Boulton, who had told him of his negotiations with the Adam brothers, were dissuaded from pursuing their plans for showrooms in the Adelphi by James Stuart, who thought he could offer something better.[85] But it is also possible that Boulton decided against extending his commitments for financial reasons. Robert and James Adam were unwilling to provide any capital for the venture other than the building or to devote any of their own time to it other than the time taken in devising the necessary designs.[86] The risks and the management would have fallen entirely on Boulton.

Instead of establishing a showroom in London Boulton appears to have contented himself in 1770 with a public exhibition and auction at James Christie's saleroom in Pall Mall. This sale took place on 6th–7th April.[87] The advertisements spoke in Boulton's true promotional style of the

valuable collection of the truly elegant production of Mr Boulton's d'or moulu manufactory, at Soho in Staffordshire. Consisting of an assortment of superb ornament ... of exquisite workmanship, and finished in the antique taste.[88]

Using James Christie's room was better than hiring a room of his own, and Boulton could be sure to attract the customers he wanted. Auction sales were a popular pastime of the fashionable world and several manufacturers of ornamental works of art sold their products in this way.[89] A month after Boulton's sale, Horace Walpole commented to his friend Horace Mann that the rage to see the exhibitions in London was 'so great, that sometimes one cannot pass through the streets where they are', and added that on show were not only pictures by Benjamin West and 'Etruscan vases, made of earthen ware in Staffordshire, from two to five guineas,' but also

or moulu, never made here before, which succeeds so well that a tea-kettle which the inventor offered for 100 guineas, sold by auction for 130. In short we are at the height of extravagance ...[90]

In spite of Boulton's own criticisms of some of the vases[91] this first sale in 1770 appears to have been successful, and Boulton arranged another in the spring of 1771. Wedgwood heard news of his intentions in December 1770 and thought that Boulton had 'not yet determined upon the mode of sale'.[92] It is possible, as Wedgwood seems to have thought, that Boulton was still toying with the plan of displaying his vases in his own showroom. But, if so, the idea was short-lived. Early in January he had decided on an auction, and asked Mayhew and Ince to make two or three cabinets to protect the ornaments from dust and handling.[93] In the middle of February he wrote to James Christie to announce his intention of using his rooms again and to ask his advice about the most suitable dates. It was a question of whether Easter week would be as good as any other – 'for I presume Passion will not do as all Christian spirits will not be so high in that week as the following' – and whether the nobility would still be in town.[94] Christie advised him to hold the sale before Easter – 'as the town will by then be in confusion by people of fashion preparing for their transmigration to the country'[95] – but Boulton replied that the things could not be ready in time and that he would rather delay than 'make a shabby appearance'.[96]

Boulton's plan was to set aside three days before the sale for viewing. On the first two the exhibition would be reserved for the nobility and on the third it would be opened to '*toute le monde*'.[97] The auction would occupy the following three days, the whole exhibition and sale thus taking a week. One of the reasons for having the private view was that it gave patrons an opportunity to place orders for vases without having to rely only on drawings, an opportunity which some of them took.[98]

Having arranged the date and ensured that his patrons would, if they attended the exhibition, do so in relative comfort, Boulton turned his attention to encouraging their attendance. Again he conducted this aspect of the preparations himself, although William Matthews did what was necessary in London. Boulton's insistence on good publicity shows him to have been well aware of the need for effective marketing.

There were two main planks to the publicity. The first was advertising, for which the planning seems to have been more successful than the execution. Boulton wrote to his friend James Keir, who was in London, about an advertisement. Keir did not choose to insert one without consulting Boulton, but he sent a draft for Boulton to approve and return to Matthews, who would see to its insertion in the papers:

Advertisement

> Mr Boulton begs leave to acquaint the nobility and gentry that, induced by the encouragement given by them last winter, he has continued his manufacture of gilt and chased vases ... and various other pieces of ornamental furniture finished in or moulû; and that he purposes to expose to sale, about the latter end of March, a collection of these, which he hopes from the improvements he has been able to make will be thought not unworthy of their attention and further encouragement.

Keir left the blank space 'for the names of such principal ornaments, as clock-cases, candlesticks, as you think proper'.[99] It appears that the plan was to put a preliminary advertisement in one of the newspapers in February, but a letter to Matthews complained that no advertisement had appeared by the 26th.[100] A few days later Boulton asked Christie to advertise every day for a week and then again about six days later,[101] but something again went wrong. After a fortnight one of his clerks wrote to Matthews:

> Mr Boulton says ... that he is still very much surprised that he has never yet been able to procure a sight of the advertisements although he has spent much time and

some money at the coffee houses with that view, that he is fearfull if it is inserted 'tis in so few papers that the publick are not well acquainted with it – but he particularly begs that either you or Mr Christie will see it regularly inserted daily in some paper or other and that he had rather have it appear in too many papers than too few.[102]

This letter appears to have had some effect and advertisements duly appeared in the papers.[103] The text of the advertisement repeated the puffery of the 1770 version and promoted 'the superb and elegant produce of Mr Boulton's or moulu manufactory', describing it as 'a variety of most beautiful and rich articles ... replete with elegance and true taste, and most elaborately finished'.[104]

Boulton's second method of publicising the sale was by letter. He had told some of his patrons about the forthcoming sale already in occasional letters,[105] but what he planned now was a methodical distribution of printed letters to a large number of possible buyers. 'I think to write a letter', he informed Christie early in March, 'to all and each of the nobility and gentry (that may likely become purchasers) ...', and he asked for a list of names of 'all and of every rank' whom Christie thought might buy.[106] Later in the month he drafted three letters, one for dukes and lords, one for ladies of the nobility and one for gentlemen, and sent them to James Keir for his advice.[107] All three letters invite 'such of the nobility and gentry as are judges and promoters of the endeavours of British artists' to attend the private view on 8th–9th April.

The final piece of written publicity was the preface to the catalogue of the sale. Boulton did not think it enough to present a mere catalogue of the ornaments even though the entries in it were reinforced with such epithets as 'rich', 'elegant', 'richly inlaid', 'most beautiful', 'richly embellished' and 'magnificent'. A suitable preface would, he hoped, convince the likely purchasers not only that his ormolu vases were rich and elegant but also that he was performing practically a public service by breaking into what had been for years a preserve of the French. His first draft of the preface overplayed this claim to public esteem, as Keir pointed out when he returned it with his various comments and amendments:

I have omitted mentioning that you are content to work without profit for the advantage of your countrymen, because in these days, such an instance of disinterestedness would not be credited, and if it was, it would rather excite admiration of your generosity than of your understanding.[108]

Boulton's final preface, which is quoted in full in Chapter 2 (see pp. 51–2), was a direct appeal to the nobility and gentry and to 'persons of taste'. It was not just a promotion of the ornaments. It was an appeal for support to enable 'further advances in elegance, correctness and execution' in order to strengthen his business and prevent expenditure on imports from abroad. He acknowledged the patronage of 'personages of the highest rank' (i.e. the King and Queen, as Keir made clear in his letter) 'and the zeal shewn by them and by many of the nobility and gentry to promote the establishment of this new branch of our manufacture'.

Preparations for the exhibition and sale in 1772 followed the same pattern, but they reveal even more clearly Boulton's determination to be as exclusive as possible in his appeal to the nobility and gentry. He saw the exhibition both as a selling opportunity and as a showcase from which they could choose designs.[109] His original intention was to exclude everyone else altogether. One of his clerks wrote to the Duchess of Portland:

Our Mr Boulton purposes to make an exhibition (and no auction) of some quite new and very elegant things about the beginning of March, which will be continued about 2 or 3 weeks for inspection and sale to the nobility and gentry only, as care

> will be taken to expell that class who do not come to purchase but expressly to incomode those that do ...[110]

Wedgwood had come to the view five years earlier that an auction room was not the answer and that exclusivity was the only way to attract the nobility and gentry, because 'everybody would be apt to stroll into an auction room', which would drive his 'present sett of customers out of it. For you well know they will not mix with the rest of the world any farther than their amusements, or conveniencys make it necessary to do so'.[111] Perhaps Boulton had gleaned the thought from him. He told Christie that he intended to invite about fifteen hundred 'persons of rank and fashion' by letter and he was anxious that the public advertisements, which Christie was to insert in the papers, should follow the wording of the draft text which he had sent and should avoid mentioning the word 'auction' or the dates of the exhibition: he proposed to send tickets with his letters, which would ensure the exclusion of

> all the dirty journeymen chasers, silversmiths etc. etc., and I think there will be few persons that may be likely to be purchasers but what will either be in my list or will be of the acquaintance of some persons in my list, so that I mean to try a private auction instead of a publick one.[112]

He was too late. The first advertisement, presumably arranged by Christie, had already appeared two days before he wrote his letter. It advertised an auction at the beginning of April. The wording was altogether more restrained than the advertisements of 1770 and 1771. The ornaments were described only as 'an elegant assortment ... with rich decorations'. Boulton was not mentioned, only the 'Soho Manufactory'. Whoever wrote it clearly believed that exaggeration did not pay. The appeal rested instead on the assurance that the designs of the ornaments were 'entirely different from those exhibited at the two former sales'.[113]

Boulton cannot have been pleased, but there is no evidence of his reaction in the archives. His plans for an exclusive exhibition prevailed about a fortnight later and a further advertisement appeared:

> **OR MOULU of SOHO MANUFACTORY**
>
> At Mr Christie's Auction-Room, late the Royal Academy in Pall-Mall. Inconveniences having arisen from the promiscuous admission in the last year's sale, on this account the proprietors have been advised to have recourse to tickets, which they have already delivered to many of the nobility and gentry, requesting the favor of their farther distribution of them amongst their friends. Such of them as are by mistake or otherwise omitted, are humbly requested to send a note, with their names, to Mr Christie, as above, may be furnished with any number. The motive of this plan being solely to prevent the Nobility and Gentry from being incommoded, and not to exclude any person of rank or fashion.[114]

These exclusive arrangements, announced rather late in the day, do not appear to have influenced the outcome of the auction. Boulton was keenly disappointed by the failure of the sale and became less inclined to concentrate on the London market. His personal sales effort decreased, or rather was deflected into the promotion of silver production and, later, of steam engines. He thus gave much less attention to the sale at Christie and Ansell's in 1778 which, as I have shown earlier, was planned more as an attempt to clear accumulated stock than to make an impact on the fashionable world. The arrangements with Christie and Ansell's were delegated to John Stuart, the clerk who had gone to London to represent the firm at the beginning of the year.[115] Boulton did, however, insist on holding the sale in May, despite the advice given to Stuart by Christie that it would be better to postpone it until after the holidays.[116] This was a mistake, probably motivated by the need to clear some of the stock. Further evidence of a decline in Boulton's personal marketing effort is the brevity both of the descriptions of the pieces in the catalogue (see Appendix III) and of his letter to his patrons.[117]

The sale was advertised, but only five days in advance of the planned date. The ornaments were described as 'an elegant assortment of the much admired or moulu, the property of Messrs Boulton and Fothergill, brought from their manufactory at Soho, in Staffordshire'.[118]

Although sales of ormolu in the mid-1770s were not on the scale that Boulton had hoped for at the beginning of the decade, and although he was now becoming preoccupied by the engine trade, he still flirted in 1776 with the idea of a showroom in London. He was thinking this time not only of ormolu but also of silver, plate and several of the firm's toys, for many of which an auction was not a suitable method of sale,[119] but ormolu formed an integral part of his plan because of its visual appeal. He appears to have been prompted to formulate his ideas by John Wyatt, who went to London from Soho to act as the firm's agent early in 1776. Wyatt was finding his task difficult. He could not ask fashionable customers to come to his inadequate lodgings up two flights of stairs, and the cost of taking samples and patterns to them was unjustifiably high – and they were usually out when he called. He found the merchants and shopkeepers as 'uncertain and haughty' as the people of fashion. All this he summarised in a letter to Boulton in which he added the suggestion of opening a showroom:

> Almost every person I have been with is desirous to know where your curious productions are to be seen and would gladly call any where for that purpose. 'Tis needless to offer to wait upon them with any particular articles, for they perhaps want nothing in particular yet if they were to see all most likely something would please. But as it is the things I have hardly have a chance for selling.
>
> If I might presume to give my opinion I think it highly necessary that a convenient place should be found where not only the people of fashion but the merchants, shopkeepers etc. etc. might see everything you have in town both to buy and to give orders from. Then it might not be amiss to have printed cards and to advertise it. In which case (from the knowledge I have gathered in the short time I have been here) I am pretty confident it would very soon become a thing of importance. If you think this worth an answer and will inform me what situation you would prefer and what rent you would go to I will make a strict search. Sam Wyatt has three spots on which he could build you a room. In Oxford Street at his own house, in Bond Street, and in Gerrard Street. But as it would be a long time, suppose by next winter, before it could be ready, a proper place should be had in the mean time. I think Bond Street an excellent situation (its between old and new Bond Street) for the exhibition room and Sam has a house adjoining to the spot in Albemarle Street that he could let you have till the new one was ready if you were determined to build. Sam would build whatever you may want upon his own foundation and if you will take a lease for 21 years he would require seven per cent for his money. If for seven years only he would have 10 per cent. The people of fashion all seem so sanguine in their wishes for your establishment of this room and so thoroughly convinced of the exorbitance of the shops that I think there is very little doubt of its meeting with immediate and great success. The temporary place I think would only require a few drawers or presses etc. which might be made so as to serve afterwards in any other place.[120]

Boulton gave the suggestion a lot of thought and, drawing on his earlier discussions with James Adam for some of his inspiration, he drew up some notes of his ideas for a showroom, or 'theka', which were a lot grander than anything Wyatt had meant to propose:[121]

My ideas of a Theka in London are to have an elegant lofty long room, suppose 700 square feet which is equal to a circle of 30 feet diameter or to a square of 26 feet, situated about Covent Garden, Southampton Street, Charing Cross, Pall Mall, St James Street or may do in New Bond Street but must not go further from the City.

I would not have it a shew to the street, as the nobility are more at their ease in a private shop; the novelty of patterns are preserved better from Birmingham Sheffield and London pimps; besides which when things have been exposed to the street walker, their value and their novelty is diminished in the opinion of fine folkes.

It may either be upon the ground or up one pair of stairs but I could wish it to be well lighted and the lights so disposed as to make it a proper room for an exhibition of pictures (for that will be one of our articles of sale) the drawers or the glasses and all the repositories of our goods should be under curtains so that when a stranger comes you may probably find him a pimp before he gains his point and if a real gentleman or fine lady bringing things out of obscurity by gentle and gentle degrees gives them time to inspect and doth not palle the eye and exhaust the curiosity of the parties in a moment, which always happens when a lady hath turned herself around and seen at once all that is to be seen. Some of the articles of sale will be such as other shops cannot procure and the general style of the shop will not have its fellow in London and without publishing one advertisement in the beginning, I could draw all the nobility and people of tast there in the first month (and them only) by genteeler means and thereby render it a more fashionable place for nobility to trifle away their time and their mony than any other in London.

1st Wrought silvor plate of all kinds
2nd Plated wares ditto
3rd Or moulu ditto
4th Clocks and cases
5th Fine steel work ditto
6th Another branch which of itself is sufficient to exclips all the shops in town in the way.[122]
7th Toys trinketts and all Birmingham Sheffield and London fine goods such as buckles of silver, pinchbeck.
8th Buttons fine for retale and curt [?] common for wholesale
9th Jewellry

Then suppose I could find a person that could advance from 2 to 6 thousand (for I will advance equal to what he will) and if he was a jeweller so much the better perhaps such a man as one of Duvall's sons or even such a one as — [inked out] provided he hath mony in that case one may get such assistance as will give strength, extention and formidableness to the Theka.

No 6 will be ready for exhibition in 3 months after such an establishment is determined upon otherwise we shall confine the article to exportation and never be seen at all in this country.

I fear if Mr Wyatt was to open a small shop in the common London style it would be injurious to the reputation of an after establishment upon the aforesaid plan. But if my plan was adopted we should at once stride over the heads of all others and totaly eclips both the Staffordshire burnt clays and the Birmingham varnished clays.[123]

If Mr Samuel Wyatt will build us such a room we will take it for 21 years upon the terms he mentions.

Query – if such a room as Athenian Stuart's painting room could not be rented. I query if he now uses his room, and Lecester fields is a good situation. Some of the back parts of the Pall Mall houses which front St James Square would be elegant and very light, or query Fords auction room – what would be the rent of it?

I shall certainly come to London this Spring and then I will do something but in the intrem beg Mr Wyatt would look and enquire. Is there a good stair case to the house in Southampton Street and could the other rooms be ready let for I think untill some thing formidable could be established that we should not go to a greater expence than 50 pounds.

Soho room[124] can lend Theka goods in the winter and Theka lend Soho in Summer.[125]

Boulton's note ended with the words '*for ready mony only*'. He had learnt how expensive it was to grant credit.

Nothing came of these ideas, although it appears that John Wyatt ordered some showcases from Mayhew and Ince[126] and that Samuel Wyatt got as far as sending Boulton the plans for the baths which he was building with a room above which he thought would be suitable for Boulton's purpose.[127]

Nearly two years later John Stuart, who succeeded John Wyatt as agent in London, was looking for lodgings and, like his predecessor, again put forward the advantages of having a showroom for the ormolu, plate and other articles in lodgings 'fit for the reception of the nobility'.[128] He found the lodgings, but any idea of a grand showroom had been shelved. Boulton was probably put off by the financial difficulties that the partnership was facing.

Drawings and samples

The firm made frequent use of drawings in the initiation of sales to customers. The drawings of ormolu ornaments which have survived in the archives, all of which are reproduced in this book, are probably typical of the sketches which were shown or sent to customers.[129] In London the agents could take the drawings to the customer[130] and invite his orders or comments. Despite the training of young draughtsmen at Soho, the quality of the drawings often left much to be desired. On one occasion, William Matthews was asked to advise the Duchess of Ancaster to choose what she wanted from the exhibition in London rather than from the book of drawings she was to be given, because the drawings were 'very irregular'.[131] Drawings were frequently sent direct to customers,[132] excuses being often made for their shortcomings.[133] At Soho, books of drawings were kept so that visiting customers could choose from a wide selection.[134]

Sometimes potential customers were shown samples, especially by Boulton himself and by the agents in London, and on occasion ormolu ornaments were sent on sale or return.[135]

Exports

Boulton did not confine himself to the English market. Born and bred in the Birmingham toy industry, he shared the typical toy manufacturer's ambitions in overseas markets. He was happy, he said in 1767, to supply all Europe with his goods.[136] He had heard from Wedgwood in the same year how receptive some of 'the German nobility' were to Wedgwood's creamware, and he must have been encouraged by Wedgwood's assessment that if he could supply the merchants adequately 'the consumption will certainly be great'.[137] It was a view very much in line with Boulton's own salesmanlike instincts. Wedgwood's subsequent successes in overseas markets must have given Boulton further encouragement when he began to produce his own lines of luxury products. Fothergill's mercantile contacts, increased by his tour of the Baltic States in 1766–8, were a useful base from which to expand the firm's network of foreign customers.

In the 1770s Boulton was conscious of the need to increase his sales of ormolu, in view of the expenses of production. He wrote in 1771:

> One country is not a large enough market for commodoties which can be bought only by persons of elegance and fortune, nay the demands of our country would scarce be sufficient to pay the expences of making our original models if I was to carry this branch of our manufacture as high as my ideas would lead me.[138]

He was also spurred on by his consciousness of competing with the French metalworkers, who dominated the market on the continent. Having fought the French on his home ground and claimed credit for preventing the expenditure of large sums abroad in the 'purchase of a foreign commodity' he hoped to establish a 'considerable branch of commerce'[139] and to carry the battle into the French camp.

It is probable that the greater part of the ormolu goods produced at Soho in the 1770s was exported. It is impossible to be certain about this because no sales ledgers from before 1776 have survived and because sales abroad were often handled by merchants with whom there was little correspondence. It is unlikely that sales overseas amounted to much during the initial years of production, when Boulton's chief aim was to capture the custom of the fashionable classes in his own country. But he was thinking of selling vases in Paris as early as 1769,[140] before he was producing them either in sufficient quantity or of sufficient quality. After 1771–2 there is evidence in the archives of increasing deliveries of ormolu to various European countries and especially to Russia. By 1776 Wedgwood could report that Boulton and Fothergill sold most of their ormolu abroad and that they were hoping to supplant the French in the Russian market both in plate and in ormolu.[141] Some countries were not worth the trouble. There was no demand for elegant things in Siberia or America, 'or even some parts of Germany'.[142] Other countries presented great difficulties, such as tariff barriers and the problems of ensuring payment. But Boulton was not deterred by problems such as these. He was particularly keen on the Russian market, where the tariff was thirty per cent,[143] and tried to establish a market for vases in Sweden,[144] where the duties amounted virtually to prohibition.[145] He also joined with his competitors in efforts to have such restrictions on trade removed[146] and carried on a similar campaign on his own when occasion demanded.[147]

This is not the place however for an account of all the problems which a manufacturer faced in overseas markets, or of the methods by which Boulton sought to surmount them. The export of hardware by the toy manufacturers of Birmingham in general, and by Boulton and Fothergill in particular, has been described elsewhere.[148] I only intend here to describe the methods by which Boulton and Fothergill set about selling their ormolu abroad. The description will give an incomplete picture of their activities, because ormolu ornaments were only a part of the hardware business and because, being luxuries, they could not appeal to the same markets as cheaper goods.

The new factory at Soho was a considerable draw. Foreign visitors were encouraged to come to look at it, and many did. The factor John Motteux, who traded with many overseas houses, introduced visitors, and came himself in 1767, probably in the company of the Spanish and Venetian ambassadors.[149] In 1767–70 visitors are recorded from America, Austria, Denmark, France, Germany, the Netherlands, Italy, Poland, Portugal, Russia, Sardinia, Spain, Sweden and Switzerland.[150] The record of visitors includes barons, counts, dukes and princes. 'Le Prince Hereditaire de Hesse Darmstadt' came in October 1771, the 'Prince of Holstein', nephew to the Empress of Russia, in 1775.[151]

Boulton put a lot of effort into entertaining his foreign visitors and was especially pleased by the visits of foreign nobles. Half his time was taken up, he said in the autumn of 1772, by the visitors we daily have at our manufactory and which cannot be avoided ... We had last week Prince Ponitowski, the nephew of the King of Poland, the French, the Danish, the Sardinian and the Duch ambassadors. We have had this week Count Orlof, one of the 5 celebrated brothers who are favourits with the Empress of Russia ...[152]

There can be no doubt whatever that he took great care to show examples of ormolu ornaments to all of them. His particular pleasure at the visit of Orloff was founded on his hopes of expanding his sales of ormolu to the Russian court: a previous Russian visitor had been Count Chernichev, to whom Boulton showed an assortment of vases which he sent to St Petersburg in 1771.[153]

More positive evidence of the display of ormolu to foreign noblemen is provided by a letter from Fothergill to his partner in May 1772 reporting the visits of two Austrian nobles and a Spanish chevalier who 'bought in vases, buttons etc. to the amount of £117 – he intends a Titus for the King of Spain, which I have ordered to be well finished ...'[154] Other foreign visitors who ordered or bought ornaments during visits to Soho included Baron Grote, who bought some Cleopatra vases in 1771, and the Count of Brahe from Sweden, who bought a pair of vases in 1776 (see Appendix I).[155] The failure of the sale at Christie's in 1772 must have made Boulton even more anxious to impress his foreign visitors. That he succeeded in impressing them is clear from two letters from Mrs Montagu, who found that all the foreigners who had visited Soho in the summer of 1772 had been charmed by Boulton's productions and by his own politeness.[156]

Another way of encouraging sales to foreign courts was to make contact with their ambassadors in London and with British ambassadors abroad. I have already quoted Boulton's report of the visits to Soho of the French, Danish, Sardinian and Dutch ambassadors in 1772. Other ambassadors who visited Soho in 1767–72 included those from Naples, Poland, Portugal, Russia, Spain and Venice (see Appendix II). It seems to have been a routine visit for successive ambassadors from Russia. Boulton also made a point of visiting foreign ambassadors when he was in London. It may have been on one such visit that he was able to ensure the approval of Moushin Pushkin, the Russian envoy in London, for his plan to send an assortment of vases for the approval of the Russian Court in 1771,[157] although this may have occurred when Pushkin visited Soho in August.[158] Two years later he asked Pushkin to provide introductions to the Russian nobility for his agent who was travelling to Russia.[159]

Russia was a particularly promising market. The Empress Catherine was an avid collector, and was much given to making bulk purchases of works of art. She was keen to see St Petersburg as a centre of artistic patronage. Apart from buying works of art, she commissioned jewellery, ceramics, silverware, tapestries and furniture from the leading craftsmen of Europe. The wealth of her court must have seemed to the manufacturers and merchants like the wealth of the industrialists and financiers of the United States at the turn of the nineteenth and twentieth centuries or the rapid wealth of the Arab states and sheikhdoms in the 1970s. St Petersburg was a 'financial honeypot' for artists, designers, architects, manufacturers and merchants.[160]

Boulton knew of Wedgwood's earlier sales to the Russian Court. Wedgwood's first shipment to Russia was in 1769. His initial contact was Lord Cathcart, the ambassador to Russia, whom he met in March 1768 with the idea of 'introducing my manufacture at the Court of Russia'. He was particularly encouraged by Lady Cathcart, who was the sister of Sir William Hamilton. Wedgwood wrote to Boulton, reporting on his meeting with Cathcart and the encouragement that he had received.[161] The introduction led to several sales, including a consignment of vases in 1770, all of which the Empress kept.[162]

It is not surprising, therefore, that in 1771 Boulton too sent a consignment of vases for the Russian Court to Lord Cathcart. This consignment, the first to be sent from Soho to Russia, was accompanied by descriptions of the geographical, sidereal and Minerva clocks, which were then being made at Soho, and by a suitably flattering letter in which Boulton drew Lord Cathcart's attention to his industrious and expensive efforts to break into a French monopoly. He hoped that the ambassador would be able to use his influence like several other men in similar positions 'whose distinguished taste, like that of your Excellency, must have great influence in introducing British productions among foreigners'.[163] Cathcart was helpful, passing the vases to a suitable commercial house[164] in St Petersburg, which unpacked them and kept them until he had mentioned them to the Empress. She bought them all. She was so full of praise for them that Cathcart suggested a second consignment, although he did not think Boulton and Fothergill could 'depend upon the duration of a demand for things so expensive and which are not necessary'. He also commented that ormolu was particularly suitable for clocks, of which the French supplied many to Russia, and ended, helpfully, with a postscript:

> French writing [sc. tables] ornamented with or moulu and ink stands, candlesticks and clocks belonging to them, of the same materials, are much used here. The great heat of the rooms where there are stoves makes it necessary to have great attention to the making of any furniture of wooden work. I showed your letter to Count Czernichoff and shall be very glad if I have been of any use in laying a foundation for the reception of your manufacture in a country where a great deal is imported from France, inferior in quality and dearer in point of price.[165]

Two years later Cathcart's successor, Sir Robert Gunning, was asked to sponsor a further consignment for the Empress. Gunning replied three months later. He had delayed doing so because the ornaments had not arrived. He had intended to tell Boulton 'how far they met with the approbation of the Empress and what are the articles most to be recommended for your sending hither in future'. Since the ornaments had not arrived, he assured Boulton that the Empress was 'perfectly satisfied' with what had already been sent and 'expected with some little impatience to see the newest productions of your invention and good taste'.[166] The purchases by the Empress Catherine and her courtiers account for many of the ormolu-mounted vases that survive today in Russia, particularly in the State Hermitage Museum and at Pavlovsk, despite sales by the Soviet Union in Berlin in the late 1920s.

Russia was not the only overseas market. One of the other ambassadors whom Boulton and Fothergill employed, or hoped to employ, as intermediaries at this time was Sir John Goodricke in Sweden. They asked him to further the sale of some samples of ormolu which they had sent to an agent in Stockholm in 1772. The samples were of 'the lowest sort in the ormoulu way' but they promised to send some 'capital things'.[167] Other ambassadors whom they approached in the early 1770s included Lord Stormont in Paris,[168] Lord Grantham, the ambassador at Madrid,[169] Sir Robert Murray Keith, the envoy in Vienna,[170] and Sir Rodney Valltravers, who was to take samples of various goods and a complete catalogue of the productions of Soho to various courts. Boulton even offered to send specimens of ormolu pieces on approval to the same courts, providing the arrangement did not involve the payment of any duties.[171]

Boulton used these contacts with ambassadors particularly for sales of ormolu because they were a means of direct access to the nobility and gentry, but he made a point of keeping in touch with ambassadors too as a means of promoting the general hardware business.[172] It was a means of promotion pursued by other manufacturers such as Wedgwood, whose wares reached, by the same means, the courts of (among others) Russia, Poland, Portugal, Denmark, Sweden, the Netherlands, Turkey, Naples, Turin and China.[173]

In other respects, too, Boulton and Fothergill's marketing of their ormolu ornaments overseas fitted in with the general hardware trade. They made extensive use of correspondents in foreign towns. The number of these correspondents increased steadily throughout the 1760s as the toy business expanded,[174] and Boulton actively encouraged new connections. Fothergill toured the Baltic countries and Northern Germany in 1766–8. His journey took him to Hamburg, Lübeck and Königsberg in Germany,[175] then through Denmark and Sweden to St Petersburg, where he spent about four months,[176] and back through Riga, Königsberg, Danzig, and perhaps Amsterdam.[177] An extended business-seeking tour such as this by one of the principals of the business was bound to risk prejudicing Boulton and Fothergill's relationship with the factors.[178] It must have enlarged the number of potential correspondents considerably, and the number of agents which the firm later employed in St Petersburg probably stemmed from contacts originally made during Fothergill's extended visit in 1767. While Fothergill was 'hunting in the nothern parts of Europe',[179] P. J. Wendler was travelling in Italy. The letters between Wendler and Boulton suggest that his chief tasks were to collect designs, models and materials, and to discover which toys were likely to find a ready demand. Boulton asked him to find out about 'the tast, the fashions, the toys, both usefull and ornamental, the impliments, vessells, etc. etc. etc. that prevail in all the different parts of Europe'. He was no doubt also enjoined before his departure to take any opportunity that occurred to recommend Boulton and Fothergill to local agents although they had to be particularly careful in the Italian market not to tread on the toes of the merchants in London.[180] In 1771 a Mr Galliard, who was emigrating to Switzerland, offered to act on behalf of Boulton and Fothergill, among others, during tours of Italy, Germany and France.[181] By 1770 Boulton could claim that he had 'established a correspondence in almost every mercantile town in Europe'.[182]

It was not easy to be sure of the credit-worthiness of these agents, but very few bad debts are recorded in the archives.[183] One of them occasioned Boulton's visit to France in 1765. He went there because of the bankruptcy of his largest customer in Paris, Moses Oppenheim.[184] This possibility of bad debts, along with other causes of loss, such as fluctuating exchange rates and the likelihood of damage, made it remarkable that Boulton and Fothergill were prepared to risk sending valuable consignments of ormolu to Europe, but such risks are the essence of commerce.

Several agents are mentioned by name in surviving letters in connection with the ormolu trade. One of the earliest is Solomon Hyman, Boulton and Fothergill's principal agent in Paris, to whom Boulton offered his vases in 1769 in the confident expectation that he would be able to sell them.[185] Others were Peter Sutter of Stockholm, to whom some sample vases were sent in 1772,[186] and J. C. Rigail and R. Roullard of Amsterdam, who were sent samples and descriptions of the geographical, sidereal and Minerva clocks in the same year.[187] They may have been the recipients of the vases sent to Amsterdam after the 1771 sale.[188] There appear to have been several agents in Russia. Some ormolu pieces were sent to Butler and Company in Moscow on sale or return in 1779.[189] In St Petersburg, Raikes and Saffree looked after the pieces that were sent to Lord Cathcart at the end of 1771,[190] and in 1779 William Porter tried unsuccessfully to sell the sidereal clock.[191] Fothergill also wanted Boulton to ask the 'great Russian house' Tompson and Peters to attend the sale at Christie's in 1771.[192] Boulton and Fothergill employed several agents in some of the more important cities such as St Petersburg[193] and Hamburg, in spite of their stated policy of dealing with only one for fear of flooding the market with similar goods.[194] In 1774 the partners also sent F. A. Müller to tour Russia with patterns of ormolu and plate, and asked the Russian ambassador in London to provide him with letters of introduction to the Russian nobility.[195]

It is difficult to trace many of the local agents who handled ormolu goods, for two reasons. First, no ledgers survive from before 1776 and letters recording the despatch of 'goods' often give no further details. Second, agents were given code names or ciphers in the firm's records, which conceal their identity.[196] Thus J. H. Ebbinghaus, who became a partner in the business for a few years (see Chapter 2, p. 28), was 'Niagara' and William Porter of St Petersburg was 'ALQ'.[197] The exotically named 'Pondicherry' was an agent in Königsberg, 'Senegall' was in Naples.[198] 'Panza', who in 1778 ordered a Titus clock, a Belisarius clock and a set of three or five vases for a chimneypiece, has not been identified.[199] 'AOQ, Iraps' was probably Charles-Raymond Grancher (or Granchez), a *marchand-mercier* who was established in Dunkirk in the 1760s and opened a shop in Paris ('Iraps') in 1767.[200] He was appointed *bijoutier du Roi* in 1774. His shop 'Au Petit-Dunkerque' was on the corner of the Quai de Conti and the Rue Dauphine and was one of the centres for the fashionable world.[201] He dealt in a wide range of goods, including jewellery of all sorts, furniture, clocks, candelabra, bronzes, silver, plate, porcelain, swords and sword hilts, saddlery, cutlery, fans, buttons, toys, snuff boxes, watch chains, ink stands, games' boards and lacquered goods. He imported many goods from England and advertised '*tout ce que l'industrie & les arts d'Angleterre font paraître journellement d'utile & de curieux*'.[202] He toured England in 1771, visiting manufacturers and buying vases, busts and medallions from Wedgwood. In 1772 he advertised a gilt bronze '*Venus qui pleure sur le tombeau d'Adonis. Cet ouvrage en Pinsbeck est avec un socle de marbre de Paros.*'[203] It sounds like one of Boulton's Venus perfume burners (Plate 359). Boulton would have been pleased perhaps to have the Derbyshire marble described as 'Paros', but would not have been happy to have his gilt ornament described as Pinchbeck.

'AOQ, Iraps' was a substantial customer and an order received from him in 1781 illustrates not only the variety of the partnership's products at this date but also some of its methods. It contains many pieces of plate and silver – coffee urns, ink stands, fish spades, candlesticks, etc. – several 'toys' such as toothpicks and sword hilts, buckles etc., and mechanical paintings, the variety of goods matching some of the variety in Grancher's advertisement. The order also included:

	£	s	d
6 pairs or moulu vases 973386 94/6	28	7	0
2 pairs ditto ditto (i.e. 977999 126/–, 978000 110/–)	11	16	0
A bronzed figure of Bellizarius with marble and or moulu ornaments and clock in the pedestal 978014 25 guineas	26	5	0
An or moulu figure of Venus with marble and or moulu ornaments and with clock in the pedestal 978016 21 guineas	22	1	0
An or moulu figure of Narcissus, bronzed rock, marble and or moulu ornaments with clock in the pedestal No 978015 £19 19	19	19	0
An or moulu triangular clock piece supported by lions, with marble and or moulu and clock piece 978017	21	0	0[204]

The numbers refer to a sequence of order numbers, recorded presumably in an order book, which has not survived. The discounts granted to 'AOQ, Iraps' varied from ten per cent on the ormolu goods and paintings to twenty per cent on the silver and plate. His order also included a pair of ormolu candlesticks and a pair of ormolu and marble candle vases, which were sent on approval. The total charge was £439 1s. 4d.

Although Boulton and Fothergill dealt principally with agents abroad they also sent goods to Europe through merchants in London. They had taken steps to establish relations with merchants who had overseas connections from the beginning of their partnership, and Fothergill in particular cultivated the trade in the early 1760s. In 1764 he gave Boulton a list of thirty-five merchants in London for Boulton to call on. The countries served by them included America, Germany, the Netherlands, Italy, Russia and Spain.[205] Evidence for sales of ormolu through London agents is, however, thin on the ground. Gilt ornaments were sent to Jean Sontag of The Hague through James Cox in 1773[206] and a clock for a European correspondent was sent to William Lewis in 1774.[207] John le Coq, who ordered some ormolu 'chandeliers' in 1781,[208] was another London merchant who had dealings with Boulton and Fothergill in the export trade.[209] John Motteux, one of the merchants who financed their Bill Account, acted for them particularly in their trade with Italy,[210] but there is no evidence that he exported any ormolu ornaments. It seems that sales of ormolu did not depend greatly on London merchants or factors, although toy manufacturers relied heavily on them from the middle of the eighteenth century for their sales abroad.[211] There is also little evidence of sales of ormolu to local merchants in Birmingham.[212]

Boulton and Fothergill employed factors regularly for the export of toys while also dealing direct with foreign agents. This made their relationship with the factors difficult at times, as did their own business at the warehouse in Birmingham where they sold other manufacturers' products, such as brassfoundry, on commission.[213] They continued, however, to sell abroad by both means, and took the risk of offending both. With ormolu, they may have found it difficult to solve the pricing problem – how to sell ornaments without discounting the price too much – which they had also encountered with shopkeepers.

The products sold abroad were sometimes modified to suit the taste in some foreign markets for more exotic decoration. Clock dials particularly were rimmed with coloured glass 'jewels'. The Narcissus clock illustrated in Plate 173 was made for a foreign buyer. The clock with a waisted case depicted in the sketch in Plate 147 also has a 'jewelled' bezel. Decoration of this sort bore an extra cost which the customer was expected to pay.[214]

In 1774 Boulton and Fothergill boasted to Patrick Robertson that the production of ormolu vases was in a flourishing state 'arising from our improvements in gilding and in their forms, as well as from the reception they meet with in every capital city in Europe'.[215] Their ornaments, while not produced in the quantity that this boast might suggest, were certainly well received, as is shown by the many ornaments that survive today in continental Europe.

This survey of marketing methods has shown how deeply Boulton himself was involved in the marketing of his ormolu products, at least in the early 1770s. His involvement, because it brought him into contact with men of wealth, position and influence, gave him a foundation on which to build the edifice of his later ventures. Financially, as I have shown earlier, the ormolu trade was a failure in spite of his effort and enthusiasm. But it enabled him to advertise his name in the most useful circles both in England and abroad, which is probably why he was so eager to be his own most active salesman. The eventual success of the steam engine business owed much to the contacts that he made and to the experience that he gained in his attempts to increase the sales of ormolu.

Survey of ornaments

In this survey I discuss the ormolu ornaments produced at Soho under generic headings in alphabetical order, beginning with candlesticks and ending with vases. The specific named designs that can safely be identified with the archives, such as the lion-faced candlestick, the King's, Minerva and Titus clock cases, and the Bacchanalian, caryatic, goat's head, sphinx and wing-figured vases, are discussed separately in alphabetical order after each essay dealing with the generic subject. Each section contains, if possible, details of when the ornaments were made and sold, and who bought them. I have dealt with the design of ornaments, where there is sufficient evidence, in Chapter 3. I have not repeated the evidence for the origin of a design in this Survey, but have referred the reader in each case to the pertinent pages in Chapter 3.

The sketches of ornaments that have survived in Boulton and Fothergill's pattern books are a useful aid to identifying vases and other ornaments. Sample pages are illustrated in Plates 122–4. All the drawings for ormolu ornaments are illustrated in this Survey.[1] Each of the drawings that relates to an object made at Soho is illustrated alongside an example of the object. The drawings of so far unidentified ornaments are illustrated in the generic sections of the survey.

It is not possible, on the evidence of the drawings alone, to deduce the chronological order of the ormolu ornaments. As explained in the Bibliography, the drawings in the first pattern book, which contains nearly all the sketches of ormolu ornaments, were cut and re-mounted in the nineteenth century and are no longer in chronological sequence. Plates 122 and 123 are the only uncut pages (apart from the large drawing of the tea urn in Plate 232 which occupies a complete page). They show what all the original pages would have looked like, with the objects in number sequence. Plate 124 shows a page of re-mounted drawings. It shows how the mutilation has destroyed the invaluable chronological sequence of the original pages. I have not attempted in this Survey to produce a chronology, but I have dated those that can be dated from the evidence of the archives, and have otherwise suggested which ornaments were earlier or later than others. I have listed in Appendix V the numbered ornaments recorded either in the pattern books or in archives. This list may give some idea of the chronological sequence of, anyway, some of the ornaments.

In countless details this Survey supplements what I have said in earlier chapters. I have tried to avoid including too much of the same information in both parts, but some repetition has been inevitable. The narrative of the earlier chapters would have been poorer for lack of evidence, and the value of this Survey as a work of reference would have been greatly reduced, if I had tried to avoid repetition completely.

Candlesticks, candelabra

Besides the many varieties of candle vase, which are discussed under the heading of 'vases', Boulton and Fothergill produced a number of ormolu candlesticks and candelabra. There were several candlesticks, for example, in the sale at Christie's in April 1771. Three pairs were described as 'table candlesticks in or moulu with triangular feet':[2] according to a manuscript annotation the last of these pairs was enamelled. A 'triangular foot' usually meant a triangular base. Two further pairs were described as 'elegant large table candlesticks with two branches, in or moulu'[3] (it is possible that these were lion-faced candlesticks) and three pairs simply as 'table candlesticks in ormoulu'.[4] The buyers included the Earl of Kerry, Lord or Lady Melbourne and Lady Cunliffe. Also in the sale were a pair of 'large sideboard alabaster candlesticks with Corinthian capitals and other ornaments in or moulu'[5] and

122. Pattern Book 1, p. 156.

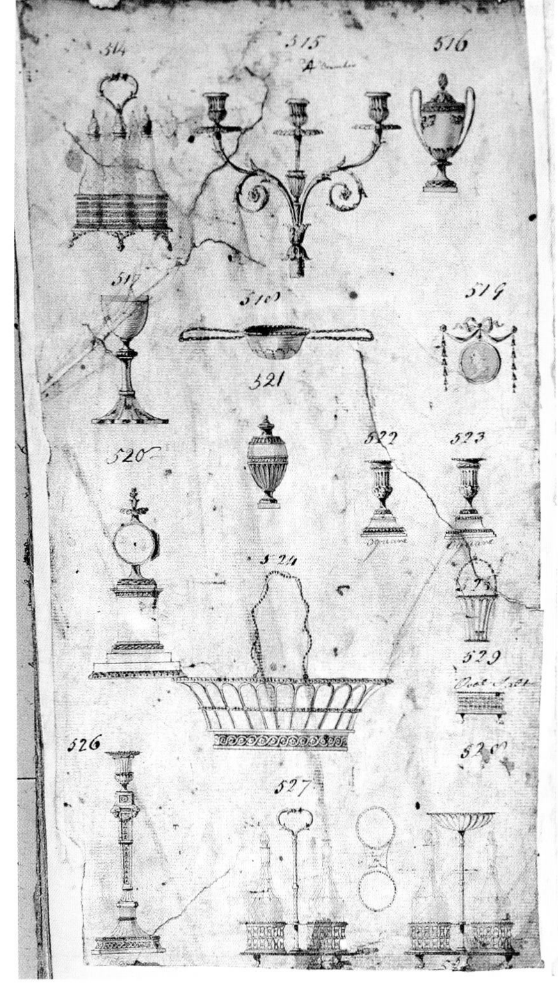

ABOVE RIGHT:
123. Pattern Book 5, p. 33.

124. Pattern Book 1, p. 19.

three or four pairs of 'wreathed Corinthian columns with branches for two candles', which I discuss below under the heading 'wreathed-column candlestick'.

Several of the pairs of candlesticks included in the sale in 1771 remained unsold,[6] and there are very few subsequent references to ormolu candlesticks in the archives. Mrs Montagu ordered some candlesticks in 1772,[7] and others may have been made in 1777 for Lord Arundell, who asked for an estimate of the cost of making them but failed to send his model.[8] There were five pairs of ormolu candlesticks in the sale in 1778, only one of which was sold.[9] 'Triangular' candlesticks were still among the firm's wares in 1781[10] and three pairs of candlesticks and a single 'tripod' candlestick with an ebony foot were listed among the stock in 1782.[11]

As these few references show, there seems to have been little demand for ormolu candlesticks at any time, perhaps because they were expensive in relation to candlesticks made of silver plate, of which Boulton and Fothergill produced large numbers. Furthermore, only six identifiable designs for ormolu candlesticks have survived in the pattern books. One of these (Plate 125) is a 'triangular' candlestick ornamented with grotesque eagles' heads and claw feet which are similar to the devices used on another curious pattern for a circular perfume burner or warming stand (Plate 126). Another is a column candlestick (Plate 127), which was made in silver or plate.[12]

The third is the candlestick illustrated in Plate 128. Candlesticks of this model have survived and one is illustrated in Plate 129. The pedestal and steps are made of white marble. The circular pedestal is, unusually, decorated with lathe-turned mouldings, but this accords with the drawing. Also unusually, but again in accordance with the drawing, only the bottom step is decorated with a pierced guilloche ring. The ring is attached to the copper base underneath the candlestick, from which the usual threaded fixing rod rises up the centre of the hollowed marble. All three steps are decorated with a beaded ring. These rings do not appear in the drawing and may be later additions. Another difference from the drawing is the plain treatment of the top of the nozzle, which in the sketch is gadrooned. This gadrooned piece was probably an insert to hold the candle. The present insert appears to be a later addition. The candlestick shares a number of features with other ornaments made in about 1770–1 – the stepped base with its guilloche ornament (Plate 346), the swags on the pedestal (Plate 327) and the candle nozzle (Plate 263).

The fourth and fifth are drawings for Apollo and Diana, and the sixth is for the triton candlestick. A seventh drawing for a lion-faced candlestick was probably a sketch for a silver version but would have served for the ormolu version too. These sketches for named candlesticks are dealt with in the following sections.

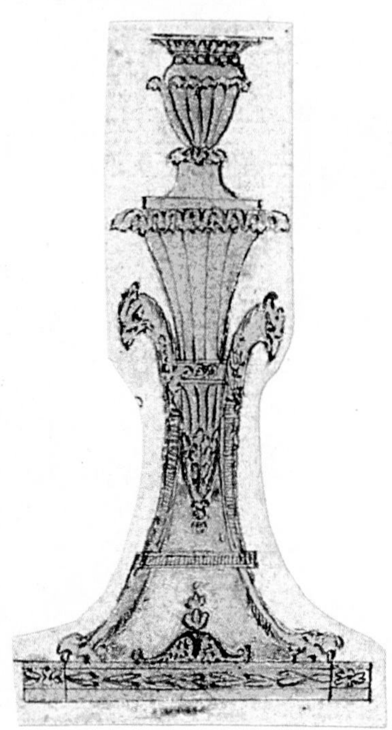

125. Pattern Book 1, p. 51.

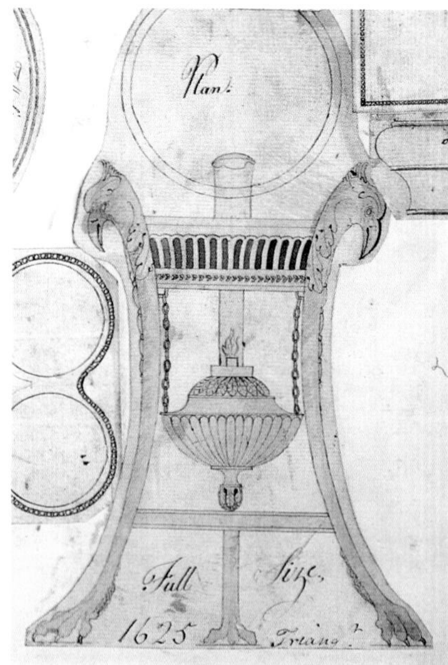

126. Pattern Book 1, p. 74.

Apollo and Diana candelabra

In the sale at Christie and Ansell's in 1778 there were two pairs of 'twelve-inch figures of Apollo and Diana in bronze, supporting branches in or moulu for three lights each'.[13] The reserve price in each case was £26 15s. 6d., and one of them remained unsold. This may have been the pair which in 1780 was booked to Boulton himself but which he returned shortly afterwards.[14] The same pair perhaps was still in stock in 1782.[15]

The description of these candelabra tallies with two drawings in the first pattern book (Plate 132.1–2). There is no clue in the archives on the source of these designs. They are entirely English in feeling but the idea of employing a figure to hold the candle branches was probably copied from French candelabra. French designers often used Apollo and Diana, representing the day and the night, as the bearers of candle branches.

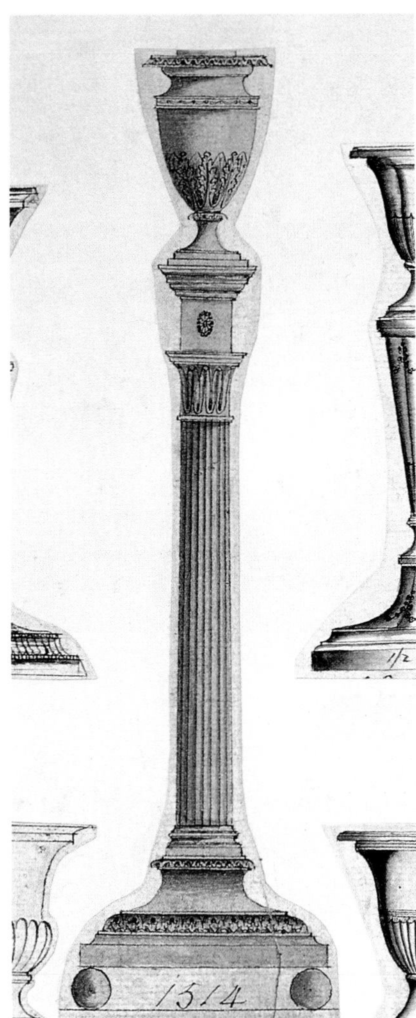

127. Pattern Book 1, p. 37.

128. Pattern Book 1, p. 171.

BELOW:
129. Candlestick, 7.2 in., Hotspur Ltd.

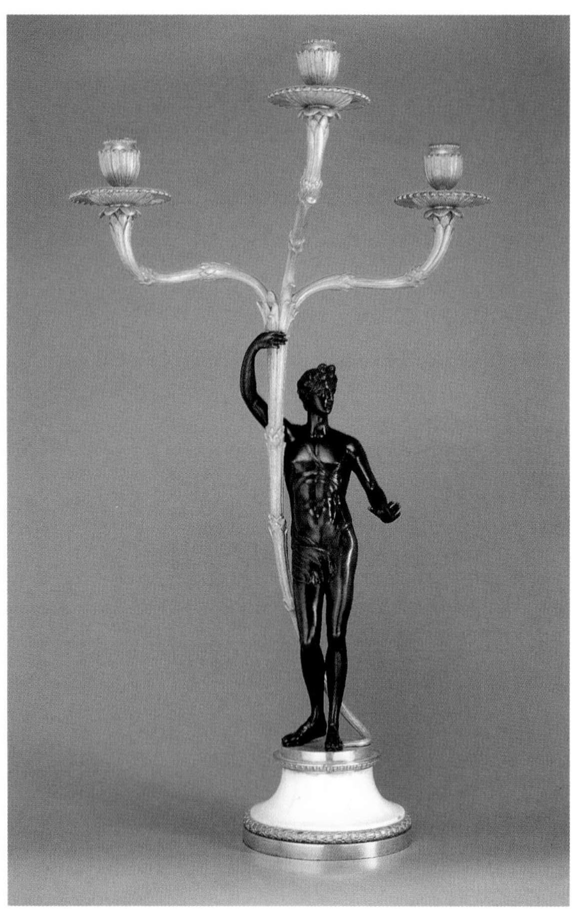

130–1. Apollo and Diana candelabra, 26.8 in., Birmingham Museum and Art Gallery, Soho House.

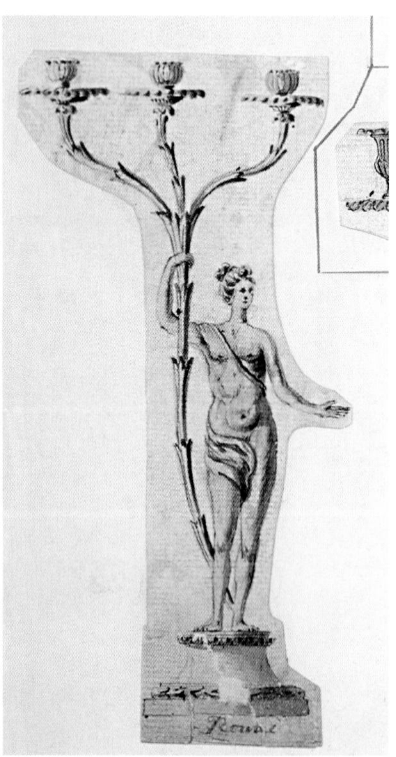

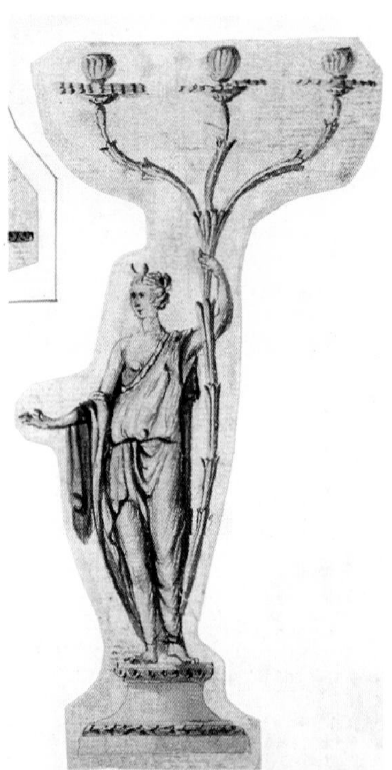

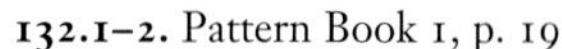

132.1–2. Pattern Book 1, p. 19.

133. Pattern Book 1, p. 41.

134. Pattern Book 1, p. 47.

The figure of Apollo owes something to classical sources, but the modeller seems to have borrowed features from classical models rather than copying a known statue.[16] The concave pedestal is reminiscent of French design, although its origins are also classical.

Two pairs of these candelabra are so far known. One pair (Plates 130–1) is now at Soho House, an appropriate home for them bearing in mind that a pair was booked to Boulton in 1780, even if he did return them.[17] They conform closely to the drawings. The circular concave pedestals are of white marble. The figures are fixed from beneath the pedestal, which is supported by a copper base plate soldered to the lower gilt mount. The palm branches are attached also from beneath and by a screw through the gods' hands. The mount below the sunflower drip rings differs from the sketch. The nozzle inserts are later replacements.

These candelabra are among the finest of the ornaments produced at Soho towards the end of the 1770s, although they lack the elaboration and sophistication of their French equivalents.

Lion-faced candlestick

I have discussed the origin of the design for Boulton's lion-faced candlestick in Chapter 3 (pp. 66–7). He probably copied it, in the true spirit of eighteenth-century invention, from a candlestick by Gouthière, and I have argued in Chapter 3 that it was one of the French models that had a big influence on Boulton's early designs for ormolu ornaments. Elements of the design appear on other ornaments – for example the lions' masks and paw feet (Plate 244), the squared branches (Plates 262, 263–4) and the splash rings below the nozzles (Plate 365).

Boulton and Fothergill produced silver versions of the design, without branches, in 1768–9 (Plate 16) and seem to have antedated the use of the design by other silversmiths. Two sketches for the candlestick appear in the first pattern book (Plates 133–4), the first without branches, the second with curling branches, which date probably from the 1780s.[18] Both of these sketches are likely to have been for silver or plate versions of the candlestick. I also discussed in Chapter 3 the possible French origins of the squared branches (Plate 17), two sketches of which (again probably for silver and plate versions) appear in the same pattern book (Plates 136–7).

There are not many references to ormolu versions of the lion-faced candlestick in the archives. The words 'lyon-faced' and 'lyon' appear in correspondence to describe the candlesticks in 1771,[19] and Boulton and Fothergill intended to put at least one pair into the sale at Christie's in that year.[20] No lion or lion-faced candlesticks are listed in the Christie's sale catalogue. Lion-faced candlesticks may have been described in the catalogue as 'elegant large table candlesticks with two branches, in or moulu'. There were two pairs in the sale.[21] At the end of 1771 The Earl of Kerry was sent a pair of 'lyon-faced' candlesticks by mistake and was charged £18 18s. od. for them.[22] Two pairs were delivered to the Earl of Sefton, including perhaps the Earl of Kerry's unwanted pair, at the sale at Christie's a few months later. He was charged £18 18s. od. for each pair.[23]

Two of the Earl of Sefton's candlesticks are now in the Walker Art Gallery, Liverpool.[24] They are not an exact pair, which suggests that the two pairs bought by Sefton in 1772 were not identical and that the Walker Art Gallery's 'pair' are rather one from each pair. The chief difference is the treatment of the central finial: in one case the drum is decorated with swags of drapery, in the other it is left plain. The construction of the candlesticks is typical of Boulton and Fothergill's work, with the many cast pieces fitting together with the guidance of flanges and notches and fixed with central threaded rods, the lions' masks bolted to their squared mounts, the tapering

135. Lion-faced candlesticks, 18 in., Blenheim Palace.

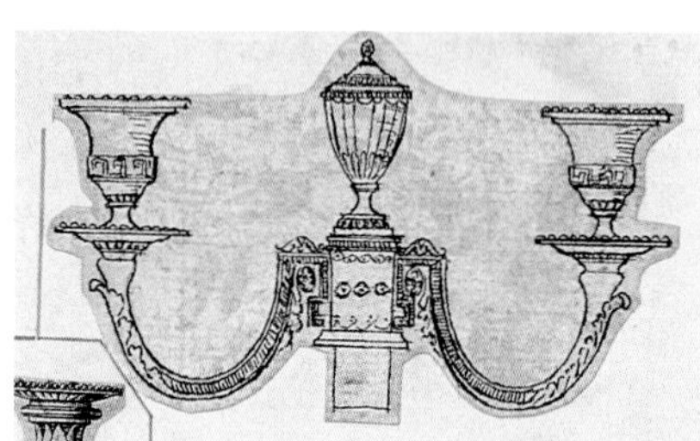

136. Pattern Book 1, p. 13.

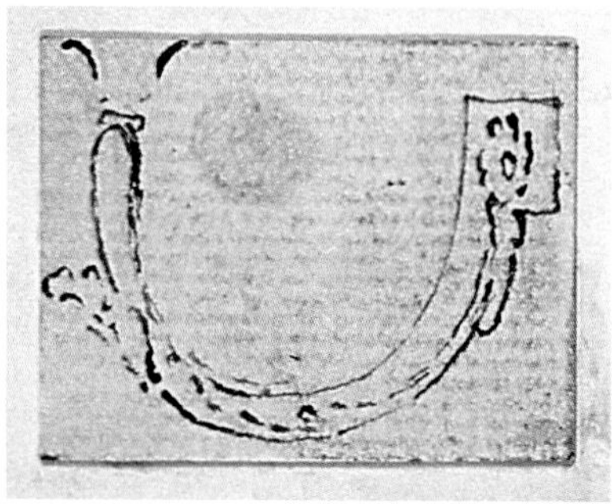

137. Pattern Book 1, p. 11.

138. Lion-faced candlestick, detail, Blenheim Palace.

part of the body made in four pieces and soldered, and sundry assembly marks.[25]

The candlesticks illustrated in Plates 135 and 138 are at Blenheim Palace. They are identical to one of the two Sefton candlesticks, the central finial being decorated with drapery swags, although they have been modified and drilled for electricity and have, therefore, lost their base plates and threaded fixing rods. The hatching of the top surface of the branches on one of these candlesticks has been polished, but whether this is an original difference or a later modification is not clear, and it will not escape the keen-eyed reader that the two candlesticks have not been identically assembled – the drapery swag beneath the lions' masks should both be as shown in the pattern book (Plate 133). These candlesticks at Blenheim were probably one of the 'two pairs of gilt candlesticks' invoiced to the Duke of Marlborough in August 1772. The four candlesticks and a 'gilt cassolete on a pedestal' cost £52 12s. 6d.[26]

Other examples of the lion-faced candlestick have survived. It is not always easy to be sure whether they came from Soho or from French workshops, but the differences in the chasing, the gilding and the construction can help to distinguish them.[27]

Triton candlestick

139. Pattern Book 1, p. 19.

In the sale at Christie's in 1771 there was a 'tryton in dark bronz, holding branches for two candles in or moulu, on a bassment of the same neatly ornamented'.[28] It was bought by General Carnack for £12. The description is close to a drawing in the pattern books (Plate 139), the colouring of which suggests that the branches and the rocky base are both of ormolu. The branches in this sketch are similar to the branches of the King's vase (Plate 339). The triton kneels on a 'bassment' of rocks and the branches emerge from a cornucopia-shaped shell.

In Chapter 3 (pp. 83–5) I have discussed the possible sources for this figure of a triton, which was designed by William Chambers. The triton in the 1771 sale was bronzed. So were the two tritons cast by Boulton and Fothergill for William Chambers in 1773. The architect had provided models for these and wrote in March 1773 to thank Boulton for the 'two bronzes which are very well cast' and to ask for the return of the models 'as they do not belong to me I must deliver them to the owner'.[29] That these two bronzes were tritons is clear from a letter from Boulton and Fothergill later in the month confirming that they had sent off the two tritons and a griffin.[30] Their casts of these two tritons were presumably the 'pair of tritons with candelabras' in the sale of Chambers's things after his death in 1796.[31] The mention of candelabra is tantalising and brings us back to the drawing in the pattern book.

Apart from the triton candelabrum in the 1771 sale and the references to William Chambers's tritons in 1773, there is only one other reference in the archives to tritons. This is in the 1782 Inventory and records '2 Triton figures 24½ lb' in the warehouse.[32]

No candelabrum corresponding to the drawing in the pattern book or to the description in the 1771 sale has yet been recorded. The examples of triton figures that are so far known have no branches, and it is very difficult to determine whether they came from Soho or not. The strongest candidate is the triton illustrated in Plate 46, but there is insufficient evidence to enable a firm attribution to Boulton and Fothergill. There is no sign that this figure was ever fitted with candle branches. The copper and zinc content of the brass of which it is made is remarkably similar to the composition of other ornaments made at Soho.[33] This proves nothing, but is useful contributory evidence. The figure is close to the sketch in the pattern book, although there is no sign of flowers on the imprecise rocks in the sketch. There are, however, flowers in Wedgwood's sketch (Plate 45), and, if my surmises about Boulton's acquisition of the model are correct, there is no reason to think that Boulton's model had no flowers. The rocks in the sketch are just badly drawn. The figure is bronzed and it stands on a red marble base, which may not be contemporary with it.

A pair of similar sized but entirely gilt tritons recently appeared in the salerooms, which look as if they came from the same model (Plate 47).[34] Again there is no sign of candle branches. It is impossible to be certain who made these figures (see Chapter 3, p. 85).[35] Other triton figures will no doubt appear, including, perhaps, a figure with branches corresponding to Boulton and Fothergill's sketch.

140. Wreathed-column candlestick, 12 in., Christie's.

Wreathed-column candlestick

In the sale in 1771 there were four pairs of 'wreathed corinthian columns with branches for two candles, on the capital a small vase in the antique taste, the whole in or moulu'.[36] The catalogue description matches the gilt candlesticks of Plates 140–1. These candlesticks share a number of features with other ornaments, notably the nozzles and drip rings (which are wrongly assembled in Plate 140 and show the upper drip ring the wrong way up in Plate 141), the splayed and reeded base, and the urn, which reappears on the Minerva clock case (Plate 168). The column is made of thin rolled copper. The Corinthian capital, also made of thinly rolled metal, is attached to a threaded iron rod mounted on a plate at the top of the splayed base. The splayed base is fixed to the square pedestal by hammering. The floral wreaths entwining the column are cast and are attached by

141. Wreathed-column candlestick, 12.2 in., Private Collection.

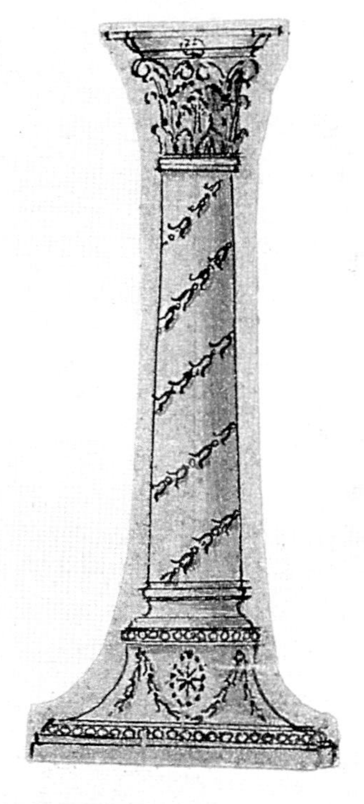

142. Pattern Book 1, p. 51.

screws fixed into the column. All the mounts above the capital are cast. The branches are attached to the lower squared piece by threads bolted to the inverted finials on either side of the capital. Once assembled, they fit into the column by means of a copper sleeve attached to the lower squared piece. The only difference between these two candlesticks is the decorative treatment of the centre of the branches.

Both of these candlesticks were said, when they were recently sold, to have come from Weston Park.[37] This was the home of Sir Henry Bridgeman, whose wife visited Soho in August 1770.[38] She must have bought candlesticks of this pattern, because the candlestick acquired her name in the Soho correspondence. In May 1771 a letter to Matthews mentions a pair of 'Lady Bridgman candlesticks with lapis pillars £12 12s od'.[39] The reference is not enough in itself to link the wreathed-column candlestick to Lady Bridgeman, but the 'lapis pillars' and the price conclusively do so when compared with the description and the reserve price of another of the lots in the 1771 sale – 'a pair of wreathed Corinthian columns the shaft of which is a curious imitation of lapis lazuli with branches for 2 candles, on the capital is a small vase in the antique taste or moulu'.[40] The imitation lapis lazuli was presumably made of lacquered glass, as in Plates 162 and 356.

Candlesticks of this pattern were also included in the sale at Christie's in 1772. A 'pair of Lady Bridgmen's candlesticks' was delivered from the sale to 'Mr Dunbar'. He was charged ten guineas.[41]

The making of the column and its base and capital is akin to the techniques used in the manufacture of silver plate. The spiral wreath is also akin to designs for plate candlestick columns. There are many examples of a spiral wreath on designs for plate in the pattern books (Plate 142).

Chimneypiece mounts

The ornamentation of stone chimneypieces with ormolu mounts was very much in accordance with James Stuart's and Robert Adam's rejection of the heavy designs of their predecessors – the 'monumental chimney-pieces', in the words of Sir John Soane, of Inigo Jones, William Kent, James Gibbs and the 'whole train of their humble imitators'.[42] Adam relied for effect on delicate and polychromatic decoration. Several lavish examples survive from the period, including, among Adam's own designs, the chimneypiece in the drawing room at Syon House, carved in white marble by Thomas Carter and with elaborate ormolu mounts of high quality,[43] and the inlaid scagliola and ormolu chimneypiece from the glass drawing room in Northumberland House, probably made by Bartoli and Richter, which is now also at Syon.[44] Boulton and Fothergill cannot be linked with either of these pieces, nor, so far, with any surviving ormolu-mounted chimneypiece. Contrary to the accepted view, they appear from the archives to have supplied very few ormolu chimneypiece mounts. Towards the end of the 1770s they were supplying pewter mounts which were meant to be painted and to simulate pieces of decorative carving,[45] and on occasion they supplied silver mounts,[46] but they did not advertise their ability to make ormolu mounts. As with door furniture and furniture mounts this may have been because chimneypiece mounts were probably classed as hardware and not thought worthy of specific mention in letters, invoices or orders. But it seems more likely that Boulton and Fothergill seldom received orders to supply them.

The archives record only two occasions on which they supplied ornaments for chimneypieces. One of these was in 1774 when two gilt figures sitting upon a 'rock or bank', which were presumably intended for each side of the chimneypiece, were supplied to Sir Robert Cunliffe at a cost of £19 1s. 0d.[47] The other occasion was three years earlier when Mayhew and Ince, who were providing furniture for the Earl of Kerry's house on the east side of Portman Square, sent Boulton and Fothergill a wooden model of a chimneypiece with a drawing showing how it was to be ornamented. The drawing, as Boulton and Fothergill pointed out in their reply, was not very clear –

> and therefore we have made a sleight sketch by a larger scale, some of yours not being very distinct from being so small. Pray are the ornaments A B and C such as you approve? and should the ram's head be placed in the front as in the drawing sent you or should it be placed at the extreame angle so as to appear both at the end and front alike? Should the claws be marble or mettle, if the latter should they appear both end and front or front only? We should be glad to have Mr Devall's opinion how the ornaments should be fixed on, whether by screws going through the gilt ornaments or by sodering pins on the back of the ornaments.[48]

It is clear from this letter that the design was some sort of pastiche of motifs in the antique taste. The design might have been initiated either by Mayhew and Ince or by Devall,[49] who was responsible for the marble parts of the chimneypiece and for its erection. The chasing of these ornaments was not completed until December[50] and they then had to be sent to London so that Devall could fix them to the marble before they could safely be gilt. They were delayed ten days at the carriers' warehouse 'for want of a carriage note'[51] on the way south, and Boulton and Fothergill expected the gilding to take about eighteen days.[52] They were not finally completed until seven months after the initial order.[53]

Clock cases, watch stands

Once he had started to make ormolu ornaments at Soho, it must have occurred to Boulton that there was a market for ormolu-mounted clock cases and watch stands. In France elaborate ormolu-mounted clock cases were in fashion and, as with vases, it must have been tempting for Boulton to try and cash in on the demand. Even so, clock cases did not figure among his first products in 1768–9. He was prompted to consider them perhaps by Thomas Pownall, who reminded him in the autumn of 1769 that ormolu clock cases of all sorts were very much in the 'mode-Francoise'.[54] Boulton does not seem to have done anything about this suggestion until the following year, when he received the request through William Chambers to make a clock case for the King (Plate 160). The patronage of the King was a promising augury, and he at once began the speculative production of clock cases. The first clock case recorded in the archives was, characteristically, a copy of the King's, which Boulton hoped to auction at Christie's in 1771. This was followed by three elaborate clock cases, for Boulton's geographical and sidereal clocks (Plates 155, 177) and for an allegorical case depicting Minerva (Plate 166), all of which reused features of Chambers's designs for the King. These clock cases are all described below. They were ambitious projects and were not typical examples of the firm's range of clock cases during the 1770s. They were too expensive to meet with the general demand for which Boulton was always hoping.

They were, however, representative of Boulton and Fothergill's work in three respects. First, they illustrate Boulton's habit of using the same cast ornaments on many different objects. Second, they were all pedestal clocks, that is to say they were made to stand on tables, brackets or chimneypieces. Boulton and Fothergill made no longcase clocks and very few wall clocks. The only certain reference to a wall clock in the archives occurs in 1780 when John Hodges informed Boulton that Joseph Dyott[55] had in his

143. Pattern Book 1, p. 78.

144. Wing-figured wall clock case, 8.5 in., Private Collection.

possession 'a wainscot clock case number 308 at 14 guineas' which was sent to him 'as a specimen of workmanship and color of gilding'.[56] The word 'wainscot' is ambiguous, but that Hodges was referring to a wall clock is confirmed by the survival of a sketch in the pattern books of a clock case decorated with two winged figures and numbered 308 (Plate 143). The following entries in the Inventory of stock in 1782 probably refer to a clock of this design:

	£	s	d
Chasing on a wing figure clock $14\frac{1}{4}$ days	2	10	0
Clock for a wing figure	4	4	0[57]

Plate 144 shows a clock case of this design. So far it is the only one known. It conforms very closely to the sketch, but has lost the finials on the winged figures' heads and the suspended beads or chains, the hanging holes for which are behind the drapery. The ornament at the bottom looks more elaborate, but this is because the bottom of the sketch was clipped before it was pasted into the pattern book. A nineteenth-century French dial and movement are fitted to the clock case, which may disqualify it from being the one noted in the 1782 Inventory and suggests that it was exported.[58] The winged figures, with their entwined tails and their awkwardly configured wings, do not appear on any other ornament. Although no record of this clock case appears in the archives before 1780, the number 308 suggests that it may have been among the earlier designs.

The third respect in which Boulton's ambitious clocks were typical of the firm's work was that, with the exception of the King's clock case, they all pointed to some moral about man's mortality or embodied some reference to philosophy, a term which in the eighteenth century included the study of astronomy and the natural sciences. Thus the Minerva clock case depicted the goddess of wisdom unveiling a plaque, which showed Prudence making a libation to Time, and pointing to the 'flying moments', while a boy sat nearby reading Gay's appropriately moral lines about Time or, in other versions, Virgil's lines about the brevity of life (Plate 170). The geographical clock showed the revolutions of the earth and the position of the sun (Plate 159), and the sidereal clock showed the movement of the sun in relation to the fixed stars, while Science explained the Laws of Nature on the pedestal (Plates 178, 181) and Urania, the Muse of Astronomy, reclined on the top (Plate 179). Such allegorical conceits were popular in France and seem to have delighted Boulton's fancy. They reflected his enthusiasm for the antique taste, which blinded him to such illogicalities as combining Minerva with John Gay and muddling the Greek and Roman pantheons.

According to the archives the earliest allegorical cases which were made in any quantity were Venus timepieces, with horizontal movements fitted in the top of the vases, three of which were included in the sale at Christie's in 1771 (Plate 359 shows a Venus vase fitted as a perfume burner), and Titus clocks (Plates 183, 185), the first of which was made for Samuel Pechell in 1772. Each of these allegorical clock cases is described separately later. Examples of both were produced for many years. They were smaller and cheaper than Boulton's more ambitious clock cases – the Titus clock case was called a 'watch-stand' on more than one occasion and Pechell's was fitted with a watch movement – and they were the most characteristic of Boulton and Fothergill's clock cases. The allegories are simple and obvious. Venus stands weeping at the tomb of Adonis, whom Time will never restore: her lament, in Greek, is inscribed on the urn (Plate 191). In later versions an obelisk takes the place of the urn, with Adonis's plaque fixed to it, and the movement is fitted into the pedestal. Titus is shown regretting that a day has passed without his having done a good deed.

Several other allegorical designs were proposed or made. Thus at the end of 1771 Samuel Pechell was given the choice of two other designs in case he did not like Titus. One of these showed 'Prudence with a motto on a scroll from Juvenal' and the other 'one of the Parca[e] with an inscription upon the altar from Virgil'.[59] Both sound as if they conformed to the general pattern of the Venus and Titus clock cases, with a figure and a pedestal, perhaps with a vase on top. No drawings of these two designs have survived. The patterns in Plates 145 and 146 may give some idea of their appearance, although both were probably drawn in the latter half of the 1770s. Plate 145 is a sketch of a clock case representing a female figure, presumably Prudence, holding an ewer and approaching an altar on the top of which is an effigy of Time. The pedestal is similar to the pedestal of the candle vases of Plate 301, with ram's heads at the corners and medallions with bowed frames set between swags. The sketch is related to the clock case depicting an offering to Diana, which is described later (Plate 153). The sketch of the medallion, while slight, looks as if it is a sacrifice group (Plate 76.4, see Chapter 3, p. 110), which depicts another religious offering. Plate 146,

145–6. Pattern Book 1, p. 18.

although it was probably not designed as a clock case, appears to be a sketch for a figure of one of the Parcae, or Fates.

In the later 1770s the number of allegorical designs appears to have increased. Lord Arundell was sent no less than fourteen sketches of vase clocks, most of which were presumably allegorical pieces, in 1777,[60] and at the beginning of the next year there were more than a dozen vases 'with figures, part with time pieces' in stock.[61] Several of these were no doubt included in the sale at Christie and Ansell's in May 1778 when, besides two Titus clocks and a Minerva, clocks of several other designs were offered. There were, for example, two clocks which depicted 'an elegant figure of Urania in bronze' (Plate 189, see p. 236), and two figures of 'Narcissus in bronze, admiring himself in a fountain', which may not have been clock cases, but could have been (Plates 173, 175, see pp. 220–2). Two further allegorical cases depicted an offering to Diana (Plate 153, see pp. 198–200). There were also two cases representing 'Cleopatra at the tomb of Marc Antony, in statuary marble, with a clock in the pedestal',[62] one of which had a bronze figure and was reserved at £21: the other was reserved at £25, which suggests that the figure of Cleopatra was gilt. Two 'or moulu clock pieces of Cleopatra' were sold to Capper, Palmer and Perkins two years later for £32 each. Each was fitted with a 'circle of stones' round the dial, at a further cost of 18s., showing that they were intended for export.[63] Yet another allegorical piece of ormolu and white marble, which was probably a clock case, depicted 'Penelope petitioning Minerva for the safe return of Telemachus'.[64] Another allegorical clock in the sale, which was not based on a classical theme, represented a group of boys supporting a watch, with the seasons depicted by emblems on the plinth.[65] Also in 1778, but not at Christie and Ansell's, Boulton and Fothergill sold 'a Belizarius with a better clock than the last' to one of their agents overseas (Plate 151, see p. 197).

Wedgwood, when he visited Boulton at Soho in 1776, observed correctly that 'most of his time pieces, and groups of figures have pyramids [i.e. obelisks], or alters of white marble to lean upon'. He suggested that they might be decorated with 'our statues etc. with blue grounds' (i.e. cameos), an idea that, he said, Boulton welcomed. He undertook to send some, and thought that 'proper subjects may be modelled for Russia or any other place whither his time pieces are to be sent'.[66] There is evidence that Boulton used Wedgwood's cameos on the pedestals of some of his white marble candle vases (Plate 80), but so far no example of a timepiece with Wedgwood cameos on the pedestal has come to light.

The archives do not suggest that Boulton and Fothergill sold clock cases other than those based on allegorical themes in any great quantity. The movements for 'vase clocks', which they bought from John Whitehurst on several occasions,[67] were probably movements for Venus clock cases, which appear to have been made in greater numbers than other types. The same can probably be said of the vase clocks purchased on occasion from William Holywell,[68] who appears to have assumed the chief responsibility for supplying movements after Whitehurst's departure to London in 1775.[69] Probably the 'horizontal time-piece' sent to Amsterdam in 1771[70] was another Venus, this being apparently the only design for which Boulton adopted the French idea of fitting a horizontal movement, with revolving hour and minute rings, into a vase. Boulton and Fothergill's preference for clocks with conventional dials reflected the conservatism of English taste. Several other references to clocks in the archives are so brief that it is impossible to say for certain that they were based on designs other than those that I have already discussed. Thus Holywell supplied movements for 'pedestal' clocks,[71] and many manuscripts refer simply to 'or moulu' or 'gilt' clock cases,[72] which might have been of almost any design.

These sparse descriptions provide no clues about the types of clock case that were produced at Soho, other than the allegorical designs discussed above. There are, however, three sketches of pedestal clock cases in the pattern books. One of these (Plate 147) shows a watch supported on a waisted marble pedestal resting on the backs of three lions. This can probably be identified with a design which was sold to 'AOQ, Iraps', probably the Paris *marchand-mercier* Charles-Raymond Grancher (see Chapter 5, p. 179), in 1781: it was described as 'an or moulu triangular clock piece supported by lions, with marble and or moulu and clock piece' and it cost £21.[73] The sketch shows that, besides using a number of familiar mounts, the clock case had a 'circle of stones' fitted round the dial, marking it as a clock intended for export. Another sketch (Plate 148), if the supporting animals balancing urns on their heads are again lions (they look more like cheetahs, but they are not unlike the famous lions of Delos), might equally be identified with this invoice, although it is less obvious from the sketch that this case has a triangular base. Both of these sketches owe something to French influence. The third sketch (Plate 149) is of a cylindrical clock mounted on a marble pedestal and base more consonant with other Soho designs. It is numbered 520, a number which does not appear elsewhere in the archives. These three clock cases were all apparently designs from the later 1770s.

Finally, there is a sketch of a pedestal clock case in Boulton's notebook for 1773, with the humorous outline of a face on the dial (Plate 150). This may be a sketch of a clock which he had seen somewhere, but the supporting lion and the distinctive foot with its spiral flutes, which appears on several pieces made for the Royal Family (Plates 160, 184, 339), suggest that Boulton was trying rather to evolve a new design and borrowing, as usual, a few well-tried motifs from previous ornaments.

The clock cases and watch stands were not always supplied with movements and patrons were sometimes expected to find their own. Many of the surviving examples have later movements, especially those that went abroad and were fitted with French movements. In spite of Boulton's ambition at one time to create a large-scale watch manufactory, watch movements were never made at Soho. Boulton and Fothergill commissioned many small movements from Whitehurst, besides the two full-scale clocks for the geographical and sidereal cases, and William Holywell supplied many movements after 1775. They also ordered two movements from Thomas Wright subsequent to their co-operation, if that is the correct word, in the making of the King's clock:[74] in 1780 a clockmaker named Ray undertook to supply movements for 'several emblematical pieces for two or three foreign orders' which had been ready for some time.[75] Movements were also bought from local watchmakers in Birmingham, but the difficulties which Boulton and Fothergill sometimes met with locally are well illustrated by a letter to Whitehurst in 1778 in which he was asked to find 'a good going clock that will strike' in London because they had 'endeavoured to procure such a clock in Birmingham' but could not.[76]

The references in the archives suggest that clock cases and watch stands were not made in large numbers at Soho, and certainly not in the quantity that Wedgwood was led to believe in 1776, when he was told that Boulton and Fothergill had sold two hundred Venus timepieces.[77] They were perhaps too expensive or too philosophical for Boulton's English patrons. Most went to Europe, but some were made for markets as far afield as China,[78] a market, which, although the clocks were 'neat and showy things', was hardly the most appropriate for the display of Boulton's Greek and Roman conceits.

147–8. Pattern Book 1, p. 78.

149. Pattern Book 5, p. 33.

150. Matthew Boulton's Notebook 1773.

151. Pattern Book 1, p. 79.

Belisarius

In 1778 Boulton and Fothergill sold 'a Belizarius with a better clock than the last' to one of their agents overseas.[79] This was yet another clock case based on a theme of classical origin. Belisarius served with notable success in wars against the Vandals and Goths during the reign of the Emperor Justinian in the sixth century AD.[80] A sketch in the pattern book (Plate 151) of an old man, who is presumably blind, holding a staff in his right hand and the lead of a seated dog in his left hand, probably represents the great general after his final disgrace in AD 563, when he was unjustly condemned for his alleged part in a conspiracy against the Emperor, and, as the unfounded tradition alleged, was deprived of his eyes and reduced to beggary.[81] The theme of his downfall was a popular one with late eighteenth-century storytellers and artists in France and Britain, who increasingly used themes from classical myth and history to convey messages on moral conduct.[82] Exemplifying as it did the vicissitudes of fortune, and the baseness of ingratitude, it would have appealed to Boulton. The sketch shows the outlines of a clock dial on the face of the obelisk and of an oval medallion on the pedestal. There is no other drawing of a clock case in the pattern books with the dial positioned on the obelisks: but it is very likely that the clock was mounted, as in the Titus clock (Plates 184–6), in the pedestal. Capper, Palmer and Perkins bought two Belisarius clocks in 1780 for £30 each. Each clock was set with a 'circle of stones' round the dial at an extra cost of 18s., indicating that the clocks were intended for export.[83] A merchant in Paris identified as the *marchand-mercier* C.-R. Grancher (see Chapter 5, p. 179), bought another in 1781 for £26 5s. 0d. This was described as 'a bronzed figure of Bellizarius with marble and or moulu ornaments and clock in the pedestal'.[84] In the 1782 inventory there was a plinth for a 'Belisarius' in stock, and 'a whole marble obelisk with or moulu ornaments and a bronzed figure of Belisarius with clock in the pedestal'.[85] So far no example of a Belisarius clock has been recorded.

Boy

In the 1771 sale at Christie's there was 'a pedestal clock case with a correct eight-day repeating clock; on the top a boy sitting on books, in a contemplative attitude, with a globe and scrole on which is delineated a small scheme of the solar system'.[86] It was the last lot on the first day. The reserve price was £42, the same as the reserve for a King's vase (Plate 339). It fetched only thirty-nine guineas and was booked to Morgan, who was probably the agent who took some of the unsold stock.[87] In 1772 General Cholmondeley bought a 'boy clock', which had been in the sale at Christie's in April of that year.[88]

The theme is typical of Boulton's liking for allegory and natural philosophy and owes its origins to French models. Emblematic of the study of astronomy, the boy represents the thirst for knowledge, or perhaps the genius of time.

Plate 152 illustrates a 'boy clock', so far the only one recorded.[89] The design conforms closely to the catalogue description, except that the boy has lost his scroll. The holes for holding the scroll can be seen in the polished surface by the books. The globe can be revolved by hand. The clock sits on a marble pedestal supported by ball feet screwed into the ormolu case. The two-train, rack-striking movement is, unusually, a pendulum movement, with an anchor escapement. The back plate is engraved but unsigned, the dial is enamel, and the hands are steel.

Many of the ormolu mounts of this clock case appear on other ornaments. Most notably, the boy and his books, and the whole of the

152. Boy clock case, 14.5 in., Christie's.

pedestal from the guilloche frieze down to the fluted frieze at the bottom, including the pierced and chased side panels, are repeated on the earlier version of the Minerva clock case (Plate 166). They were cast from the same moulds. Examples of both clocks were in the 1771 sale. Whether the boy clock preceded the Minerva clock as a design, or was a means of reusing parts designed for the Minerva, is not clear: but they are examples of the constant reuse of models on different ornaments which was typical of production at Soho.

Diana

The clock case illustrated in Plate 153 represents a classical robed female figure carrying an ewer and approaching an effigy of the goddess Diana. The ewer is decorated with burnished anthemion motifs. Diana is depicted with her customary emblems – the crescent moon in her hair, the bow and quiver of the huntress. The white marble pedestal, with its four rams' heads and other mounts, is very similar to the vases in Plates 301–2, and the white marble base with its ormolu surround is typical of Boulton's allegorical pieces. The clock, or rather watch movement, is mounted in the pedestal, with an enamelled dial. On the other three faces of the pedestal are gilt

153. Offering to Diana, 15.4 in., Schloss Fasanerie.

medallions mounted in glazed frames (Plate 154), also echoing the vases of Plates 301–2.

The design corresponds with the description of a clock case in the sale at Christie and Ansell's in 1778 – 'An offering to Diana in bronze, statuary marble and or moulu, with a clock in the pedestal'.[90] A few lots earlier there was also 'An offering to Diana in bronze, the plinth and pedestal of statuary marble and or moulu'.[91] There is no mention of a clock in the catalogue entry for this earlier lot. Both lots were reserved at £18, and both

154. Offering to Diana, detail.

remained unsold. Presumably they were returned to Soho, along with the many other ornaments which failed to reach their reserve prices in this unsuccessful sale. It is possible that the clock case illustrated in Plate 153 was subsequently sold to one of Boulton's agents in Europe, where the principal market for his allegorical clock cases seems to have been, and so found its way to Fasanerie, where it now is. There is, however, no evidence for this. Nor is there any record of the sale of a Diana clock to the probable buyer, the Elector William I of Hesse, either in the Boulton archives or at Fasanerie.[92]

There is a sketch in the first pattern book that is very similar to this clock case (Plate 145). This probably depicts Prudence approaching the shrine of Time. The positioning of the clock face is quite different, but the posture, drapery and arms of the figure are similar, as are the ewer (but not its decoration), and the mounts on the pedestal and base. The design may owe something to engravings of gems in Gori's *Museum Florentinum* (Plate 60, see Chapter 3, p. 92), but I have not yet identified an exact source.

The three medallions (Plate 154) all show Achilles Victorious and derive from a gem reproduced by James Tassie and much used by Wedgwood. It was used on several of Boulton and Fothergill's ornaments (Plates 302, 304). I have discussed in Chapter 3 Boulton's probable debt to Wedgwood for this and its companion medallions (see pp. 107–14).

Unlike other allegorical ornaments, the Diana clock case does not convey an obvious message about mortality. It may be that Boulton was thinking of her as the goddess of childbirth, in which role she had the power to ensure the survival of a child and so to help mankind to fight the inevitable victory of Time. The connection between an offering to Diana with Achilles is obscure, but I have observed in Chapter 3 that Boulton does not seem to have chosen decorative medallions with any thematic connection in mind.

OPPOSITE:
155. Geographical clock, 30.5 in., Private Collection.

Geographical clock

Boulton seems to have conceived the plan of making his geographical and sidereal clocks early in 1771. He was attracted by the idea of exploiting at once the growing interest in scientific enquiry and the fashion for the antique taste. What better means could there be of matching beauty and philosophy than the production of clocks which would be both majestic in their design and show the motions of earth, sun, planets and stars? The formula seemed certain to succeed. 'I am determined', he said in a letter to John Whitehurst, 'to make such like sciences fashionable among fine folks'.[93]

He turned for advice and help to John Whitehurst and to their mutual friend, the travelling lecturer James Ferguson, who himself was actively interested in astronomical clock movements.[94] He probably discussed the geographical clock (Plate 155) with Whitehurst early in 1771, having perhaps derived some of his ideas from discussions with Ferguson beforehand. In February 1771 he wrote to Whitehurst:

> I am not at all confined as to the size of the case for the clock which is to turn the work upside down but as I have already the modals made for a case whose size is about 9 inches wide 9 inches in perpendicular depth and 6 inches horizontal depth, i.e. from front to back, I should be glad to avail myself of that modell if the size will suit you as it will save me some expence as well as time. But I cannot touch it untill I return from London which will be about a fortnight after the Easter week and then I will have two brass hemispheres made to screw into each other so as to form a perfect globe. When I am in London I will talk to old Ferguson about the covering of the globe which are now in use [and] were his property once.[95] It's very necessary to be exact in size with the brass globe. I think you are quite right about the annual index by which the clock will show when it wants correction as to the sun's place.[96]

156. Geographical clock, detail.

It is clear from the design and measurements of the finished clock case that Boulton proposed from the beginning to copy the main features of the clock case which he was making for the King under the direction of William Chambers (Plate 160). The use of the same models was, as I have shown in Chapter 3, a frequent practice at Soho, and Boulton paid scant regard to the feelings of the customer whose design he was copying. Thus many of the decorative features of the case – the mouldings at the top and bottom of the squared case, the rams' heads with their ribbons, the swags and the ewers with their fish or dolphin handles – were cast from the same models and their quality fully matches the work on the King's clock case. Several of the models were also used for the sidereal clock at the same time (Plate 177, see pp. 222–30), including the trellis-patterned sides with their floral decoration (Plates 156, 182), which echo, in their intricate pattern, the marquetry of certain pieces of French furniture.[97] It all saved Boulton 'some expence as well as time'.

It is also clear from his letter to Whitehurst that he planned from the earliest stage to incorporate a revolving globe on top of the clock, and that he accepted the clockmaker's observation that an annual hand would help with the adjustment of the position of the sun, which moves up and down in front of the globe as it were along the line of the ecliptic, if they were driven by the same annual motion. It is very likely that he also had in mind at this stage the use of the three figures, which 'support' the globe (Plates 157–8). These figures were copies of three of the four figures on a silver gilt crucifix made by Antonio Gentile da Faenza in about 1582 (Plate 67), two of which were illustrated by William Chambers in his *Treatise on Civil Architecture* under the heading of 'Persians and Caryatides' (Plate 41, figs. 1 and 3). I have argued in Chapter 3 that the architect was not the source of the models for the geographical clock case (see p. 80) but that they came from the sculptor John Flaxman, from whom in December 1770 Boulton bought, among other models, a 'group of Hercules and Atlas' for two guineas (see Chapter 3, pp. 97–8).

That Boulton's source was Flaxman is confirmed by the use of Flaxman's phrase 'a group of Hercules and Atlas' in the description of the geographical clock which Boulton sent to Lord Cathcart in St Petersburg, along with descriptions of the sidereal and Minerva clocks, in October 1771. At this stage the geographical clock case was well on the way to completion:

> A geographical clock in a Dorick pedestal of or moulu ornamented in the Grecian taste. On one side of the dye is a circular dial shewing the hour and minute. Upon the top is a group, representing Hercules and Atlas, supporting the terrestrial globe, which latter is inclosed with a glass globe and is thereby preserved clean and the motions prevented from being incommoded. This terrestrial globe (which is one of Senex's of 6 or may be 8 inches)[98] makes a revolution in 24 hours mean time (by means of the clock beneath). It has a brass circle fixed to it and a sun connected with that circle so as to be always perpendicular to it, this circle has an annual motion given to it also by the clock which keeps the sun every day in its proper degree of declination, consequently [*sic*] you see at every instant what part of the earth is enlightened and what is in darkness. The above-mentioned circle being what is called the *terminator lucis et umbrae* you see the lengthening and shortening of the days the rising and setting of the sun and the hour in every part of the world. Although this may not be useful to a Professor of Astronomy yet it will greatly assist young astronomers in forming proper ideas of the causes of these appearances.[99]

It is convenient in the context of this description to discuss both the clock itself and the globe, both of which Boulton took a keen interest in during the process of manufacture. The clock movement is simple but elegant, and is well made and finished. The influence of James Ferguson is apparent. Ferguson knew Whitehurst well, visiting him in 1762 when

159. Geographical clock, detail of globe.

he was on a lecture tour[100] and corresponding with him subsequently.[101] He lectured in Derby, during an extensive tour of the Midlands, in November and December 1771, and in between unpacking and packing his apparatus and giving his lectures he spent his 'otherwise vacant hours' with the 'good and ingenious Mr Whitehurst, clock and watch maker here, about schemes for astronomical clocks which he has orders to make according to my plans'.[102] In several of his designs Ferguson favoured a twenty-four hour dial and a barrel without a fusee. The geographical clock shares both these features. The movement is also curiously French in many details: the omission of a fusee is typically French but the shapes of the gears and collets and the curious pivot plate mounted on the back plate, all suggest French influence or origin. I cannot explain this but it is not atypical of Whitehurst's work. It is an eight-day movement with a half-second pendulum and a thirty-tooth escape wheel,[103] the unusual recoil escapement covering three teeth. The globe turns once a day and the engraved sun (Plate 159) that traces the ecliptic, is operated by a carriage that runs to and fro on top of the movement. The sun is attached, as the description says, to a brass ring (the '*terminator lucis et umbrae*'), which gives a rough idea of the extent of night and day. The hour and minute hands are made of finely pierced blued steel and the annual hand,[104] which shows the date on the circumference of the dial, is brass. The minute hand and wheel, from which the globe is operated, and the annual hand and wheel, from which the sun is operated, can be adjusted by manual knobs mounted on the back plate.

OPPOSITE:
157–8. Geographical clock, details of figures.

The signature 'Whitehurst Derby' is engraved on the back plate.

The dial is enamelled. The original enamelling was not carried out at Soho but subcontracted to an enameller named Weston who worked in Quakers' Buildings in Smithfield, London. Like all subcontractors he was a slow worker. Whitehurst wrote to him at least twice and Boulton once to ask for delivery as soon as possible,[105] and at one time Boulton considered making do with a plated dial if the enamelled one did not arrive in time.[106]

The wording of the description of 30th October 1771 suggests that it had not been decided whether to have a six-inch or an eight-inch globe. This must be a slip, because although the globe had not been ordered the glass cover was already made and an eight-inch globe would have been too big for it.[107] A month later Boulton wrote to Whitehurst:

I think Mr Ferguson can point out the best place for buying the globe and therefore as it will save time I wish you would wrote to London for one to come direct to Derby. By this time I hope you have received the clock case and figures which were sent in one box and the globe of glass in another. Whenever you screw on the globe put thin leather between the metal and the glass least you crack it.[108]

Whitehurst ordered the globe and in February 1772 heard from James Ferguson that it was ready:[109] but when it arrived he found that it was seven-eighths of an inch smaller in diameter than he had ordered and that he had to make a 'new horizon' (i.e. the '*terminator*' ring), which he hoped to complete in a day.[110] The adjustment is clear from the lengthened spindles, level with the equator, on which the '*terminator*' ring pivots on each side of the globe (Plate 159).

The globe is in unusually good condition because it has been protected by glass for two centuries. It is signed 'N. Hill' in a cartouche of classical figures. This was Nathaniel Hill, who was a well-known land surveyor, mathematical instrument maker and globe maker and who is known to have worked in Chancery Lane between 1745 and 1765.[111] He must still have been working when this clock was made, unless his successors had some of his old gores in stock. The globe is not one of the standard sizes quoted on his trade card.[112] Whitehurst had presumably asked Ferguson to order a globe of about 6.5 inches diameter but Hill had no gores to fit this size. Its diameter is 5.6 inches, wanting '7/8 inches'.

So much for the construction of the clock. Boulton offered it for sale alongside the sidereal clock, which was finished just in time, at Christie's in April 1772. He was hoping it would fetch £180[113] but, like the sidereal clock, it remained unsold. Both clocks were taken back to Birmingham. This failure must have been a bitter disappointment, judging from Boulton's earlier enthusiasm. In a letter written from London to his wife he conveyed his feelings about the frivolity of the rich:

I find philosophy at a very low ebb in London and therefore I have bought back my two fine clocks which I will send to a markett where common sense is not out of fashion. If I had made the clocks play jiggs upon bells and a dancing bear keeping time, or if I had made a horse race upon the faces I believe they would have had better bidders. I therefore shall bring them back to Soho and some time this summer send them to the Empress of Russia who I believe would be glad of them. Everything else went tolerable yet nevertheless I am determined never to undergo such hurrys hereafter but will find another means of selling them.[114]

The Empress's purchase of the ornaments which had been sent to St Petersburg in 1771 and Lord Cathcart's enquiry about the prices of the three clocks of which Boulton had sent him a description[115] clearly gave Boulton some confidence in the sale of his fine clocks to her.[116]

He had every reason to believe that she would be interested. The clock was one of his two grandest products, fit for an Empress. The case, like the case of the sidereal clock, is an outstanding example of the best work carried out in ormolu at Soho. The gilding is rich, the chasing of higher quality than on many ornaments, and the modelling better. The superiority of the modelling is doubtless due to the acquisition of the models from Chambers and Flaxman. The contrasts between matt and burnished surfaces are typical of Boulton and Fothergill's best work. The use of tortoiseshell veneers on the wooden base adds a touch of colour to the totally gilt case. The inclusion, as the main feature of the clock case, of figures derived from the Italian *cinquecento* in a design intended to appeal to the fashionable antique taste may seem quixotic, but it accorded with eighteenth-century ideas of invention and gives the clock an appealing grandeur. Mixing styles never worried Boulton.

The geographical clock was not sent to Russia. It was delayed initially because Boulton thought it could be improved by the addition of a seconds' hand.[117] John Scale accordingly wrote to Whitehurst to ask if he could add one.[118] Whitehurst replied that it could be done on the back of the clock but that he would prefer not to do it if Boulton could do without.[119] This reply probably explains why, although the annual, hour and minute motions are complete, there are some curious holes in the back plate and why the rear end of the escape wheel arbor is squared and pierced. It would not be difficult, since the pendulum has a half-second swing, to fit a seconds' dial to the back plate and the escape wheel arbor would be altered in exactly the way it has been in order to do this. It looks as if Boulton insisted on the change but that the work was later removed because it is pointless to have a dial where it cannot be seen.

There are two further references to this clock in Boulton and Fothergill's correspondence. The firm wrote to Whitehurst in June 1772 and said in a postscript: 'The recollouring of the g'c clock case will some — — [?] besides the risks attending it and we imagine it cannot be so bad as to require it'.[120] Perhaps Whitehurst thought the gilding had suffered during his alterations. Two years later Fothergill wrote to his partner suggesting that James Watt's coming visit to Russia would be 'a fine opportunity of introducing the two clocks there',[121] but in the event the sidereal clock went alone.

I do not know who eventually bought this remarkable clock from Boulton. Until 1967 it was owned by the Philips family at Tean, near Stoke-on-Trent. Since the family was living at Tean in the 1770s it may well have been sold to either John Philips (1695–1777) or his son of the same name (1724–1813).[122] The Philips family were textile manufacturers, trading under the names of John and Nathaniel Philips and became Boulton and Watt's customers when they wanted to equip their mill at Tean with steam power.[123]

King's clock case

The King's clock case (Plate 160) provides a useful insight into some of Boulton's business methods, and particularly into his habit of unashamedly copying designs executed for one patron, even a Royal one, in his subsequent work for others.

There is unfortunately no record of the original order for the clock case. It does not appear to have been discussed during Boulton's visit to the Palace at the end of February 1770. Possibly he discussed it on the following Monday morning with William Chambers, but there is no evidence. Chambers had invited him to breakfast[124] and on the previous evening Boulton wrote to his partner, John Fothergill, who was looking after the factory at Soho during his absence, that in the morning he would receive from Chambers 'the King's design which I will send down'.[125] This tantalising remark remains unexplained in the archives. The design may

have been nothing more than 'a sketch of the King's for a better foot' for Boulton and Fothergill's '4-branched vase' (see Chapter 3, p. 79). But it is conceivable that it was a design for the clock case and that Chambers's reason for inviting Boulton to breakfast was to explain it and deliver it to him.

After breakfast with the King's architect Boulton waited at about noon on the Duke of Northumberland and stayed until three o'clock, after which he dined with Mr Wright, presumably Thomas Wright the King's Clockmaker,[126] who gave him some orders and some models.[127] But if he received a design for the clock case in the morning and if he knew that Wright was to make the clock he did not mention either fact to his wife in his account of his day's work. In spite of this, the suggestion that Chambers might have handed Boulton a design for the clock case on that morning is not improbable. The correspondence in the Boulton archives reveals that Chambers undoubtedly designed the clock case and that the craftsmen at Soho worked from his drawing during its manufacture. The letters also reveal that work on the clock case was substantially completed ten months after Boulton's breakfast with him. In January 1771, one of Boulton's clerks wrote to Thomas Wright, who was to supply the movement of the clock:

OPPOSITE:
160. King's clock case, 18.8 in., Royal Collection, Windsor Castle.

> On Monday morning our agent Mr Matthews will hand you the clock case for his Majesty (without the ornamental parts which did not think necessary to send now) and beg you will fit the clock to it as soon as you possibly can and then return it down to us by first coach after he receives it, and we shall then immediately gild and finish it and send it by the coach ... All the ornaments are compleatly finished except the gilding, so that the whole will be attended with no delay after we receive the case back from you. We hope you will be able to do it and return it to Matthews on Monday or Tuesday at longest, however beg you will use all the expedition in your power ... We hope you have made the clock of such a size as will fit the case, all that we can say or know about the matter is that we have conformed to a hair breadth to Mr Chambers drawing.[128]

On the same day a letter was sent to William Matthews, asking him to make sure that Wright finished the work as quickly as possible and explaining that if his clock did not fit the case it was not Boulton and Fothergill's fault: they had 'made it accurately to Mr Chambers's drawing'.[129]

Chambers's working drawing has not survived. There is a pencil drawing attributed to Chambers, which may or may not be a preliminary sketch for the clock case (Plate 36). I have discussed this sketch in Chapter 3 in the context of Chambers's influence on Boulton's ornaments (see pp. 79–80). It shares with the final design of the King's clock case the plan of a square clock case with rams' heads and swags and an urn on the top, but not much else. I have also discussed the final design in Chapter 3 and shown how features of it, including particularly the rams' heads and swags, the ewers with their handles in the form of fishes biting the rims, the urns on the top with their spiral flutes, Greek fret decoration and two rings, and the engraved door at the back (Plate 161), are mirrored elsewhere in other work by Chambers and appear to owe a lot to drawings which he made in Italy and France (Plates 37–8, see p. 80).

It was a vain hope that Wright would fit the movement of the clock to the case during the day on which Matthews was to take the case to him, or even by the following day. The movement did not fit, a feared possibility that can be read into Boulton and Fothergill's letters to both Wright and Matthews, in which they firmly exonerated themselves from any blame in advance. Because his movement did not fit, Wright returned the case to Matthews, who promptly sent it back to Soho. A month later it was on its way back to London,[130] with a request to Matthews to take it to Wright together with a letter which explained the alterations:

Along with this Mr Matthews will hand you the King's clock case, altered as far as we could according to your instructions communicated to us through his (Mr Matthews's) hands vizt.
1st. The inside of the rim in the front is now made widest and a rabbet is made for the plate on which the dyal is fixed, to fall against.
2nd. It cannot be altred for the glass to go in on the inside ... nor do we think it necessary, as it may be put in as well as it is and if you don't chose to do it please send the glass to us and we will put it in.
3rd. The extremity of the rim in the front is made exactly according to Mr Chambers's directions and could not be otherwise as there are thick festoons to lie upon it which could not lie properly upon such a circle, as the clock we had from you has and we dare say Mr Chambers will be satisfyed with it as it is.
4th. The spring [*sc.* the spring catch of the door] is altred according to your desire.
5th. The door behind is now pierced but this we could not well think of before, as we did not know it was to be a musical clock.
6th. We have made a metal plate for the clock to stand upon with feet etc. according to your directions and which you may fit at any height you please. These alterations we doubt not will be satisfactory, and beg you will fit the clock to the case as soon as possibly and return it to Mr Matthews who will pack and return it to us, by the coach, to be gilt and finished ...[131]

OPPOSITE:
161. King's clock case, rear, Royal Collection, Windsor Castle.

The alterations, as this letter shows, were quite extensive and mostly concerned the door at the front. It is not clear whether the door at the back (Plate 161) was engraved with its floral motifs and griffins in the first place or whether this was done subsequently at the same time as the piercing. The last alteration, the addition of an internal plate supported by four rounded 'feet' for the movement to stand on, demonstrates again the lack of liaison between the two workshops at the design stage.

If Boulton again hoped to have the case, with the movement finally fitted, back at Soho within a few days, so that it could be gilt and decked with its ornaments, he was again to be disappointed. A fortnight later Matthews was again requested to tell Wright that the case was needed immediately.[132] At the beginning of March 1771, Matthews wrote to say that he had 'again applyed to Mr Wright about the clock case' who told him that it would be the latter end of the week before it could be returned and that the alteration of the glass was 'very material'.[133] Even this promise proved optimistic and ten days later Matthews received a letter from Soho, which expressed Boulton's frustration:

Oh the clock case the clock case the clock case ... Mr Boulton says he shall certainly think some trick is playing against him if he does not receive it soon for it was impossible that Mr Wright could have more than an hour or 2s work at it, and that if it is not sent off he begs you would go to W——— and take it away done or not done ...[134]

A few days later Matthews heard again from Soho: 'Mr Boulton thinks Wright uses him d———d shabily'[135] and he wrote on the same day to say that the case was still delayed.[136]

It appears that the case eventually reached Soho on 26th March 1771,[137] when presumably the gilding was quickly put in hand and the ornaments fitted. At the beginning of April it was taken back to London and Boulton planned to take it himself to Richmond where his partner hoped to hear that he 'met a most gracious reception'.[138] It is difficult to believe that the King and Queen were anything but delighted with the clock when it was finally delivered. The ornaments reflect their chosen architect's familiar interpretation of the antique taste. The variegated panels of blue john, on the front and both sides, and the blue john of the pedestal beneath the ringed urn, make a luxurious background for the rich gilding. The chasing of the ornaments, with the contrast between matt and burnished surfaces, matches the finest work produced at Soho.

The month movement is not exceptional and has been substantially altered, probably by B. L. Vulliamy (1780–1854), who held the appointment of clockmaker to the royal household. The pendulum is characteristic of his work, and no doubt he thought that the pin-wheel escapement was a fashionable improvement on the previous verge. At a later date the bells and the striking work on the front plate have been removed, perhaps when the clock was being cleaned or repaired, and not replaced.

The clock is now at Windsor Castle.[139] George IV may have taken it to Carlton House, and it was in Buckingham House in 1817.[140] It is illustrated in George IV's 'Pictorial Inventory of Clocks etc.', a list of objects drawn up, probably by B. L. Vulliamy, in about 1827. This inventory consists mainly of clocks and candelabra and is thought to depict objects from Carlton House awaiting decisions on where they were to go. According to an annotation the clock was then in the 'room next to the throne room, St James Palace'. Further annotations say that the 'clock was made by Wright of the Poultry for his late Majesty' and that it was sent by Vulliamy to Windsor Castle on 26th January 1829.[141] Boulton's guiding role in the making of the clock was not mentioned by the compiler of the inventory. At Windsor it is the centrepiece, between the pairs of King's vases (Plate 339) and sphinx vases (Plate 355), of the *garniture de cheminée* in the Queen's private sitting room.

So, after many anxious delays, the King received his clock case, which would probably have been the end of the story if the manufacturer had been anyone else. Boulton, however, immediately thought of capitalising on the fact that his ormolu work had attracted the patronage of the first family of the land. He was well enough versed in the arts of puffery to know the significance of his success and how it might be used. His friends and rivals no doubt expected some loud boasts, aimed at potential customers among the aristocracy.

He did more than boast. He had the nerve to make an identical clock case at the same time, which he planned to put into his sale at Christie's in the spring of 1771. He asked leave of neither the King nor William Chambers. In a letter to Thomas Wright in January, Boulton's clerk wrote:

> As we are making another exactly of the same sort and dimensions for ourselves to be sold at our next auction in March next if you have another clock of the same sort beg you will fit that also to the case [i.e. the King's clock case] and save it for us.[142]

The case for this second clock was sent to Matthews in the middle of February,[143] and Wright was requested 'not to disappoint us in the clock to it which must be in the case by Lady day, and we also desire you will put your name on the dial face ...'[144] As the date of the auction drew closer Wright's delays became exasperating.[145]

No clock case of Chambers's design appeared in the catalogue of the sale in 1771. Perhaps Wright failed to deliver the movement in time, but it is more likely that Boulton thought better of his plan at the last minute, having listened to the advice of William Matthews:

> [Wright] also says that Mr Collinson who you know and with whom he hath consulted thinks your having a clock to sell at an auction of the same pattern with his Majesty's will be an affront to his Majesty as he should have given you his permission before you had copyed his drawing – this I own strikes me, as every man in common life is emulous to avver and establish himself author of what meets the approbation of the judicious, and to have it before publication as it greatly enhances its value. I therefore do think 'tis absolutely necessary to pay the King the compliment of asking leave to copy his design. I don't by this mean to impede finishing of your labours.

162–3. King's clock case, 18.8 in., Courtauld Institute Gallery.

> Contrary will expedite it as I possibly can. Yet I think by only shewing that intended for the King you may procure more orders, by which you may gain more, than if you raised one at an auction to half as much more than what you rate it; for should you receive orders for 50 everyone will think he hath the second of the sort ever made and that he was the first after his Majesty who was possessed of one – which idea an auction will set aside.[146]

Whether Boulton was persuaded by the caution that he should have asked permission to copy the design or by the remarks about those fifty potential customers we shall never know. But he refrained from auctioning the second clock in 1771. It was probably the 'King's clock-case' which was put up for auction at Christie's a year later and which remained unsold.[147]

Unfortunately Matthews's opinion proved wrong and no further orders for clock cases of the same pattern materialised. Perhaps, like most of Boulton's ormolu products, they were too expensive, for Fothergill expected even the King to baulk at the price.[148] Even so, Boulton had others made. In the firm's last sale at Christie and Ansell's in 1778 there was 'an elegant eight-day clock with chimes and quarters, the case of which is executed in ormolu and tortoise-shell, from a design of Sir William Chambers', which also remained unsold.[149] Three 'King's clock cases imperfect' and one 'clock case with clock, King's pattern' were listed in the Inventory taken at Soho in June 1782.[150]

I do not know how many of these clocks have survived, but one of them is illustrated in Plate 162. The chasing and gilding of this clock case rival the quality of that made for the King. The two cases, apart from a few obvious differences, which include the treatment of the sides (Plate 163) and the height of the feet, are practically identical. There are differences of detail in the chasing of the mounts – for example the rams' heads and the buds on the festoons beneath the dials – but most of the decorative components were clearly cast in the same moulds. The most striking difference between the

164. King's clock case of Plate 162, detail.

two cases is the use of blue john panels in one, and of blue and gold painted glass in the other. If Boulton ever intended to fit blue john panels to the second case it is likely that he rejected the idea because he could not obtain pieces of stone of the right dimensions or colour. The fine fawn-coloured piece of blue john on the top (Plate 164) was neither so large nor of such a difficult shape as the panels. But probably he never intended to fit blue john panels in the first place. The splendid pierced and chased side panels (Plate 163) have an air of planning about them, and we know from the description of the clock case which was put up for sale in 1778, that not all the cases of this design were fitted with blue john.

The movement of this clock presents a mystery. It is a simple, eight-day striking movement, scarcely in keeping with the fine garb in which it is dressed, and the 'signature' on the back plate is wrong, for two reasons. First, the name should presumably be 'John Whitehurst, Derby' and not 'John Whitehouse, Derby'. Second, the movement was not made by John Whitehurst's workshop at all. It has none of the features and none of the quality of his usual work. Yet it is a genuine enough movement and, since it has the marks of cleaners and repairers dating from 1796 and probably 1792,[151] there is little doubt that it has been in the case since its manufacture. I can only suggest one explanation. There is evidence in the archives to suggest that on occasion John Whitehurst arranged for clocks and watches to be supplied by workshops in London.[152] It is thus possible that Whitehurst was responsible for ordering the movement of this clock and that either he or someone at Soho instructed the engraver to inscribe his name on the back plate. There was nothing unusual in selling another clock-maker's clock as one's own and there are many extant clocks and scientific instruments on which the engraver has spelt the name of the 'maker' wrongly. Instructions given by word of mouth can easily be mistaken, and 'Whitehurst' and 'Whitehouse' sound very much the same. In Birmingham at any rate the latter was a common enough name.[153] Boulton himself confused the two names in 1765,[154] as did his clerk in 1778.[155]

The fact that there is no signature on the front of the dial supports the suggestion that the movement was bought separately. The dial was enamelled by Weston of Quakers' Buildings, Smithfield, whose signature is on the back of it. If the clockmaker had commissioned Weston to make the dial he would presumably have asked him to put his name on the front; it was rare for a clockmaker not to 'sign' his clocks conspicuously. It looks, therefore, as if the dial and movement were ordered separately and that, as with the dials of the geographical and sidereal clocks, which he also made, Weston was given no instructions about a 'signature'. The movement probably came from the workshop of Eardley Norton (fl.1760–94), a well-known clock- and watchmaker who worked at 49 St John Street, Clerkenwell. It matches identically another recorded movement, which is fitted in a lacquered wooden case and signed 'Yeld Notron'.[156] This mysterious signature is, in the words of F. J. Britten who recorded a bracket clock in Holland signed 'Yeldaye Notron', a 'curious jumble of Eardley Norton'.[157]

When this King's clock came to light in the early 1770s it had been owned for several years by a dealer who claimed that it came from Moccas Court, Hereford, which was built for Sir George Cornewall in 1776–83.[158] Cornewall knew Boulton and had some correspondence with him about a steam pumping engine and the state of the coinage in the 1780s.[159] He inherited the baronetcy from his father, the merchant and banker Sir George Amyand, in 1766, and assumed the name of Cornewall on his marriage in 1771 to Catherine Cornewall, the heiress to Moccas. Since the movement appears to have been supplied by Eardley Norton, the clock can safely be identified with the one mentioned in a letter from Boulton and Fothergill to William Matthews in April 1772: 'Shall also debit your account for the clock and case for Mr Amyand as agreed for £48 6s. 0d. Don't forget to see after the clock too [?]. It's from Mr Yardley Norton.'[160] A few weeks later it needed some alterations or repairs, probably because the movement had not been fitted earlier, and Matthews was asked to send it to Soho but to have a glass made in London.[161]

The exact identity of the 'Mr Amyand' mentioned in these letters is uncertain. One possibility is that Sir George was wrongly identified as 'Mr' in the Soho records and ordered the clock before he changed his name in 1771, but Boulton's clerks were not inclined to disregard titles, and for him to be still described as 'Mr Amyand' in April 1772 seems unlikely. Sir George Cornewall's uncle, Claudius Amyand (1718–74), and his brother John Amyand (1751–80), both died without any children. Either of these men might have bought the clock and left it to Sir George, or might have acted as his agent in London in respect of the purchase.[162]

Minerva

The Minerva clock case was one of Boulton and Fothergill's earliest allegorical clock cases. There was a Minerva in the sale at Christie's in 1771. The description in the catalogue was:

> A very correct repeating eight day clock, the case of which is an allegorical piece of sculpture in or moulu; representing Minerva, who with her right hand unveils a vestive vase, with her left she notes the flying moments; and on the vase is seen an oval medalian, Prudence making libations at the shrine of Time; on the other side is a boy seated on books, contemplating the following lines from Gay,
>
> 'Tis I who measure vital space,
> And deal out years to human race;
> By me all useful arts are gain'd,
> Wealth, learning, wisdom is attain'd:

In ev'ry view men ought to mind me,
For when once lost they never find me!
He spoke; the gods no more contest,
And his superior gift confest,
That Time (when truly understood)
Is the most precious earthly good.

The reserve price placed on this conceit was £150 and it was the last lot to be offered on the second day.[163] It was sold for £173 5s. 0d.[164]

A second clock was made towards the end of 1771. According to the description that Boulton sent to Lord Cathcart in St Petersburg, along with descriptions of the geographical and sidereal clocks, this second clock was the same as the first one except that the boy had less to read:

> An 8 day repeating clock with an alegorical case representing Minerva pointing to the dial with one hand and with the other she is unveiling a votive vase on which is enchased upon an oval medallion a representation of prudence making a libation at the shrine of time whilst a boy on the other side seems reading the following inscription (which is engrav'd upon a scroll he holds in his hand) Breve et irreparabile tempus Omnibus est vita[e]; sed famam extendere factis Hoc virtutis opus: all gilt in or moulu.[165]

The second clock was probably offered for sale at Christie's in 1772. It remained unsold[166] and there is no further trace of it in the archives. Boulton thought of sending it to Russia[167] but there is no evidence that it went. It might have remained in stock and been sent to Christie and Ansell's in 1778 in another attempt to sell it (the Minerva in the 1778 sale had the same inscription from Virgil).[168] This clock too remained unsold, in spite of a reserve price of only £36.[169]

The 1782 Inventory shows that there was still a Minerva in stock four years later. This was described as a 'Minerva with clock (and marble) ready to gild £9 9s 0d'.[170] Thus at least three and perhaps four clock cases of this design were made.

A drawing of a Minerva clock survives in the first pattern book (Plate 165). The drawing is very indistinct in parts and has been partly obscured by smudges and careless trimming. It shows Minerva unveiling the urn with her right hand, as described in Boulton's text and in the sale catalogue. She wears her aegis[171] – the mask of the Medusa is just visible in the sketch – and holds a spear, pointing downwards, also in her right hand. Her owl perches on the pedestal beneath the urn. The boy sits on books on the other side of the pedestal and holds a scroll. The clock face mounted in the pedestal is square and there is a faint outline of a chapter ring within it. The pedestal sits on a two-stepped base, which is supported by ball feet and decorated underneath with an acanthus mount. An alternative third step to the base is pencilled in lightly in place of the ball feet. The clock stands on a large lower pedestal, which, with its pitchers, rams' heads and tapered legs, is clearly modelled on William Chambers's designs for the King's clock case (Plate 160). Presumably this version of the Minerva clock was intended to be a pendulum clock, the pendulum and possibly even some of the mechanism being housed in the lower case. No examples of a Minerva clock with this lower case have yet come to light and it is possible that none were made. None of the written descriptions mentions it. Moreover, the design seems sufficient without it, but this may be because the drawing is not to scale. The drawing is numbered 767.

165. Pattern Book 1, p. 76.

Plates 166 and 169 show two of the known examples of Minerva clock cases. Both answer closely to the written descriptions. In the ormolu clock

166. Minerva clock case, 18.5 in., Christie's.

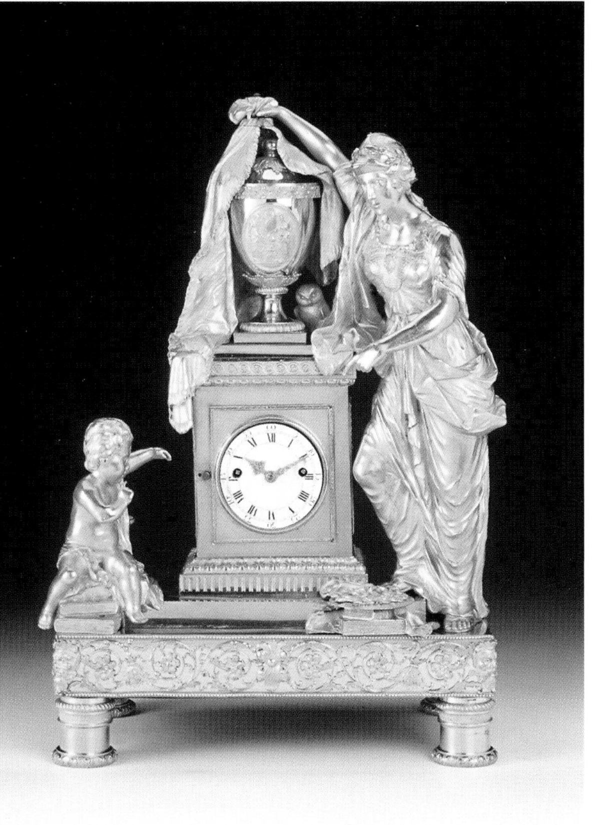

167. Minerva clock case of Plate 166, detail.

168. Minerva clock case of Plate 166, detail.

169. Minerva clock case, 18.5 in., Mallett.

case illustrated in Plates 166–8,[172] Minerva is shown in the pose described, unveiling the urn on which is the plaque of Prudence making her libation to Time. Minerva wears classical drapery, a helmet crowned with a laurel wreath (for she is also the goddess of War) and her aegis, looking like a somewhat skimpy breastplate, which is decorated with a Medusa mask (Plate 167). Her helmet has lost its crest. Also missing is the spear, shown in the drawing in her right hand. The conduit for it can be seen in Plate 167 above her thumb. Peeping out from between her and the urn is her owl, symbolic of wisdom and learning. At her feet are ranged objects related to her attributes – her shield, bearing a mask of Medusa, more laurel, a book and a scroll. The boy sits on further books and holds the scroll, which is now missing but which was engraved with the lines on Time by Gay,[173] in his outstretched left hand. Two further urns are mounted at the rear of the base (Plate 168). The sides of the pedestal have pierced panels with a scrolling ornament (Plate 168). The base is decorated with a delicate scrolling frieze and grotesque heads at the corners.

Many of the ornaments and friezes appear on other vases and clock cases. Particularly, the two ormolu urns mounted on the base are identical to the urn on the wreathed-column candlestick (Plates 140–1). The whole of the pedestal beneath the 'votive vase', with its squared door for the clock face reminiscent of the sketch (Plate 165), its pierced side frets, its decorative borders and mouldings from the guilloche frieze at the top down to the fluted decoration at its base, is echoed in the boy clock (Plate 152), as are the boy himself and his books and scroll. The measurements of these mounts indicate that they were cast from the same moulds.

Not all of this clock case came from Boulton and Fothergill's factory. At some point, probably in the 1780s, the clockmaker Benjamin Vulliamy fitted the present movement to the case. At the same time his workshop fitted a new bezel to the dial. The movement is of a type often commissioned by Vulliamy, with two trains and a half dead-beat angled escapement. The brass pendulum bob, chamfered ebony rod, enamelled dial and pierced gilt hands are also typical of Vulliamy's clocks, as is the back plate which is engraved with floral motifs, including a basket of flowers, and is signed 'Vulliamy London'. Vulliamy also, presumably, added the cylindrical ormolu feet, which bear no relation to any other product from Soho.

It is not impossible that this clock started life in the form of the drawing in the pattern book (Plate 165). The squared door reflects the drawing and the addition of the new feet suggests that there may originally have been something else under the clock. The high reserve price of £150 in the 1771 sale could even provoke the thought that this clock might have been the one in the sale and subsequently lost its large pedestal either before Vulliamy modified it or during his modifications. But this is speculation. It is equally possible that it originally had no feet. It is a pity that no record of its repair in the Vulliamy workshop seems to have survived.

170. Minerva clock case of Plate 169, detail.

Plate 169 illustrates another version of the Minerva clock case, closely similar but combining white marble and ormolu.[174] The use of marble suggests that it is a later version than the clock of Plate 166. Minerva's helmet has its crest, and she holds a spear (the wrong way up), which has been replaced, in her right hand. The boy's scroll is inscribed with Virgil's lines (Plate 170). Plates 171 and 172 show the shield with its gorgon head at Minerva's feet and the medallion on the urn. The mounts, including the frieze round the base, are identical to those on the clock case in Plate 166, except for the bezel, the spandrels flanking it on the face of the pedestal, and the feet. These feet, which look French, along with the French movement, dial and bezel, suggest that this clock case was exported by Boulton and Fothergill to France.

The sources of Boulton's design for the Minerva clock case are

171–2. Minerva clock case of Plate 169, detail.

uncertain. The modelling of the figures is not up to the standard of the best French *bronziers* and it seems likely that they were modelled at Soho, perhaps by Francis Eginton. The whole ensemble has a French feeling about it. It is likely that the modeller adopted the conceit of a female figure pointing the time and a boy (often winged in French designs) representing the genius of learning or time from French models (see Chapter 3, p. 68). The origin of the medallion representing Prudence at the shrine of Time has not yet been identified.

Narcissus

Plate 173[175] shows Narcissus gazing at his reflection, with which he had fallen in love, in a pool. The story of Narcissus, who pined away for love of his own beauty, died and was turned into a flower, was a favourite with classical authors and artists. It fitted well as one of Boulton's allegorical themes, reminding us about the futility of human vanity and the transience of human beauty. The overall design of the ornament is similar to other allegorical designs, including Belisarius, Titus and Venus (Plates 151, 186, 192). The figures of Narcissus and his dog are gilt. They stand on a bronzed base chased with rocks and vegetation. The pool is made of silver plate. The three pieces of stone making up the pedestal and obelisk are white marble. The mounts on the pedestal and obelisk, including the swags of drapery pinned to the three sides of the pedestal, are familiar from other ornaments. The clock case is constructed in the usual way, with a central threaded rod and the mounts between the stones flanged to support them (Plate 121). The medallion pinned to the obelisk depicts a variant of Hygieia or

173. Narcissus clock case, 16.5 in., Birmingham Museum and Art Gallery, Soho House.

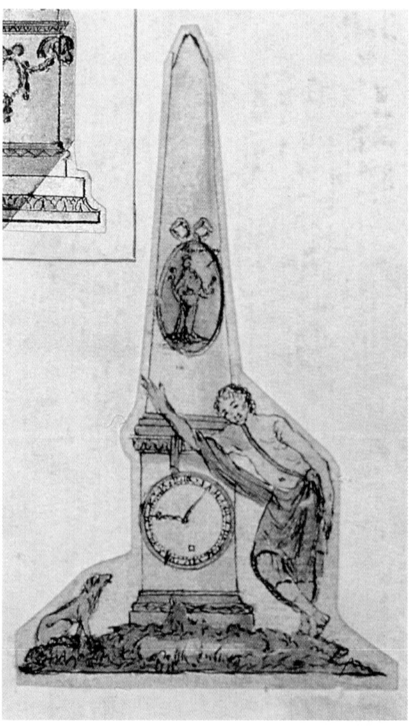

174. Pattern Book 1, p. 77.

Peace, holding what may be a branch or a firebrand but looks like a rough modification of the snake in her left hand (see Chapter 3, p. 112). The watch movement is fitted with an enamelled dial and gilt hands. The bezel is decorated with blue glass beads backed by silver foil, showing that the clock was intended for export (see Chapter 5, p. 180).

The ornament accords closely with a sketch in the pattern book (Plate 174). The treatment of the grass round the pool in the sketch is more naturalistic, and the dog stands at a different angle, but these differences are insignificant. Someone has written 'Clemency' across the top of the medallion on the obelisk. Whoever did this was clearly ignorant of the image and its origins. If the error was contemporary with the drawing, it supports my suggestion that neither Boulton nor his modellers paid much attention to the subjects depicted on many of the medallions that they fitted to their ornaments, and may even not have known what they were (see Chapter 3, p. 116).

A second Narcissus clock case is illustrated in Plate 175.[176] This has a marble base, which is fringed with a chased ormolu border attached to it by two flanges, and is more akin to other allegorical ornaments (Plates 151, 192). The forest floor is gilt rather than bronzed and has shrunk to something more akin to a suburban garden pool surround. The bezel has no beads. The obelisk, which has been renewed, is decorated with a medallion of Ceres or Plenty, another medallion that appears on earlier ornaments (see Chapter 3, p. 106). As with Hygieia, there is no obvious connection with the tale of Narcissus. The case is fitted with a later watch movement in a copper cylinder.

No mention of a Narcissus ornament appears in the surviving archives

175. Narcissus clock case, 17.2 in., Leeds City Art Gallery, Temple Newsam.

until 1778. There were two in the sale at Christie and Ansell's in that year. The first was described as 'Narcissus in bronze, admiring himself in a fountain, the vase and plinth of statuary marble decorated with or moulu'; and the second as 'Narcissus admiring himself in a fountain, in bronze, and statuary marble, perforated for essences'.[177] Both were reserved at £11 and neither was sold. Both entries suggest that the figure of Narcissus was bronzed and not gilt. Both ornaments had vases and not obelisks. Neither is described as a clock case, and one of them was described as a perfume burner. There are only two mentions of a Narcissus serving as a clock case in the archives. The first appears in Boulton and Fothergill's Day Book in 1781, when the ormolu trade was in decline. The entry records the sale of 'an or moulu figure of Narcissus, bronzed rock, marble and or moulu ornaments with clock in the pedestal'.[178] The price was £19 19s. 0d., but whether the buyer got a vase or an obelisk for his money is not recorded. The second is in the 1782 Inventory which records, among the finished stock, '1 or moulu obelisk of Narcissus with clock'.[179] It was valued at £20. Also in the Inventory, among the unfinished work there were:

	s	d
1 pedestal for Narcissus vase	4	
1 plinth for ditto ditto 8 by 5 ins	9	
1 Narcissus figure	7	6
Chasing on ditto 4½ days	15	9[180]

Like the ornaments sold in 1778, this was clearly a vase and not an obelisk.

Sidereal clock

Early in 1771 Boulton was turning over in his mind the idea of making a companion clock to the geographical clock (Plate 155). This second clock would show the movement of the sun against a celestial globe. He wrote to John Whitehurst in February, giving him directions for the making of the movement of the geographical clock, and added:

> I think I shall make another with a celestial globe on the top and turned by a clock to show the sun's place and what stars are upon the meridian. I —— [?] golden statue of Astronomy in a proper attitude on one side and a boy on the other with a roll on which is engraved a solar system and the motto, chose by the doctor,[181] engraved on a proper place 'The stars shall fade away, the sun himself grown dim with age: Nature sinks in years'. Do turn the mechanism over in your mind ...[182]

This design, related in part to the boy clock case (Plate 152), came to nothing, but Boulton's idea of a sidereal clock lingered and in August, when work on the geographical clock was proceeding, his clerk wrote to Whitehurst:

> We shall want another exceeding good clock something like the drawing Mr Ferguson gave you but with a sidereal face in the middle but believe Mr Boulton will pay you a visit in a week or two and then will give you more particular directions.[183]

No further mention of this sidereal clock appears in the archives, but by the autumn of 1771 its design was settled and a full description was sent to Lord Cathcart in St Petersburg, along with descriptions of the geographical and Minerva clocks:

> A table clock 3 feet 8 inches high. The case of it is a pedestal gilt in or moulu and decorated with a bas relief of Science explaining the laws of nature by the globe and solar system with this motto '*Felix rerum cognoscere causas*'[184] and other antique ornaments suitable to the subject, upon which pedestal is agreeably raised a circular case for the clock the front of which is environed with the 12 signs of the Zodiack

gilt fixed upon a ground of azure enamel.[185] On the top of the circle is a large and fine figure of Urania crowned with stars and resting upon a celestial globe. It has a standard pendulum of 39.2 inches – prepared in such a manner as not to contract by cold or expand by heat. The hour circle is of enamel. It is divided in 24 hours and minutes within which is a plate that compleats the face of the clock and makes a revolution in a syderial day by the means of which is shewn the month, the day of the month, the rising, southing, and setting of the sun in the latitude of London and consequently of any other place not further south. The stars are gilt of gold upon a ground of blue.[186] This clock also shews the lengthening and shortening of the days and the suns place in the ecliptic. Attention has not only been given to the ornaments and to the variety of astronomical phenomina pointed out, but also very particularly to the simplicity of the mechanism, for the whole is accomplished by so easy means that the parts of the clock are not multiplied, nay it has fewer wheels than a common 8 day clock. The only extra work in the mechanism is the addition of some of the inventions of Mr Harrison's longitudinal timekeeper[187] which are essential to the accurate performance of the clock.[188]

Further details of the star plate in the centre of the dial, and of the way in which it was manufactured, were given by Boulton in a letter to Whitehurst in December:

I mean to send to you a piece of copper plated with silver for the star plate which when you have hammered flatt and mounted upon its proper axis and stoned fine with fine pumice and then with charcoal so as to have a true surface, I will then beg the favour of Mr Ferguson to lay down the stars and circles truly upon it and you may engrave the names of some of the first rate stars contagious to them and then drill a small hole in the place of each star which will serve us to rivet our gilt stars, which stars we shall stamp to three sizes also grave the months and days. When you have thus prepared the plate please to send it to us and will polish it and throw over its surface a very thin coat of transparent sky blue varnish, and upon that put 2 or 3 coats of copal varnish which may be polished as flatt and as fine as a looking glass after which we can open the drill holes through and varnish and if any sticks in the grove of the ecliptick we can easily clear that away. By this means we shall have a beautiful star plate that I think will be a proper contrast to the hour circle as it will be only a transparent line upon the silver. If the star or hour plate was to be made white I think it would look much whiter and clearer being made of plated silver than if it was only silver ... The star plate might be made of thin metal provided you were to cut out the ecliptick and so by rivetting the two pieces upon another plate you have thereby a compleat groove – but I will send it about as thick as a crown piece and you may then turn the groove in it. The silver will be thick enough to stone with pumice if you hammer it flatt. Perhaps our hammers are finer than yours and therefore I will send it ready hammered.[189]

176. Sidereal clock on stand, Birmingham Museum and Art Gallery, Soho House.

This letter also informed Whitehurst of the despatch to him of the case for the geographical clock. The case for the sidereal clock followed two months later, when Whitehurst was asked to complete it as quickly as possible.[190] Boulton was afraid of not having the two clocks ready in time for the April sale. But, in fact, after delays with the dial[191] and plates, including the star plate,[192] a hitch with the signs of the zodiac which had to be rejected because they were too big for the dial,[193] and the last-minute fitting of the dial glass,[194] the sidereal clock was completed in time.

The completed clock (Plate 177) conforms fairly closely to these descriptions and instructions. There are no signs of the zodiac, and the star plate is silvered and not covered with a blue varnish as proposed in both manuscripts.[195] Nor is the chapter ring ('the hour circle') enamelled: it is silvered. The dial (Plate 178) is otherwise close to the description. The chapter ring is marked with twenty-four hours and sixty minutes, each minute having ten-second divisions. The silvered star plate, which revolves

OPPOSITE:
177. Sidereal clock, 41 in., Birmingham Museum and Art Gallery, Soho House.

178–80. Sidereal clock, details.

within the chapter ring, is engraved with the month, the day of the month, the names of the signs of the zodiac, a three hundred and sixty-degree scale, circles representing the Tropic of Capricorn, the Equator, the Tropic of Cancer and the Arctic Circle, and the names of the major stars and constellations. The stars are made in three sizes and are gilt. The line of the ecliptic is represented by a groove in the star plate. The gilt sun slides up and down the hour/date hand as a pin on its underside follows the groove, demonstrating the sun's position among the fixed stars. On the glass in front of the dial (Plate 179) an ellipse is drawn with black chalk.[196] This demonstrates the position of the fixed stars above the horizon at any moment to the reader of the dial. Originally drawn for London, the ellipse was redrawn for the latitude of St Petersburg, before the clock was sent there in 1776, in accordance with instructions sought from Ferguson, whose manuscript instructions for the alteration have survived.[197] The four points of the compass are noted on the glass by the letters E, S, W and N, a simplified version of Ferguson's suggestions,[198] the lines connecting them (South–North and East–West) crossing in the centre at the zenith of St Petersburg. Thus, in Ferguson's words, 'when the sun, or any star, is due east, south, west or north of Petersburg, it will appear so in the clock, under these lines; and the stars which pass vertically over that city will pass directly even with the zenith point on the glass'.[199]

The clock thus shows the minutes (by the larger of the two blued steel hands), the hours (by the smaller hand), the date (by the same smaller hand), the movement of the sun on the ecliptic, the time of sunset and sunrise (when the sun on the hour/date hand crosses the ellipse of the horizon), the 'movement' of the fixed stars in relation to St Petersburg, and the stars which should be visible at any time from St Petersburg. It does not show sidereal time. The star plate revolves three hundred and sixty-six times in each year,[200] while the hour hand revolves three hundred and sixty-five times in accordance with solar time. This comparison of sidereal and solar time, based on whole numbers and therefore on relatively simple gearing, is not an accurate indicator of the difference between the two times at any given moment. It gives only an idea of the position of the sun at any time against the background of stars. The movement is simple, as in the geographical clock. The duration is seven and a half days, there is no fusee, the escapement is dead-beat. The uncompensated pendulum is 27.18 inches long (not 39.2 inches as stated in the description sent to Lord Cathcart). There is no sign of any refinements on the lines of Harrison's timekeepers, mentioned in the same letter. It is all very close to the descriptions in the letters.

As in the case of the geographical clock, the influence of James Ferguson is apparent. Boulton's letters quoted above make it clear that he was involved with the design and the preparation of the star plate, and it was to Ferguson that Boulton turned when he wanted the horizon on the glass adapted for St Petersburg. But he was clearly involved with the design at an early stage. I have mentioned in connection with the geographical clock how Ferguson visited Derby in November–December 1771 during his lecture tour of the Midlands, and how he spent his 'vacant hours' with the 'good and ingenious Mr Whitehurst, clock and watch maker here, about schemes for astronomical clocks which he has orders to make according to my plans'. Ferguson's account continues:

> One of the clocks is to have a plate with all the stars visible in the horizon of London, to go round in a sidereal day, and a sun to go round in 24 solar hours, shifting his place daily in the ecliptic; and, together with the stars, rising and setting every day in the year, in a fixt horizon, at the time they rise and set in the heavens. – I have had the whole plan of this to draw out, and all the stars to lay down upon the plate, which you know cannot be soon done.[201]

Most of the design can therefore be attributed to Ferguson, although Whitehurst no doubt made modifications as the work proceeded.

The ormolu case answers closely to the references in the documents. The movement and dial are mounted in a copper drum, the sides of which are decorated with pierced and chased cast ornaments (Plate 179). There are glazed apertures on each side of the drum through which the movement can be seen. The back door of the drum (Plate 180), which like the bezel at the front screws off, is engraved with an elaborate flower-like star.[202] Urania, the muse of Astronomy, reclines on top of the drum, leaning her left arm on a celestial globe. The drum is supported by a case, which is decorated with classical ornament – 'other antique ornaments suitable to the subject'. Inset into the front of the case is the 'bas relief of Science explaining the Laws of Nature by the globe and solar system' (Plate 181), complete with the abbreviated line from Virgil's *Georgics*, '*Felix rerum cognoscere causas*', referring to the Epicurean poet and philosopher Lucretius. Many of the components of the case are illustrated in Plates 118–20. These illustrations show a number of the features of the construction of the case – the heavy metal internal frame set within the cast and chased rectangular mouldings at the base, some of the brackets concealed within the base (there are ten of the largest and four each of the others), the rolled copper sheet of the curved trunk and drum, the cast ornaments (Urania and the sphinxes cast by the *cire perdue* process), the economy in the gilding of the side panels, and the telltale gilding spills. The keen eye can detect the rich gilding preserved on the panels behind where the mounts are fitted, demonstrating some unfortunate past cleaning and 'conservation' of the gilded surfaces of most of the case. The very keen eye might detect in Plate 120 the notches (I–IIII) on the lower corners of the curved trunk which identify the positions of the four sphinxes and which were cut before the trunk was gilt.

The precise sources of many of the ornaments are not clear. I have so far not found the models for the two most prominent features – the figure of Urania and the plaque of Science explaining the Laws of Nature, although depictions of Science or Mathematics, with wings on her head and accompanied by a sphere and mathematical instruments and instructing youth, appear in sources that Boulton may have known.[203] Urania appears on many French clocks in a variety of reclining postures and, like other figures modelled at Soho, for example Venus and the boy on the Minerva clock case, may owe her origin to a French model. Alternatively she may, like other mounts, have been among the models that William Chambers gave to Boulton in 1770, which I discussed in Chapter 3 (see p. 79). When writing to Whitehurst to commission the geographical clock, Boulton said that he wanted to reuse the models used for the King's clock case (Plate 160), and he did so (Plate 155). The designs, and probably some of the models, came from Chambers (see pp. 79–80). For the sidereal clock he repeated again the rams' heads (without the ribbons), the cornice which they support and the swags beneath their chins, and the side panels (Plate 182) use the same diamond-pattern relief decoration used on the geographical clock. The likelihood is that Chambers was the major source of models for this clock. The six urns on the base pedestal and the four winged sphinxes have a strong flavour of Chambers's archaic classicism.

The sidereal clock was offered for sale, along with the geographical clock, at Christie's in 1772. Neither clock was sold. I have quoted Boulton's letter to his wife, expressing his disappointment, in the account of the geographical clock on p. 206. If he had made the clocks 'play jiggs upon bells or a dancing bear keeping time' or if he had made 'a horse race upon the faces', they might have sold. He would send the clocks to Russia where he hoped that their philosophical attractions would be better appreciated. He had probably been encouraged by the Empress Catherine's purchases

181–2. Sidereal clock, details.

of ornaments in 1771 and thought that she and her Court would be less frivolous than the English aristocracy. He reckoned that the sidereal clock should fetch £275.[204]

First, however, he took the clocks back to Soho and asked John Scale to suggest certain modifications to Whitehurst:

> Just at Mr Boulton's departure for London this morning he requested me to inform you that he found it a general objection (or rather remark by a many at the sale) to the 2 clocks their not having hands to shew minutes and seconds, and that he could never sell them both provided they shewed minutes and seconds but more particular the siderial, and without which we cannot sell them. He therefore desires you will consider their construction and try whether you cannot put hands to them.[205]

Whitehurst did not like the suggestion at all –

> I received Mr Scale's information concerning the clocks, which concerns me much. I can make a minute motion to the syderial clock; but it will make great alterations. Pray what do you think of showing minutes and seconds on the back side of the clock? Should that scheme be approved, I think it practical with much less alteration than the front where seconds are impracticable.[206]

– and he wanted Boulton to avoid having the alterations done at all if possible.

Although Boulton had sent a description of the clock to St Petersburg while it was being made, and thought immediately of the Empress after the sale,[207] he changed his mind for some reason, and the clock remained at Soho. Further attempts to sell it failed and a year later Fothergill, who was depressed by the state of the business following the bankruptcy of Fordyce, wrote to his partner:

> I despair of ever being able to dispose of the siderial clock at the price it ought to bring us. It is my wish and I do think it most advantageous for us to present it to

the Empress of Russia after it is properly finished and regulated for the latitude of St Petersburg. I am certain from her known noble disposition she will make us far greater amends[208] than any price we are likely ever to obtain from our own gambling nobility, but the point is to get it properly presented which must be done by the advice and means of Lord Cathcart for if it goes by the channel of a Russian of distinction it is odds but he presents it as from himself at our expence ...[209]

A few days later he wrote again to say that Dr Small entirely agreed with his suggestion.[210] A year later, in March 1774, when the clock was still in Whitehurst's workshop, Fothergill was still pursuing the idea and thought that James Watt's proposed visit to Russia would provide

a fine opportunity of introducing the [tw]o clocks there, also of explaining the different excelle[nce]s of the siderial one (of which I must request your application to Mr Whitehurst that we may obtain it without further delay) ...[211]

Eighteen months later the clock was still at Soho, when Mrs Yorke visited the manufactory and recorded in her diary that Boulton was 'making a clock for the Empress of Russia, which has more motions than I can remember. The ornaments which are very elegant are of the or moulu'.[212] Mrs Yorke can be forgiven for believing that the clock was being specially made. She was probably told so, and it was certainly true that it was being 'improved' for St Petersburg. The modifications during the four years after the sale in 1772 included the alterations necessary to add a minute hand, the re-drawing of the horizon on the glass to adapt it to the latitude of St Petersburg and the engraving of the backplate with the signature 'Boulton and Fothergill 1774'.[213] Whitehurst must have declined to fit a seconds mechanism.

The clock was finally sent to St Petersburg in the summer of 1776, part of the delay having been due presumably to the modifications which Whitehurst was carrying out: but the delay was extended by the loss of certain parts at Soho.[214] The clock was sent to 'ALQ', which appears to have been the code for William Porter, a merchant in St Petersburg. It was valued at £315.[215] It was sent not for presentation to the Empress but for sale, which proved a forlorn hope. William Porter wrote three years later:

I have now before me your esteemed favour of the 29th ultimo to which I am sorry I can not send you a more satisfactory reply. Your clock has been shewn at Court first to the Empress, afterwards to Prince Potempkin and accepted by neither though I asked only Rs2500. I left it standing in the palace for some time but finding no longer the least reason to hope for success I brought it home two days ago. They all praised it – it was very fine, an elegant piece of workmanship – but it did not strike the hours, nor play any tunes – how could a clock without such necessary requisites cost Rs2500? – from such remarks you will see the vanity of expecting to find a market in this place for anything but gewgaws and French baubles, and you have only to think of a proper place whither the time piece may be sent in the spring.[216]

So much for Boulton's idea that the Empress and her courtiers would appreciate philosophy more than the frivolous English aristocracy. Fothergill remained his usual gloomy self:

I don't know of any other method of disposing of the clock but by lottery or raffle if that species of gaming is permitted in Russia. For if we putt it up to auction I am fearfull we shall be great losers. It is too scientifical a machine for the genius of that country.[217]

A decision had still not been reached in 1781, when Porter was in London.[218] Eventually, Boulton asked him to return it but he delayed for another year because he was assured that the Academy of Arts and Sciences in St Petersburg would take it. But this hope too was dashed. In 1787, after eleven years in Russia, the clock returned to Soho, without its glass case because it was too damaged to be worth sending.[219]

Following its return to Soho, Boulton seems to have taken it to his own home, Soho House. Boulton's notebook in 1799 lists a 'blank sash behind the star clock' in a list of work for builders,[220] suggesting that the clock stood in a window recess. It stands today in Soho House, on a wooden pedestal painted in simulated porphyry with white painted ornamentation (Plate 176). This stand was not its original stand, and it was probably modified for the clock when it was taken to Soho House.[221] When Boulton's son, Matthew Robinson Boulton, bought the Tew Park estate in 1815, he moved the clock to Tew. At some time in the nineteenth century the stand was over-painted with a simulation of grained oak. This was presumably done to match either the oak furniture which M. R. Boulton commissioned from George Bullock, or, perhaps more likely, the similar oak furniture which was supplied by George Morant for the new Gothic library in the 1840s.[222]

Titus

It was apparently one of Boulton's patrons, Samuel Pechell, who suggested making an allegorical clock case depicting the Roman Emperor Titus. Boulton and Fothergill sent him four sketches for 'watch stands' at the end of 1771 and said in the accompanying letter:

> We think your idea of the emperour Titus is a very good one for the purpose and have sent you two designs of him. In the one he wears the long toga such as he represented in his triumphal arch (viz. Montfacon): the other he is in the chlamys and paludamentum which last we think distinguishes the emperor more than the other ... The likeness of the emperor we purpose copying from a deliniation of a gem in the Mideum collection which we have not attended to in the slight sketches sent you, for finished drawings require more time than the multiplicity of our business will allow nor are they necessary for one whose mind's eye supplies the deficiencies ...[223]

Blinded perhaps by this flattery to the deficiencies of the drawings, Pechell chose the sketch of Titus in the toga. Boulton and Fothergill advised him to have the enamelled dial made in London, because they had never made any themselves, and recommended 'Mr Weston, enameler in Quakers Buildings Smithfield'.[224] Weston was the supplier of the dials for the geographical, King's and sidereal clocks. Pechell was to provide the watch movement himself and he sent it to Soho in April 1772. In the event he left the provision of the dial to Boulton because he had to leave London for a month.[225] The clock case was sent to London in April 1772 but it had a small hole in the back of the figure near one of the shoulders,[226] which was perhaps the reason for its return to Soho two months later.[227] It was finally delivered, on Pechell's instructions, to General Cailland in September.[228] The price, which Pechell questioned, is not recorded, but Boulton and Fothergill claimed in support of their invoice that Pechell was paying only the prime cost and that they had sold many like it 'with a bronzed figure at £21 and with a gilt figure like yours at £25'.[229]

The sketches that were sent to Pechell have not survived, nor has it been possible to identify his clock case with any of the surviving examples, of which there are several. In each of them Titus is represented standing by a pedestal and wearing the toga and a laurel wreath. In some cases there is an urn on the pedestal. The words '*diem perdidi*', which the Emperor is supposed by tradition to have uttered when he had passed a day without doing good to anyone,[230] are engraved either on the pedestal (Plates 184, 185) or, if there is an urn, on a plaque on the urn (Plate 186).

Boulton and Fothergill's first letter to Samuel Pechell mentioned

183. Titus clock case, 14.3 in., English Heritage, Kenwood.

184. Titus clock case of Plate 183, detail.

185. Titus clock case, 15 in., Christie's.

that in one of the drawings (the one that Pechell later selected) Titus was wearing a long toga such as he wore 'in his triumphal arch', and cited 'Montfacon' as their authority. But the figure on the clock cases bears little relation to the representation of the Emperor, as carved on his triumphal arch, in Montfauçon's *L'Antiquité Expliquée* (Plate 58). It is clear from the letter to Pechell that Montfauçon was only being used as an authority for the choice of dress. I have shown in Chapter 3 (see p. 92) that the model for the figure was copied from a figure in A. F. Gori's *Museum Florentinum* (Plate 59).

It was not perhaps tactful of Boulton and Fothergill to inform Samuel Pechell in September 1772 that they had sold several Titus clocks. The idea was his in the first place, he had given them the first order and it was only completed after a considerable delay. It was, however, Boulton's constant practice to copy an object made for one patron, even if it was an exceptional commission, if he thought that he could sell it to others: and the Titus clock case was no exception. A second case was put in hand at the same time as the one for Samuel Pechell. Boulton's plan was to include this second case in the sale at Christie's in April 1772, but it proved impossible to finish it in time. Duval, who was the craftsman working on it at Soho, was waiting for Francis Eginton's instructions about the size of the door at the back of the case.[231] In the event he made it larger than the door on Pechell's case and fixed festoons 'upon the door' without waiting for Eginton's advice:[232] and the case was then gilt and presumably sent to London. If the words 'upon the door' can be construed as meaning 'above the door' this second case was probably the one that Boulton sold to the King soon afterwards.[233] The King's Titus has survived (Plate 183). It is fitted with a timepiece supplied by B. L. Vulliamy, the clockmaker to the Royal household, in 1800. An entry in Vulliamy's 'Clock Book' dated 12th July 1800 reads:

334 Fitted into a gilt case of Boulton's making

	£	s	d
Bullock the movement	5	5	0
L & [?] Drew the dial		18	0
Swift the hands		7	6

Debited to the Queen

July 12, 1800[234]

A rather fuller description of Vulliamy's work appears in his Day Book:[235]

12 July 1800 The Queen	
Made a new eight day movement name Vulliamy London No. 334 fitted to a metal case with an enamel'd dial plate and gold hands at eleven guineas	11. 11
To taking all the case to pieces and repairing it in several places and gilding it all over in the best manner at fifteen guineas and a half	16. 5. 6
Made a very large bent glass shade to cover the clock and fixed the clock upon a mahogany stand with a white holly moulding and covered with crimson velvet at three guineas and an half	3. 13. 6
Making a folding packing case for the clock and packing	14
Making a packing case for the glass and packing it into	11
	32. 15

The wooden stand and the glass shade have not survived.

The number 334 is engraved both on the finely engraved back plate of the movement (Plate 184) and on the bob of the pendulum. The dial is enamelled, with gilt numbers, and the hands are also gilt, as described in Vulliamy's Day Book. The movement is a simple eight-day timepiece without a striking train and the pendulum can be adjusted by the winding square, which nestles under the eagle's chin on the front of the case.

The case is interesting because it is one of the earliest versions of the design. It has been slightly modified since it was first made, especially underneath, where Vulliamy had to insert a plate on which to mount his movement. Vulliamy's other repairs are not obvious, but they may include the replacement of the top surface of the pedestal. The case is a fine example of Boulton and Fothergill's early allegorical clock cases, all in ormolu, like the early Minerva case (Plate 166). The components are as usual carefully fitted, and the mounts are contrived to achieve the usual contrast between matt and burnished surfaces. Vulliamy presumably repeated what he found when he re-gilt the case. The contrast can be seen, for example, on the festoons (the festoon and eagle are repeated on the back of the pedestal), the fruits of which are highly burnished, on the stamped key-pattern frieze round the pedestal, and on the spirally fluted feet, which are similar in style to the feet on the King's clock case and blue john candelabra (Plates 160, 339). The figure of Titus has a matt finish: Boulton gave special instructions that the gilders should be careful not to 'scratch off the matt' when they were gilding the faces of the first two Titus figures.[236]

The claim that 'many' of these clock cases had been made in 1772 was probably an exaggeration. Apart from the King's purchase only three other orders are recorded in the archives in 1772–3. One of these was for the King of Spain.[237] Another was for Henry Hoare, the banker, for whom 'as the figure of Titus is generally more approved of when bronzed than when gilt, the contrast being stronger, we have made yours a bronzed one and as an additional ornament added to the stand a small gilt vase perforated for an essence pot ...'[238] This was perhaps the first Titus to be decorated with such a vase. For the third customer, Mrs Montagu,[239] Boulton elected to have the figure of Titus bronzed rather than gilt because he himself preferred it.[240] He offered to change it if she wanted to, which she did, very politely:

> I am charmed with the graceful figure of Titus, and think the bronze better than if the whole piece was or moulu, considered by itself, but as this is to stand on a chimney piece where it will have a picture behind it, I find it makes no appearance, the black figure is quite lost on the dark back ground. I have therefore shut it up in its case in order to change it for one of or moulu, if it will be the same to you; if not, I will keep it, for I have your interests more at heart than the glare and the glitter of golden ornaments.[241]

The final sentiment was probably provoked by the news that Fordyce's banking business had crashed and that Boulton had had money deposited in it. Whether or not Boulton replaced the figure is not known.

Plate 185 illustrates a Titus clock case with a bronzed figure.[242] It is mounted on a plinth of variegated red marble, which may be a later addition. The ormolu plinth is decorated with a fluted frieze. Apart from this frieze, the dial bezel and the variations to swags, the case is very similar to the King's version of the clock. The motto is extended with the addition of the prefix '*Eheu*' but it is inscribed, as in the case of the King's Titus, on the pedestal. The movement, with its enamelled and gilt dial, was fitted in the nineteenth century. It is signed Arnold and Dent, London.

Two other Titus cases are recorded with a similar fluted plinth.[243] Both have bronzed figures of the Emperor and urns on the pedestals, suggesting that this was the model supplied to Henry Hoare. Each of them has the words '*Diem perdidi*' engraved on the pedestal below the dial. Each has an oval medallion of 'Clementia' (Plate 57) fixed to the front of the urn. This could be a rare example of a decorative medallion deliberately suited to the subject of the design. I have discussed its origin in Chapter 3 (see p. 91).

In later years the Titus clock case continued to be one of the regular items in the firm's range of ormolu ornaments. There were two in the sale at Christie and Ansell's in 1778.[244] The catalogue descriptions differ slightly, but in each case the figure of the Emperor was finished in bronze and the pedestal was made of 'statuary marble, ornamented with or moulu'. No vase or urn is mentioned. Both cases were reserved at £21: neither was sold.

Also in 1778 an order for a 'Titus with clock' was received from one of the merchants in Europe,[245] and in 1780 Capper, Palmer and Perkins bought '2 or moulu clock pieces of the Emperor Titus' for £31 each. These were each set with a circle of stones round the dial, at a further cost of 18s. each, and were obviously intended for export.[246] In 1782 there was only one in stock, described as '1 Titus vase with marble body ready to gild'.[247]

This last extract, and the catalogue entries in the 1778 sale, illustrate how in the later years of ormolu production more frequent use was made of white marble. There is a Titus clock case at Fasanerie[248] which has a gilt plinth decorated with a frieze of the type which bands the vases of Plate 349, and fluted feet as on the clock case of Plate 184. It has a marble pedestal and vase, and its lid is pierced for the emission of perfume. The words '*diem perdidi*' are engraved on a plaque on the vase. The swags on the vase are more delicate than in the earlier models. The rim of the vase is decorated with a guilloche band supporting two helmeted masks. The festoons and eagles that adorn the pedestal are as in Plate 184.

The clock case illustrated in Plate 186 is perhaps the latest model of the Titus. The gilt plinth and feet have gone, replaced with a marble base with a chased ormolu surround similar to other allegorical clock cases and watch stands (Plates 153, 175). There is no underplate. The festoon on the front of the pedestal has been altered, losing its eagle and curving above the

186. Titus clock case, 16.6 in., Birmingham Museum and Art Gallery.

187. Titus clock case of Plate 186, detail.

188. Pattern Book 1, p. 169.

dial instead of hanging as a swag from the corners, to allow a larger dial to be placed higher in the pedestal. The guilloche frieze, with its helmeted masks, and the swags on the vase are similar to the ornaments on the clock at Fasanerie. The figure is the same. The festoons and eagles remain on the other faces of the pedestal (Plate 187). Its quality and construction are characteristic of Boulton and Fothergill's later work in ormolu. The individual components, which fit together as in Plate 114, are exactly fashioned and the gilding is of the highest quality. The vase is fitted as a perfume burner with a pierced lid and a gilt copper lining. The watch movement, which has been replaced, is fitted in a copper case that slots and locks into the pedestal: the dial is enamelled and the hands gilt. There is no signature on the reverse of the dial or on the front plate of the watch.

This case corresponds to a sketch in Boulton and Fothergill's pattern books (Plate 188), on which a nineteenth-century wag has scrawled the name Cetawayo, a Zulu king in 1872–84. It is probably the type of case that was put up for sale in 1778, although both examples in the sale had bronze figures.

Two other similar Titus clock cases are known in collections open to the public. One, in the National Gallery, Melbourne, has a gilt figure. The watch movement is French and the enamelled dial is signed 'Fd Berthoud, Paris'. The other is at Sans Souci, Potsdam, and has a bronzed figure and a movement signed 'Jos Minutti, München'.

The Titus clock case was one of the most apt and successful of Boulton and Fothergill's many allegorical clock cases, although the modelling of the figure, as so often with figures modelled at Soho, leaves something to be desired. Titus's words, which convey the idea of time passing all too quickly, echo the clockmakers' traditional conceit of engraving on their dials such mottoes as 'Time spends' or '*Tempus fugit*'. The idea is developed in later versions to that of human mortality with the placing of a vase on the pedestal, which has the air of a funeral urn. At the same time the Emperor's words are a constant admonition that to do good is an end in itself. This moral allegory delighted Mrs Montagu who, worrying lest she had paid Boulton too little when she settled her bill, remarked

It would be worse than losing a day, it would be abusing it, to pay you short for the noble Titus, whose figure ought to admonish me of whatsoever things are just, lovely and of good report.[249]

It was an allegory calculated to please such a blue stocking.

Urania

Two of the ornaments in the sale at Christie and Ansell's in May 1778 were described as 'An elegant figure of Urania in bronze, holding a time piece against an obelisk of statuary marble, in the pedestal of which is an enamelled tablet showing the equation of time'.[250] The reserve price was £18. The description echoes other designs incorporating figures from classical mythology or history, including Belisarius (Plate 151), Narcissus (Plate 173) and Venus (Plate 192).

Three Urania watch stands have so far come to light, two of them with bronzed figures, one of which is illustrated in Plate 189, the third with a gilt figure.[251] In all three cases Urania, the muse of Astronomy, stands on a white marble base by a marble obelisk. In the bronzed versions she holds a watch, hung from a hook concealed behind the ribbon in her right hand. In the gilt version the watch is set with a chased and ornamented bezel into the obelisk (which has lost its lower supporting piece of marble), and Urania's right hand is made to seem as if it is holding the ornament above the bezel. In all three versions her left hand points in the general direction of the globe. The marble base is carved with a convex moulding and has a chased ormolu surround fixed to the underplate. The ormolu mounts and the assembly, with a central fixing rod and flanged mounts fitting together with fixed pins and holes, is standard. There are no mounts other than the equation table on the pedestal. The enamelled equation table on the pedestal has an ormolu frame.

OPPOSITE:
189. Urania watch stand, 16 in., Mallett.

There is no drawing of an ornament of this pattern in the pattern books. Whether or not any of the three known examples were in the 1778 sale is impossible to say, but there is a strong chance that one or other of them was. The equation table is mostly, but not entirely, in French, which might suggest that the ornaments were made for export, but this is not conclusive since the 1778 sale was a sale of accumulated stock and might well have included things made for markets abroad.

In the Inventory taken in 1782 there was 'an Astronomy figure in or moulu with white marble obelisk and a watch', valued at £25.[252] This was probably Urania, although the price was significantly higher than the reserve price in the 1778 sale. Perhaps the gilding made the difference, or perhaps it was a good watch.

The figure of Urania (Plate 190) is better modelled than many of Boulton's figures, which suggests that the moulds were not fashioned at Soho. It is very likely that the model came from the sculptor John Bacon, to whom Boulton paid five and a half guineas for 'a model and mould of a figure of Urania' in 1773 (see Chapter 3, p. 98).

Venus

There were three Venus clocks in the sale at Christie's in 1771.[253] Two of them were described in the catalogue as:

EQUATION DE JOURS NATURELS

190. Urania watch stand of Plate 189, detail.

191. Venus clock case, 12 in., Mallett.

An horizontal time piece representing Venus at the tomb of Adonis, in marble and or moulu, on the pedestal is a medalian of his death, and on the urn is the following inscription

> ΑἶΑῖ
> Ταὺ Κυθέρειαν
> Απώλετο
> Καλὸς 'Α΄δωνις.[254]

One of the clocks, reserved at £30, was bought by Sir Watkin Williams Wynn for £31 10s. 0d. and the others, reserved at £25, fetched £28 7s. 0d. and £26 5s. 0d.[255] The description of Sir Watkin's clock omitted any mention of marble or of a medallion on the pedestal.

There is a drawing of a Venus vase in the pattern books (Plate 360). Venus is shown in this drawing leaning on the pedestal in a posture of grief. On the pedestal is a medallion depicting Adonis and the wild boar that killed him. Cupid sits on the top step of the plinth, wiping the tears from his right eye. He holds a firebrand, which is inverted to symbolise the extinction of life. Near him on the ground are his quiver and two doves, symbols of Venus. On the pedestal is mounted the vase, or funerary urn. The drawing suggests that the ornament is made of marble and ormolu.

The Venus vase was used as a perfume burner, and I have discussed and illustrated an example of it in the section on vases (Plate 359). But it was adaptable to use as a timepiece by the insertion of a horizontal movement at the top of the vase, so that the hour and minute divisions could be seen against a fixed pointer between the sheaves of chased acanthus-leaf ornament. The vases of these perfume burners were made in two pieces to facilitate the conversion, the join being concealed behind the chased border beneath the frieze. The use of a horizontal movement in a vase was one of the many ideas that Boulton copied from French makers.

Several Venus perfume burners have survived but so far no example of an unaltered Venus clock case has been recorded. This is surprising, given the number of timepieces mentioned in the archives. Plate 191 shows a clock case that has been much restored.[256] The horizontal watch movement is housed in a gilt copper vase, the time being indicated on two revolving silvered rings. The goddess's lament is engraved on the front of the vase, with all of its eccentric breathings and accents. The pedestal is white marble. On the pedestal is mounted the gilt medallion depicting the death of Adonis. The cast figures on this medallion are set against a separate polished background, an unusual construction repeated on a Venus perfume burner at Syon (see p. 356). The other three sides of the pedestal are decorated with swags of drapery. The lid and finial on top of the clock, and Cupid's firebrand, have been replaced. The plinth is a later 'restoration', being made of Siena marble and not the expected white Derbyshire marble, and is fringed with a chased ormolu surround. There is no underplate.

I have discussed the source of the design of the Venus vase in Chapter 3 and attributed it, like so many of Boulton's allegorical figures, to French inspiration, probably through an engraving by Ravenet (see pp. 68 and 96).

The design proved comparatively successful. In April 1772 Boulton and Fothergill wrote to John Whitehurst:

> We now want three small clocks for what we call the Venus vase, pray have you not two in hand, and did not Mr Tyson bring one when he brought the globe.[257] If so imagine you packed it up to go back again as we cannot find it here. Shall send you two vases for the other two clocks next week but beg you will send one immediately and the other as soon as possible, for remember executing orders twelve months after will not do. We lost the sale of the others on that account.[258]

It is not perhaps just coincidence that three orders for Venus clocks are recorded in the archives in 1772. The King bought one[259] and Sir Harbord Harbord another, at a cost of £21.[260] Lord Sefton was sent one,[261] but returned it because it was sent too late.[262] Whitehurst's workshop was still supplying movements for the Venus vases in 1776,[263] and in 1778 he was asked to examine a Venus clock, which was intended for the Countess of Derby.[264]

There were five Venus vases in the sale at Christie and Ansell's in 1778, but none of them was described in the catalogue as a timepiece and they are discussed later in the section on vases. One of them was pierced as a perfume burner and another was mounted with candle branches. The other three were not described in sufficient detail, but were probably perfume burners: it would not have been difficult, however, to convert them into clocks with horizontal watch movements.

192. Pattern Book 1, p. 77.

Venus clocks were still in demand in 1781, when an 'or moulu figure of Venus with marble and or moulu ornaments and with clock in the pedestal' was sent to 'AOQ, Iraps' (the *marchand-mercier* Charles-Raymond Grancher, see Chapter 5, p. 179) at a cost of twenty-one guineas.[265] This is the only mention of a Venus clock with the movement fitted in the pedestal and it may well be that it incorporated an obelisk rather than a vase. I suggest this because there is a second drawing in the pattern books (Plate 192) showing Venus and Cupid with an obelisk. The clock is in the pedestal and the medallion of Adonis is on the obelisk. No examples of this pattern have yet come to light. It is wholly in accordance with other designs for allegorical pieces towards the end of the 1770s (Plates 151, 173, 186, 189). There was a Venus clock with an obelisk among the stock in 1782.[266]

In view of the poor modelling of the figure of Venus, it is surprising that this clock case appears to have been so successful. Even more surprising, perhaps, is the sale of Venus vases in Paris. Surprise was certainly the reaction of Wedgwood, who considered the sculpture inferior and the price excessive. He wrote to his partner after a visit to Soho in 1776:

> You remember a poor Venus weeping over the tomb of Adonis – a time piece. How many would you imagine they have sold of this single group? 200 at 25 guineas each, including the watch![267]

The letter is tinged with a mixture of admiration and envy of Boulton's marketing abilities. But I think Wedgwood was deceived by some impressive 'sales talk' and that the number of Venus clocks that he was told had been sold was wildly exaggerated. There is nothing in the archives to suggest that they were made in such quantities: if they had been the ormolu business might well have been a financial success.

Door furniture

Birmingham was the major centre in the eighteenth century for the production of household brassware – furniture mounts, handles, escutcheons, castors, door knobs, shutter knobs and borders, etc. Most of these components were not gilt, but some were. Boulton and Fothergill were not major producers of hardware of this sort, but they were willing to respond to commissions. There are no patterns for door knobs or escutcheons in the pattern books. They did however make door furniture. In 1771 they offered a 'specimen of our own furniture' to a firm in Wolverhampton to whom they were returning the furniture they had gilded for them.[268] Later in the same year they replied to an order for four locks with gilt furniture at 21s., that they had one pattern for the furniture alone at 21s. 'allowed to be very handsome, but none lower'. Door furniture had to be made to order.[269]

The earliest reference in the archives to door furniture concerns the set of five escutcheons and door knobs in the dining room at Kedleston Hall, Derbyshire (Plate 193). These were commissioned from Soho in July 1765, when Samuel Wyatt, who was working as clerk of the works at Kedleston, wrote to Boulton and sent with his letter 'a small box which contains the pattern of the escutcheon and knob'.[270] The commission antedates Boulton's serious interest in ormolu ornaments by some three years, which raises the question of why Boulton was approached at all. In view of Boulton's close acquaintance with the Wyatt family it was probably Samuel Wyatt's idea, but it is possible that Wyatt was directed to send the pattern to Soho by Robert Adam, the architect at Kedleston.

That Boulton was not used to producing door furniture at this date is suggested by the delay before the escutcheons and knobs for Kedleston were ready. In December 1765 Wyatt wrote to Lord Scarsdale that he had 'not yet got the escutcheons for the dining room locks and as I have heard nothing of them lately, I purpose going to Birmingham in the Christmas week ...'[271] In March 1766 he wrote to Boulton, ordering some nails of a special pattern which he wanted as soon as possible, 'though I would by no means have them any hindrance to the escutcheons etc.',[272] and in June he told Boulton that Lord Scarsdale's patience was 'quite tired out, I am afraid to mention the name of Boulton to him, so that if you think of ever seeing Kedleston House any more, you must let my Lord have the escutcheons etc. for the dining room doors ...'[273] There is no record in the archives of when the escutcheons were finally delivered, but an entry in a ledger at Kedleston records a payment in 1768 to 'Wyatt Saml by Mr Boulton's Bill £25 2s od'.[274] The door knobs are somewhat worn by nearly two hundred and forty years of use, and all but one of the escutcheons has lost the pendant that conceals the key hole for the primary door lock, as has the

193. Door escutcheon and knob, 6.3 in., National Trust, Kedleston Hall.

escutcheon illustrated in Plate 193. The other pendant operates the secondary lock. The stems of the handles are decorated with spiral flutes. Each handle is numbered.

Readers who are familiar with Adam's designs will recognise the escutcheons and knobs as one of his regular patterns. They correspond closely to a design in the *Works in Architecture* (Plate 20). They are very similar to escutcheons at Osterley Park, Middlesex, and Saltram Park, Devon (Plate 194). Since Adam was concerned with all three houses he presumably commissioned all three sets of door furniture. On the strength of the order for Kedleston, it could be supposed that they were all made at Soho, but this seems unlikely. The differences in the detail of the three sets of escutcheons suggest that they were cast in different moulds. There are also distinct differences in the chasing. There is also a lack of documentary evidence. Although Boulton supplied ormolu pieces at later dates to the owners of both Osterley and Saltram there is no evidence in the archives of any work for Adam at either house: after Boulton's inefficiency over the order for Kedleston there is every reason to suppose that Adam went elsewhere for ormolu door furniture for subsequent patrons.

Boulton was not the only available manufacturer of door furniture, although his eminence has led historians to think of him in that light.

194. Maker unknown, door escutcheons and knobs, 7 in., National Trust, Saltram House.

195. Door escutcheon and knob, silver, Ely House, Dublin.

In Chapter 2, I have mentioned Thomas Blockley, who was probably the largest producer of household hardware (see p. 34), and William Bent, who supplied the library door furniture for Adam at Nostell Priory in 1767 (see p. 40). Blockley is just as likely as Boulton and Fothergill to have been the supplier of the gilt door furniture to many of the houses then being rebuilt or refurbished, and probably more likely.

The detective story is, however, further confused by the existence of evidence that on occasion Boulton and Fothergill supplied gilt escutcheons to other suppliers, including both Blockley and Bent.[275] There is, therefore, no conclusive evidence that Boulton was not the supplier of the Osterley and Saltram escutcheons or of door furniture in other houses: it is always possible, though unlikely, that he supplied the owners direct, by cribbing Adam's earlier design. The silver escutcheons and handles that Boulton and Fothergill supplied to Ely House in Dublin in 1772 (Plate 195) may support this theory.[276]

Several patrons enquired about or ordered door furniture from the firm. Lord Shelburne asked Boulton in 1773 how much knobs and escutcheons 'finished after his best manner' would cost per dozen,[277] and in 1777 two designs for escutcheons were made for the inspection and approval of Lord Arundell,[278] on whose behalf two samples had been ordered by the architect James Paine as early as 1773:[279] the price was quoted at 31s. 6d. each. When Lord Arundell eventually ordered two escutcheons in July 1778, he forgot to return the design.[280] The Earl of Kerry may have been supplied with two escutcheons and a door handle, which for some reason the cabinet makers Mayhew and Ince returned to Boulton and Fothergill's warehouse in 1783, claiming a credit of two guineas:[281] the doors for Mrs Montagu's new house in Portman Square may well have been fitted with escutcheons from Soho, although the relevant archives mention only gilt ornaments, which were clearly patterned borders for the panels.[282]

In the Inventory of 1782 there are only two handles and escutcheons listed, one priced at £2 2s. 0d. and the other at £1 15s. 0d., but reduced to £1 8s. 0d. and £1 3s. 4d. respectively because they had been in the warehouse for many years and, like most of the other ormolu pieces, were probably damaged.[283] There were also '5 escutcheons and nobs' in Richard Bentley's workshop, valued at 15s.[284]

These somewhat scant references do not suggest that a large number of escutcheons and knobs were made at Soho, or even that they were a regular part of the ormolu trade.

The short-lived business in mechanical pictures in the 1770s opened up the possibility of setting copper-based pictures with ormolu borders into doors and shutters. In 1777 Samuel Wyatt suggested that 'panels for doors and window shutters with very narrow mouldings and ornaments in or moulu would be a good subject for Soho painting'.[285] I have not so far traced any surviving examples, but a record in the 1782 Inventory of a 'painted door panel on copper with an antique painting in the middle and with or moulu ornaments' shows that such things were made.[286]

Ewers

Boulton made a note in his diary in 1772, at the time of the sale at Christie's, that Sir Harbord Harbord wanted, among other things, 'I pair of ures such as are proper for the gods to drink necter'.[287] He also noted that he should call on his patron and show him 'a design of a ure'. In the same year the Earl of Sefton was supplied with a pair of ewers at a cost of £14 14s. 0d.[288] Apart from a 'stone lackered ewer' and a 'very good' stone body for an 'ewer vase' listed in the 1782 Inventory[289] there is no other mention of ormolu-mounted ewers in the archives.

The ewers illustrated in Plate 196 are suitably classical in design for the gods' refreshment, even if they would hold only a small amount because the stone is carved with only a meagre cavity – the copper lining measures about 5.5 x 1.5 inches. A sketch of the design has survived in the pattern book (Plate 198). It echoes both the shape of a classical ewer illustrated in d'Hancarville's book (Plate 55) and the device of placing a mask where the handle joins the back of the body of the jug, a feature that Wedgwood also

OPPOSITE:
196. Ewers, 19.2 in., Birmingham Museum and Art Gallery, Soho House.

197. Ewer of Plate 196, detail.

198. Pattern Book 1, p. 83.

199. Ewers, 19.5 in. and 18.9 in., Gerstenfeld Collection.

used.[290] The use of masks as decoration on ewers might owe something to French models (cf. Plate 15).

The construction of these ewers is typical of Boulton and Fothergill's work. The mounts beneath the blue john body are made separately and slotted together, and the whole body is held together by a nut screwed to the top of a threaded rod, which pierces the copper lining and is attached to an iron plate at the base. The masks are bolted to the stone body and the casting at the top (Plate 197) is made in one piece except for the handle, which slots into the top of the satyr mask and is screwed to the lip. The blue john bodies are assembled from several pieces cemented together and are left unpolished where they are concealed by the lower mounts.

The Earl of Sefton's ewers, supplied in 1772, are now in the Gerstenfeld Collection (Plate 199).[291] They are similar in all respects to the ewers of Plate 196 although the blue john stones are of sharply contrasting colour – one is deep purple, the other ochre and brown. There are minor differences in the chasing.

I have records of three other ewers of this design in private collections. Two of them have bodies of deeply veined blue john, the third is made of one piece of brown and grey fluorite with rough metallic patches, which can probably be identified with 'hatterel'.[292] None of the seven ewers mentioned here has the band round the body, decorated with a Vitruvian scroll motif, or the mounts at the top of the stem beneath the vase, both of which are shown in the drawing in the pattern book (Plate 198).

Fender

The Duke of Richmond ordered an ormolu fender at the beginning of 1773. Boulton and Fothergill had not made one before and were unable to estimate the cost.[293] It was finished by April and the Duke was charged £13 13s. od., which was no more than prime cost.[294] The fender was probably intended for Goodwood and the instrument maker Alexandre Tournant, who left Soho to work for the Duke at Goodwood early in 1773, had a hand in its construction.[295] The fender does not appear to be at Goodwood today. This fender was an unusual commission. Boulton and Fothergill did not like accepting commissions for single objects of this sort because they meant the expense of special models and tended, as in this case, to cost more than they thought the customer would pay.

Furniture mounts

Soho was only one of many workshops and factories in Birmingham which were capable of producing furniture mounts. Boulton and Fothergill were not among the major producers. Birmingham metalworkers supplied large quantities of handles, escutcheons, castors and other furniture mounts to furniture makers both in Britain and abroad.[296] Boulton and Fothergill were not listed in 1770 among the producers of 'brassfoundry', the definition of which included 'cabinet handles and escutcheons'.[297] There are few references in the Boulton archives to furniture mounts, which is surprising, given past habits of attributing fine-quality mounts to him. There are no drawings of furniture mounts in the pattern books.

The vast majority of furniture mounts in the eighteenth century were not gilt. They were burnished, or treated with a cleansing solution such as nitric acid, and then lacquered, a process that was known in France as '*mis en couleur d'or*'. But some of the brassfounders in Birmingham made gilt mounts for the best cabinet makers in spite of the distance from London.[298]

The distance put them at a disadvantage. It was one thing to produce standard fittings such as handles and castors, which cabinet makers bought in quantity: it was not so simple to supply finely finished mounts to fit particular pieces of furniture at a distance of about one hundred and twenty miles. There were many skilled metalworkers and gilders in London, some of whom formed close links with leading cabinet makers, for example Dominique Jean with Langlois, and it was difficult and probably unprofitable to compete with them.

For these reasons gilt furniture mounts do not appear to have been part of Boulton and Fothergill's regular stock-in-trade. They were willing, however, to carry out the work on request, as a few references show. Thus Boulton discussed with James Stuart the making of a border for a tea table for Thomas Anson in 1769,[299] and the London cabinet makers Mayhew and Ince sent some ornaments to be gilt in 1770 and 1775,[300] and some more to be gilt and repaired in 1772.[301] Mounts were supplied to a local cabinet maker, Nathaniel Dudley, on at least two occasions,[302] and in 1776 'sundree ornaments gilt for a cabinet' were supplied to a customer named W. P. N. French at a cost of £7.[303] In the same year Charles Pelham ordered some 'or moulu ornaments for a commode' through John Wyatt in London.[304] They were initially promised by Christmas and Boulton and Fothergill's lack of practice in this sort of work is demonstrated by their apologetic letter in March 1777:

> We are much concerned that we have been obliged to violate our promise in not sending the ornaments as we expected. Could we have conceived the trouble and unavoidable delays that would attend the execution thereof, we certainly should not have ventured to promise it as soon ...[305]

The ornaments were sent a few days later and cost £53 18s. 0d: this was expensive and Boulton and Fothergill felt obliged, in case Pelham thought it excessive, to point out that 'no pains nor expence hath been wanting to execute and render them as rich as possable both in workmanship and the gilding'.[306] The ornaments were presumably intended for a commode at the Pelhams' house in Arlington Street. Unfortunately the commode cannot be traced today[307] and the style of the mounts remains a mystery.

Boulton's name has been linked so often in the past with those of leading cabinet makers that it is surprising to find references to so few of them in the archives.[308] There is no reference for example to Thomas Chippendale or to John Linnell, to whom Boulton has sometimes been supposed to have supplied mounts: nor has any reference to Boulton yet been found in either of these two cabinet makers' own letters, accounts or notes. Boulton and Fothergill had a considerable correspondence with George Seddon while Mrs Montagu was building and equipping her new house in Portman Square in 1780–2, but this was concerned only with the supply of plate glass and mechanical pictures. Seddon was also asked to provide wooden stands for Boulton's copying machines, which were yet another promising but short-lived venture.[309] The only other well-known London cabinet makers whose names appear in the archives were Samuel Norman and Mayhew and Ince. Samuel Norman appears only once, and in somewhat unsatisfactory circumstances. This was in 1765, when he apparently tried to secure payment of a draft on Sir Herbert Packington twice over.[310] This incident proves no more than that Norman knew Boulton. He may have purchased mounts from Soho but there is no evidence. Several letters to Mayhew and Ince have survived,[311] and there are several others that refer to them. I have cited some of these letters elsewhere (see Chapter 5, pp. 163, 174), and it is clear that the two firms were in regular contact from 1771 at the latest. It is possible that Mayhew and Ince were responsible for several of Boulton and Fothergill's com-

200. Duchess of Manchester's cabinet, 74.2 in., Victoria and Albert Museum.

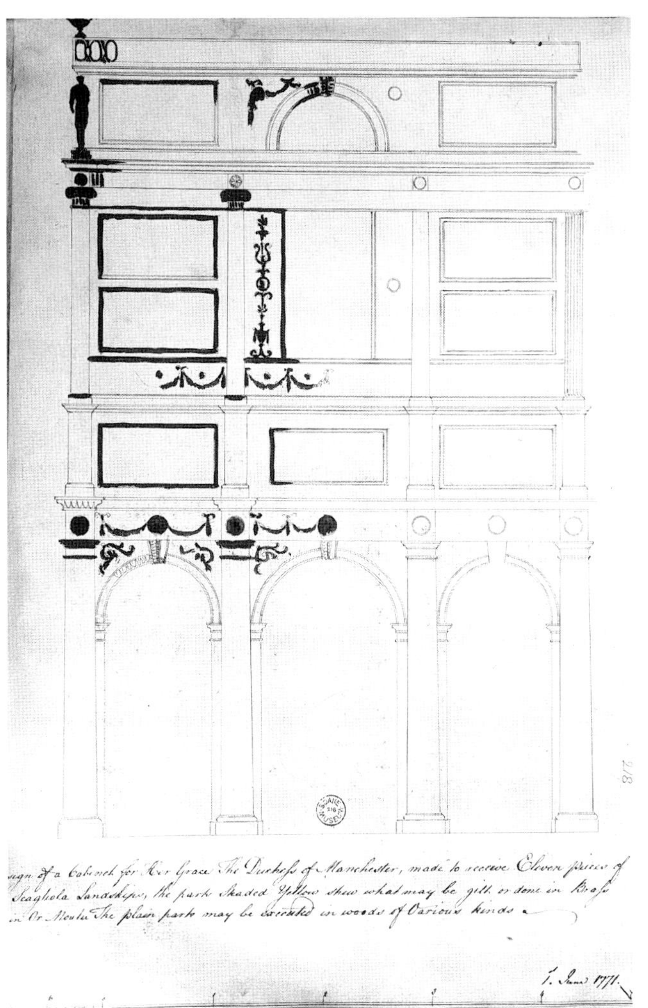

201. Robert Adam, design for cabinet, Soane Manuscripts, Vol. 17, no. 218, Sir John Soane's Museum.

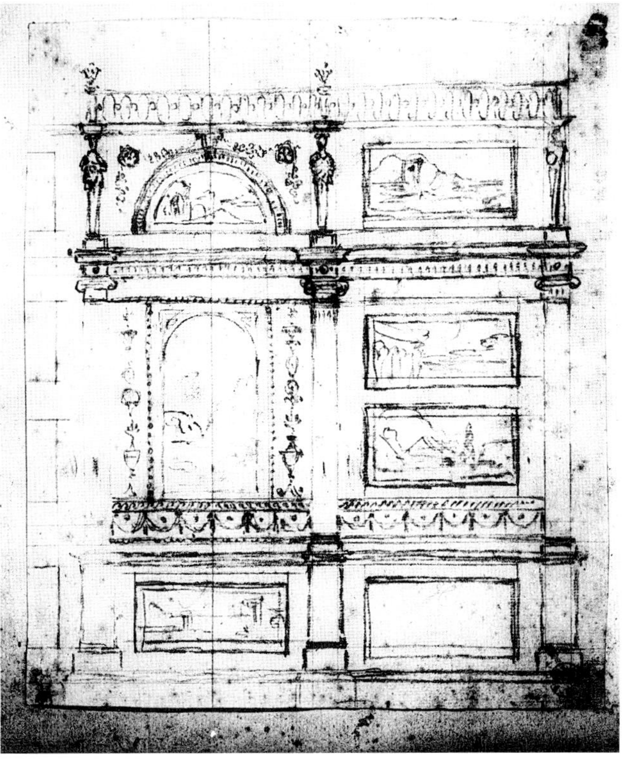

202. Robert Adam, design for cabinet, Soane Manuscripts, Vol. 27, no. 5, Sir John Soane's Museum.

FOLLOWING PAGE:
203. Duchess of Manchester's cabinet, detail of Ionic capital.

missions. They certainly commissioned work for the Earl of Kerry.

The most important single order for which they were responsible was the commission for the ormolu mounts for the Duchess of Manchester's cabinet (Plate 200).[312] This cabinet, which has been illustrated frequently elsewhere,[313] is one of the most decorative and remarkable pieces of furniture of its period. It was made as a means of displaying the eleven marble intarsia coastal and lake scenes which were made by Baccio Capelli at Florence in 1709.[314] It is not known how the Duchess of Manchester acquired these panels, but she owned them by 1771 when, presumably on her instructions, Robert Adam produced a design for a cabinet to display them. His design was inscribed – 'made to receive eleven pieces of scagliola[315] landskips, the parts shaded yellow shew what may be gilt or done in brass in or moulu, the plain parts may be executed in woods of various kinds' (Plate 201). A rougher sketch has also survived among the Adam drawings, which is closely related to this finished design and which shows that the draughtsman had seen the landscape panels themselves (Plate 202). In the event the Duchess settled for yet another design, which maintained the proposed arrangement of the marble panels but incorporated fewer, and less elaborate, mounts. Mayhew and Ince were commissioned to make the cabinet, which consists of a series of mahogany panels veneered with satinwood and rosewood and richly inlaid with classical motifs. The marble panels were set so that they looked like drawers or cupboard doors, but access to the shelves inside the cabinet is only possible through the two doors at each end. The cabinet, which is just as finally executed, was

probably designed by Adam, although his drawing for it has not survived. His authorship is suggested by the use of a capital which is modelled on a capital which he recorded from the peristyle of the temple of Aesculapius at Spalatro (Plates 21, 22), and also by features borrowed from his original design, such as the gilt frames for the marble panels and the Ionic capitals, which have been transposed to the tops of the legs (Plate 203).

Mayhew and Ince sent a drawing of the cabinet to Boulton and Fothergill in 1774, with an order for the ormolu ornaments and a request for an estimate of the cost of making them. Their instructions were by no means clear, as Boulton and Fothergill's reply shows:

> In answer to your favour of the 8th ultimo concerning the ornaments for the Duke and Dutchess of Manchester's cabinet, it is not possible to make an accurate estimate thereof, before the work is finished, but as near as we can guess they will amount to about 70 £ or 75 £. We have already begun with such parts as we are clear you intend being made in or moulu; but as there are some parts of which we are a little doubtfull have herewith returned you the drawing and request you will coulour such parts as you intend to be in gilt metal, and return it immediately. We hope to have the whole completed some time in February next.[316]

Unfortunately none of Mayhew and Ince's letters to Boulton and Fothergill concerning this cabinet have survived, but the doubts about the design were apparently resolved. In April 1775 Mayhew and Ince wrote to enquire about the progress of the work and received the reply:

> We duly received your favour of the 1st inst., and in looking into the metal ornaments for the Dutchess of Manchester's cabinet we find they will be compleat for gilding in about 9 days, when we shall immediately as they are ready forward them to you in order to try how they fit, as we think it best so to do, before they are gilt for fear there should be any alterations to make after, (when considered that the gilding part will not delay them above 3 or 4 days after we receive them back). We are sorry it has not been in our power to compleat them sooner, and hope our delay will be no great disappointment.[317]

Boulton and Fothergill were no more prompt than many of their own subcontractors, about whose delays they so often complained. The mounts were not sent to London for another eleven weeks.[318]

The compression of the circular links of the central frieze in order to make them fit the faces of the projecting columns symmetrically (Plate 205), was probably one of the alterations carried out at this stage. The ornaments were then returned to Soho, where they were gilt. They were finally sent to Mayhew and Ince in October. The invoice amounted to £73 11s. 0d.[319] This was later increased, at the request of Mayhew and Ince, and rendered to the Duchess, the increase representing a profit for the cabinet makers which they did not want to charge in their own name.[320] The charge seems high, but Boulton and Fothergill claimed that it included only a very moderate profit.[321] The manufacture of the mounts certainly entailed some lengthy and skilled work. The pierced friezes must have required a great deal of manual filing, and the ornaments, which are relatively finely chased and richly gilt, are representative of the firm's best quality work (Plates 203–7). Boulton and Fothergill's moderate profit was subsequently dented when Mayhew and Ince claimed not to have received the ninety-six stars for the central frieze (Plate 205) and they had to make a new set.[322] Nor was this the end of the commission. The two firms were still arguing about the Duchess's account eight years later. Boulton eventually paid £32 13s. to the cabinet makers, not because he thought he owed it but in order to finish the dispute about this and other accounts.[323] The cabinet was recorded in an inventory as standing in the State Bedroom at Kimbolton in 1790, when it was described as a 'cabinet of inlaid marbles, mounted in or moulu, very

OPPOSITE:
205. Duchess of Manchester's cabinet, detail.

OPPOSITE:
206. Duchess of Manchester's cabinet, detail.

PREVIOUS PAGE:
204. Duchess of Manchester's cabinet, detail of foot.

207. Duchess of Manchester's cabinet, detail.

fine'.[324] It was exhibited in the 'Great Art Treasures' exhibition in Manchester in 1857 in a group of pieces of furniture inlaid with marble and semi-precious stones. It was described at the time as a 'monument of labour and materials misapplied'.[325] Today the fashion has swung back and it is rightly seen as one of the finest examples of the craftsmanship of its day.

In addition to supplying mounts on occasion to patrons and cabinet makers, Boulton and Fothergill tried their hand at complete if minor pieces of useful furniture. Boulton conceived the idea in about 1770 of mounting some of the firm's pieces of japanned furniture with gilt borders, rims, feet and escutcheons.[326] There was a japanned knife and cutlery case in the 1778 sale at Christie and Ansell's – knife and cutlery cases were something of a speciality (see pp. 261–5) – and some 'mounts for a japanned clock' were listed among the stock in 1782.[327]

The table of Plate 208 was made for Matthew Boulton himself right at the end of the eighteenth century, some time after the ormolu business had ceased. It hardly qualifies, therefore, for inclusion in this study, but the mounts on the table frame, including particularly the lions' masks and lyres, echo models used when the ormolu business was part of the factory's regular business and are likely to have been cast in the same moulds. The table was invoiced to Boulton in 1799 by John Hodges, who had been much involved with the ormolu business in the 1770s before assuming responsibility for silver and plated wares in 1782. Boulton and Watt provided the metal and cast the ornaments at a cost of £7 16s. 1d. The table, probably the wooden frame, was made and fitted by 'IGS', who was probably a cabinet maker or joiner, at a cost of £10. Hooker and Hodges himself did the chasing for £10 2s., and William Nelson, Boulton's partner in the gilt button trade, did the gilding for £16 17s. 9d. Inclusive of burnishing the invoice amounted to £45 3s. 4d.[328]

The table is an oddity. The construction for a start is curious. The legs are solid metal, each cast in two pieces. They are attached to the table frame with heavy iron bolts. The front and sides of the legs are decorated with chased classical ornament, with paw feet and bearded satyrs' heads, but the backs of the legs are entirely plain. The sharp edges and the profile of the legs make the decoration of the sides look cramped (Plate 209). The gilt

208. Table, 29.5 in., Birmingham Museum and Art Gallery, Soho House.

209. Table, detail.

copper band on the lower legs, which is fashioned to hold a shelf, is decorated with a stamped or rolled shell motif and is not of the same quality as the other mounts. It has been modified at some point, perhaps when the frame was modified. The best and most typical mounts are the lyres, lions' masks and floral swags of the frieze. These are all separately attached by nuts and are all numbered (as are the four legs). The wooden D-shaped frame is made of pine. The curved frieze is made of laminated pine with an outer layer of hardwood on which the gesso and gilding have been applied. The back of the frame has, at some point in its history, been cut back, probably to accommodate the table to a new setting when it was moved from one house to another. The white marble slab is probably original.[329]

The design of the table can also be described as odd. It is an anachronism for 1798–9. It probably owes its origins to Boulton's own preferences. It is likely that he wanted a side table for the entrance hall at Soho House, and was indulging a taste of some thirty or forty years earlier. Sketches for console tables in the French manner, with lower shelves, delicate classical ornament and paw feet, survive in his personal papers.[330] The table shows every sign of not being designed by a professional cabinet maker or architect, and may be the result of a working sketch done by Boulton himself, or in the factory at his instigation.

The table must have been removed to Tew Park after Boulton's son Matthew Robinson Boulton moved to Tew in 1815. It was there that I first saw it, standing over a radiator.[331] After restoration, which has included the re-insertion of a tray at the lower level, it has now returned to Soho House, where it can be seen standing in the entrance hall for which it was probably first made.

Girandoles, sconces

The word 'girandole' was often used in the eighteenth century to denote a candle branch or a sconce. Thus Robert Adam could describe a vase with two candle branches as a 'girandole vase'.[332] It is, therefore, sometimes difficult to know exactly what sort of object is implied on every occasion that the word is used in manuscript sources. The situation is complicated in the case of Boulton and Fothergill by the fact that although they supplied ormolu 'girandoles' to several patrons, none have so far been identified as their work. Most of them have perhaps been disposed of following the advent of electric light.

It seems probable that Boulton and Fothergill mostly used the word 'girandole' in the accepted modern sense of a branched candle holder fitting to the wall, and it seems that production of ormolu girandoles of this sort did not begin at Soho until some time in 1771.[333] The Earl of Shelburne had suggested to Adam in 1765 that Boulton might make him 'some girandoles for holding 2 and 3 candles at Bowood',[334] but it appears that nothing came of the request. Some sconces were made, at the request of Samuel Wyatt, for glass frames at Kedleston in 1766.[335] These are, however, not described. They were probably no more than branches and sockets of the sort which Boulton and Fothergill supplied on occasion to patrons and cabinet makers.[336]

The first order recorded in the archives was at the end of 1771, when Colonel (later General) Burgoyne was sent some girandoles which were 'really of a very fine taste and of an exceeding good chasing, gilding and workmanship' for his house in Hertford Street, London: they were so good that Boulton and Fothergill were sure that he would not mind the cost exceeding the estimate of five or six guineas.[337] There were several girandoles at the sale at Christie's in 1772[338] and during 1772–3 they were

210.1 Pattern Book 1, p. 13.

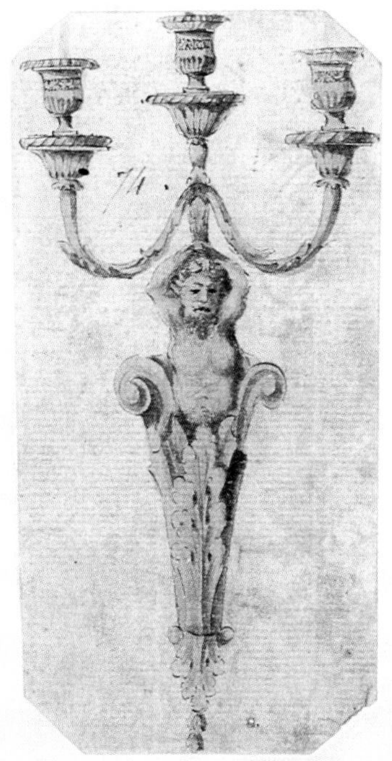

210.2 Pattern Book 1, p. 19.

supplied to various patrons. In 1772 the Earl of Kerry ordered a pair of 'great gerandoles', one of which was damaged during transport. He was also sent drawings of others.[339] The Archbishop of Canterbury was sent a drawing in the same year.[340] The Duchess of Ancaster had four copies of a girandole made,[341] and Lady Edgecumbe was sent a drawing of a two-branched girandole, which was the same as the Duchess of Ancaster's,[342] to which she duly responded with an order.[343] In 1775 Lord Nuneham bought a pair of 'precisely the pattern of Lord Edgecumbe's' which cost £12 15s. od.[344] Other patrons who bought girandoles in later years included the Earl of Ashburnham, who was sent five drawings to choose from, in 1775,[345] and General Charles Fitzroy in 1778.[346] Lord Arundell enquired about 'sconces or girandoles' in 1777. There were none ready made but he was told that there were several designs to choose from.[347] There were two pairs in the sale at Christie and Ansell's in 1778, one of which was described as 'two-branched',[348] and there were three pairs, one of which had three branches and the others two, in stock in 1782.[349]

There is no more exact description of any girandole in these references, or in the many other letters referring to orders or drawings, than 'two-branched' or 'three-branched'. There are only two drawings of girandoles in the first pattern book (Plate 210.1–2). Both are characteristic designs. It may or may not be coincidence that one is two-branched and the other three-branched. The two-branched design with the ram's head, numbered 419, has nozzles similar to those of the Apollo and Diana candelabra (Plate 130). It is an adaptation of the single branch that appears in another pattern (Plate 312.2). The three-branched design, numbered 74, incorporates nozzles of the pattern used on the goat's head and other candle vases (Plates 281, 333). The branches are supported by a triton figure which, with its raised arms and the acanthus decoration coming to the midriff, is reminiscent of the bearded figures which support the branches of the King's vase (Plate 344).

Ice pails

Ice pails were the first of the objects that Thomas Pownall, after discussion with those 'who have nothing to do but to copy or invent new modes of luxury and manificence, and who have lived amongst the French', suggested in the autumn of 1769 that Boulton might make.[350] In 1772 three drawings of ice pails were submitted to the Duke of Ancaster. The estimated price was about twenty guineas.[351] A sample was sent to the Duchess in April 1773,[352] the result of which was an order for five. They were delivered in May. The invoice described them as:

	£	s	d
3 large ice pails in ormoulu with plated linings @ 15 gns.	47	5	0
2 smaler ditto ditto ditto @ 12 gns.	25	4	0
	72	9	0[353]

The Duchess liked the form of the pails, but wanted handles so that the servants would not spoil the gilding when handling them. She thought that goats' heads with handles would be suitable, and Boulton suggested that Francis Eginton should model them.[354] Five days later, Fothergill reported that Eginton had contrived a very good handle, which he was bringing to London.[355] Other patrons who bought ice pails in later years were James Belliss, who paid £28 7s. od. for a pair,[356] the Earl of Ashburnham, who was charged £113 8s. od. for four of the pattern supplied to the Duke of Ancaster,[357] the Earl of Coventry, who bought a pair for £25 4s. od.,[358] the Countess of Derby[359] and the Earl Beauchamp.[360] In the sale at Christie and Ansell's in 1778 there were two ice pails 'in or moulu richly gilt, chased and lined with silver', one for a pint bottle (reserved at £10 10s.) and the other for a quart (reserved at £13 13s.).[361] Since neither of them reached the reserve price they were probably the two that were still in stock in 1782.[362]

There are several drawings of ice pails in Boulton and Fothergill's pattern books, but nearly all of them are designs for silver and plate. One of the drawings might have been a design for either silver or ormolu (Plate 211). When submitting drawings to the Duke of Ancaster, Boulton's clerk said that the pails could be made in ormolu or silver, which suggests that the same drawing served on occasion for work in different metals.[363]

211. Pattern Book 1, p. 177.

Several ice pails of this design that should, I think, be attributed to Boulton and Fothergill have survived. None of them have the dropping husks in the flutes of the body of the pail. The neck below the guilloche rim is plain and not fluted. Their handles are somewhat shorter than shown in Plate 211 but they all rise from the satyrs' masks as in the drawing. The fluted handles are usually decorated with a band of double twisted rope in the centre. A typical ice pail, which was owned by Sir Patrick Thomas, a direct descendant of Matthew Boulton, and can therefore be attributed with reasonable certainty to Boulton and Fothergill, is illustrated in Plate 212.[364] The construction of this pail is similar to other work carried out at Soho. The body is cast in quarter sections and soldered together. The pieces of the lower part with the acanthus decoration are cast separately from the pieces of the upper fluted part. The base is cast separately and screwed to the vase from the inside. The mask handles (Plate 213) are cast and bolted to the body. The silvered lining is cylindrical with a curved base, formed from two pieces of sheet copper, joined with a silver solder and hammered to shape (cf. Plate 97).

212. Ice pail, 8 in., Victoria and Albert Museum.

OPPOSITE:
213. Ice pail of Plate 212, detail.

214. Boulton and Fothergill (attrib.), ice pail, 9 in., Private Collection.

The ice pail illustrated in Plate 214 is constructed in similar fashion, its body cast in quarter sections and the vase screwing onto the base. The lining is formed in the same way, although it has a flat rather than a curved bottom. The cast handles are in the form of rams' heads, the horns extending to form the handles. The handles are not fluted and their central decoration is chased with acanthus and a beaded band. The base of the pail is ornamented with a chased ring. It is impossible to attribute this pail with total certainty to Boulton and Fothergill – there are no drawings of the rams' heads with their extended horns and no archival references to ormolu ice pails with rams' head handles – but it bears signs of manufacture at Soho. Could there have been some confusion following the Duchess of Ancaster's suggestion of handles in the form of goats' heads? Or could Eginton have simply preferred to make rams' heads?[365] These are intriguing questions, particularly because no ice pails with handles in the form of goats' heads have yet come to light. It is equally possible that the ice pail handles modelled by Eginton were the satyr masks illustrated in Plate 213.

The Duchess of Ancaster's invoice in 1773 listed 'large' and 'smaller' ice pails at fifteen and twelve guineas. The 1778 sale catalogue listed a pail for a quart bottle and another for a pint bottle at thirteen and ten guineas. It sounds as if there were two standard sizes. It is, therefore, interesting that the ice pail of Plate 212 is eight inches high, whereas others of the same design are nine inches. Boulton's descendant Sir Patrick Thomas had one of each. These may well have been the pails for pint and quart bottles recorded in the 1782 Inventory, which I have mentioned above.

Ink stands

Ink stands were another of Thomas Pownall's suggestions in 1769,[366] and in 1771 Boulton claimed that ink stands were among the ormolu wares being produced at Soho.[367] It seems unlikely, however, that many ormolu ink stands were made at Soho. Lord Cathcart wrote to Boulton in 1772 that French ink stands were popular in Russia,[368] but Boulton does not seem to have taken advantage of the advice. I have not found any order for an ink stand and there are no designs for ormolu ink stands in the pattern books: such drawings as have survived are designs for silver ink stands.

Knife and cutlery cases

Knife and cutlery cases made in the form of vases or urns seem to have been made at Soho from the middle 1770s. Some, if not most, of the urns were japanned. Two urns ordered by the Earl and Countess of Craven were to be japanned by Henry Clay. At the beginning of 1776 Boulton and Fothergill had to write to the Countess of Craven to say that they quite despaired 'of ever getting your knife cases done by Mr Clay and therefore think it necessary to inform you that you may no longer wait in expectation of them'. Anxious not to lose the order, they continued:

> We beg leave to observe to your Ladyship our remarks on such (viz.) the form is now become old fashion and the spoons cannot be taken out (by the servants) but by laying hold of that part which is to be put to the mouth which is a disagreeableness we have often heard. In consequence we have invented a vase, to contain knives and forks and spoons, and for your inspection we have inclosed a drawing of the same. The brown part is intended to be mahogany and the yellow, either or moulu or silver. The pedestal is to open with a number of drawers, lined with velvet, in which are to be deposed the forks and spoons, lying flatt, and the knives to be set in the vase or top part. The drawing shews on one side the top the handles of the knives, the other the cover of the vase, so that the lid or cover may be taken off at pleasure and shew all the knife handels. In our opinion this will be a handsome compleat vase for the purpose ...[369]

215. Pattern Book 1, p. 124.

Lord and Lady Craven were 'very much offended' at the delay, but ordered a knife case to correspond with the new drawing 'except that both the vase and the pedestal must be mahogany, the ornaments or moulu'. It was to contain three dozen large knives and forks and was 'for her Ladyship's inspection, which if approved she will then give orders for the rest. She adds if they cannot be done very soon she must get knife cases somewhere else, as she has not any in town to set upon her sideboard'.[370] In spite of this threat Boulton and Fothergill continued with the order. The knife case was not sent until nearly nine months later.[371] When it arrived Lord Craven complained that the drawers were too small for the spoons.[372] It was described in Boulton and Fothergill's ledger as 'a vase to contain knives, forks and spoons' and cost £36.[373] Later the same design was sent for the approval of another patron.[374]

The Craven's mahogany vase on its pedestal has not yet come to light. The description of it, however, corresponds closely to a drawing in the pattern books (Plate 215) which shows an urn mounted with lion masks, medallion and other mounts, standing on an ormolu-mounted pedestal with four drawers. The drawing is not the one sent to Lady Craven, which showed the mahogany in brown and the vase partly cut away to reveal the knife handles, but it is likely that her knife case looked very like this drawing.

216–17. Knife and cutlery urn, 22 in., Mallett.

Plate 216 shows one of a pair of urns, which closely correspond to the drawing.[375] The urns are made of copper, lacquered to simulate porphyry. The ormolu mounts – the formalised leaves cradling the vase and cresting the lid, the Vitruvian scroll and guilloche bands girdling the vase, the swags, the paterae and the ring of laurel with crossed ribbons at the base – are typical of the work at Soho, as is the assembly of the vases. As in the drawing, the medallions represent Ceres, the goddess of plenty, a very suitable deity for a dining room. I have discussed Boulton's model for this medallion in Chapter 3 (see p. 106). The lions' masks with their rings are like those on the King's vase, but they lack beards. This is to make room for the paterae beneath them (Plate 217). The lids are mounted on sprung columns and are made to spring upwards when the paterae are depressed. The knives and forks were slotted into the inner and outer of the four rings of holes revealed when the lids are opened (Plate 217). The middle two rings, with their wider apertures, were for forks, as is made clear in the letter from Wedgwood to his partner quoted below. The forks were inverted so that the handles of knives and forks were all visible. They are set in red velvet, decorated with silver braid.

These urns stood originally, as the drawing in the pattern book shows, on pedestals mounted with chased ormolu borders, drawer handles and swags. These pedestals have survived (Plate 218) and correspond, as do

218–19. Stands for knife and cutlery urns, 12.1 in., Private Collection.

220–1. Knife and cutlery urn, H. Blairman and Sons.

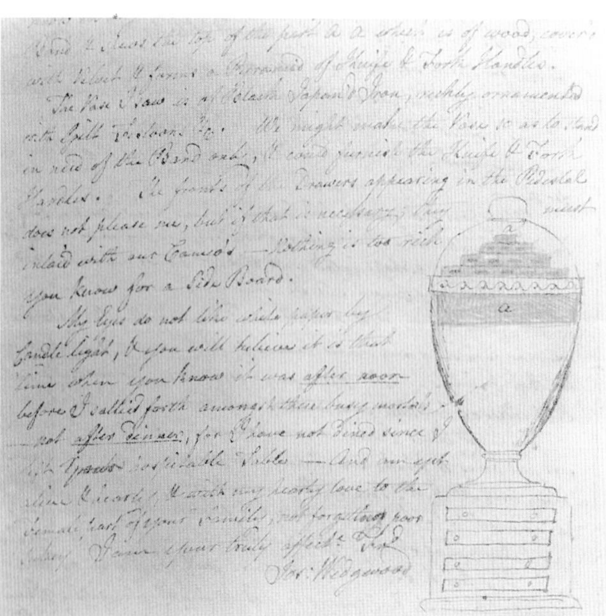

[illegible] the top of the post a a which is of wood, cover'd
with Velvet & forms a Pyramid of Knife & Fork Handles.
The Vase & [illegible] is of Black Japan'd Iron, richly ornamented
with Gilt [illegible] &c. We might make the Vase so as to stand
in [illegible] of the Board only, & could furnish the Knife & Fork
Handles. The fronts of the Drawers appearing in the Pedestal
does not please me, but if that is necessary, they must
inlaid with our Cameo's — Nothing is too rich
you know for a Side Board.
My Eyes do not like white paper by
Candle light, & you will believe it is that
time when you know it was after noon
before I sallied forth amongst these busy mortals
— not after dinner, for I have not dined since I
left [illegible] hospitable Table — And now [illegible]
[illegible] & with my hearty love to the
female part of your Family, not forgetting poor
[illegible] I am your truly affect. Friend
Jos: Wedgwood

222. Josiah Wedgwood, letter to Thomas Bentley, 25th October 1776, sketch of knife and cutlery urn, Wedgwood Museum, Barlaston.

the urns, to the details of the drawing. They are made of well-figured mahogany. The chased borders do not extend to the back of the pedestals, but are left plain, since they would have stood on a sideboard against a wall. The four drawers of one of the pedestals are designed to hold spoons and are lined with red velvet and silver braid (Plate 219), matching the interior of the knife urns. The drawers of the other pedestal are unlined, but may have originally been equipped for more spoons 'lying flatt', as proposed in Boulton and Fothergill's description to Lady Craven. The polished tops of the pedestals show the marks of the square bases of the vases and the two fixing holes for each of them. It is a pity that the urns have been separated from the pedestals and it would be good to see them reunited.[376]

One of another pair of knife urns with similar decoration is illustrated in Plates 220–1. The medallion (Plate 73) is of a female bust with an elaborate coiffure, a tiara and eardrops. She is Julia, the daughter of the Emperor Titus, and I have discussed the origin of Boulton's cast of her in Chapter 3 (see p. 107). The copper urns and stems are lacquered black. The interior fittings of the urns are missing. The urns stand on large pedestals, also lacquered black with ormolu borders and bases. Behind the doors of the pedestal are three mahogany-veneered drawers for cutlery. The drawers are lined with red velvet and silver braid. These knife cases were previously owned by the Galitzine family, and were said to have been in the Gatchina Palace, St Petersburg. There is no record of a sale to Russia of a knife or cutlery case in the archives.

Wedgwood saw a 'vase to hold knives, forks and spoons on the side board' when he visited Soho House towards the end of 1776. He enclosed a drawing of it (Plate 222) and thought there could be an opportunity to make several of the parts for it:

> The pedestal is mahogany, with drawers for spoons by which an indelicacy is avoided, that of taking hold of the bit of the spoon with the footmans fingers, which you are immediately to put into your mouth. The vase may be ornamented, you know in any manner we think proper. It takes off at the band and shews the top of the part which is of wood, cover'd with velvet and forms a pyramid of knife and fork handles.
> The vase I saw is of black japan'd iron, richly ornamented with gilt festoons etc. We might make the vase so as to stand in need of the band only, and could furnish the knife and fork handles. The fronts of the drawers appearing in the pedestal does not please me, but if that is necessary; they must inlaid with our cameo's – Nothing is too rich you know for a side board.[377]

Wedgwood's drawing misses a number of decorative features and its proportions are wrong, but it shows that the vase he saw was similar to the drawing in the pattern book and to the knife cases and pedestals of Plates 216 and 218. His description tallies closely with these vases, except that the vase he saw had a black lacquered body as in Plate 220. There is no evidence that Boulton ever took up his suggestion that Wedgwood and Bentley might provide components and ornaments.

Obelisks

The lapidaries of Derbyshire frequently used obelisks, like vases, as a means of showing off the beauties of the coloured stones from the local mines. Boulton bought an obelisk when he visited Derbyshire early in 1768.[378] There are eleven designs of obelisks in the first pattern book. Four of them are designs for unmounted stones and may represent obelisks sold in the showroom at Soho.[379] Three are designs for clock cases with figures representing Belisarius (Plate 151), Narcissus (Plate 174) and Venus (Plate

192). These designs were probably inspired by the work of French *bronziers*. I have discussed them in the section on clock cases (see pp. 197, 221, 239). Plate 189 illustrates another clock case with an obelisk, representing the muse of Astronomy Urania, which is not illustrated in the pattern book (see p. 236).

The other four sketches show ormolu-mounted obelisks without any hint of a clock or watch. They owe their stylistic origins to the obelisks with their bronze supporters and decoration in the great public spaces in Rome, but Boulton's exact source is unclear. Three of them (Plates 223.1–3) are grouped, with two of the unmounted obelisks and the Belisarius, Narcissus and Venus clock cases, under a heading 'Jewel Stands', but this was added when the sketches were pasted into the pattern book in the nineteenth century. Their function appears to be purely ornamental. They are decorated with mounts, which are similar to those on other ormolu ornaments produced at Soho. All of them appear to be made of white marble and belong to the late 1770s. The obelisk of Plate 223.1 has a two-stepped ormolu base, a marble pedestal edged with a frame of ormolu, four sphinxes beneath the obelisk and ormolu edging to the obelisk. The sphinxes and the gadrooned mount beneath the obelisk are reminiscent of the sphinx vase (Plate 357). The medallion fixed to the obelisk is annotated 'Empress of Rusia', which may indicate that it was intended for export to Russia. The obelisk of Plate 223.2 has a marble base fringed with a chased surround similar to the designs for clock cases (Plates 153, 186, 189), four lions supporting a marble pedestal which is ornamented with a medallion in a frame with a bow and swags, ball feet beneath the obelisk, an unusual foliate mount at the base of the obelisk, and a second medallion fixed to the obelisk. The medallion on the pedestal appears to be a representation of Peace with an olive branch and a dove. The medallion on the obelisk shows Hygieia or Peace, a medallion often used by Boulton and Fothergill, the origins of which I have discussed in Chapter 3 (see pp. 110–12). The sketch of Plate 223.3 shows an obelisk with a marble base and pedestal decorated with rams' heads and framed medallions like the vases of Plate 301. It too has ball feet beneath the obelisk. The fourth drawing of an obelisk (Plate 223.4) is like other designs for allegorical clock cases and watch stands. It shows an unidentified classical figure standing on a marble base, and a pedestal and obelisk with mounts similar to the obelisk of Plate 223.2, but without the foliate mount at the base of the obelisk. The bronze and ormolu figure looks Roman, but the significance of his posture and gesture is unclear, as is the addition of the Corinthian capital set on the base behind him. The medallion on the pedestal shows a woman with an altar, the medallion on the obelisk a female bust with a necklace, possibly Julia the daughter of the Emperor Titus, which I have discussed in Chapter 3 (see p. 107). There is no named ornament in the archives to which this drawing can be readily matched.

The mounts on the obelisks illustrated in Plate 224 do not correspond to any of these sketches.[380] I am inclined to attribute them to Boulton and Fothergill, although not with total conviction. The mounts, including the unusual leaf mounts rising at the four corners at the base of the obelisk and dropping from the top, are characteristic of the factory's work, the base mount beneath the obelisk and the guilloche bands particularly so.

223.1–2. Pattern Book 1, p. 77.

Picture and cameo frames

Many sales of ormolu picture frames are recorded in the archives during the late 1770s and early 1780s. These were the years when Boulton was

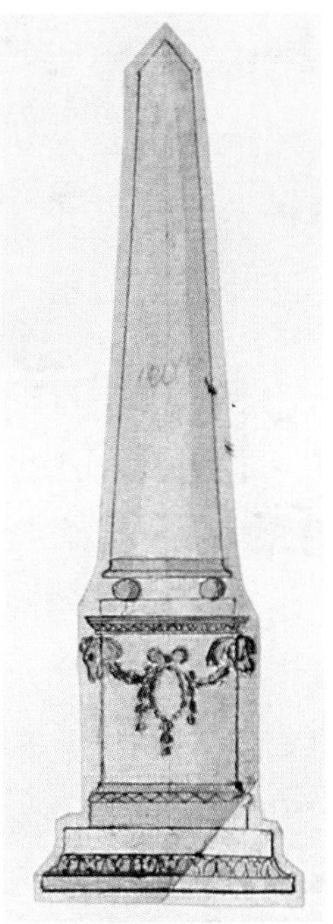

223.3–4. Pattern Book 1, p. 77 (Fig. 3), p. 79 (Fig. 4).

224. Boulton and Fothergill (attrib.), obelisks, 17 in., Ashmolean Museum, Oxford, on loan to Derby Museum.

producing mechanical pictures at Soho, and the frames were often sold in conjunction with the paintings.[381] The following is a typical extract from the records:

		£	s	d
A painting of Penelope on canvas		2	12	6
A ditto of Calypso ditto		2	12	6
2 or moulu frames to ditto	25/–	2	10	0[382]

The paintings of Penelope and Calypso were oval. Two frames were listed in the 1782 Inventory as '2 or moulu Penelope frames 11½ inches by 9½ inches £2 10s. 0d.'.[383] Penelope and Calypso, the two most captivating women in Odysseus's life, were painted in oval by Angelica Kauffmann and copied by Boulton as 'mechanical paintings'. Several versions of these two paintings are known, and there is some confusion about their authorship, let alone their identification. Most have been catalogued as by Kauffmann, and Calypso has sometimes been described as Ariadne.[384] It seems likely that

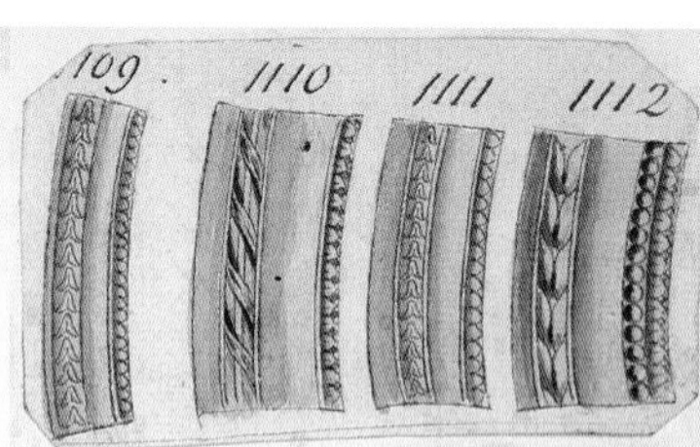

225. Picture frames, Angelica Kauffmann, *Penelope* and *Calypso*, 11.5 in., Private Collection.

226.1–2. Pattern Book 1, p. 80.

Kauffmann painted more than one version, not only on canvas but also on copper, but some versions are likely to be Boulton's mechanical paintings. There has not yet been a thorough study of the business in mechanical paintings,[385] and definite attribution will have to wait until examples can be firmly identified.

Plate 225 shows Penelope and Calypso, painted by Kauffmann on copper and mounted in ormolu frames matching the measurements quoted in the 1782 Inventory. The frames do not conform to any of the sketches in the pattern book, but there is no doubt that they came from Soho. The pictures came from Tew Park and were probably the 'small oval Penelope by Mrs Kauffmann cost 15gns, small oval Calypso by Mrs Kauffmann cost 15gns' listed in the 1782 Inventory.[386] The full titles of these two paintings were 'Penelope with the bow of Ulysses' and 'Calypso unconsolable for Ulysses'.[387] It is likely that Fothergill was referring to this painting of Penelope when he wrote to his partner early in 1778 that 'a Penelope awaits for a new sort of frame from Jee and Eginton';[388] Angelica Kauffmann herself was no doubt referring to both paintings when she wrote in June 1778:

> Mrs Angelica Kauffman presents her compliments to Mr Boulton, acquaints him that according to his desire she has done the little picture which is to be a companion to the Penelope, it represents Calypso mournful after the departure of Ulysses. Mrs Angelica flatters herself that Mr Boulton will approve of it as she has finished it with all possible care.[389]

Picture frames were sold in many sizes, as is shown by the 1782 Inventory,[390] by letters and account books, and by the several drawings in the pattern book (Plates 226–7), which give an idea of the decorative treatment. With one exception (Plate 227.3), numbered 1665, which is half size, all the drawings are said to be full size. They are therefore for small paintings or for cameos. The internal measurement of the largest oval frame (Plate 226, numbered 1663) is less than four inches. The internal measurements of the rectangular frames in Plate 227.1–2 (numbered 1695 and 1668) are 3.6 x 4.5 inches and 2.9 x 3.8 inches.

One of the sketches, numbered 1080 (Plate 226), is annotated with the words 'Lady Lucan or moulu frame full size'. Intriguingly the name 'Ld Lucan' appears in the margin against a record of '1 doz. small or moulu picture frames' in the 1782 Inventory.[391]

227.1–3. Pattern Book 1, p. 76 (Figs 1–2), p. 74 (Fig. 3).

It is likely that Boulton and Fothergill supplied gilt frames for cameos and plaques produced by Wedgwood, but there is surprisingly little evidence. Wedgwood wrote in 1776 that Boulton and Fothergill were making gilt metal frames suitable for his plaque of 'Herculaneum dancers' for sale at 15s. each,[392] but there is no evidence that Boulton supplied any to him. The numbering of the sketches in the pattern book suggests that picture and cameo frames may only have become regular products from the late 1770s. But the production of cameo frames may have continued at Soho for some time after the regular production of ormolu ornaments had ceased: they were more closely related to the button and toy trades. Wedgwood wrote to Boulton in 1786:

> I have left a few sets of my cameo buttons to be mounted, and shall be glad to increase our connection in this way, as well in selling you cameos for your own trade, as in having them mounted by you for mine, both in gilt metal and steel.[393]

There are several jasper cameos mounted in ormolu frames in the Wedgwood Museum, Barlaston. Others of identical patterns survive in other collections and appear from time to time in the salerooms. Some of these may have come from Soho, but I hesitate to ascribe any of them to Boulton and Fothergill without firm evidence

Sugar dishes

There were six sugar dishes made of blue john and ormolu and 'lined with silver' in the sale at Christie's in 1771.[394] The reserve price in each case was £5 5s. 0d. and four of them remained unsold.[395] There were three, each reserved at £1 11s. 6d., in the sale at Christie and Ansell's in 1778[396] and one was in stock in 1782.[397] Ormolu sugar dishes do not appear to be mentioned elsewhere in the archives and no example has yet come to light.

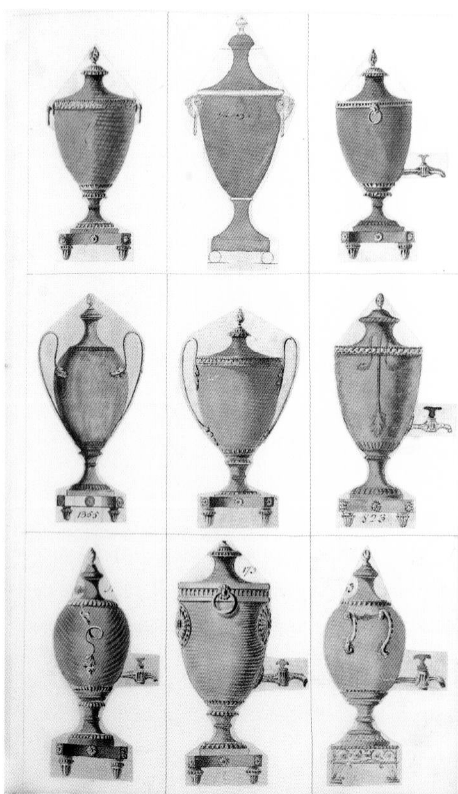

228. Pattern Book 1, p. 129, tea urns.

Tea urns

Boulton and Fothergill made tea urns of several different patterns in silver and plate.[398] They also produced them with a bronzed finish (Plate 228). Evidence in the archives for the manufacture of tea urns mounted with ormolu is somewhat thin but significant. The first commission was for a 'tripodic tea-kitchen', which the architect James Stuart designed in 1769. 'I have some sketches', wrote Stuart in December 1769, 'of the subjects we talked of at Soho, the border of the tea table, and the tripodic tea kitchen.'[399] In March 1770 Boulton wrote from London, after his first visit to the Palace, that he was 'to wait upon their Majestys again so soon as our tripod tea kitchen arrives'.[400] On the next day he asked Fothergill when the 'other tripod' would arrive and when 'a third could be sent'.[401] It is clear from the context that 'tripod' refers to a tea kitchen: later in the same letter Boulton specifies that one of the Queen's new vases could be like the 'new tea kitchen', and asks again to be informed 'what day I may expect the tripod tea kitchen'.

There was a tea urn in the sale at Christie's in 1770. Horace Walpole, writing on the extravagance of the fashionable world in London, reported to his friend Horace Mann that a 'tea-kettle' offered at the sale at Christie's fetched one hundred and thirty guineas against the expectation of its 'inventor' of one hundred guineas. The prices sound exaggerated, but Walpole was obviously struck by Boulton's urn.[402]

At the sale at Christie's in 1771 there was a 'tea vase or moulu decorated with festoons of flowers and lined with silver'. It was reserved at £18 18s. 0d. It remained unsold.[403]

Boulton had also planned late in 1770 to mount with ormolu some green porcelain bodies and necks as tea urns. He showed the porcelain to Wedgwood when the latter visited Soho and asked him to make some of them in 'Etruscan painted ware' (i.e. black basalt),[404] which Wedgwood promised to do.[405] Early in 1771 Wedgwood sent the parts of the tea vases:

> The neck is too small, but perhaps you can accommodate your moulding to it, if so, do not mount it plain (i.e. unpainted), it is not good enough, and we shall have better, but mark out the size, and form of you[r] divisions and send it to Mr Bentley to be painted. If the next will not do, we are making some larger. Be so good to let me know if it is anything near what it should be in other respects ...[406]

James Stuart had ordered one of these Etruscan ware tea urns for Mrs Montagu instead of a plated one,[407] but there is no record of the completion of the order.

In 1772 the Earl of Kerry ordered a 'tripod tea kitchen', but there is again no record of its delivery. He may not have pursued it, or he may have had a tea urn made in silver instead. He may not even have intended to order a tea kitchen[408]

Plates 229 and 231 illustrate tea urns at Syon and in the Royal Collection.[409] Their debt to James Stuart is obvious, and it is likely that they were made to the design mentioned in his letter in 1769. The tripod legs, with their fluted sides and paw feet, the two triangular guilloche stretchers with their Vitruvian scroll decoration on the inner side, and their manner of attachment with the screws hidden behind small pieces which slot into place at the backs of the legs, the shaped triangular base, and in Plate 231 the anthemion mount on the base, are all reminiscent of Stuart's tripod perfume burners (Plate 25). The fluted base in Plate 229 reappears on the candle vases which I have attributed to Anderson and which were probably made to Stuart's design (Plate 33). Other motifs appear on other vases produced at Soho at about the same time. The branches are very similar for example to the branches on the caryatic vase (Plate 324), which owes a number of its

OPPOSITE:
229. Tea urn, 20 in., Syon House.

230. Tea urn of Plate 229, detail.

231. Tea urn, 21.7 in., Royal Collection.

features to Stuart. They are identical to the branches on the vases in Plate 241, and the mounts into which they fit are also the same. The branches are repeated on the vases of Plate 244. The frieze on the upper surface of the tea urn in Plate 231 is also similar to the friezes on the vases in Plate 241 and to the frieze on the medallion vase (Plate 349). The pierced frieze round the tops of the urns has similarities to the frieze round the base of the Minerva clock case (Plate 166), although it is interrupted with vases. Both tea urns have gilt copper bodies and tinned copper linings, which are fixed by hammering to the rims of the urns. The undersides of the lids are also tinned. Each urn has three taps, two of them false, decorated with grotesque masks. One of the urns has ivory tap handles (Plate 229), the other mother-of-pearl. The heating lamps are suspended by chains and have chased covers

232. Pattern Book 7, loose sheet.

with flame finials when they are not in use. When in use, the flame bears directly onto an indentation in the copper lining of the urn. The lamp in Plate 231 is missing its wick holder. The two urns differ in the treatment of the bases, one having a fluted ormolu base mounted on a further wooden base veneered with tortoiseshell (Plate 229), the other having a shaped ebonised fruitwood base decorated with ormolu ornaments. There are other differences in the ornaments. The urn in the Royal Collection has a more elaborate frieze on the body of the urn. The top of the Syon urn is fluted; the top of the Royal urn is decorated with the pierced frieze that I have already mentioned. There is an extra lozenge band on the body of the Royal urn, and the rim of the heating inlet on its underside is decorated with a beaded band. It has three gilt rings mounted between the swags on its body. The top of its burner is plain rather than fluted, as are its three candle nozzles. The three vases set into the frieze on its body are lightly engraved with classical scenes representing Hercules and (probably) the Nemean lion, Hercules and (probably) Virtue and Pleasure, and an unidentified woman making an offering with an outsize ewer. It stands on castors, which could be contemporary, although I would have expected ormolu feet of the type shown in Plate 232. There is no sign of screw holes for such feet in the wooden base.

These two urns represent a degree of sophistication, even if their design might be described as a little fussy, which shows how far the techniques of manufacturing had advanced by the early 1770s. The Duke of Northumberland's urn may have been one of the objects that Boulton took with him when he visited Northumberland House in March 1770. Alternatively, it could have been the 'tripod' that was sent to the Duke in 1772.[410] It can probably be identified with the 'tripod vase and lamp with three branches gilt', which was recorded in the Drawing Room at Northumberland House in 1786.[411] It would be tempting to identify the Royal urn with the tea kitchen that Boulton was anxious to receive before he visited the Palace in March 1770, but it was bought by Queen Mary in 1938, and where it came from is not known.[412]

When she visited Soho in May 1770, Dorothy Richardson saw 'a very elegant silver gilt tea kitchen made for Sir Harbord Harbord, and sent down to mend. It is an embossed vase, from the middle spring three branches for candles, and under them are three heads, out of which the water is drawn. It stands upon a tripod' (see Chapter 1, pp. 24–5). The description sounds like the urns illustrated in Plates 229 and 231, and it is most likely that she was wrong in using the term 'silver gilt', a mistake that she also made in describing other ornaments.

Several sketches in the pattern books (Plate 228) suggest that other more routine tea urns may have been decorated with ormolu mounts, but equally the mounts could have been silver or plate.[413] Some of the mounts illustrated are somewhat similar to the decorative mounts on other ormolu ornaments; for example, the feet are in many cases very similar to the feet fitted to the sphinx vase (Plate 355).

The drawing illustrated in Plate 232 is subtitled 'an ornamental vase radix amethysti mounted d'or moulu but if executed in silver or d'or moulu it will serve as an ornamental vase or a tea vase, A being the spout'. The triangular base is similar to the base of the tea urn in Plate 231, with its paterae at the centre of the concave sides. The flutes and beaded feet are a familiar Boulton and Fothergill pattern. No examples of this elaborately decorated urn have yet come to light.

There was a 'gilt tea urn' valued at £15 and written down to £12 12s. 0d. among the 'very old pieces' in stock in 1782.[414]

Tripods

In February 1771 Boulton and Fothergill sold two tripods to the Earl of Shelburne for £100 5s.[415] There is no evidence that these tripods were gilt, but their price was similar to the reserve prices put on the four tripods in the sale at Christie's in 1771. Each of these tripods in the sale was described as 'for incense in or moulu, lined with silver, with three branches for candles, after a design of Mr Stuart's'.[416] Three of them were reserved at £50 and the fourth at £45. One of them apparently remained unsold[417] and was later withheld from the many unsold pieces that were to be sent to Amsterdam.[418]

It is likely that these tripods were modelled on the type of tripod illustrated in Plates 25 and 28. I have discussed in Chapter 3 my reasons for attributing the design of these tripods to James Stuart and their manufacture to the metalworker Diederich Nicolaus Anderson (see pp. 72–5). I have also suggested there that Boulton may have borrowed a tripod from Stuart or Anderson and copied it. Alternatively he may have bought one from Anderson's widow, or he may have received the models from William Chambers, who recorded one of the tripods in a slight sketch (Plate 32). The most likely source is Stuart himself, whom Boulton met in the late 1750s, and for whom he cast the massive tripod for the 'Lanthorn of Demosthenes' at Shugborough in 1770–1 (see Chapter 3, p. 72).

It is very likely that the tripod, which Dorothy Richardson saw at Soho in May 1770, was modelled on this design by Stuart. She described it as 'a gilt Egyptian embossed tripod, with a place in the middle for incense and from three sides branch candle sticks' (see Chapter 1, p. 25).

It has so far not been possible to identify any of the tripods produced at Soho in the early 1770s. The only firmly identifiable tripods based on Stuart's design that have come to light are the four 'gilt tripods with marble plinths' which were made for the Earl Gower in 1777,[419] one of which is illustrated in Plate 233. They incorporate many of the features and decorative details of Stuart's model, suggesting that Boulton and Fothergill had either taken casts of the components of one of Anderson's tripods or received moulds of them (Plates 26, 234). It is interesting that the pierced pattern on the lid (Plate 235), the only part of the tripods that was not cast, is completely different from the Stuart prototype.

These tripods, which have at some time been wired for electricity and have lost their inner bowls, incorporate many of the familiar methods of construction at Soho. The design of the branches is totally different from Stuart's version and echoes branches used on other ornaments by Boulton and Fothergill (Plates 306.2, 373). The shallower marble plinth (Plate 236) is markedly dissimilar, although it follows Stuart's scheme of decoration. The details of the chasing are perceptibly different, and not of the same quality as the chasing on the tripods at Kedleston (Plate 27), Althorp or the Victoria and Albert Museum. There are no medallions beneath the necklaces of the figures, although there are pierced rings from which they might be suspended. These tripods are another example of Boulton's frequent use of borrowed designs.

The manufacture of these four tripods was somewhat troublesome. Francis Eginton, who was in charge of the ormolu business, wrote to Boulton in April 1777 to ask 'whether Lord Gour will want his tripods before the Princes order is finished'. He despaired of getting them done unless 'a verry good and expeditious chaser' could be found who would come for two or three months.[420] They were delivered by October at a total cost of £181 1s. 6d.[421]

There were two pairs of tripods, each with three branches, in the sale at Christie and Ansell's in 1778, which were probably tripods of this design.[422]

OPPOSITE:
233. Tripod perfume burner with candle branches, 25.2 in., Private Collection.

There is only one tripod among the drawings in the pattern books (Plate 237). It is a design for a perfume burner and it owes a debt to Stuart's larger and more elegant design in its use of a triangular marble plinth with concave sides, paw feet, fluted legs and horizontal stretchers decorated with a guilloche motif. It also owes a debt to contemporary French designs in its use of a snake coiled between the legs and, as it were, supporting the bowl. This was a favoured motif of Parisian metalworkers and examples abound of perfume burners and candelabra which incorporate it. The Marquess of Granby bought a 'snake tripod' in 1774 at a cost of £16 16s.[423] Lord Digby ordered a 'or moulu snake tripod' in the same year, together with two vase candelabra to stand on each side of it.[424] All three ornaments still remain at Sherborne Castle, Dorset (Plates 238, 296). The tripod conforms closely to the drawing but the lid is missing. The ormolu bowl is cast in one piece and the inner copper bowl is gilt. It is fitted with three projections, which slot into grooves behind the scrolled tops of the legs (Plate 239). The legs are held to the bowl and to the horizontal rings by screws, and are attached to the marble base by bolts. The oval paterae are made separately and are attached by screw threads, as is the inverted finial beneath the bowl. The snake is attached by two screws to the inside surfaces of two of the legs. There is a similar tripod perfume burner at Temple Newsam, Leeds (Plate 240), but in this case the bowl is made of marble. There is a pierced lid with a finial, but the snake and one of the guilloche rings are missing. The position of the former upper ring has been altered and it has been filed to fit the smaller space lower down the legs. The original screw holes where the two rings and the snake were attached to the legs have been plugged. The paterae on the insides of the legs are modern. The construction of this second tripod is in other respects very similar to the one at Sherborne.

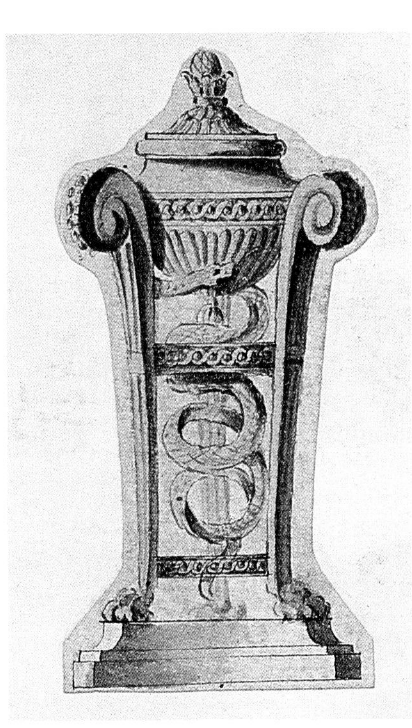

237. Pattern Book 1, p. 171.

There are other references to tripods in the archives. A tripod was among the consignment of ornaments which was sent to St Petersburg at the end of 1771 and was bought by the Empress. It may have been the Stuart tripod that was unsold in the 1771 sale and held back from the consignment of ornaments later sent to Amsterdam (see p. 56). Lord Cathcart mentioned that it was 'particularly admired'.[425] Large tripods with branches were listed among the products in 1772,[426] and one of them was made for the sale at Christie's in that year. 'Oh the branches for the tripod are not come', wrote Boulton to his partner from London, 'there was not 4 hours work to do when I came from home. I fear it will lessen my sale 50 or 60 £ ...'.[427] The price suggests that it was probably another of Stuart's tripods. There were six tripods in the sale at Christie and Ansell's in 1778. Two had marble plinths and were 'perferated for essence'. They were reserved at eight and seven guineas, prices that suggest they were smaller, possibly snake, tripods.[428] The other four were two pairs of 'tripods in or moulu, with branches for three lights each',[429] one of which was also pierced for perfume burning. The reserve prices were £27 and £25 10s. None of these tripods appears to have found a buyer.

The Earl of Kerry ordered four tripods for his house in Portman Square through the cabinet makers Mayhew and Ince in 1771. These were to hold candle branches but Mayhew and Ince's original instructions for the design of the branches were by no means clear.[430] There were twelve branches in all, so that each tripod had three, and they were eventually completed in March 1772.[431] There were also two large 'table' tripods with three branches, each of which were finished at the same time.[432] These six tripods, along with the chimneypiece mounts and vases which were made for Lord Kerry at the same time, were all gilt 'of the French colour so as to match those French ones upon your Lordship's chimney piece as near as we can remember'.[433] They were probably all sold in 1778 when Lord Kerry's furniture and works of art were auctioned by Christie and Ansell.[434] The

OPPOSITE:
234–6. Tripod perfume burner, details.

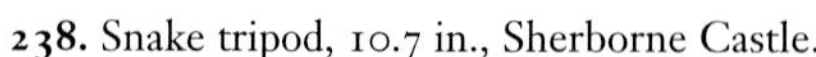

238. Snake tripod, 10.7 in., Sherborne Castle.

240. Snake tripod, 12.3 in., City of Leeds Art Gallery, Temple Newsam.

239. Snake tripod of Plate 238, detail.

descriptions in the catalogue of this sale are somewhat sparse and it is not easy to identify the ormolu objects from Soho among the many ormolu pieces listed. The four tripods for the drawing room are, however, probably the four small girandoles 'for three lights each',[435] and the two table tripods were one of the two pairs in the saloon.[436]

A drawing of a tripod with a marble plinth 'to hold six candles' was sent with an estimate of £55 to Lord Arundell in 1777.[437]

There were several vases and other objects among the range of Boulton and Fothergill's products whose supports were devised in the form of a tripod (e.g. Plates 229, 304, 324). The tea urns were even referred to sometimes as 'tripods'. I have described these 'tripodic' products under other headings.

Vases

Boulton's plans for developing the ormolu business centred largely on vases. They were by far the most numerous of Boulton and Fothergill's ormolu ornaments.

Vases usually took the form of candle holders, candelabra or perfume burners (or cassolettes or essence pots, as Boulton and Fothergill sometimes called them), but some were made simply as ornaments. It is impractical to discuss candle vases and perfume burners separately. Some designs, such as the sphinx vase (Plate 355), were invariably made as perfume burners. Others, such as the Cleopatra and goat's head vases (Plates 327, 331), were always made as candle vases. But this was not true of many designs, which were adaptable at the whim of the client. Thus the vase with the round pedestal illustrated in Plate 268, which was normally a perfume burner with a pierced lid, could be fitted instead with candle branches (Plate 270), and even the Venus vase, which was made both as a clock case and as a perfume burner, was fitted on at least one occasion with candle branches. Other vases could either hold one candle or be fitted with branches for two (Plates 261, 262). Vases were often made to serve a dual purpose. In the sale at Christie and Ansell's in 1778, for example, there was 'a pair of cassolettes in or moulu, with branches for three lights each'.[438] Usually the priority was reversed and descriptions of candle vases often ended with the words 'perferated for essence'.

Boulton's clerks used two distinct methods of identifying the various types of ornament. The first method, employed chiefly within the factory and in correspondence with agents, was the use of an identifying name. Most of the clock cases discussed earlier in this Survey had clearly identified names. So too did several vases. The second method was the use of a stock number, probably derived from the sequence of the drawings of the ornaments in the pattern books.[439] The sketches which were sent to potential customers were often marked with these numbers in order to make it easier for them to indicate their preference, and in some cases objects were identified by the same numbers in orders, invoices and letters.

Unfortunately the loss of the numbering sequence in the first pattern book (see Bibliography, manuscript sources, p. 478), and the lack of any other key to the names or stock numbers which were applied to the various vases, make it impossible to identify all the named or numbered vases mentioned in the archives with surviving vases. In some cases there is no doubt. These include the vases that can be identified with a numbered sketch and vases whose features clearly reflect the names given to them, such as the Bacchanalian, goat's head and sphinx vases (Plates 313, 332, 355). They also include vases that survive today and can be identified with references to their original purchase or delivery in the archives, such as the

King's vase (Plate 339), the medallion vase (Plate 349) and the wing-figured vases supplied to Robert Child in 1772 (Plates 365–9). The named vases over which there are no doubts are described in alphabetical order in separate sections after this introductory survey.

A pair of large medallion vases was listed among the unsold stock in Boulton and Fothergill's letter to William Matthews after the sale in 1771. Mystery surrounds some of the other vases mentioned by name in the same letter. Among them there were, for example:

	£	s	d
4 pairs sadle vases gilt bodies 63/–	12	12	0
5 pairs ditto ditto stone ditto 73/6[440]	18	7	6
A pair of little naked vases 42/–, a pair of pine apple ditto 84/–	6	6	0[441]

The 'pine apple' vase, of which there is no trace in the sale catalogue, was presumably given this name in recognition of some sort of pineapple ornament. The 'little naked' vase likewise cannot be traced, but a year later a pair was sold with sockets for candles.[442] The 'sadle' vases might be identified, judging from the prices, with the many pairs of 'candle vases with laurel festoons' that were included in the sale, but this is speculation, and the reason for the name is obscure. A pair of small saddle vases with gilt metal bodies was sold at Christie's a year later. They were not a pair, and were 'returned by a damned swearing chap'.[443] A pair of saddle vases with marble bodies was sold for £4 14s. 6d. to a visitor to Soho in 1775.[444] The name was still current in 1780,[445] and three saddle vases, including a pair with marble bodies, remained in stock in 1782.[446]

Other vases whose names presumably reflected some feature of their design were listed among the stock in 1782. There were, for example, a broken white marble 'lyre essence vase' (see pp. 342–4), and a broken marble Bacchanalian vase and a Bacchus vase 'ready to gild' (see pp. 319–23). Also in stock in 1782 were a small 'dancing boy' vase and a pair of bronzed metal 'dancing boy' vases,[447] which might perhaps have been the pair of 'small vases in or moulu, with a bas relief of boys dancing' which was included in the sale at Christie and Ansell's in 1778 and failed to sell.[448]

Vases were sometimes named after patrons or retailers, presumably because they had either provided or first chosen or commissioned the design, and even after certain craftsmen at Soho. Thus a large japanned vase was named after Lord Shelburne. Boulton asked his partner to send Lord Shelburne's 'enriched laquered vase' to London in March 1770, and at the same time wanted 'a pair of Lord Shelburne's large green vases' put in hand. When 'mounted, chased, remounted and then taken to pieces' the bodies were to be sent to Baskerville 'to be japand of the opaque blew'.[449] Mrs Beckford wanted four Lord Shelburne's vases in 1771, which could not be delivered before the sale at Christie's.[450] The vase was made on occasion with a blue john body.[451] The specification of blue lacquer for the bodies, the parallel use of blue john, and Boulton's description of the vase as 'enriched', suggest that Lord Shelburne's vase may have been the type of vase illustrated in Plate 258. But as yet there is no proof. Equally it is impossible to identify for sure the 'Digby's' vase, which was probably named after Lord Digby, an example of which was listed among the stock in 1782.[452] Perhaps it was the type of candle vase that he bought in 1774 (Plate 296).

The 'Burgoyne's' vase, which was named perhaps after Colonel (later General) Burgoyne, might be more readily identifiable. A 'branched metal Burgoyne' remained unsold in 1771[453] and might, judging from its price, have been one of the vases described in the catalogue as 'an altar richly embellished in the antique taste, on which is a vase with three branches for candles in the same taste'.[454] The bodies of these vases differed – one was recorded as entirely ormolu, one was blue john and one white marble. Lady Sandys bought one of these vases, the body unspecified, for £26 15s. 6d. and in 1772 she returned a 'Burgoyne's vase' for repair.[455] Boulton and Fothergill were still making Burgoyne's vases in 1775[456] and the stones for five of them remained in stock in 1782.[457] These records might refer to vases of the type illustrated in Plates 263–6, which, with their 'richly embellished' altar and three branches, match the description in the sale catalogue well.

Similarly the four-branched 'Egginton's vase' with a gilt body, which also remained unsold at the 1771 sale and was valued at £21,[458] may be identifiable with the caryatic vase (see pp. 323–4). It was also made with a blue john body.[459] One of the four-branched caryatic vases in the 1771 sale had a gilt body, and an annotation in the sale catalogue suggests that the amended reserve price was £21.[460] The name 'Egginton' may have been in recognition of Francis Eginton's modelling of the figures.

A two-branched 'Bingley's' vase, recorded in the same letter as returned to Soho, may also be identifiable. It was presumably named after the manager of the plated department, William Bingley. It seems nearly always to have had two candle branches and usually a pedestal.[461] These vases cost £15 15s. od. each[462] and pairs were sold at this price to Sir John Griffin Griffin in 1771,[463] and Mr Thynne in 1772.[464] A pair described as 'lyon-faced' was lent in the same year to the banker Robert Child while he was waiting for the wing-figured vases that he wanted.[465] The combination of pedestal, two branches and lions' faces suggests that Bingley's vase is likely to have been the type of vase illustrated in Plate 244 (see pp. 287–92), which in turn was probably the type of vase described in the 1771 sale catalogue as 'a rich vase lined with silver and branches for two candles, standing on a square pedestal of radix amethysti and or moulu'.[466]

According to the summary of ornaments which remained unsold at the sale in 1771, there were several other vases named after people. There were, for example:

	£	s	d	
3 of Harrach pattern 2 branched vases at £10 10s	31	10	0	
5 of Morrison's 4 leaved vases with drapery at £6	30	0	0	4 only
1 ditto ditto lined for essence	6	0	0	
5 Kentish essence potts stone bodies lined at 70s	17	10	0	
1 ditto ditto ditto ditto not lined	3	3	0	
2 ditto ditto green chinea at 70s	7	0	0	
5 pairs of Morrison's gilt bodies	15	15	0	
1 ditto ditto stone ditto	3	13	6	
5 pairs ditto enamel bodies at 63s a pair	15	15	0[467]	

These can mostly be linked, but without much confidence, to entries in the 1771 sale catalogue. Some of them can be linked, with even less confidence, to vases which have survived. The two-branched vases of 'Harrach pattern', which were presumably named after the London jeweller, were probably the vases 'of the radix amethysti and or moulu, with branches for two candles', which were reserved at £10 10s. od.[468] General Carnack bought two.

The 'Kentish' vase was presumably named after the goldsmith John Kentish, who had premises in Cornhill, London. Boulton and Fothergill supplied him with some vases in 1769.[469] It is clear from the summary of the pieces which remained unsold in April 1771 that this vase was a perfume burner and that its body was made variously of stone or china.[470] According to the archives it was one of the earliest patterns devised at Soho: a Mr Smith ordered a pair with gilt bodies in 1769 'but not with the same figures as the pattern'.[471] There is not enough evidence in the archives to enable the identification of this vase with any surviving vase. It might, however, judging from its price and from the variety of materials of which it was made, be identified with the 'essence pot radix amethysti and or moulu lined with silver' of which there were forty-one examples in the sale in 1771.[472] Some of these had china bodies, and others were enamelled, at least two of them with green enamel and one with blue.[473]

There seem to have been two types of 'Morrison's' vase. One was described in the list of unsold pieces as '4-leaved' and was decorated with drapery. It was a perfume burner and was priced at £6.[474] It was probably catalogued in the sale as a vase or 'essence pot radix amethysti and or moulu, lined with silver and ornamented in the antique taste'.[475] Among the purchasers were the Earl of Kerry and Lord Melbourne. The other vase was smaller and priced variously at £3 3s. 0d. and £3 13s. 6d. It was fitted with a gilt, stone or enamel body. There were many vases reserved at these prices in the sale in 1771 but most of them are insufficiently described in the catalogue. Sir John Griffin Griffin bought a pair of Morrison's vases with blue enamelled bodies in 1771,[476] but they do not appear to have survived. There is otherwise no record of an identifiable purchaser in the archives. There were at least two pairs of Morrison's vases with stone bodies in the sale in 1772,[477] and the name was still in use at Soho ten years later.[478]

Three other vases named after people are recorded in the archives but cannot be identified. A 'Hancocks' vase with candle branches, named presumably after the Soho workman William Hancock (see Chapter 4, p. 150), and a three-branched 'Colmores' vase were made for the sale in 1772, although in the event the latter was not ready in time.[479] The stones for a pair of 'Smith's pattern' vases were among the stock in 1782.[480]

Vases identified by stock numbers in the correspondence and accounting records are fewer. Most of the records of stock numbers date from about 1780 or later. Thus Sir Joshua Reynolds was sent, by mistake, a pair of 'white marble or moulu essence vases no. 834 at 280/– each vase' in 1780.[481] In the same year the Earl of Chesterfield was supplied with:

	£	s	d
1 Venus or moulu essence vase white marble no. 108	15	15	0
1 pair white marble pedestal or moulu vases no. 59	14	14	0
1 pair ditto ditto small vases no. 349	4	14	6[482]

The Venus vase is discussed later (Plate 359, see pp. 351–6). The number 349 coincides with the number on a sketch of a small vase in the firm's pattern books (Plate 257) and a closely related vase is illustrated in Plate 256. Also in 1780 Duncan Macalester bought:

	£	s	d
1 pair of or moulu essence vases with radix amethysti stones no. 11 at £12 12s	12	12	0
1 pair of or moulu candle vases with white marble bodies no. 55 [at] 94/6	4	14	6[483]

Several numbered vases were listed in Richard Bentley's workshop in 1782, including another '55':

	£	s	d
1 pair vases 859 blue john bodies ready to gild	2	3	0
1 pair ditto 212 marble ditto ditto	2	14	0
6 pairs ditto 55 ditto ditto ditto 31/6	9	9	0[484]

and the following were listed in one of the warehouses:

	£	s	d
1 two handled vase, stone body no. 76	4	4	0
1 two ditto ditto ditto no. 75	5	5	0
1 old round step foot candlestick vase no. 86	3	13	6
1 small candlestick vase each 67, 68, 67 pair 52/6	6	11	3[485]

In another warehouse there were 'a pair of vases, white marble no. 295' valued at £11 11s. 0d., and a pair of 'small or moulu marble vases for candles no. 1013' valued at £4 4s. 0d.[486]

The reference to the 'old round step foot candlestick vase' is interesting because it implies that the vases of the types illustrated in Plates 260, 262, 264 and 346, examples of which I have suggested were included in the sale in 1771, were no longer made at the end of the decade. The number 859 is also interesting because there is a sketch marked with this number in the pattern books (Plate 275). This is one of six numbered sketches which I have so far been able to identify with surviving vases (Plate 276). The others are numbered 863 (Plates 290 and 288), 860 (Plates 297 and 296), 238 (the wing-figured candle vase, Plates 370 and 367), 399, which is the sketch for the King's vase (Plates 341 and 339), and 1241 (plates 294 and 293). Only four other sketches are numbered, of which one (349, Plate 257) can be linked, as I have said above, to a purchase by the Earl of Chesterfield in 1780, and another (1013, Plate 309.2) can be linked to a reference in the 1782 Inventory, which I have mentioned above. I have so far not discovered any vases to match these two sketches or the remaining two numbered sketches, 516 (Plate 311) and 1237 (Plate 307).

The sketches incorporate many of the characteristic features of Boulton and Fothergill's designs. They make it clear that many of the mounts were interchangeable. It is because Boulton and Fothergill asked their patrons to choose from this limited repertoire of motifs that each vase seems to carry their trademark. The best way in which to demonstrate these repetitive motifs is to describe the vases which, using the evidence of the archives, the pattern books and stylistic comparison, can safely be attributed to Boulton and Fothergill.

241. Candle vases, 16.5 in., Blenheim Palace.

In Chapter 2 I have mentioned some of the vases, which, on the evidence of the archives, were probably among the firm's products in 1769–70 and were included in the sale in 1771. They included the Cleopatra and goat's head candle vases (Plates 327, 331) and the two-branched candle vases with spiral fluted stems of the type illustrated in Plate 241. These vases stand on ebonised wooden bases. The blue john bodies are made in two pieces and are lined with silvered copper bowls made in the usual way from two pieces of rolled copper soldered vertically and round the bottom. The rims are pierced for the emission of the perfume. The lining is also, unusually, pierced, as can be seen in Plate 242. The lids, with their flame finials, do not have a third nozzle on the underside. The spiral-fluted stem is cast in two pieces, the loose floral collar covering the join. The ornaments demonstrate the variety in the quality of the chasing which is typical of Boulton and Fothergill's work. The fine chasing of the anthemion frieze on the body of the vase (Plate 242) contrasts with the rather crude Vitruvian scroll of the pierced rim. In Chapter 3, I have mentioned how much the design of the mounts on these vases probably derives from James Stuart (see p. 76) – the spiral stem with its guilloche base and floral collar, the anthemion frieze, the branches, and the acanthus mount to which the branches are fixed. The spiral stem is echoed on the caryatic vase of Plate 324, the anthemion frieze on the lid of the tea urn attributed to Stuart (Plate 231). The branches also are repeated on the tea urn. The branches slot into the top of the acanthus-carrying mount in exactly the same way on both objects, and the acanthus mount is the same. There is no record in the archives of the purchase of these vases, which are at Blenheim, but the fourth Duke of Marlborough did buy other ornaments in 1772.[487]

242. Vase of Plate 241, detail.

243. Candle vases, 16 in., David Collection, Copenhagen.

Several vases of this design are known. There is a pair at Harewood House which have candle nozzles on the undersides of the lids of the type illustrated in Plates 243 and 263: each vase also has a rim carved in the stone just below the anthemion frieze.[488] Another pair survives at Frogmore, with the same reversible nozzles.[489] I have records of two other pairs with reversible nozzles. There is a further pair with no extra nozzles in the City of Birmingham Museum.[490] Other pairs are recorded in private collections or have appeared on the market in recent years.[491] A single vase, which was recently sold,[492] can be identified with the vase bought by the fourth Earl Fitzwilliam at Boulton and Fothergill's sale at Christie's in 1771. It was described in the catalogue as 'a vase radix amethysti and or moulu, lined with silver and perferated for essence, with ornaments in the antique taste and branches for two candles'.[493] It was reserved at £15 15s. 0d. and Lord Fitzwilliam paid £18 17s. 6d. There were four other vases in the 1771 sale of the same description.[494] All were reserved at £15 15s. 0d.

Also in the 1771 sale was a vase almost identically described as a 'vase radix amethysti and or moulu line with silver and perforated for essence, with ornaments in the antique taste and branches for three candles'.[495] This was reserved at £16 16s. 0d. It must surely be the same model of vase with the addition of a third branch. I have records of nine of these vases with blue john bodies and two with white marble bodies. The pair of marble vases is illustrated in Plate 243.[496] The mounts are all closely similar to the two-branched versions and the finials are reversible, as the illustration shows. The only unusual feature is the triangular marble base. All the other examples so far recorded, all with blue john bodies, have square bases, usually of ebonised wood and usually on four ball feet.[497] The exceptions are the two vases once owned by the Earl of Ashburnham, which have two-stepped square marble bases.[498]

I have suggested earlier (see p. 283) that vases of the type illustrated in Plates 244–5 should be identified with the 'Bingley's vase', and that they were probably the vases with square pedestals in the sale at Christie's in 1771. Like the vases just discussed, these vases were offered singly and were also reserved at £15 15s. 0d. each. The two designs were among the earliest mounted stone vases of some size produced at the Soho Manufactory. The branches on the vases of Plate 244 are the same as the branches on the vases of Plate 241 and on the tea urns (Plates 229, 231). The lions' masks and the

paw feet beneath the vase echo the lion-faced candlestick (Plate 135), which Boulton copied from a French model (see Chapter 3, pp. 66–7). The lions' masks and their square mounts are of the same dimensions as their counterparts on the candlestick and appear to have been cast from the same moulds. Most of the extant vases of this pattern have blue john panels in the square pedestals, although there is a pair at Shugborough that have black japanned glass panels. Sometimes the vases were sold without pedestals. A pair of Bingley's vases without pedestals was delivered to Sir Gregory Page in 1771,[499] and a two-branched pair with square ebonised wood bases, instead of pedestals, survives at Harewood House.

244. Lion-faced candle vases, 17.5 in., Private Collection.

The assembly of these vases is typical of the work at Soho. The components slot together with the use of projecting pegs and holes and closely fitted rims. The vase is held together by a threaded rod, with a nut at the base of the inside of the stone body. A circular plate measuring about one inch holds the threaded rod and is screwed into the base plate. Identification marks for attaching the branch to the vase can be seen on the top surface of the lion mask's square mount in Plate 245. The undersides of the blue john lids and the internal linings are silvered or gilt (silvered in the case of the vases of Plate 244). All the vases have the Greek fret band, floral swags suspended from paterae or rounded knobs, laurel mounts with crossed ribbons beneath the paw feet, and a crossed ribbon rim at the top of the body. The body mounts are pinned or bolted. All of the pedestals are decorated with guilloche and lozenge and acanthus mounts. As with so many of Boulton and Fothergill's blue john vases, the bodies are usually

OPPOSITE:
245. Vase of Plate 244, detail.

made of more than one piece of stone. They are usually mounted with two branches of the type illustrated in Plate 244, but the pair at Harewood has simpler branches without the loop. The vases at Shugborough have no branches. The vases in the Royal Collection (Plate 246) also have no branches.[500] Whether these vases ever had branches is doubtful, but the square blocks on which the lions' masks are mounted have slots for the fitting of branches. The linings of the Royal Collection vases are silvered.

Several vases of this type survive in private collections, and there is a two-branched pair in the Metropolitan Museum, New York.[501] A vase with a white marble body, lid and pedestal, but with the same mounts and branches, appeared on the London market some years ago.

These vases demonstrate, like the vases with the spiral-fluted stems, the enthusiasm that Boulton had for the use of blue john in vases of some size from the early years of production. They also demonstrate the different treatment, from vase to vase, of the chasing, suggesting that not all the work on the ornaments that make up a complete vase was necessarily done by the same chaser. This varied work can be seen for example in the inconsistent dimensions of the hatched lines on the sides of the lions' masks' square mounts on the pair of vases in the Royal Collection (Plate 246).

246. Lion-faced vases, 13.5 in., Royal Collection.

247. Vase perfume burners, 10 in., Christie's.

248. Candle vases, 7.7 in., Christie's.

249. Candle vases, 7.7 in., Howard Antiques Ltd.

250. Pattern Book 1, p. 170.

This vase is perhaps the most French in feeling of all Boulton's vases. Not only does it owe some of its components to French models, it also reflects the somewhat archaic style of early French designs in the antique taste.

The blue john vases shown in Plate 247 are also among the earlier ormolu products at Soho.[502] They are one of three patterns of vase based on a classical urn. The sphinx vase (Plate 355) is clearly closely related to them. The other urn-shaped vase is the Bacchanalian vase (Plate 313), which was made some years later. Despite the apparent similarity to the sphinx vase, most of the mounts differ. The chased mount below the stem is laurel, the fluted cradle holding the vase is solid, the guilloche band above it is unpierced, the acanthus leaf mounts on the vase have no masks and there are more of them, and the mounts on the blue john lid also differ. The copper internal lining is gilt, as is the underside of the lid. The blue john of these vases is rhomboidal in shape, the illusion of a complete urn being created by the cast cradle, which is presumably why the cradle is solid and not open work like the sphinx vase. There was a saving in not mounting a complete vase. A number of these vases, all with blue john bodies and some with blue john stems, are recorded, not all completely alike.[503] Among them is a pair very similar to the sphinx vase, with grotesque masks in place of the acanthus mounts, a pierced vase cradle, a shallower lid and a fluted stem, which may have been assembled using mounts originally intended for a sphinx vase.[504]

Another early type of candle vase is illustrated in Plate 248.[505] These vases are simple and fairly crudely made, and they repeat motifs used on other vases. Several vases of this design are recorded with either gilt or enamelled copper bodies (Plate 249). Examples have also survived with blue john and white marble bodies and copper inner linings.[506] Their assembly, which is typical of Boulton and Fothergill's earlier ormolu ornaments, is shown in Plate 108. As in other early vases, for example the goat's head vase (Plate 106), there is no base plate with a long threaded rod rising from it. Instead the cast and chased stem is fixed to the base by hammering, and the vase and lining are held together by a short threaded bolt, screwed down into the top of the stem piece. Some examples of these vases have a more convincing guilloche band at the top of the body. Others have laurel swags and pendants of the type that decorate the Cleopatra vases in Plate 327 instead of the drapery swags and pendants.[507] The reversible finials are almost exactly repeated in the vase in Plate 261.

There is a corresponding sketch in the pattern book (Plate 250) with the laurel swags and pendants. The vase can perhaps be identified with the candle vases described in the sale at Christie's in 1771 as 'with drapery and other ornaments'. There were ten pairs in the sale.

Plate 251 shows another ornament, a perfume burner, which is probably among the earlier ormolu products at Soho.[508] It, too, corresponds to a drawing in the pattern book (Plate 252), although it has lost the cover to the burner suspended below the bowl. This would have been similar to the covers on the burners of the wing-figured perfume burners of Plate 362. The pierced pattern of the lid, and the pierced band beneath the finial, also differ from the drawing; this band does not fit elegantly with the mount that carries the finial and it may have been added or altered. The sphinxes and the laurel swags and pendants, with their rather poorly chased flowers, are bolted to the triangular pedestal. The bowl is screwed to the heads of the sphinxes. The inside of the bowl is gilt, its underside left as plain copper where it receives the heat of the wick.

The sphinxes on this perfume burner, with their draped headdresses and the shaped and engraved copes which hang round their shoulders and down their backs, reappear on a silver coffee pot made at Soho in 1769–70

251. Perfume burner, 10.7 in., Christie's.

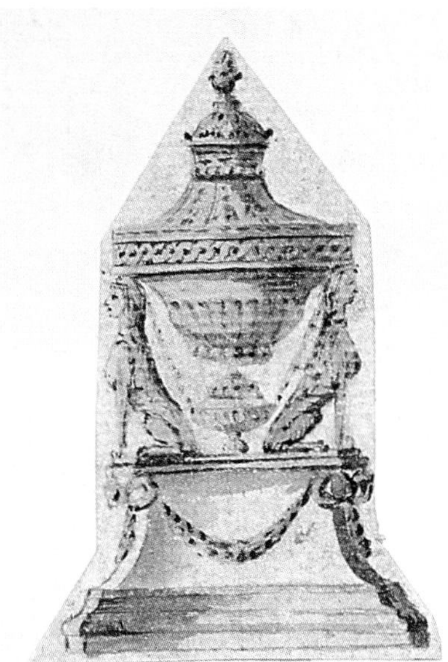

252. Pattern Book 1, p. 171.

(Plate 95), reinforcing the theory that this is one of the earliest of Boulton and Fothergill's ormolu ornaments. In Chapter 3, I have recorded that the three sphinxes appear to be closely related to a drawing by James Wyatt (see p. 87).

The theme of a gilt pedestal, decorated with swags and pendants, is repeated in the vase of Plate 253, which is mounted on a square pedestal. This vase is a perfume burner, with a blue john body of richly coloured stone, a gilt copper lining and a lid pierced with a simple six-part anthemion motif. It has several of the features of a sketch in the pattern book (Plate 254) which shows a vase on a pedestal decorated with similar mounts. The lid in the sketch is decorated with leaves and appears not to be pierced, and the pedestal looks round rather than square. The pinned mounts on the pedestal on the vase in Plate 253, which are soldered together to form a single four-sided mount, follow the sketch, as do most of the other mounts, including the swags on the body, the guilloche frieze, and the scroll handles. The construction of this vase is a typical example of Boulton and Fothergill's technique, the vase support being made up of no less than twelve separate pieces, excluding the decorative swags and pendants on the pedestal. All the pieces are neatly rimmed or fitted with supporting flanges and pins, and many of them are marked for identification during the process of assembly. The vase is held together, in typical manner, by screwing characteristic nuts onto a threaded rod, which is fixed to the square base plate. One nut holds the vase, the other, chased and gilt and with two fixing holes as in Plate 97, holds the gilt copper lining. A vase of the same model, but with a white marble body and pedestal, is illustrated in Plate 255. A pair of white marble vases was sold during the disposal of works of art by the Soviet Union in 1929.[509]

Another vase with scroll handles is numbered 349 in the pattern book (Plate 257). It was described in 1780 as 'a small white marble vase' when a pair was supplied to the Earl of Chesterfield (see p. 284). The candle vases of Plate 256 closely match the sketch, although the handles in the sketch are set at a sharper angle. The finials and nozzles are reversible; the lower edge

253. Vase perfume burner, 10.7 in., Birmingham Museum and Art Gallery.

254. Pattern Book 1, p. 171.

255. Vase perfume burner, 10 in., Private Collection.

256. Candle vases, 6.5 in., Hotspur Ltd.

257. Pattern Book 1, p. 170.

258. Vase perfume burners, 13 in., Syon House.

of the guilloche band round the top of the body is toothed as in Plate 267. The pair supplied to Lord Chesterfield in 1780 may have had pedestals, depending on the interpretation of the 'ditto ditto' in the record of his purchase (see p. 284). There is a gilt copper lining and the assembly is typical, with an iron rod attached to the square base plate. The vase was also made with a blue john body.[510]

Swags and pendants similar to those on the vase of Plate 253 appear on the bases of the vases of Plate 258, with the addition of bucrania in the centre of each side. There have always been some doubts about attributing these vases to Boulton and Fothergill. The arguments for not doing so are that several of the mounts do not appear in precisely the same form on other vases, for example the four medallions, the fluted band round the lower part of the body, and the handles with their dolphin heads, and that there are subtle differences in the design of some of the mounts that do appear elsewhere. Nor is there a corresponding drawing in the pattern books. But these criticisms can be levied against other vases and I can see no argument at present for attributing them to a different workshop. Indeed there is a strong case for identifying these vases with the references in the archives to 'Lord Shelburne's vase', as I have suggested above (see p. 282). They are the only vases that match the descriptions 'japand of the opaque blew', 'large' and 'enriched', which were applied to Lord Shelburne's vases in 1770. The Duke of Northumberland, furthermore, was one of Boulton's earliest patrons. The vases may have been two of the '7 ornamental vases' listed on the chimneypiece in the drawing room at Northumberland House in 1786.[511]

The bodies of these vases are of copper, and the lacquer, which has become discoloured over the years, was originally blue and is applied to a silvered surface, probably silver plate. The lids of the vases are cast, with a decoration of fluted rays, and are not pierced. The copper linings are gilt and are fashioned, as is the case with many of the inner linings of Boulton's vases, from rolled and hammered copper, soldered vertically (cf. Plate 97). A cast copper piece is attached to them which screws onto the vertical rod housed in the base. The medallions and the paterae are attached to the vase by characteristic nuts, and the ribbons of the medallions 'hang' from small

259. Vase perfume burners, 13.5 in., Partridge Fine Arts.

flowers, which are also bolted to the vase. The handles are attached from the inside by screws. The dolphin heads on the handles may well have been among the models given to Boulton by William Chambers in 1770 (see Chapter 3, p. 85).

Four pairs of these vases have so far been recorded, all with identical mounts. In the case of the second pair the bodies are also blue lacquer, the lacquer having been restored.[512] The bodies of the third pair are white marble (Plate 259). The fourth pair is in the State Hermitage Museum in St Petersburg.[513] These vases have blue john bodies, strengthening the case for believing that this pattern can be identified with Lord Shelburne's vase. They stand on later square pedestals with a further ormolu base of a green stone that is probably from one of the Russian lapidary works. These vases may well have been part of the consignment of vases sent to the Empress Catherine in 1771, although they are catalogued as having come from a 'private collection'. All three of these pairs have lids pierced with a similar four-part pattern, for the emission of perfume.

The four medallions (Plate 62) are identical on all four pairs. I have shown in Chapter 3 (p. 92) that these derive from the second volume of A. F. Gori's *Museum Florentinum* although it is not certain that Boulton's modeller copied them direct from Gori's illustrations.

There were two 'essence vases', one with a blue john body and the other marble, 'with handles terminating in dolphins' in the sale at Christie and Ansell's in 1778.[514] These may have been vases of this type. There are no other vases so far recorded with dolphin handles.

The vases that I have so far discussed, along with the Cleopatra vase (Plate 327), the goat's head vase (Plate 331) and the wing-figured perfume burner (Plate 362) can all be included among the earlier products of 1769–70, and it is not difficult to detect how other vase designs evolved from them. The candle vases of Plate 260[515] clearly owe some of their origin to the Cleopatra vase. The vase itself is the same, and it sits on the same fluted stem and Greek fret base. But it is now mounted on a circular blue john pedestal, or 'altar', decorated with lions' masks, reminiscent of the lions' masks on the vases of Plate 244, and laurel swags. The pedestal, being larger than the vase, presents an opportunity to show variegated blue john to better advantage. The pedestal sits on a two-stepped blue john base decorated with pierced guilloche bands. This is the 'old round step' mentioned in the Inventory in 1782.[516] It is repeated on the lyre vase, which must have been made at about the same time (Plate 346). The finial and nozzle are the same as those on the vases in Plate 249. There is a copper lining. There are many known examples of this vase. Some have two steps, but have gadrooned caps to cover the candle nozzle when it is not in use, in the place of the reversible finial (Plate 261).[517] Others have two or three gilt steps, some with gilt pedestals.[518] All have blue john vase bodies of the Cleopatra model.

Vases of this design were sometimes fitted with two candle branches of the type fitted to the lion-faced candlesticks (Plate 135). Plate 262 shows a pair of these candelabra.[519] I have discussed the French origins of the design of the branches in Chapter 3 (p. 67). They reappear on other candle vases (Plate 264), as do the nozzles and splash rings (Plate 365). The vases are necessarily larger in view of the size and weight of the branches, the curve of the laurel swags on the body of the vase is shallower, and a plain cast mount takes the place of the Greek fret base below the vase. The branches are fixed to the base of the lid, which fits into the vase by means of a copper sleeve. The pedestal or altar stands on three blue john steps, decorated with pierced guilloche bands, instead of only two. The richly veined blue john is shown to good advantage in the two pedestals and was obviously chosen with great care. Other examples of this candle vase are known, all with blue

260. Candle vases, 11.5 in., Royal Collection.

261. Candle vases, 10.5 in., Gerstenfeld Collection.

262. Candle vases, 15 in., Gerstenfeld Collection.

OPPOSITE:
263. Candle vases, 15.7 in., City of Leeds Art Gallery, Temple Newsam.

264. Vase of Plate 263, detail.

john pedestals and three steps,[520] and there is a somewhat damaged single vase at Pavlovsk which may have been in the consignment of vases sent to the Empress Catherine in 1771.[521]

Plate 263 illustrates a type of vase that I have tentatively identified as 'Burgoyne's' vase (see pp. 282–3). Its debt to the previous vase discussed is obvious. The body of the vase is bigger still, in order to cope with the physical and stylistic weight of the three branches, and the whole design is altogether grander. The central finial reverses into a nozzle of the type used on the vases of Plate 243. The branches (Plate 264), again of the type used for the lion-faced candlesticks (Plate 135), are fixed into the rams' head mounts, which are linked by a scrolling decorative frieze echoing the frieze round the base of the sphinx vase (Plate 357). There are three floral swags on the body. The pedestal is decorated with caryatids, drapery swags and paterae. There are three marble steps decorated with unpierced guilloche bands. Inside the vase is a cylindrical gilt copper lining.[522]

Other examples of this vase with white marble bodies, pedestals and steps are recorded.[523] Blue john versions, with the same branches, are also known.[524] A different blue john version is illustrated in Plate 265.[525] These vases have three undecorated gilt steps. They are otherwise similar to the marble version. They are probably the earlier version of the design, carrying as they do the looped branches of earlier vases (Plates 241, 244) and of the tea urn, the design of which I have tentatively attributed to James Stuart (Plate 229). There are no paterae on the pedestal, and the keen-eyed reader will notice that the scrolling floral frieze round the top of the bodies is upside down (Plate 266).

The construction of all these three-branched vases is typical in its precision, in the make-up of the various components and in their identification for the purpose of assembly. Unless 'restored', the vases are held together by the usual threaded rod fixed to the base plate, with a typical chased and two-holed nut at the top inside the gilt copper lining and a plain nut inside the vase. The mounts are pinned in the usual manner. The way in which the weight of the branches of the vase shown in Plate 265 is supported by the rams' heads, which are in turn fixed to the fragile stone, is an uncharacteristically weak feature of the design. A more satisfactory solution, in which the weight of the branches is supported by the metal rim, is illustrated in Plate 262.

There is no drawing in the pattern books corresponding to the candle vases illustrated in Plate 267, but they must clearly be attributed to Boulton and Fothergill. These vases may have had caps similar both in construction and design to the cap illustrated in Plate 328. The stamped guilloche band appears frequently on vases from Soho (Plates 253, 269). This band is not usually serrated along its lower edge but this feature appears both on other vases (Plate 255) and in one of the numbered sketches (Plate 309.2). The form and decoration of the stem are also typical. Apart from the casting of the socket and handles in one piece, to which the small copper lining is welded, the construction also gives these vases away. Each separate piece is carefully rimmed and fitted, and most are marked with the customary identification marks. The bodies of these vases are made of a rich pink-veined stone. I have records of several pairs of these vases, including one pair with marble bodies.[526]

A relatively common vase, which was usually made as a perfume burner with a gilt copper lining and a pierced lid, is illustrated in Plate 268.[527] The quality of most of these vases suggests that the model may date from after 1770, reflecting Boulton's call for an improvement in the quality of the ormolu work. The circular pedestal, which was usually made of white marble even if the body of the vase was made of blue john, appears in at least four sketches in the pattern books. Other characteristic features are

265. Candle vases, 19 in., Christie's.

267. Candle vases, 8 in., Private Collection.

266. Vase of Plate 265, detail.

the laurel swags and oval paterae which are pinned to the pedestal, the swags of husks pinned to the body, the elegant loop handles, the guilloche frieze, the fluted stem and its concave four-sided support, also decorated with a guilloche pattern. This was repeated in some of Boulton's designs for silverware (Plate 91). The construction of a vase of this type is demonstrated in Plate 110,[528] which shows that they are built in the typical manner, with the vase and the gilt copper lining bolted to the threaded rod with typical nuts. In this illustration the nut that fastens the vase body is misplaced above the lining. Most of the vases of this design have identical chased nuts both holding the lining and on the underside of the lid. There are three of these vases in the State Hermitage Museum, St Petersburg,[529] and a pair at Pavlovsk,[530] and I have records of many other pairs.[531] Many pairs with white marble bodies and pedestals also survive, including a pair at Harewood House (Plate 269) and another pair at Sandringham.[532] There is a pair at Pavlovsk. Plate 270[533] shows one of a marble pair fitted with candle branches of the type illustrated in Plates 296, 298 and 301 and in the pattern book (Plate 312.1), underlining the range of choice offered to purchasers of Boulton and Fothergill's vases.

A similar pair of vases is illustrated in Plate 271.[534] These are candle vases, with reversible finials and nozzles. They are modelled approximately on one of the sketches in the pattern book (Plate 272). The stone is of a striking violet colour. In all other respects these vases are characteristic of Boulton and Fothergill's work. The vases have gilt copper linings and the individual mounts are, as usual, neatly turned and fitted and marked for identification. The Vitruvian scroll frieze at the top of the body is an uncommon feature in the sketches of ormolu vases but it was used on other vases (Plate 298) and on silverware (Plate 90). Models of this vase usually have blue john bodies and white marble pedestals.

268. Vase perfume burners, 9 in., Christie's.

Plate 273 shows a variant of this design, with a guilloche band at the top of the vase, squatter handles, a laurel mount beneath the stem, and no pedestal.[535] This vase, with its acanthus ornament spreading from the branches, is similar to the drawing numbered 516 in the pattern books (Plate 311), but it has a two-stepped base with ball feet and no spreading mount above the stem. As is often the case, the blue john does not reach the top of the guilloche rim. The lining is gilt copper, fixed with the usual chased nut. This design was also made in white marble.

The small candle vases of Plate 274[536] are made of brilliant reddish stone, illustrating the variety, texture and beauty of blue john. This stone is probably from the 'Bull Beef' vein of the blue john mine. The design of the vase follows the sketch numbered 859 (Plate 275) almost precisely. The finials are reversible, the nozzles being similar to the nozzles on other vases (Plates 296, 298). I have already mentioned that a pair of these vases was in stock at Soho in 1782 (see p. 284). The very neat construction is illustrated in Plate 111, showing the rims, pegs and holes of the flat mounts, the pins which hold the body mounts, the standard nuts, the notches in the top rim into which the finial and nozzle lock, and the gilding spills. A detail of the handles is shown in Plate 112. The cylindrical copper lining is gilt on the inside and made of two pieces of copper soldered in the usual way (Plate 97). One of a pair of these vases with white marble bodies standing on round marble pedestals is shown in Plate 276.[537] These vases correspond fairly closely to another sketch in the pattern books (Plate 309.3), but the loop handles are not split, the lid and finial are different, and the rim at the top of the body is not decorated with a guilloche pattern. The white stone has been stained by careless cleaning, the vases having been washed at some point without being taken to pieces, with the result that the rust of the pins that fix the mounts to the bodies has penetrated the marble. They are thus an object lesson in restoration, but the colour is not unattractive. Several of

270. Candle vase, 12.5 in., Christie's.

269. Vase perfume burners, 9.2 in., Harewood House.

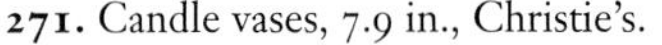

271. Candle vases, 7.9 in., Christie's.

272. Pattern Book 1, p. 171.

273. Candle vases, 6.5 in., Christie's.

274. Candle vases, 6.5 in., Private Collection.

BELOW:
276. Candle vases, 7.6 in., Private Collection.

275. Pattern Book 1, p. 170.

277. Candle vases, 7.5 in., Christie's.

278. Pattern Book 1, p. 171.

279. Vase perfume burners, 9.5 in., Private Collection.

the mounts on these vases appear on other vases, but the anthemion motif between the splayed acanthus decorations of the handles is unusual.

The reversible finials and nozzles of the vases of Plate 277 are closely similar to those on these candle vases. But there are many differences in the other mounts. The vase cradle is chased with an acanthus motif, the rim is decorated with a guilloche pattern, there are oak leaf and ribbon swags and pendants, and the handles are more elaborate, with their scrolls resting on rams' heads. The construction is, however, the same. The lining is copper. These vases also have their parallel in a sketch in the pattern books (Plate 278).[538]

The same handles with the scroll resting on rams' heads appear on the perfume burners in Plate 279.[539] The swags and pendants are similar but the other mounts are different. The fluted stem with its bead ring is similar to the stem of the vases in Plate 268. The splayed pedestal, in this case of white marble, is unique to this pattern and is decorated with a guilloche band at the base, mounted on a copper base plate. The lining is gilt copper and is now soldered to the pierced rim. The construction is normal, the holding rod fixed to the base plate, with the various pieces notched, pegged, rimmed and marked for identification during assembly. The fixing nuts are standard (cf. Plate 97). The rams' heads are pinned to the vase body. These vases were also made with white marble bodies and pedestals,[540] and marble pairs are recorded with fluted ormolu pedestals.[541] Vases of this type also survive with branches for two candles, with both blue john and marble bodies and fluted ormolu pedestals (Plate 280). These branches are the same as those fitted to other vases (Plates 270, 296, 298, etc.) and mirror the sketch in the pattern book illustrated in Plate 312.1.

Another vase that closely resembles a sketch in the pattern book is illustrated in Plate 281. The sketch is shown in Plate 282. This candle vase is very like the goat's head vase (Plate 332), except that it has elaborate double handles in place of the goats' heads, the swags and the pendants.

280. Candle vases, 13.5 in., M. Turpin.

281. Candle vases, 9 in., Birmingham Museum and Art Gallery, Soho House.

282. Pattern Book 1, p. 170.

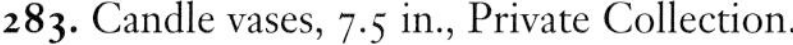

283. Candle vases, 7.5 in., Private Collection.

284. Pattern Book 1, p. 171.

285–6. Vase perfume burners, 12 in., Mallett.

287. Pattern Book 1, p. 170.

288. Candle vases, 12.5 in., Norman Adams.

289. Vase of Plate 288, detail.

The construction is different. Instead of the stem being fixed to the square piece beneath it, with a short threaded rod (Plate 106) there is a base plate into which a longer threaded rod with a slotted head is screwed. The cylindrical lining is copper.[542]

A pair of small candle vases with truncated scroll handles is illustrated in Plate 283. These vases, too, conform to a sketch in the pattern book (Plate 284). The finials and nozzles are reversible, and many of the mounts, including the guilloche band round the body of the vase, appear on other ornaments. The lining is gilt copper. There is a pair of these vases in the State Hermitage Museum, St Petersburg.[543]

The vases of Plates 285–6 have beautifully veined red and purple blue john bodies.[544] They conform to a sketch in the pattern books (Plate 287). The lid is pierced; the lining is of gilt copper. The construction is typical. The scroll handle, a feature that appears in a number of vases made in the later years of production, is pinned to the body, and the laurel swags are bolted. The fluted stem echoes the vases of Plates 268 and designs for silverware (Plate 91).

290. Pattern Book 1, p. 170.

Plates 288–9 illustrate a pair of similar vases, also made of finely coloured and veined blue john. But there are several differences. They are candle vases. The finials echo the finials of the wing-figured vases of Plate 367. They are reversible, the nozzles being similar to the nozzles on the Apollo and Diana candelabra (Plates 130–1). There are no swags on the bodies; the scroll handles (Plate 289) are decorated with a slighter acanthus motif at the bottom, husks on the outer surface, and a rosette on the scroll at the top. These vases are close to a drawing in the pattern books numbered 863 (Plate 290) although the sketch suggests that there may have been other mounts on the body of the vase. The number of the sketch, and the likeness of the nozzles to those on the Apollo and Diana candelabra, suggest that these vases were made in the later 1770s.

Plate 291[545] illustrates a perfume burner with a body of red blue john, which matches the drawing in Plate 292, the only noteworthy differences

291. Vase perfume burner, 14.6 in., Hotspur Ltd.

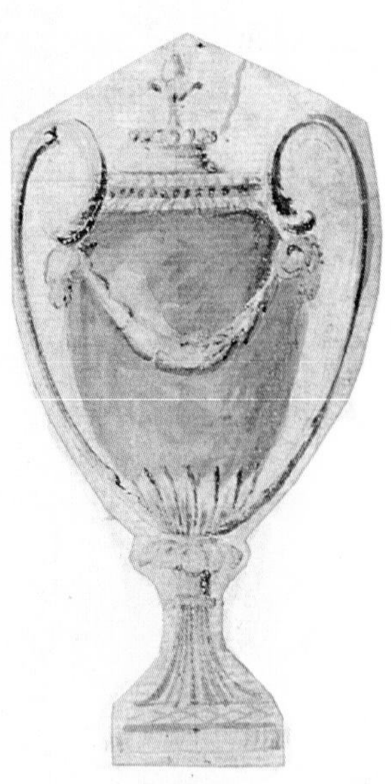

292. Pattern Book I, p. 137.

293. Vases, 11 and 11.4 in., Private Collection.

294. Pattern Book 1, p. 124.

295. Vases of Plate 293.

being the length of the laurel leaves cradling the vase and the treatment of the pierced rim and the stem of the finial. The handles are more slender than those on the previous vases, relying entirely on an acanthus motif, and the finial is more pronounced. The rams' heads and the laurel swags and pendant reappear, and the stem is a characteristic shape but is chased with stylised leaves. The pierced rim, with its double row of beads, is reminiscent of the Persian vase (Plate 351), but is not as decorated. A pair of these vases was sold by the Soviet Union in Berlin in 1928.[546]

The vases of Plate 293 share their lid, with its pinecone finial, leaf motif and gadrooned rim, with the vases of Plate 244. They conform in most respects to the sketch numbered 1241 in the pattern books (Plate 294). These vases are ornamental, and are designed to show off the highly figured blue john. Because of this, there are no oak-leaf swags and pendants on the bodies, as suggested by the drawing. Plate 295 shows that the left-hand vase is made of carefully cut pieces of stone. Plate 295 also shows the satyr's mask on the handle, with rather tame horns in the centre of his forehead, and the elegant treatment of the voluted scroll at the top of the handle. The mounts beneath the body are typical. The vases are slightly larger than double the size of the drawing, which is annotated 'half size'. The two vases are slightly different in height owing to the different sizes of the stones, and the handles are mounted on the wrong vases, as is evident from the way in which, on the left-hand vase, they overlap the cradling mount at the bottom of the vase, whereas on the right-hand vase they stop short of it. Another pair of these vases, with opaque white glass bodies similar to the bodies of the wing-figured vases of Plates 365 and 367, this time with the swags and pendants shown in the drawing, survives at Pavlovsk.[547] James Keir supplied the glass bodies from his glassworks in Stourbridge (see Chapter 4, p. 151). It is possible that these vases were the same model as those described after the sale at Christie's in 1772 as a '2 handled mask face',[548] although the number 1241 might suggest that they were made at a later date.

As the 1770s wore on, Boulton and Fothergill used white marble more often for their ormolu ornaments, as they did for clock cases. The vases illustrated in Plate 296 correspond with a drawing in the pattern books (Plate 297), although the treatment of the stem and feet has not in this case followed the sketch, and the vases have been supplied with branches of the pattern frequently fitted when the patron wanted candle vases (Plates 270, 298, 301, 312.1). The sketch is numbered 860, suggesting that this vase is virtually contemporaneous with the vases of Plates 274 (859) and 288 (863). Apart from the stem and the feet, the vase is close to the sketch, even down to the loose pieces of ribbon hanging from the swags and the shape of the handle where it joins the ram's head. Inside each vase is a shallow lining that suggests that these vases were designed to hold a single candle when the branches were not in use. One of the swags is missing, as is one of the nozzle inserts. Two of the acanthus ornaments and beaded rings beneath the splash rings are also missing. The construction of the branches is illustrated in Plate 113. The branches are fixed to a copper sleeve, which fits into the copper lining of the vase. The construction of the rest of the vase is similar to Plate 114, with the usual base plate, threaded rod and nuts, the mounts fitting neatly together with the use of integral pegs, holes and rims. Lord

296. Candle vases, 12.2 in., Sherborne Castle.

297. Pattern Book 1, p. 170.

299. Pattern Book 1, p. 171.

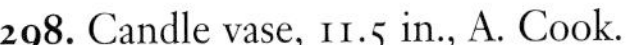
298. Candle vase, 11.5 in., A. Cook.

Digby bought these vases in 1775,[549] along with the tripod perfume burner illustrated in Plate 238. All three ornaments are at Sherborne Castle. Boulton and Fothergill sent four drawings of candle vases in September 1774 for Lord Digby to choose from, and advised him that 'the branch on one of the drawings may be applied to any of the others'.[550] They sent Lady Digby the prices of the four patterns 'as near as we can remember them' a week or so later,[551] but apparently Lord Digby did not like any of the suggestions sufficiently and he was sent a further design.[552] The cost was not quoted.[553]

The candle vase of Plate 298, which is one of a pair, repeats the Vitruvian scroll frieze which was used to decorate the vases of Plate 271, and which was used more frequently for pieces of silverware (Plate 90). The four-sided base with its guilloche decoration is also a design which Boulton and Fothergill used on pieces of silverware in almost identical form (Plates 90, 95). The handles are distinctive and are decorated where they join the body with an acanthus motif. This vase is based on a sketch in the pattern books (Plate 299) and has been fitted with the same branches for two candles as the previous vases. The pieces beneath the splash rings on each branch are later additions. Otherwise the vase retains many of the characteristic features – the method of construction, the pinning of the mounts, the gilt copper lining and the chased gilt nut which fastens it – which stamps it as a product of Soho.[554] The medallion does not feature in the drawing. A vase of a closely related design, with a patera in place of the medallion, no Vitruvian scroll frieze, and a two-stepped squared base with ball feet is shown in Plate 300.[555]

300. Candle vase, 11.2 in., Christie's.

301. Candle vases, 15.3 in., Weston Park Foundation.

Candle branches of the same pattern are fitted to the vases illustrated in Plate 301. The simpler form of this vase is illustrated in Plate 302. It conforms closely to a drawing in the pattern books (Plate 303), although the cap that fits into the candle holder when it is not in use is less elaborate than the drawing. Plate 114 reveals the details of the construction of one of the vases in Plate 302. It is an object lesson on the normal method of construction of many of the vases at Soho. Apart from the components, which need no further explanation, Plate 114 shows the careful notching (I, II, III and IIII) on the marble pedestal to ensure that the four rams' heads, whose shafts are similarly notched, are fitted in their correct holes. The rams' heads, swags and medallions recur on a number of ornaments, including clock cases and obelisks (Plates 153, 223.3), indicating that they were all made at about the same time from the same moulds.

The eight oval medallions on the vases of Plate 302 (Plate 76) are framed behind glass. They represent, in the upper row from the first vase, Pomona, Neptune, Venus Victorious and a Sacrifice Group and, in the lower row from the second vase, Achilles Victorious, a seated Heroic Figure, Hygieia and Aesculapius. I have discussed the source of these medallions in Chapter 3 (see pp. 107–12), where I have illustrated another pair of these vases (Plate 80) in order to show Boulton's likely debt to Wedgwood. The vases of Plate 80 have simpler caps and only four of the medallion images (Venus Victorious, Sacrifice Group, the Heroic Figure four times, and

302. Candle vases, 11.9 in., Private Collection.

303. Pattern Book 1, p. 171.

Hygieia twice), all of the medallions being gilt except the two ceramic medallions shown in Plate 80.

Boulton used nine medallions on the vases of this type that are so far recorded. The ninth, Filial Piety (Plate 77), is among the medallions mounted on the pair of vases illustrated in Plate 301. I have discussed its origin with the other medallions in Chapter 3 (see p. 112). The other three medallions on the first vase are Neptune, Achilles Victorious and Hygieia, and on the second vase Pomona, the Heroic Figure (twice) and Aesculapius. These vases are at Weston Park. Like many other candle vases, they have been wired for electricity, but unlike others no holes have been drilled in them and the construction has been left unaffected. There is no record in the archives of their purchase. It is, however, highly probable that Sir Henry Bridgeman, who succeeded to the Weston estate in 1764, knew Boulton and visited Soho. His estate was near Birmingham, and Boulton would scarcely have neglected a local Member of Parliament. I have recorded elsewhere that Lady Bridgeman visited Soho in 1770, and had the distinction of having the wreathed-column candlestick named after her (see p. 191). Perhaps she bought these vases some years later.

Several of these vases are known. There was a single vase at Pavlovsk in the 1970s, but it was not there in 2001.[556]

Three of the oval medallions recur on each of the vases illustrated in Plates 304 and 305.[557] These vases share features with other examples of

304. Vase perfume burners, 14.8 in., City of Leeds Art Gallery, Temple Newsam.

Boulton and Fothergill's work. The scrolled handles echo the handles of other vases, but they are decorated at their bases with an anthemion motif and a pendant of husks, which are unusual features on handles of this type. The floral swag on the vase body is identical to the swags used on the vases of Plate 264. The triangular ormolu base, with its concave fluted border, is similar to the base of the caryatic vase of Plate 324. The floral frieze at the top of the body echoes the vases of Plate 258 and appears on silverware made at Soho (Plate 92). The medallions are clearly cast from the same moulds as those on the vases of Plates 301 and 302. The same three medallions are used on all three of the vases illustrated. They represent (from left to right in the two illustrations) a Sacrifice Group, Achilles Victorious, and the Heroic Figure (see Chapter 3, p. 110). The two vases in Plate 304 have lost the two top mounts on their lids, which would have been like those in Plate 305. The linings of these vases are gilt copper, and the construction is typical. Despite the triangular design of the vases, the

305. Vase perfume burner, 15.5 in., Christie's.

lids are pierced with a four-part pattern with a prominent anthemion motif. There are other examples of the surprising combination of four-part pierced lids and three-sided vases (Plate 94).

I have discussed in Chapter 3 (see pp. 68–70) the debt that Boulton may have owed to the architect James Wyatt for certain designs, including the female figures supporting this triangular vase. Wyatt's wingless figures supporting a stand for a silver ewer (Plate 53) are very close to Boulton's versions. They feature the same claw feet, the acanthus decoration, the bead necklaces and the hairstyle. Wyatt's whole drawing is virtually the same as the sketch for an ewer and stand in Boulton and Fothergill's pattern book (Plate 52).

It is likely that two vases of this type were included in the sale at Christie and Ansell's in 1778, described in the catalogue as 'essence vases, in marble mounted in or moulu, supported by a tripod'.[558] They were reserved at £16 16s. 0d.

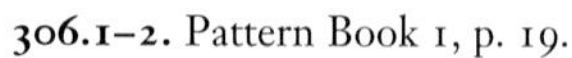

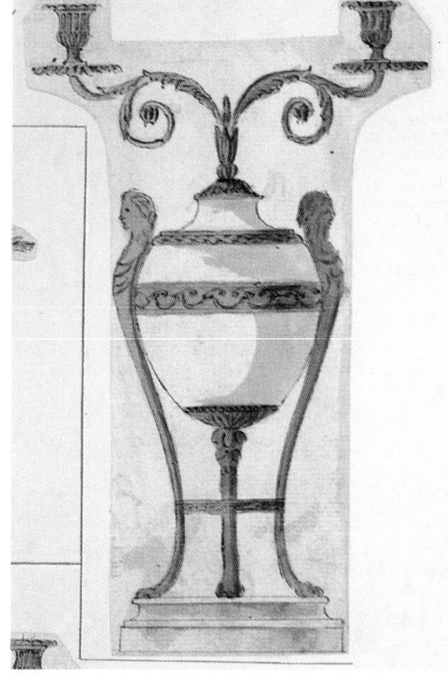

306.1–2. Pattern Book 1, p. 19.

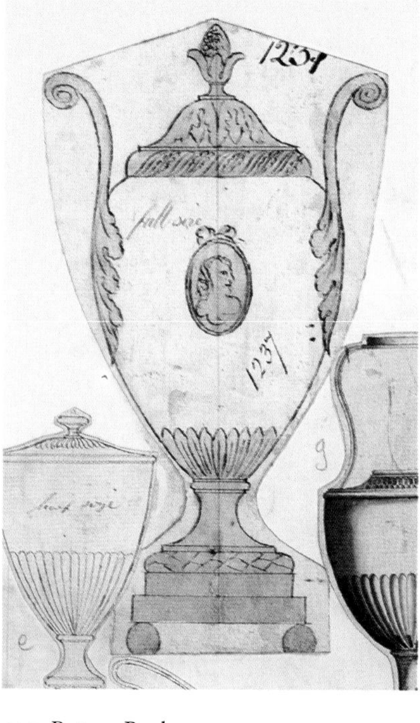

307. Pattern Book 1, p. 124.

308. Pattern Book 1, p. 135.

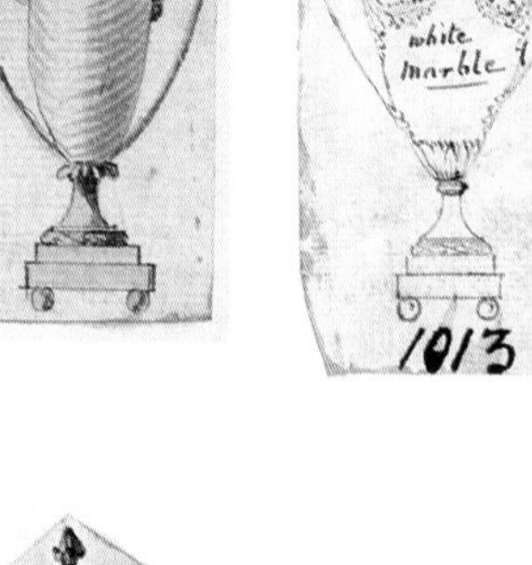

309.1–3. Pattern Book 1, p. 170.

310.1–3. Pattern Book 1, p. 171.

311. Pattern Book 5, p. 33.

Unidentified drawings of vases

During this survey of vases and in the sections that follow on named vases, I have identified most of the sketches in the pattern books with surviving examples. Eleven sketches remain unidentified. These are illustrated in Plates 306–11. It is possible that some of these vases were never made in precisely the forms shown in the sketches. Sketches were sent to potential customers to choose from, or even to choose components from – there are many mounts in the sketches that can be recognised on vases illustrated in this book – and some of the sketches may have been of designs that did not appeal. But the weight of evidence suggests that most of the drawings in the pattern books were of designs that were made. The vase numbered 1013 (Plate 309.2), for example, was certainly made (see p. 285). It is most unlikely that the other two numbered sketches (Plates 311, which is close to the vase in Plate 273, numbered 516, and Plate 307, numbered 1237) were never realised. My guess is that vases of all these designs will be found in due course.

The most noteworthy of the unidentified sketches are the three-branched candle vase resting on the backs of four sphinxes, with feet of the type fitted to several earlier vases (Plate 306.1), the two-branched triangular marble vase with a Vitruvian scroll band round the body and three female supports with claw feet (Plate 306.2), the vase with scroll handles, a medallion and ball feet, numbered 1237, and measuring just over seven inches high (Plate 307), the vase with two masks fixed to the rims (Plate 309.1), and the blue john vase with split handles standing on a pedestal (Plate 310.2), which is very close to the vases in Plate 276. The drawing of the perfume burner in Plate 308 may be a design for silver despite its colouring.

312.1–2. Pattern Book 1, p. 11.

Drawings for candle branches

Plate 312 shows two designs for candle branches. The first of these I have mentioned on several occasions, since it matches branches fitted to several vases (Plates 298, 300, 301), often as an option instead of a pierced lid (Plate 270). An example of a double branch of this type, dismantled, is illustrated in Plate 113. No branch corresponding to the second drawing, showing a branch resting on a ram's head, has yet been recorded. It is very similar to another drawing, which I have discussed under the heading of girandoles (Plate 210.1, p. 257), and it may be a drawing for a sconce. But it may equally be a sketch for a vase branch and is reminiscent of the manner in which the branches are fitted to the vase of Plate 263. Rams' heads were frequently used on vases.

This survey of vases has shown the way in which Boulton and Fothergill used identical or very similar mounts for many different types of vase. It was as if they designed vases like children making faces out of those cardboard kits of eyes, noses, mouths and hair. The variety of vase designs was wide, but the component parts were frequently the same. The customer thus had a wide range of choice, but the manufacturing process was, in theory, more streamlined. These remarks are also true of several of the named vases, to which I now turn.

Bacchanalian vase

The Bacchanalian or Bacchus vase (Plates 313–14) is a classic example of Boulton's eclectic methods of 'adopting the most elegant ornaments of the

313–14. Bacchanalian vase perfume burners, 16 in., Private Collection.

315. Bacchanalian vase, detail.

most refined Grecian artists ... humbly copying their style, and making new combinations of old ornaments without presuming to invent new ones'.

Two of these vases were included in the unsuccessful sale at Christie and Ansell's in 1778. The first was catalogued as:

> an elegant vase in statuary marble and or moulu after the antique, on which is a bas relief representing Mercury delivering the infant Bacchus to the care of Ino. This piece turns round upon a swivel for the conveniency of viewing the bas relief, and is perforated and lined for essences.[559]

Both vases were reserved at £16 16s. od. Neither was sold. A 'Bacchanalian vase, broken marble' and a 'Bacchus vase ready to gild' were recorded in the Inventory of stock in 1782,[560] and an 'or moulu Bacchanalian vase' was sold to Lord Stormont in 1783, also for £16 16s. od.[561] These references suggest that the Bacchanalian vase was a design of the second half of the 1770s, when Boulton and Fothergill were increasingly using white marble for vase bodies. If the vase had been one of the stock patterns at the beginning of the 1770s when the ormolu trade was more active, some reference to it would surely have survived.

The two vases of Plate 313[562] differ from the vases in the 1778 sale in not being (or no longer being) mounted on a swivel 'for the conveniency of viewing the bas relief'. Plates 313–14 show between them the entire relief, fulfilling, I hope, the function of the swivel. The vases also differ from a sketch of a Bacchanalian vase in the pattern book (Plate 316) in that the vase in the sketch has no lid. It is clear from the sale catalogue that the vase was fitted with a pierced lid for the emission of perfume, and the sketch is incomplete. The sketch also shows what looks like a female figure carrying an ewer walking alone between two vine stems, whereas the equivalent figure on the vase is male and one of two figures framed by the vine.

The construction of these vases, with their carefully fitted and richly gilt ormolu mounts and their gilt copper linings (Plates 97, 315) fixed by the customary two-holed chased nuts, is typical of the work at Soho. The lid is cast, the cone finial and the leaf mount beneath it being separate pieces. The marble body is widened to fill the pierced cradle. The threaded fixing rod rises from a square base plate. The mounts are bolted to the body, the frieze of figures being cast in a number of separate pieces.

The design is striking and is one of the most satisfying of all Boulton's

316. Pattern Book 1, p. 171.

318. Caryatic candle vase of Plate 317, detail.

317. Caryatic candle vase, 24 in., Gerstenfeld Collection.

vase designs. It is one of the few vases based on the classic urn, and it is the only vase that incorporates a complete pictorial frieze of classical figures. In Chapter 3 (see pp. 116–20) I have shown that the origin of this frieze of Mercury delivering the infant Bacchus to the care of Ino, lies in the Athenian sculptor Salpion's 'Gaeta' vase, and I have suggested that although Boulton may have copied the frieze from Wedgwood (Plate 85), a more likely source was the Roman bronzeworker Zoffoli (Plate 86).

Other Bacchanalian vases survive at Syon and at Soho House, both of them identical to the vases illustrated here.[563] The frieze, copying Boulton and Wedgwood's configuration of the celebrants, was used by later metalworkers, but the Gaeta vase never attained the popularity with metalworkers and collectors of the Borghese, Medici or Warwick vases.

Caryatic vases

In the sale at Christie's in 1771 there were four large vases that were described in the catalogue as 'lined with silver and perferated for insence with four branches for candles, supported by two caryatides standing on an ornamented ebony plinth'.[564] Three of them had blue john bodies and one was described as 'the whole in or moulu'. Two were reserved at £25 and two at £26 5s. 0d. Three of the vases were sold, one to Pinchbeck for £25 4s. 0d., and another to General Carnack for £31 10s. 0d. Another four-branched 'large caryatic vase radix amethysti and or moulu ... standing on a plinth richly inlaid' was offered on the first day.[565] This was reserved at £31 10s. 0d. and appears to have remained unsold, since a '4-branched Carryatic vase' at the same price was listed among the unsold stock in May.[566]

The use of caryatids as the chief ornamental feature of the design was calculated to appeal to the fashion for the antique taste. Boulton was familiar with the use of both male and female figures as decorative supports for entablatures in classical architecture from his general study of classical sources. He owned a copy of William Chambers's *Treatise on Civil Architecture*, in which 'Persians and Caryatides' were discussed in a chapter of their own.

Several caryatic vases are known. None of them can yet be identified with references in the archives. One of them is illustrated in Plates 317 and 318.[567] The vase is ornamented with two female figures with arms stretched above them, gripping with both hands the rings attached to the upper sides of the candle branches. The branches are very similar to those on the King's vase (Plate 339). The body is hollowed to receive the silvered lining, and is decorated with fulsome swags of fruits and foliage and a cradle of spaced acanthus leaves. The double-beaded rim, which is typical of Boulton and Fothergill's larger vases, is pierced to allow the emission of the perfume. The lid and the stem are of blue john. The plinth is made of ebonised wood, stands on simple ball feet, and is decorated with a formalised ormolu acanthus-leaf moulding. I have suggested earlier that the caryatic vase should probably be identified with 'Egginton's' four-branched vase and that

319. Caryatic candle vase, 24 in., Hotspur Ltd.

Francis Eginton may have modelled the figures. The plinth and feet of the King's vase (Plate 345) were probably developed, with the help of William Chambers, as an improvement to the plinth of this vase (see Chapter 3, p. 79).

Examples of caryatic vases of this type, all with four branches, blue john bodies, lids and stems, ebonised plinths and ball feet can be seen in the Metropolitan Museum, New York (a pair),[568] Warwick Castle (a single vase), and Badminton House (a pair).[569] There is no record of the purchases of the vases at Warwick or Badminton in the archives.

One of the four vases in the 1771 sale, which I have mentioned above, was described as wholly of ormolu. Plates 319 and 320 show one of a pair of caryatic vases with gilt bodies, lids and stems, and with bases made of red Derbyshire limestone. These are the only wholly gilt vases of this type so far recorded.[570]

Plates 321–2 show a caryatic vase, one of a pair, of a different type. This model of vase was probably a precursor of the caryatic vases already discussed. The caryatids are very similar in most respects – hairstyle and ornament, gathered drapery and clasp, tapered trunks decorated with patterns of guilloche and tapering husks – but the scrolls of the split

320. Caryatic candle vase of Plate 319, detail.

handles, which slot into grooves cut in their shoulders, take the place of their up-stretched arms. Many of the other mounts differ. The finial, for example, is a cone and not a flame, the lid is shallower, the pierced rim has a very different decoration and larger holes, the leaves cradling the vase are more formalised, the collar at the top of the stem is plain and the ring at its base has no crossed ribbons. The stepped ebonised wooden base is cruciform. On the bodies, instead of swags, there are medallions depicting a sacrifice group. I have discussed this medallion, which also appears on the medallion vase (Plate 349) in Chapter 3 (Plate 81, see p. 114). These vases have been drilled at various points for electricity, and have lost their linings.

Plate 323 illustrates a wholly gilt version of this vase. Three branches, chased with acanthus motifs, spiral upwards from the lid. Their splash rings and nozzles are similar to those on the Persian vase (Plate 351).

321. Caryatic vase perfume burner, 14 in., Private Collection.

322. Caryatic vase perfume burner of Plate 321, detail.

A third version of the caryatic vase is illustrated in Plates 324–6. This vase is also one of a pair. It answers well to another catalogue entry in the 1771 sale:

A large caryatic vase radix amethysti and or moulu lined with silver and perferated for insence, with branches for three candles, standing on a triangular plynth of statuary marble.[571]

Several of the features of this vase are repeated from the vase of Plate 321. The scrolls at the bottom of the branches slot into the shoulders of the figures in place of the upstretched arms of Plate 317. The figures are the same. The pierced rim, however, echoes the rim of the vase of Plate 317. The mounts cradling the vase are again different, with a stylised anthemion mount between the acanthus leaves. The branches are of a familiar type and there is a central nozzle to make four lights in all. The spiral stem, with its floral collar concealing the join, occurs in the vases of Plate 241, which were made at about the same date. The triangular base reappears in the tea urn of Plate 229 and the vases of Plate 304. The combination of the spiral stem, the scrolling tripod legs, and the triangular base with its concave fluted edge, derive from a design that I have attributed to James Stuart and to Diederich Nicolaus Anderson (Plates 33–4, see Chapter 3, p. 76). I have suggested in Chapter 3 that Boulton may have acquired the models for these mounts from Anderson's widow or his estate in 1768 or 1770. These vases are so far the only recorded vases by Boulton and Fothergill incorporating this combination of ornaments. The mounts are characteristically bolted to the bodies of the vases and the branches are indented with identification marks to aid correct assembly. These caryatic vases are typical of Boulton and Fothergill's earlier work on a grand scale. They have been converted for electricity and have lost their linings and acquired modern screw threads.

323. Caryatic candle vase, 22.7 in., Hotspur Ltd.

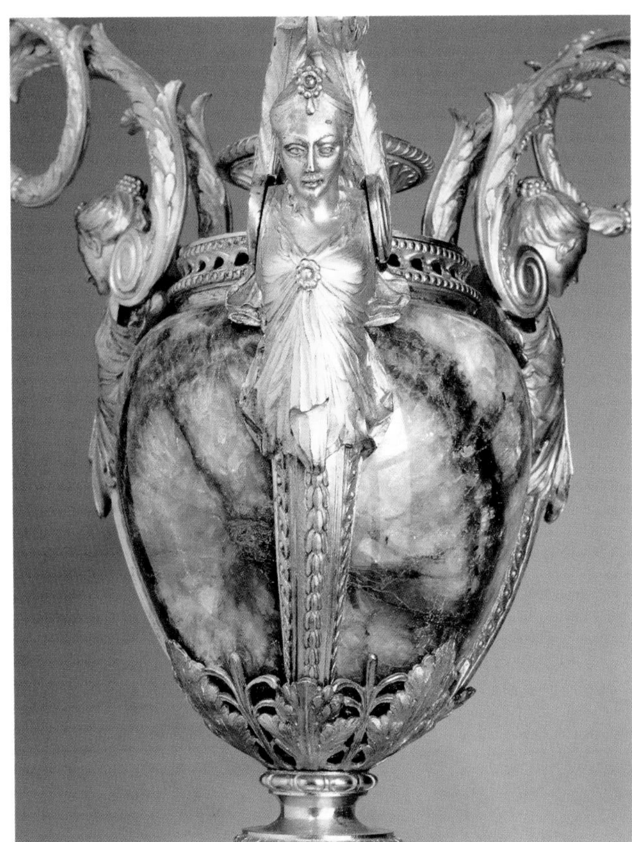

324. Caryatic candle vase, 23.7 in., Private Collection.

325–6. Caryatic candle vase of Plate 324, details.

Cleopatra vase

Early in 1770 Boulton thought that the Dowager Princess of Wales might be persuaded to buy a pair of Cleopatra vases, but his letter to his partner gives no clue about their appearance or function apart from a hint that they were probably (on this occasion) candle vases.[572] Later in the same year the Marquess of Rockingham bought another pair at a cost of £5 10s. 0d.[573] Several Cleopatra vases were included in the sale in 1771 at Christie's. The name was not used in the catalogue but it appears in the subsequent letter to William Matthews, which listed the unsold stock. This included:

	£	s	d
4 pairs of Cleopatra vases with philosopher[574] pedestals £5 5s.	21	0	0
1 pair ditto ditto lapis ditto	5	5	0
1 pair ditto ditto metal ditto	5	5	0[575]

327. Cleopatra candle vases, 8.8 in., Michael Winner.

328. Cleopatra candle vases, 10.2 in., Private Collection.

The prices and the mention of pedestals decorated with gilt metal, philosopher's stone and lapis suggest that these vases may have been some of the six pairs listed in the sale catalogue as 'candle vases radix amethysti and or moulu on a square pedestal of a curious composition',[576] and the four listed as 'candle vases radix amethysti and or moulu, on a square pedestal of artificial lapis lazuli'.[577] The pedestals would have been made of painted glass simulating lapis, agate, etc., and not of stone. The simulated 'lapis' and 'agate' panels in the pedestals of the sphinx vases (Plates 355–6) were made in the same way.

That Cleopatra vases were sometimes ornamented with medallions is confirmed by an order from Baron Grote, which was recorded at the end of 1771:

1 pair of vases Cleopatra with medalls and a plain rim round to engrave a name which he will send as per pattern	£6 6s. 0d.[578]

The Earl of Catherlough bought a pair of Cleopatra vases in 1771.[579] After 1771 the name does not re-appear in the archives until 1782, when a few parts, including eleven pairs of stone bodies, were listed among the stock.[580]

The vases of Plates 327–9 are Cleopatra vases. It may seem odd to suggest this when it is the portrait of Ceres, and not of Cleopatra, that generally appears on vases of this type when they have medallions on the pedestal (Plate 328). But these are the only vases that answer closely to the descriptions in the letter to William Matthews. Furthermore, Plate 327 shows two vases with gilt pedestals, as described in the letter to Matthews, and medallions of Cleopatra, wearing a diadem and a veil and with an asp at her breast. I have discussed the origin of this medallion in Chapter 3 (see Plate 71, p. 106). These vases are so far the only recorded examples of vases from Soho with a depiction of Cleopatra and are clearly early, if not the first, examples of this type of vase. Perhaps, having named the vase after Cleopatra, Boulton's workmen fixed medallions of Ceres, whose image I have also discussed in Chapter 3 (Plate 72, see p. 106), without knowing the difference: but it is also entirely possible that the later use of the portrait

329. Cleopatra vases, 10.5 in., Christie's.

of Ceres set against panels of simulated stone was due to the loss of, or damage to, the die used for making the original Cleopatra panels, in which the portrait is integral to the gilt panel. Ceres was probably the nearest approximation to the lost portrait of Cleopatra.

The Cleopatra vase was a candle vase, and was among the earliest of the vases made at Soho. Many of them survive. All have the same stamped three-step pedestal with ball feet, the stamped Greek fret frieze round the top of the pedestal, the stem with spiral flutes, the acanthus-leaf cradle holding the vase body, and, decorating the body, the laurel swags, pendants and flowers. All have the same convex and fluted candle nozzle. Some have cast and chased lids with finials, others have simpler gadrooned caps, yet others have neither. Nearly all have blue john bodies,[581] usually with inner linings of copper, and most have painted glass panels as described above. Some have panels entirely gilt, or, rarely, of blue john. They do not all have portrait medallions, but the lack of a portrait did not stop them being called 'Cleopatra vases' any more than being decorated with a portrait of Ceres.

Plate 327 shows the pair with the medallions of Cleopatra.[582] The pedestals are gilt, suggesting, along with the portrait medallion, that this is the earliest version of the design. The portrait is integral to the gilt panel, which is the same on all four sides. There are no caps. The portrait is shown in detail in Plate 71.

Plate 328 shows a pair of Cleopatra vases with the portrait of Ceres mounted on panels of simulated malachite.[583] These vases have caps, as do the vases in Plate 329, which have no medallions and panels of simulated granite.[584] Other pairs are recorded with panels of simulated lapis,[585] agate and aventurine,[586] and I have seen two pairs with entirely blue john pedestals without the gilt fillets, which hold the glass panels, down the sides. Both were mounted with portrait medallions of Ceres.[587]

These vases are closely similar to a drawing in the pattern books (Plate 330), which has a cap like the vases in Plate 329 and a medallion, which looks more like Ceres than Cleopatra.

330. Pattern Book 1, p. 171.

Goat's head vase

This vase proved to be one of the most persistent and popular of Boulton and Fothergill's small candle vases. The first recorded orders for goat's head vases date from 1769 when a Mrs Yeats ordered '1 pair of goat's head vauses light blue cheny or enamelled'.[588] A month later a Mrs Balfour ordered a pair of vases with green, presumably china or enamelled, bodies,[589] and Sir William Guise a pair with blue john bodies 'of the purpel stone no medals on'.[590] Other vases of the same pattern with blue john bodies are mentioned in the archives in ensuing months. Boulton sold a number of them in London during his visit early in 1770,[591] and reckoned that if he had some more 'with blew john and some with the leopard or tyger stone' he could sell a pair to the Princess of Wales.[592] There were several pairs in the sale at Christie's in 1771. They were not listed in the catalogue as goat's head vases, but can perhaps be identified with the many 'candle vases radix amethysti and or moulu' which were included in the sale. Some of them were listed by name in the record of unsold pieces that was sent afterwards to William Matthews. This included –

		£	s	d
3 pair of goats head vases gilt bodies at	73/6	11	0	6
3 pair ditto ditto enamel	73/6	11	0	6
6 pairs goats head stone bodies	84/–	25	4	0[593]

The quantity of unsold vases suggests that the ornaments in the sale catalogue most likely to be goat's head vases were the 'candle vases with laurel festoons', of which there were twenty-eight pairs in the sale. Eighteen of them were priced at £3 13s. 6d., including three that were annotated as enamelled and five as gilt. The other ten, nine of them on the third day of the sale, were priced at £3 3s. 0d.[594] Several of the vases appear to have been sold.

Several more pairs with stone, i.e. blue john, and green enamelled bodies were included in the sale at Christie's in 1772,[595] at least one of them being mounted not with ormolu but with silver.[596] Several purchases of goat's head vases are recorded in the same year, the buyers including Lord Scarsdale, who paid £4 4s. 0d. a pair,[597] Joseph Didier and Mrs Balfour (again), who bought a pair with green bodies for £3 13s. 6d.[598] The vase was usually made with only one socket for a candle, but in 1774 Lord Digby was sent a drawing and informed that with branches for two candles a pair would cost about £10 10s. 0d.[599]

The goat's head vase was still among the firm's wares in later years. In 1782 seventeen vases were listed among the stock, most of them with gilt or green or blue enamelled bodies.[600]

It is clear from these references in the archives that, as with so many of the smaller vases, Boulton and Fothergill made goat's head vases with a wide assortment of bodies. The order for Sir William Guise in 1769 suggests that, at any rate in the earlier years, they were usually decorated with medallions.

Plate 331 illustrates a pair of goat's head vases with blue john bodies and medallions of Alexander the Great.[601] I have discussed the origin of this medallion, which is the only medallion applied to goat's head vases, in Chapter 3 (Plate 70, see p. 106). This pair of vases may have been part of the set of vases that Boulton supplied to the King and Queen in 1770. It could be significant that when the King's clock (Plate 160), King's vases (Plate 339) and sphinx vases (Plate 355) were moved to Windsor Castle in 1829, the deliverer recorded two of the 'Derbyshire spar vases mounted in or moulu' as 'very small in suite with the clock by Wright'.[602] The goat's head vases are now the only blue john vases in the Royal Collection that

331. Goat's head candle vases, 8.2 in., Royal Collection.

can be described as very small and as *en suite* with the clock.

Plate 332 illustrates a goat's head vase with a blue john body. It is shown in Plate 333 with the candle nozzle upwards. All goat's head vases have this reversible finial and nozzle, just as they all have the same mounts. The vase is shown in pieces in Plate 106. This illustrates the method of construction, with a threaded rod screwed from above through the copper lining into the top of the stem, and the stem fixed by hammering to the upper piece of the square base. Plate 106 also shows how the vase body is made of two distinctive but quite different pieces of attractively veined blue john, and how the cradle piece is marked with nine dots for identification during assembly. The hole in the rim suggests that this vase would originally have had medallions, but not all surviving vases have them, and the rims of some have no holes in them.

Plate 334 shows a pair with gilt copper bodies.[603] A medallion is suspended from the rim of each vase: there are no medallions on the reverse side, but the rims are holed for them. The construction is very similar to the construction of the blue john vase illustrated in Plates 332–3.

Many other examples of goat's head vases are recorded both in salerooms and in private collections, including pairs with white marble, lacquered and silver plate bodies.[604]

All of these goat's head vases correspond to a sketch in the pattern books, which shows a vase without medallions (Plate 335). The mounts beneath the vase body in this sketch differ in detail from the executed mounts, which correspond more closely with the mounts drawn in another sketch (Plate 282) and with the related vase of Plate 281. This is yet another example of the way in which the mounts on particular vases could be chosen from several almost standard patterns. The candle sockets might be used as evidence of the same methods of design. They reappear on other objects (Plate 281) and, in yet another context, in the pattern books (Plate 210.2).

332–3. Goat's head candle vase, 8.2 in., Private Collection.

334. Goat's head candle vases, 7.6 in., Norman Adams.

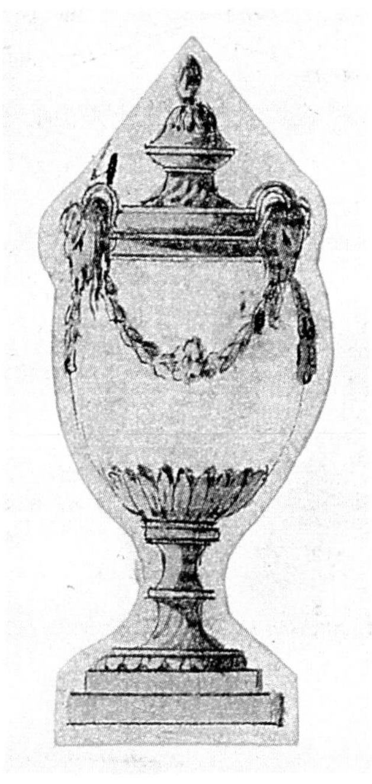

335. Pattern Book 1, p. 171.

Griffin vases

There were eight vases in the sale at Christie's in 1771 which were described in the catalogue as being 'of radix amethysti and or moulu lined with silver and perferated for essence, supported by three griffins upon a round pedestal of the same materials, the whole in the antique taste'.[605] They were all reserved at £10 10s. 0d., and seven of them were sold at prices of between £11 0s. 6d. and £15 4s. 6d. Lady Godolphin and a Colonel William were among the buyers. The unsold vase was presumably the griffin vase valued at £10 10s. 0d. which William Matthews was later instructed to send, together with some other unsold vases, to Amsterdam.[606] At the end of the same year Sir John Griffin Griffin appropriately bought another griffin vase for £10 10s. 0d.[607] There was a 'small' one in the sale at Christie's in 1772,[608] and a pair of 'griffin' vases with stone bodies, a 'griffin or moulu essence vase, white marble, and three round stone plinths for griffin vases', were listed among the stock in 1782.[609]

The description in the 1771 catalogue fits the vase illustrated in Plate 336.[610] This is a perfume burner with a pierced rim and a silvered copper lining. The plinth, vase body and lid are made of blue john and the underside of the lid is gilt. The design of the plinth is characteristic, although it is larger in diameter than other rounded pedestals. Many of the mounts are also characteristic, including the cone finial, the rams' heads, laurel swags,

336. Griffin vase perfume burner, 12 in., Gerstenfeld Collection.

337. Griffin vase perfume burner, 22 in., National Trust, Hinton Ampner.

OPPOSITE:
338. Griffin vase of Plate 337, detail.

and the acanthus cradle below the body. The vase stands on an unusual hexagonal base with concave indentations. Above it there is a gadrooned mount similar to the mount on the lyre vase of Plate 347.

The 1782 Inventory quoted above mentions a marble version of this vase. It was also made with a gilt body and gilt lid, but still with a blue john plinth.[611]

Plate 337 shows a very much larger blue john vase supported by three griffins standing on a triangular gilt plinth. This vase is pierced for the emission of perfume, although it no longer has a lining. The lining would have been silvered, the evidence being the silvered surface on the underside of the lid. As Plate 337 shows, the vase body is made of more than one piece of blue john. The vase originally had three candle branches. There are three filled up holes in the blue john body about 1.25 inches below the upper rim, through which the branches would have been bolted to the body, and each griffin has a filled hole on the top of his head, which would have been the supports for the bases of the branches. The branches possibly echoed the branches on the Persian vase (Plate 351). In its original form the vase would have been a very grand ornament.

This vase is similar in many respects to the Persian vase, an example of which was included in the sale in 1771. The pierced rim with its beaded decoration, for example, the finial, the shape of the blue john body, the hexagonal column which supports it, and the decoration of the upper surface of the triangular plinth all afford close parallels. The griffins are clearly based on the same design as those that support the smaller vase.

There is no corresponding sketch for either of these vases in the pattern books, although several drawings incorporate features that appear in them. The origin of the models for the griffins is also mysterious. I have argued in Chapter 3 (see p. 85) that the most likely source of the model is the architect William Chambers, although the griffin that he designed (Plate 50) differs in important respects.

OPPOSITE:
339–40. King's candle vase, 22.1 in., Royal Collection.

King's vase

In Chapter 5, I have related how, when Boulton visited the Palace in March 1770, the Queen told him that the china vases on the chimneypiece in her bedroom were to be taken away and asked him how many of his vases would be needed in their place (see pp. 164–5). The answer, according to a subsequent letter from Boulton to Fothergill, was seven. They were to be 'some of them about as large as the 4-branched vase …' and the largest were to be 'feneered with blew john and like the new tea kitchen'.[612] After March 1770 there are no further letters in the archives which give any information about work on the manufacture of these vases or about their eventual delivery to the King and Queen. Boulton seemed to think that they would be ready very soon after his first instructions to his partner.[613]

From the documents alone it would not be possible to know beyond doubt what any of these vases to be supplied to the Queen looked like. Fortunately, however, there is plenty of evidence about the largest vases, not least the description in the catalogue of the sale at Christie's in 1771 of two similar vases, each reserved at £42:

> A large vase of radix amethysti and or moulu, perferated for incence, with two double branches, supported by demy satyrs, with festoons, etc. standing on a plynth richly inlaid, after a model that hath been executed for his majesty.[614]

Following the sale in May 1771, Boulton and Fothergill sent a top, some screws and a branch for 'the king's vase' to William Matthews, their agent in London. These parts may have been either for one of the vases supplied to the King and Queen or for one of Barton's purchases.[615] Nearly two years

later, Fothergill reported to Boulton that Eginton and Scale had calculated the cost of the '6 king's vases and clock case' and that they had already cost £412 and more. He thought it unlikely that the King would allow them much profit.[616]

The vases illustrated in Plates 339–40,[617] together with the clock case of Plate 160 and the two sphinx vases of Plate 355, form a *garniture de cheminée* in the Queen's private sitting room at Windsor Castle. These vases, with their rim 'perferated for incence', their two double branches 'supported by demy satyrs', their 'festoons' of oak leaves and acorns, and their 'richly inlaid' plinths, match the description of the vases in the 1771 sale catalogue. Each vase has a large blue john body of fine variegated colour and a lid and a stem of the same stone. There is a gilt copper lining. The plinth is made of wood veneered with tortoiseshell. The overall design of the vase is not unlike the design of the caryatic vase illustrated in Plate 317. The branches and nozzles are similar, but most of the decorative mounts are different. Some of the mounts occur on other vases. The lid is very similar to the lid of the vases which I have suggested might be identified with Bingley's vase (Plate 244), and the oval paterae on the body of the vase and the plinth occur on other vases (Plate 268). The turned feet with their twisted flutes can be seen supporting the Titus clock case of Plate 184 and, in an extended form, the King's clock case (Plate 160). The use of this foot for so many Royal commissions is significant. In Chapter 3 (see p. 79) I have attributed its design to William Chambers, the King's architect, who did a drawing from a sketch of the King's for a better foot to Boulton and Fothergill's '4-branched vase', probably the caryatic vase.

It seems that Chambers was responsible for a great deal more of the design than just the foot, and I have discussed his role in it in Chapter 3 (see Plate 42 and pp. 80, 82). Like the King's clock case, these vases are key evidence of the relationship between Chambers and Boulton, illustrating the strong influence that Chambers had on Boulton's designs.

There are two further King's vases at Windsor, with darker and more uniform stone bodies, which may have been supplied to the King and Queen at the same time.[618] When worrying about the cost, Fothergill mentioned six vases and the clock case costing £412. If four of these were King's vases and two were sphinx vases, the reserve prices of which in the 1771 sale were £42 and £12 12s. 0d. respectively, the clock would have been estimated at about £220, which is not unrealistic. The other candidates for inclusion among the six vases are the goat's head vases also in the Royal Collection (Plate 331), but the inclusion of these at the expense of two King's vases would push the cost of the clock probably too high. The four King's vases were for some years at Buckingham House, and were moved to Windsor in 1829.[619]

Boulton repeatedly turned specific commissions to advantage by offering ornaments of the same designs to other patrons. The King's vase was no exception. As I have said earlier, two vases of this pattern, each with two double branches, were included in the sale in 1771, a piece of marketing cheek that Boulton seems to have got away with.

The vase was offered to patrons as one of the firm's standard patterns, and is recorded in a sketch, numbered 399, in the pattern books (Plate 341). This is one of the few surviving sketches inscribed with a stock number. It follows the original design for the King fairly closely except in the more elaborate treatment of the branches. There are vases that have branches close to those in this sketch, with the extra loop in the outside branch. One is at Harewood House[620] and another is in the Art Institute of Chicago.[621] Neither of these vases has the ormolu mounts on the sides of the ebonised projections on which the lions' masks are fitted, which can be clearly seen in the sketch. Another pair of vases with the same double

341. Pattern Book 1, p. 19.

branches has white marble bodies, lids and stems.[622] Other vases with the less elaborate double branches for four candles, more on the lines of the vases at Windsor, are also recorded.[623]

The existence of a pair of white marble vases is of some interest. There is only one reference in the archives to King's vases with white marble bodies. In 1772 Fothergill referred to Lord Kerry returning a pair of King's vases because he intended to have white ones instead.[624]

The King's vase was also mounted with double branches for three candles each. One was made for Lord Grantham in 1771. He probably ordered it after seeing the two vases in the exhibition before the sale in April. It was ready in August[625] and was sent to William Matthews nearly three months later. Boulton and Fothergill had resisted Lord Grantham's wish to reduce the cost of manufacturing and had in fact done the opposite for the best of reasons:

> When Lord Grantham gave the order to Mr Boulton he pressed very much to have one for 30 guineas even if he made some alteration to reduce it to that price, but as that can not be done without spoiling the whole beauty of the vase it was not attempted and indeed instead of diminishing any part we have made an addition. The branches were not thought quite so perfect as they should be and therefore we have had new ones modeled for 6 lights instead of four which in general are much better. However as Mr Boulton gave his Lordship to understand that he would undertake one for 30 guineas it is not charged any more though they cannot be afforded at the price in general. Forty guineas is the common price, and at which price his Lordship will not find any difficulty in recommending others.[626]

Perhaps Boulton was happy to keep the price down in the hope that Lord Grantham would recommend the vases to the noblemen at the Spanish court, where he was the ambassador from 1771, or perhaps he was influenced by his Lordship's order 'for a friend of his' for four Persian vases. This was a valuable order amounting to £500 even after a substantial concession.[627]

342. King's candle vase on pedestal, National Trust, Saltram House.

In the event this order was altered. It was for Lord Grantham's sister, Mrs John Parker, who was busy with the furnishing of the new saloon that Robert Adam had designed at Saltram Park in Devon.[628] It is quite likely that she, or more probably her other brother Frederick Robinson, saw the King's vase which had been made for Lord Grantham and preferred it to the Persian vases which had been ordered for her. Boulton and Fothergill wrote to Matthews that they would willingly comply with her request to alter the order, although it would not be easy to sell the Persian vases elsewhere, and to send her instead four vases 'made like that we sent Lord Grantham'. At the same time they sent a drawing of the size of the plinth of the vases for Matthews to deliver to Adam.[629] The vases were completed in March 1772 and were sent to Matthews with an invoice for £126 7s. od.[630] Mrs Parker was pleased with them. She wrote to her brother Frederick after she had visited Boulton and Fothergill's display at Christie's in that year:

> I was at the exhibition of ormolu this week. There are some new things but nothing that I wished much to have, being satisfied with four of these urns you bespoke for lighting the great room.[631]

Two months later she bought a fifth vase for £31 14s. od.[632] It is not clear which room this extra vase was intended for.

All five vases have survived at Saltram. Four stand in the saloon, one in each corner on gilt pedestals, which were probably intended for their support from the beginning (Plate 342). I do not know who made these pedestals but they were probably designed by Robert Adam.[633] It was no doubt in order to make their tops of the right diameter that he needed the measurements of the plinth of the vase from Boulton. The fifth vase now

OPPOSITE:
343. King's candle vase, 22.5 in., National Trust, Saltram House.

344–5. King's candle vase of Plate 343, details.

stands on a pier table in the dining room. All five vases are identical in design. Each is mounted with double branches for three candles on either side (Plate 343), and is therefore similar to the vase supplied to Lord Grantham. The decoration and mounts are otherwise similar to those of the vases made for the King. The plinths are made of wood veneered with tortoiseshell (Plate 345) and the vases are lined with gilt copper bowls for perfume. The undersides of the lids are also gilt.

Over the years these five vases have been moved round and their branches have been muddled. It would be logical to expect that when Boulton and Fothergill sent Matthews four vases and eight branches they would have marked them in some way to ensure that he fitted the branches to the vases in the correct sequence. And so they did. On four of the vases, including the one now in the dining room, the mounts into which the branches are slotted are numbered. The branches are numbered accordingly, but they are not now fitted to the correct vases.[634] The fifth vase is unnumbered and is presumably the one supplied later: both it and its unnumbered branches are now in the saloon, but not together.

The splendour and quality of these vases are shown to excellent effect in the grand saloon at Saltram, and it is a happy fact that they have escaped the fate of many other elaborate candle vases, which have been wired for electricity.

Other King's vases with double branches for six candles survive at Hinton Ampner and in private collections.[635]

OPPOSITE:
346. Lyre vase perfume burners, 12.5 in., Private Collection.

Lyre vase

There was a 'lyre essence vase, white marble, in parts broken' listed among Boulton and Fothergill's stock in 1782,[636] and a 'small lyre vase' was recorded in the Day Book in 1780.[637]

Several perfume burners with a prominent lyre mount on each face of the body are known (Plate 346). All stand on round stone pedestals mounted on two-step bases. These circular stepped bases, decorated with pierced guilloche rings, were described in the 1782 Inventory as the 'old round step'.[638] They are characteristic of a number of vases made in about 1771–2 (Plates 261–2). The pedestals are decorated with base and cornice mounts, similar to those on the vases in Plate 260 and other vases, and with four bucrania with drapery hanging from their horns, and laurel swags. The stem is plain and burnished, the lower mount being chased with laurel and crossed ribbons, the upper mount with a guilloche motif. The vase cradle, with a double ring above the formal leaves holding four flowers, is unusually fitted inside with four projections which slot into holes in the blue john body and hold it in position. Laurel swags hang from the lyres and the rams' heads. The rim of the vase is decorated with a gadrooned pattern, and the lid, which is made of stone and is gilt on the underside, is not pierced. The lining (Plate 97) is gilt and held in place by the usual holed nut, unusually finely chased. The lining is made of unusually thick brass and appears to have been formed by pressing and hammering, although it is difficult to tell because it was subjected during manufacture to much filing as well as hammering. The fixing rod rises from the copper base plate, which is integral with the lower guilloche ring on the base. These vases are richly gilt and better proportioned than some of their contemporaries, the vase bodies being proportionally larger in relation to the pedestals. Some of the mounts, notably the lyres and the bucrania, may well owe their origin to William Chambers or to Anderson. Blue john versions of the lyre vase are rare, and this is the only pair so far recorded with stone lids. A blue john vase with a gilt lid pierced for the emission of perfume is in the State Hermitage Museum, St Petersburg.[639]

OPPOSITE:
347. Lyre vase perfume burners, 11 in., Christie's.

Several lyre vases survive with white marble bodies and pedestals and pierced gilt lids decorated with acanthus leaves spreading from the cone finial.[640] In some cases the guilloche rings round the base are not pierced.[641]

Plate 347 shows a pair of white marble vases with different mounts beneath the vase.[642] The plain burnished stem is supported by a round gadrooned mount, which echoes the griffin vase (Plate 336), and a fluted square base. These mounts appear together in the large drawing of the tea urn in the pattern books (Plate 232). There are other, more subtle differences from the earlier lyre vase. The drapery hanging from the horns of the bucrania on the pedestal hang behind the laurel swags. The lyres are cast from different moulds. They have no acanthus decoration at the bottom, a different motif at the top, and diamond-shaped holes in their frames. Versions of this design, with blue john bodies and pedestals and pierced lids, are recorded.

Medallion vase

There were two vases in the catalogue of the sale at Christie's in April 1771, each described as 'a large vase in or moulu in the antique taste, with medalians and other ornaments'. The catalogue is annotated 'not come' against each of the lots.[643] No reserve price appears in the catalogue against either vase. The two vases were listed among the unsold vases after the sale as 'a pair of large medallion vases, gilt vases' at twelve guineas each.[644]

Fothergill had warned Boulton, who was in London preparing for the sale, early in April that 'you will not receive the 2 medallion vases while in London owing to some of the wrought work which goes up the hollows being broke'. Some of the pieces needed to be filed and chased afresh, and then gilt, and would not be ready for ten days. Fothergill added a sketch in the margin of the letter (Plate 348) to illustrate what he was talking about.[645] It seems clear from this sketch, and from the mention of 'wrought' work in the 'hollows', that he was referring to vases of the type illustrated in Plate 349. These vases have two medallions each, depicting a sacrifice to Aesculapius, and the 'hollows' of the lower part of the vase are decorated

themselves the whole day among whom was Bradbury the Gilder
whom Tyson says (in Excuse) was so drunk as oblig'd him to
stay to assist in bringing him home. I am afraid you will
not receive the 2 Medallion Vases while in London owing to
some of the wrought work w.d goes up the hollows being broke
& which has occasion'd Tarr to leave work as he says they
there must bee some fresh fil'd & chas'd besides Gilding so will
not be finish'd these 10 days as Bradbury is determin'd on a Weeks
play &c and as I found but few hands at work this morning
who I observ'd came chiefly to extort more then they perhaps
might earn by Saturday night I thought proper to order
the doors as to be lock'd this evening & to continue till monday
morning except to the 3 following viz
Marsfeat to finish Lady Cravens boxes

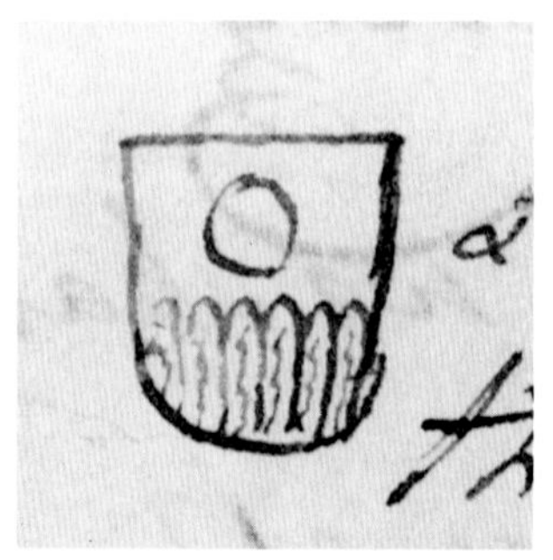

348. John Fothergill letter to Matthew Boulton, 4th April 1771, sketch of medallion vase, Central Reference Library, Birmingham.

349. Medallion vase perfume burners, 15 in., State Hermitage Museum, St Petersburg.

350. Medallion vase of Plate 349, detail.

with 'wrought' pendants. It is very likely that these two vases are the only surviving medallion vases, and these were the two intended for the sale in 1771. What happened to them after they were delivered to William Matthews in April or May 1771 is not recorded, but they probably formed part of the consignment of vases sent to Lord Cathcart in St Petersburg and bought by Catherine the Great later in the year (see Chapter 5, p. 177). They are now in the State Hermitage Museum in St Petersburg.[646]

It is difficult to know, in the absence of documentary evidence, what purpose these vases were intended for. In the Hermitage Museum's records they are described as wine coolers. In defence of this, the lids are made in two parts, the cone finial and its supporting leaf and gadrooned mounts lifting off separately from the lower plain burnished part. It could be argued that this unusual design was intended to allow a wine bottle to stand in the vase with its neck sticking up through the lid. But there are several objections to this interpretation. First, not many wine bottles would have fitted easily into the inside of the vase. Second, it would not be easy either to replace the lower lid over a bottle or to remove it again. Third, the silvered lining is holed at the bottom so that it can be fixed with a nut to the central threaded rod, which holds the vase together. The lining is therefore not a suitable receptacle for ice or any liquid falling from a bottle. Fourth, there is no documentary evidence that these vases were intended as wine coolers or ice pails. It seems likely, therefore, that they were intended, like many other vases, as perfume burners, the unusual lid being a way of arranging for the emission of the perfume without taking the whole lid off. Other vases intended as perfume burners had unpierced lids (Plate 346), reflecting the fact that patrons keen on vases bought some of them purely as ornaments and had no intention of using them.

The vases share a number of features with other vases. The use of an entirely metal body is characteristic of the earlier years of production. The frieze round the top of the body is reminiscent of the tea urn (Plate 231) and the candle vases with the spiral fluted stem (Plate 241), both strongly influenced by James Stuart (see Chapter 3, p. 76). Even closer is the frieze of the gilt base of the Titus clock case at Fasanerie, which appears to be identical (see p. 234). The medallion (Plate 350) reappears on the early caryatic vases (Plates 321–2). I have discussed this medallion, the origin of which has so far eluded me, in Chapter 3 (see p. 114), where I have illustrated one of Wedgwood's versions of it. The lower part of the vase, with its fluted decoration, reflects other vases even if the treatment of the motif is different, and the 'wrought work' in the 'hollows' echoes other ornaments (Plate 160) and the sketch of the ice pail in the pattern books (Plate 211). Boulton and Fothergill frequently used this device of husks in fluted hollows on pieces of silverware. The acanthus decoration of the stem, with the ends of the leaves upturned, is unusual. The rather prominent blued pins that now fix the mounts in the 'hollows' are later replacements for what would originally have been small gilt headed screws. Similar pins can be seen in Plate 349, on each side of a crack in the frieze at the top of the body, of the vase on the left. The lining is silvered and is constructed out of two pieces of rolled copper soldered together in the same way as the lining of the Bacchanalian vase illustrated in Plate 97.

Persian vase

The final and most lavish piece in the sale at Christie's in 1771 was catalogued as:

A magnificent Persian candelabra for 7 lights, in which is inserted a vase of the largest and most beautiful piece of radix amethysti the mines hath ever produced,

> which with the double branches etc. is suported by three Persians, finely modelled, standing on triangular plynth of statuary marble ornamented with military trophies proper for the subject.[647]

It was reserved at £200 and was apparently sold for £199 10s. 0d.[648]

Later in the same year Lord Grantham ordered 'for a friend of his four large vases of beautifull spar supported by three naked Persian slaves with 3 double branches for 6 lights'. Boulton and Fothergill claimed to have sold such vases for £150 each, but agreed to reduce the price of four to £500. The vases were being made and they hoped that Lord Grantham would confirm the order.[649] In the event his 'friend', who was his sister Mrs John Parker, preferred to order four King's vases, and Boulton and Fothergill were left with the problem of disposing of four very expensive Persian vases. They wrote to Matthews:

> You'll please to acquaint Mr Adam the architect that although the 4 candelabras for Lord Grantham's sister are almost entirely finished we shall nevertheless comply with her request and dispose of them otherwise (although we put ourselves under some difficulties thereby) ...[650]

One of the vases was probably the Persian vase, which was sent to Christie's for the sale in 1772.[651] It failed to sell.[652] There is no subsequent record of any order for a Persian vase in the archives. It may well have been the same vase, therefore, which appeared in the sale at Christie and Ansell's in 1778 and which was catalogued as –

> A superb candelabra with six branches, radix amethisti, supported by three Persian figures finely modelled in bronze after M. Angelo, the plinth suitably ornamented and richly gilt in or moulu.[653]

This vase was bought in at fifty-two guineas. It did not, however, remain among the stock recorded in the Inventory taken in 1782, when there were two pairs of stone bodies for Persian vases in stock but no completed vases.[654]

Two of the vases that Mrs Parker declined to take were probably sold to Sir Lawrence Dundas. In January 1772 Boulton and Fothergill wrote to him:

> In conformity to the orders you were kind enough to favour us with at the last sale we had in London we have this day forwarded to you per waggon 2 boxes marked D nos. 1 and 2 to be delivered at your house in Arlington Street containing a large radix amethysti vase supported by three Persian slaves and amounting as per invoice on the other side to £150 6s. We doubt not of its reaching your hands safe and shall be happy in hearing at your conveniency that it proves satisfactory, as also in seeing ourselves favoured with your further commands ...[655]

This letter mentions only one vase, but apparently Sir Lawrence Dundas found it satisfactory and bought a second one. Both have survived, and one of them is illustrated in Plate 351.[656] They stand on a pair of carved and painted pedestals, six of which were designed for the saloon of Dundas's house in Arlington Street by Robert Adam.[657]

These Persian vases have three branches each, with two candle holders on each branch (the vase in the sale in 1771 was probably fitted with a seventh socket in place of the lid and finial). The branches are similar, but not precisely so, to branches on other vases: the sockets and splash rings are unusual, but are similar to the nozzles and splash rings on the early caryatic vase of Plate 323. The component parts of the branches (Plate 107) are marked for ease of identification during assembly, and each branch is numbered so that it can be matched with the correct mount on the body of the vase. The lid of each vase is made of blue john. The interior is lined on the inside with a silvered copper bowl, probably silver plate under the later

351–4. Persian candle vase, 32 in., Victoria and Albert Museum.

silvering, made of two pieces soldered together as in Plate 97. The cast rim is pierced and conforms to a pattern used in other vases. The large blue john bodies are supported by a hexagonal column (Plate 354). The same column appears on the large griffin vase of Plate 337. The three male figures (Plate 354) are hatched with a fine chisel to give them a rough matted finish to contrast with the burnished gilt surfaces of the column and plinth. The gilding on them is not in the best of conditions. Their backs are hollowed to accommodate the fitting of the branches. The triangular marble pedestal is decorated on each side with an ormolu mount representing a collection of military trophies (Plate 353), an idea that Boulton probably borrowed from French models. Several of the components have been drilled in order to adapt the vases for electric lights and the original fixing rod and nuts have been replaced for the same reason.

The catalogues of the sales in 1771 and 1778 described the three supporting figures as 'Persians', and Boulton and Fothergill's letter to Sir Lawrence Dundas called them 'Persian slaves'. They clearly derive from William Chambers and I have discussed them in Chapter 3 (see p. 80).

Sphinx vase

There were ten vases in the sale at Christie's in 1771, which were described as 'in the antique taste radix amethysti and or moulu, lined with silver and perferated for essence, supported by four sphinxes upon an ornamented base of ebony'.[658] According to the list of unsold pieces sent to Matthews afterwards, one of these vases was returned because the new owner wanted a lapis pedestal and not an agate one,[659] but the others were all sold at or above the reserve of £12 12s. od. The highest price was £26 5s. od., and the buyers included Lord (or Lady) Sandys, General Carnack, and Pinchbeck, presumably the clockmaker.

The chief material for the bodies was blue john (Robert Bradbury was asked to supply six blue john 'sphinx' vases a month before the sale),[660] but the materials used for the pedestals varied. Pedestals of lapis, agate and marble are mentioned in the archives.[661] The many sphinx vases that have survived embody few differences from each other apart from the treatment of the pedestals, and the differences are certainly not enough to justify the widely divergent prices at the sale. It is thus probable that at least two lots in the sale consisted of pairs of vases and were wrongly catalogued.[662]

The vases illustrated in Plate 355[663] form, with the clock case of Plate 160 and the King's vases of Plates 339–40, the *garniture de cheminée* in the Queen's private sitting room at Windsor Castle. They were probably two of the vases which Boulton ordered to satisfy the Queen's request for some vases for the chimneypiece in her bedroom in 1770. The design could have been one of the 'various vases etc., to be executed in ormoulu by Mr Bolton for their Majesties', which William Chambers exhibited at the Royal Academy in 1770 (see Chapter 3, pp. 80, 82–3). The construction is typical, with interlocking mounts and the usual pins and nuts. The blue john on both vases is well veined on one side and a plainer honey-coloured stone on the other. Blue john is also used for the lids and the stems. The vases share a number of features with other vases. The feet, for example, echo several patterns for tea urns in the pattern books (Plate 228), including the drawing for the tea urn which Boulton was probably referring to when he told Fothergill that some of the Queen's vases should be 'feneered with blew john like the new tea kitchen'. The scrolling decoration of the base was used also on the vases of Plates 263 and 265. The sphinxes and the feet reappear in a sketch for another vase (Plate 306.1) and the sphinxes, together with the gadrooned mount that rests on their backs, in a sketch of an obelisk (Plate

223.1). The upper of the two plinths ('the pedestal') is decorated with glass panels painted to simulate stones, which echo the use of painted glass in the Cleopatra vases (Plates 328–9) and the copy of the King's clock case in Plate 162.

The pierced rim has parallels, although not precise, in several other vases. The shape of the body, like the Bacchanalian vase, is based on a classical urn. The earlier vases of Plate 247 hint at some of the sphinx vase's mounts, including the guilloche band and the fluted cradle, which on the sphinx vase becomes more elegant. The grotesque masks, bearded and moustached, do not appear on other ornaments. The sources of these and of the sphinxes are uncertain, but the likely source is again William Chambers.

The upper plinths are faced with panels of brown and gold lacquered glass, simulating aventurine, and the lower plinths consist of wood veneered with tortoiseshell. The interiors are lined with gilt copper bowls for the perfume, and the undersides of the lids are similarly gilt.

Several other sphinx vases have survived. Two further vases are in the Royal Collection at Windsor Castle.[664] These are very similar to the vases in Plate 355, but one of them (Plates 356–7) has floral mounts at the corners of the upper plinth and lapis glass panels, a gilt stem and a gilt lining, and the other has an unbeaded rim, lapis glass panels, drapery festoons mounted on the glass panels and a silvered lining.[665] Most of the surviving vases have blue john bodies and wooden plinths veneered with tortoiseshell. The upper plinth is usually faced with panels of lacquered glass of various colours – brown and gold (aventurine),[666] blue and gold (lapis),[667] a combination of these two,[668] pink and white (agate or marble),[669] etc. – simulating the various stones, which in letters and invoices they were said to be made of. A pair of vases with flecked white glass panels simulating agate and with drapery festoons is illustrated in Plate 358.[670] The lids of these vases are ormolu and not stone, as are the stems. On some vases the upper plinth is made of white marble.[671] The mounts are usually very similar to those of the vases illustrated in Plate 355, but sometimes the feet are not decorated with the bead moulding, or the upper plinth is decorated either with chased oval rosettes fixed to the corners (Plate 357) or with swags of drapery fixed to the faces (Plate 358) or with both, or the mounts which cradle the body are not pierced,[672] or the guilloche band round the body is pierced. A different leaf mount also appears on some of the lids.

The sphinx vase continued in favour after 1771. Colonel St John paid £10 10s. 0d. for a 'good sphinx vase' in 1772[673] and Lady St John bought another for £7 7s. 0d. in the same year.[674] Other purchasers in 1772 were Robert Child[675] and 'Mr Calcraft',[676] who was probably John Calcraft, the protégé of the Marquess of Granby, who later became the devoted follower of William Pitt. Both vases cost £12 12s. 0d. The Marquess of Granby himself bought a pair of sphinx vases for £25 4s. 0d. in 1774,[677] and a 'sphynx or moulu cassolete' was sold to Sir Charles Cocks in 1777 for £11 11s. 0d.[678] There were one sphinx vase 'upon marble, broken' and three stones, presumably blue john vase bodies, in stock in 1782.[679]

Venus vase

I have already discussed the Venus vase in some detail during my earlier account of its use as a clock case, and I have discussed the origins of its design in Chapter 3 (see pp. 68, 96). From the archives it appears to have been used often as a clock case, but there is a sketch of it in the pattern books which shows it without a clock (Plate 360), and many of the entries in the archives are ambiguous. There is no way of telling, for example, whether the 'Venus vase' which was sent to Robert Hyman in 1776 was fitted with a

355. Sphinx vase perfume burners, 12.5 in., Royal Collection.

356. Sphinx vase perfume burner, 12.7 in., Royal Collection.

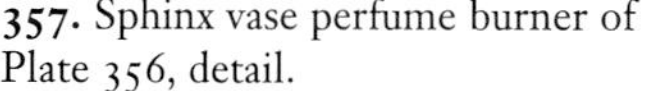

357. Sphinx vase perfume burner of Plate 356, detail.

358. Sphinx vase perfume burners, 12.5 in., Christie's.

movement or not, although the price of £23 12s. 6d. might suggest that it was.[680] Other references are equally vague. Surviving vases suggest that more Venus vases were sold as perfume burners than as clock cases, but as I have said in the earlier account of Venus clock cases, the copper vase bodies were usually made in two pieces and soldered together, the upper piece being easily cut to allow the display of horizontal hour and minute rings at the front of the vase (Plate 191).

There were two Venus vases in the sale at Christie's in 1771 which were explicitly described as perfume burners. The description of the first was similar to the descriptions of the clock cases in the same catalogue:

> Venus at the tomb of Adonis in statuary marble and or moulu: on the dye of the pedestal is a medalian representing his death, and upon it an urn lined with silver and perferated for essence, and may be occasionally used for a lamp.[681]

This vase was presumably supplied with detachable branches. It was bought by the Earl of Kerry for £17 17s. 0d. The second vase was described more briefly and was bought by Lord, or Lady, Melbourne for £21.[682] Later in 1771 another 'Venus essence pott' was sent to Charles Dunbar in Hill Street, London.[683] Many were exported. In 1772 the Paris *marchand-mercier* Charles-Raymond Grancher was advertising for sale a Venus weeping at the tomb of Adonis on a white marble base (see Chapter 5, p. 179).

None of the five Venus vases included in the sale at Christie and Ansell's in 1778 was described as a timepiece in the catalogue.[684] They were described simply as 'Venus and Cupid in or moulu, at the tomb of Adonis' and were made of 'richly decorated' or 'ornamented' marble. One of them, the figures of which were made of bronze, was described as 'perforated for essences' and another was fitted with branches for two candles. This last vase was the only one to find a buyer, in the person of Sir Patrick Crawford, who paid £13 10s. 0d. The reserve prices of between £12 12s. 0d. and £13 10s. 0d. suggest that none of these vases was fitted with a timepiece although they could clearly be adapted if the buyers wished.

The Venus vase proved a relatively popular product – I have quoted earlier the tall story about the number of Venus timepieces that Wedgwood was told had been sold when he visited Soho in 1776 (see p. 140) – and Venus vases were still being supplied in 1780. Boulton himself took a 'Venus essence vase ormoulu and white marble', although he returned it to stock later, presumably because a prospective purchaser disappointed him,[685] and the Earl of Chesterfield bought '1 Venus or moulu essence vase white marble no. 108' for £15 15s. 0d. in the same year.[686] This is the only record of the vase's stock number at Soho. There was an 'or moulu Venus essence vase, white marble' still in stock in 1782, valued at £15 15s. 0d.[687]

Plate 359 illustrates a Venus perfume burner.[688] It lacks the inscribed lament on the vase of the clock case (Plate 191), as does the sketch in the pattern book (Plate 360), but the moral of the frailty of life is clear without it. The base is decorated with an acanthus-leaf border. The vase and hollowed pedestal and mounts are fastened with the usual threaded iron rod and nuts. The medallion of Adonis and the wild boar, cast in one piece, is mounted on the face of the pedestal (Plate 361): the other three sides are decorated with drapery festoons. The stem is chased with spiral flutes with guilloche and rope rings below and above it. The gilt vase body sits in an acanthus-leaf cradle. The formal acanthus mounts below the rim are individually screwed to the body. The pierced lid is decorated with a cone finial with acanthus leaves spreading from it. There is a gilt lining. The figures, along with Venus's doves and Cupid's quiver, are close to those in the sketch except that in the sketch Venus's right hand rests on the pedestal and Cupid appears to be looking away. Cupid's bow, inverted to symbolise the extinction of life, has been replaced.

359. Venus vase perfume burner, 11.5 in., Private Collection.

360. Pattern Book 1, p. 171.

361. Venus vase perfume burner of Plate 359, detail.

Several other Venus vases are known, all with white marble bases and pedestals. There is one at Syon, somewhat damaged and missing its lid and Cupid's bow and brand, but interesting because the medallion of the death of Adonis is made by setting the separately made pictorial relief against a polished gilt oval, as on the clock case of Plate 191. On another recently exhibited Venus perfume burner Venus's right hand was resting on the pedestal as shown in the drawing.[689]

I have discussed the inferior modelling of Venus, which was criticised by Wedgwood in the context of Venus timepieces after his visit in 1776, in Chapter 3 (see p. 120).

Wing-figured vases

Three types of wing-figured vase were produced at Soho. The earliest mention of a 'winged' vase in the archives is in a letter from Fothergill to his partner early in 1772, when he reported that the Earl of Stamford had visited Soho and bought 'the winged vase'.[690] The price was £12 12s. 0d.[691] Fothergill's words, and the fact that the cost of the vase was being calculated at the time by John Scale,[692] suggests that it was a new design. The partners were obviously confident about it, and several examples were included in the sale at Christie's in April 1772. They seem to have sold well, as Boulton and Fothergill's subsequent account with William Matthews shows:

	£	s	d
To cash received of Prince of Wales a pair wing figured cassolettes	12	12	0
For Mr Thyne, delivered from the sale … 1 wing figure vase purple stone	14	14	0
For Mr Child, delivered from the sale –			
a pair of wing figured cassolettes with pedestals	29	8	0
a pair of ditto ditto vases white bodies on ditto	37	16	0
a pair of ditto ditto ditto without pedestals not delivered when I came	29	8	0
For the Duke of Northumberland, delivered at the sale … 1 wing figured vase without a pedestal	14	14	0[693]

The pair that had not been delivered to Robert Child had blue john bodies. Christie had apparently delivered them to the wrong buyer.[694] Another pair was sent from Soho to replace them three months later.[695]

Also in 1772 Lady Gower bought a 'pair' of 'wing figured casolettes' for £12 12s. 0d.[696] and the Earl of Sefton a single vase for £14 14s. 0d.[697] The wing-figured vase remained among the firm's patterns thereafter. Several stones fashioned to the pattern were listed among the stock in 1782,[698] as well as a 'wing-figured vase, stone body with 2 branches, in parts imperfect' which was valued at £11 11s. 0d. and depreciated to £8 8s. 0d.[699]

These references clearly imply two types of vase. The Prince of Wales and Lady Gower each paid twelve guineas for a pair of cassolettes, but the Earl of Stamford paid the same price for a single vase. The Duke of Northumberland, the Earl of Sefton and Mr Thyne each paid fourteen guineas for a single vase, the Duke of Northumberland's vase being described as 'without a pedestal'. Robert Child paid twenty-eight guineas for two vases without pedestals. But he also paid thirty-six guineas for two with pedestals and twenty-eight guineas for two cassolettes with pedestals.

Neither the Prince of Wales's perfume burners nor Lady Gower's have survived in the possession of their descendants. We can, however, be certain what they looked like. Several wing-figured perfume burners are known which readily match the description of 'wing-figured cassolettes'. Two of them are illustrated in Plate 362. These vases have pierced lids with a simple leaf decoration and beaded rims, and gilt copper linings. Their bodies are decorated with guilloche and Vitruvian scroll bands and formalised leaves. Beneath the vase, suspended by gilt chains fastened to the breasts of the winged figures as if continuing their necklaces, there is an oil burner with a gadrooned bowl. Its lid is decorated with leaves and lifts off to allow access for filling the bowl with oil. The lid is holed so that the wick can heat the base of the vase's lining through the circular hole at the bottom of the vase body. The chains are not original. Beneath the burner there is a triangular gilt plinth on which the three winged figures stand, and on which there is a decorative mount chased with acanthus leaves. The three figures have a band of beads encircling the buns of their coiffures and beaded necklaces. Drapery falls over their shoulders, but their breasts are bare. Below their breasts, their bodies become fluted legs ending in claws.

There are parallels between these vases and the vases of Plate 304. Both are tripods, both have female figures with stylised trunks ending in claw feet. On the plinth in each case there is a central chased mount. But the parallels stop there, and they are somewhat stretched. A nearer parallel lies in the vase of Plate 251, another perfume burner on a triangular plinth with a hanging oil burner, and in the silver perfume burner of Plate 94, which has now lost its oil burner and chains. I have argued in Chapter 3 (see p. 87) that these vases with their suspended burners may owe something to the influence of James Wyatt.

Perfume burners of this design survive in private collections and at Pavlovsk[700] and the Manchester Art Gallery.[701]

The pair of wing-figured perfume burners illustrated in Plate 363 is identical in all respects to those of Plate 362, except that they stand on elaborate pedestals and have their original faceted and gilt chains (Plate 364). They can be safely identified with the 'pair of wing figured cassolettes with pedestals' delivered to Robert Child after the sale at Christie's in 1772 at a cost of twenty-eight guineas.[702] It is easy to see from these vases and their pedestals why Boulton was pleased with his exhibition in 1772 and thought that the designs of the objects on show approached more closely the 'models of Grecian antiquity'. The triangular pedestals with the panels depicting three Bacchic figures, the rams' heads with pendants of husks, and, on the base, the bucrania and swags, are derived directly from de Caylus's *Recueil d'Antiquités* and I have discussed them in Chapter 3 (Plate 64, see p. 95). They illustrate yet again Boulton's eclectic methods of design.

These two vases were recorded in the inventory taken at Osterley Park on the death of Robert Child in 1782. They were then in the drawing room, and were recorded as 'two elegant or molee tripods'.[703] It seems to have been Boulton's fate never to be recorded in patrons' inventories.

These were clearly not the only perfume burners of this type made with pedestals. At least one pedestal survives, without its vase,[704] and the Duke of Marlborough's purchase of a 'gilt cassolete on a pedestal' for Blenheim in 1772 may well have been a wing-figured vase.[705] It does not survive at Blenheim.

The other wing-figured vases mentioned in the archives cost twelve or fourteen guineas each, and Robert Child paid thirty-six guineas for a pair of white-bodied vases on pedestals. These two vases stand today in the tapestry room at Osterley, where Child presumably put them when they were delivered. They and their stands were recorded in the tapestry drawing room in the inventory of the furniture at Osterley after his death in 1782 as 'two exceeding elegant tripod stands richly carved and gilt in burnish gold with three oval paintings and green baize covers' and 'two very elegant or molee vases and pedestals which carry two lights each for the before mentioned stands'.[706]

362. Wing-figured vase perfume burners, 8.5 in., Birmingham Museum and Art Gallery, Soho House.

363. Wing-figured vase perfume burners, 15.2 in., Christie's.

364. Wing-figured vase perfume burner of Plate 363, detail.

365. Wing-figured candle vase, 20.7 in., National Trust, Osterley Park.

366. Wing-figured candle vase of Plate 365, detail.

367. Wing-figured candle vase, 14.5 in., National Trust, Osterley Park.

368. Wing-figured candle vase of Plate 367, detail.

369. Wing-figured candle vase, 14.6 in., National Trust, Osterley Park.

370. Pattern Book 1, p. 156.

Plate 365 shows one of these vases. The winged figures differ more markedly than they may seem to do at first sight from the winged figures on the perfume burners. Their wings are raised, they have an extra bead necklace, and there is a bead ring where the candle branch is inserted into the top of each figure's head. Perhaps to compensate for these extra beads, the buns of their coiffure are left unbeaded. The vases, as usual, share some of their mounts with other ornaments. The candle sockets and drip rings reappear for instance on the lion-faced candlesticks (Plate 135) and on the vases of Plate 244, and the finial and lid are repeated on the vase of Plate 288. The lid can be inverted so that a third candle socket, similar to the sockets of the caryatic vase of Plate 324, can be used. The stamped copper guilloche band reappears on several other vases, and the pedestal (Plate 366), which is panelled with pieces of blue john, is reminiscent of the vases of Plate 244. The beaded chains are not original. These wing-figured vases are typical of Boulton's techniques of design and construction, although the quality of the workmanship is of the best. In one respect, however, they differ from most other vases, namely in the composition of their bodies. These look like statuary marble but they are made of white opaque glass. James Keir supplied them from his glassworks at Stourbridge. Boulton and Fothergill asked him, in April 1772, to make twelve vases in each of two moulds[707] and it is likely that one of the moulds was made with the wing-figured vase in mind (see Chapter 4, p. 151). These vases have been wired for electricity in the recent past.

There is a second pair of wing-figured vases at Osterley with the same white glass bodies (Plates 367–8). These stand on square white marble plinths but are otherwise almost identical to the pair that I have already discussed. The figures have no beaded crowns. The construction of these vases, some of whose mounts have unfortunately been drilled for electric flex, is shown in Plate 109. The inner lining is gilt. The chains have again been replaced. These vases cannot readily be identified with any entry in the inventory taken after Robert Childs's death in 1782, but they may then have been at his house in Berkeley Square or at Upton.

A pair of wing-figured candle vases with blue john bodies and marble plinths have also survived at Osterley (Plate 369), which can probably be identified with the vases described in the inventory as 'two elegant spar vases mounted in or moulee with double branches and statuary pedestals', or with two of the 'four spar vases mounted with or molee' listed in the drawing room.[708] Despite the description of the marble base as a pedestal, the former sounds more likely. These vases are closely similar in design and in execution to the other two pairs and are mounted on small plinths of white marble as in Plate 367. The figures and branches are numbered so that they can be assembled correctly. Boulton and Fothergill asked Matthews to tell Robert Child, when he delivered these vases, 'that the numbers marked on the bottom squares of the branches serve to shew the holes they are to be fixed into which are marked with the very same numbers'.[709] They also remarked that the 'bead rings' were tied to the branches, which probably referred to the crowns of beads which would have decorated the heads of the figures (cf. Plate 365). The chains, as on the other two pairs of vases at Osterley, have been replaced.

There are two sketches in the pattern books of wing-figured vases. The first, which is numbered 238 (Plate 370), shows the vase in its commonest form as a double-branched candle vase on a simple base. This sketch shows that the crown of beads was not always, or perhaps even usually, part of the design.

Several candle vases with double branches have survived, all of the same pattern and all with virtually the same mounts. None have the beaded crowns on the heads of the figures and most, but not all, are mounted on

371. Pattern Book 1, p. 133.

plain marble pedestals. There is a pair of vases with damaged white glass bodies at Pavlovsk,[710] and others have been exhibited or sold in recent years.[711]

The third type of wing-figured vase is illustrated in Plate 372.[712] The body and plinth are of white marble. The second sketch in the pattern book (Plate 371) shows a vase very close to this model, without candle branches and with chased handles and a closely related finial. The handles are attached to the rim of the vase behind the heads of the figures, both in the drawing and in Plate 372. Other features of the vase in Plate 372 differ from the drawing, notably the different treatment of the stem with its laurel ring base, the longer flutes and beaded ring and acanthus mount beneath the

372. Wing-figured vase, 18.5 in., Christie's.

vase (this appears to be upside down in the photograph), the lack of a stone plinth and the very different mount on the body of the vase. This mount is close to part of the decoration on a silver ewer elsewhere in the pattern books (Plate 198), a design that is modelled on a differently decorated drawing by James Wyatt.

This vase was also made with elaborate candle branches.[713] A vase with a fine reddish blue john body is illustrated in Plate 373. Its branches, which echo those used on Boulton's three-branched version of James Stuart's tripod (Plate 233), have some similarities to the drawing in Plate 312.1, but they grow out of a basin of leaves shaped almost like a tulip and have a pronounced anthemion mount at the centre. The mount on the body is missing its central piece with its somewhat Egyptian flavour.

373. Wing-figured candle vase, 20.2 in., Hotspur Ltd.

Notes

NOTES TO CHAPTER I
Birmingham and Soho
Notes to pp. 9–30
Notes 1–147

1. Sold Christie's, 27th–29th May 1987 (Tew Park), lot 403. Schaak's bill to Matthew Boulton, or rather receipt, dated 13th October 1770, for 'painting two portraits £10 10s. 0d.' survives in the Boulton archives. The second portrait was probably of Fothergill. It survives in a private collection in Australia.
2. Hutton, *History of Birmingham* (1835), p. 77. By 1791 the figure had increased by a further 47 per cent.
3. Timmins, *Resources, Products and Industrial History of Birmingham* (1866), p. 216. Burke visited Soho on 15th October 1770 (Register Book, Great Tew Archive).
4. The 'street' was Deritend.
5. Leland, *Itinerary* (1538), Vol. iv, p. 89, quoted by Hamilton, *English Brass and Copper Industries* (1926), pp. 122–3.
6. Camden, *Britannia* (1586), Vol. 1, p. 609, quoted by Hamilton, *English Brass and Copper Industries* (1926), p. 123.
7. Hamilton, *English Brass and Copper Industries* (1926), p. 123. This book contains a good account of the rise of Birmingham's brass and copper trades. My own brief account in this chapter is largely based on it and on Court, *Rise of the Midlands Industries* (1938), which places the metal trades of Birmingham in a wider context. See also Hopkins, *Birmingham* (1989).
8. Hutton, *History of Birmingham* (1781), p. 63.
9. The first of these two Acts made the use of the Book of Common Prayer compulsory in all churches. The second effectively banned non-conformists from practising their religions within five miles of any incorporated town or borough represented in Parliament (Hamilton, *English Brass and Copper Industries* (1926), p. 125).
10. Page (ed.), *Victoria History of the County of Warwick* (1908), Vol. 2, p. 458ff.
11. Hopkins, *Birmingham* (1989), pp. 4–7 is sceptical about putting too much emphasis on dissenters as a central cause of Birmingham's growth, pointing out that the experience of other towns does not corroborate the argument. Wolverhampton was also an unincorporated town, and Coventry succeeded in developing industries despite being incorporated.
12. Prosser, *Birmingham Inventors and Inventions* (1881), p. 3.
13. Hutton, *History of Birmingham* (1835), p. 169.
14. Sketchley and Adams, *Tradesman's True Guide* (1770), p. 10.
15. A large number of patterns of furniture mounts made in Birmingham have survived. See Goodison, 'The Victoria and Albert Museum's Collection of Metal-Work Pattern Books' (1975).
16. Gill and Briggs, *History of Birmingham* (1952), Vol. 1, p. 64.
17. These were all alloys, the last three being forms of brass, i.e. alloys of copper and zinc, their colours varying with the quantities of the constituent metals. They are defined in Chapter 4 (see pp. 127–8). 'White metal' was an alloy of about fifty parts of tin, three or four parts of antimony and one of copper: it was later known as 'Britannia metal' and was much used by cutlers because it resembled silver.
18. Tutenag, an alloy of copper, zinc and nickel with some iron, silver or arsenic, but sometimes also used as a word for zinc alone.
19. Sketchley and Adams, *Tradesman's True Guide* (1770), p. 12.
20. Sketchley and Adams, *Tradesman's True Guide* (1770), p. 14.
21. Sketchley and Adams, *Tradesman's True Guide* (1770), p. 54.
22. Hopkins, *Birmingham* (1989), pp. 7, 20, 85. Hopkins draws an interesting contrast with the textile industry which was subject to different commercial and technical pressures and so needed more advanced mechanisation.
23. Hopkins, *Birmingham* (1989), p. 20 suggests that it was 'the fastest growing industrial town in the country'.
24. Hutton, *History of Birmingham* (1835), p. 190.
25. Fitzmaurice, *Life of William, Earl of Shelburne* (1912), pp. 276–8.
26. Hamilton, *English Brass and Copper Industries* (1926), pp. 137–8.
27. Defoe, *Plan of the English Commerce* (1728), p. 291.
28. Although better known to historians as an industrial chemist and an influential businessman, Garbett (1717–1803) was a manufacturer of buttons and hardware.
29. It is significant that all three were listed in Sketchley and Adams's *Tradesman's True Guide* (1770) under the heading of 'Merchants' (pp. 40–1) and were not recorded as button, buckle or toy makers.
30. Fitzmaurice, *Life of William, Earl of Shelburne* (1912), p. 398.
31. Connell, *Portrait of a Whig Peer* (1957), p. 26.
32. For further details of his business and achievements see Robinson, 'Boulton and Fothergill 1762–1782' (1959), pp. 62–3; Samuel Lloyd, *The Lloyds of Birmingham* (1907), pp. 42–3; Hutton, *History of Birmingham* (1835), p. 169; Gill and Briggs, *History of Birmingham* (1952), Vol. 1, p. 100ff; Hamilton, *English Brass and Copper Industries* (1926), p. 272; Court, *Rise of the Midlands Industries* (1938), p. 234ff; Hopkins, *Birmingham* (1989), pp. 84–5.
33. Robinson, 'Boulton and Fothergill 1762–1782' (1959), pp. 62–5. The evidence given by Garbett and Taylor is summarised in the House of Commons Journals, 20th March 1759. There must be some doubt about the precision of their figures.
34. Lord Shelburne considered that the button and toy trades owed their success to the development of stamping and the division of labour. See Fitzmaurice, *Life of William, Earl of Shelburne* (1912), p. 277.
35. Mare and Quarrell, *Lichtenberg's Visits to England* (1938), pp. 98–9.
36. Thus Gill and Briggs *History of Birmingham* (1952), Vol. 1, p. 103 calls Boulton 'the most famous captain of industry in Birmingham during the eighteenth century ... a man of many enterprises, who is universally remembered for one of them, his support of James Watt in carrying through and perfecting the invention of the steam-engine': and Paul Mantoux in his classic, *Industrial Revolution in the Eighteenth Century* (revised edition, 1964), gives a brief account of Boulton's business at the Soho Manufactory but only by way of background to his promotion of the steam engine. One recent writer who has given space to Boulton's earlier businesses is Hopkins, *Birmingham* (1989), and 'Boulton before Watt' (1984). James Watt (1736–1819) first visited Soho in 1767: he moved to Birmingham in 1774 after the bankruptcy of his previous backer, John Roebuck, the founder of the Carron Iron Works. His partnership with Boulton dated from 1775, when the term of his patent was extended for twenty-five years by Act of Parliament.
37. Robinson, 'Matthew Boulton's Marketing Techniques' (1963), p. 39. In his several papers about Boulton, Eric Robinson has shown how important his earlier partnership was. He rightly observes (p. 40) that Boulton would have been a significant figure in the Industrial Revolution even if he had not promoted a single steam engine.
38. Matthew Boulton (hereafter abbreviated to M.B.) to John Scale, 18th September 1778, quoted by Robinson, 'Matthew Boulton's Marketing Techniques' (1963), p. 39.
39. The only published biography of Boulton is Dickinson, *Matthew Boulton* (1937). Details of his life can also be found in Schofield, *Lunar Society of Birmingham* (1963), and in many other books concerned with Birmingham and industrial history in the eighteenth century.
40. Smiles, *Lives of Boulton and Watt* (1865), p. 130. Smiles's work was published in 1865, but as Quickenden points out, *Boulton and Fothergill Silver* (1989), p. 37, note 24, he is probably a reliable authority.
41. James Watt, 'Memorandum concerning Mr Boulton', 17th September 1809, p. 1.
42. Robinson, 'Boulton and Fothergill, 1762–82' (1959), pp. 61–2.
43. Robinson, 'Boulton and Fothergill, 1762–82' (1959), p. 61.
44. M.B. to his wife, n.d. [3rd March 1770].
45. Watt, 'Memorandum concerning Mr Boulton', p. 10.
46. Schofield, *Lunar Society of Birmingham* (1963), p. 18.
47. James Keir, 'Memorandum of Matthew Boulton', 3rd December 1809, p. 1.

48. James Keir (1735–1820) is best known as an industrial chemist, but his early business career, after studying medicine at Edinburgh and serving in the army for seven years, was in the glass trade. He became a partner in a glassworks at Stourbridge in 1772. He was offered a partnership by Boulton and Fothergill but declined. He founded the alkali works at Tipton in 1783. He was an able businessman and an accomplished scientist and Boulton turned to him for advice on several occasions. Court and Schofield both give details of his career.
49. Keir, 'Memorandum of Mr Boulton', p. 9. Keir's judgement is supported by many of Boulton's letters. He wrote, for example, to James Watt on 7th February 1769 that it was not worth his while to make steam engines 'for three counties only; but I find it well worth my while to make for all the world'.
50. Wedgwood to Bentley, 23rd May 1767 (E25-18147). Wedgwood visited Soho on 14th May 1767 (Register Book, Great Tew Archive). He became a close friend of Boulton, in spite of a somewhat uneasy rivalry between their businesses. As I shall show later, there were many parallels between the two firms, notably in the eclecticism of their designs and their marketing techniques.
51. Keir, 'Memorandum of Mr Boulton', p. 5.
52. Keir, 'Memorandum of Mr Boulton', p. 6.
53. Keir, 'Memorandum of Mr Boulton', p. 7.
54. M.B.'s Notebook, 1751–9, pp. 44–54.
55. M.B.'s Notebook, 1768–75. The recipes are discussed in Chapter 4, pp. 143–8.
56. M.B.'s Notebook, 1751–9.
57. Keir, 'Memorandum of Mr Boulton', p. 7.
58. The most complete account of the Lunar Society and its origins is Schofield, *Lunar Society of Birmingham* (1963), where the lives and work of the scientists whom I have mentioned are amply described. Schofield's book is indispensable reading for anyone who wants to study Boulton's life and affairs.
59. John Whitehurst (1713–85) was an able clockmaker and worked in Derby. He took a keen interest in natural philosophy and was a notable geologist. He moved to London in 1775 to take up an appointment at the Royal Mint. See Schofield, *Lunar Society of Birmingham* (1963); Hutton, *Works of John Whitehurst* (1792); White, *Whitehurst Family* (1958); and Craven, *John Whitehurst of Derby* (1996).
60. James Ferguson (1710–76) was a talented writer and lecturer in natural philosophy, well known for his work on globes and astronomical clocks. See Henderson, *Life of James Ferguson* (1867); Taylor, *Mathematical Practitioners of Hanoverian England* (1966), pp. 176–7; and Ferguson's own autobiographical note prefixed to his *Select Mechanical Exercises* (1775).
61. William Small (1734–75) came to Birmingham in 1765 after six years as Professor of Natural Philosophy at the College of William and Mary, Williamsburg, Virginia. He became Boulton's family physician and until his early death was his most constant adviser. He was probably the most influential of the early members of the Lunar circle. See Schofield, *Lunar Society of Birmingham* (1963).
62. M.B. to William Matthews, 31st August 1781. Anne's younger brother, Luke, died in 1764, which meant that Boulton effectively gained control of the entire Robinson family fortune.
63. Notes endorsed 'Case between Boulton and Fothergill' (J. Fothergill Box), compiled by Boulton, probably in 1781.
64. M.B. to T. Hollis, 3rd February 1761 (Charles Roberts Autograph Letters Collection, Haverford Collection Library, Pennsylvania), quoted by Schofield, *Lunar Society of Birmingham* (1963), p. 26.
65. M.B. to John Fothergill (abbreviated hereafter to J.F.), 9th May 1772.
66. M.B. to T. Hollis, 15th January 1757.
67. 'Case between Boulton and Fothergill' (J. Fothergill Box).
68. The partnership agreement is summarised more fully by Cule in his unpublished thesis, *Financial History of Matthew Boulton* (1935).
69. See Robinson, 'Boulton and Fothergill 1762–1782' (1959), pp. 67–8. According to Boulton's 'Case between Boulton and Fothergill', Fothergill approached Boulton in 1762, having quarrelled with Duncumb.
70. These included H. F. Bargum, the Danish financier who founded the Royal Danish Guinea Company (Robinson, 'Boulton and Fothergill 1762–1782' (1959), p. 68). On 5th August 1767 Boulton wrote to Bargum, who had agreed to advance £5,000 to the partnership, asking for part of the loan immediately. Although subsequent letters show that Bargum in fact only advanced part of the loan, the connection with him must have seemed very hopeful and potentially lucrative. In 1763 Fothergill left, wanting to dissolve the partnership with Boulton, but he returned after two months.
71. J.F. to M.B., 7th May 1762.
72. M.B. to 'Montreal', 6th July 1763. 'Montreal' was a code name for one of the firm's overseas agents: see Chapter 5, p. 179.
73. Cule, *Financial History of Matthew Boulton* (1935), pp. 9–10. The decision may also have resulted from Boulton's accretion of wealth following his brother-in-law's death in 1764.
74. The manufactory was probably designed and the construction masterminded by William Wyatt (1734–83). Several members of the Wyatt family of builders worked in various capacities for Boulton and Fothergill. See Colvin, *Biographical Dictionary of English Architects* (1995), pp. 1101ff; Quickenden, 'Boulton and Fothergill Silver' (1989), pp. 19–20, and other mentions of the family in this book.
75. Fitzmaurice, *Life of William, Earl of Shelburne* (1912), pp. 274–5.
76. J.F. to M.B., 7th May 1762.
77. M.B.'s Notebook, 1765, p. 26.
78. Rowe, *Adam Silver* (1965), p. 53, says that Boulton was one of the very few makers of fused plate on any scale outside Sheffield and was almost certainly the biggest single producer of it of his day.
79. J.F. to M.B., 11th February 1764. See Quickenden, 'Boulton and Fothergill Silver' (1989), p. 18 and note 93 (p. 40). Quickenden notes that the partners had sheets of plate rolled for them in Derby (B. and F. to William Richardson, 7th August 1764). Zacchaeus Walker, in a letter to M.B. dated 10th December 1765, reported that a Dutch merchant had returned some plated candlesticks. Plated candlesticks also appear in a list of candlesticks in M.B.'s Notebook, 1765, p. 40.
80. M.B.'s Notebook, 1765, p. 26, 'We must buy ... Tovey's brassfoundry'.
81. M.B.'s Notebook, 1765, p. 40, where there is a list of objects including brass, plated, iron and silvered candlesticks.
82. M.B.'s Notebook, 1765, pp. 40–1.
83. S. Wyatt to M.B., 31st July 1765.
84. Watt, 'Memorandum concerning Mr Boulton', p. 1.
85. M.B. to P. J. Wendler, n.d. [1767].
86. 'Tagebücher des Grafen von Zinzendorf und Pottendorf' (State Archives, Vienna), Vol. 13 (1768), quoted in Eric Robinson 'Birmingham seen by an Austrian Nobleman', *Birmingham Post*, 12th August 1958.
87. M.B.'s Notebook, 1768–75, pp. 11ff: no ormolu objects are mentioned in this list, which appears to have been compiled in about November 1768.
88. M.B. to J. H. Ebbinghaus, 2nd March 1768.
89. Wedgwood to Bentley, 23rd May 1767 (E25-18147).
90. M.B. to Wedgwood, 10th July 1767.
91. M.B. to Richard Tonson, 21st June 1769.
92. B. and F. to Thomas Craig, Dublin, 26th March 1772. I have replaced stops in the manuscript with semicolons.
93. Pattern Book 1, pp. 160, 171 (vases), pp. 77, 79 (obelisks).
94. Langford, *A Century of Birmingham Life* (1868), p. 272. The best account of Boulton's silver is Quickenden's unpublished thesis, *Boulton and Fothergill Silver* (1989): see also Quickenden, 'Boulton and Fothergill Silver: Business Plans and Miscalculations' (1980) and other articles published by Quickenden and cited in the Bibliography. The opening of the Birmingham Assay Office on 31st August 1773, which came about largely as a result of Boulton's own efforts, was a significant event. Silver no longer had to be sent to Chester to be hallmarked. The volume of articles produced in Birmingham could be increased and there was less risk of damage during travel.
95. Keir, 'Memorandum of Mr Boulton', p. 2. The clock business was concentrated on the

production of William Small's remarkable one-wheeled clock, the perfection of which Small reported to James Watt in a letter dated 3rd February 1771. A copy of the specification of Small's patent (no. 1048) dated 28th June 1773 survives in the Boulton papers, along with a series of Small's letters about it (William Small Box).

96. There are many references in the archives to the production of mechanical paintings, but the venture lost money. It was yet another business in which Boulton misjudged his market. It has been discussed briefly by Robinson and Thompson in 'Matthew Boulton's Mechanical Paintings' (1970).

97. Keir, 'Memorandum of Mr Boulton', p. 2.

98. For the importance of the rolling mill in the evolution of the eighteenth-century metal trades, see Hamilton, *English Brass and Copper Industries* (1926), and Court, *Rise of the Midlands Industries* (1938). The rolling mill encouraged the use of the stamp and the press instead of hammering. Boulton's manager, John Scale, wrote to Boulton on 7th February 1773 sending a silver candle-stick made with the use of stamps and dies. It was much cheaper than if made by the traditional methods. The London silversmiths thought such methods of manufacture distinctly unfair. See Rowe, *Adam Silver* (1965), pp. 53–5, for comments on the use of rolling mills, stamps and dies in the production of silver in Birmingham and Sheffield; also Quickenden, *Boulton and Fothergill Silver* (1989).

99. Watt, 'Memorandum concerning Mr Boulton', pp. 1–2.

100. M.B. to James Adam ('Adams Esq., Architect'), 1st October 1770.

101. Roll, *An Early Experiment in Industrial Organisation* (1930), pp. 186, 194, 201; Berg, *Age of Manufactures* (1985), pp. 283–4, 302.

102. Dorothy Richardson, 'Tours', Vol. 2, pp. 208–17 (John Rylands University of Manchester Library, Ryl.Eng.MSS 1123). I am grateful to Lucy Peltz for drawing my attention to this manuscript and for providing me with a transcript. Dorothy Richardson (b.1748) was the daughter of the Reverend Henry Richardson, rector of Thornton in Craven, Yorkshire, and lived at Bierley Hall, near Bradford. She toured Britain extensively. She was particularly interested in antiquarian objects and collections and in factories, and recorded the details of many factory visits. She travelled on this tour with her uncle John Richardson. The Register Book (Great Tew Archive) records him as 'Richardson Esq.' of Kildwick in Craven, York, on 31st May 1770, but omits his niece.

103. 'Congealed water' was a name vulgarly given to a number of crystallised minerals, in this case blue john.

104. 'Measurement of shops in the Soho Manufactory Xmas 1777', but headed 'Dimension of all the shops in the Soho Manufactory taken in November 1776' (J. Bownas & Co. Box). The document was drawn up as an aid to valuing the manufactory and accompanies other similar summaries. It has no relevance to J. Bownas & Co., later successors to the Matthew Boulton and Button Co., and was presumably mis-filed when the archives were first assembled in the Assay Office.

105. Inventory, 1782.

106. Wilcox (ed.), *Papers of Benjamin Franklin* (1974), Vol. 18, p. 116, 28th May 1771. After the visit to Birmingham the travellers went to Burton-on-Trent which, said Williams, was 'remarkable for good ale'. Franklin's visit is recorded in the Register Book (Great Tew Archive).

107. G. C. Lichtenberg to J. A. Schernhagen, 16th October 1775. See Mare and Quarrell, *Lichtenberg's Visits to England* (1938), p. 97. Lichtenberg's name does not appear in the record of visitors to Soho (Register Book, Great Tew Archive). The record however is incomplete and often records the presence of 'others' with certain visitors.

108. M.B. to J. H. Ebbinghaus, n.d. [June 1766].

109. M.B. to James Adam, 5th October 1770.

110. Wedgwood to Bentley, 24th–26th December 1770 (E25-18334).

111. M.B. to the Earl of Dartmouth, 10th November 1772 (Dartmouth MSS, copy in the Assay Office Library, Birmingham).

112. Swinney, *New Birmingham Directory* (1773).

113. M.B. to J. H. Ebbinghaus, 18th November 1767.

114. M.B. to J. H. Ebbinghaus, 2nd March 1768.

115. Morgan (ed.), *An American Quaker in the British Isles* (1992), pp. 254–5. I am grateful to Nick Molyneux for drawing my attention to these journals.

116. M.B. to J. H. Ebbinghaus, 2nd March 1768. See Quickenden, *Boulton and Fothergill Silver* (1989), p. 22.

117. Their problems are discussed by Robinson, 'Boulton and Fothergill 1762–1782' (1959), pp. 73–5.

118. M.B. to the Earl of Warwick, 30th December 1770.

119. Robinson, 'Boulton and Fothergill 1762–1782' (1959).

120. Robinson, 'Boulton and Fothergill 1762–1782' (1959), p. 72, suggests that this need was partly responsible for the use of code names in the firm's books to denote certain continental agents.

121. The financial affairs of Boulton and Fothergill have not been fully unravelled. There are a large number of references in the archives that need to be collated and interpreted. Cule traced the history of the partnership in his *Financial History of Matthew Boulton* (1935). The brief account here largely follows Cule's thesis and must be regarded as correct in general thrust but tentative in detail.

122. The figures for capital, trading profits, etc., which follow are largely derived from a memorandum headed 'Statement of Affairs 1763–80' (J. Fothergill Box).

123. Cule, *Financial History of Matthew Boulton* (1935), p. 7, suggests that the loss might have been due to Fothergill's absence for two months, but this of itself seems an insufficient cause.

124. Cule, *Financial History of Matthew Boulton* (1935), p. 15.

125. M.B. to J. H. Ebbinghaus, n.d. [June 1766].

126. Cule, *Financial History of Matthew Boulton* (1935), p. 12.

127. B. and F. to Henry Morris, 2nd December 1771.

128. J.F. to M.B., 22nd May 1772. Zacchaeus Walker became Boulton's clerk in 1760 and looked after the accounting from an early stage (M.B. to J. H. Ebbinghaus, 1st December 1766). He worked with Fothergill in the warehouse in Birmingham at 38 Snow Hill and after 1777 at New Hall. He married Mary Boulton, and died in 1808.

129. M.B. to J. H. Ebbinghaus, 2nd March 1768. In this letter Boulton said that the journeymen's wages were £260 each week and that materials such as gold, silver, brass, iron etc., had to be paid for within six weeks.

130. J. H. Ebbinghaus to M.B., 30th December 1766.

131. M.B. to H. F. Bargum, 18th November 1767.

132. John Baskerville to M.B., 24th October 1764. Baskerville, the famous japanner and printer, persuaded Tonson, who did not know Boulton, to make the loan.

133. M.B. to John Motteux, 17th October 1766. Motteux, who was later Chairman of the East India Company, was one of the merchants who regularly accepted Boulton and Fothergill's bills.

134. J. H. Ebbinghaus to B. and F., 26th August 1768.

135. Cule, *Financial History of Matthew Boulton* (1935), pp. 28–9.

136. M.B. to the Earl of Dartmouth, 10th November 1772.

137. J. H. Ebbinghaus to M.B., 24th May 1772.

138. The loss in 1773 was £2,316 6s. 9d. Profits were recorded in 1774 and 1776 but no accounts were made up for the other years.

139. Cule, *Financial History of Matthew Boulton* (1935), p. 74. Quickenden, *Boulton and Fothergill Silver* (1989), pp. 218ff., shows that Boulton's borrowings in the 1760s and 1770s were far greater than Cule's thesis suggests. Towards the end of the 1770s he borrowed substantial sums which were not fully paid back until the success of the engine business in the late 1780s.

140. Cule, *Financial History of Matthew Boulton* (1935), p. 101.

141. Memorandum headed 'Mr Keir's remarks on partnership', n.d. [*c.*1775].

142. M.B. to James Watt, 26th November 1780.
143. Morgan (ed.), *An American Quaker in the British Isles* (1992), p. 255.
144. John Scale (1737–92) was in charge of the manufactory from the early 1770s. He was in partnership with Boulton and Fothergill in the button business in 1778 (Ledger, 1778–82, p. 84) but was in effect the manager of it.
145. See Cule, *Financial History of Matthew Boulton* (1935), pp. 38ff: Scale's document was an attempt both to defend himself against Fothergill's unjustified suspicions and to suggest improvements.
146. There is a large number of letters in the archives asking patrons to pay outstanding bills.
147. J. H. Ebbinghaus to M.B., 24th May 1772.

NOTES TO CHAPTER 2
The ormolu trade at Soho
Notes to pp. 31–62
Notes 1–279

1. Swinney, *New Birmingham Directory* (1773).
2. See Verlet, *Bronzes Dorés Français* (1987); Eriksen, *Early Neo-Classicism in France* (1974); Hughes, *Wallace Collection Catalogue of Furniture* (1996). Verlet's book is an invaluable source book for the work of the metalworkers in France in the eighteenth century and for the role of others connected with the trade, including the Paris *marchand-merciers*. Philippe Caffieri (1714–74) appears to have been an important figure in the 1760s. Gouthière was born in 1732 and died in 1813–14. Verlet pointed out in 'The Wallace Collection and the Study of French Eighteenth-Century Bronzes d'Ameublement' (1950) that Gouthière happens to be the best known of eighteenth-century metalworkers but that there were many others, such as Pitoin, who were just as competent, if not more so. From 1776 the *fondeurs-ciseleurs* and the *ciseleurs-doreurs*, whose guilds merged in that year, obliged their members to mark their work, which greatly helps the process of attribution.
3. M.B. to various patrons, 18th May 1778.
4. Verlet, *French Royal Furniture* (1963), pp. 192–3. Heavy penalties were imposed when *ébénistes* occasionally infringed the regulation.
5. Verlet, *French Royal Furniture* (1963), pp. 11–12.
6. Hayward, 'English Brass-Inlaid Furniture' (1965), and 'The Channon Family of Exeter and London' (1966); Gilbert and Murdoch, 'John Channon and Brass-Inlaid Furniture' (1993).
7. Smith, *Buckingham Palace* (1931), pp. 265–7 and Plates 350–1; de Bellaigue, Harris and Millar, *Buckingham Palace* (1968), pp. 148–9.
8. Smith, *Buckingham Palace* (1931), p. 255 and Plate 330; de Bellaigue, *Buckingham Palace* (1968), p. 159. Pinchbeck bought several of Boulton and Fothergill's mounted vases in 1771 but there is no evidence that he bought any gilt mounts for clock cases at any time. The mounts may have been supplied by Diederich Nicolaus Anderson, but he died in 1767.
9. Sketchley and Adams (1770), *Tradesman's True Guide*, p. 10.
10. See Goodison, 'The Victoria and Albert Museum's Collection of Metal-Work Pattern Books' (1975).
11. Dickinson, *Matthew Boulton* (1937), p. 54, mentions a reference (in the *English Gazetteer* of 1762) which spoke of Birmingham ormolu being highly esteemed in Europe: Robinson, 'Boulton and Fothergill 1762–1782' (1959), p. 65, quotes evidence given to Lord Shelburne by Capper and Garbett in 1766 to the effect that before 1760 all sorts of 'necessarys' in metal were exported to Portugal including gilt metal toys of all sorts.
12. His workshop was at 30 Park Street. By 1773 his business was trading as Tovey & Son at the same address (Swinney, *New Birmingham Directory*, 1773).
13. Z. Walker to M.B., 10th December 1765. This letter contains a copy of a letter to Norman complaining that he had attempted to encash a draft on Sir Herbert Packington twice over. A postscript addressed to Boulton, which reads 'Do you remember what Mr Tovey said of Norman's pay?' suggests that the cabinet maker had been one of his creditors. Samuel Norman (*fl.*1746–67) was one of the leading London cabinet makers but was bankrupt in 1767. See P. A. Kirkham, 'Samuel Norman: a study of an eighteenth-century craftsman', *Burlington Magazine*, August 1969.
14. See Lane, 'Thomas Blockley of Birmingham' (1991).
15. Harewood MSS 492, p. 4 (Leeds City Archives). I am grateful to the late Christopher Gilbert for drawing my attention to this reference. The bill includes 60 gilt escutcheons, 86 gilt door knobs, 178 gilt drops for doors, 22 gilt sash knobs, 22 gilt roses for shutters with 24 spindles and 24 handles and 22 sash fittings ('not gilt').
16. Alnwick MSS, U.1.44,46. On 2nd January 1766, Brimingham was paid £2 2s. od. on account for the door ornaments and on 7th January 1767, £30 on account for the shutter ornaments. Like so many fine gilt metal ornaments of the period the door mounts at Syon House have been attributed to Boulton: see for example Hussey, 'Syon House, Middlesex' (1950). It has also been suggested that Mr Bermingham or Brimingham might have been Boulton himself. But I agree with Lane, 'Thomas Blockley of Birmingham' (1991), that Blockley is the more likely supplier. He was more established in the line of trade than Boulton at the time, and there is no reference in the Boulton archives to the Northumberland commission. Brimingham, or Bermingham, whose name also appears in the Syon House accounts as Brimmingham, is not recorded in any of the contemporary London directories.
17. The most up-to-date account of Cox's career is Smith, 'James Cox: a Revised Biography' (2000). See also le Corbeiller, 'James Cox, a Biographical Review' (1970); Pagani 'Clocks of James Cox' (1995); Young (ed.), 'Genius of Wedgwood' (1995), pp. 122–4. Cox was working from 1749 and died in 1791.
18. 'A Descriptive Catalogue of the Several Superb and Magnificent Pieces of Mechanism and Jewellery, Exhibited in the Museum at Spring-Gardens, Charing Cross' (London 1772). In 1773 Cox enlarged the exhibition and an Act of Parliament was passed permitting him to dispose of the pieces by lottery. The enlarged collection was described in 'A Descriptive Inventory of the several Exquisite and Magnificent Pieces of Mechanism and Jewellery, comprised in the Schedule annexed to an Act of Parliament made in the Thirteenth Year of his present Majesty, George the Third' (London 1773). I shall return in Chapter 5 to Cox's show in 1772 in the context of Boulton and Fothergill's own exhibition and sale at Christie's in the same year.
19. See Smith, 'James Cox' (2000), Figs. 17–18, le Corbeiller, 'James Cox' (1970), Plates 4–7.
20. The sale took place on 1st–2nd July. The catalogue is preserved among the archives at Christie's. Another sale, of which the catalogue also survives, took place on 16th–17th December 1772.
21. He boasted in his 'Descriptive Catalogue' ('Advertisement', p.v.) that he had given employment to many artists including the painter, the goldsmith, the jeweller, the lapidary, the sculptor and the watchmaker.
22. M.B.'s Diary, 1769.
23. 'Gerard Terkinder, son of John, to Charles Magniac of St Clements Danes, chaser, £10.' (Inland Revenue Books, Public Record Office).
24. Hilary Young, 'A drawing from the circle of James Cox, possibly by Charles Magniac', *Burlington Magazine*, June 1996, pp. 402–4, tentatively attributes a drawing in the Victoria and Albert Museum (Accession no. E.3985-1906) to Magniac, but this is largely on the basis of my mention of him in *Ormolu* (1974).
25. Jean's marriage to 'Mary Francoise Joseph Angolois', who signed her name 'Mai Francis Langlois', took place on 20th October 1764 at St Pancras-in-the-Fields: Pierre Langlois was one of the witnesses. Jean's full name is given in the register as Peter Dominique Jean (St Pancras-in-the-Fields Marriage Register, reference kindly supplied by Mrs Beryl Cross). Beard and Gilbert, *Dictionary of English Furniture Makers* (1986), p. 482, gives his address as near Windmill Street, Tottenham Court Road.
26. It is not clear whether the man's name was Dominique Jean or Jean Dominique. Boulton seems to have thought it was the latter, but in most of the archives cited here it is given as the former.
27. See Beard and Gilbert, *Dictionary of English Furniture Makers* (1986), pp. 526–7. Pierre Langlois was working in London by 1759, producing furniture in the French manner. See also Edwards and Jourdain, *Georgian Cabinet-Makers* (1955), p. 103; Coleridge, 'Pierre Langlois, his œuvre and some recent discoveries' (1967); Coleridge, *Chippendale Furniture* (1968), pp. 35ff; a series of articles published by Peter Thornton and William Rieder in *Connoisseur*, December 1971 pp. 283–8, February 1972 pp. 105–12, March 1972 pp. 176–88, April 1972 pp. 257–65, May 1972 pp. 30–5; and Rieder, 'More on Pierre Langlois' (1974).
28. Dorothy Stroud found that Daniel Langlois was apprenticed to Dominique Jean, water gilder, in March 1771 (Apprenticeship

Lists, Public Record Office): see *Furniture History*, Vol. 1 (1965), p. 62.
29. Edwards, 'Patrons of Taste and Sensibility' (1965), p. 458, suggested that Daniel Langlois was the maker of the mounts. His argument was based on Langlois's apprenticeship to Dominique Jean. He was, however, unaware at the time of the evidence in the Boulton archives of Dominique Jean's relationship to, and close working association with, the Langlois family. It seems likely now that Dominique Jean supplied the mounts. Daniel Langlois's exact part in the making of the commode is unclear: he might have assisted Dominique Jean or the cabinet maker. In Goodison, 'William Chambers's Furniture Designs' (1990), I have suggested that William Chambers may have been responsible for the design of the commode.
30. Edwards, 'Patrons of Taste and Sensibility', p. 458, and Fig. VIII. The Duke of Bedford patronised Langlois during the refurnishing of Woburn in 1760 (Edwards and Jourdain, *Georgian Cabinet-Makers* (1955), p. 103). One of the commodes is also illustrated in C. Musgrave, *Adam and Hepplewhite Furniture* (London 1966), Plate 124.
31. Hayward, 'Christopher Fuhrlogh' (1969).
32. The close relationship of the mounts on these various pieces of furniture is discussed by Hayward, p. 651: he concludes that they were the work of the same bronze founder. The work of John Linnell (*c.*1737–96) has been frequently discussed, but see especially Hayward and Kirkham, *William and John Linnell* (1980); Edwards and Jourdain, *Georgian Cabinet-Makers* (1955), pp. 75–8; Hayward, 'The Drawings of John Linnell in the Victoria and Albert Museum' (1969); and Kirkham, 'The Careers of William and John Linnell' (1967).
33. Windsor Castle Archives 25050. Jean's bill on this occasion (October–December 1783) amounted to £483 18s. od. and was mainly for supplying, cleaning and gilding mounts, candle branches and sockets, etc. His total bill for work at Carlton House between 1783 and 1786 amounted to £1,409 16s. od. (Windsor Castle Archives 34953). His name is given as Dominique Jean and he was working by direction of William Gaubert, who appears to have been responsible for commissioning several of the Prince of Wales's suppliers.
34. In May and June 1786 he was paid £28 for doing some gilding at Audley End, including ornaments for two commodes and five sets of locks, and gilding and furnishing five rings for a cabinet delivered to Mr Fuhrlogh (Audley End Accounts, Essex Record Office D/Dby/A44/7-8). See Williams, 'Audley End' (1966), p. 35.
35. Soane MSS, Vol. 54, no. 262, which is a design for a 'deershead' lamp, as made for Kenwood, 'to be executed by Dominique'.
36. In January and February 1775 he submitted four bills for gilding work to the Duke of Northumberland, variously spelled Lord Duc Nortemberlant, Lord Douck Nortemlant and Nortemlan: the bills list 'ornaments', branches and nozzles and total £28 7s. od. (Alnwick MSS, U.III, no 6 (8), (9), (10), (14)). On 27th May 1784 he was paid £11 for 'gilding the ball on Coleshill House' (Longford Castle Account Book, 1768–95).
37. Smith, *Buckingham Palace* (1931), p. 114. He provided the gilt ornaments for four chimneypieces which were probably intended for Carlton House.
38. The inscription beneath the lid of the plate warmer reads 'Diederich Nicolaus Anderson made this plate warmer in 1760'. Harris, *Robert Adam and Kedleston* (1987), p. 34, illustrates the drawing and dates it *c.*1757. He suggests that it may well be by James Stuart, who was active at Kedleston. There are differences of detail between the drawing and the finished object, notably in the treatment of the top. A more accurate drawing survives in the Soane MSS Vol. 25, p. 93. Harris suggests that this is likely to have been a drawing of record. If it is, it must have been drawn soon after the warmer was made because it is inscribed 'for Sir Nathaniel Curzon Bart' and must date before 1761.
39. Probate Records, Public Record Office, 11/379/331. Anderson, who was described as a chaser, died on 20th July 1767 and left all his effects to his wife Penelope. His Danish origin was confirmed in his wife's will, which was proved in 1779. The will referred to her late husband's brother and sister in 'Flensbury [sic], Denmark' (Prob. 11/1053/230). I am grateful to Roger Smith for this reference.
40. Harris, *Sir William Chambers* (1996), pp. 66–7, 204. The Charlemont Correspondence is in the possession of the Royal Irish Academy, Dublin, and is reported in the Historical Manuscripts Commission 12th Report, Appendix, Part X, Vols. I–II.
41. William Chambers to Lord Charlemont 25th August 1767, 2nd October 1767 (Charlemont Correspondence, Vol. II).
42. Harris, *Sir William Chambers* (1996), p. 667. Lord Charlemont's commissions were completed by Anderson's 'man', his workshop being continued for a time by his wife. The 'triton' candlestick can be identified with a pattern made later by both Wedgwood and Boulton (see Chapter 3, pp. 83–5 and Plates 45, 139).
43. See O'Connor, 'The Charlemont House Medal Cabinet' (1989); Goodison, 'William Chambers's Furniture Designs' (1990), pp. 74–5, Figs. 17–19; Roberts, 'Sir William Chambers and Furniture' (1996), pp. 172–4, Figs. 258–61.
44. Beard, *Georgian Craftsmen* (1966), p. 82. Anderson was paid £10 on account on 24th January 1767: the identification with Diederich Nicolaus Anderson is proved by the payment of the balance of £7 11s. 6d. to Mrs Anderson, the widow of Mr Anderson, on 24th November 1767 (Syon House Accounts, Alnwick Castle MSS U.I. 44). An earlier payment of £50 to 'Nich Anderson' (Hoare's Bank, Ledger C, p. 325, 4th July 1765), may also refer to Diederich Nicolaus Anderson. The mosaic tables with gilt borders, in the form of fasces bound by recurring chased leaves, also survive at Syon.
45. M.B.'s Diary, 1768 (October).
46. M.B. to J.F., 25th February 1770.
47. Goodison, 'Mr Stuart's Tripod' (1972).
48. J.F. to M.B., 5th November 1765.
49. J.F. to M.B., 22nd December 1765.
50. See Michael Wilson, *The English Chamber Organ, History and Development 1650–1850* (Oxford 1968), pp. 35, 80, 137.
51. Pyke was presumably the son of John Pyke the clockmaker (*fl.*1710–d.1762) and became a member of the Clockmakers' Company in 1753. Both he and his father made musical clocks. See Baillie, *Watchmakers and Clockmakers of the World* (1951), p. 260.
52. The movement is signed on the musical barrel 'George Pyke, Bedford Road, London': various names and dates are inscribed inside the movement, the earliest date being 1763. Similar clocks are recorded at Wentworth Woodhouse and Kensington Palace.
53. Pyke's trade label is stuck onto one of the barrels.
54. Robert Adam to Sir Rowland Winn, 18th August and 15th September 1767: Sir Rowland reported the arrival of the 'locks and furniture for the library doors' in a letter to Adam on 27th September 1767 (Nostell Priory Archives C/3/1/5/2/1-3). Bent's shop was in St Martin's Lane.
55. M.B.'s Diary, 1768. Harrache was probably the son, or at any rate a relation, of Pierre Harrache, the first Huguenot silversmith to gain admittance to the Goldsmiths' Company: see Hayward, *Huguenot Silver in England* (1959), p. 16. He had premises in St Martin's Lane until 1751, when they were taken over by the cabinet maker William Vile (Westminster Parish Rate Books, Parish of St Martin's F. 527).
56. Register Book (Great Tew Archive), 2nd June 1769, 'Mr Harash Pall Mall London'.
57. When he retired in 1778 his stock-in-trade was sold in two sales at Christie and Ansell's rooms on 13th March (a four-day sale) and 9th May. Both catalogues have survived in Christie's Archives.
58. The invoice, dated 23rd April 1771, survives at Corsham. So do the vases, which stand on the marquetry pedestals supplied by William Vile's partner John Cobb: see Harris, *Furniture of Robert Adam* (1963), Plate 61.
59. Mallet, 'Two Documented Chelsea Gold-Anchor Vases' (1965), p. 29, touched briefly on the fashion for decorative vases in the eighteenth century. See also Rackham, 'Vases or the Status of Pottery in Europe' (1943), especially pp. 4ff., where the author cites

instances of vases being bought in England, for ornament rather than use, from the first half of the seventeenth century and discusses the way in which the potteries such as Chelsea, Derby and Longton Hall took advantage of the fashion from the 1750s onwards.

60. Wedgwood to Bentley, January 1769 (E25-18216).

61. Wedgwood to Bentley, 1st May 1769 (E25-18240).

62. Wedgwood to Bentley, 2nd August 1770 (E25-18314).

63. Wedgwood to Bentley, 15th March 1768 (E25-18193).

64. Eriksen, *Waddesdon Manor: Sèvres Porcelain* (1968), p. 232. The vases were sold unmounted. Other sales of vases for mounting are recorded in 1768, 1770, 1773 and 1775.

65. This is Eriksen's suggestion, *Waddesdon Manor: Sèvres Porcelain* (1968), p. 232. He bases the identification of the ewers with the vases reported in the sale records on the price, 42 livres, which is inscribed on the base of each vase.

66. Eriksen, *Waddesdon Manor: Sèvres Porcelain* (1968), pp. 236–7, a pair of green Sèvres vases mounted as pot-pourri jars, dating from *c.*1767–70. Verlet, *Bronzes Dorés Français* (1987), p. 28, Plate 16, illustrates a Chinese vase, also at Waddesdon, mounted as a pot-pourri vase *c.*1745–9. He illustrates many other examples.

67. Havard, *Dictionnaire de l'Ameublement* (1887–90), col. 603, recorded entries listing cassolettes in the inventories of Marguerite d'Autriche (1524) and Catherine de' Medici (1589). There were several at Versailles in 1682 (Havard, col. 604), but the real vogue came later.

68. Boulton acknowledged the loan in a letter to Mrs Montagu dated 16th January 1772.

69. Mrs Montagu to M.B., 23rd January 1773.

70. Eriksen, *Waddesdon Manor: Sèvres Porcelain* (1968), pp. 70, 234.

71. Dickinson, *Matthew Boulton* (1937), p. 54; Edwards and Macquoid, *Dictionary of English Furniture* (1954), Vol. I, p. 98, etc. Robinson, in 'Matthew Boulton's Marketing Techniques' (1963), p. 50, seems to have been the first author to give the correct date, i.e. 1768 or 1769.

72. Thus Dickinson, *Matthew Boulton* (1937), p. 54, referring to a statement about Birmingham ormolu in the *English Gazetteer* of 1762, said that 'this must refer to Boulton because at the time he took it up it was not being made elsewhere in England': several authors, labouring under a similar conviction, have attributed to Boulton ormolu pieces which were made long before his factory had the necessary skills.

73. There is a reference to ormolu clock cases in part of a letter from M.B. to J. H. Ebbinghaus, n.d. [1766]: but the page belongs to another letter written several years later.

74. But see previous note.

75. M.B.'s Notebook, 1765, p. 26.

76. M.B.'s Notebook, 1765, p. 16.

77. M.B. to Lord Cathcart, 30th October 1771.

78. Watt, 'Memorandum concerning Mr Boulton', p. 1.

79. Lord Shelburne to Adam, 16th April 1765.

80. M.B.'s Notebook, 1765, p. 26. This was probably William Tovey.

81. M.B.'s Notebook, 1765, p. 26.

82. J.F. to M.B., 5th November 1765 and 22nd December 1765.

83. M.B. to P. J. Wendler, n.d. [July 1767].

84. P. J. Wendler, Venice, to M.B., 4th July 1767.

85. M.B. to P. J. Wendler, n.d. [July 1767].

86. M.B. to Wedgwood, 10th July 1767.

87. B. and F. to Wooley and Hemming, 19th January 1771.

88. It would be wrong to imply that there were no imports during the Seven Years' War.

89. Wedgwood to Bentley, 21st November 1768 (E25-18215).

90. Wedgwood to Bentley, 15th March 1768 (E25-18193).

91. Wedgwood to Bentley, 3rd January 1768 (E25-18222).

92. M.B. to Wedgwood, 10th July 1767.

93. Miss Apphia Witts bought two pairs of marble candlesticks at the warehouse in 1768 (Miss A. Witts to B. and F., 4th November 1768).

94. Wedgwood to Bentley, 21st November 1768 (E25-18215).

95. Edward Pardoe and Joseph Burton. Their indentures were dated 31st August 1768 and 27th September 1768, respectively. See Appendix VI.

96. Wedgwood to Bentley, 15th March 1768 (E25-19193).

97. Wedgwood to Bentley, 21st November 1768 (E25-18215).

98. M.B. to Wedgwood, 20th December 1768.

99. M.B. to Wedgwood, 17th January 1769.

100. M.B. to Wedgwood, 20th December 1768.

101. M.B. to Wedgwood, 17th January 1769.

102. M.B. to Wedgwood, 17th January 1769.

103. Wedgwood to Bentley, 27th September 1769 (E25-18261). James Cox was the jeweller of Shoe Lane who has been mentioned earlier in this chapter.

104. Charleston (ed.), *English Porcelain* (1965), article by J. V. G. Mallet, 'Chelsea', pp. 37–8, in which the author suggests that Cox was probably attracted to the purchase of the Chelsea factory by hopes of a link with Boulton for the production of ormolu-mounted porcelain. But apart from Wedgwood's letters there is no evidence for this. Cox re-sold the factory to William Duesbury in February 1770.

105. Wedgwood to Bentley, 27th September 1769 (E25-18261).

106. Wedgwood to Bentley, 1st October 1769 (E25-18264) (Rylands Manuscripts Eng.1104, p. 521, Rylands Library, Manchester).

107. Wedgwood to M.B., 19th February 1771.

108. Wedgwood to M.B., 19th February 1771.

109. A brief account of the mineralogy of blue john and of the varieties of stone mined at Castleton is given in Chapter 4, p.154. See Ford, *Derbyshire Blue John* (2000).

110. Ford, *Derbyshire Blue John* (2000), pp. 58–9, 61. Ford suggests that mining started on top of the hill at Treak Cliff in about 1765 but that others may have mined the stone as a by-product of lead mining as early as 1753.

111. Watson, *Catalogue of Furniture in the Wallace Collection* (1956), p. 93, says that the French developed the use of blue john, importing large quantities and mounting it with gilt bronze: he also says that Boulton began using it in emulation of the French. The theory rests on the survival of vases which might date from the 1760s (e.g. *Catalogue* nos. F.345–7) and on suggestions made in a letter to *The Times* from Sir Buxton Browne, 24th May 1934. But the evidence is unconvincing.

112. M.B. to John Whitehurst, 28th December 1768.

113. Wedgwood to Bentley, 6th June 1772 (E25-18376).

114. M.B.'s Diary, 1769: the fashioned stones were '3 pair of bodys, 1 pair vases, 1 top £2 9s. 6d.' Mrs Hall was perhaps the widow of Joseph Hall from whom Boulton bought stones in 1768.

115. The Howe family were connected with the mining industry in Derbyshire for a long period. Miss Nellie Kirkham has kindly supplied me with several references to Robert Howe from her records of the Derbyshire lead mines. It appears that there were at least two and probably three men of the same name concerned with the mines at Castleton between 1750 and 1838.

116. Bradbury and his son became Boulton's most important suppliers of stone.

117. M.B. Diary, 1769 (October). 'Tyger' is presumably shorthand for a type of veined blue john, probably hatterel. See Chapter 4, p. 152.

118. Receipt dated 2nd March 1769: 14 tons ¾ cwt of blue john cost £81 1s. 6d. John Platt (1728–1810) was the son of the mason architect George Platt (1700–43) and continued his father's business when he was old enough. The work of the two men has been summarised by Potts in *Platt of Rotherham* (1959). The discovery of blue john is attributed to Platt by one tradition (Ford, *Derbyshire Blue John* (2000), p. 61) but this seems unlikely. He rented the marble quarries at Ashford (Potts, *Platt of Rotherham*, p. 9) and the blue john mines at Castleton in the late 1760s. His journal records the sale of stone to Boulton on 25th February 1769 – 'Mr Boulton of Birmingham sold him 14 tons

of Blue John at £5 15s. 6d. ton delivered at Castleton'. Boulton paid £81 on 2nd March (Potts, *Platt of Rotherham*, p. 13). See also Gunnis, *Dictionary of British Sculptors* (1953), p. 308.
119. Robert Howe to M.B., 31st December 1769.
120. Presumably silver plate.
121. i.e. Wedgwood black basalt. See Reilly, *Wedgwood* (1989), Vol. I, pp. 397–9.
122. The meaning of this is made clear in a letter from Boulton to Solomon Hyman dated 23rd January 1769, in which he asked his correspondent to obtain the recipe 'pour metter le cuiver jaun en couleur ou pour saucer la foundry comme en fait a Paris. If you remember I paid a guinea to your friend in the garrett for teaching me to boyl brass work en couleur ...' (saucer = to drench, souse, etc.).
123. M.B.'s Notebook, 1768–75, p. 1.
124. M.B.'s Notebook, 1768–75, p. 2.
125. M.B. to Solomon Hyman, 23rd January 1769.
126. M.B. to Solomon Hyman, 23rd January 1769.
127. For Mainwaring, Bath, 15th July 1769.
128. For Mr Smith, 4th August 1769.
129. For Mrs Yeats, n.d. [but 28th August 1769], Mrs Balfour, 4th September 1769. Mrs Balfour visited Soho on 4th September (Register Book, Great Tew Archive).
130. For Sir William Guise, 9th September 1769: the vases were addressed to Sir William at Rencombe (i.e. Redcombe), Cirencester. Goat's head vases with blue john bodies were also mentioned in an undated letter from Boulton to Fothergill, which was probably written in London in 1770. 'Sir Willm Guyse and two sisters' from 'Rendcomb abt 4 miles from Cirencester' visited Soho on 9th September (Register Book, Great Tew Archive).
131. Lord Willoughby de Broke to M.B., 28th November 1769.
132. M.B. to J.F., n.d. [7th or 8th March 1770]: also a bill submitted to the Marquess of Rockingham on 19th October 1770 (Fitzwilliam MSS, Sheffield City Library).
133. M.B. to J.F., n.d. [7th or 8th March 1770].
134. M.B. to J.F., n.d. [4th March 1770].
135. M.B. to J.F., n.d. [4th March 1770].
136. Pownall (1722–1805) had been Governor of the colonies New Jersey and South Carolina. In 1769 he was MP for Tregony, Cornwall.
137. Thomas Pownall to M.B., 8th September 1769. Pownall had visited Soho on 17th or 18th August (Register Book, Great Tew Archive) and had been giving thought to Boulton's enterprise. It is not clear whether the dessert service was to be made of ormolu or plate. There are some good examples of ink stands made with Sèvres plaques and ormolu mounts in the James A. Rothschild Collection at Waddesdon: see Eriksen, *Waddesdon Manor: Sèvres Porcelain* (1968), pp. 182–7, where three are illustrated, one dating from 1765 and the others from about the same time.
138. The references are given in Appendix I.
139. Wedgwood to Bentley, 24th–26th December 1770 (E25-18334). Wedgwood supplied a sample vase and neck.
140. M.B. to his wife, 6th March 1770.
141. The names are clearly descriptive of types of fluorspar. See note 117.
142. M.B. to J.F., n.d. [7th or 8th March 1770].
143. The patronage of the Royal Family gave great support to Boulton's marketing plans and he used the connection to good effect: his account of this visit is given in Chapter 5, p. 165.
144. M.B. to J.F., n.d. [7th or 8th March 1770].
145. Wedgwood to Bentley, 1st October 1769 (E25-18264, Rylands MSS Eng.1104, p. 522).
146. M.B. to J.F., n.d. [4th March 1770].
147. See Chapter 5, pp. 168–70 for further comments on the sale and the preparations for it.
148. *The Public Advertiser*, 13th March 1770 and several later dates in March and April (Burney 571B, British Library). The sale appears to have taken place on 6th–7th April.
149. James Adam to M.B., 14th August 1770.
150. M.B. to J.F., n.d. [probably end of February 1770].
151. i.e. in London.
152. M.B. to J.F., n.d. [4th March 1770].
153. M.B. to the Earl of Warwick, 30th December 1770.
154. Wedgwood to Bentley, 24th–26th December 1770 (E25-18334).
155. One of three draft letters to patrons advertising the sale dated 25th March 1771. This one was intended for dukes. Lords and gentlemen had different letters.
156. This preface was drafted by Boulton and revised by James Keir.
157. See Chapter 5, pp. 168–70 for further comments on the sale and the preparations for it.
158. *The Gazetteer and New Daily Advertiser*, 26th March 1771 and several later dates in March and April (Burney 581B, British Library). The sale took place on 11th–13th April.
159. Two price catalogues of the sale have been preserved in the archives of Christie's. See Appendix III.
160. B. and F. to Nathaniel Jefferys, 16th February 1771.
161. B. and F. to William Matthews, 2nd March 1771.
162. B. and F. to Sir John Griffin Griffin, 27th March 1771.
163. First day, lots 2, 7, 16, 21, 25, 33, 39, 44, 50, 57, 61, 70, 74; second day, lots 2, 6, 12, 19, 25, 35, 39, 44, 50, 54, 65, 73, 78; third day, lots 2, 6, 11, 16, 21, 31, 38, 43, 48, 53, 63, 70, 74. In two cases (second day, lots 19, 35) annotations give the colour of the enamel as green and in one (second day, lot 54) as blue. Two of the lots were pairs although not listed as such.
164. I am assuming that the margin prices in the first catalogue were reserve prices: see Appendix III.
165. First day, lots 12, 15, 20, 24, 28, 32, 37, 43, 49, 56, 60, 69, 73, 77; second day, lots 5, 11, 15, 18, 24, 29, 34, 38, 43, 49, 53, 58, 64, 72, 77, 83; third day, lots 5, 10, 12, 15, 20, 25, 30, 37, 39, 42, 47, 52, 57, 62, 69, 73, 77.
166. First day, lots 3, 8, 17, 26, 34, 45, 51, 62, 71; second day, lots 3, 7, 13, 20, 36, 40, 51, 55, 66, 79; third day, lots 3, 7, 17, 22, 32, 44, 49, 64, 71.
167. Some were £3 13s. 6d., £3 10s. od., and £3 3s. od.
168. Some were £3 3s. od.
169. First day, lots 35, 52; second day, lots 4, 21; third day lots 34, 65.
170. First day, lot 27; second day, lots 46, 61; third day, lot 55.
171. First day, lot 81; second day, lot 76; third day, lot 66.
172. Second day, lot 62: the reserve price was £18 18s. od.
173. Third day, lot 61.
174. Third day, lots 35, 36.
175. Mrs Delaney to the Viscountess Andover, 11th April 1771, Llanover (ed.), *Autobiography and Correspondence of Mary Granville, Mrs Delaney* (1862), Vol. I, p. 335.
176. The arrangements are discussed in detail in Chapter 5.
177. M.B. to James Christie, 22nd March 1772.
178. M.B. to James Christie, 22nd March 1772.
179. John Scale to M.B., 6th February 1772.
180. M.B. to Mrs Montagu, 16th January 1772.
181. *The Gazetteer and New Daily Advertiser*, 20th March 1772 (Burney 587B, British Library). The sale took place on 10th–11th April. See Chapter 5, pp. 168–70, for further comments on the sale and the preparations for it.
182. B. and F. to William Matthews, 27th April 1772.
183. B. and F. to William Matthews, 4th April 1772.
184. B. and F. to William Matthews, 4th April 1772.
185. B. and F. to the Duchess of Portland, 6th November 1771.
186. Wedgwood to Bentley, 11th April 1772 (E25-18365).
187. Cox's exhibition was extensively advertised in *The Gazetteer and New Daily Advertiser* (Burney 587B, after May 588B, British Library) from 22nd February to the end of 1772, and in *The Public Advertiser* (Burney 584B) from 3rd March. It received extensive comment in *The London Magazine* Vol. 41 (1772), pp. 125–8. Admission was by ticket, and the catalogue was printed in English and in French. Cox also held sales at Christie's, but these contained very little

ormolu. They were held on 1st–2nd July and 16th–17th December.
188. *The Gazetteer*, 10th March 1772 (Burney 587B, British Library).
189. Act 2, Scene 1.
190. Countess of Craven to M.B., 12th January 1771, etc.
191. B. and F. to William Matthews, 23rd February 1771.
192. B. and F. to William Matthews, 19th October 1771. The order, which was intended for Mrs Parker at Saltram, was later altered to vases of the pattern supplied to the King (Plate 343).
193. B. and F. to the Earl of Kerry, 5th March 1772.
194. It was delivered in January 1772: B. and F. to Sir Lawrence Dundas, 4th January 1772.
195. B. and F. to the Duke of Northumberland, 4th January 1772. The cost of the objects was £95 5s. od.
196. J.F. to M.B., 23rd January 1772.
197. B. and F. to Sir John Griffin Griffin, 27th March 1771; B. and F. to William Matthews, 19th September 1771.
198. B. and F. to Thomas Craig, Dublin, 26th March 1772.
199. Wedgwood to Bentley, 11th April 1772 (E25-18365).
200. Mrs E. Montagu to M.B., 12th December 1772.
201. It is not easy to deduce exactly what was sold. The summary of prices in the catalogues (Appendix III) suggests that only £1,412 out of the recorded total of £2,905 10s. 6d. represented actual sales: bids for the remaining lots failed to reach the reserve prices. However, in a letter from Boulton and Fothergill to William Matthews dated 6th May 1771 the unsold vases were invoiced at £608 18s. od. The difference may have been accounted for by deliveries, subsequent to the sale, to Amsterdam and to a certain Morgan, whose name appears in the catalogue against several of the unsold lots. Some unsold lots can be identified with objects listed in the letter to Matthews (e.g. third day, lot 81, which in the letter is invoiced as 'A Venus clock £26 5s. od.') but others, such as the Persian candelabrum which was reserved at 190 guineas (third day, lot 84), are not mentioned subsequently at all.
202. M.B. to John Scale, n.d. [April 1771].
203. B. and F. to William Evill, Bath, 16th May 1771. On the same day several more objects were sent to Matthews for inclusion in the consignment for Amsterdam including a sphinx vase, a griffin vase and a clock (B. and F. to William Matthews, 16th May 1771). The real reason for not sending more to Evill was probably Boulton's dislike of dealing with shopkeepers, who usually took goods only on sale or return. Evill's signature occurs on clocks and watches (e.g. Sotheby's, 22nd March 1971, lot 138): Baillie, *Watchmakers and Clockmakers of the World* (1951), records that he was active before 1762.
204. B. and F. to William Matthews, 27th April 1772. Christie paid £834 15s. 4d. to Matthews, after deducting commission of £80 16s. od. Boulton and Fothergill reckoned that the net amount should have been £842 10s. 6d.
205. M.B. to Lady Dashwood, n.d. [April 1772]. Lady Dashwood had bid for a vase which was 'nock down to her' but she only bid for it because she thought it was going too low and she offered to return it [Lady Dashwood to M.B., n.d.]: Boulton thanked her for her 'obligeing offer' but managed to decline it.
206. M.B. to his wife, n.d. [12th April 1772]. The whole passage in the letter is quoted on p. 206 during the account of the geographical clock.
207. M.B. to his wife (12th April 1772). The Titus clock is illustrated in Plate 183.
208. J.F. to M.B., 28th March 1772.
209. J.F. to M.B., 20th May 1772.
210. B. and F. to James Todd, York, 1st August 1771; B. and F. to William Evill, Bath, 26th October 1771; etc.
211. Wedgwood to Bentley, 6th June 1772 (E25-18376). Wedgwood was referring to a shopkeeper in Bath, presumably William Evill or Mainwaring.
212. Boulton knew Fordyce and the bankruptcy hit him hard. 'Fordice Esqr' and his lady visited Soho on 17th September 1771 (Register Book, Great Tew Archive), and Mrs Fordyce bought a sphinx vase at the 1771 sale.
213. M.B. to the Earl of Warwick, November 1772; the paragraph was repeated in a letter to the Earl of Dartmouth dated 10th November.
214. B. and F. to Sir J. Dalrymple, 7th July 1772.
215. M.B. to the Earl of Dartmouth, 10th November 1772 (Dartmouth MSS, copy in Boulton archives).
216. See Appendix I: e.g. Mrs John Parker, Lady Gower, General Cholmondeley.
217. See Appendix I: e.g. Duke of Ancaster, Mrs E. Montagu, Earl of Sefton.
218. B. and F. to William Matthews, 6th May 1771.
219. M.B. to his wife, n.d. [12th April 1772].
220. M.B. to Rodney Valltravers, November 1772; B. and F. to Sir John Goodricke, Stockholm, 16th December 1772.
221. J.F. to M.B., 22nd May 1772. The Spanish gentleman appears to have been the ambassador, the Duke of La Villa Hermosa, who is recorded as visiting Soho on 12th May 1772 (Register Book, Great Tew Archive).
222. J.F. to M.B., 2nd March 1773.
223. Wedgwood to Bentley, 13th July 1772 (E25-18380).
224. For an account of the establishment of the Assay Office see Quickenden, *Boulton and Fothergill Silver* (1989), pp. 26–31; Westwood, *The Assay Office at Birmingham* (1936).
225. The events leading up to Boulton's partnership with Watt are summarised by Schofield, *Lunar Society of Birmingham* (1963), pp. 66ff.
226. See Appendix I: e.g. Duke of Ancaster, Earl of Ashburnham, Sir Robert Cunliffe, Lord Digby, Earl of Findlater, Marquess of Granby, Charles Pelham, Lord Algernon Percy.
227. B. and F. to William Lewis, 6th March 1775.
228. B. and F. to Robert Bradbury jun., Bakewell, 12th March 1775.
229. e.g. B. and F. to the Earl of Findlater, 11th October 1776.
230. Sir Robert Gunning, St Petersburg, to M.B., 13th September 1774. Gunning (1731–1816) was ambassador at St Petersburg 1772–5.
231. B. and F. to the Marquess of Granby, 19th November 1774.
232. Ledger, 1776–8, pp. 120, 138, 174, etc.
233. Wedgwood to Bentley, 14th July 1776 (E25-18684). Wedgwood was quoting what he was told at Soho: a less ebullient picture emerges from the Boulton papers.
234. Journal, 1776–8. The first entries summarise an inventory taken on 31st December 1775. The various activities, e.g. buttons, gilt boxes and instrument cases, etc., are recorded separately. The trade in 'Silver, plated and or moulu goods etc.' was carried on in partnership with Francis Eginton.
235. B. and F. to John Taylor, 25th June 1777.
236. John Hodges to M.B., 31st January 1778. Hodges was first employed at Soho in 1768, when he was taken on as an apprentice from a charity school. By the late 1770s he was working in some sort of executive capacity and there are many letters from him to Boulton from 1777–8, reporting on the state of the hardware trade and giving details of sales made from Soho. The exact division of duties between him and John Scale at this time is not clear, but after 1782 he became manager of the silver and plated departments while Scale was managing the button company.
237. John Hodges to M.B., 6th February 1778.
238. John Hodges to M.B., 6th February 1778.
239. J.F. to M.B., 14th February 1778. The sale of Lord Kerry's furniture, which was carried out by Christie and Ansell at his house in Portman Square, was advertised for 25th February but was postponed to 23rd–31st March.
240. B. and F. to John Stuart, 25th March 1778.
241. B. and F. to John Stuart, 25th March 1778.
242. *Morning Post and Daily Advertiser*, 9th May 1778 (Burney 662B, British Library). The sale was planned for 14th May, but was postponed to 20th May.
243. *Morning Post*, 18th–20th May 1778.
244. *Morning Post*, 15th May 1778.
245. According to the Journal of 1779–81,

p. 4, the proceeds of the sale amounted to £182. Addition of the sums raised by the lots which appear to have been sold (see Appendix III) brings the amount to £209 3s. 0d. Most of the difference is accounted for by the £20 cash paid from the proceeds by John Stuart to Boulton (Cash Debtor Book 1772–82, 17th June 1778). The lots that do not appear to have been sold add up to £933 17s. 0d. in the catalogue, but according to the firm's Ledger, 1776–8, p. 326, John Stuart returned goods to a total value of £1,239 2s. 3d. between 24th June and 31st July.

246. The details of the preparations are given in Chapter 5, pp. 171–2.

247. John Stuart to M.B., 31st March 1778.

248. John Stuart to M.B., 31st March 1778.

249. Lots 97–115.

250. Lots 91, 93, 127.

251. Lots 2, 8, 13–17, 21–3, 28–9, 32–3.

252. Lots 11, 27, 30–1, 40–3, 48, 50–2, 57, 64, 87.

253. Lots 27, 40–1.

254. Lots 42–3.

255. Lot 92.

256. John Hodges to M.B., 8th June 1778.

257. The picture trade had at least some connection with the ormolu business. Besides being made for shutter and door panels pictures were also sold in ormolu frames.

258. Day Book, 1779–81.

259. John Hodges to M.B., accompanying a note headed 'Sales from Soho 23–30 May 1778'.

260. Ledger, 1778–82, p. 128.

261. B. and F. to Robert Bradbury, 26th July 1781.

262. B. and F. to John Stuart, 20th October 1781.

263. Inventory, 1782, pp. 133–4.

264. Inventory, 1782, p. 156.

265. Inventory, 1782, p. 181.

266. Inventory, 1782, pp. 83–4.

267. Many sales are entered in the ledgers as 'goods'. Any of these may have been ormolu pieces, but this seems unlikely because (a) few orders are mentioned in the firm's letters, and (b) orders for pieces of silver and plate are recorded in detail.

268. The 'Button Co.' and the 'Plated Co.' were the two chief businesses recorded in the ledgers at this time. In 1789 the Button Company occupied 14,000 sq. ft. of space and the Plated Company, including the toy room and the wire drawing yard, 10,436.5 sq. ft. (paper entitled 'Particulars of the Houses, Workshops and Mills at Soho 1789').

269. B. and F. to Robert Bradbury, 16th December 1783.

270. B. and F. to Lord Stormont, 14th October 1783, M.B. and Co. Ledger 1782–9, p. 35, 25th November 1783.

271. e.g. B. and F. to the Earl of Shelburne (?), 13th September 1784. The letter enclosed drawings of girandoles, vases and candlesticks.

272. Wedgwood to M.B., 14th June 1786.

273. See Prosser, *Birmingham Inventors* (1881), p. 59.

274. M.B.'s Notebook, 1799, p. 27. The table illustrated in Plates 208–9 and 254, which was made for Boulton himself in 1799, was a one-off product.

275. Hunt, *Bombelles in Britain* (2000), p. 29. Bombelles presumably saw some ornaments on display in the toy room.

276. Keir, 'Memorandum of Mr Boulton', p. 5.

277. J.F. to M.B., n.d. [probably 1773].

278. Keir, 'Memorandum of Mr Boulton', p. 4.

279. Smith, *Buckingham Palace* (1931), pp. 107–8.

NOTES TO CHAPTER 3

Design

Notes to pp. 63–124

Notes 1–293

1. M.B. to P. J. Wendler, n.d. [July 1767].
2. M.B. to Mrs E. Montagu, 16th January 1772.
3. M.B. to Earl of Findlater, 20th January 1776.
4. M.B. to his wife, n.d. [11th April 1772].
5. Patte, *Cours d'Architecture* (1777), Vol. V, pp. 86ff. Patte's work was a continuation of J. F. Blondel's work of the same name. The translation by Peter Thornton is from Eriksen, *Early Neo-Classicism in France* (1974), pp. 21–2.
6. See Quickenden, *Boulton and Fothergill Silver* (1989), pp. 162–3.
7. M.B. to Mrs E. Montagu, 16th January 1772.
8. Sir Joshua Reynolds, *Discourses on Painting and the Fine Arts* (1837), Sixth Discourse, pp. 91, 96. Honour sums up the attitude of contemporary artists to 'imitation' in *Neo-Classicism* (1968), p. 107.
9. A supplement appeared later in thirty sections published between 1772 and 1777.
10. See Harris, *Furniture of Robert Adam* (1963), Plate 1. A related design, undated, is illustrated in Harris, *Newly Acquired Designs by James Stuart* (1979), Plate 16B, also in Lever, *Architects' Designs for Furniture* (1982), Plate 14.
11. See Eriksen, 'Lalive de Jully's Furniture "à la grecque"' (1961), pp. 340–7; Harris, 'Early Neo-Classical Furniture' (1966), pp. 1–6. See also Stuart's drawings for an unidentified room *c.*1757, Lever, *Architects' Designs for Furniture* (1982), Plates 13a, 13b.
12. *Correspondence Litteraire* (Paris 1813), Part I, Vol. III, p. 362, quoted in Harris, *Furniture of Robert Adam* (1963), p. 9.
13. M.B. to the Earl of Findlater, 20th January 1776. Boulton goes on to qualify his comment by saying that he had not seen any of the best work of Robert-Joseph Auguste (1723–1805), the celebrated goldsmith. The word 'trop' is transcribed as 'troy' in the manuscript of this letter. This was presumably a mistake by the clerk who copied Boulton's original into the letter book.
14. Lord Cathcart to B. and F., 21st February 1772.
15. Verlet, *Bronzes Dorés Français* (1987), p. 198, Fig. 227; Verlet records signed candlesticks with Gouthière's address in 'Quai Peltier', which suggests that they date from after 1758, when he moved to Quai Pelletier and became a *maître ciseleur-doreur.*
16. Quickenden, 'Lyon-Faced Candlesticks and Candelabra' (1999), pp. 198–9.
17. The four silver candlesticks by Thomas Heming at Harewood are hallmarked 1774–5. Quickenden, 'Lyon-Faced Candlesticks and Candelabra' (1999), pp. 198, 204, records other examples by Heming, including two pairs dated 1771–2 with later branches by Benjamin Laver 1777–8.
18. The candelabra are now in Warsaw Castle. Prieur's design is discussed and illustrated in Eriksen, *Early Neo-Classicism in France* (1974), p. 352, Plates 405, 408. Eriksen, *Waddesdon Manor: Sèvres Porcelain* (1968) illustrates several examples of squared handles fitted to Sèvres vases (pp. 190–1, 198–9, 234–5, etc.).
19. De Bellaigue, *Waddesdon Manor: Furniture, Clocks and Gilt Bronzes* (1974), Vol. II, Plate 207.
20. François Vion, *Livre de Desseins*, no. 13 (Bibliothèque Doucet, Paris, VI E 15, Rés. Fol. 20/1). See also Ottomeyer, Pröschel and Augarde, *Vergoldete Bronzen* (1986), p. 247, Figs. 4.6.9 and 4.6.10. Clock cases based on this design sold Christie's, 9th December 1993, lot 166; Christie's, New York, 24th May 2001, lot 8. Christie's dated these clock cases *c.*1780, but they seem to me to be earlier in style. Vion became a *maître-fondeur* in 1764. Geoffrey de Bellaigue has kindly adduced evidence from other objects supporting a date before 1770.
21. Verlet, *Bronzes Dorés Français* (1987), p. 35, Colour Plate 25, illustrates a clock by Lepaute 1769–70 at Fontainebleau, modelled by de Wailly, which shows the muse Clio pointing to the time on a revolving terrestrial globe, accompanied by a winged boy described as *'le génie du Temps'*.
22. Eriksen, 'Lalive de Jully's Furniture "à la grecque"' (1961), p. 344. The identification of this clock as that originally made for Lalive de Jully, which rests partly on a contemporary description and partly on the name of the clockmaker, Julien le Roy, is convincing. Other clock cases of this design have survived.
23. Soane, *Lectures on Architecture* (ed. Bolton, 1929), Lecture XI, 'Decoration and Composition', pp. 172, 180.
24. Samuel Wyatt to M.B., 31st July 1765.
25. Earl of Shelburne to Adam, 16th April 1765.
26. Earl of Shelburne to Adam, 16th April 1765.
27. Robinson, 'Matthew Boulton's Marketing Techniques' (1963), p. 57.
28. See Eriksen and Watson, 'The "Athénienne" and the Revival of the Classical Tripod' (1963), p. 108; according to an advertisement in 1773 the 'Athénienne' had six possible uses besides candelabra and perfume burners.
29. M.B.'s Diary 1768 (October) – 'Paid Mr Ryder at Lord Shelburne's for a pattern of tripod £15 15s. od.'. Thomas Ryder exhibited at the Free Society in 1766 and 1777, giving his address as 'at Mr Brasire's, Great Queen Street, Lincolns Inn Fields'. This was the address of the engraver James Brasire, who interestingly exhibited engravings after designs of James Stuart at the Free Society in 1764 and 1766 (Royal Academy Archives).
30. James Stuart to Thomas Anson, 23rd September 1769 – 'The tripod is in great forwardness, I think it will be best to have it cast at Birmingham, my friend Mr Boulton will cast it there, better and cheaper far than it can be done in London' (Staffordshire County Record Office MSS, D615/P(5)1/6); James Stuart to M.B., 26th December 1769. The bowl was made by Wedgwood (J. Stuart to Wedgwood, 24th January 1771, Wedgwood to J. Stuart, 29th January 1771, both in the Wedgwood MSS at Barlaston); Wedgwood to Bentley, 24th–26th December 1770 (E25-18334), etc.
31. Goodison, 'Mr Stuart's Tripod' (1972): see also Thornton and Hardy, 'The Spencer Furniture at Althorp' (1968), p. 449.
32. B. and F. to William Matthews, 9th January, 2nd February 1771.
33. The Adams' two drawings for the west end of the dining room at Kedleston and for the sideboard, both of which are dated 1762 (Kedleston MSS), also show the tripod, indicating that it was made before that date. Both drawings are illustrated in Goodison, 'Mr Stuart's Tripod' (1972), Figs. 60–1, and Harris, *Robert Adam and Kedleston* (1987), pp. 30–1.
34. Possibly George Richardson: see Goodison, 'Mr Stuart's Tripod' (1972), p. 700.
35. Stuart's drawings from the Kedleston MSS were illustrated in Goodison, 'Mr Stuart's Tripod' (1972), Figs. 62, 69–71, and Harris, *Robert Adam and Kedleston* (1987), pp. 26–31 (in colour).
36. British Museum, Inventory no. 1955-4-16-13; also illustrated in Goodison, 'Mr Stuart's Tripod' (1972), Fig. 63.
37. Duchess of Northumberland's Diary 1763–7 (Alnwick MSS no. 121). The Duchess's description tallies with the Adams' drawings of the sideboard in the Kedleston MSS.
38. Accession no. M46-1948.
39. Stuart and Revett, *Antiquities of Athens*, Vol. 1 (1762), preface.
40. Rockingham, Spencer and Stuart were all members of the Society of Dilettanti – Stuart from 1751, Rockingham from 1755 and Spencer from 1765. See Cust, *History of the Society of Dilettanti* (1914), pp. 257, 258, 263.
41. Stuart and Revett, *Antiquities of Athens*, Vol. 1 (1762), p. 29.
42. Stuart's evidence for this is summarised in Goodison, 'Mr Stuart's Tripod' (1972), p. 699.
43. Boulton's usual alloy contained about 8–10 per cent zinc (see Chapter 4, p. 128). This tripod is made of brass with a zinc content of 26–7 per cent. I am grateful to Dr Peter Northover for carrying out the testing of the metal and to the Victoria and Albert Museum for permitting the test.
44. Goodison, 'Mr Stuart's Tripod' (1972), pp. 73–4.
45. Free Society, 1761, no. 102, catalogued under 'Sculpture and Models'. The exhibitor is listed as 'Mr Anderson', but in my view the attribution is sound. It is not clear whether

the tripod was made of metal or plaster.
46. Department of Prints and Drawings, Victoria and Albert Museum, Accession no. 5712. The drawing is on the back of p. 1. Among Boulton's papers there are two sketches by his natural son John Phillp, who became a draughtsman at Soho, of a tripod leg with its female head and paw foot. The detail is faithful to the examples illustrated in Plates 25 and 28. The significance of these sketches, which are dated 1795, is unclear.
47. Sold Sotheby's, 26th June 1953, lot 71 and now in the Metropolitan Museum of Art, New York (Morris Loeb Bequest). The tripods are not an exact pair. Their 'hyacinth' candle branches and ebony-veneered triangular oak bases were added by Vulliamy in 1812–13, when they were also re-gilt. A complete list of Vulliamy's work on them, with details of the craftsmen and prices, survives in Vulliamy's Day Book, pp. 246–7, 282 (Public Record Office, C 104-58). Vulliamy had previously, in November 1803, billed Ashburnham for 'taking entirely to pieces two very large Metal tripods carrying 3 lights each, cleaning all the gilt work and making it look like new and cleaning and repairing the marble plinths' (Day Book, p. 58).
48. The perfume burner, Wedgwood Museum, Accession no. 1153, is illustrated in Robin Reilly, *Wedgwood: the New Illustrated Dictionary* (Woodbridge, 1995), p. 146; the candelabrum is illustrated in Meteyard, *Wedgwood and his Works* (1873), Plate XXIII (one of a pair). In the Wedgwood Museum there are three picture clay models of the tripod legs, two of them fragmentary.
49. Victoria and Albert Museum, Accession no. 4790A-1901; Wedgwood Museum, Accession no. 5164. Both were illustrated in Goodison, *Ormolu* (1974), Plates 31, 32.
50. Wedgwood probably received the design from Stuart: see Goodison, 'Mr Stuart's Tripod' (1972), p. 700.
51. James Stuart to M.B., 26th December 1769.
52. Robinson, 'Matthew Boulton's Marketing Techniques' (1963), p. 57. Stuart's most notable design for silverware was for the Admiralty tureens (B. and F. to James Stuart, 5th October 1771): see Rowe, *Adam Silver* (1965), pp. 81–2 and Plate 47. Wedgwood supplied the clay models for the dolphins on these tureens (Wedgwood to M.B., 19th February 1771). The second tureen was supplied to the order of 'Athenian Stuart' in 1781 (M.B. to John Hodges, 1st April 1781). A drawing of it survives in Pattern Book 1, p. 111 (Plate 96).
53. The pair from Spencer House is now at Althorp. Other pairs are in the Royal Collection (Inventory no. 985) and at Spencer House (probably from Norfolk House), bought from a house in Yorkshire. A similar vase with handles and no branches sold Sotheby's, 9th July 1976, lot 17.
54. The composition of the brass is however not the same as that of the tripod of Plate 28. The zinc content falls within the range of 7½–8½ per cent, much less than the zinc content of the brass used in the tripod. This does not prove that Anderson was not the maker – he may well have used different alloys at different dates. But it sows a seed of doubt. I am grateful to Dr Peter Northover for carrying out the testing of the metal and to the Victoria and Albert Museum for permitting the test.
55. See Harris, *William Chambers* (1970); Harris and Snodin (ed.), *Sir William Chambers* (1996), for general surveys of the architect's work. The latter accompanied the exhibition of Chambers's life and work at the Courtauld Institute Gallery in 1997, which included a number of Boulton and Fothergill's ornaments.
56. Harris, *William Chambers* (1970), pp. 19–20.
57. Harris, *William Chambers* (1970), pp. 20ff: Harris lists among Chambers's acquaintances Louis-Joseph le Lorrain, Charles-Michel-Ange Challe, Nicholas-Henri Jardin, Gabrielle-Pierre-Martin Dumont, and Ennemond-Alexandre Petitot. He also knew Gabriel-François Doyen, Claude Vernet and Hubert Robert, and many other artists who shared his leanings towards the classical idiom. See also Harris, 'Early Neo-Classical Furniture' (1966), pp. 1–5.
58. Harris, *William Chambers* (1970), pp. 21–2, quotes Chambers's letter to his pupil Edward Stevens in 1774 in which his judgements of Italian architects are summarised.
59. Roberts, 'Sir William Chambers and George III' (1996), pp. 41–54.
60. Harris, *William Chambers* (1970), pp. 10ff. Chambers was knighted by King Gustav III of Sweden in April 1770.
61. Harris, 'Early Neo-Classical Furniture' (1966), p. 4. De Wailly made designs for ormolu which were carried out by R.-J. Auguste.
62. Jacques-François Saly, *Vases Inventés et Gravés par Jacobus Saly* (1746).
63. J. Beauvais, *Livre de Vases* (Paris, 1760).
64. Charles de Wailly, *Suite de Vases* (1760).
65. Joseph-Marie Vien, *Suite de Vases Composée dans le Goût de l'Antique* (Paris, 1760).
66. Ennemond-Alexandre Petitot, *Suite de Vases Tirés du Cabinet de Monsieur du Tillot Marquis de Felino* (Parma and Milan, 1764).
67. Jean Laurent le Geay, *Collection de Divers Sujets de Vases, Tombeaux, Ruines, et Fontaines Utiles aux Artistes* (1770).
68. Department of Prints and Drawings, Accession no. 5712. The 507 drawings by Chambers are listed in Snodin (ed.), *Sir William Chambers* (1996), pp. 33–101, and discussed in the introductory essay by Barrier, 'The Franco-Italian Album and its Significance', pp. 20–6. Barrier, p. 20, notes that Chambers probably bought the album in Rome, perhaps with its title '*Receuil de Divers Dessein*' already stamped on the spine.
69. Harris, Snodin and Astley (ed.), *Drawings of William Chambers* (1996), p. 13.
70. Barrier, 'The Franco-Italian Album and its Significance' (1996), p. 25, gives several examples.
71. M.B. to his wife, 6th March 1770.
72. Harris, 'Early Neo-Classical Furniture' (1966), p. 5 and Plate 6.
73. Franco-Italian Album, 5712-150, p. 25 (verso), Snodin (ed.), *Sir William Chambers* (1996), Plate 29 (no. 166); Goodison, 'William Chambers's Furniture Designs' (1990), Fig. 2.
74. Snodin (ed.), *Sir William Chambers* (1996), Plates 11 (no. 9), 17 (no. 56), 27 (no. 143).
75. There is no evidence of a connection between Chambers and Langlois or Dominique Jean. But Chambers must have come across Dominique Jean at least through his official duties, and his Swedish background and contacts brought him the acquaintance of Georg Haupt, the Swedish cabinet maker. Haupt was closely associated with another Swede, Christopher Fürloh, who became his brother-in-law and who worked very near the Langlois workshop in Tottenham Court Road. Fürloh was probably the leading maker of inlaid cabinet work in London after Langlois, and Dominique Jean supplied him with mounts. The exact working relationship of these craftsmen, and Chambers's place in the chain, need to be unravelled.
76. Goodison, 'William Chambers's Furniture Designs' (1990); Roberts, 'Sir William Chambers and Furniture' (1996); Young, 'Silver, Ormolu and Ceramics' (1996).
77. M.B. to J.F., n.d. [4th March 1770].
78. The drawing is inserted into George IV's 'Pictorial Inventory of Clocks etc.', which was compiled in about 1827 and which survives in the Royal Collection (Stable Yard House).
79. The drawing has been identified by John Harris.
80. Franco-Italian Album, 5712-195, p. 37, no. 156.
81. Franco-Italian Album, 5712-216, p. 49, and 5712-148, p. 25.
82. Franco-Italian Album, 5712-113, p. 19, a sketch after Petitot of an urn with a Greek fret frieze. See Snodin (ed.), *Sir William Chambers* (1996), Plate 16, no. 33.
83. Franco-Italian Album, 5712-204, p. 39; 5712-207, p. 40; 5712-416, p. 251. See also Chambers, *Treatise on Civil Architecture* (1759), facing p. 21, 'Doric Entablature Imitated from the Theatre of Marcellus' and Harris, *Catalogue of British Drawings for Architecture* (1971), Plate 46 (a pier glass).
84. Department of Prints and Drawings, Victoria and Albert Museum, Accession no. E4994-1910. See Young, 'Sir William Chambers and John Yenn: designs for silver' (1986), p. 32, Fig. 40.
85. Reilly, *Wedgwood* (1989), Vol. I, Plate 545

illustrates a pair. Reilly dates this *c.*1772 but also records an order for '350 of the Dolphin ewers' dated 15th February 1769 (Plates 444A–B and pp. 348–9).
86. Franco-Italian Album, 5712-290, p. 61. The same horse features in Piranesi, *Le Antichità Romane* (1756), Vol. II, Plate XXX and elsewhere in Piranesi's works.
87. Chambers, *Treatise on Civil Architecture* (1759), p. 37.
88. Lot 126.
89. Boulton bought a 'Persian candlestick' from Anderson's widow in 1768 (M.B.'s Diary, 1768). It is always possible that this was the means of securing the Persian figure, but even if this was so, the source was still William Chambers.
90. Exhibition at the Royal Academy, 1770, Catalogue, p. 6, no. 39 (Royal Academy Archives).
91. Department of Prints and Drawings, Victoria and Albert Museum, C. J. Richardson Collection, Accession no. E3436-408. Young, 'Sir William Chambers and John Yenn: designs for silver' (1986), p. 31, suggests that this drawing was likely to have been a presentation drawing after one by Chambers. It may even have been one of the drawings exhibited at the Royal Academy in 1770 under Chambers's name.
92. Department of Prints and Drawings, Victoria and Albert Museum, Accession no. E5031-1910.
93. William Chambers to Lord Charlemont, 25th August 1767 (Charlemont MSS, Historic Manuscripts Commission, 12th Report, 1891, I.283) quoted in Harris, *William Chambers* (1970), p. 66.
94. Department of Prints and Drawings, Victoria and Albert Museum, Accession no. E4969-1910.
95. Harris, *William Chambers* (1970), pp. 66–7.
96. Wittkower, *Gian Lorenzo Bernini* (1956), Plates 59, 88, 123–4; Barrier, 'Chambers in France and Italy' (1996), p. 21. If Chambers did not design the triton himself, he may have bought a model or a bronze in Rome. A bronze triton, described as an '*elegante modello di una fontana*', was in the Museo Torlonia, Rome. See Visconti, *Monumenti del Museo Torlonia* (1885), p. 135, no. 193. It was illustrated in Reinach, *Répertoire de la Statuaire Grecque et Romaine* (1897), Vol. I, p. 429, Plate 745. Reinach's drawing shows the triton on rocks, without flowers, with a large bowl resting above the shell. Reinach thought that the triton might have been an 'antique' model (*Répertoire*, Vol. I, p. LVII).
97. B. and F. to William Chambers, 23rd March 1773.
98. An example survives at Temple Newsam, City of Leeds Art Gallery. See also Reilly, *Wedgwood* (1989), Vol. I, p. 463, Plate 666.
99. Wedgwood Museum, Accession no. 61.30635. The book consists of drawings largely in ink, cut and pasted in. The triton is numbered 337.
100. Department of Prints and Drawings, Accession no. E5029-1910. The illustration in the 1791 edition of the *Treatise on Civil Architecture* is, of course, much later than the drawing. Ormolu versions of the griffin were made in the 1760s, as implied by the fact that the two plates of 'ornamental utensils' in the *Treatise* in which the griffin appears contained unspecified ornaments for Lord Charlemont. The design or a model could easily have been available to Boulton in 1770.
101. Goodison, 'William Chambers's Furniture Designs' (1990), p. 75. Two griffin candlesticks, almost identical to those illustrated in Plates 5, 13, 50, but with nozzles missing and mounted on porphyry bases, survive at Hinton Ampner (National Trust, from the estate of Ralph Dutton). Other pairs sold Sotheby's, Florence, 6th–7th April 1987, lot 590; Christie's, 12th November 1998, lot 5; Christie's, New York, 19th April 2001, lot 250.
102. There is a pearwood model in the Wedgwood Museum, Accession no. 3118.
103. Boulton's griffins have a plain medallion. The griffins at Blenheim have a medallion of Diana (Plate 14) which is derived from a gem reproduced in Tassie's collection of gems. See Raspe, *Descriptive Catalogue* (1791), Vol. I, p. 157, no. 2148.
104. Franco-Italian Album, 5712-18, p. 4.
105. M.B. to J.F., n.d. [March 1770].
106. e.g. B. and F. to James Wyatt, 29th October 1771, Ledger, 1776–8, p. 230, 18th March 1777 – 'sundries sent to Robert Milne Esq. £26 8s. 9d.'.
107. M.B. to Robert Mylne, 4th November 1775 (silver candlesticks, and silver mounts for a mantelpiece); John Wyatt to B. and F., 8th March 1776 (an ink stand for Lady Morton); B. and F. to Sir Harbord Harbord, 1st August 1772, and many other references. See Quickenden, *Boulton and Fothergill Silver* (1989), pp. 174–7; also Rowe, *Adam Silver* (1965), p. 66, and Robinson, 'Matthew Boulton's Marketing Techniques' (1963), p. 57.
108. Ferguson, 'Wyatt Silver' (1974), pp. 751–5.
109. Ferguson, 'Wyatt Silver' (1974), Fig. 56.
110. National Art Collections Fund, *Review* (1995), p. 67.
111. Quickenden, 'Boulton and Fothergill Silver: an Épergne designed by James Wyatt' (1986), pp. 417–21.
112. M.B. to Peter Elmsley, 2nd October 1771: 'Along with the 5 volumes of the Herculinium you will receive some other books which are also to be bound ...'. Only five volumes were published by 1771.
113. Early Accounts 1768: the subscription was £1 11s. 6d. and was paid to a bookseller named Mainwaring.
114. B. and F. to William Matthews, 4th May 1773. 'Mr Hoare' was probably Henry Hoare who bought some vases in 1770.
115. Robert Wood, *Ruins of Palmyra, otherwise Tedmor, in the Desert* (London, 1753) and *Ruins of Balbec, otherwise Heliopolis, in Coelosyria* (London, 1757).
116. Thomas Major, *The Ruins of Paestum, otherwise Posidonia, in Magna Graecia* (London, 1768).
117. Piranesi, *Le Antichità Romane* (1756), Vol. III, Plate XXVIII; *Diverse Maniere* (1769), Plate I, by p. 31 ('Etruscan Monuments of Various Kinds').
118. 'Books from the Library of Matthew Boulton and his Family', Christie's, 12th December 1986, lots 63, 69.
119. B. and F. to William Matthews, 2nd February 1771.
120. Society of Artists, 1769, no. 192, and 1771, no. 56 (Royal Academy Archives). Darly called himself 'Professor and Teacher of Ornament'. He was at 33 The Strand in 1769 and 39 The Strand in 1771.
121. 'A New Book of Ornaments in the Present (Antique) Taste as now used by all Professors' (1772).
122. Baron d'Hancarville was the name adopted by Pierre François Hugues, the son of a bankrupt cloth merchant in Nancy. The narrative in his volumes bears little relationship to Hamilton's vases, being more concerned with d'Hancarville's wish to promote himself as an antiquary of the stature of Winckelmann, but the plates are beautiful. They include vases that were never in Hamilton's collection. See Haskell, 'Adventurer and Art Historian' (1987); Jenkins, 'Contemporary Minds: Sir William Hamilton's Affair with Antiquity' (1996). According to Wendler's letter to Boulton, which was written on 4th July 1767, the first volume did not appear in 1766: it was due 'in about 2 or 3 weeks'.
123. Vol. I, preface, p. xviii.
124. P. J. Wendler to M.B., 4th July 1767.
125. M.B. to P. J. Wendler, n.d. [July 1767]. It is unlikely that he passed on Wendler's recommendation to his competitors.
126. 'Tagebücher des Grafen von Zinzendorf und Pottendorf', Vol. 13 (1768), 6th September 1768 (State Archives, Vienna). According to the Register Book (Great Tew Archive) he visited Soho on 5th September.
127. The third and fourth volumes were not completed until 1776. Wendler wrote to Boulton on 31st July 1776: 'Sir William Hamilton ... will inform you of the true state of the publication of d'Anguerville's Etruscan Vases ... I heard lately that Mr d'Anguerville was again chased away from Florence, so as he was from Naples, through jealousie, and that his creditors rendered themselfs masters of his publication; but I think the subscribers are likewise creditors. I wrote about it to Florence, but have not yet answer ...'. Sir William Hamilton went to Florence where he found d'Hancarville in gaol and his creditors in possession of the plates. He organised them into a publishing syndicate and the volumes eventually reached subscribers in the early 1780s, too late to have any influence on Boulton's ormolu

ornaments. See Jenkins, 'Contemporary Minds: Sir William Hamilton's Affair with Antiquity' (1996).
128. See Reilly, *Wedgwood* (1989), Vol. I.
129. See Rowe, *Adam Silver*, Plates 40–56 and p. 65: Rowe suggests that d'Hancarville was the most useful of Boulton's sources of designs for silverware.
130. D'Hancarville, *Collection of Etruscan, Greek and Roman Antiquities* ... (1766–7), Vol. II, Plate 106.
131. D'Hancarville, *Collection of Etruscan, Greek and Roman Antiquities* ... (1766–7), Vol. II, Plate 23.
132. Early Accounts 17th December 1764 – 'From J. Sketchley's sale ... Montfacon's Antiqt. £8 8s. od'.
133. A second edition was published in Paris in 1722–4 and an English edition by D. Humphreys in London in 1721–5. Supplements to each volume were published in 1757.
134. Montfauçon, *Antiquité Expliquée* (1719), Vol. III, Part 1, Plate XXIV, no. 3.
135. Montfauçon, *Antiquité Expliquée* (1719), Vol. III, Part 1, p. 42.
136. Montfauçon, *Antiquité Expliquée* (1719), Vol. II, Part 1, Plate XCII, no. 4.
137. Montfauçon, *Antiquité Expliquée* (1719), Vol. I, Part 2, Plate CCXI, no. 15.
138. Plate CCXII, of which no. 5 is the most likely image.
139. B. and F. to Samuel Pechell, 11th December 1771.
140. Montfauçon, *Antiquité Expliquée* (1719), Vol. IV, Part 1, Plate XCIX.
141. P. J. Wendler to M.B., 14th April 1767. Wendler also offered him prints of 'Rome in paintings al fresco', which are not so easy to identify.
142. B. and F. to Mayhew and Ince, 26th August 1771.
143. M.B. to Peter Elmsley, 28th September 1771. Elmsley (1736–1802), whose bookshop was in the Strand, was one of James Christie's co-owners of *The Morning Chronicle*.
144. They had not arrived by 5th October (B. and F. to William Matthews, 5th October 1771).
145. Gori, *Museum Florentinum, Statuae Antiquae*, Vol. III (1734), Plate LXXXV.
146. Gori, *Museum Florentinum, Gemmae Antiquae*, Vol. II (1732), Plate LXXV.
147. Gori, *Museum Florentinum, Gemmae Antiquae*, Vol. II (1732), Plates XVI, LXIX, LXXIII, LXXVII.
148. Polyxena, daughter of Priam and Hecuba, was said in Euripides's *Hecuba* (ll.220ff.) to have been sacrificed on the tomb of Achilles by Neoptolemus to appease Achilles's ghost and so to secure winds to take the Greeks home from Troy. Gori, *Museum Florentinum*, Vol. II (1732), pp. 123–4, argues that the image shows her about to kill herself.
149. A copy was sold among 'Books from the Library of Matthew Boulton and his Family', Christie's, 12th December 1986, lot 43.
150. De Caylus, *Recueil d'Antiquités*, Vol. VII (1767), Plate XLIII.
151. De Caylus, *Recueil d'Antiquités*, Vol. VII (1767), pp. 187–8. De Caylus bought the altar from Lambert-Sigisbert Adam (*'Adam l'ainé'*), who restored a number of sculptures excavated in Rome under the direction of Cardinal de Polignac. Adam kept for himself several pieces which were of no use to the Cardinal.
152. An English edition was published by George Marshall in London in 1771.
153. M.B.'s Diary, 1767 – 'Less Antiquite, Des Godetz'.
154. 'Books from the Library of Matthew Boulton and his Family', Christie's, 12th December 1986, lot 115.
155. Sayer, *Compleat Drawing Book* (third edition, 1762), Plate 61 (Aubrey Toppin Library, English Ceramic Circle). The engraving does not appear in every copy of the *Compleat Drawing Book*. Cyril Cook, 'James Gwin and his Designs on Battersea Enamel' (1952), in which the author attributed the engraving to Ravenet, illustrated it (p. 67) and said that it appeared in the 5th edition (1786) of the *Compleat Drawing Book*, but it is not in the copy of the 5th edition in the British Library. This may not be surprising because the drawing masters and sellers of jobbing prints were often erratic in the collections that they issued, probably making up 'books' from material available as orders occurred. Books of prints were heavily used and mutilated by craftsmen, which means that surviving copies, which are anyway rare, have sometimes lost parts of their contents. I am grateful to Antony Griffiths and Kim Sloan of the Department of Prints and Drawings, British Museum, for this guidance. Sayer sold prints at 53 Fleet Street. The most complete catalogue of his stock was an *Enlarged Catalogue of New and Valuable Prints* published by Sayer and Bennett in 1775 (reprinted by Holland Press, London, 1970). The print of Venus does not appear separately in this catalogue.
156. Victoria and Albert Museum, Schreiber Collection, III.60. The same image occurs on a snuff box also in the Schreiber Collection, III.52. See Rackham, Catalogue (1924), Vol. III, pp. 22–3 and Plate 33.
157. There is a bill in the archives from Sayer and Bennett, dated 24th April 1780, for prints etc. delivered in 1777–8, but these are irrelevant to the Venus vase, which was designed in about 1770. Nevertheless the bill shows that Boulton and Fothergill were aware of Sayer. They might have bought prints from him earlier.
158. Robinson, 'Matthew Boulton, Patron of the Arts' (1953), p. 373.
159. Gunnis, *Dictionary of British Sculptors* (1953), pp. 146–7. The elder Flaxman was born in 1726 and died in 1795.
160. This invoice was sent by William Flaxman, John Flaxman's elder son, to his younger brother John who was to give it to Boulton.
161. Christie and Ansell's sale, 1778, lots 56, 73.
162. Montagu in 'A Renaissance Work Copied by Wedgwood' (1954), p. 380, discusses whether Gentile copied models by Michelangelo.
163. Chambers, *Treatise on Civil Architecture* (1759), p. 37.
164. Other examples of these lamps in black basalt can be seen at Stourhead, Wiltshire, the Wedgwood Museum, Barlaston, and the Victoria and Albert Museum. See Reilly, *Wedgwood* (1989), Vol. I, p. 472, Plates 678–9. Later Wedgwood used the same figures in jasperware (Reilly, Vol. I, Colour Plate 184).
165. An anonymous drawing of two of the figures mounted on a triangular architectural frame and annotated on the back 'Stuart's sale 1788' survives in the Department of Prints and Drawings, Victoria and Albert Museum, Accession no. 7757/7. It looks like a sketch of a ceramic version of the figures. The young man with the cap has a belt across his chest, as in Flaxman's model. 'Stuart' was presumably James Stuart, who died in 1788. I do not attach any significance to his ownership or authorship of the drawing.
166. J. Bacon to M.B., 11th June 1773.
167. Clifford, 'John Bacon and the Manufacturers' (1985), p. 299, draws a parallel between the figures in a study for a wine cooler by Bacon (Royal Academy Archives, E. B. Jupp's 'Catalogue of Royal Academy Exhibitions', Vol. I, p. 18, illustrated in Clifford, Fig. 35) and the triton supporters on Boulton's King's vase (Plate 343). There is a similarity. Bacon's tritons are bearded, but their arms are stretched horizontally and not above their heads, and their lower bodies taper into what look like scales. Clifford also records Bacon's work for Wedgwood in modelling a companion to the Triton candlestick (Clifford, p. 294, Fig. 11). He also suggests that Bacon may have had a hand in designing and modelling door furniture for Boulton (Clifford, p. 298, Fig. 39). This rests on a drawing by Bacon, which could well be a sketch of someone else's design and not necessarily Bacon's own. Copies of Bacon's sketches, in the ownership of the Bacon family, are in the Witt Library at the Courtauld Institute of Art. The escutcheon discussed by Clifford is no. 212648.
168. Daniel Pincot to M.B., 24th June 1771. Pincot, who was working in Goulston Square, Whitechapel, in 1767, was working for Mrs Coade in Lambeth by 1771: see Kelly, *Mrs Coade's Stone* (1990). He exhibited a copy of the Borghese vase in artificial stone at the Society of Artists in the same year. He made these for subscribers, and told Boulton in the same letter that 'the second subscription for 8 only' at 25 guineas each was 'filling apace'.

169. Possibly Thomas Wright, clockmaker to the King, the supplier of the movement for the King's clock case (Plate 160).
170. M.B.'s Diary, 1768.
171. Clifford, 'The Plaster Shops of the Rococo and Neo-Classical Era in Britain' (1992). Clifford has rescued a number of plaster shops from obscurity and underlined their importance in what today is called the supply chain.
172. Clifford, 'The Plaster Shops of the Rococo and Neo-Classical Era in Britain' (1990).
173. Wedgwood to Bentley, 21st November 1768 (E25-18215).
174. B. and F. to William Matthews, 27th April 1772: 'To cash received of Mr Boulton of Harrach sundries £9 4s. 6d.' Some of the goods in Harrache's sales at Christie and Ansell's in 1778 could also have come from Soho: there were for example several 'Derbyshire' vases mounted in ormolu.
175. M.B.'s Diary, 1768 (October).
176. John Motteux, the factor and banker.
177. M.B.'s Diary, 1768 (October).
178. M.B. to J.F., 25th February 1770. Some of 'Wyatt's candlesticks and vases' also sold well at this auction.
179. M.B. to J.F., n.d. [4th March 1770].
180. Dr John Ash to M.B., 30th December 1769.
181. M.B. to J.F., 30th April 1773.
182. Wedgwood to Bentley, 21st November 1768 (E25-18215).
183. M.B.'s Diary, 1769.
184. M.B. to J.F., n.d. [4th March 1770].
185. Duke of Richmond to M.B., 3rd April 1770.
186. Earl of Dartmouth to M.B., 10th December 1768.
187. M.B. to Mrs E. Montagu, 16th January 1772.
188. P. J. Wendler to M.B., 14th April 1767.
189. M.B. to Solomon Hyman, 23rd January 1769.
190. John Hunter to M.B., 3rd December 1772.
191. Wedgwood to Bentley, 24th December 1770 (E25-18334).
192. Wedgwood to Bentley, 24th December 1770 (E25-18334). The body would have been black basalt: see Reilly, *Wedgwood* (1989), Vol. I, pp. 397–9.
193. Wedgwood to M.B., 19th February 1771.
194. B. and F. to Wedgwood, 9th June 1770, Wedgwood Museum Archives, 30392-4. Boulton's handwritten note to 'Mr Wedgwood' is inserted in Boulton and Fothergill's letter ordering some ceramics.
195. Wedgwood to Bentley, 19th November 1769 (E25-18269).
196. Invoice from 'Hoskings and Oliver' to 'Wedgewood and Bentley', dated May 1770, Wedgwood Museum, 30950-2. The invoice carries the date 13th August 1770 at the bottom, presumably the date when it was rendered. James Hoskins (d.1791) was 'moulder and caster in plaster' to the Royal Academy.
197. Meteyard, *Life of Josiah Wedgwood* (1865–6), Vol. II, pp. 212, 218. Wedgwood reported to his partner in December 1770 that Boulton had promised to make some branches, but these may not have been for a triton – Wedgwood to Bentley, 24th–26th December 1770 (E25-18334).
198. Wedgwood and Bentley advertised 'a pair of tritons, from Michael Angelo, 11 inches high' in their *Catalogue* (1773), p. 50. no. 23, and made triton candlesticks not only in black basalt but also later in jasper – see Reilly, *Wedgwood* (1989), Vol. I, p. 463 and Colour Plate 174). There is a pair of master models in the Wedgwood Museum (illustrated in Young, 'Silver, Ormolu and Ceramics' (1996), p. 159, Fig. 237). The biscuit and jasper versions of Wedgwood's triton have skins and nets slung over the shoulders and wrapped round the waists. Wedgwood appears to have had only one figure and needed to find a way of making a matching one, facing the other way. See Clifford, 'John Bacon and the Manufacturers' (1985), pp. 292, 294. The Derby factory also produced a triton candlestick of the same model, without the skins and nets of Wedgwood's versions, in soft-paste porcelain (Victoria and Albert Museum, Schreiber Collection, I.347).
199. Reilly, *Wedgwood* (1989), Vol. I, p. 474.
200. Gray, *James and William Tassie* (1894). See also Smith, *James Tassie* (1995), in which there is a useful bibliography.
201. Royal Academy Archives.
202. The catalogue was an update of Raspe's earlier catalogue of 1786 which was compiled following an order from Catherine II of Russia for a complete set of Tassie's gems. I shall refer to the catalogue in this discussion of Boulton's sources even though its publication post-dates Boulton's use of many of the gems. The core of it reproduces, in more extended form, the material in his earlier catalogues, and there is no reason to suppose that the gems used by Wedgwood and Boulton were not among Tassie's stock in the late 1760s and early 1770s. The catalogue, furthermore, has the advantage of listing the complete collections of Tassie's gems that survive in the Victoria and Albert Museum and in the National Portrait Gallery, Edinburgh. A complete photographic record of the collection is in the Ashmolean Museum, Oxford (Beazley Archive). Raspe records the owners of gems, and the stones from which they were cut, and adds commentaries, which are entertaining and calculated to distract the researcher.
203. Bill, receipted by James Tassie, dated 11th November 1769 for '70 impressions in sulfer' (11s. 8d.) and 'two enamel impressions' (2s.), Wedgwood Museum, L1/34.
204. Raspe, *Descriptive Catalogue* (1791), Vol. I, p. 238, no. 3526. Raspe comments that if Kallimorphos is 'the name of the master, the work does him no real credit'.
205. Raspe, *Descriptive Catalogue* (1791), Vol. I, p. 447, no. 7699.
206. Raspe, *Descriptive Catalogue* (1791), Vol. I, p. 491, no. 8350. There are several adjacent gems in the collection with a similar image.
207. Raspe, *Descriptive Catalogue* (1791), Vol. II, p. 554, no. 9508. There are two gems in the collection.
208. Raspe, *Descriptive Catalogue* (1791), Vol. II p. 563, no. 9682.
209. Montfauçon, *Antiquité Expliquée* (1719), Vol. I, Part 1, Plate XIV, illustrated a gem of 'Jupiter Hammon' with rams' horns.
210. Wedgwood and Bentley, *Catalogue* (1773), p. 9, no. 743 (the 1774 catalogue makes it clear that it was a cameo); *Catalogue* (1774), p. 27, no. 240. Most of the cameos and intaglios mentioned hereafter as appearing in the 1773 *Catalogue* reappear in the later catalogues.
211. Wedgwood Museum, Accession no. 403. In the Museum's Accession Register the mould is listed as Lysimachus, a head of whom is listed as no. 753 in the 1773 *Catalogue* (p. 9). Lysimachus was one of Alexander's successors, and there was confusion among cataloguists about the attribution of this image to Alexander or Lysimachus who, according to Raspe, *Descriptive Catalogue* (1791), Vol. II, p. 563, issued the first medals of Alexander with Ammon's horns.
212. Raspe, *Descriptive Catalogue* (1791), Vol. II, p. 573, nos. 9860-9.
213. Raspe, *Descriptive Catalogue* (1791), Vol. II, p. 573, no. 9867.
214. Wedgwood and Bentley, *Catalogue* (1773), p. 30, also Appendix, p. 14, no. 1614.
215. Reilly and Savage, *Portrait Medallion* (1973), p. 107; *Adams, Dwight and Lucille Beeson Collection* (1992), p. 150, Colour Plate 140.
216. Raspe, *Descriptive Catalogue* (1791), Vol. II, p. 139, no. 1822. Raspe illustrated the image in Plate XXVII.
217. Wedgwood and Bentley, *Catalogue* (1773), p. 6, no. 201, also Appendix, p. 15, no. 1636; *Catalogue* (1774), p. 22, no. 35, and p. 24, no. 120.
218. Meteyard, *Choice Examples of Wedgwood's Art* (1879), frontispiece.
219. Raspe, *Descriptive Catalogue* (1791), Vol. II, p. 643, nos. 11, 521. It was also illustrated and described in Stosch, *Pierres Antiques Gravées* (1724), Plate XXXIII and p. 49.
220. Wedgwood and Bentley, *Catalogue* (1773), p. 31.
221. Raspe, *Descriptive Catalogue* (1791), Vol. I, p. 148, no. 2017.
222. Wedgwood and Bentley, *Catalogue* (1774), p. 8, nos. 213–14, and p. 25, no. 153.
223. Wedgwood Museum, Accession no. 239. The mould is impressed with the catalogue number '214' (see previous note).
224. Raspe, *Descriptive Catalogue* (1791), Vol. I, p. 182, no. 2570.

225. Wedgwood and Bentley, *Catalogue* (1773), p. 6, no. 178. The gem was a rock crystal from 'Duke Strozzi', described by Raspe as 'Cab. Strozzi, Rome'.
226. Wedgwood and Bentley, *Catalogue* (1774), p. 8, no. 152.
227. Wedgwood Museum, Accession no. 212. The mould is impressed with the catalogue number '110', but this number is ascribed to a 'Council of the Gods' in the *Catalogue* in 1774 and 1777.
228. From the Greek word *callipygos*, meaning with beautiful buttocks. The Callipygian Venus was (and is) a renowned marble statue in the Farnese collection. It is now in the Museo Nazionale, Naples. See Haskell and Penny, *Taste and the Antique*, no. 83, pp. 316–18. The statue is not related to Tassie's gem, which he copied from an 'antique paste' in the collection of Lord Algernon Percy. Much closer is 'Venus Felix' (Haskell and Penny, no. 87. pp. 323–5), also known as 'Victorious Venus', which depicts the goddess with drapery over her left arm and Cupid stretching his arm upwards to her, presumably offering her Mars's helmet which has been broken.
229. Raspe, *Descriptive Catalogue* (1791), Vol. I, p. 377, no. 6383.
230. Wedgwood and Bentley, *Catalogue* (1773), p. 8, no. 511; *Catalogue* (1774), p. 11, no. 518, p. 24, and p. 25, no. 148. The image is confused in the Museum's Accession Register with Wedgwood and Bentley's cameo of Venus and Cupid. The intaglio of Venus Victrix is illustrated in Reilly, *Wedgwood* (1989), Vol. I, p. 475, Plate 683.
231. Wedgwood Museum, Accession no. 217. It is impressed with the catalogue number '111'. This is one of six moulds for cameos or intaglios, only one of which shows Venus naked as in Tassie's collection.
232. Raspe, *Descriptive Catalogue* (1791), Vol. I, pp. 261–2, no. 4177.
233. British Museum, illustrated in Luke Syson and Dora Thornton, *Objects of Virtue: Art in Renaissance Italy* (London, 2001), p. 111, Fig. 81.
234. e.g. Wedgwood and Bentley, *Catalogue* (1773), p. 8, nos. 598, 603; *Catalogue* (1774), p. 11, no. 605; *Catalogue* (1777), p. 29, nos. 313, 319, and p. 30, no. 335. Boulton would have been familiar with the impression from Wedgwood's vases. He may also have seen the painted roundel above the dining room door at Kedleston, which appears in Robert Adam's drawing on the end wall of the room in 1762 – Kedleston MSS, see Harris, *Robert Adam and Kedleston* (1987), p. 30 – before it was removed some time before 1778.
235. Wedgwood Museum, Accession no. 302. The Accession Register describes the cameo mould as 'a sacrifice group'. The mould is impressed with the catalogue number '112', but this number is ascribed to Janus in the *Catalogue* in 1774 and 1777.
236. Raspe, *Descriptive Catalogue* (1791), Vol. I, p. 456, no. 7846.
237. Wedgwood and Bentley, *Catalogue* (1773), Appendix, p. 14, no. 1622. Their 1777 catalogue records intaglios of an 'Offering to Victory', p. 29, no. 300 and p. 30, no. 344.
238. Wedgwood Museum, Accession no. 226. The mould is impressed with the catalogue number '70'. A jasperware gem is illustrated in Meteyard, *Choice Examples of Wedgwood Art* (1879), Plate XVI.
239. Raspe, *Descriptive Catalogue* (1791), Vol. I, p. 427, no. 7363, Vol. II, p. 138, no. 9272.
240. Wedgwood and Bentley, *Catalogue* (1773), p. 14, no. 1623. Other cameos and intaglios listed in the catalogues as 'Perseus' and 'Diomedes' may also have been of this image. An intaglio is recorded as 'Diomedes or Perseus' in the Catalogue of 1777, p. 29, no. 301. A mould of it survives in the Wedgwood Museum (Accession no. 693). See Reilly, *Wedgwood* (1989), Vol. I, Plate 683 and Colour Plate 132.
241. Wedgwood Museum, Accession no. 213. The mould is impressed with the catalogue number '1623'.
242. Raspe, *Descriptive Catalogue* (1791), Vol. II, p. 724, no. 13829, illustrated in Plate LVII.
243. Raspe, *Descriptive Catalogue* (1791), Vol. II, pp. 724–5.
244. 'Seventh Wedgwood International Seminar' (Art Institute of Chicago, 1962), p. 22. 'Esculapius and Hygia' are listed in Wedgwood and Bentley's *Catalogue* (1773), Appendix, p. 14, no. 1620.
245. Victoria and Albert Museum, Accession no. C.2611-1910.
246. Reilly, *Wedgwood* (1989), Vol. I, p. 406, Plate 552. Wedgwood produced a jasper cameo of the same scene with fewer figures. See 'Seventh Wedgwood International Seminar' (Art Institute of Chicago, 1962), pp. 22–3; Meteyard, *Wedgwood Handbook* (1875), p. 101.
247. Wedgwood and Bentley, *Catalogue* (1773), p. 14, no. 1621; *Catalogue* (1774), p. 11, no. 592, p. 22, no. 27, pp. 28–9, nos. 279, 289. The *Catalogue* (1777) added two more intaglios, p. 29, no. 310 and p. 30, no. 340.
248. Wedgwood Museum, Accession no. 304. It is impressed with the catalogue number '190'. Not all the moulds show Hygieia with the altar. Some show her without it and holding a bowl.
249. Wedgwood and Bentley, *Catalogue* (1773), p. 8, no. 583; *Catalogue* (1774), p. 11, nos. 579, 586, and p. 25, no. 169. The *Catalogue* (1777) added a fourth intaglio, p. 29, no. 309. Reilly, *Wedgwood* (1989) illustrates jasper cameos, Vol. I, Colour Plate 132, and Vol. II, Plate 1227.
250. Wedgwood Museum, Accession no. 346.
251. Raspe, *Descriptive Catalogue* (1791), Vol. I, p. 486, no. 8291.
252. Wedgwood Museum, Accession no. 285.
253. The only letters from James Tassie to Boulton are dated 5th January 1790 (asking to resolve a bet on the manufacturing process involved in adding the inscription to the rim of Boulton's halfpennies) and 5th March 1791 – 'By Mr Raspe's order, I have sent you a copy of our Catalogue of Engraved Gems …'. Boulton was not a subscriber to the volumes.
254. Inventory, 1782, pp. 159, 172.
255. P. J. Wendler to M.B., 14th April 1767.
256. Wedgwood to Bentley, 30th September 1769 (E25-18263).
257. He anxiously asked his partner whether Lord Bessborough had 'sold all his casts from antique gems, or the gems themselves, to the Duke of Marlborough', because they 'had leave from Lord Besborough to take casts from all his casts'. Reilly, *Wedgwood* (1989), Vol. I, p. 474, says that some 240 of the first 414 intaglios catalogued were from antique gems lent by Sir Watkin Williams Wynn. See Wedgwood to Bentley, 31st May 1773 (E25-18464).
258. Wedgwood had written to his partner ten days earlier that he had nothing at Etruria to match the Sacrifice medallion and that Bentley should send something from London – 'you are in the only place in the world for artists' – Wedgwood to Bentley, 20th September 1769 (E25-18258). In his letter of 30th September (E25-18263) he recommended Bacon or Tassie.
259. Wedgwood and Bentley, *Catalogue* (1773), p. 3.
260. Wedgwood to Bentley, 18th May 1773 (E25-18461).
261. Wedgwood to Bentley, 7th June 1773 (E25-18469).
262. Toy makers, 8 Temple Street, Birmingham. They were presumably among the recipients of the fifty dozen seals sent to Birmingham in May.
263. Wedgwood to Bentley, 21st–22nd November 1773 (E25-18500). Boulton and Fothergill supplied a large number of tortoiseshell boxes with cameos to Wedgwood and Bentley in the mid-1770s – Wedgwood Museum, 28-4746, 4747, 4749, 4756, 4757, 4759; 4-3157, etc.
264. Wedgwood to Bentley, 27th November 1773 (E25-18502).
265. Inventory, 1782, pp. 159, 172 (see Appendix IV).
266. Wedgwood to Bentley, 2nd December 1773 (E25-18504).
267. Wedgwood to Bentley, 30th December 1773 (E25-18512).
268. Wedgwood to Bentley, 25th October 1776 (E25-18707).
269. Reilly, *Wedgwood* (1989), Vol. I, Figs. 481, 547, 549, 550.
270. Raspe, *Descriptive Catalogue* (1791), Vol. I, p. 261, nos. 4172–4.
271. '33 metal cameos, cast, sorted sizes' and '1lb. 8oz. metal mounts to set cameos etc. in' were recorded in one of the warehouses in the 1782 Inventory, p. 172.
272. The vase is illustrated in Anthony Blunt, *Nicolas Poussin* (London and New York, 1958), Vol. 1, Plate 131a.
273. Montfauçon, *Antiquité Expliquée* (1719),

Vol. I, Part 2, Plate CXLII, facing p. 230 – *'Le beau vase de Gaiete nous represent Mercure de forme peu ordinaire presentant le petit Bacchus nouveau né a nourir à une Nymphe, que Spon croit être Leucothée'*. Leucothea was identified in classical mythology with Ino.

274. Vol. I, Part 2, Plate CLIII.

275. Manchester Museum, Haworth Bequest, no. 6. The figures correspond to the plaque illustrated in Plate 85, except that there is an extra figure between the ewer-carrier and Mercury, and a tree between the urn-carrier and the bacchante with the thyrsus. See Reilly, *Wedgwood* (1989), Vol. I, Fig. 563.

276. Wedgwood to Bentley, 6th January 1776 (E25-18641), 21st February 1776 (E25-18655), 10th March 1776 (E25-18660). Plaques of the 'Birth of Bacchus' are listed in Wedgwood's catalogues of 1773 (no. 1), 1777 (no. 118) and 1779 (no. 206). See Reilly, *Wedgwood* (1989), Vol. I, p. 593, Vol. II, pp. 727, 733, 738; Meteyard, *Choice Examples of Wedgwood's Art*, pp. 266–7; Macht, *Classical Wedgwood Designs* (1957), pp. 45–6.

277. The Zoffolis' bronzes were discussed, and many of them illustrated, in Honour, 'Bronze Statuettes by Giacomo and Giovanni Zoffoli' (1961).

278. Torrie Collection, University of Edinburgh, National Galleries of Scotland, Catalogue no. 138.

279. This type of handle was probably derived from a Pompeiian model. See for example the neo-Attic vase from Stabiae in the Museo Nazionale, Naples, Inv. no. 6778. Examples of eighteenth-century marble vases by Lorenzo Cardelli and Vincenzo Pacetti *c.*1783–5 with similar scroll handles, bodies, reeded decoration on the lower part of the body and gadrooned rims like Boulton's vases, are in the Villa Borghese, Rome. They are illustrated in Alvar Gonzalez Palacios, 'The Stanza di Apollo e Daphne in the Villa Borghese', *Burlington Magazine*, August 1995, pp. 543–4, Figs. 88–91. See also Italo Faldi, *Galleria Borghese: Le Sculture del Secolo XVI al XIX* (Rome, 1954), pp. 58–9.

280. C. H. Tatham to Henry Holland, 15th February 1795 (Department of Prints, Victoria and Albert Museum, D.1479-1898).

281. C. H. Tatham to Henry Holland, 10th July 1795. The drawing's Accession number is D.1533-1898.

282. Francis Eginton (1737–1805) is better known as a painter of stained glass. He was working for Boulton and Fothergill from 1764 as a decorator of japanned ware and did not leave to become an independent painter until 1781. Besides superintending the production of japanned ware he also modelled objects to be cast in metal. From 1st January 1776, until 31st December 1778, he was in partnership with Boulton and Fothergill in 'Silver, Plated and Or Moulu Goods' (Ledgers, 1776–8, 1778–81) and he was thereafter concerned more with the production of mechanical paintings. See *Journal of the British Society of Master Glass-Painters*, Vol. II, no. 2 (October 1927), p. 63; Robinson, 'Matthew Boulton, Patron of the Arts' (1953), pp. 369–71; Robinson and Thompson, 'Matthew Boulton's Mechanical Paintings' (1970), p. 503.

283. M.B. to J.F., n.d. [4th March 1770]; M.B. to J.F., 30th April 1773.

284. John Eginton (d.1796) worked at Soho as an engraver and chaser (Ledger 1776–8 etc.). In 1776 Boulton and Fothergill entered into partnership with him and Edward Jee or Gee (Jee and Eginton) for the production of mechanical paintings. This venture failed and Eginton reapplied for work as a chaser in 1780 (W. Bingley to M.B., 12th April 1780). See Robinson, 'Matthew Boulton, Patron of the Arts' (1953), pp. 371ff; Robinson and Thompson, 'Matthew Boulton's Mechanical Paintings' (1970), p. 503.

285. M.B. to James Adam, 1st October 1770.

286. Robinson, 'Matthew Boulton, Patron of the Arts' (1953), p. 372.

287. B. and F. to Mayhew and Ince, 9th January 1771.

288. B. and F. to James Todd, 1st August 1771.

289. B. and F. to Lord Arundell, 14th July 1777.

290. M.B. to Lord Cathcart, 30th October 1771.

291. e.g. memorandum of order for 'Mr Smith' dated 4th August 1769; B. and F. to Lord Digby, 30th September 1774.

292. Mrs E. Montagu to M.B., 23rd January 1773.

293. Wedgwood to Bentley, 14th July 1776 (E25-18684).

NOTES TO CHAPTER 4
Manufacture
Notes to pp. 125–156
Notes 1–131

1. Inventory, 1782, p. 102.
2. Quickenden, *Boulton and Fothergill Silver* (1989), p. 104. The reader who wants a more detailed account of the production processes in the related silver business should refer to Quickenden, *Boulton and Fothergill Silver* (1989), pp. 101–35. Several of the processes were identical and several of the craftsmen were the same.
3. I am grateful to Dr Peter Northover of the Department of Materials, Oxford University, for carrying out these analyses for me, and to the Victoria and Albert Museum and the City Museum and Art Gallery, Birmingham, for agreeing to take part in the sampling process. The summary in my text also includes a sample from the Narcissus clock case of Plate 173, taken when it was in the possession of Hotspur Ltd.
4. Interestingly, brass with low zinc content is known today as 'commercial bronze'.
5. Hamilton, *English Brass and Copper Industries* (1926), pp. 162–3.
6. Ledger, 1776–8.
7. Samuel Glover to M.B., 7th December and 23rd December 1769. These letters concern the despatch of between 10 and 20 tons of 'b.j.', i.e. black jack, an ore of zinc, to Boulton from Cornwall. The ore was to be sent in casks via the Port of Bristol. Glover hoped to tell Boulton the terms on which 'considerable parcells may be regularly delivered' and reckoned that he would want the transactions to remain 'as secret as possible'. This was probably because William Champion of Bristol had obtained a patent in 1766 for making brass with black jack. See Hamilton, *English Brass and Copper Industries* (1926), pp. 154–5.
8. Hamilton, *English Brass and Copper Industries* (1926), pp. 217ff; Gill and Briggs, *History of Birmingham* (1952), Vol. I, p. 111. Boulton was by 1780 very much involved in the copper mining industry through the engine trade.
9. In his letter to James Adam on 1st October 1770 Boulton said that the motive power was provided by his two water mills. Rolling was sometimes done at Hofford Mill, which was owned by a certain Kellet (Ledger 1776–8) and was offered on a lease to Boulton and Fothergill in 1780.
10. M.B. Notebook, 1751–9, p. 53.
11. B. and F. to Benjamin Huntsman, 9th August 1764 (steel rolls 7¼ inches wide, 3⅝ diameter for copper and silver); B. and F. to Abraham Darby & Co., 14th December 1771.
12. M.B.'s Notebook, 1768–75, p. 95.
13. Quickenden, *Boulton and Fothergill Silver* (1989), pp. 110–14 gives an account of the process. His 'Lyon-Faced Candlesticks and Candelabra' (1999), p. 205, describes the application of the process to the silver versions of the lion-faced candlestick (Plate 137). The Inventory of 1782 records a stamping shop and a die-sinking shop: it also records the workshops of two men, John Jerom and John Vale, who carried out the stamping process.
14. Hamilton, *English Brass and Copper Industries* (1926), pp. 346–8; Young, *Old English Pattern Books of the Metal Trades* (1913), pp. 12–13.
15. M.B.'s Notebook, 1768–75, p. 96. The fly press is described by Quickenden, *Boulton and Fothergill Silver* (1989), pp. 108–9.
16. John Scale to M.B., 7th February 1773. Boulton and Fothergill made some of their steel dies and bought others from Benjamin Huntsman and other makers. See Quickenden, *Boulton and Fothergill Silver* (1989), p. 111.
17. John Scale to M.B., 7th February 1773: many dies were listed in the stamping shops in the Inventory in 1782.
18. B. and F. to E. Roche, 26th November 1771. See Quickenden, *Boulton and Fothergill Silver* (1989), pp. 114–15.
19. Quickenden, *Boulton and Fothergill Silver* (1989), p. 109.
20. See Hamilton, *English Brass and Copper Industries* (1926), pp. 342–4, for a description of these processes. Boulton thought of adapting both processes to the manufacture of silverware (Notebook, 1768–75, p. 96).
21. Hamilton, *English Brass and Copper Industries* (1926), p. 346.
22. This was the use attributed to the process both by Diderot, *Encyclopédie* (1751–7), and Rees, *Cyclopaedia* (1788).
23. B. and F. to William Matthews, n.d. [26th February 1771], J.F. to M.B., 4th April 1771. These references are concerned with buttons.
24. Samuel Wyatt to M.B., 31st July 1765.
25. Inventory, 1782, p. 5
26. M.B.'s Notebook, n.d. [1770?], p. 34; M.B. to Wedgwood, 20th December 1768.
27. e.g. B. and F. to William Matthews, 12th September 1772 (the 'best' plaster for Francis Eginton) and an invoice from John Flaxman dated 16th November 1770 which included – 'To 2 cwt of fine plaister £1 4s. od.'.
28. Mayhew and Ince sent some examples of branches, candle sockets etc., which they wanted copied, in 1781 – B. and F. to John Stuart, 20th October 1781.
29. M.B. to 'Soho' (J.F.), n.d. [4th March, 1770].
30. Inventory 1782, p. 102. The chief caster was probably Isaac Riley or Ryley (Ledger, 1778–82).
31. e.g. B. and F. to Wedgwood, 17th January 1769, which contains a request that certain china vases should be made to precise measurements because the mounts could not be altered.
32. Wedgwood to Bentley, 24th–26th December 1770 (E25-18334).
33. B. and F. to William Matthews, 21st July 1772.
34. See Appendix IV, pp. 126–7.
35. Diderot, *Encyclopédie*, Plates Vol. III (1763), '*Ciseleur et Damasquineur*', Plates I–II; Vol. VIII (1771), '*Sculpture en Or et en Argent*', Plate III.
36. M.B. to the Earl of Shelburne, 7th January 1771.
37. M.B. to John Scale, 31st March 1772.
38. It is clear from M.B.'s Notebook, 1768–75, pp. 1, 14, etc., that leaf gilding was also practised by button manufacturers. Boulton and Fothergill bought their gold in London: letters to a refiner named Robert Albion Cox survive (27th August, 14th December 1774, etc.).
39. Or, according to several authors, water or beer: e.g. Stalker and Parker, *Treatise of Japanning and Varnishing* (1688), p. 65; Rees, *Cyclopaedia* (1788), s.v. 'Gilding'.
40. See previous note.
41. Herman Boerhaave, *A New Method of Chemistry* (trans. P. Shaw and E. Chambers, London, 1727), p. 74; *Elements of Chemistry* (trans. T. Dallowe, London, 1735), pp. 347–8.
42. Peter Shaw, *Chemical Lectures* (London, 1755), pp. 105–6.
43. G. Smith, *The Laboratory or School of Arts* (4th edition, London, 1755), pp. 13–27.
44. Pierre-Joseph Macquer, *Dictionnaire Portatif des Arts et Metiers* (Paris, 1766–7).
45. Early Accounts, 26th September 1758 – an account sent to Boulton for the purchase of several books including 'Boorhaave £1 4s. od.'; also 'Webster £0 1s. 6d.', which was possibly John Webster, *Metallographia or An History of Metals* (London, 1671). Boulton also owned parts of Diderot's *Encyclopédie* – James Keir to M.B., n.d. [March 1771] – and a manuscript copy of six volumes of Joseph Black's lectures on chemistry (Christie's, 12th December 1986, lot 24). His copy of Boerhaave, *A New Method of Chemistry*, was sold Christie's, 12th December 1986, lot 26.
46. M.B.'s Notebook, 1768–75, p. 7.
47. Many of the contemporary books, such as those cited in previous notes, contain accounts of these recipes.
48. M.B.'s Notebook, 1768–75, p. 33: the note, which I have translated, was written in 'Bad French' and was possibly a transcription of instructions given to Boulton by an immigrant French craftsman such as Dominique Jean. On p. 119 of the same notebook Boulton noted that 'redness may be obtained by absorbing the gold more into the metal by repeated and greater heats'.
49. Ledger, 1776–8, for example contains many debits for 'drugs': no earlier accounts have survived.
50. Some of the recipes are very similar to recipes in G. Smith, *The Laboratory or School of Arts* (1755).
51. M.B.'s Notebook, 1768–75, p. 31.
52. M.B.'s Notebook, 1768–75, p. 127. A similar recipe is noted on p. 32: in this recipe 1 oz of sodium chloride is proposed, and a little calcined potassium nitrate (sal prunell) is suggested, which would make little difference.

53. M.B.'s Notebook, 1768–75, p. 121.
54. i.e. suitable for clearing 'dead' work (Notebook, p. 123).
55. Boulton observed that 'ethiops martial' might be a useful ingredient and made notes of a recipe for making it in the same notebook (p. 120).
56. M.B.'s Notebook, 1768–75, p. 128.
57. M.B.'s Notebook, 1768–75, p. 32.
58. M.B.'s Notebook, 1768–75, p. 32.
59. M.B.'s Notebook, 1768–75, p. 128.
60. M.B.'s Notebook, 1768–75, p. 127.
61. M.B.'s Notebook, 1768–75, p. 127.
62. Argil, or cream of tarter, is used in many plating processes as a stabiliser, forming complexes with unwanted elements such as dissolved iron.
63. M.B.'s Notebook, 1768–75, p. 31, a recipe for 'Bradbury's yellow couler', which appears to rely on the presence of chlorides in its ingredients as the solving agents; p. 32, a similar recipe.
64. M.B.'s Notebook, 1768–75, p. 34, a recipe which, assuming 'gros' (a French unit of weight) as equivalent to 144 grains, consisted of potassium aluminum sulphate 27.8 per cent, potassium nitrate 27.8, zinc sulphate 27.8, cupric sulphate 7, ferrous sulphate 4.6, ochre 2.1, copper acetate 1.1, ammonium chloride 1.1 and saffron 0.7.
65. J.F. to M.B., 5th November 1765.
66. M.B.'s Diary, 1769.
67. M.B. to Solomon Hyman, 23rd January 1769. Boulton was referring to a dipping recipe.
68. Preface to Sale Catalogue, 11th April 1771. In this preface French gilding is described as 'too near' to the colour of brass. Boulton's admiration of French gilding, however, is clear from his private letters: this public statement was an attempt to promote his own wares.
69. Alexandre Tournant to M.B., 2nd April 1773, 29th May 1774 and 13th April 1775. Tournant (*c.*1730–92) worked at Soho 1770–2 and was then recommended by Boulton to the Duke of Richmond in a letter dated 4th December 1772. He was an accomplished glass-grinder and later became one of the opticians to the King in France: see Taylor, *Mathematical Practitioners of Hanoverian England* (1966), p. 247. Tournant's letter to Boulton on 29th May 1774 contains a recipe for a reddish 'dead' colour, and that of 13th April 1775, a recipe for a colouring solution containing ochre and directions for its preparation. He had obtained these recipes from Paris.
70. B. and F. to the Earl of Ashburnham, 2nd November 1775; B. and F. to the Earl of Findlater, 11th October 1776.
71. John Scale to M.B., 3rd March 1785.
72. M.B. to J.F., n.d. [probably February 1770], in which Boulton complained that the ornaments were tarnishing for lack of proper wiping and drying up after burnishing.
73. Inventory, 1782, pp. 2–3.
74. Quickenden, *Boulton and Fothergill Silver* (1989), pp. 317–19. In the 'Measurement of Shops' taken in 1776 (J. Bownas & Co. Box) he is recorded as having a chasing shop and a warehouse.
75. M.B. to 'Soho' (J.F.), n.d. [4th March 1770], M.B. to J.F., 30th April 1773, J.F. to M.B., 5th May 1773.
76. Quickenden, *Boulton and Fothergill Silver* (1989), p. 318.
77. Quickenden, *Boulton and Fothergill Silver* (1989), p. 307. John Scale criticised his workmanship in 1773 (Proposals to B. and F. by J. Scale, 1773). Quickenden records that he cast parts for the manufacture of clocks in 1776 (Ledger 1776–8, 4th May 1776), but these may not have been mounts. He is recorded in the 'Measurement of Shops' in 1776 (J. Bownas & Co. Box) as having a casting shop and a silver casting shop.
78. Ledger, 1778–82. He is also recorded as having a casting shop in the 1776 'Measurement of Shops' (J. Bownas & Co. Box).
79. Quickenden, *Boulton and Fothergill Silver* (1989), p. 329.
80. Quickenden, *Boulton and Fothergill Silver* (1989), pp. 327, 329.
81. Inventory 1782, pp. 8, 104.
82. Quickenden, *Boulton and Fothergill Silver* (1989), p. 321. In the 1776 'Measurement of Shops' (J. Bownas & Co. Box) he is recorded as having a die-sinking shop.
83. B. and F. to William Matthews, 4th April 1772.
84. The indentures are dated 31st August and 27th September 1768. See Appendix VI.
85. W. Bingley to M.B., 12th April 1780.
86. B. and F. to William Matthews, 4th April 1772, 8th April 1772, M.B. to J.F., n.d. [received 9th April 1772].
87. Quickenden, *Boulton and Fothergill Silver* (1989), p. 316.
88. Quickenden, *Boulton and Fothergill Silver* (1989), pp. 324–5. He is recorded in the 1776 'Measurement of Shops' as having a 'sodering' shop.
89. Inventory 1782, pp. 133–4: see Appendix IV. There was also a John Bentley, who was later responsible for gold, gilt, silver and plated chains (Ledger, 1776–8, p. 1). See Quickenden, *Boulton and Fothergill Silver* (1989), pp. 308–9.
90. John Scale to M.B., 6th February 1772, B. and F. to M.B., 4th April 1772.
91. Quickenden, *Boulton and Fothergill Silver* (1989), p. 310.
92. Quickenden, *Boulton and Fothergill Silver* (1989), p. 311.
93. Journal 1776–8, Ledger 1778–82.
94. M.B.'s Notebook, 1768–75, p. 31.
95. J.F. to M.B., 4th April 1771.
96. Three 'Enamel Manufacturers' were listed in Sketchley and Adams, *Directory* (1770), p. 25. James Keir was also a producer of enamelled bodies (see note 104).
97. Wedgwood to Bentley, 11th February 1769 (E25-18228).
98. M.B. to James Adam, 1st October 1770.
99. B. and F. to Samuel Pechell, 18th January 1772. Watney and Charleston have summarised evidence of the enamelling trade in Birmingham in 'Petitions for Patents concerning Porcelain, Glass and Enamels' (1966). The trade was well established in Birmingham by 1767 and included the manufacture of candlesticks, snuff boxes, ink stands, tweezers, toothpick cases, clock and watch dials, etc. (Watney and Charleston p. 63): Boulton's role in the industry is described as obscure (p. 82).
100. M.B. to Wedgwood, 20th December 1768 and 17th January 1769.
101. Wedgwood to Bentley, 24th December 1770 (E25-18334); Wedgwood to M.B., 19th February 1771.
102. M.B. to J.F., n.d. [4th March 1770].
103. M.B. to J.F., n.d. [7th or 8th March 1770].
104. B. and F. to James Keir, 1st April 1772. It appears that Keir sent enamelled vases by mistake, and he was reminded that they should have been flint glass (B. and F. to Keir and Co., 7th April 1772). Keir became a partner in the glassworks in 1772. See Court, *Rise of the Midlands Industries* (1938), p. 221; Schofield, *Lunar Society of Birmingham* (1963), pp. 81–2; Francis Buckley, 'Notes on the Glasshouses of Stourbridge 1770–1830', *Transactions of the Society of Glass Technology* (1927), Vol. II, pp. 110–11.
105. B. and F. to William Duesbury, 17th October 1772.
106. B. and F. to Scott, Keir & Co., 27th May 1773.
107. M.B.'s Diary, 1768.
108. M.B.'s Diary, 1768.
109. B. and F. to Robert Bradbury jun., 26th September 1774.
110. Ford, *Derbyshire Blue John* (2000), p. 37. Boulton used the term 'tiger stone' on several occasions, also the term 'leopard stone', which clearly described some stone with the same sort of colouring. He bought some tiger stone in 1769 (M.B.'s Diary, October 1769).
111. The mineralogy of blue john is discussed in detail by Trevor Ford in *Derbyshire Blue John* (2000), pp. 24ff.
112. Ford, *Derbyshire Blue John* (2000), p. 7.
113. Ford, *Derbyshire Blue John* (2000), p. 53.
114. Ford, *Derbyshire Blue John* (2000), pp. 44ff, describes the processes of working the stone in greater detail.
115. Receipt dated March 1769, Robert Howe to M.B. 31st December 1769. See Chapter 2, notes 123, 126.
116. M.B.'s Diary, 1769.
117. B. and F. to the Marquess of Granby, 19th November 1774, B. and F. to Scott, Keir & Co., 27th May 1773.
118. e.g. B. and F. to Robert Bradbury jun., 20th September 1774.
119. Robert Bradbury and his son of the same name were presumably stone workers rather than agents or lessees of the blue john mines. They appear in the Boulton archives between 1769, when Boulton visited Derby-

shire and probably first made contact with them (M.B.'s Diary, 1769), and at least 1785. In the 1780s unmounted stone ornaments were sold at Soho on their behalf (B. and F. to Robert Bradbury, 11th August 1780, 30th November 1784, etc.).
120. B. and F. to Robert Bradbury, n.d. [February 1771].
121. Memorandum headed 'Ordered from Mr Bradbury junior', 7th March 1771.
122. B. and F. to Robert Bradbury, 6th August 1772; B. and F. to Robert Bradbury jun., 20th May 1771, 19th October 1772 ('feet, pedestals and covers'), 26th September 1774, 12th March 1775 (twelve pairs of stones for each of the drawings 8, 9 and 11, six pairs for drawing 10), etc.
123. B. and F. to Robert Bradbury jun., 17th August 1771, 20th September 1774.
124. B. and F. to Robert Bradbury sen., 23rd June 1774.
125. B. and F. to Robert Bradbury jun., 26th September 1774.
126. B. and F. to Robert Bradbury jun., 12th March 1775.
127. M.B. to Wedgwood, 17th January 1769; B. and F. to William Duesbury, 17th October 1772; B. and F. to Scott, Keir & Co., 27th May 1773.
128. The suppliers are mentioned later during my discussion of the various clock cases produced at Soho. See Survey of ornaments.
129. Charles Wyatt was a first cousin of the architects James and Samuel and married their sister Jane. He was a clerk at Soho for some time, and was a partner in the button business in 1776 (Journal 1776–8, p. 1). He was dismissed in 1777 for misappropriating materials. See Quickenden, *Boulton and Fothergill Silver* (1989), p. 332.
130. Andrew Cabrit worked for many years as a clerk at Soho: in 1772 he was threatened with dismissal, but he remained there all his life and became head of the firm's foreign business, dying in 1792.
131. The annual inventory usually took place at the end of the year: in 1771 it was expected to take ten or twelve days to complete – B. and F. to the Earl of Kerry, 26th December 1771.

NOTES TO CHAPTER 5

Marketing

Notes to pp. 157–180

Notes 1–215

1. Quickenden, *Boulton and Fothergill Silver* (1989), pp. 51–81, gives an account of the firm's marketing methods and achievements in the silver and plate businesses.
2. M.B. to J. H. Ebbinghaus, n.d. [26th June 1766].
3. B. and F. to William Evill, 14th August 1771.
4. B. and F. to Henry Morris, 2nd December 1771. Morris's shop was at 82 Fleet Street.
5. B. and F. to Wooley and Hemming, 19th January 1771.
6. M.B. to James Adam, 1st October 1770.
7. James Adam to M.B., 5th November 1770.
8. John Kentish jun. to M.B., 14th December 1769.
9. Memorandum of order for 'Mr Smith', 4th August 1769; B. and F. to William Matthews, 6th May 1771, etc.
10. B. and F. to Christopher Pinchbeck, 14th December 1771. Pinchbeck was the son of the maker of astronomical clocks and inventor of the 'Pinchbeck' alloy of copper and zinc that resembled gold (see Chapter 4, p. 127). He bought a caryatic vase in the 1771 sale (second day, lot 89). Baillie, *Watchmakers and Clockmakers of the World* (1951), records that Pinchbeck (1710–83) worked in Fleet Street, but the vases from Soho were addressed to him 'at the bottom of the Haymarket'. He can presumably be identified also with the C. Pinchbeck who described himself as a 'toyman and mechanician' and who worked in St Martin-in-the-Fields. See Watney and Charleston, 'Petitions for Patents' (1966), p. 57.
11. B. and F. to William Evill, 14th August 1771. The vases were sent two months later (B. and F. to William Evill, 26th October 1771). It is not clear what Evill's new 'mode of sale' consisted of.
12. B. and F. to James Todd, 1st August 1771.
13. B. and F. to Thomas Wilkinson, 75 Cornhill, 25th October 1771.
14. B. and F. to Patrick Robertson, 19th October 1771. Robertson was an Edinburgh silversmith with a considerable local reputation. See Baker, 'Patrick Robertson's Tea Urn and the Late Eighteenth-Century Edinburgh Silver Trade' (1773), and Quickenden, *Boulton and Fothergill Silver* (1989), pp. 74–5.
15. B. and F. to Patrick Robertson, 12th November 1771. He planned to send the vases abroad, which entailed 'more expences', and Boulton and Fothergill gave him a further 5 per cent discount to allow for it.
16. B. and F. to William Matthews, 27th November 1771.
17. B. and F. to William Matthews, 1st April 1772.
18. J.F. to M.B., 16th February 1772.
19. This was presumably William Bent whose workshop was in St Martin's Lane. He supplied door furniture to Sir Rowland Winn at Nostell Priory in 1767 and was sent goods from Soho on at least two occasions in 1771 (B. and F. to William Bent, 9th February and 23rd July 1771). These consignments were the sixth and seventh of a series and the contact with Bent probably went back to the earliest days of the partnership. In 1762 Bent was handling the sale of Boulton and Fothergill's chapes in London (J.F. to M.B., 1st June 1762).
20. e.g. Patrick Robertson on 17th October 1767, 12th September 1770 and 13th May 1775, 'Harrash' (presumably Thomas Harrache) on 2nd June 1769, and Parker, a jeweller in St Paul's on 28th June 1770 (Register Book, Great Tew Archive).
21. B. and F. to Wooley and Hemming, 19th January 1771, and many other letters.
22. B. and F. to Patrick Robertson, 17th January 1771. Wooley and Hemming were offered 10 per cent two days later (see previous note).
23. Ledger, 1776–8, p. 103 (28th March 1776, James Belliss, William Webb); Day Book, 1779–81 (25th October 1780, John J. Appach); etc. The same discount was offered to certain merchants, e.g. to Capper, Palmer and Perkins of Great Charles Street, Birmingham (Day Book, 1779–81, p. 465, 24th October 1780) and to John le Coq, a merchant in London (B. and F. to John le Coq, 6th July 1781).
24. B. and F. to Wooley and Hemming, 19th January 1771.
25. This 5 per cent discount remained their normal practice, e.g. B. and F. to John Stuart, 3rd November 1781.
26. B. and F. to William Moore, Dublin, 9th June 1773.
27. B. and F. to Henry Morris, 2nd December 1771; B. and F. to Thomas Craig, Dublin, 26th March 1772.
28. Inventory, 1782. Discounts varied between 10 per cent on, for example, paintings, to 20 per cent on plate.
29. Possibly William Evill, or Mainwaring.
30. Wedgwood to Bentley, 6th June 1772 (E25-18376).
31. B. and F. to Henry Morris, 2nd December 1771.
32. McKendrick, 'Josiah Wedgwood' (1960), p. 412.
33. Wedgwood to Bentley, 19th June 1779 (E25-18898).
34. Colvin, *Biographical Dictionary of English Architects* (1995), pp. 1103–5. Colvin prints a family tree on p. 1102.
35. Colvin, *Biographical Dictionary of English Architects* (1995), pp. 1124–8.
36. S. Wyatt to M.B., 6th March and 12th June 1766.
37. S. Wyatt to B. and F., 9th September 1769.
38. S. Wyatt to B. and F., 9th September 1769.
39. Later (1784–6) he built the ill-fated Albion Mills at Blackfriars for Boulton and Watt.
40. Colvin, *Biographical Dictionary of English Architects* (1995), pp. 1107–21. James Wyatt worked with the family firm from 1768 but rocketed to fame as an architect when his designs for the Pantheon in London were realised.
41. Earl of Shelburne to Adam, 16th April 1765.
42. Lord Arundell to M.B., 3rd September 1773.
43. M.B. to Robert Mylne, 4th November 1775.
44. Ledger, 1776–8, p. 230, 18th March 1777; B. and F. to Robert Mylne, 28th June, 13th November 1777.
45. Mrs Montagu to M.B., 22nd November 1779. Mrs Montagu turned to Boulton for more than just the ormolu decorations, following her dissatisfaction with James Stuart's lack of diligence, and there are many letters in the archives referring to Boulton's work for her on the supply of glass, etc. See Kerry Bristol, '22 Portman Square', *British Art Journal*, Vol. II, no. 3, Spring/Summer 2001.
46. Register Book (Great Tew Archive). This record of visitors starts in 1767 and goes to the end of the century, but there are lacunae, and not all visitors are recorded. See Appendix II.
47. Register Book (Great Tew Archive). Many visits are also recorded in correspondence.
48. B. and F. to Wooley and Hemming, 19th January 1771.
49. M.B. to J. H. Ebbinghaus, 20th October 1767.
50. James Keir, 'Memorandum of Mr Boulton', p. 5.
51. M.B. to J. H. Ebbinghaus, 20th October 1767.
52. B. and F. to William Matthews, 9th January 1771.
53. B. and F. to Mayhew and Ince, 9th January 1771: two of the cabinets were needed first for the sale at Christie's in the spring.
54. M.B. to John Scale, n.d. [April 1771].
55. B. and F. to Mayhew and Ince, 8th June 1771.
56. Wedgwood to Bentley, 13th July 1772 (E25-18380).
57. J.F. to M.B., 30th January 1772.
58. B. and F. to G. and T. Otley, 27th July 1775. See Quickenden, *Boulton and Fothergill Silver* (1989), p. 60.
59. John Hodges to M.B., n.d. [after 30th May 1778]. The letter contains a list of sales made at Soho from 23rd to 30th May. There is no ormolu in the list. The 1782 Inventory pp. 145–62 shows that there were a wide variety of goods in the toy room.
60. According to the 1776 'Measurement of Shops' (J. Bownas & Co. Box), the toy room measured 49 ft. x 15 ft.
61. Morgan (ed.), *An American Quaker in the British Isles* (1992), p. 255.

62. M.B. to his wife, 6th March 1770.
63. M.B. to his wife, n.d. [3rd March 1770].
64. Wedgwood to Bentley, 21st November 1768 (E25-18215). Some of Boulton and Fothergill's toys had found their way into the Palace in earlier years: see Robinson, 'Matthew Boulton's Marketing Techniques' (1963), p. 49.
65. M.B. to his wife, 3rd March 1770.
66. M.B.'s Notebook, 1773, pp. 7–8. The titles are all abbreviated in the manuscript.
67. Matthews was at 5 Castile Court, Bartholemew Lane, in 1768. By February 1770 he was at 10 Walbrook, where Boulton stayed with him. By March 1771 he was at 14 Cannon Street. Boulton stayed there during his visits to London in 1771–3. Matthews entered into partnership with Barton by 1777 and was at 6 Green Lettice Lane, Cannon Street. He died in 1792.
68. M.B. to John Motteux, 15th January 1768.
69. M.B. to J.F., 25th February 1770.
70. See Cule, *Financial History of Matthew Boulton* (1935), pp. 44–6.
71. B. and F. to Sir Harbord Harbord, 15th February 1776.
72. John Wyatt to M.B., 27th February 1776, and to B. and F., 8th March 1776.
73. John Stuart to B. and F., 7th January 1778.
74. B. and F. to John Wyatt, 9th February 1776: Wyatt was to receive 10 per cent on sales of ormolu. Chippindall received a 5 per cent commission, but nothing if the sale resulted in a bad debt (B. and F. to Richard Chippindall, 24th April 1784).
75. See Appendix I, e.g. Earl of Craven, Lady Morton, etc.
76. McKendrick, 'Josiah Wedgwood' (1960), p. 419; Finer and Savage, *Selected Letters of Josiah Wedgwood* (1965) p. 45 and introduction, p. 13; Baker, 'A Rage for Exhibitions' (1995), pp. 118ff. The showroom was probably in Charles Street. In 1768 Wedgwood acquired the premises in Newport Street to which the showroom was moved.
77. McKendrick, 'Josiah Wedgwood' (1960), pp. 419–20, discusses the establishment of this showroom and the methods of display by which Wedgwood increased his sales: he was taking £100 a week in cash sales in London by the spring of 1769 besides many orders.
78. Wedgwood to Bentley, 27th September 1769 (E25-18261).
79. M.B. to J.F., 25th February 1770.
80. James Adam to M.B., 14th August 1770.
81. M.B. to James Adam, 1st October 1770.
82. M.B. to James Adam, 1st October 1770.
83. James Adam to M.B., 5th November 1770.
84. James Adam to M.B., 28th January 1771.
85. Wedgwood to Bentley, 24th December 1770 (E25-18334). Stuart was apparently attempting to interest Boulton and Wedgwood in some houses over which he had control between the Adelphi and the Strand.
86. James Adam to M.B., 5th November 1770. In this letter Adam goes on to discuss the staff necessary to run the showroom and their remuneration, to suggest the possibility of another partner, to ask Boulton for his estimate of the likely profit on capital employed and to mention the risk of competitors getting hold of and copying their designs (a problem from which Wedgwood regularly suffered).
87. *The Public Advertiser*, 4th April 1770 (Burney 571B, British Library). See Chapter 2, p. 50, where I have quoted the list of the ornaments mentioned in the advertisements for the sale. Catalogues were available, but no surviving catalogue has yet come to light.
88. *The Public Advertiser*, 13th March 1770. The advertisement appeared in *The Public Advertiser* on several later dates in March and April. The date of the sale was not given in the early advertisements, presumably to encourage people to view the show.
89. In April 1771, for example, William Duesbury held a four-day sale at Christie's (17th–20th April) of the previous year's produce of the Chelsea and Derby porcelain factories.
90. Horace Walpole to Horace Mann, 6th May 1770, Lewis, Hunting Smith and Lam (ed.), *Horace Walpole's Correspondence with Horace Mann* (1967), p. 211.
91. Sale catalogue 11th April 1771, Preface (quoted in Chapter 2, pp. 51–2).
92. Wedgwood to Bentley, 24th December 1770 (E25-18334).
93. B. and F. to Mayhew and Ince, 9th January 1771.
94. M.B. to James Christie, n.d. [13th February 1771].
95. B. and F. to William Matthews, n.d. [26th February 1771].
96. M.B. to James Christie, 2nd March 1771.
97. M.B. to James Christie, n.d. [13th February 1771].
98. e.g. B. and F. to Sir Laurence Dundas, 4th January 1772: Dundas had seen the Persian vase in the exhibition and ordered a pair.
99. James Keir to M.B., n.d. [February 1771]. A modified version of Keir's draft appears in Boulton and Fothergill's letter book, in Boulton's handwriting, on 27th March. In the event the advertisements did not follow this wording.
100. B. and F. to William Matthews, n.d. [26th February 1771].
101. M.B. to James Christie, 2nd March 1771.
102. B. and F. to William Matthews, 16th March 1771.
103. M. Hobster to M.B., 31st March 1771: Hobster wrote from the Bedford Coffee House and had seen the sale advertised.
104. *The Gazetteer and New Daily Advertiser*, 26th March 1771 (Burney 581B, British Library). The advertisement reappeared in the *Gazetteer* and in *The Public Advertiser* on several later dates in March and April. The sale was advertised right up to 13th April, the last date of the auction. I have quoted the list of the ornaments mentioned in the advertisement in Chapter 2, p. 52.
105. M.B. to the Earl of Warwick, 30th December 1770; M.B. to the Earl of Shelburne, 7th January 1771.
106. M.B. to James Christie, 2nd March 1771.
107. The drafts are dated 27th March 1771. Keir did not alter them substantially – James Keir to M.B., n.d. [April 1771].
108. James Keir to M.B., n.d. [April 1771].
109. B. and F. to William Matthews, 29th February 1772.
110. B. and F. to the Duchess of Portland, 6th November 1771.
111. Wedgwood to Bentley, n.d. [May/June 1767], (E25-18149).
112. M.B. to James Christie, 22nd March 1772. Boulton thought that the experiment might be useful to Christie on other occasions. The failure of the sale no doubt persuaded Christie otherwise.
113. *The Gazetteer and New Daily Advertiser*, also *The Daily Advertiser*, both 20th March 1772 (Burney 587B, British Library). The same advertisement appeared on several days in March and early April (see next note). I have quoted the list of ornaments mentioned in the advertisement in Chapter 2, p. 54.
114. *The Gazetteer and New Daily Advertiser*, *The Daily Advertiser*, both 6th April 1772. This advertisement was printed for the next five days up to 11th April, the second and last day of the sale.
115. B. and F. to John Stuart, 18th March 1778 and 25th March 1778; John Stuart to M.B., 31st March 1778, etc.
116. John Stuart to M.B., 31st March 1778. The sale had already been postponed from early April for fear of clashing with two private sales, which contained several ormolu pieces. Boulton was, however, impatient and preferred to hold the sale at the earliest possible date: this represented a change of mind since a fortnight previously, when he was in favour of postponing the sale until 1779 if it could not be held before 12th April (B. and F. to John Stuart, 18th March 1778).
117. Dated 18th May 1778.
118. *Morning Post and Daily Advertiser*, 9th May 1778 (Burney 662B, British Library). The advertisement was printed every day until 20th May, the day of the sale. The sale was originally planned for 14th–15th May, as advertised on the 9th, but was postponed. I have quoted the list of ornaments mentioned in the advertisement in Chapter 2, p. 60. Copies of the catalogue were dated erratically (Appendix III).
119. It is perhaps odd that Boulton never tried to sell silver by auction, apart from a few pieces in the 1778 sale, but production did not build up until after 1773 and his experience of auctions by then had not been happy.

120. John Wyatt to M.B., 27th February 1776.
121. John Wyatt to B. and F., 8th March 1776. Wyatt did not want to open a shop but to have a place where he could keep a boy assistant and show a few samples to the visiting gentry.
122. This probably refers to mechanical pictures.
123. A punning reference to Henry Clay, the japanner and inventor of papier mâché.
124. i.e. the showroom at Soho.
125. Paper in Boulton's hand, 'My Ideas of a Theka in London are', n.d. [March 1776], (John Fothergill Box).
126. Mayhew and Ince to B. and F., 16th January 1779. Boulton and Fothergill were mystified by Mayhew and Ince's bill (B. and F. to Mayhew and Ince, 6th March 1779) and asked John Stuart to discover from Wyatt what had happened to the cases (B. and F. to John Stuart, 29th January 1779). The account was still in dispute in 1783 (John Hodges to John Wyatt, 2nd August 1783).
127. John Wyatt to B. and F., 8th March 1776.
128. John Stuart to M.B., 7th January 1778.
129. See Bibliography, introduction p. 478, for a description of the Pattern Books.
130. B. and F. to William Matthews, 22nd January 1772, 29th February 1772, 16th September 1772, 19th December 1772, B. and F. to John Wyatt, 22nd June 1776, etc.
131. B. and F. to William Matthews, 29th February 1772.
132. B. and F. to the Duke of Ancaster, 11th July 1772; B. and F. to Lord Digby, 30th September 1774; B. and F. to the Countess of Craven, 10th January 1776; B. and F. to the Earl of Findlater, 20th January 1776, etc; also the letters cited in the next note.
133. B. and F. to Samuel Pechell, 11th December 1771; B. and F. to Lord Arundell, 22nd March 1777 and 14th July 1777, when no less than 12 drawings of clocks were sent to Lord Arundell: however slight these drawings were they must have taken some time, which was in the event time wasted because Lord Arundell had enquired not after clocks but locks (B. and F. to Lord Arundell, 13th November 1777). He only received two drawings of locks, i.e. escutcheons for doors.
134. B. and F. to Mayhew and Ince, 9th January 1771. Boulton and Fothergill wanted Mayhew and Ince to find a draughtsman who could copy three books of ornaments for them.
135. B. and F. to Lord Nuneham, 12th March 1775; John Hodges to M.B., 23rd April 1777.
136. M.B. to P. J. Wendler, n.d. [April 1767].
137. Wedgwood to M.B., 7th August 1767. In this letter Wedgwood welcomed a scheme mooted by Boulton for producing engravings of their manufactures as a means of publicising them abroad.
138. M.B. to Lord Cathcart, 30th October 1771.
139. Sale catalogue 1771, preface. See Chapter 2, pp. 51–2.
140. M.B. to Solomon Hyman, 23rd January 1769.
141. Wedgwood to Bentley, 14th July 1776 (E25-18684).
142. M.B. to Mrs Montagu, 16th January 1772.
143. Lord Cathcart to M.B., 21st February 1772.
144. M.B. to Sir John Goodricke, 16th December 1772.
145. Robinson, 'Boulton and Fothergill 1762–82' (1959), p. 66. In 1766 Fothergill had reported to Boulton during his tour of the Baltic countries that the only means of sharing in the hardware trade to Sweden was to smuggle it (J.F. to M.B., 31st July 1766).
146. e.g. in an appeal to the Earl of Shelburne to ask the new ambassador to Portugal to press for the removal of prohibitions on the import into Portugal of English hardware (Robinson, 'Boulton and Fothergill 1762–82' (1959), pp. 65–6).
147. M.B. to Sir John Goodricke, 1st May 1769. Goodricke was ambassador to Sweden.
148. Robinson, 'Boulton and Fothergill 1762–82' (1959). See also Quickenden, *Boulton and Fothergill Silver* (1989), Chapter 2.
149. 28th September 1767, Register Book (Great Tew Archive).
150. Register Book (Great Tew Archive). See Appendix II.
151. Register Book (Great Tew Archive), October 1771, 30th August 1775.
152. M.B. to J. H. Ebbinghaus, 24th October 1772: Boulton was making excuses for not sending Ebbinghaus, who had invested money in the partnership, any account. Ponitovski came on 16th September 1772, the Danish ambassador ('Baron Deiden' or 'Deide', who had previously visited on 11th July 1769 and 28th July 1770) on 23rd September 1772, the French ambassador ('Count de Guines') on 22nd September. No visit by the Dutch ambassador is recorded, but this may have been General Bentinck, who came on 20th October. 'Monsr le Comt Orlow', the 'youngest brother of that family', came on 22nd October (Register Book, Great Tew Archive).
153. M.B. to Lord Cathcart, 30th October 1771.
154. J.F. to M.B., 22nd May 1772. The visitors were 'Le Comte d'Oetting et de Wal', 'Le Comte Lamburg' (who later sent other visitors) and the 'Duke and Duchess of La Villa Hermosa'. They came on 12th May (Register Book, Great Tew Archive).
155. Their visits were in November 1771 and on 29th March 1776 (Register Book, Great Tew Archive).
156. Mrs Montagu to M.B., 26th October 1772 and 23rd January 1773.
157. M.B. to Lord Cathcart, 30th October 1771.
158. Register Book, 31st August 1771 (Great Tew Archive).
159. B. and F. to Moushin Pushkin, 15th October 1774.
160. Norman, *Hermitage* (1997), p. 23.
161. Wedgwood to B. and F., 19th March 1768 (dated by Wedgwood 1767, but Cathcart did not receive his appointment until January 1768).
162. Young (ed.), *Genius of Wedgwood* (1995), p. 214.
163. M.B. to Lord Cathcart, 30th October 1771.
164. Raikes and Saffree – J.F. to M.B., 28th January 1772.
165. Lord Cathcart to B. and F., 21st February 1772.
166. Sir Robert Gunning to M.B., 2nd/13th September 1774. This was probably the consignment which was described in a letter in November as a 'very large order … destined for St Petersburg' (B. and F. to the Marquess of Granby, 10th November 1774). Boulton had apparently also offered to mount stones for the Empress. Gunning wrote that she was 'unlikely to give you any employment in that way'.
167. B. and F. to Sir John Goodricke, 16th December 1772.
168. B. and F. to Lord Stormont, 13th August 1774.
169. B. and F. to William Matthews, 19th October 1771.
170. Keith visited Soho on 15th July 1772 (Register Book, Great Tew Archive). He was recommended to Boulton by his friend Joseph Yorke, who said that Keith wished to 'shew as far as he is able specimens of your elegant and useful manufactures' (Joseph Yorke to M.B., 10th July 1772).
171. M.B. to Sir Rodney Valltravers, November 1772.
172. e.g. the Duke of Richmond, Sir William Hamilton, Sir Robert Murray Keith – Robinson, 'Boulton and Fothergill 1762–82' (1959), p. 42; also Sir Patrick Crawford who wrote offering his assistance in Holland on 5th September 1777.
173. McKendrick, 'Josiah Wedgwood' (1960), pp. 426–7.
174. M.B. to J. H. Ebbinghaus, n.d. [after May 1766]. Robinson has given an account of the firm's overseas agents in 'Boulton and Fothergill 1762–82' (1959), pp. 68ff.
175. In 1767 Boulton claimed that over half the letters received at Soho were in German (M.B. to William Daniel, 10th July 1767). If true, it was fortunate that Fothergill was fluent in the language.
176. M.B. to J. H. Ebbinghaus, 20th October 1767: Fothergill had been ill in Sweden for several weeks.
177. Robinson, 'Boulton and Fothergill 1762–82' (1959), p. 67; Quickenden, *Boulton and Fothergill Silver* (1989), p. 22.
178. Robinson, 'Boulton and Fothergill 1762–82' (1959), p. 67; Robinson cites a letter to Lewis Baumgartner, an important merchant in London, dated 27th March 1766, in which the partners assured him that Fothergill would not go to France, Spain or Italy.

179. M.B. to P. J. Wendler, n.d. [July 1767].
180. Wendler was in Italy again in 1776. He wrote to Boulton and Fothergill from Rome on 31st July: he was proposing to go to Naples in September where he hoped to recommend them particularly to a Mr Raiola.
181. J.F. to M.B., 4th April 1771.
182. M.B. to James Adam, 1st October 1770.
183. Robinson, 'Boulton and Fothergill 1762–82' (1959), p. 76. The usual method of enquiry was a letter to established customers.
184. M.B. to his wife, 18th November and 24th November 1765. He managed to smuggle some patterns into France, and was not at all impressed by Parisian fashions.
185. M.B. to Solomon Hyman, 23rd January 1769.
186. B. and F. to Sir John Goodricke, 16th December 1772.
187. B. and F. to J. C. Rigail and R. Roullard, 25th March 1772. The descriptions, in French, were a translation of the descriptions sent to Lord Cathcart on 30th October 1771.
188. B. and F. to William Matthews, 22nd April 1771, 4th May 1771, 6th May 1771, 16th May 1771, 4th June 1771. The consignment included a 'horizontal timepiece' (presumably a Venus vase), a three-branched Burgoyne's vase, a griffin vase, a sphinx vase, and sundry small vases and essence pots. Other vases, including a caryatic vase, a tea vase and a large medallion vase were to be sent but were held back.
189. B. and F. to G. Thompson Rowand, 6th December 1780. This was not the only occasion on which Boulton and Fothergill sent ormolu goods abroad on sale or return but it was done rarely, for obvious reasons: on this occasion the pieces were spoiled and had to be sold at reduced prices.
190. Lord Cathcart to B. and F., 21st February 1772. Timothy Raikes and James Saffree were import and export merchants. See Cross, *By the Banks of the Neva* (1997), p. 87.
191. J.F. to M.B., 16th December 1779. Lord Cathcart recommended William Porter as an agent to Wedgwood in 1771. See J. Cathcart to Wedgwood, 9th March 1771 (Wedgwood Museum, Wedgwood Mosley Collection, 1442). Porter was a Scottish merchant and was well established in St Petersburg. See Cross, *By the Banks of the Neva* (1997), pp. 35–6.
192. J.F. to M.B., 3rd April 1771. John Thomson was another Scottish merchant. See Cross, *By the Banks of the Neva* (1997), p. 71.
193. They were dealing with at least eleven agents there in 1780. See Robinson, 'Boulton and Fothergill 1762–82' (1959), p. 77.
194. Robinson, 'Boulton and Fothergill 1762–82' (1959), p. 77.
195. B. and F. to Moushin Pushkin, 15th October 1774.
196. Robinson, 'Boulton and Fothergill 1762–82' (1959), p. 72. Robinson suggests that these codes arose from the customers' desire to have exclusive patterns and from the firm's wish to conceal from one customer the sort of discount that it was allowing to another.
197. Ledger 1776–8, p. 17, 9th May 1776 '... for a siderial clock sent to ALQ £315'.
198. See Robinson, 'Boulton and Fothergill 1762–82' (1959), p. 72, where these two are identified.
199. J.F. to M.B., 20th May 1778.
200. I am grateful to Geoffrey de Bellaigue for making this suggestion and for supplying me with excerpts from *L'Avant Coureur* and *Mercure de France*, in which Grancher advertised his business. See de Bellaigue, *Waddesdon Manor: Furniture, Clocks and Gilt Bronzes* (1974), Vol. I, pp. 227–8, Vol. II, pp. 860–1; also Verlet, *Bronzes Dorés Français* (1987), pp. 444–5; Sargentson, *Merchants and Luxury Markets* (1996), pp. 119–27.
201. De Bellaigue, *Waddesdon Manor: Furniture, Clocks and Gilt Bronzes* (1974), Vol. I, p. 208; Verlet, *Bronzes Dorés Français* (1987), p. 444.
202. *L'Avant Coureur*, 28th December 1767.
203. *Mercure de France*, 30th November 1772.
204. Day Book, 1779–81, p. 648, 5th May 1781.
205. J.F. to M.B., 8th February 1764. The list was in addition to other merchants listed in Boulton's own memorandum book. See Quickenden, *Boulton and Fothergill Silver* (1989), p. 17.
206. B. and F. to James Cox, 31st July 1773.
207. B. and F. to William Lewis, 25th February 1774.
208. B. and F. to John le Coq, 6th July 1781 and 4th August 1781. Drawings were sent to le Coq with both letters. He had bought ormolu vases before, and returned two in 1771 (B. and F. to William Matthews, 27th November 1771).
209. Robinson, 'Boulton and Fothergill 1762–82' (1959), p. 69.
210. Robinson, 'Boulton and Fothergill 1762–82' (1959), p. 70.
211. Gill and Briggs, *History of Birmingham* (1952), Vol. 1, p. 113. The factors, who were commission agents, not only collected orders but also arranged or provided credit and saw to the problems of shipping and insurance.
212. There were seventy such merchants in Birmingham in 1770. See Gill and Briggs, *History of Birmingham* (1952), p. 114.
213. This subject is discussed by Robinson in 'Boulton and Fothergill 1762–82' (1959), pp. 74–5.
214. Day Book, 1779–81, p. 465, 24th October 1780, recording the sale to Capper, Palmer and Perkins of two Titus, two Cleopatra and two 'Bellizarius clock pieces' with 'a circle of stones' costing 18s. extra each.
215. B. and F. to Patrick Robertson, n.d. [between 5th and 9th November 1774].

NOTES TO SURVEY OF ORNAMENTS
Notes to pp. 181–364
Notes 1–713

1. I have made the assumption that the drawings of objects that are coloured with a wash clearly intended to indicate gold are of objects made in ormolu. In most cases there is little doubt. In one or two cases, however, e.g. the candlestick illustrated in Plate 127, the intention may have been to make the ornament in silver gilt. Patrons were sometimes offered the choice between ormolu and silver gilt when they were sent a design – e.g. B. and F. to the Duke of Ancaster, 11th July 1772 (ice pails); B. and F. to the Countess of Craven, 10th January 1776 (knife and cutlery cases).
2. First day, lot 4; second day, lot 10; third day, lot 4.
3. First day, lot 83; second day, lot 63.
4. First day, lots 9, 48; second day, lot 23.
5. Third day, lot 61.
6. B. and F. to William Matthews, 6th May 1771. They were probably sent to Holland with some of the other unsold pieces.
7. Mrs E. Montagu to M.B., 23rd January 1773.
8. B. and F. to Lord Arundell, 22nd March 1777; John Hodges to M.B., 23rd April 1777.
9. Lots 19, 66, 67, 68, 70.
10. Day Book, 1779–81, p. 649, 5th May 1781 – '1 pair triangular or moulu candlesticks 978002 – 189/– £9-9s-0d.'.
11. Inventory, 1782, pp. 180–1.
12. It is not impossible that this is a drawing for a silver gilt candlestick, and not ormolu at all. See note 1.
13. Lots 79, 124.
14. Day Book, 1779–81, p. 230, 1st May 1780 – '1 pair bronze figures Apollo & Diana with ormoulu branches for 3 lights, no. 975325, 30 guineas, £31-10s'.
15. Inventory, 1782, p. 134: the patterns were also recorded in the inventory (p. 94).
16. One of the most celebrated statues from antiquity was the Apollo Belvedere, which inspired large numbers of copyists. Boulton's Apollo owes some features to this famous statue, notably the left-looking stance with outstretched left arm, the bared chest and quiver strap, but differs too in many respects. See Haskell and Penny, *Taste and the Antique* (1981), pp. 148–51, Fig. 77.
17. They were sold at Christies (Hill Court), 13th December 1982, lot 53, and subsequently on 5th October 1991, lot 211, and 3rd July 1997, lot 10. The other pair were sold by Koller, 2nd December 1999, lot 1136, catalogued as 'spätes Louis XVI' with no hint of Apollo or Diana. They later appeared on the London market.
18. Snodin, 'Matthew Boulton's Sheffield Plate Catalogues' (1987), p. 25, Fig. 2.
19. Usually in relation to silver or plate versions – B. and F. to William Matthews, 22nd April 1771, B. and F. to Parker Wakelin, etc.
20. B. and F. to William Matthews, 13th February 1771. One candlestick was mislaid. B. and F. asked Matthews to look in his 'press' because that would be easier than to 'hunt all the shops' at Soho or to check all the entries in Matthews's account. They wanted the candlestick in order to 'clean it against the sale'.
21. First day, lot 83; second day, lot 63.
22. B. and F. to the Earl of Kerry, 7th December and 26th December 1771.
23. B. and F. to William Matthews, 27th April 1772.
24. They were sold as a pair by the executors of the late Countess of Sefton, Christie's, 19th June 1980, lot 5.
25. Quickenden, 'Lyon-Faced Candlesticks' (1999), p. 203 publishes a useful drawing showing the construction of one of these candlesticks.
26. B. and F. to the Duke of Marlborough, 22nd August 1772.
27. Pairs attributed to Boulton and Fothergill, with reason, include the pair at Soho House (City of Birmingham Museum and Art Gallery), exhibited in Mallett, 'The Age of Matthew Boulton' (2000), illustrated catalogue pp. 76–9; and a pair sold Christie's, Monaco, 28th–29th April 2000, lot 33, attributed in the catalogue to Gouthière.
28. Third day, lot 28.
29. British Library, Additional Manuscripts 41134, p. 94.
30. B. and F. to William Chambers, 23rd March 1773.
31. Christie's, 20th–22nd June 1796, lot 33. Lot 34 was 'a pair of ditto of Wedgwood's manufactory'.
32. Inventory, 1782, p. 93. They were valued at 8d. per pound and the value was 16s. 4d.
33. I am grateful to Brian and Robin Kern of Hotspur Ltd for sharing with me the results of the metallurgical tests carried out by Dr Peter Northover of the Department of Materials, Oxford University, in 1992. The figure was sold at Christie's, 11th December 1990, lot 89.
34. Sotheby's, New York, 9th December 1995, lot 102. Unfortunately I have not seen these figures, and cannot be confident about their attribution.
35. The same applies to a pair of bronzed tritons with candle nozzles similar to those in Wedgwood's sketch (Plate 45) sold Sotheby's, 10th November 1995, lot 146, and Christie's, New York, 21st October 1999, lot 138.
36. First day, lot 23, reserved at £12 12s. 0d; second day, lot 32, which is catalogued as a single piece but which judging from the reserve price of £12 12s. 0d. must have been a pair; third day, lot 45, reserved at £21, which although catalogued as a single piece was two pairs, as an annotation in the margin of the second catalogue makes clear.
37. Christie's, 20th November, lot 3 (Plate 140), the other candlestick through a London dealer.
38. Register Book (Great Tew Archive), 21st August 1770.
39. B. and F. to William Matthews, 6th May 1771.
40. Second day, lot 71, reserved at £12 12s. 0d.
41. B. and F. to William Matthews, 27th April 1772. See Appendix I.
42. Soane, *Lectures on Architecture* (ed. Bolton, 1929), p. 172.
43. Bolton, *Architecture of Robert and James Adam* (1922), p. 262; Harris, *Genius of Robert Adam* (2001), p. 78 and Plate 115.
44. Hussey, *English Country Houses: Mid-Georgian* (1963), p. 95, Plate 176; Harris, *Genius of Robert Adam* (2001), p. 102 and Plate 151.
45. Kelly, *Decorative Wedgwood in Architecture and Furniture* (1965), p. 65; *Book of English Fireplaces* (1968), pp. 62–3.
46. e.g. M.B. to Robert Mylne, 4th November 1775.
47. B. and F. to Sir Robert Cunliffe, 5th October and 18th October 1774.
48. B. and F. to Mayhew and Ince, 26th August 1771.
49. John Devall the elder (1701–74) and younger (1728–94) were well-known masons. Apart from large-scale building works they supplied statuary pieces, including chimneypieces, to many houses. The name was sometimes spelt Duval, as in Boulton and Fothergill's letter to Mayhew and Ince, 25th December 1771. See Gunnis, *Dictionary of British Sculptors* (1953), pp. 128–9. It was probably the younger man who was supplying the Earl of Kerry's chimneypiece.
50. B. and F. to the Earl of Kerry, 7th December 1771.
51. B. and F. to Mayhew and Ince, 25th December 1771.
52. B. and F. to the Earl of Kerry, 29th December 1771.
53. B. and F. to the Earl of Kerry, 5th March 1772.
54. Thomas Pownall to M.B., 8th September 1769.
55. Joseph Dyott was probably related to Boulton, whose grandfather married Elizabeth Dyott. He set up in London as a retailer in 1778 and offered Boulton his assistance and some space in his warehouse (John Stuart to M.B., 7th January 1778).
56. John Hodges to M.B., 1st May 1780.
57. Inventory, 1782, pp. 133–4.
58. The movement is stamped 16731/Lepine/Paris/14/4/62/2Medaille d'or/Paris 1827. The clock was sold Christie's, 17th November 1994, lot 7.
59. B. and F. to Samuel Pechell, 11th December 1771.
60. B. and F. to Lord Arundell, 14th July 1777.
61. John Hodges to M.B., 31st January 1778.
62. Lots 118, 119.
63. Day Book, 1779–81, p. 465, 24th October 1780.
64. Lot 120: reserve price £12 12s. 0d.
65. Lots 56, 73: reserve price £18.

66. Wedgwood to Bentley, 25th October 1776 (E25-18707).
67. e.g. John Whitehurst to M.B., 16th June 1771 (two vase clocks); B. and F. to John Whitehurst, 7th May 1772 (one), 22nd September 1774 (six), 19th October 1774 (six, to be fitted in 'metal vase bodies').
68. e.g. Journal, 1776–81, pp. 88, 564, 30th April 1776 and 6th August 1778; Journal, 1778–81, p. 238, 23rd November 1779.
69. Holywell lived at Soho, and debits in the Ledger, 1776–8, include rent for his house, etc. Whitehurst continued to advise Boulton after 1775 and to procure movements for him on occasion (e.g. B. and F. to John Whitehurst, 20th October 1778). Furthermore his workshop in Derby remained active: the Ledger, 1776–8, p. 88, records that two of the movements supplied by Holywell for Venus clocks on 30th April 1776 came from Whitehurst.
70. B. and F. to William Matthews, 16th May 1771.
71. e.g. Journal, 1776–8, pp. 64, 121, 25th March and 18th June 1776.
72. e.g. Ledger, 1776–8, pp. 174, 214, 9th September and 30th December 1776; Inventory, 1782, p. 83.
73. Day Book, 1779–81, p. 648, 5th May 1781.
74. B. and F. to Thomas Wright, 15th July 1773: Wright not only took three years to complete the two movements but even tried to charge Boulton and Fothergill for the King's movement.
75. John Hodges to M.B., n.d. [probably September 1780].
76. B. and F. to John Whitehurst, 20th October 1778.
77. Wedgwood to Bentley, 14th July 1776 (E25-18684).
78. B. and F. to Captain Arthur, 16th August 1781.
79. J.F. to M.B., 20th May 1778.
80. Gibbon, *Decline and Fall of the Roman Empire* (1898), Vol. IV.
81. Gibbon, *Decline and Fall of the Roman Empire* (1898), Vol. IV, p. 430.
82. See Smith, 'The Suffering Hero' (1989).
83. Day Book, 1779–81, p. 465, 24th October 1780.
84. Day Book, 1779–81, p. 647, 5th May 1781.
85. Inventory, 1782, pp. 133, 156. The plinth (p. 133) measured 10 x 6.5 inches and was valued at 13s. The clock (p. 156) was valued at £26 5s. 0d.
86. First day, lot 88.
87. B. and F. to William Matthews, 6th May 1771.
88. B. and F. to William Matthews, 24th June 1772. The clock is previously referred to in B. and F. to William Matthews, 19th April 1772. Both letters talk of the missing key and advise Matthews to have it made in London.
89. Sold Christie's, 17th November 1994, lot 45.
90. Lot 121.
91. Lot 116.
92. I am grateful to the late Prince Philipp of Hesse-Cassel for his advice on the likely buyer of the clock and for helping me with other queries.
93. M.B. to John Whitehurst, 23rd February 1771.
94. Some of his designs are given in his *Select Mechanical Exercises* (1775), pp. 11ff.
95. Ferguson (1710–76) bought John Senex's (d.1740) copper globe plates and moulds etc. at auction when Mary Senex gave up her late husband's business in October 1755. Ferguson set himself up as Senex's successor in the Strand, but did not stick to globe making, and by July 1757 the business had been sold to Benjamin Martin. See Taylor, *Mathematical Practitioners of Hanoverian England* (1966), p. 176, Millburn; 'James Ferguson's Lecture Tour of the English Midlands' (1985), p. 402.
96. M.B. to John Whitehurst, 23rd February 1771.
97. e.g. de Bellaigue, *Waddesdon Manor: Furniture, Clocks and Gilt Bronzes* (1974), Vol. I, p. 295.
98. See note 95.
99. M.B. to Lord Cathcart, 30th October 1771. A French translation of this description was sent on 25th March 1772 to J. C. Rigail and R. Roulland in Amsterdam.
100. Henderson, *Life of James Ferguson* (1867), p. 268: according to Henderson, Whitehurst gave Ferguson 'several curious papers and drawings of escapements, pendulums and hydraulic engines'.
101. White, 'The Whitehurst Family' (1958), says that in 1925 he saw some correspondence between Ferguson and Whitehurst which included '20 or so beautifully executed coloured drawings of clock parts, such as escapements, complicated astronomical movements and perpetual calendars'. These drawings, all signed by Whitehurst, were sold to a buyer in America and have disappeared.
102. John Whitehurst to James Beresford, Bewdley, 9th December 1771, quoted in Millburn, 'James Ferguson's Lecture Tour of the English Midlands' (1985), p. 414.
103. The wheel count is: escape wheel 30, pinion 6, third wheel 72, pinion 7, centre wheel 70, pinion 12, intermediate wheel 84, pinion 18, great wheel 96.
104. The description of 30th October 1771 omitted to mention this.
105. John Whitehurst to M.B., 11th February 1772; M.B. to Mr Weston, 11th March 1772.
106. M.B. to John Whitehurst, 2nd December 1771.
107. M.B. to John Whitehurst, 26th August 1771 – 'we have not yet received the glass globes but expect them every day and as soon as they arrive will send them'.
108. M.B. to John Whitehurst, 2nd December 1771.
109. John Whitehurst to M.B., 11th February 1772.
110. John Whitehurst to M.B., 12th February 1772.
111. Taylor, *Mathematical Practitioners of Hanoverian England* (1966), p. 208.
112. Science Museum, London: the advertised diameters were 3, 9, 12 and 15 inches. Boulton's specification of a 6-inch or 8-inch globe, and the likely request by Whitehurst for a globe slightly exceeding 6 inches, bore no relation to the standard sizes of Senex's globes, which were 3, 9, 12, 17 and 28 inches. It was unreasonable to expect a globe maker to incur the expense of drawing and engraving new copper plates for unusual sized gores. In a letter to me John Millburn has said that it is unlikely that 6-inch globes were available before about 1775. He suggests that Hill may have produced the globe by doubling the dimensions on the plates for a 3-inch globe. He argues that the latter were generally nearer 2.75 inches than 3 inches, which could account for the actual measurement of 5.6 inches.
113. M.B.'s Notebook, 1772, p. 11: this was the value that Boulton put on the clock when he was thinking of sending it to Russia. The note was probably made in response to Lord Cathcart's letter of 21st February 1772 enquiring about the price.
114. M.B. to his wife, n.d. [11th April 1772].
115. Lord Cathcart to M.B., 21st February 1772.
116. That it was his declared intention to send the clocks to Russia is confirmed by a letter from Wedgwood to Bentley dated 18th April 1772 (E25-18367).
117. M.B.'s Notebook, 1772, p. 1 – 'Memorandum to write to Whitehurst to make 2d and minutes'. The note about minutes refers to the sidereal clock.
118. B. and F. to John Whitehurst, 7th May 1772.
119. John Whitehurst to M.B., 12th May 1772. Ferguson, *Select Mechanical Exercises* (1775), p. 11, stated that 'seconds are of very little use in common clocks not made for astronomical observations; and table clocks never have them'. He probably influenced the decision not to fit a seconds' movement in the first place.
120. B. and F. to John Whitehurst, 25th June 1772.
121. J.F. to M.B., 20th March 1774.
122. The inside of the backplate of the movement is incised 'JW Derby cleaned Nov 24 1810'. The Whitehurst clockmaking business was then in the hands of John Whitehurst's nephew, also John.
123. There are drawings of the double-acting crank engine supplied to them, dated 1822 with later modifications in 1866–70, in the Boulton and Watt papers (Central Library, Birmingham).
124. M.B. to his wife, n.d. [3rd March 1770].
125. M.B. to J.F., n.d. [4th March 1770].
126. Thomas Wright (fl. 1770–d. 1792) was, according to Baillie, *Watchmakers and Clockmakers of the World* (1951), Watchmaker to the King. Baillie's source was probably Britten, *Old Clocks and Watches and their*

Makers (1911), in which it is recorded that the words 'Maker to the King' appear on one of Wright's bracket clocks. Wright's workshop was in Poultry.
127. M.B. to his wife, 6th March 1770.
128. B. and F. to Thomas Wright, 17th January 1771.
129. B. and F. to William Matthews, 17th January 1771. Chambers is also mentioned in the letter to Wright dated 14th February 1771, which is quoted below.
130. B. and F. to William Matthews, 14th February 1771.
131. B. and F. to Thomas Wright, 14th February 1771.
132. B. and F. to William Matthews, n.d. [26th February 1771].
133. William Matthews to M.B., 6th March 1771.
134. B. and F. to William Matthews, 16th March 1771.
135. B. and F. to William Matthews, 21st March 1771.
136. B. and F. to William Matthews, 23rd March 1771.
137. B. and F. to William Matthews, 27th March 1771.
138. J.F. to M.B., 4th April 1771.
139. Royal Collection, Inventory no. 30028.
140. It was illustrated by Pyne, *Buckingham House* (1819) on the mantelpiece in the Crimson Drawing Room in a print dated 1817 (Royal Collection, Stable Yard House).
141. Pictorial Inventory, Vol. B, no. 26 (Royal Collection, Stable Yard House). The removal of the clock to Windsor is recorded in Jutsham Deliveries, Vol. III (1820–30), p. 170, as 'No. 32 A spring clock, name Wright, in a Derbyshire spar case. From Buckingham House, but lastly from the stores at St James's, under the care of Mr Vulliamy' (26th January 1829). The entry is annotated 'Intended for Windsor Castle. Sent there by Mr Vulliamy by His Majesty's command given through me BJ no. 29. See Query Book [i.e. the Pictorial Inventory] Page 26' (Royal Collection, Stable Yard House). The King's vases and the sphinx vases went to Windsor at the same time.
142. B. and F. to Thomas Wright, 17th January 1771.
143. B. and F. to William Matthews, 16th February 1771.
144. B. and F. to Thomas Wright, 14th February 1771.
145. B. and F. to William Matthews, 26th February 1771.
146. William Matthews to M.B., 6th March 1771.
147. B. and F. to William Matthews, 27th April 1772.
148. J.F. to M.B., 28th March 1772.
149. Lot 74: the reserve price was £35.
150. Inventory, 1782, p. 83: '3 King's clock cases imperfect, 90lb 12 oz waste @ 8d. £3 0s. 6d.'; p. 180: '1 clock case with clock, King's pattern £40', the value being reduced to £31 10s. 0d. because most of the ormolu pieces had been in stock for many years and were damaged.
151. The signatures inside the clock are as follows:
(a) Inside the back plate: E. G. Dawes (?) 28th Dec. 99; John Watson 1802; Rd Warner Jan. 1822 and Jan. 1824; T. Mills, Gloucester, 1839; W. Husband 16th May 1933, 1934.
(b) Inside the front plate: F. St C. R. 4th Aug. 1902, 4th Nov. 1910. (c) Behind the dial plate: Smith 25th Jan.92; R. Jones 23rd Aug. 1814; Davison 8th Mar. 1814; R. Boundy 30th Mar. 1820; William Husband 1934, 38.
(d) On the going barrel: R. Smith 5th Aug. 1799; J. Davison 8th Mar. 1814; Rob – (?).
(e) On the striking barrel: S. (?) Smith 6th Nov. 93 (cleaned); G. Grimson 22nd Dec. 1796; Rob – (?). Daniel Parkes has suggested that the large number of signatures probably indicates provincial work. Baillie, *Watchmakers and Clockmakers of the World* (1951), is of no help in identifying any of the repairers.
152. B. and F. to John Whitehurst in London, 20th October 1778.
153. The name occurs frequently in Birmingham directories of the period and the indenture of a John Whitehouse as an apprentice at Soho, dated 8th March 1767, is preserved in the Boulton archives.
154. M.B.'s Notebook, 1763–8, 30th January 1765: 'paid Mr. Whitehous of Derby for a wheel barometer…'.
155. B. and F. to John Whitehurst, 20th October 1778.
156. I am grateful to Daniel Parkes for this information.
157. Britten, *Old Clocks and Watches and their Makers* (1911), p. 720.
158. Colvin, *Biographical Dictionary of English Architects* (1995), p. 60.
159. The letters survive in the Boulton and Watt papers, Central Library, Birmingham.
160. B. and F. to William Matthews, 27th April 1772.
161. B. and F. to William Matthews, 24th June 1772.
162. A 'Mr Amiens' visited Soho on 16th July 1770 (Register Book, Great Tew Archive).
163. Second day, lot 93.
164. The second copy of the catalogue gives the proceeds as £165, but this must have been an error for 165 guineas. The buyer was Morgan, who was probably a dealer.
165. M.B. to Lord Cathcart, St Petersburg, 30th October 1771. The lines are taken from Virgil, *Aeneid* X.467–9.
166. B. and F. to William Matthews, 27th April 1772 – '1 Minerva' is listed among the items to be returned.
167. M.B.'s Notebook, 1772, p. 11 – 'Minerva with an 8 day repeating clock – 90 guineas. To the Empress'. This note was probably made in response to Lord Cathcart's letter of 21st February 1772 asking for the prices of the clocks described by Boulton in his letter of 30th October 1771.
168. Lot 125. The catalogue entry calls the boy a 'genii' and spells '*vitae*' correctly.
169. John Hodges to M.B., 8th June 1778 – 'all the ormulu goods are arrived [i.e. back from London] except the King's clock case and Minerva'.
170. Inventory, 1782 p. 133. Also listed in the inventory were 'Dial plates and fingers for 2 Minerva movements £0 10s. 0d.' (p. 94), '1 small figure of Minerva 9d.' (p. 133).
171. The aegis was given to Athena (Minerva) by Zeus. Homer, *Iliad* V.741, relates that it was a golden tasselled goatskin with a gorgon's head. The gorgon's head was given to Athena by Perseus. It is shown on 6th-century BC vases fringed with snakes and covered with scales and, towards the end of the century, with the gorgon's head. Probably the best known classical model of the aegis was on the chryselephantine statue made by Phidias for the Parthenon in Athens, known only through a Roman copy, which appears to have had both a gorgon's head and snakes. See Carpenter, *Art and Myth in Ancient Greece* (1991), figs. 73, 85, 300.
172. Sold from the collection of Sir Michael Sobell, Christie's, 23rd June 1994.
173. The scroll was shown in a photograph of the clock when it was in the possession of the London dealer Moss Harris.
174. Exhibited Mallett 'The Age of Matthew Boulton' (2000), illustrated in the catalogue pp. 58–61.
175. Sold Sotheby's, 20th November 1981, lot 86; Sotheby's, New York, 5th–6th December 1991 (Keck Collection), lot 15.
176. Sold Auktionsverkets, Stockholm, 11th–14th April 1978, lot 145.
177. Lots 55, 78.
178. Day Book, 1779–81, p. 648 (5th May 1781).
179. Inventory, 1782, p. 156.
180. Inventory, 1782, pp. 133–4.
181. Probably William Small.
182. M.B. to John Whitehurst, 23rd February 1771.
183. B. and F. to John Whitehurst, 26th August 1771.
184. The motto is a misquotation of Virgil, *Georgics* II.490 – '*Felix qui potuit rerum cognoscere causas*', a reference to the poet Lucretius who expounded the Epicurean philosophy of materialism in his poem *De Rerum Natura*.
185. The words 'gilt … enamel' are deleted in the MS.
186. The words 'upon … blue' are deleted in the MS.
187. John Harrison (1693–1776) won the Board of Longitude's prize of £20,000 for an accurate marine timekeeper. His fourth and prize-winning chronometer was tested on voyages in 1761 and 1764. See R. T. Gould, *The Marine Chronometer: its History and Development* (London 1923); H. Quill, *John Harrison* (London 1966); W. J. H. Andrewes (ed.), *The Quest for Longitude* (Harvard 1996).
188. M.B. to Lord Cathcart, 30th October 1771.
189. M.B. to John Whitehurst,

2nd December 1771.
190. B. and F. to John Whitehurst, 6th February 1772.
191. Weston made the dial. He also made the dials of the geographical and King's clocks.
192. John Whitehurst to M.B., 12th February 1772 – 'I must confess I was much distressed about the plates not coming, nor do I think it proper to make the star plate of common cast brass, therefore wrote immediately to Soho to desire a plate of — — [?] gilt metal'. Whitehurst also said in this letter that Weston was sending 'the head for the syderial clock'. He received the plates a month later (John Whitehurst to M.B., 12th March 1772).
193. M.B. to J.F., 23rd January 1772.
194. M.B. to John Scale, 31st March 1772.
195. This probably accounts for the deletions in the description sent to Lord Cathcart. See notes 185 and 186.
196. The glass is a recent replacement, following the breakage of the original glass during a burglary at Soho House in 2000.
197. Ferguson's manuscript instructions include a scale diagram (Great Tew Archive). They are undated, but were written between 1773 and 1776. The present glass is a replacement but the horizon is an accurate reproduction of the original, thanks particularly to the survival of Ferguson's drawing.
198. In his instructions Ferguson said that 'the word Zenith [the zenith of St Petersburg] may be written on the glass, and likewise the four words *Oriens*, *Meridies*, *Occidens*, *Septentro* for East, West, South, North'. Boulton, or more probably Whitehurst, must have decided not to complicate still further an already complex dial.
199. Ferguson's manuscript concludes with the observation; 'the north point of the horizon is 60 degrees from the Pole A [i.e. the centre of the dial which represents the North Pole] and the south point is 120 degrees from it, the east and west points 90'.
200. The precise sidereal day contains 23 hours, 56 minutes and 4.1 seconds.
201. John Whitehurst to James Beresford, Bewdley, 9th December 1771, quoted in Millburn, 'James Ferguson's Lecture Tour' (1985), p. 414.
202. The hinged door on the back of the body of the clock has lost its lock and the original decorative key hole cover. The four small holes visible in Plate 180 were presumably the fixing holes for the lock.
203. Jennifer Montagu has pointed out to me that John Croker's medal of Newton (1726) has a similarly winged female figure holding a simplified plan of what looks like the solar system, with Virgil's line reduced to '*Felix cognoscere causas*'. Croker (1670–1741) was chief engraver to the Royal Mint from 1705. Perhaps his medal provides a clue to the source of Boulton's plaque. Personifications of Science and Mathematics were shown in source books on iconography with wings on their temples or heads – see Ripa, *Iconologia* (1645), Book 3, p. 554, which shows a woodcut in which Scienza holds a mirror in her right hand and a globe and a triangle in her left. An English edition of this influential book was published in London in 1709 (ed. P. Tempest), in which Science is described on p. 67 and illustrated in Fig. 269. (I am grateful to Jennifer Montagu for these references.) In Richardson, *Iconology* (1779), Vol. I, Plate XXXIV, Fig. 132, Mathematics is shown with wings on her head and is accompanied by an armillary sphere. She applies a pair of compasses to a scroll held by a naked child 'whom she seems to be instructing' (Vol. I, p. 71). Boulton was a subscriber to Richardson's book.
204. M.B.'s Notebook, 1772, p. 11: this was the value that Boulton put on the clock when he was thinking of sending it to Russia earlier in the year. The note was probably made after receiving Lord Cathcart's letter of 21st February 1772 enquiring about the price.
205. B. and F. to John Whitehurst, 7th May 1772.
206. John Whitehurst to M.B., 12th May 1772.
207. He seems to have told others of his intention besides his wife. Wedgwood wrote to Bentley on 18th April 1772 (E25-18367) that he wished Boulton 'success with his clocks at St Petersburg'.
208. Fothergill was hoping for a reward in the shape of orders for other goods.
209. J.F. to M.B., 2nd March 1773.
210. J.F. to M.B., 10th March 1773.
211. J.F. to M.B., 20th March 1774. The second clock was the geographical clock.
212. Diary of the Hon. Mrs Charles Yorke, 6th September 1775 (Wimpole Family Papers): I am grateful to John Hardy for supplying me with this reference.
213. Some of the alterations made at this time can be deduced from the movement. Before the minute hand was added there would have been little of the movement in front of the front plate, and the large holes cut in it would not have been there. Before the alterations the movement would indeed have had 'fewer wheels than a common 8-day clock'. The first intermediate wheel appears to have been moved about three-eighths of an inch. This may have been connected with alterations to the pendulum. The description sent to Lord Cathcart in October 1771 mentioned a standard pendulum of 39.2 inches (i.e. a seconds' pendulum) 'prepared in such a manner as not to contract by cold or expand by heat'. The present pendulum is a crude piece of work, quite uncharacteristic of Whitehurst's usual refinement, with a large leaden bob and a wooden rod. It measures 27.18 inches and beats seventy-two times per minute. There is no reason to doubt that originally the clock had a compensated seconds pendulum, and the thirty-tooth escape wheel perhaps supports this theory. But if it did, the clock must have stood on a stand that allowed the pendulum to protrude below the case. Perhaps, before sending it to Russia, and realising it would go without a stand, Whitehurst substituted a shorter pendulum that fitted into the case. This may account for the moving of the intermediate wheel and a change in the wheel counts. But if this theory is right, surely the present crude pendulum must have been put in later. Maybe Whitehurst's shorter pendulum was lost on the way to, or the way back from Russia or during the move to Great Tew in the nineteenth century.
214. B. and F. to John Whitehurst, 1st October 1774: the lost parts were 'the brass plate and the stays'.
215. Ledger, 1776–8, p. 17, 9th May 1776 – 'General a/c Sales for a siderial clock sent to ALQ £315'. There is an entry in the same Ledger, p. 214, 31st December 1776, which probably refers to a repair carried out before the clock was sent – 'By Profit & Loss, for gilding a figure over again for siderial clock £3. 4s. 0d.'.
216. William Porter to B. and F., 29th October 1779: see next note.
217. J.F. to M.B., 16th December 1779. Fothergill enclosed a copy of Porter's letter.
218. B. and F. to William Porter, 18th April 1781.
219. William Porter & Co. to M.B., 2nd November 1787: Cabrit forwarded the letter to Boulton on 12th December. Porter sent the clock from Cronstedt to Boulton's usual shippers in Hull, J. and C. Broadley, on board the 'Nottingham'.
220. M.B. Notebook 84, p. 8, 14th October 1799.
221. The pedestal may well have been designed for a different purpose, appropriate as it looks under the clock. It was extended at some point at the back by about 2¼ inches. The extension has been cut subsequently to accommodate a skirting board. Giles Ellwood, 'James Newton', *Furniture History* Vol. XXXI (1995), p. 137, suggests that the pedestal was 'almost certainly' supplied to Boulton by Newton, a London cabinet maker, in 1797, but no account survives.
222. Christie's Sale Catalogue, Tew Park, Great Tew, 27th–29th May 1987. The clock, on its simulated oak stand and without the six urns, was illustrated in Christopher Hussey, 'Great Tew, Oxfordshire II', *Country Life*, 22 July 1949, p. 257.
223. B. and F. to Samuel Pechell, 11th December 1771.
224. B. and F. to Samuel Pechell, 18th January 1772.
225. Samuel Pechell to M.B., 8th April 1772. Boulton wrote to Fothergill from London a few days earlier to say that Pechell had given him a week to complete the clock and that Fothergill was to send it and not 'let it be delayed by any of Duval's schemes for

fastening the watch', M.B. to J.F., n.d. [received 9th April 1772].
226. B. and F. to William Matthews, 15th April 1772.
227. B. and F. to William Matthews, 18th June 1772.
228. B. and F. to Samuel Pechell, 17th September 1772. Pechell had asked for it to be delivered to Cailland in his letter of 8th April. The two men seem to have been near neighbours in George Street, Hanover Square.
229. B. and F. to Samuel Pechell, 17th September 1772.
230. The original source of this tradition is Suetonius's *De Vita Caesarum*, Titus, 8, which was written in the second century AD.
231. B. and F. to William Matthews, 8th April 1772.
232. B. and F. to William Matthews, 9th April 1772. The doubt about the size of the door was probably because the movement had not been chosen.
233. M.B. to his wife, n.d. [11th April 1772].
234. Vulliamy's Clock Book 1797–1806, British Horological Institute.
235. Public Record Office, C104-58, p. 232.
236. M.B. to John Scale, 31st March 1772.
237. J.F. to M.B., 22nd May 1772.
238. B. and F. to Henry Hoare, 27th October 1772. The clock is mentioned again in J.F. to M.B., 27th January 1773. It cost £23 12s. 6d.
239. Mrs Montagu asked Boulton to remember 'the clock case' in a letter dated 20th October 1772.
240. M.B. to Mrs E. Montagu, 14th December 1772.
241. Mrs E. Montagu to M.B., 23rd January 1773. The final sentiment was probably provoked by the news that Fordyce's banking business had crashed and that Boulton had had money deposited with it.
242. Sold Sotheby's, 9th June 1978, lot 103, Christie's, 7th November 1988, lot 24.
243. The movement of the watch in one of them is signed 'Harrison Audlem no. 114'. The other case was sold Christie's, 29th March 1984, lot 16. The urn was fitted with square handles and a lid that look like later additions.
244. Lots 96, 117.
245. His code name was 'Panza': J.F. to M.B., 20th May 1778.
246. Day Book, 1779–81, p. 465, 24th October 1780.
247. Inventory, 1782, p. 133: it was valued at £8 8s. od.
248. This clock case can be seen in an illustration in Philippe Jullian, 'Fasanerie', *Connaissance des Arts*, November 1965, p. 111.
249. Mrs E. Montagu to M.B., 16th January 1773.
250. Lots 95, 122. The first was bought in, the second sold to 'Fitzgerald' for eighteen guineas.
251. The other Urania with a bronzed figure was sold Sotheby's, 19th November 1987, lot 5. Its globe was missing. The gilt Urania was illustrated in Goodison, 'Urania Observed' (1985), p. 242. The figure may originally have been bronzed: the globe has been replaced.
252. Inventory, 1782, p. 156.
253. First day, lot 85; second day, lot 68; third day, lot 81.
254. The entries do not exactly correspond and the accentuation of the Greek words is eccentric. This is the lot sold on the second day.
255. The third, booked to 'Mr Price' at £26 5s. od., appears not to have been a genuine sale (B. and F. to William Matthews, 6th May 1771 – 'A Venus clock £26 5s. od.'). It was probably the clock sent to Amsterdam with several other unsold pieces in June (B. and F. to William Matthews, 4th June 1771).
256. Sold Christie's, 26th February 1954, lot 112; exhibited Lunar Society Exhibition, City Museum and Art Gallery, Birmingham, 1966, Catalogue no. 102; Mallett, 'The Age of Matthew Boulton', (2000) pp. 48–9.
257. Presumably the globe for the geographical clock.
258. B. and F. to John Whitehurst, 30th April 1772.
259. M.B. to his wife, n.d. [11th April 1772].
260. M.B.'s Diary, 1772 – 'Sir Harbord Harbord, 1 Venus clock £21 os. od.'.
261. B. and F. to Lord Sefton, 29th October 1772.
262. B. and F. to William Matthews, 19th November 1772. Boulton and Fothergill planned to send it to Paris and Matthews was debited £25 1s. od.
263. Journal, 1776–8, p. 88, 30th April 1776. The clockmaker William Holywell was credited as follows: 'April 6th 2 Venus clocks finished only by Holywell, the movements he says came from Whitehurst £5 5s. od; April 20th A Venus clock £4 4s. od.'
264. John Hodges to M.B., 31st January 1778.
265. Day Book, 1781, p. 647, 5th May 1781.
266. Inventory, 1782, p. 156.
267. Wedgwood to Bentley, 14th July 1776 (E25-18684).
268. B. and F to Corson and Pountney, Wolverhampton, 27th April 1771.
269. B. and F. to Jefferys and Drury, 23rd September 1771.
270. Samuel Wyatt to M.B., 31st July 1765.
271. Samuel Wyatt to Lord Scarsdale, 21st December 1765 (Kedleston Papers 5/158).
272. Samuel Wyatt to M.B., 6th March 1766.
273. Samuel Wyatt to M.B., 12th June 1766.
274. This amount probably also covered some sconces and nails ordered by Samuel Wyatt at the same time as the door escutcheons. Further payments to Boulton of £1 2s. od. and £7 6s. od. are recorded in the ledgers on 29th October 1770 and 13th February 1776. I am grateful to Leslie Harris for noting these references.
275. Ledger 1776–8, p. 174, an entry dated 6th September 1776 'for an or moulu scutcheon sent Blockley £1 2s. od.'. Other sales of door furniture to retailers may of course be concealed under such general descriptions as 'Goods', which appear often in letters, ledger entries, etc. Bent was supplied with various goods from Soho between 1762 and 1772, most of which are unspecified.
276. Goodison, 'The Door Furniture at Ely House' (1970).
277. Earl of Shelburne to M.B., 8th December 1773.
278. B. and F. to Lord Arundell, 13th November 1777.
279. Lord Arundell to M.B., 3rd September 1773. Paine had seen and ordered the patterns 'a great while ago'.
280. B. and F. to Lord Arundell, 16th July 1778.
281. B. and F. to Mayhew and Ince, 11th August 1783.
282. Mrs Montagu to M.B., 22nd November 1779, and other letters.
283. Inventory 1782, p. 181.
284. Inventory 1782, p. 133.
285. F. Eginton to M.B., 23rd April 1777 (Great Tew Archive).
286. Inventory 1782, p. 206.
287. M.B.'s Diary, 1772.
288. B. and F. to the Earl of Sefton, 19th May 1772; B. and F. to William Matthews, 28th November 1772.
289. pp. 180, 83.
290. Reilly, *Wedgwood* (1989), Vol. I, Plates 544, 544A, Colour Plate 78. Wedgwood's mask is also of a horned and bearded satyr. Boulton and Fothergill used the device also in designs for silver jugs – Pattern Book 1, p. 81, Rowe, *Adam Silver* (1965), Plates 40, 41.
291. Sold Christie's, 17th–21st September 1973, lot 115 (Executors of the late Countess of Sefton), and again Sotheby's, 1st December 1978, lot 143 (Gerald Hochschild Collection). They are illustrated in Lennox-Boyd (ed.), *Masterpieces of English Furniture: the Gerstenfeld Collection* (1998), Plate 128.
292. The pair were catalogued and illustrated in Anna Maria Massinelli, *The Gilbert Collection: Hardstones* (London 2000), pp. 196–7, catalogue no. 84, where they were wrongly described as being the Earl of Sefton's ewers. The single ewer was illustrated in Goodison, 'Matthew Boulton's Ornamental Ormolu' (1971), p. 1136, Fig. 6.
293. B. and F. to the Duke of Richmond, 9th January 1773.
294. B. and F. to the Duke of Richmond, 10th June 1773.
295. B. and F. to William Matthews, 1st April 1773.
296. See Goodison, 'The Victoria and Albert Museum's Collection of Metal-Work Pattern Books' (1975). These pattern books include a wide variety of handles, escutcheons, castors, etc. for furniture and several sets of commode mounts.
297. Sketchley and Adams, *Tradesman's True Guide* (1770), p. 10.
298. I have suggested earlier that one was

William Tovey (see Chapter 2, p. 34).
299. James Stuart to M.B., 26th December 1769.
300. B. and F. to Mayhew and Ince, 9th January 1771, 5th January 1776.
301. B. and F. to Mayhew and Ince, 14th October 1772.
302. Ledger, 1776–8, p. 103, 25th May 1776 ('knife case furniture'); Day Book, 1779–81, p. 28, 4th November 1779. 'To sundry ormoulu mounts and 1 centrepiece for 2 wood vases £1 13s. od.'. Dudley is recorded in directories as working at 1 New Meeting Street in 1770, 69 High Street in 1773 and 8 New Street in 1781.
303. Ledger, 1776–8, p. 2, 12th February 1776; Cash Debtor Book, 1772–82, 9th February 1776.
304. Charles Pelham to M.B., 28th January 1777.
305. B. and F. to Charles Pelham, 13th March 1777.
306. B. and F. to Charles Pelham, 16th April 1777. Pelham gave a further order for 'ornaments' in 1778, which cost £12 13s. 10d; B. and F. to Mrs Pelham, 10th January 1778; B. and F. to Charles Pelham, 24th February 1778.
307. It may have been among the furniture sold by the Earl of Yarborough from 17 Arlington Street in 1929. The sale at Christie's on 11th July 1929, for example, included several ormolu-mounted commodes, but all were catalogued as 'Louis XV' or 'Louis XVI'.
308. Some decades ago it was customary to attribute the finest mounts to Boulton. Thus Osbert Sitwell, *Left Hand Right Hand* (1957), p. 244, describes the Renishaw commode as executed by Chippendale and Haigh with ormolu mountings by Matthew Boulton. He was echoing a common habit in the antiques trade.
309. Most of the correspondence with Seddon and with his partner in the glass trade, John Mackintosh, is recorded in the Letter Books for 1777–82, 1780–1, and 1781–3, and in the Mrs Montagu Box.
310. Z. Walker to M.B., 10th December 1765.
311. Most of Boulton and Fothergill's letters to Mayhew and Ince were reproduced in full by Boynton in 'An Ince and Mayhew Correspondence' (1966), pp. 23–6.
312. Victoria and Albert Museum, Accession no. W43-1949.
313. e.g. McQuoid and Edwards, *Dictionary of English Furniture* (1954), s.v. 'Cabinets', Plate VI opposite p. 191; Harris, *Furniture of Robert Adam* (1963), Plate 41; Boynton, 'Italian Craft in an English Cabinet' (1966); Baker and Richardson, *A Grand Design* (1997), pp. 322–3.
314. The signature '*Baccio Cappelli fecit Fiorenza anno 1709*' is scratched on the back of the central upright panel.
315. An error.
316. B. and F. to William Ince, 3rd December 1774.
317. B. and F. to Mayhew and Ince, 6th April 1775.
318. B. and F. to Mayhew and Ince, 28th June 1775.
319. B. and F. to Mayhew and Ince, 16th October 1775. Boulton and Fothergill also charged £3 3s. od. for a framed drawing, presumably of the cabinet, which was sent to the Duchess in 1774.
320. B. and F. to Mayhew and Ince, 8th December 1775, 5th January 1776. The two firms' collusion came to grief because the Duke appears to have seen both bills (B. and F. to William Matthews, 9th November 1776, in which the original charge was given as £75 1s. od.).
321. B. and F. to Mayhew and Ince, 8th December 1775.
322. B. and F. to Mayhew and Ince, 23rd February 1776, 23rd March 1776.
323. B. and F. to Mayhew and Ince, 6th March 1779, 11th August 1783, 6th December 1784.
324. Kimbolton Inventory, March 1790, County Record Office, Huntingdon, Manchester Collection, Accession no. 255.
325. Baker and Richardson, *A Grand Design* (1997), p. 323. The Victoria and Albert Museum bought the cabinet in 1949.
326. M.B.'s Notebook, 1768–75, p. 120: he was also considering mounts of brass and platinum. No study has yet been made of Boulton and Fothergill's japanned ware, which included trays, tea tables and knife cases. Some of the pieces were supplied by the japanner Henry Clay, the inventor of *papier mâché*, who trained as a japanner with John Baskerville and patented his paperboard process in 1772: see Gill and Briggs, *History of Birmingham* (1952), Vol. 1, p. 102; Court, *Rise of the Midlands Industries* (1938), pp. 233ff.
327. Inventory, 1782, p. 83: they were valued at 2s. 6d.
328. 'Statement of the cost of an or moulu table made for M. Boulton by Mr John Hodges.'
329. B. Wyatt account book – half a day 'polishing a marble table', August 1798, and two days 'altering a marble slab for side table', September 1798. I am grateful to Rita McLean for drawing my attention to these entries. She has also found an account from James Newton, the London cabinet maker (see p. 393, note 221) who supplied furniture to Soho House, in August 1798 for 'a damasked leather cover for a marble slab'.
330. Great Tew Archive.
331. It can be seen in the corner of the dining room in the catalogue of Christie's sale at Tew Park, 27th–29th May 1987, p. 51.
332. Soane MSS Vol. 6, p. 15.
333. M.B. to Lord Cathcart, 30th October 1771.
334. Earl of Shelburne to Robert Adam, 16th April 1765.
335. Samuel Wyatt to M.B., 6th March and 12th June 1766.
336. In Goodison, *Ormolu* (1974), Plates 14, 15, I illustrated a pair of giltwood torchères, the ormolu nozzles and splash rings of which were typical of Boulton and Fothergill's work.
337. B. and F. to Colonel Burgoyne, 10th December 1771.
338. B. and F. to William Matthews, 17th March 1772.
339. B. and F. to the Earl of Kerry, 14th May, 21st May, 22nd June 1772.
340. B. and F. to William Matthews, 16th September 1772.
341. B. and F. to the Duke of Ancaster, 11th July 1772, 13th February 1773, etc.
342. B. and F. to William Matthews, 19th December 1772. The writer remarked that the same design would 'serve Mr Riley'.
343. B. and F. to William Matthews, 3rd January 1773.
344. B. and F. to Lord Nuneham, 12th March, 23rd March 1775.
345. B. and F. to the Earl of Ashburnham, 5th April, 2nd November 1775. The girandoles cost £72 9s. od.
346. B. and F. to General Fitzroy, 20th June 1778.
347. B. and F. to Lord Arundell, 22nd March 1777.
348. Lots 38, 90.
349. Inventory, 1782, pp. 83, 133, 181. There were also '32¾ lbs cast work, parts for girandoles, at 8d' valued at £1 1s. 1d. (p. 93).
350. Thomas Pownall to M.B., 8th September 1769.
351. B. and F. to the Duke of Ancaster, 11th July 1772. The pails could be made in ormolu or silver, but not in plate.
352. B. and F. to William Matthews, 24th April 1773.
353. B. and F. to William Matthews, 22nd May 1773.
354. M.B. to J.F., 30th April 1773.
355. J.F. to M.B., 5th May 1773.
356. Ledger, 1776–8, p. 103, 28th March 1776.
357. B. and F. to Lord Ashburnham, 22nd May 1776; Journal, 1776–8, p. 107, 28th May 1776; B. and F. to Lord Ashburnham, 1st June 1776.
358. Ledger, 1776–8, p. 269, 1st November 1777.
359. John Hodges to M.B., 31st January 1778.
360. John Stuart to M.B., 31st March 1778.
361. Lots 44, 45.
362. Inventory, 1782, p. 181.
363. Although Boulton's clerk said that the pattern could not be made in plate, I have seen a pair made entirely of stamped gilt copper, the pieces soldered together. They could as readily have been made of rolled and stamped plate.
364. It is not easy to distinguish Boulton and Fothergill's pails from others made in France. I illustrated four in Goodison, *Ormolu* (1974), Plate 63, which I believed to be by Boulton and Fothergill. Other examples, some of which cannot be firmly attributed, sold Parke

Bernet, New York, 19th April 1969, lot 70 (catalogued as 'Louis XIV'); Sotheby's, 8th December 1983, lot 434; 23rd April 1989, lot 40; 19th November 1993, lot 15 (catalogued as 'Louis XVI', I think correctly); Sotheby's, New York, 12th–13th April 1996, lot 348. Another pair sold Christie's, 8th December 1994, lot 68 (collection of Sir Philip Sassoon, sold by the Marquess of Cholmondeley from Houghton Hall). The decoration of the base and other features suggest that these were French, as the catalogue suggested. It is a temptation to connect them with the Duchess of Ancaster, since Georgiana, daughter of the third Duke (1756–79) married the fourth Earl of Cholmondeley, later the first Marquess, in 1791. It is not a temptation I fall for.

365. There are several drawings in the first pattern book of silver or plate ice pails with ring handles attached to rams' heads.

366. Thomas Pownall to M.B., 8th September 1769.

367. M.B. to Lord Cathcart, 30th October 1771.

368. Lord Cathcart to M.B., 21st February 1772. He was probably referring to ink stands made of porcelain and mounted with ormolu of the type illustrated in Eriksen, *Waddesdon Manor – Sèvres Porcelain* (1968), pp. 182–7.

369. B. and F. to the Countess of Craven, 10th January 1776.

370. John Wyatt to M.B., 1st February 1776.

371. B. and F. to the Earl of Craven, 2nd November 1776: according to a letter to Lord Craven dated 7th August 1776 the 'large knife case is under hand and being sent as soon as possible'.

372. B. and F. to the Earl of Craven, 4th November 1776.

373. Ledger, 1776–8, p. 189, 30th October 1776. Two small shagreen travelling cases were also sent to Lord Craven at a cost of £7 12s. 5½d. – B. and F. to the Earl of Craven, 16th September 1776. These had been mentioned in a letter of August when Lord Craven was told that two 'small cases' were delayed because the workman who was making them had a riding accident in July (B. and F. to Lord Craven, 7th August 1776).

374. B. and F. to John Wyatt, 22nd June 1776.

375. One of these urns was shown in Jourdain, *English Decoration and Furniture of the Later 18th Century* (1922), Fig. 300. The illustration was of a 'painted pedestal surmounted by a metal brass-mounted urn' (Collection of Lord Leverhulme). The urns were sold abroad in 1978.

376. These pedestals can be seen in the catalogue of Christie's sale at Tew Park, 27th–29th May 1987, p. 51. This suggests that the urns were almost certainly at Soho House in the eighteenth century.

377. Wedgwood to Bentley, 25th October 1776 (E25-18703). Was the urn and pedestal Wedgwood saw one of the pair mentioned in the previous note? (Plate 216). If so, the porphyry decoration would have been added later, perhaps to match the porphyry decoration of the stand beneath the sidereal clock case (Plate 176). But this is all speculation.

378. M.B.'s Diary, 1768 (January).

379. Two unmounted blue john obelisks were put into the sale at Christie's in 1771 (first day, lot 66).

380. They are illustrated in Nicholas Penny, *Catalogue of European Sculpture in the Ashmolean Museum 1540 to the Present Day* (Oxford 1992), Vol. III, p. 13, nos. 451–2. Penny comments that the parts have been reassembled in the twentieth century 'in a manner that makes examination impossible'.

381. But not always, e.g. Ledger, 1776–8, pp. 248, 263, 269, sales of frames costing between £2 18s. 6d. and £3 17s. 6d. to the Marquess of Exeter, Earl of Dartmouth and Countess of Derby, all in 1777.

382. Day Book, 1779–81, p. 231, 1st May 1780.

383. Inventory, 1782, p. 181.

384. e.g. Sotheby's, 16th December 1981, lot 190 (Penelope); Sotheby's, 13th July 1988, lot 195 (Penelope and Ariadne); Phillips, 4th July 1995, lot 78 (Penelope and Ariadne); Sotheby's, 8th November 1995, lot 122 (Penelope and Calypso).

385. An initial study was published by Robinson and Thompson, 'Matthew Boulton's Mechanical Paintings' (1970).

386. Inventory, 1782, p. 191.

387. B. and F. to Baron de Watteville de Nidan, 23rd December 1780.

388. J.F. to M.B., 7th February 1778.

389. Angelica Kauffman to M.B., 12th June 1778.

390. Inventory, 1782, pp. 181, 206.

391. Inventory, 1782, p. 168.

392. Wedgwood to Bentley, 7th May 1776 (E25-18667).

393. Wedgwood to M.B., 14th June 1786.

394. First day, lots 14, 23; second day, lots 8, 28; third day, lots 8, 23.

395. B. and F. to William Matthews, 6th May 1771.

396. Lots 4, 9, 10.

397. Inventory, 1782, p. 180.

398. Pattern Book 1, pp. 129, 131, 133, 137.

399. James Stuart to M.B., 26th December 1769.

400. M.B. to his wife, n.d. [3rd March 1770].

401. M.B. to J.F., n.d. [4th March 1770]. A few days earlier he had asked Fothergill for a drawing (M.B. to J.F., 25th February 1770).

402. Lewis, Hunting Smith and Lam (ed.), *Walpole's Correspondence with Horace Mann* (1967), p. 212. Walpole did not mention Boulton by name, but the identification is obvious from the context.

403. Second day, lot 62; B. and F. to William Matthews, 6th May 1771. 'Lined with silver' probably meant that the inside was tinned. A correspondent in 1772 was told that the linings of tea urns were tinned (B. and F. to Thomas Craig, Dublin, 26th March 1772).

404. See Reilly, *Wedgwood* (1989), Vol. I, pp. 397–9.

405. Wedgwood to Bentley, 24th December 1770 (E25-18334).

406. Wedgwood to M.B., 19th February 1771.

407. Wedgwood to Bentley, 24th December 1770 (E25-18334).

408. B. and F. to the Earl of Kerry, 21st May 1772. He had apparently enquired after a tripod, but Boulton and Fothergill's only record of an order was for a 'tripodic tea kitchen'.

409. Royal Collection, Inventory no. 55429.

410. B. and F. to the Duke of Northumberland, 4th January 1772. The invoice also included an 'essence pot' and totalled £95 5s. od.

411. Inventory, Northumberland House, 1786, quoted by Owsley and Rieder, *The Glass Drawing Room from Northumberland House* (1974), p. 28.

412. It is described and illustrated in Queen Mary's 'Catalogue of Bibelots, Miniatures and other Valuables', Vol. IV (1938–45), p. 6, no. 10 (Royal Collection, Stable Yard House).

413. See also Pattern Book 1, p. 131: the numbers by the urns on pp. 125 and 131 suggest that they date from the late 1770s and 1780s.

414. Inventory, 1782, p. 181.

415. B. and F. to William Matthews, 9th January and 2nd February 1771.

416. First day, lot 87: second day, lots 69, 92; third day, lot 83. The buyers were listed as Messrs Wright, Barratt, Fellows and Brittingham. 'Lined with silver' meant that the inside of the bowl was either plated or tinned.

417. B. and F. to William Matthews, 6th May 1771.

418. B. and F. to William Matthews, 4th June 1771.

419. John Hodges to M.B., 23rd April 1777.

420. Francis Eginton to M.B., 23rd April 1777 (Great Tew Archive).

421. B. and F. to the Earl Gower, 23rd October 1777.

422. Lots 46, 49.

423. Cash Debtor Book, 1772–82, 8th August 1774.

424. B. and F. to Lord Digby, 30th September 1774.

425. Lord Cathcart to B. and F., 21st February 1772.

426. B. and F. to Sir J. Dalrymple, 7th July 1772.

427. M.B. to J.F., n.d. [received 9th April 1772].

428. Lots 25, 26.

429. Lots 46, 49.

430. B. and F. to Mayhew and Ince, 26th August 1771.

431. B. and F. to the Earl of Kerry, 29th December 1771, 8th March 1772.

432. B. and F. to the Earl of Kerry, 26th December 1771, 5th March 1772, etc.

433. B. and F. to the Earl of Kerry, 5th March 1772.
434. The catalogue is dated 25th February 1778 and survives in Christie's archives. The sale was postponed to 23rd–31st March.
435. Lot 12.
436. Lot 10.
437. B. and F. to Lord Arundell, 13th November 1777.
438. Lot 47.
439. This method of numbering was applied to other products at Soho from an early date. M.B.'s Notebook, 1768, pp. 11ff, contains a list of articles under various headings, each object being numbered and priced.
440. '3 pair' is interpolated before the price in the MS.
441. B. and F. to William Matthews, 6th May 1771.
442. B. and F. to William Matthews, 8th April 1772.
443. B. and F. to William Matthews, 27th April 1772.
444. Cash Debtor Book, 1772–82, 3rd September 1775. The name of the customer looks like Christian van Munck. No corresponding name appears in the Register Book of visitors to Soho (Great Tew Archive).
445. Day Book, 1779–81, p. 230, 1st May 1780.
446. Inventory, 1782, pp. 156, 181.
447. Inventory, 1782, pp. 180–1.
448. Lot 3: the reserve price was £3 13s. 6d.
449. M.B. to J.F., n.d. [4th March 1770].
450. B. and F. to William Matthews, 20th January 1771.
451. Memorandum of order placed with Robert Bradbury, 7th March 1771.
452. Inventory, 1782, p. 83.
453. B. and F. to William Matthews, 6th May 1771.
454. First day, lot 27; second day, lots 46, 61; third day, lot 55. All were reserved at £16 16s. od. The wording differs in the catalogue entries.
455. B. and F. to William Matthews, 5th September 1772.
456. B. and F. to Robert Bradbury, 28th June 1775.
457. Inventory, 1782, p. 84.
458. B. and F. to William Matthews, 6th May 1771.
459. Memorandum of order placed with Robert Bradbury, 7th March 1771.
460. Second day, lot 90.
461. Memorandum dated 22nd April 1771 to send a pair of Bingley's vases 'without the pedestal' to Sir Gregory Page.
462. Sir Gregory Page's cost £12 12s. od. each (B. and F. to William Matthews, 13th May 1771).
463. Invoice dated 19th December 1771, presented through William Matthews – '2 Bingleys 2 branched vases at £15 15s. od. £31 10s. od.' (Audley End MSS DDBy, A.29/11).
464. B. and F. to William Matthews, 27th April 1772. See Appendix I.
465. B. and F. to William Matthews, 26th April 1772, and other letters.
466. First day, lots 40, 78; second day, lots 59, 84; third day, lots 26, 58.
467. B. and F. to William Matthews, 6th May 1771: the entries quoted here are not consecutive.
468. First day, lots 35, 52; second day, lots 4, 21; third day, lots 34, 65. Some of the lots in the sales of Harrache's stock at Christie and Ansell's in 1778 sound as if they may have come from Boulton and Fothergill's factory, e.g. 14th March 1778 (second day), lot 64, 'A pair of large Derbyshire vases for perfume, finely variegated, and elegantly mounted in or moulu' and a similar pair on the third day, lot 60, and two similar pairs on 9th May, lots 86–7.
469. John Kentish to M.B., 14th December 1769.
470. B. and F. to William Matthews, 6th May 1771: the same alternatives were available in 1772 (B. and F. to William Matthews, 4th April 1772, 5th September 1772).
471. Memorandum of order dated 4th August 1769.
472. Two of the lots were clearly pairs although not listed as such.
473. Margin notes in the first catalogue describe five of the bodies as enamelled and nine as china. Notes in the second catalogue imply that three of the china bodies were enamelled.
474. B. and F. to William Matthews, 6th May 1771. It was also described as four-leaved in a letter to William Matthews dated 17th July 1771.
475. First day, lots 10, 31, 63, 75; second day, lots 17, 41, 56.
476. Invoice dated 19th December 1771, presented through William Matthews – '1 pair Morrisons blue enamell £3 3s. od.' (Audley End MSS DDBy, A 29/11).
477. B. and F. to William Matthews, 4th April 1772.
478. Inventory, 1782, p. 83.
479. B. and F. to William Matthews, 4th April and 8th April 1772.
480. Inventory, 1782, p. 83.
481. Day Book, 1779–81, p. 274, 30th May 1780; B. and F. to Sir Joshua Reynolds, 7th August 1780.
482. Day Book, 1779–81, p. 332, 8th July 1780.
483. Day Book, 1779–81, p. 440.
484. Inventory, 1782, p. 133.
485. Inventory, 1782, p. 180. I have not shown here the reduced prices, for which see Appendix IV.
486. Inventory, 1782, p. 156.
487. B. and F. to the Duke of Marlborough, 22nd August 1772. See Appendix I.
488. It is not known when or by whom these vases were acquired. There is no record of them in the Boulton archives.
489. Royal Collection, Catalogue no. 53114. The vases came from the H. H. Mulliner Collection – see Mulliner, *Decorative Arts in England* (1924), Plate 164. The vases were sold Christie's, 10th July 1924, lot 37, and were given to George V and Queen Mary by the Prince Regent and Princess Paul of Jugoslavia in May 1937. They are illustrated in Queen Mary's 'Catalogue of Bibelots, Miniatures and Other Valuables', Vol. III (1932–7), p. 77, no. 343 (Royal Collection, Stable Yard House).
490. Illustrated in Goodison, *Ormolu* (1974), Plate 74.
491. A pair sold Christie's, New York, 13th October 1994, later exhibited at Partridge (Fine Arts) 'Summer Exhibition' (1995), illustrated in the catalogue, p. 17. They stood on square marble bases. A further pair were sold Christie's, June 1919, from Bothwell Castle and were sold again at Anderson Galleries, New York, 10th February 1926, lot 165 (Collection of the First Viscount Leverhulme).
492. Christie's, 8th July 1998, lot 61 (Olive Countess Fitzwilliam Chattels Settlement). The vase had been wired for electricity, had pieces added to the branches, and had lost its lining. The finial was not reversible to a nozzle.
493. Third day, lot 60.
494. First day, lots 29, 42; second day, lot 75; third day, lot 41.
495. Second day, lot 85.
496. Sold Sotheby's, 18th February 1972, exhibited Hotspur 'Golden Jubilee Exhibition' (1974), p. 2, Plate 5, now in The David Collection, Copenhagen, accession nos. 15a–b/1972.
497. For example Christie's, 9th May 1941, lot 64 (Earl Temple, Newton Park); Hotspur 'Golden Jubilee Exhibition' (1974), Plate 4, later exhibited at the Somerset House Art Treasures Exhibition, 1979; Phillips, New York, 5th December 2001, lot 15.
498. Sotheby's, 26th June 1953, lot 69. The vases had lost their branches and the floral friezes on the lower parts of the bodies. None of the vases bought by the Earl of Ashburnham at Boulton and Fothergill's sale in 1778 corresponds adequately to these vases. The nearest is lot 7, if the marble bases can be described as 'pedestals'.
499. Memorandum, 22nd April 1771.
500. Royal Collection, Catalogue no. 83. The vases were bought by Queen Mary in 1938 and are listed and illustrated in her 'Catalogue of Bibelots, Miniatures and Other Valuables', Vol. IV (1938–45), p. 1, no. 2 (Royal Collection, Stable Yard House). Another pair of these vases, without branches, was sold Christie's, 12th March 1947, lot 311, from the collection of the Duchess of Kent.
501. Illustrated Goodison, *Ormolu* (1974), Plate 102, also in Metropolitan Museum of Art, *Bronzes, Other Metalwork and Sculpture in the Irwin Untermyer Collection* (1962), Plate 190.
502. These vases were owned by Averys Ltd and were at the Soho Foundry when I

illustrated them in *Ormolu* (1974), Plate 95. They were sold Christie's, 25th June 1981, lot 6, and again 17th November 1994, lot 90.

503. e.g. Sotheby's, 26th May 1967, lot 68 (with blue john stems); Christie's, 27th November 1975, lot 5; Christie's, 26th September 1996, lot 73 (blue john stems, the lid missing).

504. Sold Sotheby's, 12th February 1988, lot 7.

505. Sold Christie's, 6th July 1995, lot 5.

506. Blue john examples sold Bonham's, 6th June 1975; Sotheby's, France, 27th June 2001, lot 173: a marble pair sold Christie's, 10th April 1986, lot 2. All three pairs had laurel swags and pendants.

507. A gilt pair was illustrated in Goodison, *Ormolu*, Plate 115; also Hotspur 'Golden Jubilee Exhibition' (1974), Plate 7. See previous note.

508. Sold Christie's, 5th December 1991, lot 209.

509. Lepke, Berlin, 4th–5th June 1929, lots 254–5.

510. Etude Tajan, Paris, 27th March 1995, lot 397. A white marble pair sold Christie's, 19th November 1992, lot 2, and 16th November 1995, lot 8.

511. Inventory, Northumberland House, 1786, quoted in Owsley and Rieder, *The Glass Drawing Room from Northumberland House* (1974), p. 28.

512. H. de Young Museum, San Francisco, gift of Mr and Mrs Robert A. McGowan, 1982. One of the vases has lost its gilt lining and one of the dolphin handles was also missing when I saw these vases in 1982.

513. State Hermitage Museum, St Petersburg, Inventory no. 1561–2.

514. Lots 58, 62, reserved at £11 11s. od. and £4 11s. od., respectively, and both bought in.

515. Royal Collection, Catalogue no. 5946. The vases were bought by Queen Mary in 1927 and are listed and illustrated in her 'Catalogue of Bibelots, Miniatures and Other Valuables', Vol. II (1921–31), p. 49, no. 171 (Royal Collection, Stable Yard House). Other examples with reversible finials sold Christie's, 28th May 1964, lot 7; 11th June 1985, lot 89, now at Heaton Hall, Manchester.

516. Inventory, 1782, p. 180.

517. Lennox-Boyd (ed.), *Masterpieces of English Furniture: the Gerstenfeld Collection* (1998), p. 253, no. 122, and p. 173, Plate 123. Others sold Sotheby's, 26th June 1953, lot 68 (Earl of Ashburnham) (cap missing); Christie's, 7th July 1994, lot 15.

518. Hotspur 'Golden Jubilee Exhibition' (1974), Plate 5 (three steps); Sotheby's, 18th November 1993, lot 99 (Moller Collection), later exhibited Partridge 'English Furniture and Objets d'Art' (1994), p. 38, no. 13; Christie's, New York, 14th October 1994 (two steps); Sotheby's, 13th June 2001, lot 43 (single vase, three steps). All these vases had reversible finials.

519. Sold Sotheby's, 1st December 1978, lot 142, now in the Gerstenfeld Collection. See Lennox-Boyd (ed.), *Masterpieces of English Furniture: the Gerstenfeld Collection* (1998), p. 252, no. 120, and p. 174, Plate 124.

520. e.g. Christie's, 19th November 1992, lot 28 (a pair).

521. Maria Feodorevna's Library, illustrated in Koutchoumov, *Pavlovsk* (1976), Plates 58, 65.

522. These vases were probably the pair sold from the collection of 'Comte Stroganoff' by the Soviet Union at Lepke's, Berlin, 11th–13th May 1931, lots 127–8. They were sold Christie's, 19th March 1964, lot 85, and were exhibited B.A.D.A. 'Golden Jubilee Exhibition' (May 1968), no. 169, and Hotspur 'Golden Jubilee Exhibition' (1974), Plate 10.

523. A pair was illustrated in *Treasures of Art in Russia* (Petersburg 1903), pp. 338–9, when they were in the 'Cabinet de Grand Duc Paul' at Pavlovsk, but there was no sign of them at Pavlovsk in 1979. They could be the pair sold at Lepke's in 1931 (see note 522), or they could have been destroyed in the Second World War. A vase is illustrated in Jean-Bernard Naudin and Christiane de Nicolay-Mazercy, *The Finest Houses of Paris* (New York, 2000), in a room at Hotel Lambert (Baron Guy de Rothschild); it looks as if it has lost its central finial and has a stem to hold an electric light in its place. Another pair, lacking the decorative frieze and mounted with a later central cluster of ormolu candle sockets and lily buds, was sold by the Leningrad Museum in 1928 (Lepke's, Berlin, 6th November 1928, lots 206–7). A single vase, the central nozzle filled with an electrical fitting, sold Sotheby's, 30th November 2001, lot 26.

524. e.g. Goodison, *Ormolu* (1974), Plates 103, 106, and Hotspur 'Golden Jubilee Exhibition' (1974), Plate 9.

525. Sold Christie's, 3rd July 1997, lot 75. Previously sold Christie's, 12th–14th March 1947, lot 314A (Duchess of Kent); Christie's, 7th June 1956, lot 7 (Princess Royal); Christie's, New York, 29th October 1983, lot 31; Christie's, New York, 22nd April 1989, lot 32.

526. A blue john pair sold Christie's, 15th April 1982, lot 1. The marble pair is illustrated in Goodison, *Ormolu* (1974), Plate 133. Except for the marble pair, none of the candle vases so far recorded have had caps.

527. Sold Christie's, 6th July 1995, lot 27.

528. This is one of a pair of vases, which were at Weston Park and were illustrated in Goodison, *Ormolu* (1974), Plate 134.

529. Inventory nos. E6480, E7549-50. E6480 and E7549 were exhibited in 'Treasures of Catherine the Great' (inaugural exhibition of the Hermitage Rooms, Somerset House, London, 2000–1), catalogue no. 315, p. 161. The lining and fixing nut of E7550 are missing.

530. Illustrated in a general view in Koutchoumov, *Pavlovsk* (1956), Plate 92.

531. e.g. pairs sold Sotheby's, 2nd December 1966, lot 73; Christie's, 24th April 1980, lot 89 (exhibited 'International Art Treasures Exhibition', Bath (1973), no. 281b, Hotspur 'Golden Jubilee Exhibition' (1974), Plate 28); Arcole, Paris, 13th June 1988, lot 101; Christie's, 4th July 1996, lot 278. A vase was illustrated in Mulliner, *Decorative Arts in England* (1924), Fig. 169: it was then owned by the Duchess of Manchester. A pair of vases with fine purplish veined stone bodies and pedestals, containing bands of hydrothermal minerals – iron, copper, calcium, etc. – and without mounts on either the bodies or the pedestals was exhibited Mallett, 'The Age of Matthew Boulton' (2000), pp. 62–3.

532. Royal Collection, Catalogue no. 7644, 1–2. Other pairs sold Christie's, 23rd May 1968, lot 4; Sotheby's, 9th June 1978, lot 91. Like the blue john versions, other pairs are in private collections.

533. Sold Christie's, 28th June 1984, lot 2 and illustrated Partridge (Fine Arts) 'Summer Exhibition' (1986), p. 86.

534. When I illustrated these vases in *Ormolu* (1974) they were in the possession of Averys Ltd at the Soho Foundry. They were sold Christie's, 25th June 1981, lot 5.

535. Sold Christie's, 14th June 2001, lot 2.

536. Sold Sotheby's, 11th April 1975, lot 41, exhibited Hotspur, 'Golden Jubilee Exhibition' (1974), Plate 27.

537. Another pair was sold AB Stockholm Auktionsverk, 13th–17th November 1979, lot 328.

538. These vases sold Christie's, 19th November 1992, lot 4, and 6th July 1995, lot 10. Other examples of this vase, with blue john bodies, sold Sotheby's, 19th March 1982, lot 108 (previously exhibited Spink 'An Exhibition of Candlesticks', 1974, no. 85), with a taller and restored finial; Christie's, 7th February 1991, lot 3.

539. These vases were exhibited in 'Treasures from West Country Collections', City Art Gallery, Bristol (1967), Catalogue no. 122. A single vase sold Christie's, 25th June 1987, lot 2 (the lid remade).

540. A pair sold Christie's, 16th November 1995, lot 121, and 13th November 1997, lot 455; another pair Christie's, New York, 12th April 1996, lot 10, with remade marble lids.

541. e.g. Mallett, 'The Age of Matthew Boulton' (2000), pp. 68–9.

542. Other vases of this type sold Christie's, 1st December 1977, lot 12a (now National Trust, Mompesson House, Salisbury); Sotheby's, 18th November 1993, lot 105 (Moller Collection); Sotheby's, 13th June 2001, lot 5.

543. State Hermitage Museum, Inventory nos. E1675-6. One of the vases was exhibited in 'Treasures of Catherine the Great' (inaugural exhibition of the Hermitage Rooms, Somerset House, London, 2000–1) catalogue no. 317, p. 183. The other vase has lost its finial and nozzle.

544. Sold Sotheby's, Zurich, 1st June 1994, lot 430; exhibited Mallett, 'The Age of Matthew Boulton' (2000), pp. 56–7.

545. This vase was exhibited Hotspur 'Golden Jubilee Exhibition' (1974), Plate 29.
546. Lepke's, Berlin, 6th–7th November 1928, lots 201–2. The illustration in the catalogue shows them without the square base mount.
547. Illustrated in a general view of the Ancient Cabinet in Koutchoumov, *Pavlovsk* (1976), Plate 190, but in the 'Raspberry' room in 2001.
548. '1 pair of 2 handled mask face came from the Duke of Manchester' – B. and F. to William Matthews, 27th April 1772. They were listed among the ornaments not charged to Matthews after the sale.
549. B. and F. to Lady Digby, 6th February 1775.
550. B. and F. to Lord Digby, 30th September 1774.
551. B. and F. to Lady Digby, 8th October 1774.
552. B. and F. to Lord Digby, November 1774.
553. Another vase of this pattern was sold Sotheby's, 8th December 1978, lot 135.
554. These vases were sold Sotheby's, 2nd December 1966, lot 72; Christie's, 28th June 1979, lot 5. They were illustrated in Goodison, *Ormolu* (1974), Plate 146, with modern circular marble bases and bun feet.
555. Sold Christie's, 16th September 1999, lot 126 (a pair).
556. Illustrated in a general view of Maria Feodorevna's State Dressing Room in Koutchoumov, *Pavlovsk* (1976), Plate 92. One medallion was missing when I saw the vase in 1979: the others were Venus Victorious, Hygieia and Aesculapius. Pairs of vases sold Christie's, 2nd July 1965, lot 145; Christie's, 19th June 1980, lot 92; Christie's, New York, 31st January 1981, lot 76. A related pair of green stained bodies and pedestals, satyr masks instead of handles, and coloured medallions, was sold Sotheby's, 18th May 1973, lot 30, and exhibited at Hotspur, 'Golden Jubilee Exhibition' (1974), Plate 31.
557. The two vases in Plate 304 were sold Christie's, 6th July 1967, lot 48 and are now at Temple Newsam, Leeds. The vase in Plate 305 was sold Christie's, 7th July 1994, lot 28. Other vases of this design sold Christie's, 4th July 1996, lot 208 (with a lacquered metal body, the swags between the figures missing); Christie's, 23rd April 1998, lot 6 (the lid modified).
558. Lot 60. The vases were unsold. Another 'essence vase in radix amethysti and or moulu, on a tripod', lot 65, was also unsold.
559. Lot 80. The wording differs slightly for the other vase, lot 123.
560. Inventory, 1782, pp. 180 (also Day Book 1779–81, p. 230), 133.
561. B. and F to Lord Stormont, 5th December 1783.
562. Sold Christie's, 3rd July 1980, lot 10 (a sale of French objects).
563. The vase at Syon was illustrated in Goodison, 'Matthew Boulton's Bacchanalian vase' (1977). It then had a later pierced piece inserted between the beaded leaf mount and the pierced lid, which has since been removed. There is no trace of the acquisition of this vase in the Northumberland archives. It is unlikely to be the 'essence pot' sold to the Duke in 1772 (see Appendix I): the date is too early. The vase was recorded in an inventory in 1930 as a 'Gaeta' vase (Alnwick MSS). The vase at Soho House sold Christie's, 7th July 1988, lot 5 (Fermor Hesketh Collection) and 16th November 1995, lot 120, exhibited Mallett, 'The Age of Matthew Boulton' (2000), pp. 44–7.
564. First day, lot 84; second day, lots 89, 90; third day, lot 82.
565. Lot 79.
566. B. and F. to William Matthews, 6th May 1771.
567. This vase was bought by the first Viscount Leverhulme, 24th June 1919, and was sold Anderson Galleries, New York, 10th February 1926, lot 166. It is catalogued and illustrated in Lennox-Boyd (ed.), *Masterpieces of English Furniture: the Gerstenfeld Collection* (1998), p. 253, Plates 122, 126.
568. Illustrated in Metropolitan Museum of Art, *Bronzes, Other Metalwork and Sculpture in the Irwin Untermyer Collection* (1962), Plate 191, and in Goodison, *Ormolu* (1974), Plate 76.
569. Other caryatic vases sold Christie's, 12th March 1947, lots 312 (Duchess of Kent) and 312A (a pair, Lady Sheffield); Christie's, 7th June 1956, lot 8 (Princess Royal); Sotheby's, 19th July 1974, lot 28 (without ebonised plinths and ball feet).
570. These vases were sold Il Ponte Casa d'Este, Milan, 2nd December 1999, lot 698. One of the branches has been replaced. One of the vases has an original silvered lining, the other a replacement. The stone bases are made of a carboniferous sedimentary limestone similar to Duke's Red stone, which is found near Alport, Rowseley.
571. Second day, lot 87. The purchaser was Mr Barret or Barratt at £25 4s. od.
572. M.B. to J.F., n.d. [7th or 8th March 1770].
573. Invoice dated 19th October 1770. Fitzwilliam MSS, Sheffield City Library.
574. i.e. 'philosopher' stone, or agate.
575. B. and F. to William Matthews, 6th May 1771.
576. Second day, lots 22, 42, 57, 70; third day, lots 75, 79.
577. First day, lots 5, 22, 36, 59.
578. Memorandum of order dated 12th November 1771.
579. B. and F. to William Matthews, 4th December 1771.
580. Inventory, 1782, pp. 83–4.
581. A rare pair with white marble bodies and white glass panels, with portrait medallions of Ceres, is in the collection of the Knights of Malta, Venice.
582. Sold Christie's, 24th June 1982, lot 3. Another pair with gilt metal pedestals but with images of Ceres was illustrated in 'The Works of Matthew Boulton from the Collection of James C. Cordell Jr.' (Headley Whitney Museum, Kentucky, 1990), p. 12.
583. Sold Sotheby's, 19th June 1981, lot 4.
584. Sold Sotheby's, 5th October 1993, lot 95; Christie's, 16th November 1995, lot 9.
585. Sotheby's, 18th November 1993, lot 98 (Moller Collection, the caps like Plate 329). Another pair, without caps, sold Christie's, 26th May 1972, lot 22.
586. Mallett, 'The Age of Matthew Boulton' (2000), pp. 72–3, now at Soho House, City of Birmingham Museum and Art Gallery. The vases have no caps. Another pair, with caps like Plate 329 was exhibited Hotspur, 'Golden Jubilee Exhibition' (1974), Plate 8. Other vases with indeterminate glass panels (it is difficult to tell from monochrome photographs) sold Christie's, 29th November 1979, lot 1 (caps like Plate 329); Christie's, New York, 16th January 1999, lot 536 (the panels may be a simulation of what Boulton and Fothergill called 'tiger stone'), no caps.
587. Another pair with blue john pedestals but without medallions sold Sotheby's, New York, 20th May 1994, lot 18.
588. Memorandum of order, n.d. [28th August 1769].
589. Memorandum of order, 4th September 1769.
590. Memorandum of order, 9th September 1769.
591. M.B. to J.F., n.d. [February 1770].
592. M.B. to J.F., n.d. [7th or 8th March 1770].
593. B. and F. to William Matthews, 6th May 1771. Two notes in the manuscript suggest that there might have been four pairs of vases with gilt bodies and only two pairs with enamelled bodies.
594. It may not support this identification that lot 26 on the third day is annotated 'goats head' and described in the catalogue as a pair of candle vases 'with drapery and other ornaments', but the goat's head vase cannot be described as 'with drapery', and the annotation must be a correction to the catalogue entry rather than a description.
595. B. and F. to William Matthews, 4th April 1772.
596. B. and F. to William Matthews, 27th April 1772.
597. Cash Debtor Book, 1772–82, 18th April 1772.
598. B. and F. to William Matthews, 29th February and 16th September 1772. Lord Morton also bought a pair with green bodies [Memorandum of order, n.d.].
599. B. and F. to Lord Digby, 8th October 1774.
600. Inventory, 1782, p. 83.
601. Royal Collection, Inventory no. 6828.
602. Jutsham Deliveries, Vol. III (1820–30), p. 171, no. 36 (Royal Collection, Stable Yard House).
603. Sold Christie's, 22nd May 1969, lot 26.
604. A white marble pair illustrated

Goodison, *Ormolu* (1974), Plate 124. Other blue john examples, in varying states of repair, sold Sotheby's, 20th October 1972, lot 37 (single vase, rim not holed); Sotheby's, 11th April 1975, lot 40; Sotheby's, 28th February 1986, lot 5 (no medallions but holed rims); Christie's, 7th July 1988, lot 3 (with medallions, and later marble bases in place of ball feet); Sotheby's, 17th November 1989, lot 10 (no medallions or holes in rims); Christie's, 8th February 1996, lot 156 (no holes in rims, nozzle uncharacteristic); Christie's, 4th July 1996, lot 207 (no medallions, holed rims); Christie's, 5th June 1997, lot 7 (no medallions, holed rims); Phillips, 21st November 2000, lot 7. Vases with gilt bodies sold Christie's, 28th June 1979, lot 6 (no medallions, holed rims); Sotheby's, New York, 12th May 2000, lot 115 (medallions). A pair with lacquered bodies, probably originally blue but now brown, sold Sotheby's, 4th July 1997, lot 3. Another pair with re-lacquered bodies sold Sotheby's, 26th May 2000, lot 146, and Christie's, New York, 16th April 2002, lot 260.

605. First day, lots 13, 46; second day, lots 14, 37; third day, lots 19, 29, 56, 76.

606. B. and F. to William Matthews, 6th May ('1 griffins vase'), 16th May and 4th June 1771.

607. Invoice dated 19th December 1771, presented through William Matthews (Audley End MSS DDBy A29/11).

608. B. and F. to William Matthews, 4th April 1772.

609. Inventory 1782, pp. 84, 156, 180.

610. Sold Sotheby's, New York, 21st November 1981, lot 150. It is catalogued and illustrated in Lennox-Boyd, *Masterpieces of English Furniture: the Gerstenfeld Collection* (1998), p. 252, Plate 125.

611. Christie's, 16th November 1995, lot 3. Some of the mounts, including both finials, restored.

612. M.B. to J.F., n.d. [4th March 1770].

613. M.B. to J.F., n.d. [7th or 8th March 1770].

614. First day, lot 86; second day, lot 88. The buyer in each case was Barton and he paid £52 10s. od. and £40 19s. od. respectively.

615. B. and F. to William Matthews, 19th April, 28th April, 2nd May and 4th May 1771.

616. J.F. to M.B., 28th March 1772.

617. Royal Collection, Inventory nos. 21669, 1–2.

618. Royal Collection, Inventory nos. 21669, 3–4.

619. Pyne, *Buckingham House* (1819), illustrated a pair on pedestals in Queen Charlotte's Blue Velvet Room in a print dated 1817. In 1825 a pair stood in 'Her Late Majesty's Apartments' in Buckingham Palace, in the 'State Dressing Room'. The other pair stood in the 'Warm Room'. Each pair was described as 'a pair of or moulu spar vase lights each for 4 candles' (Inventory of the Household Furniture at Buckingham Palace taken 2nd May 1828, pp. 8, 10, Royal Collection, Stable Yard House). A single vase is illustrated in George IV's 'Pictorial Inventory' (referred to in other Royal Collection records as the Query Book) *c.*1827, Vol. B, no. 37. The drawing is annotated 'One pair stood on the chimney piece in the drawing room at Buckingham House', and 'Sent by Mr Vulliamy to Windsor Castle Jany 26th 1829'. The delivery to Windsor of all four vases is recorded in Jutsham Deliveries, Vol. III (1820–30), p. 171, as 'No. 35 Four Derbyshire vases mounted with or moulu branches to carry four lights each. NB. these vases are in suite with the clock by Wright ...'. The entry is annotated – 'I gave orders to Mr Vulliamy to send these vases to Windsor Castle by command of the King, BJ', and 'Jan 26th 1829 Sent to Windsor Castle in the early part of the year 1829. Did belong to Buckingham House, but lastly from the stores at St James's. See Query Book for sketch page B37' (Royal Collection, Stable Yard House). It is interesting that none of these records mention Boulton and Fothergill.

620. Probably the vase sold by the Duchess of Kent, Christie's, 12th March 1947, lot 313.

621. Gift of Mr and Mrs Medard W. Welch, illustrated in Goodison, *Ormolu* (1974), Plate 83; Hotspur, 'Golden Jubilee Exhibition' (1974), Plate 16.

622. Christie's, 7th November 1988, lot 25 (Lord Elphinstone). The vases have lost their plinths and stand on later square green marble bases.

623. Christie's, 11th July 1929, lot 119, a pair (Earl of Yarborough). There is no record of the purchase of King's vases by Charles Pelham, who is recorded as buying 'ornaments' in 1778 (see Appendix I).

624. J.F. to M.B., 23rd January 1772.

625. B. and F. to William Matthews, 7th August 1771.

626. B. and F. to William Matthews, 19th October 1771.

627. B. and F. to William Matthews, 19th October 1771.

628. Adam's first design is dated 1768 (Soane MSS Vol. 50, no. 68): see Bolton, *Architecture of Robert and James Adam* (1922), Vol. II, p. 159, and Topographical Index, p. 27; Harris, *Genius of Robert Adam* (2001), pp. 235–7.

629. B. and F. to William Matthews, 27th November 1771.

630. B. and F. to William Matthews, 4th March 1772.

631. Mrs Parker to Frederick Robinson, 9th April 1772 (Morley MSS, British Museum).

632. John Parker's Account Book – '18th June 1772 To Mr Draper for a vase from Mr Boulton £31 14s. od.'.

633. Harris, *Genius of Robert Adam* (2001), p. 237, suggests that they were adapted from another of Adam's designs.

634. The number 4 is the only number missing from the sequence.

635. A vase with a marble base sold Christie's, 7th July 1988, lot 7 (Fermor Hesketh Collection).

636. Inventory, 1782, p. 180.

637. Day Book, 1779–81, p. 230, 1st May 1780.

638. Inventory, 1782, p. 180.

639. Inventory no. Z1.12614. The vase was exhibited 'Treasures of Catherine the Great' (inaugural exhibition, Hermitage Rooms, Somerset House, London, 2000–1), catalogue no. 316, pp. 162, 183.

640. Goodison, *Ormolu* (1974), Plate 117. Another pair – or perhaps the same pair – were sold by the Soviet Union at Lepke's, Berlin, 4th–5th June 1929, lots 250–1. A further pair is at Firle Place, Sussex.

641. Sold Christie's, New York, 17th October 1997, lot 218.

642. Sold Christie's, Godmersham Park, 6th–9th June 1983, lot 97.

643. First day, lot 82; third day, lot 80.

644. B. and F. to William Matthews, 6th May 1771.

645. J.F. to M.B., 4th April 1771.

646. Inventory nos. E.1573-4. They were exhibited in 'Treasures of Catherine the Great' (inaugural exhibition, Hermitage Rooms, Somerset House, London, 2000–1), catalogue no. 318, p. 184, and described there as formerly in the Yusupov Collection.

647. Third day, lot 84.

648. The buyer was Barton: this may have been one of the 'buying-in' names, but the vase was not listed among the unsold pieces in B. and F. to William Matthews, 6th May 1771.

649. B. and F. to William Matthews, 19th October 1771.

650. B. and F. to William Matthews, 27th November 1771.

651. B. and F. to William Matthews, 4th April 1772.

652. B. and F. to William Matthews, 27th April 1772 – '1 large Persian slave (sc. vase)'.

653. Lot 126.

654. Inventory, 1782, p. 84.

655. B. and F. to Sir Lawrence Dundas, 4th January 1772.

656. The two vases were sold with the other contents of 19 Arlington Street by Dundas's descendant, the Marquess of Zetland, at Christie's, 26th April 1934, lot 53. The catalogue described the figures as 'three ormolu figures of Hercules' and stated that the vases were fitted for electric light. They have been illustrated frequently by previous writers, e.g. Bolton, *The Architecture of Robert and James Adam* (1922), Vol. II, p. 297; Jourdain, 'Matthew Boulton: an Artist in Ormolu' (1950), p. 52, Fig. 1; Archer, 'Elegance for the Mantelpiece' (1963), p. 1387, Fig. 5; Hotspur, 'Golden Jubilee Exhibition' (1974), Frontispiece, etc. Most writers, following Bolton, have suggested that the candelabra were made originally for Dundas's country house, Moor Park. Boulton and Fothergill's letter to Dundas shows this to be wrong.

657. Harris, *Furniture of Robert Adam* (1963), pp. 99–100 and Fig. 131.
658. First day, lots 38, 65, 76; second day, lots 33, 52, 67, 82; third day, lots 14, 51, 72.
659. B. and F. to William Matthews, 6th May 1771: the vase was returned by 'Mr Willett', who does not appear in the catalogue among the buyers (B. and F. to William Matthews, 2nd May 1771).
660. Memorandum of order date 7th March 1771 – 'Ordered from Mr Bradbury junior – 6 sphinx [sc. vases] complete …'.
661. B. and F. to William Matthews, 2nd May 1771; Inventory, 1782, p. 83.
662. First day, lot 38; second day, lot 67.
663. Royal Collection, Inventory no. 21668. One of the vases was illustrated in George IV's Pictorial Inventory *c.*1827 (called the Query Book in other records), Vol. B, no. 38 (Royal Collection, Stable Yard House). They were then on the chimneypiece of the drawing room in Buckingham House. According to an annotation they were sent to Windsor Castle by 'Mr Vulliamy' on 26th January 1829, along with the clock and the four King's vases. The delivery is recorded in Jutsham's Deliveries, Vol. III (1820–30), p. 171, as 'No. 36 Four Derbyshire spar vases, mounted in or molu festooned, with handles etc. NB two of these very small in suite with the clock by Wright…'. The entry is annotated as for the entry for the King's vases (see Note 619), referring to p.36 of the Query Book, an error for p.38. The 'very small vases' could have been the goat's head vases of Plate 331.
664. These two vases were in the H. H. Mulliner Collection. They were illustrated in Mulliner, *Decorative Arts in England* (1924), Plate 163, and were sold Christie's, 10th July 1924, lot 75. They were given to George V and Queen Mary in 1937 by the Prince Regent and Princess Paul of Jugoslavia. They are recorded in Queen Mary's 'Catalogue of Bibelots, Miniatures and Other Valuables', Vol. III (1932–7), p. 77, nos. 344–5 (Royal Collection, Stable Yard House).
665. Illustrated Goodison, *Ormolu* (1974), Plate 97.
666. e.g. a pair at Anglesey Abbey.
667. e.g. a pair in the Bundessammlung Alter Stilmöbel, Vienna, Inventory nos. HV-1444-5; a single vase missing the guilloche band sold Christie's, 30th June 1977, lot 6.
668. e.g. a pair exhibited B.A.D.A. 'Golden Jubilee Exhibition' (1968), Catalogue no. 168, Plate 120; a pair sold Humberts, Roche Court, Salisbury, 25th October 1978, lot 1036; a pair sold Sotheby's, 11th July 1986, lot 17.
669. e.g. three vases sold Sotheby's, New York, 14th January 1978, lots 21–2.
670. Sold Christie's, 28th June 1984.
671. There is a pair in the Metropolitan Museum, New York: see *Bronzes, Other Metalwork and Sculpture in the Irwin Untermyer Collection* (1962), Plate 192, Fig. 216.
672. Sotheby's, 26th May 1967, lot 67; Christie's, 11th April 1773, lot 42; Christie's, 18th July 1975, lot 33. According to an engraved plate on the upper plinth this vase was given by the Earl of Shelburne (as Marquess of Lansdowne) to a friend named Dennis Kelly in 1781. It was restored in 1866 by D. H. Kelly who probably inserted the plate and replaced certain parts.
673. M.B.'s Diary, 1772.
674. B. and F. to William Matthews, 27th April 1772.
675. B. and F. to Robert Child, 12th September 1772. This was possibly the vase illustrated by Jourdain, 'Matthew Boulton: an Artist in Ormolu' (1950), p. 53, Fig. 6, and described as 'from Osterley', which was Child's house. It was also illustrated, but inaccurately attributed to the Mulliner Collection, in McQuoid and Edwards, *Dictionary of English Furniture* (1954), sv. 'Perfume Burners', Fig. 1.
676. B. and F. to William Matthews, 16th September 1772.
677. B. and F. to the Marquess of Granby, 19th November 1774.
678. Ledger, 1776–8, p. 269, 1st November 1777.
679. Inventory, 1782, p. 83.
680. Journal, 1776–8, p. 106, 25th May 1776 – 'A Venus vase sent Robert Hyman £23 12s. 6d.'.
681. First day, lot 64.
682. Second day, lot 86.
683. B. and F. to William Matthews, 11th November 1771.
684. Lots 54, 72, 75, 76, 77.
685. Day Book, 1779–81, p. 230, 1st May 1780.
686. Day Book, 1779–81, p. 322, 8th July 1780.
687. Inventory, 1782, p. 156.
688. This vase was sold Sotheby's, 7th October 1966, lot 62.
689. Sold Sotheby's, 20th October 1972, lot 35; exhibited Hotspur, 'Golden Jubilee Exhibition' (1974), Plate 19; sold Christie's, 17th November 1983, lot 6; Sotheby's, 10th July 1987, lot 8; Christie's, New York, 16th April 1998, lot 23; exhibited Mallett, 'The Age of Matthew Boulton' (2000), pp. 50–1, Cupid's bow missing.
690. J.F. to M.B., 23rd January 1772.
691. B. and F. to the Earl of Stamford, 6th February 1772.
692. John Scale to M.B., 6th February 1772.
693. B. and F. to William Matthews, 27th April 1772: the entries are not consecutive. The price of Mr Thyne's vase was later corrected to £12 12s. 0d. (B. and F. to William Matthews, 19th June 1772).
694. B. and F. to William Matthews, 26th April 1772.
695. B. and F. to William Matthews, 21st July 1772.
696. B. and F. to William Matthews, 19th June 1772.
697. B. and F. to William Matthews, 28th November 1772.
698. Inventory, 1782, pp. 83–4, 133.
699. Inventory, 1782, p. 180.
700. A single vase on a three-step marble plinth, State Bedroom of Maria Feodorevna, illustrated in a general view in Koutchoumov, *Pavlovsk* (1976), p. 115, Plate 84.
701. A single vase, Accession no. 1982.117. Others sold AB Stockholm Auktionsverk, 10th–14th November 1981, lot 387 (a single vase, missing the top of the oil burner); exhibited Mallett, 'The Age of Matthew Boulton' (2000), pp. 66–7 (a pair); Temple Newsam, Leeds (a single vase missing burner and chains, and with a modern lid and lining soldered to the finial), illustrated Gilbert, *Furniture at Temple Newsam and Lotherton Hall* (1978), Vol. II, p. 385, Fig. 510.
702. Sold Christie's, 17th November 1994, lot 26 (Viscount Villiers), illustrated MacQuoid and Edwards, *Dictionary of English Furniture* (1954), Vol. III, p. 16, Fig. 2, and Edwards, *Shorter Dictionary of English Furniture* (1964), p. 407, Fig. 3. In Christie's catalogue, the winged figures are described as if in a fashion magazine as 'lightly clad figures *en chignon* each with a necklace of beads supporting two chains in their cleavage'.
703. Tomlin, 'The Inventory at Osterley Park' (1986), p. 119.
704. Metropolitan Museum of Art, New York.
705. B. and F. to the Duke of Marlborough, 22nd August 1772.
706. Tomlin, 'The Inventory at Osterley Park' (1986), p. 118. The tripod stands conform to a drawing in the Soane MSS, Vol. 17, no. 62, which is dated 13th November 1776. See Harris, *Furniture of Robert Adam* (1963), pp. 101–2 and Plate 138.
707. B. and F. to James Keir, 1st April 1772.
708. Tomlin, 'The Inventory at Osterley Park' (1986), p. 119. Also in the drawing room there were the two perfume burners of Plate 363 and 'one spar vase elegantly mounted on a double pedestal with or molee'.
709. B. and F. to William Matthews, 21st July 1772.
710. Library of Paul I, illustrated in general views in Koutchoumov, *Pavlovsk* (1976), p. 69, Plate 41 and p. 72, Plate 44, also in Audrey and Victor Kennet, *The Palaces of Leningrad* (1973), Plate 108 (chains missing).
711. Christie's, 12th March 1947, lot 312 (Duchess of Kent, a pair, blue john bodies, tortoiseshell plinths, chains missing); Sotheby's, 14th April 1984, lot 734, illustrated in 'The Works of Matthew Boulton from the Collection of James C. Codell Jr.' (Headley Whitney Museum, Kentucky, 1990), p. 12; Christie's, Amsterdam, 21st December 1989, lot 276 (single vase, blue john, chains missing, no plinth); Sotheby's, 10th July 1998, lot 61 (a pair, blue john bodies and plinths); a single vase

exhibited Mallett, 'The Age of Matthew Boulton' (2000), pp. 64–5 (blue john, missing chains and mount below guilloche band); Christie's, 29th November 2001, lot 40 (a pair, white glass, chains missing), sold previously Bukowski (Sweden), 4th November 1986, lot 687, now City of Birmingham Museum, Soho House.
712. Sold Christie's, 17th April 1997, lot 4.
713. A pair of white marble vases with branches sold Christie's, 16th November 1995, lot 10.

Appendices

APPENDIX I **LIST OF PATRONS**

It is impossible to compile a complete list of the people who bought ormolu ornaments from Boulton and Fothergill. The firm's archives are incomplete (see Bibliography, Manuscript sources) and the sales recorded in surviving documents were probably concealed sometimes under the title of 'goods'. With these limitations the following list is, I hope, a useful record of people who, according to the archives, bought or enquired about ormolu ornaments up to about 1782. It does not include retailers or other agents, e.g. ambassadors and agents overseas, whose orders or enquiries were not for their own accounts. These will be found in the Index. Nor does it include all the buyers listed in the catalogues of the sales at Christie's in 1771 and Christie and Ansell's in 1778, many of whose names cannot readily be identified (see Appendix III).

Under each name I have given brief biographical notes, if this has been possible. I have kept these notes to the bare minimum necessary for the purposes of identification, seldom, for example, giving any details of occupation and not mentioning a patron's wife unless she entered into the relevant correspondence. I have shown only the addresses, if any, recorded in the archives. Fuller information about many of the patrons can be found in the usual reference books such as *The Dictionary of National Biography*, Cokayne's *The Complete Peerage*, Burke's *Peerage*, etc., and in the Appendices of such books as Bolton's *Architecture of Robert and James Adam*. The biographical notes are followed in each case by a brief reference to the ornaments that the patron bought. Beneath these notes I have listed the documents in which the patron or his purchase is mentioned. Most of these documents are among the Matthew Boulton papers in the Birmingham City Archives (see Bibliography, Manuscript sources).
I have listed these in three categories:

(1) Incoming letters, i.e. written by the patron and received by Boulton and Fothergill or by Matthew Boulton, unless otherwise stated.
(2) Outgoing letters, i.e. written to the patron by Boulton and Fothergill or by Matthew Boulton unless otherwise stated.
(3) Miscellaneous, i.e. memoranda, accounting documents, letters from Boulton to his partner or his clerks, and vice versa, etc.

Many of the documents listed are quoted or at least referred to in the text of the book. The catalogues of Boulton and Fothergill's sales at Christie's in 1771 and Christie and Ansell's in 1778, which are often mentioned in this Appendix, are reproduced in full in Appendix III. References to visits to Soho mostly come from the 'Register Book' (Great Tew Archive) (Appendix II).

I have used the following abbreviations:

C.L.B.	Birmingham City Achives, Central Library, Birmingham
M.B.	Matthew Boulton
J.F.	John Fothergill
B. and F.	Boulton and Fothergill
W.M.	William Matthews

Amyand, Mr

There is no information in the relevant archives about the identity of Amyand. I have suggested in the Survey of ornaments (see p. 215) that he might have been either Claudius Amyand (1718–74) or John Amyand (1751–81), the uncle and brother respectively of Sir George Cornewall (1748–1819), who succeeded his father Sir George Amyand as second baronet in 1766, and assumed the name of Cornewall on his marriage to Catherine Cornewall, the heiress to Moccas Court, Herefordshire, in 1771. Amyand bought, or perhaps took delivery of on behalf of Sir George, a King's clock and case in 1772 (Plate 162). He can probably be identified with the Mr Amiens who visited Soho on 16th July 1770. Sir George and Lady Cornewall went there in 1778.

C.L.B.	*Outgoing letters*	Letter Book E – 27th April 1772, 16th May 1772, 24th June 1772 (all to W.M.).

Ancaster, Duke (and Duchess) of

Grimsthorpe, Lincolnshire.

1714–78, succeeded as third Duke 1742, married Mary Panton (second wife) 1750. Bought a pair of vases, several girandoles and six ice pails in 1772–3.

C.L.B.	*Outgoing letters*	Letter Book E – 29th February 1772 (to W.M.), 4th March 1772 (to W.M.), 17th March 1772 (to W.M.), 8th April 1772 (to W.M.), 19th April 1772 (to W.M.), 24th June 1772 (to W.M.), 27th June 1772 (to W.M.), 11th July 1772, 26th September 1772 (to W.M.), 19th December 1772 (to W.M.), 3rd January 1773 (to W.M.); Letter Book 1773 (Boulton and Watt papers) – 24th April 1773, 22nd May 1773, 25th May 1773 (all to W.M.).
	Miscellaneous	M.B.'s Notebook (1772); J. Scale Box – 28th January 1773 (J. Scale to M.B.); J. Fothergill Box – 13th February 1773 (J.F. to M.B.), 30th April 1773 (M.B. to J.F.), 5th May 1773 (J.F. to M.B.); Z. Walker Box – 26th April 1773 ('Inland Debts').

Anson, George

Shugborough Park, Staffordshire.

1731–89, son of Thomas Anson's sister Janette Adams, assumed the name of Anson on inheriting his uncle's estates of Shugborough 1773. Invoiced for his deceased uncle's account in 1773; and for cleaning and repairing of a girandole in 1777.

C.L.B	*Outgoing letters*	Letter Book F – 28th October 1773.
	Miscellaneous	Ledger 1776–8, 6th December 1777.

Anson, Thomas

Shugborough Park, Staffordshire.

1695–1773, brother of the admiral Lord Anson, succeeded by his sister's son, George Anson. Letters survive in both the Boulton and Wedgwood archives concerning the manufacture of the tripod and bowl which James Stuart designed to surmount his 'Lanthorn of Demosthenes' at Shugborough (see Chapter 3, p. 72). Stuart asked Boulton about the making of an ormolu border for a tea table in 1769. Probably the 'Mr Anson' who visited Soho on 14th September 1767, and the 'Anson Esqr' who did likewise on 22nd September 1770.

C.L.B.	*Incoming letters*	S3 Box – 26th December 1769 (James Stuart).
	Miscellaneous	Z. Walker Box – 26th April 1773 ('Inland Debts').

Arundell of Wardour, Lord
Wardour Castle, Dorset; Portman Square, London.
1740–1808, succeeded as eighth Baron 1756. Bought vases in 1771, corresponded about candlesticks, girandoles and a tripod candlestick in 1777, and ordered door furniture in 1778 after correspondence in 1773 and 1777.

C.L.B.	*Incoming letters*	A Box – 3rd September 1773.
	Outgoing letters	Letter Book E – 10th December 1771 (to Colonel Burgoyne); Letter Book G – 22nd March 1777; Letter Book I – 27th May 1777, 14th July 1777, 9th September 1777, 13th November 1777, 16th July 1778.
	Miscellaneous	J. Hodges Box – 23rd April 1777 (J. Hodges to M.B.).
CHRISTIE'S		Sale, Christie's 1771, second day, lots 19, 27, 35.

Ashburnham, Earl of
Dover Street, London.
1724–1812, succeeded as second Earl 1737. Bought girandoles in 1775, ice pails in 1776 and five vases in 1778. Visited Soho in July 1772.

C.L.B.	*Outgoing letters*	Letter Book G – 5th April 1775, 2nd November 1775, 22nd May 1776, 1st June 1776.
	Miscellaneous	Z. Walker Box – 26th April 1773 ('Inland Debts'); Journal 1776–8, 28th May 1776.
CHRISTIE'S		Sale, Christie and Ansell's, 1778, lots 7, 83, 86.

Aylesford, Earl of
1751–1812, succeeded as fourth Earl 1777. Bought a pair of ormolu branches 1778. Visited Soho in June 1778.

C.L.B.	*Miscellaneous*	A Box – 27th June 1778 (memorandum of order); Ledger 1776–8, 29th June 1778; Journal 1776–8, 29th June 1778.
HOARE'S BANK		Ledger G, p. 69, 30th December 1779.

Balfour, Mrs
Bought a pair of goat's head vases in 1769, ordering them at Soho during her visit on 4th September.

C.L.B.	*Outgoing letters*	Letter Book E – 16th September 1772 (to W.M.).
	Miscellaneous	B.1 Box – 4th September 1769 (memorandum of order).

Beauchamp, Lord
Probably son of first Earl of Hertford (*q.v.*), succeeded as second Marquess of Hertford 1794 (d.1822). Bought ice pails and enquired about ormolu monteiths in 1778. Visited Soho on 14th August 1769 and 24th May 1770.

C.L.B.	*Incoming letters*	S.3 Box – 31st March 1778 (John Stuart).

Beckford, Mrs
Possibly Maria Beckford, daughter of Hon. George Hamilton, wife of the Lord Mayor William Beckford (d.1770). Bought vases (probably seven) in 1771: vases cleaned and repaired in 1781.
C.L.B. *Outgoing letters* Letter Book E – 20th January 1771, 6th February 1771 (both to W.M.); Letter Book I – 18th June 1781 (to John Stuart).

Bessborough, Earl of
1704–93, succeeded as second Earl 1758. Bought two pairs of vases in 1771.
CHRISTIE'S Sale, Christie's 1771, second day, lot 44; third day, lot 39.

Brahe, Count of
Bought a pair of vases in 1776, during a visit to Soho on 29th March.
C.L.B. *Miscellaneous* Ledger 1776–8, 30th March 1776.

Bridgeman, Lady
Weston.
Elizabeth Simpson (d.1806), married Sir Henry Bridgeman (1725–1800), who succeeded as fifth Baronet 1764 and was created first Baron Bradford 1794. Appears to have bought one or more wreathed-column candlesticks by 1771 (Plates 140–1), the design being named after her in correspondence. Visited Soho on 21st August 1770 and on 23rd September 1780.
C.L.B. *Outgoing letters* Letter Book E – 6th May 1771, 27th April 1772 (both to W.M.).

Burgoyne, Colonel
Hertford Street, London.
Probably General John Burgoyne (1722–92), son-in-law of the eleventh Earl of Derby and famous for his defeat at Saratoga in 1778. Bought 'goods' in 1771, including girandoles: may have been the patron after whom Boulton and Fothergill named their 'Burgoyne's' vase. Visited Soho on 1st November 1771, and again as General Burgoyne in August 1778.
C.L.B. *Outgoing letters* Letter Book E – 10th December 1771.

Cailland, Mrs
George Street, Hanover Square, London.
Wife of John Cailland (d.1810), active in India with Clive 1753–*c*.1775. A Titus clock delivered to General Cailland for her, on instructions from Samuel Pechell, in 1772.
C.L.B. *Incoming letters* P.1 Box – 8th April 1772 (S. Pechell).
Outgoing letters Letter Book E – 17th September 1772 (to S. Pechell).

Calcraft, Mr
Probably John Calcraft (1726–72), cousin of Henry Fox, first Lord Holland, and protégé of Marquess of Granby. Bought vases, a sphinx vase, etc. in 1772. Visited Soho on 4th October 1771.
C.L.B. *Outgoing letters* Letter Book E – 16th September 1772 (to W.M.).

Campbell, Lord Frederick
Second son of fourth Duke of Argyll: was sent drawings of ormolu pieces in 1776.
C.L.B. *Outgoing letters* Letter Book G – 20th March 1776 (to John Stuart).

Campbell, Samuel
Bristol.
Bought vases in 1771.
C.L.B. *Outgoing letters* Letter Book E – 17th September 1771.

Canterbury, Archbishop of – see Frederick Cornwallis.

Carnack, General
John Carnack (1716–1800), served in India from 1758. Bought several ornaments in 1771 including perfume burners and candle vases, a triton candlestick, a caryatic vase, a sphinx vase, and an 'altar', i.e. a vase on a pedestal.
CHRISTIE'S Sale, Christie's, 1771, third day, lots 28, 34, 59, 65, 70, 72, 82.

Catherine II (the Great), Empress of Russia
1729–96, married Peter III of Russia and became Empress after his murder in 1762. Bought a consignment of vases etc. in 1772: a further consignment was sent for her approval in 1774. Boulton thought also of sending the geographical, Minerva and sidereal clocks in 1772, but in the event only the sidereal clock was sent, in 1776, which the Empress did not want. An obelisk in Boulton and Fothergill's Pattern Books is inscribed 'Empress of Russia' (Plate 223.1).
C.L.B. *Incoming letters* C Box – 21st February 1772 (Lord Cathcart); G.2 Box – 13th September 1774 (Sir Robert Gunning).
Outgoing letters Letter Book E – 30th October 1771 (to Lord Cathcart).
Miscellaneous M.B.'s Notebook 1772; Private Box – n.d. [11th April 1772] (M.B. to his wife); J. Fothergill Box – 2nd March 1773, 10th March 1773, 20th March 1774, 16th December 1779 (all J.F. to M.B.); Ledger 1776–8, 9th May 1776.

Catherlough, Earl of
1702–72, created first Earl 1763, previously Lord Luxborough (created 1745). Bought a pair of Cleopatra vases for 'Mrs Davies' in 1771. Visited Soho in November 1771.
C.L.B. *Outgoing letters* Letter Book E – 4th December 1771 (to W.M.).

Chas(?), Colonel
Was sent a design for a knife case, pattern as for Countess of Craven, in 1776.
C.L.B. *Outgoing letters* Letter Book G – 22nd June 1776 (to John Wyatt).

Chesterfield, Earl of
Eythrope, Buckinghamshire.
1755–1815, succeeded as fifth Earl 1773. Bought a Venus perfume burner, a pair of white marble pedestal vases no. 59 and a pair of vases no. 349 in 1780, probably all

during his visit to Soho on 6th July.

C.L.B.	*Outgoing letters*	Letter Book I – 24th July 1780.
	Miscellaneous	Day Book 1779–81, 8th July 1780.

Child, Robert

Berkeley Square, London; Upton, Banbury.

1739–82, banker, grandson of the goldsmith Francis Child, founder of Child's Bank; inherited Osterley Park 1763. Borrowed a pair of Bingley's vases, and bought three pairs of wing-figured vases (Plates 365, 367, 369) and a sphinx vase in 1772, and a pair of vases in 1779.

C.L.B.	*Outgoing letters*	Letter Book E – 26th April 1772 (to W.M.), 27th April 1772 (to W.M.), 16th May 1772 (to W.M.), 21st July 1772 (to W.M.), 12th September 1772, 16th September 1772 (to W.M.); Letter Book I – 27th December 1779.
	Miscellaneous	Day Book 1779–81, 23rd December 1779: Ledger 1779–82, 23rd December 1779: Journal 1778–81, 23rd December 1779.

Cholmondeley, General

Probably James Cholmondeley (1708–75), second son of the second Earl of Cholmondeley. Bought a vase in 1771, perfume burners and a boy clock in 1772.

C.L.B.	*Outgoing letters*	Letter Book E – 21st June 1772, 24th June 1772 (both to W.M.).
CHRISTIE'S		Sale, Christie's, 1771, first day, lot 58.

Cockburn, Sir James

Soho Square.

Died 1780, succeeded as third Baronet 1751. Bought vases in 1771, probably ordered during his visit to Soho on 31st August.

C.L.B.	*Outgoing letters*	Letter Book E – 19th September 1771 (to W.M.).

Cocks, Sir Charles

1725–1806, created Baronet 1772 and Baron Somers 1784. Bought a sphinx vase in 1777.

C.L.B.	*Miscellaneous*	Ledger 1776–8, 1st November 1777.

Coke, Lady Mary

1726–1811, daughter of second Duke of Argyll, married Hon. Edward Coke. Her *Letters and Journals* published in 1889–96. Bought two pairs of vases in 1778.

CHRISTIE'S		Sale, Christie and Ansell's, 1778, lots 8, 31.

Cornwallis, Frederick

1713–83, son of fourth Lord Cornwallis, Archbishop of Canterbury 1768–83. Was sent a drawing of a girandole, and placed an order for unspecified goods in 1772.

C.L.B.	*Outgoing letters*	Letter Book E – 16th September 1772, 26th September 1772 (both to W.M.).

Coventry, Earl of
1722–1809, succeeded as sixth Earl 1751. Bought a pair of ice pails in 1777.
C.L.B. *Miscellaneous* Ledger 1776–8, 1st November 1777.

Craven, Earl (and Countess) of
Charles Street, Berkeley Square, London; Combe Abbey, Warwickshire.
1738–91, succeeded as sixth Earl 1769, married Elizabeth, daughter of fourth Earl of Berkeley, 1767. Bought vases and dressing boxes in 1771, a pair of vases ('no. 71') in 1775, and a knife case in 1776. Visited Soho on 11th July 1769, 11th August 1769 (Lady Craven), 13th July 1773 and 5th August 1780.
C.L.B. *Incoming letters* C.3 Box – 12th January 1771.
Outgoing letters Letter Book E – 13th February 1771, 14th February 1771 (to W.M.), 16th October 1771; Letter Book G – 10th January 1776, 7th August 1776, 16th September 1776, 2nd November 1776, 4th November 1776.
Miscellaneous J. Fothergill Box – 4th April 1771 (J.F. to M.B.); J. Scale Box – n.d. [April 1771] (M.B. to J. Scale); M.B.'s Diary 1773; Cash Debtor Book 1772–82, 23rd September 1775; Wyatt Box – 1st February 1776 (John Wyatt to M.B.); Ledger 1776–8, 30th October 1776.

Crawford, Sir Patrick
Bought a Venus vase in 1778.
CHRISTIE'S Sale, Christie and Ansell's, 1778, lot 77.

Cunliffe, Lady
Probably Mary Wright (d.1791), married to Sir Robert Cunliffe 1752. Bought a pair of candlesticks, probably lion-faced, in 1771.
CHRISTIE'S Sale, Christie's, 1771, first day, lot 83.

Cunliffe, Sir Robert
Chester.
1719–78, succeeded as second Baronet 1767. Commissioned two figures for the decoration of a chimneypiece in 1774. Visited Soho on 30th May 1776.
C.L.B. *Outgoing letters* Letter Book G – 30th September 1774, 5th October 1774, 18th October 1774.

Dashwood, Lady
Grosvenor Square, London.
Probably the wife of Sir James Dashwood, second Baronet of Kirtlington (d.1779), whom she married in 1738–9, and mother-in-law of fourth Duke of Manchester. Bought a vase in 1772 and two pairs of vases in 1773.
C.L.B. *Incoming letters* D.1 Box – n.d. [April 1772] (three letters, two from, and one to, Lady Dashwood).
Outgoing letters Letter Book F – 20th October 1773; Letter Book 1773 (Boulton and Watt papers) – 29th May 1773.

Derby, Countess of
Grosvenor Square, London.
Elizabeth (d.1797), daughter of sixth Duke of Hamilton, married twelfth Earl of Derby (1752–1834) 1774. Bought ice pails and a Venus clock in 1778.
C.L.B. *Miscellaneous* J. Hodges Box – 31st January 1778 (J. Hodges to M.B.).

Digby, Lord (and Lady)
Lower Brook Street, London; Sherborne Castle, Dorset.
1731–93, succeeded as seventh Baron 1757, married Mary Knowler (d.1794) 1770. Bought a tripod perfume burner (Plate 238) and a pair of vases (Plate 296) in 1774.
C.L.B. *Outgoing letters* Letter Book G – 30th September 1774, 8th October 1774, November 1774, 6th February 1775.

Dillon, Lord – see Dyllon.

Downes, Lady
Probably Lora Burton (1740–1812), married fifth Viscount Downe (1728–81) 1763. Bought a pair of vases in 1778.
CHRISTIE'S Sale, Christie and Ansell's, 1778, lot 11.

Dunbar, Charles
Hill Street, London.
Bought a pair of vases and a Venus perfume burner in 1771, probably ordered during his visit to Soho on 4th October, a pair of 'Lady Bridgeman's' candlesticks in 1772 and vases in 1773.
C.L.B. *Outgoing letters* Letter Book E – 11th November 1771, 22nd January 1772, 27th April 1772, 9th January 1773 (all to W.M.).

Dundas, Sir Lawrence
Arlington Street, London.
*c.*1710–81, created Baronet 1762. Bought a Persian vase in 1772 (Plate 351).
C.L.B. *Outgoing letters* Letter Book E – 4th January 1772.
Miscellaneous M.B.'s Notebook 1773.

Dundass, Mrs
Enquired about a wing-figured vase in 1772.
C.L.B. *Outgoing letters* Letter Book E – 26th February 1772 (to W.M.).

Dyllon, Lord
Probably eleventh Viscount Dillon (1705–87) who succeeded 1741. Bought a pair of vases in 1771.
CHRISTIE'S Sale, Christie's, 1771, second day, lot 77.

Edgecumbe, Lady
Emma (d.1807), daughter of John Gilbert, Archbishop of York, married third Baron Edgecumbe (d.1795) 1761: Lord Edgecumbe was created Earl of Mount Edgecumbe 1789. Ordered girandoles in 1773.
C.L.B. *Outgoing letters* Letter Book E – 19th December 1772, 3rd January 1773 (both to W.M.).

Edgeworth, R. L.
Edgeworthstown, Mulbingar, Ireland.
Richard Lovell Edgeworth (1744–1817), author and inventor, friend of Erasmus Darwin and William Small. Was sent vases in 1774.
C.L.B. *Incoming letters* E.1 Box – 24th November 1774.

Elliott, Lady
Possibly the wife of Sir Gilbert Elliot (1722–77), third Baronet of Minto and father of first Earl of Minto. Bought a pair of vases and a perfume burner in 1771.
CHRISTIE'S Sale, Christie's, 1771, first day, lots 62, 70.

Exeter, Earl of
1725–93, succeeded as ninth Earl 1754; succeeded by nephew, who became first Marquess of Exeter. Bought a pair of vases in 1771 and a framed painting in 1777. Visited Soho on 6th September 1776.
C.L.B. *Miscellaneous* Ledger 1776–8, 4th August 1777.
CHRISTIE'S Sale, Christie's, 1771, third day, lot 69.

Farnham, Lord
Dublin.
Died 1800, succeeded as third Baron 1779, created Earl of Farnham 1785. Bought vases in 1777 which had tarnished in 1780. Visited Soho on 26th July 1771.
C.L.B. *Outgoing letters* Letter Book I – 12th August 1780.

Findlater, Earl of
1750–1811, succeeded as seventh Earl of Findlater and fourth Earl of Seafield 1770. Bought a clock case in 1776. Visited Soho on 15th May 1770.
C.L.B. *Outgoing letters* Letter Book G – 20th January 1776, 11th October 1776.
Miscellaneous Ledger 1776–8, 9th October 1776.

Fitzroy, General Hon. Charles
Stanhope Street, London.
1737–97, son of Lord Augustus Fitzroy and grandson of second Duke of Grafton: created Baron Southampton 1780. Had some branches re-gilt and bought a pair of girandoles in 1778.
C.L.B. *Outgoing letters* Letter Book I – 13th June 1778 (to John Stuart), 20th June 1778, 26th September 1778.
Miscellaneous J. Hodges Box – 23rd May 1778 (J. Hodges to M.B.).

Fitzwilliam, Earl
1748–1833, succeeded as fourth Earl 1756. Bought four vases in 1771.
CHRISTIE'S Sale, Christie's, 1771, third day, lots 52, 60, 68.

Fordyce, Lady Margaret
Lady Margaret Lindsay, second daughter of fifth Earl of Balcarres, married in 1770 the banker Alexander Fordyce, a partner in Neal, James, Fordyce and Down (failed 1772). Bought a sphinx vase in 1771. 'Fordice Esqr' and his wife visited Soho on 17th September 1771.
CHRISTIE'S Sale, Christie's, 1771, second day, lot 82.

Fredericks, Baron
Bought a clock in 1776.
C.L.B. *Miscellaneous* Ledger 1776–8, 9th September 1776.

Freeman, —
Clifford Street, London.
Bought two pairs of vases in 1779.
C.L.B. *Miscellaneous* Day Book 1779–81, 2nd November 1779.

French, W. P. N.
Bought ornaments for a cabinet in 1776.
C.L.B. *Miscellaneous* Cash Debtor Book 1772–82, 9th February 1776; Ledger 1776–8, 12th February 1776; Journal 1776–8, 12th February 1776.

Gale, William
Bruton Street, London.
Bought a vase in 1771.
C.L.B. *Outgoing letters* Letter Book E – 11th November 1771 (to W.M.).

George III, King of Great Britain (and Queen Charlotte)
1738–1820, succeeded 1760, married Princess Sophia Charlotte (1744–1818), daughter of Charles I, Duke of Mecklenburg-Strelitz, in 1761. Bought the first King's clock case (Plate 160) and at least six vases, including at least two King's vases (Plate 339) and probably two sphinx vases (Plate 355), in 1770–1, and a Titus clock case (Plate 183), a Venus clock and a pair of perfume burners in 1772.
C.L.B. *Incoming letters* W. Matthews Box – 6th March 1771.
Outgoing letters Letter Book E – 17th January 1771 (to Thomas Wright), 17th January 1771 (to W.M.), 14th February 1771 (to W.M.), 14th February 1771 (to Thomas Wright), n.d. [26th February 1771] (to W.M.), 21st March 1771 (to W.M.), 23rd March 1771 (to W.M.), 24th March 1771 (to W.M.).
Miscellaneous Private Box – n.d. [3rd March 1770], 6th March 1770, 11th April 1772 (all M.B. to his wife); J. Fothergill Box –

	n.d. [4th March 1770] (M.B. to J.F.), n.d. [7th or 8th March 1770] (M.B. to J.F.), 4th April 1771 (J.F. to M.B.), 28th March 1772 (J.F. to M.B.).
BRITISH HOROLOGICAL INSTITUTE	B. L. Vulliamy's Clock Book 1797–1806, 12th July 1800.

Gloucester, Bishop of – see William Warburton.

Godolphin, Lady

Probably Lady Anne Fitzwilliam (1722–1805), daughter of second Earl Fitzwilliam, who married Lord Godolphin (d.1785) in 1766. Bought a griffin vase in 1771.

CHRISTIE'S	Sale, Christie's, 1771, second day, lot 37.

Gower, Earl (and Countess)

Whitehall, London.

1721–1803, succeeded as second Earl Gower 1754: created Marquess of Stafford 1786. Married Susannah (d.1805), daughter of sixth Earl of Galloway 1768. Bought a pair of 'wing-figured' vases in 1772, vases and four tripods (Plate 233) in 1777. Visited Soho on 21st April 1770 and in August 1776.

C.L.B.	*Outgoing letters*	Letter Book E – 19th June 1772 (to W.M.); Letter Book I – 23rd October 1777.
	Miscellaneous	J. Hodges Box – 23rd April 1777 (J. Hodges to M.B.); Ledger 1776–8, 20th October 1777; Journal 1776–8, 20th October 1777.
GREAT TEW ARCHIVE		F. Eginton to M.B., 23rd April 1777.

Granby, Marquess of

Knightsbridge.

1754–87, succeeded as second Marquess 1770 and as fourth Duke of Rutland 1779. Bought a pair of perfume burners, a pair of sphinx vases and a serpent tripod in 1774.

C.L.B.	*Outgoing letters*	Letter Book G – 19th November 1774.
	Miscellaneous	Cash Debtor Book 1772–82, 8th August 1774.

Grantham, Lord

1738–86, succeeded as second Baron 1770. Ambassador to Madrid 1771–9. Bought a King's vase and ordered four Persian vases for his sister Mrs John Parker (*q.v.*) in 1771, the order being later changed to King's vases (Plate 343).

C.L.B.	*Outgoing letters*	Letter Book E – 7th August 1771, 19th October 1771, 27th November 1771 (all to W.M.).

Grevill, Mrs

Probably Frances Macartney, the wife of Richard Fulke Greville (d., *c.*1806), authoress and one of Mrs Montagu's rivals as a hostess. Bought two vases in 1771.

C.L.B.	*Outgoing letters*	Letter Book E – 25th February 1771 (to W.M.).

Griffin, Sir John Griffin
Audley End, Essex.
1719–97, assumed the name Griffin (previously Whitwell) on the death of his aunt the Countess of Portsmouth 1749: succeeded as fourth Baron Howard de Walden 1784 and created Baron Braybrooke 1788. Bought a pair of Bingley's vases, a pair of Morrison's vases and a griffin vase in 1771. Visited Soho on 22nd July 1776.

C.L.B.	*Outgoing letters*	Letter Book E – 27th March 1771.
ESSEX RECORD OFFICE		(Audley End Papers) DDBy.A29/11 – Receipt dated 19th December 1771.

Grote, Baron
Ordered a pair of Cleopatra vases, during his visit to Soho in November 1771.

C.L.B.	*Miscellaneous*	G.2 Box – 12th November 1771.

Guise, Sir William
Redcombe, Cirencester.
Died 1783, succeeded as fifth Baronet 1769. Ordered a pair of goat's head vases during his visit to Soho on 9th September 1769. Visited Soho again on 18th September 1770.

C.L.B.	*Miscellaneous*	G.2 Box – 9th September 1769.

Hall,—
Bought vases in 1771.

C.L.B.	*Outgoing letters*	Letter Book E – 11th September 1771 (to W.M.).

Harbord, Sir Harbord
Gunton Park, Norfolk.
1754–81, created Baron Suffield 1786. Returned a tea urn for repair 1770. Ordered a Venus clock and a pair of ewers in 1772, and had a pair of candlesticks gilt in 1778.

C.L.B.	*Outgoing letters*	Letter Book G – 15th February 1776; Letter Book N – 6th February 1783, 8th March 1783, 25th July 1783.
	Miscellaneous	M.B.'s Diary 1772.
JOHN RYLANDS LIBRARY UNIVERSITY OF MANCHESTER		English MSS 1123 – Dorothy Richardson 'Tours', Vol. 2, 1770, p. 217.

Harcourt, Earl of
Harcourt House, Oxford.
1736–1809, succeeded as second Earl 1777, formerly Viscount Nuneham. Purchased a pair of girandoles in 1775, and later had some re-gilt.

C.L.B.	*Outgoing letters*	Letter Book I – 12th March 1775, 23rd March 1775, 20th June 1778 (to General Charles Fitzroy).

Harrowby, Lord
Park Street, Grosvenor Square, London.
1735–1803, created Baron Harrowby 1776, father of first Earl of Harrowby. Bought vases in 1776 and 1777. Visited Soho on 28th November 1776, 14th May 1777 and in

1778.

C.L.B.	*Outgoing letters*	Letter Book G – 16th January 1777, 1st February 1777; Letter Book I – 20th October 1778.
	Miscellaneous	Ledger 1776–8, 1st February 1776; Journal 1776–8, 1st February 1776.

Hertford, Earl (and Countess) of
Grosvenor Street, London.
*c.*1717–94, created Earl of Hertford 1750, Marquess of Hertford 1793, married Lady Isabella Fitzroy (d.1782), daughter of second Duke of Grafton 1741. Had some ice pails re-gilt in 1774.

C.L.B.	*Outgoing letters*	Letter Book G – 13th July 1774, 13th August 1774.

Hoare, Henry
Stourhead, Wiltshire; Fleet Street, London.
1705–85, partner in Hoare's Bank 1726, succeeded to his father's estate at Stourhead on the death of his mother 1741. Bought a Titus watch stand in 1772; lent Boulton and Fothergill a 'book of vases' in 1773.

C.L.B.	*Outgoing letters*	Letter Book E – 27th October 1772; Letter Book 1773 (Boulton and Watt papers) – 4th May 1773, 3rd June 1773 (both to W.M.).
	Miscellaneous	J. Fothergill Box – 27th January 1773 (J.F. to M.B.).
WILTSHIRE COUNTY RECORD OFFICE		(Hoare Papers) 383/6 – Account for 'vases and cand.' (i.e. candle vases ?), 8th August 1770.

Holland, Lady
Kensington.
Lady Mary Fitzpatrick (d.1778), daughter of Earl of Upper Ossory, married second Baron Holland (d.1774) *c.*1772. Bought ormolu 'goods' in 1775.

C.L.B.	*Outgoing letters*	Letter Book G – 21st March 1775.

Hunloke, Sir Henry
Wingerworth, Chesterfield.
Bought vases in 1774, probably during his visit to Soho.

C.L.B.	*Outgoing letters*	Letter Book G – December 1774.

Kerry, Earl of
Portman Square, London.
1740–1818, succeeded as third Earl 1747, first cousin of second Earl of Shelburne. Bought two perfume burners, three table candlesticks and a Venus vase in 1771; chimneypiece ornaments, a pair of King's vases (later exchanged), six tripod candelabra, a pair of white marble vases, some girandoles and figures to hold candle branches in 1772; and door furniture. Also corresponded about other pieces, including a tea urn, candlesticks, etc. His furniture etc., including ormolu, sold in 1778. Visited Soho on 4th September 1769.

C.L.B.	*Outgoing letters*	Letter Book E – 26th August 1771 (to Mayhew and Ince), 7th December 1771, 26th December 1771, 29th December 1771, 8th January 1772, 26th February 1772,

5th March 1772, 7th March 1772, 8th March 1772, 11th March 1772, 14th May 1772, 21st May 1772, 22nd June 1772, 9th July 1772; Letter Book N – 11th August 1783 (to Mayhew and Ince).

Miscellaneous Mrs E. Montagu Box – 16th January 1772 (M.B. to Mrs Montagu); J. Fothergill Box – 23rd January 1772 (M.B. to J.F.), 23rd January 1772 (J.F. to M.B.), 2nd March 1773 (J.F. to M.B.), 14th February 1778 (J.F. to M.B.); J. Scale Box, 6th February 1772 (J. Scale to M.B.); Z. Walker Box, 26th April 1773 ('Inland Debts'); S.3 Box – 31st March 1778 (John Stuart to M.B.); M.B.'s Notebook 1772.

CHRISTIE'S Sale, Christie's, 1771, first day, lots 9, 48, 64; second day, lot 17; third day, lot 48; sale of Earl of Kerry's 'Magnificent Furniture' etc., Christie and Ansell's, in his house in Portman Square, 25th February 1778 and eight following days (postponed to 23rd–31st March).

Lane, Joseph

Bought vases in 1771.

C.L.B. *Outgoing letters* Letter Book E – 30th January 1771, 19th June 1771.

Lyttelton, Lord

1744–79, succeeded as second Lord Lyttelton 1774, married Apphia Witts (*q.v.*) 1771. Had a pair of vases repaired and re-gilt in 1776. Visited Soho on 13th August 1775.

C.L.B. *Miscellaneous* Journal 1776–8, 27th June 1776.

Macalester, Duncan

Bought a pair of perfume burners 'no. 11' and a pair of candle vases 'no. 55' in 1780, delivered through J. Vanneck, New Bond Street.

C.L.B. *Miscellaneous* Day Book 1779–81, p. 440.

Macclesfield, Countess of

Mary Heathcote (d.1812), daughter of Sir William Heathcote, married third Earl of Macclesfield (1723–95) 1749: he succeeded 1764. Bought a pair of vases in 1778.

CHRISTIE'S Sale, Christie and Ansell's, 1778, lot 36.

Manchester, Duke (and Duchess) of

1737–88, succeeded as fourth Duke 1762, married Elizabeth Dashwood (d.1832), daughter of Sir James Dashwood (see Lady Dashwood). Bought a pair of 'mask face' and a pair of goat's head vases in 1772 (later returned), and mounts for a cabinet in 1774–6 (Plate 200).

C.L.B. *Incoming letters* M.1 Box – 16th January 1779 (Mayhew and Ince).

Outgoing letters Letter Book E – 27th April 1772 (to W.M.); Letter Book G – 3rd December 1774 (to William Ince), 6th April 1775, 28th June 1775, 16th October 1775, 8th December 1775, 5th January 1776, 23rd February 1776, 23rd March

1776 (all to Mayhew and Ince), 9th November 1776 (to W.M.); Letter Book H – 6th March 1779 (to Mayhew and Ince); Letter Book N – 11th August 1783, 6th December 1784 (both to Mayhew and Ince).

Miscellaneous Journal 1776–8, 13th May 1776 (Mayhew and Ince).

Marlborough, Duke of
Blenheim.
1739–1817, succeeded as fourth Duke in 1758. Bought two pairs of gilt candlesticks and a 'gilt cassolete on a pedestal' in June 1772.

C.L.B. *Outgoing letters* Letter Book F – 22nd June 1772 (Mayhew and Ince), 22nd August 1772.

Melbourne, Lord (and Lady)
Peniston Lamb (1748–1819), created Viscount Melbourne 1770, married Elizabeth Milbanke (d.1818), daughter of Sir Ralph Milbanke, 1769. Bought two perfume burners, four table candlesticks, including probably a pair of lion-faced candlesticks, a 'candelabrum' and a Venus vase in 1771.

CHRISTIE'S Sale, Christie's, 1771, first day, lot 10; second day, lots 6, 23, 63, 80, 86.

Milsington, Lord
*c.*1747–1823, styled Viscount Milsington from 1756, succeeded as third Earl of Portmore 1785. Bought four candle vases and two 'candelabra' in 1771.

CHRISTIE'S Sale, Christie's, 1771, first day, lots 68, 69, 72, 80; second day, lot 81.

Montagu, Duchess of
Lady Mary Montagu (1711–75), daughter and sole heir of second Duke of Montagu, married fourth Earl of Cardigan (1712–90) 1730. He was created Duke of Montagu 1766. Bought candle vases in 1771.

C.L.B. *Incoming letters* W. Matthews Box – 6th March 1771.
Outgoing letters Letter Book E – 23rd February 1771, 2nd March 1771, 9th March 1771 (all to W.M.).

Montagu, Lord C.
Probably Lord Charles Montagu (b.1741), second son of the third Duke of Manchester, brother of the fourth Duke (*q.v.*). Bought a pair of wreathed-column candlesticks in 1771.

CHRISTIE'S Sale, Christie's, 1771, first day, lot 23.

Montagu, Mrs
Hill Street, London; Tunbridge Wells; Bulstrode.
Elizabeth Montagu (1720–1800), daughter of Matthew Robinson of Rokeby, related to Matthew Boulton's wives, married Edward Montagu (d.1775), grandson of first Earl of Sandwich, 1742. Authoress and leader of society. Commissioned a tea urn through James Stuart in 1770, bought a Titus clock in 1772, candlesticks in 1773, and ornaments for the doors of her new house in Portman Square in 1779.

C.L.B.	*Incoming letters*	Mrs E. Montagu Box – 16th January 1772, 20th October 1772, 12th December 1772, 16th January 1773, 23rd January 1773, 1st October 1778.
	Outgoing letters	Mrs E. Montagu Box – 16th January 1772 (M.B. to Mrs Montagu); Letter Book D – 14th December 1772.
	Miscellaneous	Day Book 1779–81, 31st December 1779.
WEDGWOOD MUSEUM		J. Wedgwood to T. Bentley, 24th December 1770 (E25-18334).

Montagu, Admiral

Probably John Montagu (1719–95), son of James Montagu of Lackham, Wiltshire, great-great grandson of first Earl of Manchester, Rear-Admiral 1770. Bought a pair of candle vases in 1771. Visited Soho in 1779.

CHRISTIE'S — Sale, Christie's, 1771, first day, lot 15.

Morton, Earl of

The fifteenth Earl (1732–74) who succeeded 1768. Ordered a goat's head vase (date uncertain). Visited Soho on 28th July 1768.

C.L.B. — *Incoming letters* — M.2 Box – n.d. 'memorandum of order'.

Morton, Sir B.

Bought a pair of candle vases in 1771. See also Sir W. Ponting.

CHRISTIE'S — Sale, Christie's, 1771, third day, lot 73.

Morton, Lady

Probably the wife of Sir B. Morton; or possibly Bridget (d.1805), daughter of Sir John Heathcote, of Normanton, Rutland, who married the fourteenth Earl of Morton (1702–68) in 1755; or Katherine (d.1823), daughter of Hon. John Hamilton, who married the fifteenth Earl (1732–74) in 1758. Bought a watch stand and a pair of candle vases in 1778.

C.L.B.	*Incoming letters*	Wyatt Box – 8th March 1776 (John Wyatt).
	Outgoing letters	Letter Book I – 20th October 1778 (to John Whitehurst).
	Miscellaneous	Ledger 1776–8, 26th March 1778.
CHRISTIE'S		Sale, Christie and Ansell's, 1778, lot 13.

Mountstuart, Lord

South Audley Street ('Lord Bute's').

1744–1814, succeeded as fourth Earl of Bute 1792 and created Marquess of Bute 1796. Bought vases in 1771, probably ordering them during his visit to Soho on 30th August.

C.L.B. — *Outgoing letters* — Letter Book E – 19th September 1771 (to W.M.).

Northumberland, Duke (and Duchess) of

Northumberland House, Charing Cross.

Sir Hugh Smithson (1714–86), fourth baronet, married Lady Elizabeth Percy (d.1776), heiress of first Earl of Northumberland, 1740. Assumed name of Percy 1750 and created Duke of Northumberland 1766. Inspected examples of ormolu ware in 1770, bought a tripod (possibly the tea urn illustrated in Plate 229), a perfume burner, a pair of small two-handled vases and a wing-figured vase without a pedestal in 1772.

C.L.B. *Outgoing letters* Letter Book E – 4th January 1772, 27th April 1772 (to W.M.), 16th May 1772 (to W.M.).

Miscellaneous Private Box – n.d. [February 1770], 6th March 1770 (both M.B. to his wife).

ALNWICK CASTLE MSS Payments to B. and F. dated 13th December 1772, 1st December 1774.

HOARE'S BANK Ledger E, p. 166, 10th January 1772.

Nuneham, Lord – see Harcourt, Earl of

Ormsby, Lord

Probably of the Irish baronetcy (extinct by 1833). Bought a pair of candle vases in 1771.

CHRISTIE'S Sale, Christie and Ansell's, 1771, first day, lot 1.

Orwell, Lord

*c.*1715–83, created Baron Orwell 1762 and Earl of Shipbrook 1777. Bought two perfume burners and a pair of candle vases in 1771.

CHRISTIE'S Sale, Christie's, 1771, first day, lots 5, 7, 25.

Page, Sir Gregory

1685–1775, last baronet. Bought a pair of Bingley's vases in 1771.

C.L.B. *Outgoing letters* Letter Book E – 8th May 1771, 13th May 1771 (both to W.M.).

Miscellaneous P.1 Box – 22nd April 1771 (memorandum).

Parker, Mrs John

Saltram Park, Devon.

Theresa Robinson, daughter of first Baron Grantham and sister of second Baron (*q.v.*), married John Parker (d.1788) 1769. He was created Baron Boringdon 1784. Lord Grantham ordered four Persian vases for her in 1771: the order was later changed to King's vases (Plate 343). Bought a fifth King's vase in 1772.

C.L.B. *Outgoing letters* Letter Book E – 7th August 1771, 19th October 1771, 27th November 1771, 4th March 1772 (all to W.M.).

BRITISH LIBRARY Morley MSS, 9th April 1772 (Mrs Parker to Frederick Robinson).

SALTRAM PARK (Morley MSS) John Parker's Account Book, 18th June 1772.

Pechell, Samuel

George Street, Hanover Square, London.

Ordered the first Titus clock case in 1772, to be delivered to Mrs Cailland (*q.v.*). Visited Soho ('Saml Pichell Esqr') on 19th September 1770.

C.L.B. *Incoming letters* P1 Box – 8th April 1772.
Outgoing letters Letter Book E – 11th December 1771, 18th January 1772, 15th April 1772 (to W.M.), 18th June 1772 (to W.M.), 17th September 1772.
Miscellaneous J. Fothergill Box – n.d. [received 9th April 1772] (M.B. to J.F.).

Pelham, Charles (and Mrs)
Arlington Street, London; Brocklesby, Lincolnshire.
Charles Anderson (1749–1823), great-nephew of Charles Pelham of Brocklesby, succeeded to his estates 1763 and assumed name of Pelham, married Sophia (d.1786), daughter of George Aufrere, 1770, created Baron Yarborough 1794. Had four pairs of gilt candlesticks repaired and cleaned in 1772, bought ornaments for a commode in 1777 and further ornaments in 1778.
C.L.B. *Incoming letters* P1 Box – 28th January 1777.
Outgoing letters Letter Book E – 25th July 1772; Letter Book G – 13th March 1777, 16th April 1777; Letter Book I – 9th December 1777, 10th January 1778, 24th February 1778.
Miscellaneous J. Hodges Box – 23rd April 1777 (J. Hodges to M.B.); Ledger 1776–8, 17th March 1777; Journal 1776–8, 17th March 1777.

Percy, Lord Algernon
Northumberland House, London.
1750–1830, son of first Duke of Northumberland (*q.v.*), succeeded as second Baron Lovaine 1786 and created Earl of Beverley 1790. Bought vases in 1775, probably ordering them during his visit on 11th September.
C.L.B. *Outgoing letters* Letter Book G – n.d. [27th September 1775].

Plymouth, Earl of
Whewell (i.e. Hewell) Grange, Bromsgrove.
1751–99, succeeded as fifth Earl 1771. Bought a pair of vases in 1777.
C.L.B. *Outgoing letters* Letter Book I – 17th November 1777.

Ponting, Sir W. (?)
Bought a sphinx base in 1771: in the second copy of the sale catalogue Sir B. Morton (*q.v.*) is recorded as the buyer.
CHRISTIE'S Sale, Christie's, 1771, third day, lot 14.

Portland, Duchess of
Lady Dorothea Cavendish (d.1794), daughter of fourth Duke of Devonshire, married third Duke of Portland (1738–1809) 1766. Bought vases in 1771.
C.L.B. *Outgoing letters* Letter Book E – 17th July 1771 (to W.M.), 16th November 1771.

Richmond, Duke of
Richmond House, Whitehall; Goodwood House, Sussex.
1735–1806, succeeded as third Duke 1750. Ambassador to Paris 1765. Commissioned a fender in 1773. Mentioned that he might order copies of Horace Walpole's vases in 1770.

C.L.B.	*Incoming letters*	R.1 Box – 3rd April 1770.
	Outgoing letters	Letter Book D – 4th December 1772; Letter Book E – 9th January 1773; Letter Book 1773 (Boulton and Watt papers) – 1st April 1773 (to W.M.), 10th June 1773.

Riley, Mr
Enquired about girandoles in 1772.

C.L.B.	*Outgoing letters*	Letter Book E – 19th December 1772 (to W.M.).

Rockingham, Marquess of
1730–82, succeeded as second Marquess 1750. Bought a pair of Cleopatra vases and a perfume burner in 1770.

SHEFFIELD CITY LIBRARY	(Fitzwilliam MSS) invoice dated 19th October 1770.

Rumbold, Mr
Queen Anne Street, Cavendish Square, London.
Probably Thomas Rumbold (1736–91), administrator in the East India Company, created Baronet 1779. Bought vases in 1771.

C.L.B.	*Outgoing letters*	Letter Book E – 19th September 1777 (to W.M.).

St John, Colonel
Probably a relation by marriage of Lady St John (*q.v.*). Bought a sphinx vase in 1772.

C.L.B.	*Miscellaneous*	M.B.'s Diary 1772.

St John, Lady
Probably Susannah Louisa (d.1805), daughter of Peter Simond, married eleventh Baron St John (1725–67) 1755. Bought a sphinx vase and sugar basin (later returned) at the sale at Christie's in 1772. 'Hon. Mr and Lady St John' visited Soho on 21st September 1775.

C.L.B.	*Outgoing letters*	Letter Book E – 27th April 1772 (to W.M.).

Sandys, Lord (and Lady)
1726–97, succeeded as second Baron Sandys 1770, married Anna Maria (d.1806), daughter of James Colebrooke and widow of William King. Bought a sphinx vase, three other vases and an ornamented piece of blue john in 1771, and two goat's head vases in 1772; had a Burgoyne's vase repaired in 1772. Visited Soho on 27th August 1776.

C.L.B.	*Outgoing letters*	Letter Book E – 5th September 1772 (to W.M.).
CHRISTIE'S		Sale, Christie's, 1771, third day, lots 35, 40, 51, 55, 78.

Scarsdale, Lord
Kedleston Hall, Derbyshire.
Sir Nathaniel Curzon (1726–1804), fifth Baronet, created first Baron Scarsdale 1761. Bought, through Samuel Wyatt, door furniture (Plate 193) and girandoles in 1766, ordered a blue john cup for the Duchess of Portland (*q.v.*) in 1769, and bought a pair of goat's head vases in 1772.

C.L.B.	*Incoming letters*	Wyatt Box – 31st July 1765, 6th March 1766, 12th June 1766, 9th September 1766 (all Samuel Wyatt).
	Miscellaneous	Cash Debtor Book 1772–82, 18th April 1772.
KEDLESTON HALL		Papers: 5/158 – 21st December 1765 (Samuel Wyatt to Lord Scarsdale).

Scott, Mrs
Bought vases in 1776.

C.L.B.	*Miscellaneous*	Ledger 1776–8, 30th November 1776; Journal 1776–8, 30th November 1776.

Sefton, Earl of
Hill Street, London.
1748–95, succeeded as eighth Viscount Molyneux 1759, created Earl of Sefton 1771. Bought two pairs of lion-faced candlesticks, a perfume burner, a pair of ewers (Plate 199), a Venus clock (later returned) and a wing-figured vase or vases in 1772.

C.L.B.	*Outgoing letters*	Letter Book E – 27th April 1772 (to W.M.), 19th May 1772, 29th October 1772, 19th November 1772 (to W.M.), 28th November 1772 (to W.M.).

Shelburne, Earl of
Bowood House, Calne, Wiltshire; London.
William Petty (1737–1805), succeeded as second Earl of Shelburne 1764, created Marquess of Lansdowne 1784, cousin of third Earl of Kerry (*q.v.*). Requested Robert Adam to order girandoles, branches or tripods in 1765, and lamp chains in 1770, shown samples of ormolu ware in 1770, bought tripods in 1771, requested price of door furniture in 1773, shown drawings of ornaments in 1784.

C.L.B.	*Incoming letters*	S.1 Box – 8th December 1773; A.4 Box – 14th August 1770 (James Adam).
	Outgoing letters	Letter Book D – 1st October 1770 (to James Adam); Letter Book E – 7th January 1771, 9th January 1771 (to W.M.), 2nd February 1771 (to W.M.); Letter Book N – 13th September 1784.
	Miscellaneous	S.1 Box – 16th April 1765 (Earl of Shelburne to Robert Adam); J. Fothergill Box – n.d. [February 1770] (M.B. to J.F.); Private Box – 6th March 1770 (M.B. to his wife).

Sidley, Sir Charles
Princes Buildings, Bath.
Probably the last Baronet of Great Chart, Kent (Baronetcy extinct '*temp.* Geo. III').

Pair of branches repaired and gilt in 1775. Visited Soho on 31st July 1769 (from 'Nuthall Temple, Nottingham') and probably in July 1775 ('Sir Charles Sildley').

C.L.B. *Outgoing letters* Letter Book G – 9th January 1775.

Stamford, Earl (and Countess) of

Enville, Stourbridge.

1737–1819, succeeded as fifth Earl 1768, married Lady Henrietta Cavendish-Bentinck (d.1827), daughter of second Duke of Portland, 1763. Bought a wing-figured vase and two other vases in 1772, a vase for Lady Weymouth (*q.v.*) in 1773 and a pair of branches and a vase in 1778. Visited Soho on 1st June 1780.

C.L.B. *Outgoing letters* Letter Book E – 6th February 1772, 12th January 1773.
Miscellaneous J. Fothergill Box – 23rd January 1772 (J.F. to M.B); Ledger 1776–8, 17th November 1778.
CHRISTIE'S Sale, Christie and Ansell's, 1778, lot 85.

Stewart, John, M.P.

A clock case gilt unsatisfactorily.

C.L.B. *Outgoing letters* Letter Book E – 23rd September 1772.

Stormont, Lord

1727–96, succeeded as seventh Viscount 1748, nephew of the first Earl of Mansfield, whom he succeeded 1793. Bought vases in 1774, a Bacchanalian vase and a picture frame in 1783.

C.L.B. *Outgoing letters* Letter Book G – 13th August 1774; Letter Book N – 14th October 1783, 5th December 1783.
Miscellaneous Ledger 1782–9 (Matthew Boulton & Co.), 25th November 1783.

Stovin, Mrs Mary

139 Cheapside, London.

Bought two pairs of vases in 1771.

C.L.B. *Outgoing letters* Letter Book E – 19th January 1771, 4th February 1771.

Talbot, Mr

Probably the Hon. J. C. Talbot (1750–93), to whom 'sundries' were sent in 1776, succeeded as third Baron Talbot of Hensol and created Earl Talbot 1782. Bought vases in 1773. 'Honble Mr Talbot and Lady', nephew to Lord Talbot, visited Soho in May 1772. Visited Soho again in June 1778.

C.L.B. *Miscellaneous* J. Fothergill Box – 13th February 1773 (J.F. to M.B.); Journal 1776–8, 17th August 1776.

Thyne, Mr

Probably Henry Frederick Thynne (1735–1826), younger son of second Viscount Weymouth and brother of third Viscount (see Lady Weymouth), created Baron Carteret 1784. Bought a pair of Bingley's vases and a wing-figured vase in 1772.

C.L.B. *Outgoing letters* Letter Book E – 27th April 1772, 19th June 1772 (both to W.M.).

Udney, Mr
Probably Robert Udney (1722–1802), City merchant, succeeded to family estates (Udney Castle, Aberdeen, etc.) 1786. Bought a pair of vases in 1771.
CHRISTIE'S Sale, Christie's, 1771, second day, lot 15.

Wales, Prince of
1762–1830, later George IV, King of Great Britain. Bought a pair of wing-figured vases in 1772.
C.L.B. *Outgoing letters* Letter Book E – 27th April 1772 (to W.M.).

Wales, Princess of
Princess Augusta (1719–72), daughter of Frederick II, Duke of Saxe-Gotha-Altenburg, who married Prince Frederick, Prince of Wales (1707–51), eldest son of George II. Bought two pairs of candle vases in 1770.
C.L.B. *Miscellaneous* J. Fothergill Box – n.d. [February 1770] (M.B. to J.F.); Private Box – 6th March 1770 (M.B. to his wife).

Warburton, William
1698–1779, Bishop of Gloucester 1760–79. Bought a vase in 1771. Visited Soho on 19th July 1770.
C.L.B. *Outgoing letters* Letter Book E – 9th March 1771 (to W.M.).

Weddell, William
1724–92, owner of Newby Hall, Ripon, Yorkshire. Bought a perfume burner and a pair of vases in 1776.
C.L.B. *Outgoing letters* Letter Book G – 30th March 1776 (to John Wyatt).
Miscellaneous Cash Debtor Book 1772–82, 1st October 1776.

Weymouth, Lady
Lady Elizabeth Cavendish-Bentinck (d.1825), daughter of second Duke of Portland, married third Viscount Weymouth (1734–96) 1759: he was created Marquess of Bath 1789. A vase ordered for her by Countess of Stamford (*q.v.*) in 1773.
C.L.B. *Outgoing letters* Letter Book E – 12th January 1773 (to Lady Stamford).

Willet, Mr
Possibly Ralph Willet (1719–95), collector of books and pictures, who owned a house in Dean Street, London, and an estate at Canford, Dorset. Bought a sphinx vase in 1771.
C.L.B. *Outgoing letters* Letter Book E – 2nd May 1771, 6th May 1771, 11th May 1771 (all to W.M.).

William, Colonel
Bought a pair of vases and a griffin vase in 1771.
CHRISTIE'S Sale, Christie's, 1771, first day, lots, 45, 46.

Willoughby de Broke, Lord
Compton Verney, Warwick.
1738–1816, succeeded as fourteenth Baron Willoughby de Broke 1752. Ordered two pairs of 'candlestick urns' and a perfume burner in 1769.
C.L.B. *Incoming letters* W.2 Box – 28th November 1769.

Witts, Miss Apphia
Chipping Norton; 42 Friday Street, London.
Died 1840, daughter of Broome Witts of Chipping Norton, married firstly Joseph Peach, formerly Governor of Calcutta, and secondly second Baron Lyttelton (*q.v.*) 1771. Bought a pair of marble candlesticks in 1768.
C.L.B. *Incoming letters* W.3 Box – 4th November 1768.

Wrottesley, Sir John
1744–87, succeeded as eighth Baronet 1769. Bought a candle vase in 1771. Visited Soho on 26th July 1771.
CHRISTIE'S Sale, Christie's, 1771, first day, lot 29.

Wynn, Sir Watkin Williams
*c.*1742–89, succeeded as fourth Baronet 1749. Bought a vase and a Venus clock in 1771.
CHRISTIE'S Sale, Christie and Ansell's, 1771, first day, lots 18, 85.
NATIONAL LIBRARY OF WALES, ABERYSTWYTH Wynnstay Documents, Box 115/3, Sir Watkin Williams Wynn's Account Book, 9th May 1771.

Yeats, Mrs
Ordered a pair of goat's head vases in 1769.
C.L.B. *Miscellaneous* XYZ Box – n.d. [28th August 1769]. Memorandum of order.

APPENDIX II

VISITORS TO SOHO ('REGISTER BOOK')

The names in this Appendix are extracted from a bound book ('Register Book') in the Great Tew Archive. It is a list of visitors to the Soho Manufactory. Several of the pages have been trimmed, probably when the sheets were rebound, and dates and other details have been shaved or lost. The book is unpaginated and the following page numbers are mine.

Each page of the book has the headings 'Persons Names' and 'Places of Abode'. The book starts (p. 1) with an undated page. On the reverse of this first page the record continues with a list of visitors from May to July 1767, followed by seven pages (i.e. four sheets), which are undated but may continue with 1767. These are followed by pages displaced in the rebinding of the volume and recording visitors from June 1st 1780 to July 1787 (pp. 10–66, the first pasted to the back of p. 9). On p. 67 the record reverts to 28th July 1767 and is continuous from there to p. 146 (1779). There are four loose sheets (8 pp.) from October 1771 to August 1772. From p. 147 the record continues from 1788 through to 1799.

The record is not complete. It does not include some of the known visitors recorded in other archives. On some sheets the clerk appears to have composed the record of visitors afterwards and not recalled or recorded precise dates. The records for 1773–5, for example, are sketchy. Stretches of record in other years do not look like a meticulous daily record. Often no dates are given against lists of names.

The list of visitors in this Appendix is selective. I have tried to pick out those who are known elsewhere in the Boulton archives for purchases of, or an interest in ornaments, or who could have been expected to show some interest, for example aristocracy, foreigners and ambassadors. I have included some to show that not all visitors fell into these categories. A large number of army officers and many churchmen for example came to Soho. So did many Members of Parliament and other prominent people – William Pitt, Edmund Burke, Sir William Hamilton, Dean Swift and Samuel Johnson among them – and members of the Lunar Circle and business associates of Boulton's, including Erasmus Darwin, Joseph Priestley, Josiah Wedgwood, John Whitehurst, William Small, Samuel Garbett, William Withering. Some of them, being local friends, brought other visitors. So did the japanners John Baskerville and Henry Clay. Retailers and merchants came from Britain and abroad. The book also shows that the local landowners were frequent visitors – Lords Aylesford, Craven, Dartmouth, Gower, Harrowby, Lyttelton and Warwick, Dr Digby and Lady Bridgeman among them. Many of these were Boulton's customers both for ormolu ornaments and other products. Some of them bought or ordered ornaments during their visits. These are recorded in Appendix I.

I have probably misspelt some names because it is never easy to read every piece of eighteenth-century writing accurately. In a very large number of cases the record does not tell where visitors came from. I have shown under each page the places of origin that are recorded, but these are misleadingly few since so many names are homeless. The towns and counties recorded show that visitors came to Soho from far and wide.

There are about thirty names listed on each page. Many men were accompanied by their wives, and vice versa, and many brought family and friends or groups of attendants. So the number of visitors per page is rather larger than it appears.

This summary stops in 1782, when Fothergill's death brought an end to the Boulton and Fothergill partnership. There are no specific entries in the book for 1782, but a torn page (p. 37) may refer to visitors for that year. The next entries are for June 4th 1783.

p. 1 [n.d.]: Lord and Lady Shelbourne (with many people), Lady Louisa Farmour (France), Lady Bridgman, Vancitert Esqr, Sir Edwd Winington, The Duke of Roxburgh, Sir Charles Frederick (of Wales), Lord and Lady Hopton, Lady Harriott Hope, Doct. Hope, Sir James Nasmith, Lord Donegall, Lord Spencer Hamilton, Generall Elliot (London), Generall Frytag (the last three bracketed – Governors of Gibraltar), Mr Dingley, Mr Hollis, Sir Henry Gough, Mr George Garrick, John Taylor Esq (Strand, London), Captn and Mrs Tunpenny, Mr and Mrs Turnpenny junr.

p. 2 (1767) May 8th: Dr Darwin (Lichfield), Mr Whitehurst (Derby), Mr Alcon (Refiner to the Mint). May 14th: Mr Wedgwood (potter to her Majesty at Baselom). May 16th: Tho. Taylor (North Carolina), Abraham Redwood junr (Newport Rhode Island, North America). May 18th: Lady Littleton (near Stafford, Hagley), Miss Bouverie (London), Adderley Esqr, Sir Edwd Littleton (Hagley). July 9th: Lord Dartmouth. Others from London, Yorkshire, Norwich, Dover, Worcester, Bucks.

p. 3 [n.d.]: J Teysset ? (Amsterdam), Lord Dalrymple, Lady Throgmorton and family. Others from London, Banbury, Cornwall, Edinburgh, Oxon, Birmingham, Henlow, Leicestershire.

p. 4 [n.d.]: Fras Freshfield (baize maker Colchester), Lord Valentia, Lady Peshall, the Venetian Ambassador and Mr Poly, Lord Dartmouth's son, Captain Cornwall and Lady, Lady Dartmouth and Lady Bagot. Others from Worcester, Birmingham, Brentford, Coventry, Lichfield, Leicestershire.

p. 5 [n.d.]: Mr Fitzgerald (Grays Inn, London), Mr Cary (Torr Abbey), John Bertrand (Geneva). Others from London, Ireland, Liverpool, Aston, Cambridge, Ludlow, Coatbridge, Oxford.

p. 6 [n.d.]: Leonard (America), Major Morrison (ditto). Others from 19 Light Dragoons, Rochdale, 11 Regt Dragoons, Dublin, Burton upon Trent, Turley, Alcester, Bristol.

p. 7 [n.d.]: Miss Maria Coker and Mrs Coker (Tottenham), Lady Biddolph and family. Others from London, Cambridge, Bristol, Geneva [?], Birmingham, Edinburgh, Northamptonshire, Warwick, Glasgow, West Bromwich, Canterbury.

p. 8 [n.d.]: Mr Porter (America),The Princess of ? (Russia) (crossed out), The Honble George Manners Esqr. Others from London, Hull, Coventry, Tewkesbury, Birmingham, Ireland, Flintshire, Newcastle upon Tyne, Richmond, Halifax, Norwich, Manchester.

p. 9 [n.d.]: Sir John Anstruther (brought compliments from Judge Buller to Mr Bolton), Princess of Daschkaw of Russia with her son and daughter, Sir John Gordon. Others from London, Hawbury, Northampton, Bristol, Huntingdon, Stilton, Cork, Scotland, Chirk, Warwick, Bromsgrove.

p. 67 (1767) August 25th: Mr Ploemer (refiner, London). September 2nd: Lord

Windsor. September 7th: Mr Suther (Member of Parliament for the County of Essex). August 24th: Count de Sarsfield avec Mr Garbett. September 9th: Mr Matthew and his Lady and Mrs Critchley (London with the Doctor Small). September 14th: Dr Burton (he was Master of Winchester School), Lord Clare, Mr Anson (London), Mr Pennick (Master of the British Museum London), Doctor Digby (Coleshill), Colnel Neugent (Ld Clare's son). September 17th: Mr Collins (relation of Lord Warick, Edinburgh). September 18th: Lord North & Lord Dartmouth and 4 other Gentlemen. September 18th: Sir Jno Guise (Glostershire). Others from London, Birmingham, Denby, Lichfield, Coleshill, Norwich.

p. 68 (1767–8) September 28th: Mr Motteux, the Spanish Ambassador Le Comt de Lavagne, the Venetian ditto Monsr de Vigniola. October 17th: Mr Patrick Robertson (Goldsmith in Edinburg). Others from London, Birmingham. (1768) February 8th: Mr Shroder (Hanover). April 13th: Mr Sullivan (Wallbrooke London), Baron de Gadde [?] (Stockholm), The Marquess Ximenes d'Aragone (at Florence), Baron Nabliz (Germany), a Dn Miguel D'Olemendi Ofrical (first Secretary of State to Madrid). May 6th: Le Marquis De Riveroli, Le Comte Dal Tiere. Others from London, Bordeaux, Derby, Exeter, Newcastle.

p. 69 (1768) May 31st: Sir Charles Shuckburgh Bart (Warwick). June 18th: Francis Richardson (Philadelphia). July 10th: Lord and Lady Napier. July 19th: Mr Gough (Edgbaston), Sir Jno Palmer (married Miss Gough). July 28th: Earl of Morton, Thomas Forsyth (both Brook Street London). August 17th: Mr Drake with his two sons & others (he is Membr of Pt for Agmondesham). Others from London, Birmingham, Dunquerke, Nottingham, Royal Navy Marazion Cornwall, Hants, Shrewsbury.

p. 70 (1768–9) August 20th: Rennis Esqr with Lord Dartmouth. September 5th: Count Zenzendorf (Germany), Mr Bentham (London). September 19th: Sansom (?) Ried (New York), Chevalier de Sauserre and his Lady. Others from London, Birmingham, Buckland. (1769) March 10th: Duke De Rochefaucault, Duke De Liancourt, 24th May: Paul Dieterich Gisesce (Hamburg). June 2nd: Le Marquis Devoyer d'Argenson (*Lieutenant General des armies du Roy en son hotel rue des Bons enfans a Paris, a Londres demeure* Castle Street Oxford Road No. 8) [all in presumably the general's writing], le Vicomte de Vibraye (Great George Street London) Mr Harash (Pall Mall London). June 1st: Mr Pitt (Arlington Street London, Membr Pt).

p. 71 (1769) June 13th: Lady Grisley and Miss Grisley (Draklow), Col Hay (Memb Parmt) (Warwick). July 11th: Lord and Lady Craven, Ch Gerichew (the Russian Ambassadeur Soho Square), Baron Diede the Danish Envoy, Prince Cantimess (or Cantimen [?]) (Russia). July 25th: Dean of Gloucester Dr Tucker. Others from London, Falmouth, Amsterdam, Malvern, Warwick, Liverpool, Shropshire, Bath, Bewdley, Newcastle, York, Sheffield.

p. 72 (1769) July 31st: Sir Charles Sidley (Nuthall Temple near Nottingham). August 11th: Lady Craven and her mother Lady Barkley. August 14th: Lord and Lady Beauchamp. August 21st: Mr Dundas (Lord President of Scotland) and his Lady, Mr Crawford (Perrthshire), Lady Hindford. Others from Ringwood, Warwick, Handsworth, Sutton, Fourmark, Hingesworth, Weston, Stoney Stratford, Scotland.

p. 73 (1769) August 17th–18th: Mr Pownall (Member of Pt) (London). August 23rd: Henning Legg Esqr (near Shipston Warwickshire), North Esqr with Ld Dartmouth.

September 4th: Mrs Balfour, Genl Haviland, Lord and Lady Kerry (Portman Square London), Lord and Lady Carbery, Sir Edward and Lady Littleton. September 8th: Monr De Mello Di Castro (South Audley Street, London Ambassador from Portugal). September 9th: Sir Willm Guyse and two sisters (Rendcomb abt 4 miles from Cirencester), Chevalier d'Erizzo (Coppenoles Suffolk, Ambassador from Venice), Baron Swieton, Sir Edmond Thomas. Others from London, Oxford.

p. 74 (1769) September 11th: Mr Angelo (the firework maker and fencer), Mr Baldwin (a bookseller, London), Mr Addams and his Brother (a relasion of Mr Addams the architect), Lady Dartmouth. Others from London, Oxfordshire, Wiltshire, Edinburgh, Bath, Bristol, America.

p. 75 (1769–70) September or October: Major Wm Ogle (or such a name he is aquainted wth the Duke Northumberland), Miss Taylor (of Birmingham say the Jew's daughters), Colnal Burgoyne, Colnal Harcourt, Mr Halsey (member for Hertfordshire). October 24th: General Paoli (London). Others from London, Birmingham, Stafford, Hopenhend. (1770) March 3rd: Jacob Watson (New York America), Mr Pinto (musician). Others from London, Ireland.

p. 76 (1770) March 21st: Dr Hillmore (Berlin). April 9th: Capn Bertram (America). Others from Worcester, Birmingham, Bath, Liverpool.

p. 77 (1770) April 21st: Duke of Bridgwater, Lord and Lady Gower. April 23rd: Mr Adams (London), Dr Harris (London). Others from London, Birmingham, Nottingham, Stourbridge, Derby, Bath.

p. 78 (1770) May 10th: Generall Murray and his attendants. May 14th: Edmond Afflick (London). May 15th: Earl of Findlater and his Lady. May 16th: Lady Holt and Miss Holt (near Sutton). Others from London, Worcester, Birmingham, Dorsetshire, Wolverhampton, Liverpool.

p. 79 (1770) May 24th: Lady Beauchamp and Capn Beauchamp (Windsor). May 26th: Sir Robt Bernard (Member for Westminster). May 31st: Mr Greyhouse (London) and Mr Ason's Clerk (Birm) (were deny'd permission by Mr Scale to see the works – they made a complaint to Mr Boulton that they were not us'd like Gentn). Others from London, Birmingham, Newcastle on Tyne, Rochester, Kildwick in Craven.

p. 80 (1770) June 1st: Myneer Payrote [?] and Madam Parrote [?] (damd rogues). Others from London, Buckley, Lichfield, Worcestershire, Islington, Bath.

p. 81 (1770) June 28th: Mr Parker (Jeweller St Paul's Church Yard). June 29th: a Gentn who wou'd not tell their name refus'd admittance. June 30th: Mr Smith (brassfounder Birmingham), Mr Woodley (iron merchant London). Others from Birmingham, Dublin, West Bromwich, Bristol.

p. 82 (1770) July 2nd: Major Kirkpatrick (upon the tour of Great Britain). July 3rd: John Bapt Eichberger (Merchant in Mainz Germany) Count of Holstein (one of the Lords of the Bedchamber to the King of Denmark). July 10th: Jno Carnack Esqr (Bath) and Master Carnack. Others from Walsall, Birmingham, Stafford, Bath, Bristol, Stourbridge.

p. 83 (1770) July 21st [should be 12?]: Marquis of Can[?]aciollo (Neapolitan Envoy),

M De Mello (Portegese), Count De Weldoren (Dutch), Count Scarnafis (Sardinian) (all recommended by Motteux). July 13th: Lord Wenham, Lord Summers. July 14th: Lord Deshford (son to the Earl of Findlater). Others from Dudley, Surrey, Birmingham.

p. 84 (1770) July 16th: Lady Dowager Northampton, Mr Amiens, with several Gent & Ladys and Mr Crafts. July 19th: Bishop of Gloucester and Lady viz Mrs Warburton, son and miss. July 21st: Lord and Lady Montague. Others from London, Worcester, Macclesfield, Birmingham.

p. 85 (1770) July 28th: Count and Countess of Wintisgraatz (near Viena), Count de Reveultay [?], Baron de Suttishaw, Baron Deide (Danish Ambassador), Sir Jno Goodricke Bart. Others from London, Sutton, Newcastle upon Tyne, Birmingham, Winchester.

p. 86 (1770) August 3rd: Sir Wm Dolben (St James's London), General Honywood and his Lady and son (Charles Street, Berkley Square). August 15th: Sir Jno Every. August 16th: Lord and Lady Waldgrave and son, Lady Bridgman. August 21st: Sir Piercy and Lady Brett. Others from London, Loxley, Dursley.

p. 87 (1770) August 23rd: Lord and Lady Aylsford, Lord Gurnesy, Lord and Lady Plymouth, Lord and Lady Archer. August 25th: Sir Thomas and Lady Griffin. Others from London, Edgbaston.

p. 88 (1770) September 8th: Scipworth Esqr (Member for Warwickshire). Others from London, Worcester, Birmingham, Shenstone.

p. 89 (1770) September 12th: Mr Robertson (Goldsmith Edinburgh). September 17th: Marquis Ximenes (France). September 18th: Guise and Mrs and Miss (Glocester), Dalrymple Esqr. September 19th: Signior Gordini, Saml Pichell Esqr and Mrs (George St, Hanover Sq). Others from London, Lichfield, Birmingham, Worcester.

p. 90 (1770) September 22nd: Anson Esqr and Lady. October 3rd: Gentn with Mr Baskerville. October 8th: Mr Orsell (Paris). Others from London, Dublin, Birmingham.

p. 91 (1770) October 9th: Mr Henry Thomas (Exchequer). October 15th: Mr E. Burke Esqr (Member for Wendover). October 23rd: Smith (engraver, Worcester). Others from London, Birmingham, West Bromwich, Worcester.

p. 92 (1770) October 26th: Sir Wm and Lady Bagott. November: Captn Taylor and five other officers. December 1st: Captn W. Hamilton (63 Regt). Others from London, Worcester, Gibralter, Birmingham.

p. 93 (1771) January: Mr Walker (America), Mr S. Loyd and Master Loyd (Worcester), Lord Donegall, Mr Nesbit (Bishopsgate Strt, London). January 27th: Mr Melvil (Merchant Dublin). January 29th: Mr King (St Kitts West Indies), Mr John Dimock Griffith (Merchant Chester). February: Sir Charles Shuckburgh (Paradise Row, Birmingham). February 6th: Sir Thos Gouch, Mr Day (South Carolina). Others from Birmingham, Black Brook, Worcester.

p. 94 (1771) March 4th: Lord Huntingdon. March 16th: Inge Esqr. April: Franz Heinrich Maltz (Hamburg), Hon Miss Grisley, Master Hart and other young Gentn from Shrewsbury, Mr and Mrs Kirbey (Royall Academy London). Others from London, Worcester, Birmingham, Derby, Lichfield, Gloucester.

p. 95 (1771) May 4th: Lady Dowager Craven with Mr and Mrs Lydiard and Mrs Tayler. May 10th: Mr Boswell (Amsterdam). May 13th: Mr and Mrs Birch, Mrs Clay and Master Clay, all with Mr Clay (Manufacter Birmingham). Others from London, Barrowby, Birmingham, Worcester, Uxbridge, Dorsetshire.

p. 96 (1771) [n.d.]: Doctor Franklin (Craven Street, Strand, London), Mr Ripley (Mathematical Instt Maker Wapping). 7th [i.e. June?]: Lord and Lady Marchmont, Littleton Esqr (Studley Castle), Lord and Lady Clermont (Dublin), Sir George Colebrooke. Others from Croxall, Longmer, Birmingham, 4th Regiment Dragoons, Condover, Worcester, Edinburgh, Dublin, Hagley.

p. 97 (1771) [n.d.]: Baron Bender (Viena), Mr Richd Allnut (Merchant, Minchin Lane, London), Honble Mr Greville. Others from London, Worcester, Edinburgh, Stratford, Hereford, Newark, Midleton.

p. 98 (1771) July 20th: Lord Besbory, Mr Harris with Mr Wilkinson. July 26th: Lord Farnham, Sir Jno Wrottesley (Wrottesly near Ho [?] Hampt). Others from London, Birmingham, America, York, Derby, Worcester, Lichfield, Ludlow.

p. 99 (1771) August 17th: Sir Charles Bunbury. August 20th: Mr Alcock (No. 134 Cheapside, London). August 22nd: Polish Ambassador with Generall Paoli. Others from London, Edinburgh, Dublin, Worcester, Alston, Birmingham, Bucknall, Hampshire, Bath, Lichfield.

p. 100 (1771) August 30th: Lord Mount Stuart, Sir Alexr Gillmour, Mrs Montague sister his Grace the Duke of Mont. August 31st: Sir Geo Griffith and Lady, His Excellency Moushkin Poushkin Russian Envoy and his Lady, Sir Jas Cockburn Bart (Soho Square) and Lady. September: Le Comte de Belgioioso (Envoye Extraordinaire de l'Empereur), Lord and Lady Ailsford. Others from London, Redburn.

p. 101 (1771) September 13th: Honble Miss Harriet Bouverie, Lord and Lady Greville. September 17th: Fordice Esqr and Lady, Lady Machartney, Mr and Mrs Cox, Mr and Mrs Collier (Quakers with Mr Galton). Others from London, Bedford, Worcester, Edinburgh, Lichfield, Birmingham.

p. 102 (1771) September: George Clifford Esqr and Pancrass Clifford Esqr (Amsterdam). October 3rd: Mr Friedburgh (with an Israelite merchant in Germany, Dudley Street). October 4th: Chas Dunbar Esqr and Mrs Dunbar (Hill Street, Berkley Square), Lord Irnhon (Coll Lutterel's father), Calcraft Esqr. Others from London, Fulham, Worcester, Birmingham, Shrewsbury, Manchester, Oxford, Dartford.

p. 103 (1771, LOOSE SHEET) October: Le Prince Hereditaire de Hesse Darmstadt, M Le Baron de Ratzenhove. October 8th/9th: Willm Gale Esqr (Bruton Street, Berkley Square). October 10th: Mr Henrick Rucker (Hambro). November 1st: Lord Littleton (Hagley), Colln Burgoine. Others from London, Paris, America, Ireland, Glamorganshire, Bath.

p. 104 (1771) November: Foley Esqr (Witley Court, Worcestershire), Lord Chas and Lady Spencer, Barron Grote of —, Baron von Saldern of the Duchy of Holstein, Mr

Khaln (Polish Prusia), Mr Youngschultz (from Dantzik), Mr H. Schopenhauer, Mr J. D. Eggeling (all three recommended Mr Hardy's friends), Messrs Campbell and Gault (New York), Earl of Catherlough and Mrs Davies, Mr Drake (Bengall). Others from London, Birmingham, Portsmouth, Leeds.

p. 105 (1772, LOOSE SHEET) February 15th: Honble Blunt Esqr (brother to Sir Walter Blunt), John Paynter Esqr (Harod House in Wales). April: Mr Furnivall (watchmaker Sheffield). Others from London, Bromley, Cork.

p. 106 (1772) May [?]12th: Le Comte d'Oetting et de Wal, Le Comte Lamberg, the Duke and Duchess of La Villa Hermosa, Sir John Sinclair (Stephenson near Haddington), Lord Craven and his Lady, Honble Mr Talbot and his Lady (he is nephew to Lord Talbot). Others from London, Paris, Dublin, Stratfordd upon Avon, Hull, Birmingham, Normanton, Worcester, Bridgnorth, Doncaster.

p. 107 (1772, LOOSE SHEET) June: Baron vom Sacken, Count of Reuss, Sir Joseph York, Lord Garnsee. July 17th: Le Baron de Dietrich (Strasbourg en Alsace Cons Noble au Magistrat de Strasb). July 13th: Lord De Spencer. July 15th: Sir Robert Murray Keith (Kt of the Bath). Others from London, Worcester, Sutton, Coleshill, Derby, Shrewsbury, Italy (Italians recommended by Count Lamberg).

p. 108 (1772) July: The Right Honble the Earl of Ashburnham and Lady and Honble Miss Ashburnham, Richd Morrison (Goldsmith No.15 Cheapside, London), Honble Mr Stuart (second son to Ld Bute), Lady Margt Macdonald (Welbeck Street, Cavendish Square), His Grace the Duke of Grafton and Duchess. Others from London, Worcester, Dublin, Bath, Wroxall, Warwick.

p. 109 (1772, LOOSE SHEET) August 1st: Sir Chas Holte Bart and Lady and Miss, Mr Barker (a brass founder – not admitted: but by his recommendation were admitted – Mr — upholster in High St Birmm, Miss Halwell of Hagley, and other ladies). August 4th: Doctr N (bishop of Chester), Bishop of Chester's Lady, son etc. August 6th: Lady Dowager Craven. August 7th: Lady Dudley and niece, Honble Mr Ward. August 10th: Sir Chas Shuckburgh and Lady (Warwick). Others from London, Lichfield, Cotheridge, Dublin, Worcester, Herefordshire.

p. 110 (1772) August: Lord and Lady Archer, Honble Rigby Esqr (Pay Master), Le Marquiss de Sezay (Suffolk Street No. 34), Thos and Mrs Ridell (Swinbourne Castle Northumberland). Others from London, Dublin, Ireland, Ludlow, Birmingham, Epsom, Gloucestershire, Lichfield.

p. 111 (1772) August 20th: Mr Arfwedson (Stockholm). August 21st: Lord Lewisham & his two Honble brothers (sons to Ld Dartmth). August 22nd: Scipworth Esqr (Member for Warwick). August 26th: Honble Master Ailsford, Baruk Lousada and Madam Lousada (Adelphi Buildings, Strand, London) with another lady. Others from London, Birmingham, Warwick, Bath.

p. 112 (1772) August 28th: Lady Whalmsley, Captain and Mrs Whalmesley (Bath), Lady George. Others from London, Sedgley, Worcester.

p. 113 (1772) September 2nd: General and Madm Newton (by the introduction of Lady Dartmouth). September 3rd: Messrs Saydes (Paris). September 8th: Bianchy Primavesi (Amsterdam). September 12th: Lord Paget, Lord Boston with other

Gentlemen. Others from London, Bromyard, Worcester, Northampton, Stafford, Lichfield, Chillington.

p. 114 (1772) September 14th: Lord Cranbourne (Lower Grosvenor Street, London). September 15th: Lady Ing and Miss Ing. September 16th: His Royal Highness Poniotawsky (nephew to the King of Poland), Montague Esqr, Her Grace the Duchess of Bedford. September 22nd: His Excellency Count De Guines (French Ambassador), Right Honble Lord Valentia and Lady, Governor Littleton. Others from London, Coleshill, Stone.

p. 115 (1772) September 23rd: Lord and Lady Shrewsbury. September 24th: His Excellency Baron Deiden (Danish Ambassador), Count Callenberg (at the Danish Envoy's Harery St, Cavendish Sq), Marquss de S[?]ezay. September 28th: Sir Richd Westley Bart. Others from London, Dudley, Dublin.

p. 116 (1772) October 2nd: Lord Guernsey, Honble Miss Ailsford, Right Honble Lady Finch, Honble Miss Finch. October 15th: Mr Firmin (Merchant near Somerset House Strand Londn). October 19th: Mr Weideman (Hanover). October 20th: General Bentinck (Holland). Others from London, Worcester, Notts, Ireland, Bristol.

p. 117 (1772) October 22nd: Monsr Le Comt Orlow (youngest brother of that family in Russia). Others from London, Gloucestershire, Dantzig [Carl Gottfried Grischord?, pasted in]. (1773) June 28th: Sir Jno Nelthorpe (Barton, Lincolnshire). July 13th: Lord and Lady Craven, Lord Powis. Others from London, Belfast, Liverpool, Glamorganshire.

p. 118 (1773) July 20th: Mr Sanford (New College Oxford), Edd Maxwell (Univ Coll Oxford). Others from London, Stafford, Drayton Manor, Bewdley, Winchester, Ireland.

p. 119 (1774) [n.d.]: Lady Webb Seymour, Lord and Lady Gormanston, Lord Graham, Sir Philip Hales Bart, The Honble the Earl of Ely, Sir Henry and Lady Hunlock, The Honble Mr Villiers, Sir Thomas and Lady Egerton, Sir Thomas Ward. Others from London, Shrewsbury.

p. 120 (1775) April 29th: Lord Knapton (Ireland). May 13th: Mr Robertson, Mr Keith and Mr Tyller from Edinburgh. May 31st: Sir Thomas and Lady Champneys, Sir Charles Sildley. [n.d.], but after July 20th: His Grace the Duke of Athol and Duchess. Others from London, Tobago, Dublin, Kilkenny.

p. 121 (1775): Order for Lord Valentia dated 17th August 1775 (silver) crossed out; order for Sir Charles Bingham Bart in Charles Street, Berkley Square (buttons, silver, sword handles, 20 picture frames such as Mr Egginton knows of) crossed out. See p. 122.

p. 122 (1775) August 13th: Lord and Lady Valentia, Lord Lyttleton, Lord and Lady Selkirk. August 17th: Sir Charles Bingham Bart, Lady Middleton, Lady Dashwood, Lord Dartmouth, Lord Bishop of Hereford, Honble Mr North. August 19th: Sir Walter Rawlinson. August 21st: Lord Ross. August 25th: Lady Dartmouth, Lady North and 2 daughters and a son, Lady Gray. August 30th: The Prince of Holstein (nephew to the Empress of Russia). September 11th: Lord Algernon Percy and Lady. Others from Bristol, Cardiff.

p. 123 (1775) September: Le Comte de Baudiasin (at Messrs Battier & Zourbin?). September 21st: Honble Mr St John and Lady (Hampshire and brother to Lord Viscount Bolingbroke), Deane Swift (Dublin). September 27th [Oct written in]: the Bishop of Worcester and Lady, Lord Viscount Dudley. October 19th: The Earl of Ferrers, Mons de Beaumarchier, Mons Danchny [?] Baron of Vinset etc. etc. Others from London, Hants.

p. 124 (1776) March 6th: Sir Eyre Coote (Berners Street London). March 16th: Honble Capt Nevill and Lady. March 29th: The Count of Brahe (a Swede), Mr Gyldenstolpe, Mr Wittersquist (all three recommended by Bethmann and Meinicken Merchants at Bordeaux). April 2nd: Mr Wedgwood (Staffordshire). April 13th: Lord Viscount Hereford and Lady. April 29th: Sir John Fry (London). Others from London, Limerick, Cambridge, Ireland, Bath, Lichfield, Dublin, Kells, Bristol.

p. 125 (1776) May 11th: Mr Cox (London). May 20th: Charles Amcotts Esqr and Lady (MP for Boston, Lincolnshire). May 28th: Lady Gresley (Drakelow near Burton upon Trent, Stafford). May 30th: Sir Robt Cunliffe and Lady Liverpoole. May 31st: Lady Hopetoun, Lady Margt Hopetoun. June 12th: Lady Vale (Bath). Others from London, Darlaston, Thenford, East Indies, Hampton.

p. 126 (1776) June 20th: Duchess Dowager of Athol & 3 sons. Others from Lincoln, Loughborough, Norwich, Wirksworth, Spilby, Afford, Ireland, Liverpool, Northampton, Cambridge, Oxford.

p. 127 (1776) July 12th: Sir Jno Trevelyan and Lady (Nettlecomb, Somersetshire). July 20th: Lord and Lady Aylesford. July 22nd: Sir Jno Griffin Griffin and Lady. July 26th: Sir Charles Whitwort Kt. August 1st: Gilbert Esqr (MP for Lichfield) and some other Gentlemen. August: Sir Jno Mordaunt Cope Bart (Hampshire), Lord and Lady Gower. Others from London, Devonshire, Cambridge, Andover, Oxford, Lichfield, Dublin.

p. 128 (1776) August 15th: Baron de Reden, Baron de Veltheim. August 27th: Lord and Lady Sands. August 28th: Sir Herbert Packington Bart (Westwood Worcestershire). Others from London, Henley, Cambridge, Worcester, Limerick, Kent, Hackney, Lichfield, Dublin.

p. 129 (1776) September 6th: Lord and Lady North and family, Lord and Lady Dartmouth, Honble Mr Legg, Lord Exeter, Honble Mr Cecil and Lady. Others from London, Stroud, Monmouth, Birmingham, Exeter, Worcester, Cambridge.

p. 130 (1776) September 23rd: Earl of Clerridon, Lord Hide, Honble Mr Villiers. September 25th: Sir Geo Shuckburgh Bart (Warwick). September 27th: Sir – Mackworth Bart (Lynn Regis Norfolk). October 10th: Honble Mr Grevill, Sir William Hamilton. October 22nd: Lady Ann Cecil, Honble Mr Cecil, Baron de Victinghoff (Ambassador from Russia) and Lady and daughter. Others from London, Bucks, Mitcham, Oxford.

p. 131 (1776) November 28th: Lord and Lady Harrowby. December 21st: The Marquis of Tanzy. (1777) January 8th[?]: The Earl of Antim and Lady. Others from London, Frodsham, Cirencester, Guernsey.

p. 132 (1777) February/March: Visitors from London, Aston, Handsworth, Ludlow,

Monmouth, Worcester, Stafford, Kendal, W'Haven, Dronfield, Salop, Penrith, Ireland, Liverpool.

p. 133 (1777) May 14th: Lord and Lady Harroby. May 29th: Le Baron De Lingen. June 2nd: Lady Devonshire. June 10th: The Bishop of Lichfield. June 11th: The Earl of Upper Ossory and Lady, Mr Banks (Kingston Hall, Dorset). June 20th: Lord Glincairn, the Duke de Lisle (Paris). Others from London, Cornwall, Bristol, Edinburgh, Lichfield.

p. 134 (1777) July 14th: Baron van der Brugghen, Lord Valentiam. July 17th: Lord Abingdon. Others from London, Northampton, Bath, Bramford, Oxford, Aylesbury, Coventry, Birmingham.

p. 135 (1777) [n.d.]: Rt Hon Descart and 2 Gentlemen with him, Mr Westmacote (statuary London), Mr Vardy (London), Lady Ann Cecil. Others from London, Shrewsbury, Longford, Dublin, Shropshire.

p. 136 (1777) [n.d.]: Mr Cocks (Spring Garden, London), Lady Dartmouth, Mr Legg. Others from London, Dublin, Cambridge, Manchester, Dartmouth, Warwick.

p. 137 (1777) [n.d.]: Lord Famonberg [?], Lord Mar[llend?], Mr and Mrs Holloway (Lee Place, Oxfordshire). Others from London, Edinburgh, Coventtry, Coxwold, Dublin, Bedforshire, Shropshire,

p. 138 (1777) September 24th: Visitors from London, Ormskirk.

p. 139 (1777) [n.d.]: Visitors from London, Cambridge.

p. 140 (1778[?]) n.d. [end June]: Earl of Aylesford, Honble Mr Talbot. June 30th: Sir Thos and Lady Clavering, Mr Oliver (formerly Governor in America), Sir Cornwallis and Lady Maude.

p. 141 (1778[?]) [n.d.]: Mr Dawkins MP. August: General Burgoyne, Lord and Lady Webb Seymour, Lord and Lady Harrowby, Mr Lascelles.

p. 142 (1778[?]) [n.d.]: Sir George and Lady Cornwall, Lord and Lady Hillsborough, Lady Thomas, Lord Harrowby (Bath).

p. 143 (1778 [or 1779?]) [n.d.]: Lord and Lady Carysfoot, Sir John and Lady Pool, Lord and Lady Dartmouth. Others from London, Warwick, Isle of Wight, Windsor.

p. 144 (1779) [n.d.]: Andrew de Scherbinin (Russia). Others from London, Newcastle, Atherstone, Bath, Uxbridge, Stourbridge, Hagley, Edinburgh, Harlaston, Cheshire, Cambridge, Ireland, Bruxelles, Herefordshire, Oxford, Dudley, Jamaica, Bristol, Kingsbury, Copington.

p. 145 (1779) July 23rd: DeLoose, Drasseur (Ghent, Flanders). August 2nd: Lord Colville, Baron de Watteville (Bern in Switzerland). Others from London, Herefordshire, Liverpool, Westminster Abbey, Buildwas Abbey, Salop, Norwich, Oxford, Manchester, Dublin, Bradford Wilts.

p.146 (1779) [n.d.]: Mr Lyttleton (Hagley), Admiral Montague and his Lady,

Le Comte de Grabowski, Mr Beckford (Fonthill). Others from London, Henley, Coventry, Dublin, Liverpool, Oxfordshire, Middlesex, Shropshire, Cambridge, Stourbridge.

p. 10 (1780) June 1st: Lady Stamford. June 8th: Lord Monboddo (Scotland), Sir Henry Hay (Scotland). Others from London, Dublin, Berwick, Tamworth, Rugby, Witherley, Manchester, Stockport, Hereford, Oxford, Newcastle upon Tyne, Worcester, Salop, Wolverhampton.

p. 11 (1780) June 15th: Lord Aldborough (Stratford Place London). Others from London, Cambridge, Rugby, Coventry, Birmingham, Leicester, Canterbury.

p. 12 (1780) June 3rd: Mr Vagner (Swedish Consul at Trieste). Others from London, Salop, Hammersmith, Teddington, Birmingham, Cheshire, Manchester, Gloucester, Shardlow, Branston, Thuraston, Quorndon.

p. 13 (1780) July 1st: Jas Christie Esqr (London). Others from London, Hagley Row, Birmingham, Newcastle, Drogheda, Liverpool, Coventry, Bath, Wimbledon, Gloucester, Tewkesbury.

p. 14 (1780) July 1st: Sir John and Lady Irvine (Commander in Chief, Dublin). July 4th: Messrs Wahrendorff. July 6th: Lord Lucan, Lord Chesterfield with his Lady and sister. Others from London, Birmingham, Bristol.

p. 15 (1780) July 12th: Mr Shuckburgh (Warwick). Others from London, Dublin, Lichfield, Norfolk, Coventry, Oxford, Bath, Northamptonshire, Castle Bromwich, Chesterfield, Warmington.

p. 16 (1780) July: Visitors from London, Boston (America), Worcester, Lichfield, Gloucestershire, Dublin, Falmouth, Birmingham, Newnham Gloucester.

p. 17 (1780) August 5th: Lord Craven. Others from London, Farcham Hants, Handsworth, Ellesmere, Whitchurch, Birmingham, Bradford, Worcester, Exeter, Ross Herefordshire, Norfolk, Durham, Witney, Bristol, Bridgnorth.

p. 18 (1780) August: H. Stuart [?] Esqr (Critchill, Dorset). August 10th: Sir Philip Gibbes & Ladies (Hilton Park), Count Dewelderen (St James's Square). August 17th: Lord and Lady Colvill. Others from London, Bermondsey, Worcester, Shrewsbury, Birmingham, Bewdley, Salisbury, Harrow.

p. 19 (1780) August 18th: Mr Maskelyn. Others from London, Gosport, Denbighshire, Birmingham, Worcester, Guys Cliff, Warickshire, Milton Cambridgeshire, Stourbridge, Colnbrook.

p. 20 (1780) August 25th: His Excellency Baron von Gurdeirthral. Others from London, Bristol, Leicestershire, Hadham, Bath.

p. 21 (1780) August 29th: Honble Mr and Mrs Cecil, the Bishop of St Asaph with his Lady and Family. Others from London, Dublin, Heytesbury, Hanbury, Flaxley, Warwick, Camberwell, North Cray, Moreton Dorset.

p. 22 (1780) September: Dr Withering (Birmingham), Mrs Laing (Petersburg), James

Byfeld (carver, Soho, London). Others from London, Bath, Manchester, Birmingham, Oxford, Berne, Geneva, Alcester, Bristol, Dublin.

p. 23 (1780) September: Archbishop of Cork and Lady, Honble Mr Hewett and Lady (Wroxall), Count Viscounti a Millameage [?] (Milan). September 10th: Bishop of Peterborough. Others from London, Exeter, Oxford, Wales, Dublin, Derry, Cambridge, Winchester.

p. 24 (1780) September 23rd: Lady Bridgman and family (Weston), J. Kayser & Co (Ostende). Others from London, Solihall, Campden, Evesham, Bristol, Coventry, Pershore.

p. 25 (1780) October 27th: Sir Robert Herries (London). October 31st: Honble Chas Hope Weir and Lady, Lady Charlote Irskine. Others from London, Hereford, Halesowen, Beckenham, Dublin, India, Solihall, Ireland.

p. 26 (1780) December 7th: Fried Lundin (Sweden), Mr MacLean (Dantzig). Others from London, Cork, Limerick, Dublin, Bridgenorth, Warwick.

p. 27 (1781) February 24th: Honble Herculis Rowley Esqr (Dublin), Sir Mich Cromie Bt (Dublin). March 12th: Westphalen (Berlin). Others from London, Bristol, Dublin, Ireland, Oxford, Scotland, Birmingham.

p. 28 (1781) March–April: Visitors from London, Oswestry, Birmingham, Worcester, Andover, Leicester, Edgbaston, Monmouth, Hereford, Ireland, Liverpool.

p. 29 (1781) April: Lord Bishop North and Honble Mrs North, Lord Binning (Edinburgh). April 17th: the Earl of Rochford. Others from London, Osweatry, Bath, Manchester, Leicester, Ireland, Worcester, Kidderminster.

p. 30 (1781) May: Visitors from London, Oxford, Cornwall, Ireland, Whitchurch, Hereford.

p. 31 (1781) June 19th: Dr Johnson etc. June 30th: Visitors from London, Warwick, Gloucester, Leek, Manchester, Birmingham, Lynn Norfolk, Sutton Shropshire, Stourton, Leicestershire.

p. 32 (1781) n.d. [July/August]: Mr Archdeacon Carver etc., Sir Robert Lawley and family, Bishop of Chester and Lady. Others from London, Uxbridge, Warwick, Dublin.

p. 33 (1781) n.d. [July/August]: Sir Henry Gough (Egbaston), Lord Torphicken [?], Honble Mr Cecil. Others from London, Liverpool, Brackley, Wolverhampton, Monmouthshire.

p. 34 (1781) n.d. [July/August]: Visitors from London, Canterbury, Quorndon, Leicester, Birmingham, Dublin, Bristol, Wigan.

p. 35 (1781) n.d. [July/August]: Dr Hoare (Oxford), Sir John Chetwode, Lord Coventry with co., Lady Cavendish. Others from London, Birmingham, Manchester, Ireland.

p. 36 (1781) August 20th: Visitors from London, Charlestown, Hackney, Warrington, Manchester, Derry (Ireland), Edinburgh, Worcester, Oxford.

p. 37 (1781–2[?]): Mr Trubeteskoy (Petersburg), Mr Sawlowsky (Kiow), Mr Flavianow (Ukraine). Others from London, Plymouth, Royston, Dublin.

APPENDIX III

SALE CATALOGUES OF 1771 AND 1778

Annotated catalogues of Boulton and Fothergill's sales at James Christie's saleroom in 1771 and at Christie and Ansell's in 1778 have survived among the archives of Christie's. Two copies of each catalogue have survived. One of each is reproduced here, with notes summarising the differences, if any, which appear in the duplicates. In this edition of the catalogues I have followed the methods of editing archives, which I have used throughout this book. I have extended abbreviations where the extended form is obvious and altered punctuation and capitalisation where necessary. I have preserved the spelling of the original, and have only noted differences of spelling in the duplicate catalogues if the differences cause some doubt.

The 1771 sale

The title page of the catalogue reads:

A
Catalogue
Of the
Superb and elegant produce
Of
Messrs Boulton and Fothergill's,
Or moulu
Manufactory,
At Soho, in Staffordshire;
Consisting of
A variety of most beautiful and rich articles,
comprehending vases of exquisite shapes,
clock-cases, candle-branches, essence pots,
and many other ornaments,
Which will be sold by auction,
By Mr Christie,
At his Great Room next Cumberland-House,
in Pall-Mall,
On Thursday, April 11, 1771, and
the two following days.
To be viewed on Wednesday the 10th instant, and
till the time of sale, which will begin each
day at twelve o'clock.
Catalogues may be had as above.

There follows a preface, which is reproduced in Chapter 2 (see pp. 51–2).

The first copy of the catalogue, which for the purposes of this Appendix I have called 'Catalogue A', appears to have been the auctioneer's copy, the reserve prices being inscribed in the margin by each lot. The buyers and the prices that they paid are inscribed on the blank pages facing the text of the catalogue. The duplicate catalogue ('Catalogue B') appears to have been used for accounting. It is inscribed with the names of the buyers, in neater writing than in the first catalogue, and with the prices bid, but not with the reserve prices. It includes instead of these a second column of figures that repeats the prices paid by some of the buyers. This column appears to be a record of the lots that were actually sold and to exclude those that were bought in: in most cases the prices fetched by the lots listed in it exceed the reserve prices.

This is not true in every case, however. It is thus possible that the column is a record of sales for which cash was due to Boulton and Fothergill from Christie and that some of the 'unsold' lots were taken by agents not bound perhaps to pay for their purchases through Christie or to pay immediately. It appears for example that 'Nixon', 'Price', 'Barton' and probably 'Captain Thompson' were names invented for the purpose of buying in: but 'Morgan' might well have been the agent who was mentioned shortly afterwards in a letter from Boulton and Fothergill to William Matthews as having in stock certain of the unsold ornaments from the sale (B. and F. to William Matthews, 6th May 1771). Several other names besides these are recorded in the catalogue against lots that according to the second column of prices remained 'unsold'. The two columns are totalled in the duplicate catalogue as follows:

First day:

	£	s	d	£	s	d
p. 3	73	12	0	37	11	0
p. 4	173	7	6	91	19	0
p. 5	169	16	0	87	8	0
p. 6	192	16	0	106	10	0
p. 7	220	0	0	127	1	0
	829	11	6	450	9	0

Second day:

	£	s	d	£	s	d
p. 7	11	12	0	7	7	0
p. 8	149	16	0	55	11	0
p. 9	170	11	0	90	3	0
p. 10	241	5	0	119	13	6
p. 11	413	16	6	182	5	0
p. 12	173	5	0			—
	1,160	5	6	454	19	6

Third day:

	£	s	d	£	s	d
p. 12	48	7	0	19	8	0
p. 13	142	0	6	77	13	6
p. 14	212	19	6	171	1	0
p. 15	196	5	6	148	2	6
p. 16	316	1	0	90	6	6
	915	13	6	506	11	0

The summary of the account of bids received, including the lots that were bought in, is inscribed on the page facing the preface:

	£	s	d
1st day	829	11	6
2	1,160	5	6
3	915	13	6
	2,905	10	6
Commission	145	5	0
	2,760	5	6
Debit To Mr Stuart out of catalogue			
a pair large vases	50	0	0
a pair candlesticks	6	6	0
General Carnack—an altar	16	16	0
	2,833	7	6

From this it appears that Boulton and Fothergill actually received from the sale only £1,266 14s. 6d. (the total raised by actual sales less Christie's commission), plus £73 2s. 0d. from the sales to Stuart and General Carnack, making a total of £1,339 16s. 6d. Under no circumstances, therefore, could they pretend that financially the sale was a success.

FIRST DAY Thursday, April 11th, 1771	CATALOGUE A				CATALOGUE B	
	Anno-tations	Margin Price (i.e. Reserve) £ s d	Price Paid £ s d	Buyer	*Price recorded in second column (i.e. actual sales)	Notes on differences from entries in Catalogue A
1 A pair of candle vases radix amethysti and or moulu ornamented in the antique taste					*	Buyer Lord Ormsby £4 10s 0d
2 An essence pot ditto lined with silver					*	Buyer Mr Gasbyn £4
3 A pair ditto candle vases with laurel festoons						Buyer Mr Nixon £4 5s 0d
4 A pair of table candlesticks in or moulu with triangular feet		3 10	5 5	Dr Maden	*	
5 A pair of candle vases radix amethysti and or moulu, on a square pedestal of artificial lapis lazuli		3 10	5 15 6	Ld Orwell	*	Price £5 15s 0d
6 A pair of candle vases radix amethysti, and or moulu ornamented in the antique taste		3 13 6	4 1			Buyer Mr Barton
7 An essence pot ditto lined with silver		3 10	4 8	Ld Orwell	*	
8 A pair ditto candle vases with laurel festoons		3 13 6	4 3	Price		
9 A pair of table candlesticks in or moulu		8 8	7 7	Lord Cary	*	Buyer Lord Kerry
10 An essence pot radix amethysti and or moulu lined with silver and ornamented in the antique taste		6 6	6 6	Ld Melborn	*	Buyer Lady Melbourne
11 A pair of candle vases radix amethysti and or moulu with drapery and other ornaments	Enamel	3 13 6	4	Captain Thompson		'Radix amethysti' deleted
12 A pair of candle vases radix amethysti and or moulu		4 4	4	Nixon		
13 A vase of radix amethysti and or moulu lined with silver and perferated for essence, supported by three griffins upon a round pedestal of the same materials the whole in the antique taste		10	12	Barclay		Buyer Mr Barton
14 A pair of candle vases radix amethysti and or moulu with drapery and other ornaments	Enamel	3 13 6	3 12	Nixon		'Radix amethysti' deleted
*14 A sugar dish radix amethysti and or moulu lined with silver		5 5	4 17 6	Tassarl [?]		Buyer Mr Tassel

FIRST DAY Thursday, April 11th, 1771	CATALOGUE A				CATALOGUE B	
	Anno- tations	Margin Price (i.e. Reserve) £ s d	Price Paid £ s d	Buyer	*Price recorded in second column (i.e. actual sales)	Notes on differences from entries in Catalogue A
15 A pair of candle vases radix amethysti and or moulu		4 4	4 1		*	Buyer Admiral Montagu
16 An essence pot ditto lined with silver		3 10	4 4		*	Buyer Money
17 A pair ditto candle vases with laurel festoons		3 13 6	3 15	Pinchbeck	*	
18 A vase in or moulu, the form of which is an exact copy from an antique, and ornamented in the same taste		6	7 17 6	Sir W W— [?]	*	Buyer Sir W. W. Wynn
19 A pair of candle vases in or moulu with drapery and other ornaments		3 3	3 7		*	Buyer Money
20 A pair of candle vases radix amethysti and or moulu	Enamel	4 4	4	Bradburn		'Vases radix' deleted: annotated 'enamelled'. Buyer Barton
21 An essence pot ditto lined with silver		3 10	4 1	Ing	*	Price £4 3s od
22 A pair of candle vases radix amethysti and or moulu on a square pedestal of artificial lapis lazuli		5 15 6	6	Captain Thompson[1]		
23 A pair of wreathed corinthian columns with branches for two candles, on the capital a small vase in the antique taste, the whole in or moulu		12 12	12 12		*	Buyer Lord C. [?] Montagu
***23** A sugar dish radix amethysti and or moulu lined with silver		5 5	5 10	Captain Thompson		Price £5 5s od
24 A pair of candle vases radix amethysti and or moulu		4 4	4	Lesage	*	
25 An essence pot ditto lined with silver		3 10	3 19	Ld Orwell	*	
26 A pair of ditto candle vases with laurel festoons		3 13 6	3		*	Buyer Money price £3 13s od
27 An altar richly embellished in the antique taste, on which is a vase with three branches for candles in the same taste, the whole in or moulu		16 16	16 5 6			Buyer Barton
28 A pair of candle vases radix amethysti and or moulu		4 4	4 3	Greenwood	*	

1. Here abbreviated in the original, as frequently later, to 'C. Thompson'.

FIRST DAY Thursday, April 11th, 1771	CATALOGUE A Anno-tations	Margin Price (i.e. Reserve) £ s d	Price Paid £ s d	Buyer	CATALOGUE B *Price recorded in second column (i.e. actual sales)	Notes on differences from entries in Catalogue A
29 A vase radix amethisti and or moulu, lined with silver and perferated for an essence pot, with ornaments in the antique taste and branches for two candles		15 15	15 15	Sir J. Rothly [?]		Buyer Sir John Wrotesley
30 A pair of candle vases enamelled and or moulu, with drapery and other ornaments	Enamel	3 3	3 5	Nixon		
31 An essence pot radix amethysti and or moulu lined with silver, ornamented in the antique taste		6	6 5	Price		
32 A pair of candle vases radix amethysti and or moulu		4 4	4 1	Barton		
33 An essence pot ditto lined with silver		3 10	4 4	Price		
34 A pair ditto candle vases with laurel festoons		3 13 6	3 13	Barton		
35 A vase of the radix amethysti and or moulu, with branches for two candles		10 10	10 10	Fordice	*	Buyer Mr Crawford
36 A pair of candle vases radix amethysti and or moulu on a square pedestal of artificial lapis lazuli		5 15 6	5 15	ditto	*	Buyer Mr Crawford price £5 15s 6d
37 A pair of candle vases radix amethysti and or moulu		4 4	4 4	Deard	*	
38 A vase in the antique taste radix amethysti and or moulu, lined with silver and perferated for essence supported by four sphinxs upon an ornamental bass of ebony		12 12	23 12 6	Barton		
39 An essence pot lined with silver		3 10	3 19	Fitzgerald	*	
40 A rich vase lined with silver and branches for two candles, standing on a square pedestal of radix amethysti and or moulu		15 15	22 1	Barton		
41 A pair of candle vases enamelled and or moulu with drapery and other ornaments		3 3	3 10	Pinchbeck	*	
42 A vase radix amethysti and or moulu lined with silver and perferated for essence, with ornaments in the antique taste and branches for two candles		15 15	15 10	Morgan		
43 A pair of candle vases radix amethysti and or moulu		4 4	4 10	Robinson	*	
44 An essence pot ditto lined with silver		3 10	4	Deard	*	

FIRST DAY Thursday, April 11th, 1771	CATALOGUE A				CATALOGUE B	
	Anno- tations	Margin Price (i.e. Reserve) £ s d	Price Paid £ s d	Buyer	*Price recorded in second column (i.e. actual sales)	Notes on differences from entries in Catalogue A
45 A pair ditto candle vases with laurel festoons		3 13 6	4 4	C	*	Buyer Colonel William
46 A vase of radix amethysti and or moulu lined with silver and perferated for essence, supported by three griffins upon a round pedestal of the same materials, the whole in the antique taste		10	12 12	ditto	*	Buyer Colonel William
47 A pair of candle vases in or moulu with drapery and other ornaments		3 3	3 18		*	Annotated 'Lord Dun-killon': buyer 'Lord Orwell' deleted
48 Two pair of table candlesticks in or moulu	Say £16 the pair	8	16 16	Lord Cary	*	Buyer Lord Kerry
49 A pair of candle vases radix amethysti and or moulu		4 4	4 3	Barton		
50 An essence pot ditto lined with silver		3 10 3 3	4 6 3 15	Price Barnsale	*	
51 A pair ditto candle vases with laurel festoons		3 3	3 15	Barnsale	*	
52 A vase of radix amethysti and or moulu with branches for two candles		10 10	10 10	Barton		
53 A pair of candle vases radix amethysti and or moulu with drapery and other ornaments		3 13 6	4	Morgan		
54 A small vase for a candle upon an antique altar of radix amethysti and or moulu		3 3				
55 A candelabrum of radix amethysti and or moulu in the antique taste		10 10	10 10	Barton		
56 A pair of candle vases radix amethysti and or moulu		4 4	4 1	Morgan		
57 An essence pot ditto lined with silver		3 10	3 12 6	Price		
58 A rich vase lined with silver, and branches for three candles standing on a square pedestal of radix amethysti and or moulu		16 16	16 16	General Chomley	*	Buyer General Cholmondley
59 A pair of candle vases radix amethysti and or moulu on a square pedestal of artificial lapis lazuli		5 15 6	5 17 6		*	Buyer Mr C. Bowes
60 A pair of candle vases radix amethysti and or moulu		4 4	4 2	Fitzgerald	*	

FIRST DAY Thursday, April 11th, 1771	CATALOGUE A Anno- tations	Margin Price (i.e. Reserve) £ s d	Price Paid £ s d	Buyer	CATALOGUE B *Price recorded in second column (i.e. actual sales)	Notes on differences from entries in Catalogue A
61 An essence pot ditto lined with silver		3 10	3 10	Barton		
62 A pair of ditto candle vases with laurel festoons		3 13 6	3 13		*	Buyer Lady Elliott
63 A vase of radix amethysti and or moulu, lined with silver and ornamented in the antique taste		6	6 12 6	Barton		'Lined with silver' deleted
64 Venus at the tomb of Adonis in statuary marble and or moulu; on the dye of the pedestal is a medalian representing his death, and upon it an urn lined with silver and perferated for essence, and may be occasionally used for a lamp		15 15	17 17	Lord Cary	*	Buyer Lord Kerry
65 A vase in the antique taste, radix amethysti and or moulu, lined with silver and perferated for essence, supported by four sphinx's upon an ornamented bas of ebony		12 12	15 15	Barton		
66 A pair of obelisks of radix amethisti		4 4	3 19	Nixon		
67 A vase ditto		1 11 6	2 10	Fleming	*	
68 A vase radix amethysti and or moulu lined with silver standing on a round altar of the same materials, the whole richly embellished in the antique taste		6 6	6 16	Lord Millsent	*	Buyer Lord Milsington, price £6 16s 6d
69 A pair of candle vases radix amethysti and or moulu		4 4	4 4	D[itto]	*	Buyer Lord Milsington
70 An essence pot ditto lined with silver		3 10	3 14			Buyer Lady Elliott
71 A pair ditto candle vases with laurel festoons		3 13 6	3 12	Pinchbeck	*	
72 A vase radix amethysti and or moulu, lined with silver and perferated for essence with ornaments in the antique taste, and branches for three lights		16 16	15 4 6	Lord Millnson	*	Buyer Lord Milsington
73 A pair of candle vases radix amethysti and or moulu		4 4	4		*	Buyer Mr Webb
74 An essence pot ditto lined with silver		3 10	3 13	Lesage	*	
75 A vase of radix amethysti and or moulu lined with silver, ornamented in the antique taste	'Lined with silver' deleted	6	5 17 6	Price		

FIRST DAY Thursday, April 11th, 1771	CATALOGUE A Anno- tations	Margin Price (i.e. Reserve) £ s d	Price Paid £ s d	Buyer	CATALOGUE B *Price recorded in second column (i.e. actual sales)	Notes on differences from entries in Catalogue A
76 A vase in the antique taste radix amethysti and or moulu, lined with silver, and perferated for essence supported by four sphinx's upon an ornamented bass of ebony		12 12	14 14	Seenor [?]	*	Buyer Mr Senior
77 A pair of candle vases radix amethysti and or moulu		4 4	4		*	Buyer Mr C. Bowes
78 A rich vase lined with silver and branches for two candles, standing on a square pedestal of radix amethysti and or moulu		15 15	15 15	Senor	*	Buyer Mr Senior
79 A large caryatic vase radix amethysti and or moulu, lined with silver and perferated for incence, with four branches for candles, standing on a plinth richly inlaid		31 10	30 9[1]	Barton		Price £30 9s 6d
80 A candelabrum of radix amethysti and or moulu, in the antique taste		10 10	10 10	Lord Millnsenton	*	Buyer Lord Milsington
81 A large marbled vase of an antique form, or moulu, ornaments in the antique taste		21	23 12 6	Nixon		
82 A large vase in or moulu in the antique taste, with medalians and other ornaments	Not come					
83 A pair of elegant large table candelsticks with two branches, in or moulu		15 15	16 16	Ld Cundliff	*	Buyer Lady Cunliffe
84 A large vase of radix amethysti and or moulu, lined with silver and perferated for incence with four branches for candles, supported by two caryatides standing on an ornamented ebony plinth		26 5	26 5		*	Buyer Mr Southwell
85 An horizontal time piece, in or moulu representing Venus at the tomb of Adonis, and on the urn is engraved the following inscription. ΑἶΑἶ Τὰν κυθέρειαν Απώλετο Χαλος 'Α'δωνις		30	31 10	Sir W. W. Win	*	Buyer Sir W. Williams Wynn
86 A large vase of radix amethysti and or moulu, perferated for incence, with two double branches, supported by demy satyrs, with festoons, etc. standing on a plynth richly inlaid, after a model that hath been executed for his majesty		42	52 10	Barton		

1. The price appears as '29' (i.e. guineas) with the name of the buyer and not in column.

FIRST DAY Thursday, April 11th, 1771	CATALOGUE A				CATALOGUE B	
	Anno- tations	Margin Price (i.e. Reserve) £ s d	Price Paid £ s d	Buyer	*Price recorded in second column (i.e. actual sales)	Notes on differences from entries in Catalogue A
87 A tripod for incence in or moulu, lined with silver, with three branches for candles, after a design of Mr Stuart's		50	52 10	Wright	*	
88 A pedestal clock case with a correct eight day repeating clock; on the top a boy sitting on books, in a contemplative attitude, with a globe and scrole on which is delineated a small scheme of the solar system		42	40 9[1]	M		Buyer Morgan, price £40 9s od

1. The price appears as '39' (i.e. guineas) with the initial of the buyer and not in column.

SECOND DAY Friday, April 12th, 1771	CATALOGUE A				CATALOGUE B	
	Anno- tations	Margin Price (i.e. Reserve) £ s d	Price Paid £ s d	Buyer	*Price recorded in second column (i.e. actual sales)	Notes on differences from entries in Catalogue A
1 A pair of candle vases radix amethesti and or moulu the ornaments in the antique taste		4 4	4 5	Price		
2 An essence pot ditto lined with silver		3 10	3 10	Money	*	
3 A pair of ditto candle vases with laurel festoons		3 13 6	3 17	Hopkinson	*	
4 A vase radix amethysti and or moulu with branches for 2 candles		10 10	12 1 6	Captain Thompson		
5 A pair of candle vases radix amethysti and or moulu		4 4	3 18	Morgan		
6 An essence pot ditto lined with silver		3 10	3 11	Ld Melburn	*	Buyer Lady Melbourne
7 A pair of ditto candle vases with laurel festoons		3 13 6	3 13 6	Stanton	*	
8 A sugar dish radix amethysti and or moulu lined with silver		5 5	5 15	Nixon		Price £5 12s 6d
9 A pair of candle vases radix amethysti and or moulu with drapery and other ornaments		3 13 6	3 9		*	Buyer Mr Hearne
10 A pair of table candlesticks or moulu triangular feet		5 5	5 7 6	Price		
11 A pair of candle vases radix amethysti and or moulu		4 4	4 4	Captain Thompson		
12 An essence pot ditto lined with silver	Chinea	3 10	3 10	Hopkinson	*	Annotated 'Green enamelled'
13 A pair of ditto candle vases with laurel festoons		3 13 6	3 12	Barret		Buyer Mr Barratt
14 A vase radix amethysti and or moulu lined with silver and perforated for essence supported by three griffins on a round pedestal of the same materials, the whole in the antique taste		10 10	11 6	Morgan		
15 A pair of vases radix amethysti and or moulu		4 4	3 10	Hudney	*	Buyer Udney
16 A pair of candle vases or moulu with drapery and other ornaments		3 3	3 6	Nixon		
17 An essence pot radix amethysti and or moulu lined with silver and ornamented in the antique taste		6	6	Lord Cary	*	Buyer Lord Kerry

SECOND DAY Friday, April 12th, 1771	CATALOGUE A				CATALOGUE B	
	Anno-tations	Margin Price (i.e. Reserve) £ s d	Price Paid £ s d	Buyer	*Price recorded in second column (i.e. actual sales)	Notes on differences from entries in Catalogue A
18 A pair of candle vases radix amethysti and or moulu		4 4	3 12	Wiston	*	Buyer Mr Weston
19 An essence pot ditto lined with silver	Chinea	3 3	4 5	Lord Arandale	*	Annotated 'green enam-elled', buyer Lord Arundel
20 A pair of ditto candle vases with laurel festoons		3 13 6	3 12	Morgan		
21 A vase radix amethysti and or moulu with branches for two candles		10 10	10 15	Ditto		
22 A pair of candle vases radix amethysti and or moulu on a square pedestal of a curious composition		5 5	5	Price		
23 A pair of table candlesticks in or moulu		6 6	6 6	Ld Melborn	*	Buyer Lady Melbourne
24 A pair of candle vases radix amethysti and or moulu		4 4	3 13	Spooner	*	Price £3 13s 6d
25 An essence pot ditto lined with silver	Enamel	3 10	3 9	Ditto	*	
26 A pair of candle vases radix amethysti and or moulu with drapery and other ornaments	Goats head	3 13 6	3 10	Pinchbeck	*	
27 A vase and radix amethysti, and or moulu lined with silver and perferated for essence	Chinea	3 10	3 10	Lord Arandale	*	Buyer Lord Arundel
28 A sugar dish radix amethysti and or moulu lined with silver		5 5	4 16	Price		
29 A pair of candle vases radix amethysti and or moulu		4 4	3 12		*	Buyer Mr Scroope
30 A rich vase lined with silver and branches for two candles standing on a square pedestal of radix amethysti and or moulu		15 15	24	Morgan		
31 A pair of candle vases or moulu		3 3	3 10	Bateman	*	
32 A wreathed corinthian column with branches for two candles, on the capital a small vase in the antique taste, the whole finished in or moulu		12 12	12 1 6	Barton		
33 A vase radix amethysti and or moulu in the antique taste, lined with silver and perferated for essence supported by 4 sphinx's, on an ornamented ebony base		12 12	19 8 6	Morgan		

SECOND DAY Friday, April 12th, 1771	CATALOGUE A Anno-tations	Margin Price (i.e. Reserve) £ s d	Price Paid £ s d	Buyer	CATALOGUE B *Price recorded in second column (i.e. actual sales)	Notes on differences from entries in Catalogue A
34 A pair of candle vases radix amethysti and or moulu		4 4	3 12	Price		
35 An essence pot ditto lined with silver	Chinea	3 10	3 10	Lord Arandale	*	Annotated 'green enamelled', buyer, Lord Arundel
36 A pair of ditto candle vases with laurel festoons		3 13 6	3 13	Palk	*	
37 A vase radix amethysti and or moulu lined with silver and perferated for essence, supported by 3 griffins on a round pedestal of the same materials, the whole in the antique taste		10 10	12 12	Ld G.	*	Buyer Lady Godolphin
38 A pair of candle vases radix amethysti and or moulu		4 4	3 10	Barton		
39 An essence pot ditto lined with silver	Enamel	3 10	3 9	Pinchbeck	*	
40 A pair of ditto candle vases with laurel festoons		3 13 6	3 14	Blackwell	*	Annotated 'enamelled'
41 A vase radix amethysti and or moulu lined with silver, and ornamented in the antique taste		6 6	6[1]	Price		
42 A pair of candle vases radix amethysti and or moulu on square pedestals of a curious composition		5 5	5	Barret		Buyer Mr Barratt
43 A pair of candle vases radix amethysti and or moulu		4 4	3 14	Pratt	*	
44 An essence pot ditto lined with silver	Chinea	3 10	3 10	Barton		
45 A pair of candle vases or moulu		3 3	2 19	Ditto		
46 An altar of statuary marble richly embellished in the antique taste, on which is a vase with 3 branches for candles		16 16	15 15	Barton		
47 A vase radix amethysti and or moulu		8 8 }	16 16	Palk	*	
48 Ditto its companion		8 8 }				
49 A pair of candle vases radix amethysti and or moulu		4 4	3 13 6	Leith [?]	*	
50 An essence pot ditto lined with silver	Enamel	3 10	3 12	Price		

1. The number sequence of the marginal notes in the original is confused from lot 41 to lot 48. It is shown correctly in Catalogue B.

SECOND DAY Friday, April 12th, 1771	CATALOGUE A				CATALOGUE B	
	Anno-tations	Margin Price (i.e. Reserve) £ s d	Price Paid £ s d	Buyer	*Price recorded in second column (i.e. actual sales)	Notes on differences from entries in Catalogue A
51 A pair of ditto candle vases with laurel festoons		3 13 6	3 14	Pinchbeck	*	
52 A vase in the antique taste radix amethysti and or moulu lined with silver and perferated for essence, supported by 4 sphinx's on an ornamented ebony base		12 12	15 4 6	Ditto	*	
53 A pair of candle vases radix amethysti and or moulu		4 4	3 12	Lesage	*	
54 An essence pot ditto lined with silver	Enamel	3 10	3 9	Palk	*	Annotated 'blue enam-elled'
55 A pair of ditto candle vases with laurel festoons	Enamel	3 13 6	3 12	Haughton	*	Buyer Mrs Orton
56 A vase radix amethysti and or moulu, lined with silver and ornamented in the antique taste		6 6	6	Palk	*	
57 A pair of candle vases radix amethysti and or moulu on a square pedestal of a curious composition		5 5	5	Barton		
58 A pair of candle vases radix amethysti and or moulu		4 4	3 15	Barton		
59 A rich vase lined with silver and branches for two lights, standing on a square pedestal of radix amethysti and or moulu		15 15	15 15		*	Buyer Mr Senior
60 A pair of candle vases enameled and or moulu		3 3	3 10	Fellows		
61 An alter radix amethysti and or moulu richly decorated in the antique taste on which is a vase of the same with three branches for candles		16 16	17 6	Palk	*	Price £17 6s 6d
62 A tea vase or moulu decorated with festoons of flowers and lined with silver	Sell at £15	18 18	15 15	Barret		Buyer Mr Barratt
63 Two pair of large elegant table candlesticks in or moulu		25 4	26 5	Ld Melborn	* *	Buyer Lady Melbourne
*63 A vase radix amethysti and or moulu lined with silver, standing on a round alter of the same materials, the whole richly decorated in the antique taste		6 6	9 9	Pinchbeck	*	

SECOND DAY Friday, April 12th, 1771	CATALOGUE A Anno- tations	Margin Price (i.e. Reserve) £ s d	Price Paid £ s d	Buyer	CATALOGUE B *Price recorded in second column (i.e. actual sales)	Notes on differences from entries in Catalogue A
64 A pair of candle vases radix amethysti and or moulu	All or moulu	4 4	3 7		*	'Radix amethysti' deleted, buyer Mr Herbert
65 An essence pot ditto lined with silver	Chinea	3 10	3 11	Price		Annotated 'enamelled'
66 A pair of ditto candle vases with laurel festoons		3 13 6	3 10	Lesage	*	
67 A vase in the antique taste, radix amethesti and or moulu lined with silver and perforated for essence supported by 4 sphinx's on an ornamented ebony bass		12 12	26 5	Morgan		
68 An horizontal time piece representing Venus at the tomb of Adonis, in marble and or moulu, on the pedestal is a medalian of his death, and on the urn is the following inscription Αἶ Αἶ Ταὺ κυθέρειαν Απωλετο Καλος Ἀδωνις		25	28 7	Veale	*	
69 A tripod for insence in or moulu lined with silver and 3 branches for candles after a design of Mr Stuart		50	56 14[1]	J. Barret		Buyer Mr Barratt, price £56 14s
70 A pair of candle vases radix amethysti and or moulu on a square pedestal of a curious composition		5 5	4 19		*	Buyer Mr Streatfield [?]
71 A pair of wreathed corinthian columns the shaft of which is a curious imitation of lapis lazuli with branches for 2 candles, on the capital is a small vase in the antique taste or moulu		12 12	12 1 6	Captain Thompson		
72 A pair of candle vases radix amethysti and or moulu		4 4	3 15		*	Buyer Money
73 An essence pot ditto lined with silver		3 10	3 14	Fitzroy	*	
74 A pair of candle vases enameled and or moulu		3 13 6	3 6	Ditto	*	

1. The price appears as '54' (i.e. guineas) with the name of the buyer and not in column.

SECOND DAY Friday, April 12th, 1771	CATALOGUE A Anno-tations	Margin Price (i.e. Reserve) £ s d	Price Paid £ s d	Buyer	CATALOGUE B *Price recorded in second column (i.e. actual sales)	Notes on differences from entries in Catalogue A
75 A vase radix amethysti and or moulu lined with silver and perforated for essence, with ornaments in the antique taste and branches for two candles		15 15	17 6 6	Barton		
76 A large pair of marble vases or moulu ornaments in the antique taste	Sell for £30 or 35	40	40 9[1]	Captain Nixon		Price £40 9s 6d
77 A pair of candle vases radix amethysti and or moulu		4 4	4 1	Lord Dyllon	*	Buyer Lord Dillier [?]
78 An essence pot ditto lined with silver		3 10	3 10	Fitzroy	*	
79 A pair of ditto candle vases with laurel festoons		3 13 6	3 15	Senor	*	Buyer Mr Senior
80 A candelabrum radix amethysti and or moulu in the antique taste		10 10	10 10	Ld Melborn	*	Buyer Lady Melbourne
81 A ditto its companion		10 10	10 10	Milington	*	Buyer Lord Milsington
82 A vase in the antique taste radix amethysti and or moulu lined with silver and perforated for essence, supported by 4 sphinx's, on an ornamented ebony pedestal		12 12	12 12	Ld M. Fordice	*	Buyer Lady Margaret Fordyce
83 A pair of candle vases radix amethysti and or moulu		4 4	3 15	Senor	*	Buyer Mr Senior
84 A rich vase lined with silver and branches for two lights standing on a square pedestal of radix amethysti and or moulu		15 15	15 15	Price		
85 A vase radix amethysti and or moulu lined with silver and perforated for essence, with ornaments in the antique taste and branches for 3 candles		15 15	15 4 6	Ditto		'3' deleted, '2' inserted, price £14 14s
86 Venus at the tomb of Adonis in marble and or moulu, on the pedestal is a medalion of his death and the urn perforated for essence		15 15	21	Ld Mellborn	*	Buyer Lady Melbourne
87 A large caryatic vase radix amethysti and or moulu lined with silver and perferated for insence, with branches for three candles, standing on a triangular plynth of statuary marble		25	25 4 6	Barret		Buyer Mr Barratt, price £25 4s

1. The price appears as '39' (i.e. guineas) with the name of the buyer and not in column.

SECOND DAY Friday, April 12th, 1771	CATALOGUE A Anno- tations	Margin Price (i.e. Reserve) £ s d	Price Paid £ s d	Buyer	CATALOGUE B *Price recorded in second column (i.e. actual sales)	Notes on differences from entries in Catalogue A
88 A large vase radix amithysti and or moulu perferated for insence with two double branches supported by demy satyrs with festoons, etc. standing in a plynth richly inlaid after a model that hath been executed for his majesty		42	40 9[1]	Barton		Price £40 19s
89 A large vase radix amethysti and or moulu lined with silver and perferated for insence with four branches for candles, supported by two caryatides standing on an ornamented ebeny plynth	21	25	25 4	Pinchbeck	*	
90 A ditto equally elegant, the whole in or moulu	21[2]	25	24 13 6	Barret		Buyer Barratt
91 Two pair of large elegant silver candlesticks at per oz		7/9 oz		Lord Cary	*	Buyer Lord Kerry, price £87 8s
92 A tripod for insence in or moulu lined with silver and three branches for candlesticks after a design of Mr Stuart		50	52 10	Fellows		
93 A very correct repeating eight day clock, the case of which is an allegorical piece of sculpture in or moulu; representing Minerva, who with her right hand unveils a vestive vase, with her left she notes the flying moments; and on the vase is seen an oval medalian, Prudence making libations at the shrine of Time; on the other side is a boy seated on books, contemplating the following lines from Gay. 'Tis I who measure vital space, And deal out years to human race; By me all useful arts are gain'd, Wealth, learning, wisdom is attain'd: In ev'ry view men ought to mind me, For when once lost they never find me! He spoke; the gods no more contest, And his superior gift confest, That Time (when truly understood) Is the most precious earthly good.		150	165	Morgan		

1. The price appears as '39' (i.e. guineas) with the name of the buyer and not in column.
2. This figure is probably a reduced reserve.

THIRD DAY Saturday, April 13th, 1771	CATALOGUE A Anno- tations	 Margin Price (i.e. Reserve) £ s d	 Price Paid £ s d	 Buyer	CATALOGUE B *Price recorded in second column (i.e. actual sales)	 Notes on differences from entries in Catalogue A
1 A pair of candle vases radix amethysti and or moulu ornamented in the antique taste		4 4			*	Buyer Money, price £4 5s
2 An essence pot ditto lined with silver		3 10	3 13	Barton		
3 A pair ditto candle vases with laurel festoons		3 3	3 19	McClane	*	Buyer Mr MacLeane
4 2 pair table candlesticks in or moulu with triangular feet		16 16	14 3 6	Morgan		
5 A pair of candle vases radix amethysti and or moulu	Enamel	4 4	4 4	Frank [?]	*	'Radix amethysti' deleted; annotated 'green enamelled', buyer Mr Fox [?]
6 An essence pot ditto lined with silver		3 10	7	Smart	*	Annotated 'a pair'
7 A pair ditto candle vases with laurel festoons	Gilt	3 3	3 5	Barton		
8 A sugar dish radix amethysti and or moulu lined with silver		5 5	7 17 6	Morgan		Annotated 'a pair'
9 A vase radix amethysti and or moulu lined with silver, standing upon a round altar of the same materials, the whole richly ornamented in the antique taste		6 6	6 2		*	Buyer Money, price £6 2s 6d
10 A pair of candle vases radix amethysti and or moulu	Gilt	4 4	3 9	Barton		
11 An essence pot ditto lined with silver		3 10	3 9	Pinchbeck	*	
12 A pair of candle vases radix amethysti and or moulu	Gilt	4 4	3 4	Nixon		'Radix amethysti' deleted
13 A vase of radix amethysti		1 1	1 16	Fleming		Annotated 'returned'
14 A vase in the antique taste radix amethysti and or moulu lined with silver and perferated for essence supported by four sphinx's upon an ornamented ebony bass		12 12	12 12	Sir W. Ponting [?]	*	Buyer Sir B. Morton [?]
15 A pair of candle vases radix amethysti and or moulu	Gilt	4 4	3 2		*	'Radix amethysti' deleted, buyer Mr Middleton

THIRD DAY Saturday, April 13th, 1771	CATALOGUE A				CATALOGUE B	
	Anno-tations	Margin Price (i.e. Reserve) £ s d	Price Paid £ s d	Buyer	*Price recorded in second column (i.e. actual sales)	Notes on differences from entries in Catalogue A
16 An essence pot ditto lined with silver		3 3	3 9	Lesage	*	'Ditto lined with silver' deleted
17 A pair ditto candle vases with laurel festoons	Enamel	3 3	4 4	Fox	*	Annotated 'enamelled'
18 A candelabrum radix amethysti and or moulu in the antique taste		10 10	10 10	Ditto	*	
19 A vase, radix amethysti and or moulu lined with silver and perferated for essence supported by three griffins on a round pedestal of the same materials, the whole in the antique taste		10 10	15 4 6	Barton		
20 A pair of candle vases radix amethysti and or moulu	Enamel	3 13 6	3 9	Morgan		'Radix amethysti' deleted, annotated 'enamelled'
21 An essence pot ditto lined with silver		3 10	3 13	Nixon		
22 A pair ditto candle vases with laurel festoons	Gilt	3 13 6	3	Fitzroy	*	
23 A sugar dish radix amethysti and or moulu lined with silver		3 3				
24 A vase radix amethisti and or moulu, lined with silver, standing upon a round altar of the same materials, the whole richly ornamented in the antique taste		6 6	10[1]	Britingham	*	
25 A pair of candle vases radix amethysti and or moulu	Enamel	4 4	3 13	Morgan		Price £3 13s 6d
26 A rich vase lined with silver and branches for two candles, standing on a square pedestal of radix amethysti and or moulu		15 15	26 5	Barton		
27 A pair of candle vases enamelled in or moulu		3 13 6	3 13	Nixon		Buyer Price
28 A tryton in dark bronz, holding branches for two candles in or moulu, on a bassment of the same neatly ornamented		15 15	12	General Carnack	*	
29 A vase radix amethysti and or moulu, lined with silver and perferated for essence, supported by three griffins on a round pedestal of the same materials, the whole in the antique taste		10 10				

1. Although the number sequence of the marginal notes from lot 23 to lot 31 is continuous in the original, it is clear that the notes relating to lots 23 and 29 are omitted and that these prices belong to lot 24. There are also no details for lots 23 and 29 in Catalogue B, which suggests that the objects never reached the sale.

THIRD DAY Saturday, April 13th, 1771	CATALOGUE A Anno- tations	 Margin Price (i.e. Reserve) £ s d	 Price Paid £ s d	 Buyer	CATALOGUE B *Price recorded in second column (i.e. actual sales)	 Notes on differences from entries in Catalogue A
30 A pair of candle vases radix amethysti and or moulu	Gilt	3 13 6	3 5	Pinchbeck	*	
31 An essence pot ditto lined with silver	Chinea	3 10	6	Fitzroy	*	'lined with silver' deleted, annotated 'A pair', 'and 53', 'china', 'faulty'
32 A pair ditto candle vases with laurel festoons		3 3	4 1		*	Buyer Money
33 A candelabrum radix amethysti and or moulu, in the antique taste		10 10	10 10	Stuart	*	
34 A vase radix amethysti and or moulu, with branches for two candles		10 10	12 1 6	General Carnack	*	
35 A most beautiful piece of radix amethysti with or moulu ornaments, in the antique taste		10 10 }	30 9[1]		*	Buyer Lady Sands
36 Ditto its companion		10 10 }				
37 A pair of candle vases radix amethysti and or moulu	Gilt	3 10	3 7	Price		
38 An essence pot ditto lined with silver	Enamelled	3 10	7 10	Fitzroy	*	
39 A pair of candle vases radix amethysti and or moulu	Gilt	3 13	3 9	Ld Besborough	*	Annotated 'green enamelled'
40 A vase in or moulu, the form of which is an exact copy from an antique, and ornamented in the same taste		6 6	7 10	Ld Sands	*	Buyer Lady Sands
41 A vase radix amethysti and or moulu, lined with silver and perferated for essence, with ornaments in the antique taste and branches for two candles		15 15	27 16 6	Barton		
42 A pair of candle vases radix amethysti and or moulu		3 13 6	4 5	Veale	*	
43 An essence pot ditto lined with silver		3 10				
44 A pair ditto candle vases with laurel festoons	Gilt	3 3	3 14	Ld Besborough	*	

1. This price is entered against lot 35 but refers to lots 35 and 36, as is clear from Catalogue B. The number sequence of the marginal notes is consequently wrong in the original down to lot 54, but has been adjusted here. Lots 43, 46, 50 and 53 probably never reached the sale.

THIRD DAY Saturday, April 13th, 1771	CATALOGUE A Anno- tations	Margin Price (i.e. Reserve) £ s d	Price Paid £ s d	Buyer	CATALOGUE B *Price recorded in second column (i.e. actual sales)	Notes on differences from entries in Catalogue A
45 A wreathed corinthian column with branches for two candles, on the capital a small vase in the antique taste, the whole or moulu		21	21 10 6	Fitzroy	*	Annotated '2 pairs'
46 A small vase radix amethysti and or moulu, on an antique altar of the same	Last					'Radix amethysti' deleted
47 A pair of candle vases radix amethysti and or moulu	Enamel	3 3	3 18	Morgan		'Radix ameth-ysti' deleted, annotated 'a pair' and 'enamelled'
48 An essence pot ditto lined with silver		3 10	7	Ld Cary	*	Buyer Lord Kerry
49 A pair ditto candle vases with laurel festoons	Gilt	3 3	3 7	Nixon		
50 A vase radix amethysti and or moulu lined with silver and perferated for essence		3 10				
51 A vase in the antique taste, radix amethysti and or moulu, lined with silver and perferated for essence, supported by four sphinx's on an ornamented ebony basss		12 12	16 5 6	Ld Sands	*	Buyer Lady Sands
52 A pair of candle vases radix amethysti and or moulu	Gilt	3 3	3 8	Ld Fitzwilliam	*	'Radix ameth-ysti' deleted
53 An essence pot ditto lined with silver	Chinea	3 10				
54 A pair of candle vases or moulu		3 3	3 10	Nixon		
55 An altar richly ornamented in or moulu in the antique taste, on which is a vase with branches for three candles		16 16	26 15 6	Ld Sands	*	Buyer Lady Sands, 'Gen-eral Carnack' deleted
56 A vase radix amethysti and or moulu, lined with silver, perferated for essence, supported by three griffins on a round pedestal of the same materials, the whole in the antique taste		10 10	12 12	Williams	*	
57 A pair of candle vases radix amethysti and or moulu	Gilt	3 13 6	4	Captain Thompson		
58 A rich vase lined with silver and branches for two lights, standing on a square pedestal of radix amethysti and or moulu		15 15	17 17	Ditto		
59 A pair of candle vases or moulu		3 3	3 4	General Carnack	*	

THIRD DAY Saturday, April 13th, 1771	CATALOGUE A Anno- tations	Margin Price (i.e. Reserve) £ s d	Price Paid £ s d	Buyer	CATALOGUE B *Price recorded in second column (i.e. actual sales)	Notes on differences from entries in Catalogue A
60 A vase radix amethysti and or moulu, lined with silver and perferated for essence, with ornaments in the antique taste and branches for two candles		15 15	18 17 6	Ld Fitzwilliam	*	
61 A pair of large sideboard alabaster candle-sticks with corinthian capitals and other ornaments in or moulu		10 10	9 19 6		*	Buyer Mr Duntze
62 A pair of candle vases radix amethysti and or moulu		3 13 6	4 6	Barton	*	Buyer Mr Barkley
63 An essence pot ditto lined with silver	Chinea	3 10	[1]			
64 A pair ditto candle vases with laurel festoons	Gilt	3 3	3 6	Price		
65 A vase radix amethysti and or moulu with branches for two candles		10 10	11 11	General Carnack	*	Price £12 1s 6d
66 A large marble vase of antique form and or moulu ornaments in the same taste	2	30	31 10	Fox	*	Annotated 'a pair'
67 A pair of candle vases enamelled and or moulu		3 13 6	3 7	Captain Thompson		
68 A vase radix amethysti and or moulu lined with silver and perferated for essence		6	6 6	Ld Fitzwilliam	*	
69 A pair of candle vases radix amethysti and or moulu		3 13 6	4 1	Ld Exeter	*	Buyer Lady Exeter
70 An essence pot ditto lined with silver		3 10	4	General Carnack	*	
71 A pair ditto candle vases with laurel festoons		3 3	3 5	Price		
72 A vase in the antique taste radix amethysti and or moulu, lined with silver, and perferated for essence, supported by four sphinx's on an ornamented ebony bass		12 12	15 15	General Carnack	*	
73 A pair of candle vases radix amethysti and or moulu		3 13 6	4 6	Sir B	*	Buyer Sir B. Morton
74 An essence pot ditto lined with silver	Chinea	3 10	3 16	Captain Thompson		
75 A pair of candle vases radix amethysti and or moulu on a square pedestal of a curious composition		3 13 6	5		*	Buyer Mr Duntze

1. The number sequence of the marginal notes is confused in the original from lot 63 to lot 72, but adjusted here.

THIRD DAY Saturday, April 13th, 1771	CATALOGUE A Anno-tations	Margin Price (i.e. Reserve) £ s d	Price Paid £ s d	Buyer	CATALOGUE B *Price recorded in second column (i.e. actual sales)	Notes on differences from entries in Catalogue A
76 A vase radix amethysti and or moulu lined with silver and perferated for essence supported by three griffins on a round pedestal of the same materials, the whole in the antique taste		10 10	12 12	Barton		
77 A pair of candle vases radix amethysti and or moulu		3 3	4 8	Stuart	*	
78 A vase enameled and or moulu ornamented in the antique taste		6	6	Ld Sands	*	Buyer Lady Sands
79 A pair of candle vases radix amethysti and or moulu square pedestal of a curious composition		3 13 6	5 5	Stuart	*	
80 A large vase in or moulu in the antique taste, with medalians and other ornaments	Not come				[1]	
81 A horizontal time piece representing Venus at the tomb of Adonis, in marble and or moulu, on the pedestal is a medalian on his death, and on the urn the following inscription Αἲ Αἲ, Ταν̀ Κυθὲρειαν Απώλετο Χαλοϛ ’Α`δωνις		25	26 5	Price		
82 A large vase radix amethysti and or moulu lined with silver and perferated for insence with branches for 4 candles supported by caryatides standing on an ebony ornamented plynth		26 5	31 10		*	Buyer General Carnack
83 A tripod for insence in or moulu lined with silver and branches for three candles after a design of Mr Stuart		45	58 16	[2]	*	Buyer Mr Brittingham
84 A magnificent Persian candelabra for 7 lights, in which is inserted a vase of the largest and most beautiful piece of radix amethysti the mines hath ever produced, which with the double branches etc. is supported by three Persians, finely modelled, standing on triangular plynth of statuary marble ornamented with military trophies proper for the subject.		200	199 10[3]	G. Barton		

1. There is an annotation after lot 80: ‘Fox candlestick—[?]’, which is clarified in Catalogue B: ‘A pair—[?]—[?] 3 branches Mr Fox £13-13s’. See also lot 66.
2. ‘General Carnack’ deleted.
3. The price appears as ‘190’ (i.e. guineas) with the name of the buyer and not in column.

The 1778 sale

The title page of the catalogue is more restrained than the version of 1771:

A
Catalogue
Of the produce of
Messrs Boulton and Fothergill's
Manufactory,
At Soho in Staffordshire,
Comprehending
A variety of superb vases, clocks, candelabrums,
girandoles, figures exquisitely modelled and
elegantly designed, with many other tasteful
ornaments, etc. etc.
Which will be sold by auction,
By Messrs Christie and Ansell,
At their Great Room
Next Cumberland House, Pallmall
On Saturday, May 16, 1778.
To be viewed on Thursday the 14th, and to the sale,
which will begin at twelve o'clock.
Catalogues may be had as above.

There is no preface.

The first copy of the catalogue ('Catalogue A') was presumably the auctioneer's copy, the reserve prices being inscribed in the margin. The second copy ('Catalogue B') was presumably an accounting copy. The bid prices are recorded in it twice, as in 1771, but the lots which failed to reach the reserves are more obvious because 'Nixon' is used more often as a pseudonym and, more especially, because the price of each lot is crossed through in the duplicate column if it was not sold.

There is no summary of account in the duplicate catalogue, but the lots which were sold totalled £209 3s. 0d. and the total bids added up to £933 17s. 0d.

The sale was advertised for Saturday 16th May, but was postponed and took place on Wednesday 20th May. Both catalogues are dated Saturday May 16th, 1778, on the title page, but in Catalogue B the date is crossed out and 'Wednesday May 20th' is written in ink. On the first page of each catalogue the date is given as Saturday May 18th, which is clearly a misprint.

SATURDAY, MAY 16th, 1778.	CATALOGUE A				CATALOGUE B	
	Anno-tations	Margin Price (i.e. Reserve) £ s d	Price Paid £ s d	Buyer	*Price recorded in second column (i.e. actual sales)	Notes on differences from entries in Catalogue A
1 Three small candle vases in or moulu		3 3	3 3	Simon [?]		Buyer Sim
2 One pair ditto in marble and or moulu		4	4	Price		
3 One pair small vases in or moulu, with a bas relief of boys dancing		3 13 6	3 13 6	Nixon		
4 A radix amethisti sugar bason mounted in or moulu and lined with silver		1 11 6	1 11 6	Farmer	*	
5 One pair statuary marble vases on pedestals, mounted in or moulu and perforated for essences		7	6 16 6	Price		
6 One pair statuary marble vases on pedestals mounted in or moulu and perforated for essences		7	7		*	Buyer Tenant
7 One pair radix amethisti vases on pedestals, mounted in or moulu, and perforated for essences		7	7	Ld Ashburnham	*	
8 One pair small candle vases, or moulu and marble		4	4	Lady M. Coke	*	
9 A radix amethisti sugar bason mounted in or moulu and lined with silver		1 11 6	1 11 6	Farmer	*	
10 A sugar bason, radix amethisti mounted in or moulu and lined with silver		1 10	1 10	Nixon		Buyer Price
11 One pair vases, statuary marble and or moulu, with branches for two lights each	Sold by private contract	10 10			*	Buyer Lady Downes price £10 10s
12 One pair statuary marble vases on pedestals, mounted in or moulu, and perforated for essences		9 9				Price £8 15s
13 One pair small candle vases, or moulu and marble		3 12	4	Lady Morton	*	
14 Ditto		4 10	4 9	Nixon		
15 Ditto		4 10	4 8	Ditto		
16 Ditto, radix amethysti and or moulu		4 10	4 9	Ditto		
17 Ditto		4 10	4 10	Ditto		
18 One pair vase candlesticks in or moulu		2 2	2 2	Ditto		

SATURDAY, MAY 16th, 1778.	CATALOGUE A Anno-tations	Margin Price (i.e. Reserve) £ s d	Price Paid £ s d	Buyer	CATALOGUE B *Price recorded in second column (i.e. actual sales)	Notes on differences from entries in Catalogue A
19 One pair of or moulu candlesticks		4 4	4	Ditto		
20 A vase in radix amethysti and or moulu for a candle		2 2	2	Ditto		
21 One pair small candle vases, marble and or moulu		3 3	3	Ditto		
22 Ditto		4	3 17 6	Ditto		
23 Ditto		4	3 17 6	Ditto		
24 One pair statuary marble vases on pedestals, with or moulu for essences		7				Annotated 'part'
25 One or moulu tripod with marble plinth, perforated for essence		8 8				
26 Ditto		7 7				
27 One pair vases, statuary marble and or moulu, on pedestals with branches for two lights		16 16	16 5 6	Nixon		
28 One pair small candle vases, or moulu and marble		4				
29 Ditto		4	4	Nixon		
30 One pair vases, statuary marble and or moulu, with branches for two lights		15	14	Ditto		Price £14 14s
31 Ditto		9 10	11 6	Lady Mary Coke	*	
32 One pair small candle vases, marble and or moulu		4 4	4	Nixon		
33 Ditto		4 14 6	4 14 6	Ditto		
34 One pair vases, statuary marble and or moulu perforated for essences		7	7	Ditto		
35 One ditto on a pedestal		4 14 6	4 14 6	Ditto		
36 One pair vases, statuary marble and or moulu pedestals, with sockets for candles occasionally		5 5	5 5	Money	*	Buyer Lady Macclesfield
37 Ditto		5 5	5 5	Nixon		

SATURDAY, MAY 16th, 1778.	CATALOGUE A Annotations	Margin Price (i.e. Reserve) £ s d	Price Paid £ s d	Buyer	CATALOGUE B *Price recorded in second column (i.e. actual sales)	Notes on differences from entries in Catalogue A
38 One pair or moulu two branched girandoles		12	11 11	Ditto		
39 A beautiful vase in radix amethysti		3 3	3	Ditto		
40 A pair of vases on square pedestals, of statuary marble and or moulu with branches for two lights each		16 16	16 5 6	Ditto		
41 One pair statuary marble vases on square pedestals, mounted in or moulu for candles occasionally		11	11 6	Mewer [?]	*	Buyer Mear [?]
42 Ditto with round pedestals		7	7	Nixon		
43 Ditto		7	7	Ditto		
44 A pint ice pail in or moulu richly gilt, chased and lined with silver		10 10	9 19 6	Ditto		
45 Ditto for a quart-bottle		13 13	13 2 6	Ditto		
46 A pair of tripods in or moulu, perforated for essence, with branches for three lights each		27	26 15 6	Ditto		Price £26 15s
47 A pair of cassolettes in or moulu, with branches for three lights each		15 15	15 4 6	Ditto		
48 A beautiful vase in radix amethist and or moulu, with double branches		14	14 3 6	Ditto		
49 A pair of tripods in or moulu, with branches for three lights each		25 10				Price £25 4s
50 A vase in radix amethisti and or moulu with branches for two lights		5	5 5	Mrs Wedderburn	*	
51 Ditto larger, for three lights		6	6	Nixon		
52 A pair of large or moulu vases in statuary marble with branches for two lights each		28	27 16 6	Ditto		
53 A pair of or moulu vases, radix amethisti, perforated for essence		9 9	8 18 6	Ditto		
54 Venus and Cupid in or moulu, at the tomb of Adonis, of marble richly decorated		13	12 12	Ditto		
55 Narcissus in bronze, admiring himself in a fountain, the vase and plinth of statuary marble decorated with or moulu		11	10 10	Ditto		

SATURDAY, MAY 16th, 1778.	CATALOGUE A Annotations	Margin Price (i.e. Reserve) £ s d	Price Paid £ s d	Buyer	CATALOGUE B *Price recorded in second column (i.e. actual sales)	Notes on differences from entries in Catalogue A
56 A group of boys and ornaments in bronze and or moulu, supporting a watch, on the plinth are represented (by emblems) the four seasons		18	17 17	Ditto		
57 One pair statuary marble vases ornamented with or moulu, and branches for two lights each		9 9	9 14	Mrs Wedderbourne	*	
58 An essence vase, radix amethisti in or moulu, with handles terminating in dolphins		11 11	11 6	Nixon		
59 One large radix amethisti vase mounted in or moulu, perforated for essence		10 10	10 10	Bond	*	
60 One pair essence vases, in marble mounted in or moulu, supported by a tripod		16 16	16 5 6	Ditto	*	
61 A beautiful radix amethisti vase in or moulu, perforated for essence		5 15 6	5 15 6	Ditto	*	
62 An essence vase, statuary marble and or moulu, with handles terminating in dolphins		4 11	4 10	Nixon		
63 A vase in radix amethisti mounted in or moulu		3 12	3 10	Ditto		
64 A small radix amethisti vase, with branches for two lights		6 6	6	Ditto		
65 An essence vase in radix amethisti and or moulu on a tripod		8 8	8	Nixon		
66 One pair or moulu candlesticks with triangular bases		2 12 6	2 12 6	Ditto		
67 A pair of ditto		2 12 6	2 12 6	Ditto		
68 One pair or moulu candlesticks		2 12 6	2 12 6	Ditto		
69 One pair enamelled vases mounted in or moulu		7 17 6	7 17 6	Ditto		
70 Three or moulu candlesticks with triangular bases		3 3	3 3	Mr Fitzgerald	*	
71 One pair of radix amethisti vases mounted in or moulu		7 17 6	7 17 6	Nixon		
72 Venus and Cupid in or moulu, at the tomb of Adonis, statuary marble ornamented		13 10	13 2 6	Ditto		

SATURDAY, MAY 16th, 1778.	CATALOGUE A Anno-tations	Margin Price (i.e. Reserve) £ s d	Price Paid £ s d	Buyer	CATALOGUE B *Price recorded in second column (i.e. actual sales)	Notes on differences from entries in Catalogue A
73 A group of boys and ornaments in bronze and or moulu, supporting a watch; on the pedestals are represented by emblems, the four seasons		18	17 17	Ditto		
74 An elegant eight day clock with chimes and quarters, the case of which is executed in or moulu and tortoiseshell, from a design of Sir William Chambers		35	30 9	Ditto		
75 Venus and Cupid at the tomb of Adonis in bronze, the pedestal and vase of statuary marble, and or moulu, perforated for essence		12 12	12 1 6	Ditto		
76 Ditto, with the figures in or moulu		13 10	12 12	Ditto		
77 Ditto, with branches for two lights		13 10	13 13	Sir Patrick Crauford	*	
78 Narcissus admiring himself in a fountain, in bronze and statuary marble, perforated for essences		11	10 10	Nixon		
79 A pair of twelve-inch figures of Apollo and Diana in bronze, supporting branches in or moulu for three lights each		26 15 6	27 6	Storer	*	
80 An elegant vase in statuary marble and or moulu after the antique, on which is a bas relief representing Mercury delivering the infant Bacchus to the care of Ino. This piece turns round upon a swivel for the conveniency of viewing the bas relief, and is perforated and lined for essences		14 6	14 3 6	Nixon		
81 A large vase in imitation of the verd antique, ornamented with or moulu		9 19 6	10 10	Storer	*	
82 One pair large vases, marble and or moulu with branches		28	27 6	Nixon		
83 One pair small vases, radix amethysti and or moulu		4 4	4	Ditto	*	Buyer Ld Ashburnham, price £4 4s
84 Ditto		4 4	4 4	Stater [?]	*	
85 Ditto		4 4	4 4	Ld Stamford	*	

SATURDAY, MAY 16th, 1778.	CATALOGUE A Anno-tations	Margin Price (i.e. Reserve) £ s d	Price Paid £ s d	Buyer	CATALOGUE B *Price recorded in second column (i.e. actual sales)	Notes on differences from entries in Catalogue A
86 A pair of statuary marble ditto with or moulu ornaments		4 4	4 4	Ld Ash-burnham[1]		Buyer Nixon
87 One large vase, radix amethysti, and or moulu with two branches		10 14	10 10	Ditto [*sc.* Nixon]		
88 A pedestal in statuary marble and or moulu designed for a clock		3 3	3 3	Ditto		
89 A ditto its companion		3 3	3 3	Ditto		
90 A pair or moulu girandoles		10	10 10	Storer	*	
91 An elegant obelisk in radix amethysti	Deleted					
92 An elegant japan vase on a mahogany pedestal, mounted in or moulu to contain knives, forks and spoons		20	19 19	Nixon		
93 One pair small bronzed vases		2 2	2	Ditto		
94 A small or moulu essence vase		1 5	1 4	Ditto		
95 An elegant figure of Urania in bronze, holding a time piece against an obelisk of statuary marble, in the pedestal of which is an enamelled tablet shewing the equation of time		18	17 17	Ditto		
96 The emperor Titus in bronze, lamenting the loss of a day, the pedestal is statuary marble, ornamented with or moulu for a time piece, the motto 'diem perdidi'		21	19 19	Ditto		
97–115[2]						
116 An offering to Diana in bronze, the plinth and pedestal of statuary marble and or moulu		18	17 17	Nixon		
117 The Emperor Titus in bronze, lamenting the loss of a day: the pedestal of statuary marble, ornamented with or moulu, in which is a clock with the motto 'diem perdidi'						
118 Cleopatra at the tomb of Marc Anthony, in statuary marble, with a clock in the pedestal		25	24 3	Ditto		
119 Ditto, the figure in bronze		20	19 19	Ditto		

1. 'Nixon' deleted.

2. Lots 97 to 115 were various 'elegant articles in Fillagree', i.e. silver: none were sold except lot 111, Nixon being recorded as the buyer in every other case.

SATURDAY, MAY 16th, 1778.	CATALOGUE A Annotations	Margin Price (i.e. Reserve) £ s d	Price Paid £ s d	Buyer	CATALOGUE B *Price recorded in second column (i.e. actual sales)	Notes on differences from entries in Catalogue A
120 Penelope petitioning Minerva for the safe return of Telemachus, the figures are in bronze, and the pedestal, etc. of statuary marble and or moulu		12 12	12 12	Ditto		
121 An offering to Diana in bronze, statuary marble and or moulu, with a clock in the pedestal		18	17 17	Ditto		
122 An elegant figure of Urania in bronze, holding a timepiece against an obelisk of statuary marble, in the pedestal of which is an enamelled tablet shewing the equation of time		18	18 18	Fitzgerald	*	
123 An elegant vase in statuary marble and or moulu after the antique, on which is a bas relievo representing Mercury delivering the infant Bacchus to the care of Ino. This piece turns on a swivel, and is perforated for essence		14 6	14 3 6	Nixon		
124 A pair of twelve inch figures, Apollo and Diana, in bronze, supporting branches in or moulu for three lights each		26 15 6				
125 An emblematical clock case representing Minerva as uncovering a votive vase, with one hand, on which is a bas relief of Prudence making a libation to time, with the other hand she points to the dial, whilst the genii on the other side seems contemplating the following remarkable passage from Virgil, Lib. X.— Breve et irreparabile tempus omnibus est vitae: Sed famam extendere factis hoc virtutis opus.		36	36 15	Nixon		
126 A superb candelabra with six branches, radix amethisti, supported by three Persian figures finely modelled in bronze after M. Angelo, the plinth suitably ornamented and richly gilt in or moulu		55	54 12[1]	Ditto		
127 An elegant library bookcase comprized of mahogany neatly painted, the ornaments beautiful and accurate, of a new invented and durable composition		40				

1. The price appears as '52 guineas' with the name of the buyer and not in column.

APPENDIX IV **INVENTORY 1782**

Only one bound Inventory of Stock at the Soho manufactory – tools, equipment, finished goods and work-in-progress – has survived. This was taken by John Scale on 22nd June 1782. Following John Fothergill's death on 19th June, Boulton dissolved the partnership of Boulton and Fothergill and started a new business under the name of Matthew Boulton & Co. with a new set of books. The Inventory was taken to facilitate this transition.

I have selected the extracts reproduced in this Appendix for the light they shed on the ormolu business. I have concentrated on the finished and partly finished ormolu ornaments in the warehouses, the toy room and Richard Bentley's workshop. They are listed as they appear in the Inventory, with the values attributed to them.

Warehouse (*pp.* 83–4)	£	s	d
1 pair—[?] lion-faced vases, all metal, made and chased		10	6
1 cover for Lord Shelburne's vase		1	4
3 pairs Morrison's vases, not perfect		10	6
4 pairs small two handled vases		12	0
4 stone sugar dishes		3	0
Part of a Cleopatra vase (old metal)		1	2
1 ditto gilt (old metal)		10	6
1 pair goat's head vases, not gilt		3	6
5 pairs ditto with green and blue bodies, gilt, at 15/–	4	2	6
2 pairs ditto all metal, at 15/–	1	10	0
1 sphinx vase upon marble, broken		10	0
3 King's clock cases imperfect, 90 lb 2 oz waste, at 8d	3	0	6
1 metal model for a French clock weight 10½ lb		6	10
1 clock-case gilt		6	2
1 pair 3 branched girandoles, ready to gild, 13 lb		8	8
24 odd French candlesticks and branches	5	0	0
Mounts for a japanned clock		2	6
2 brass lens candlesticks		5	0
1 pair gilt capitals for Stewart's candlesticks (Mr Boulton's own)			
2 pairs purple stone bodies, 7 inches high	1	4	0
1 stone body for ewer vase, very good		8	0
3 stone ditto for wing figure vase	1	4	0
1 ditto for ditto, waste			
3 stones for sphynx vase	1	4	0
2 ditto for ditto, waste			
62 necks and covers, different sizes		5	0
1 pair very large stones for Persian vase	2	2	0
1 pair ditto for ditto, waste			
1 pair large tabby coloured stones, 7 inches high		15	0
1 streaked stone, 7½ inches high		10	0
2 pairs stones for Digby's vase		16	0
2½ pairs ditto for Burgoyne's ditto	1	10	0
1 pair ditto for Smith's pattern		12	0
2 pairs round pedestal bodies	1	4	0
1 pair purple bodies, 6½ inches high		16	0
1 pair hollow pedestal bodies		14	0
2 pairs stones for candelabra		6	0
1 pair purple stones, 6 inches high		12	0
4 pairs Cleopatra bodies		16	0
7 pairs ditto, worse stone		8	0
5 small odd vase bodies		5	0
56 ditto ditto, very bad		5	0
1 light-coloured vase body, 7 inches high		4	0
3 stones, 6½ inches high and 6½ inches diameter		6	0
1 pair tabby stones for wing figure vase		12	0
10 bodies, 6 inches high, very bad		5	0
10 bodies 3½ by 3½ inches, very bad		5	0
3 round stone plinths for griffin vase		1	0
17 metal vase bodies		8	6
5 oval backs for picture frames at 4d		1	8
23 insides for 373 tea urns			
18 square tea urn bottoms			
3 ditto ditto			
3 ditto fronted with tortoiseshell		2	0

Warehouse (extracts) (*pp.* 88, 90)	£	s	d
9 lb glass & enamel vase bodies		1	6
1 bason for a tripod			

Warehouse no. 25 (extracts) (*pp.* 93–4)	£	s	d
2 large statuary marble vase bodies		10	0

	£	s	d
$32\frac{3}{4}$ lb cast work, parts for girandoles, at 8d	1	1	10
2 Triton figures $24\frac{1}{2}$ lb, at 8d		16	4
$13\frac{1}{2}$ pairs bronzed tea urn handles, at 4/–	2	14	0
20 lb copper stamped work, all in use, at 1/–	1	0	0
Stamping on ditto		3	6
1 figure of Urania, $12\frac{1}{2}$ lb, at 8d		8	4
$6\frac{1}{2}$ pairs Doric capitals, all good, at $\frac{1}{2}$		7	7
1 pedestal clock	3	13	6
1 small watch	2	12	6
2 vase clocks	1	1	0
Dial plates and fingers for 2 Minerva movements		10	0
2 clock glasses		1	6
Pattern shop, Apollo and Diana figures included	35	0	0

Casting shop (*p.* 102)	£	s	d
58 lb cast figures, at 2/–	5	16	0

Richard Bentley's shop (*pp.* 133–4)	£	s	d
1 pair cassolets with branches 8 lb		13	4
Work on ditto	1	10	0
1 pair triangle cassolets, marble pedestals	4	4	0
1 pair ditto ditto, metal ditto	4	4	0
1 small figure of Minerva			9
Chasing on ditto			
6 figures intended for a pair blue john vases Work on ditto } weight 18 lb, at 8d		12	0
5 escutcheons and nobs		15	0
1 pair vases 259 blue john bodies ready to gild	2	3	0
1 pair ditto 212 marble ditto ditto	2	14	0
6 pairs ditto 55 ditto ditto ditto, 31/6	9	9	0
1 Titus vase with ditto ditto	8	8	0
1 Bacchus vase ready to gild	8	5	0
1 pair vases in part with branches	1	10	0
6 odd parts of vases		10	0
1 pair girandoles, 2 lights, ready to gild	1	10	0
Cast work all good, $190\frac{1}{2}$	9	10	6
Pincebeck strips, $17\frac{1}{4}$ lb, at 1/1		18	8
Waste metal, $98\frac{1}{2}$ lb	4	2	1
1 Belisarius plinth 10 by $6\frac{1}{2}$ inches		13	0
1 pair bodies for hollow pedestal vases		8	0
1 pair squares for square pedestal		3	0
1 pedestal for Narcissus vase		4	0
1 plinth for ditto ditto 8 by 5 inches		9	0
1 astronomy figure		8	0
Chasing on ditto	1	8	0
Ditto on a bottom ornament for an astronomy vase		8	0
Ditto on a wing figure clock, $14\frac{1}{4}$ days	2	10	0
Ditto on 2 pedestal squares		1	3
Ditto on a wing figure vase, $5\frac{1}{4}$ days		18	6
1 Narcissus figure		7	6
Chasing on ditto, $4\frac{1}{2}$ days		15	9
1 Clock for a wing figure	4	4	0
Marble for a wing figure vase		15	0
Chasing on a picture frame		3	0
3 pairs vases with blue john bodies, parts of the mounts made by Chamberlain	3	15	0
1 Diana and Apollo with branches, gilt	19	8	0
1 circophicus finished, made by W.R. Hancock	2	16	0
1 Minerva with clock (and marble) ready to gild	9	9	0

Toy room (*pp.* 145–62)

The Inventory of Plated Wares (toy room) is extensive. It mostly consists of silver, plate, filigree, and some toys including smelling cases, toothpick cases, pearl enamelled and gilt smelling bottles, runners for hair, shagreen and japanned toothpick cases, plated and steel buckles, chains, watch keys, etc. The following are listed on pp. 156 and 159:

(*p.* 156)	£	s	d
1 or moulu Venus essence vase, white marble	15	15	0
1 Griffin or moulu essence vase, ditto ditto	7	17	6
An Astronomy figure in or moulu with white marble obelisk and a watch	25	0	0
A white marble obelisk with or moulu ornaments and bronzed figure of Belisarius with clock in the pedestal	26	5	0
1 or moulu cloak pin		4	6
1 pair vases, white marble no.295	11	11	0
1 pair Saddle vases, marble bodies	4	14	6
1 or moulu obelisk of Narcissus with clock	20	0	0
1 ditto ditto of Venus and Cupid, with ditto	22	1	0
1 pair or moulu vases, marble bodies, hollow pedestal	9	9	0
1 pair small or moulu marble vases for candles no.1013	4	4	0
	147	1	6
Disct 10 p cent	14	14	$1\frac{1}{2}$
	132	7	$4\frac{1}{2}$

(*p.* 159)	£	s	d
2 Tasseys seals 3/–		6	0
8 ditto ditto 2/–		16	0
121 Wedgwood's seals 2/–	12	2	0

Warehouse no. 17 (*pp.* 157–95)

The stock in Warehouse no. 17 was also extensive. On pp.

168, 172 and 180–1 there are the following:

(*p.* 168)	£	s	d
1 doz. small or moulu picture frames 5/–	3	0	0
discounted 10 p cent		6	0
	2	14	0
[annotated in left hand margin 'Ld Lucan']			

(*p.* 172)	£	s	d
104 black Wedgwood's impressions for seals, various sizes, were 4/– doz. But being mostly small ones say 2/6 p doz.	1	1	8
64 frames, sorted sizes; mostly damaged – quite out of date and suppose will scarcely bring any thing, were 6/– p doz. But say 1s p doz.		5	0
41 glass Tassie's seal impressions, sorted sizes 4/– doz.		13	0
33 metal cameos, cast, sorted sizes 1d		2	9
1 lb 8 oz old metal mounts to set cameos etc. in			9

(*pp.* 180–1)	£	s	d	£	s	d
Or moulu, vizt: A Bacchanalian vase, broken marble	16	16	0	11	11	0
1 pair two handled vases, white opake bodies, the stones cracked	11	11	0	7	7	0
A knife and spoon case	31	10	0	21	0	0
A dancing boy vase, small	2	2	0	1	5	0
1 two handled vase, stone body No. 76	4	4	0	3	3	0
1 two ditto ditto ditto No. 75	5	5	0	4	4	0
1 clock case with clock, King's pattern	40	0	0	31	10	0
1 lyre essence vase, white marble, in parts broken	6	6	0	4	14	6
1 wing-figured vase, stone body with 2 branches, in parts imperfect	11	11	0	8	8	0
1 two handled vase, stone body, No. 75	5	5	0	4	4	0
1 pair griffin vases, stone bodies	15	15	0	14	14	0
1 gilt tea urn	15	0	0	12	12	0
1 small essence vase, imperfect	1	11	6		10	6
1 two handled vase, opake body	6	6	0	5	5	0
1 pair old heavy candlesticks No. 63	4	4	0	3	3	0
1 old round step foot candlestick vase No. 86	3	13	6	1	5	0
1 sugar bason, stone body 49	2	0	0	1	10	0
1 small candlestick vase each 67 68 67, pair 52/6	6	11	3	2	5	0
1 entire radix vase	3	13	6	1	15	0
1 stone lackered ewer	6	16	6	3	13	6
1 ice pail for quart bottle	15	15	0	10	10	0
1 ditto for pint ditto	12	12	0	8	8	0
1 door handle and escutcheon	2	2	0	1	8	0
1 ditto ditto ditto	1	15	0	1	3	4
1 pair 2 light or moulu girandoles	12	12	0	8	8	0
1 pair ditto ditto ditto French gilt	6	6	0	4	4	0
1 tripod candlestick, ebony foot	2	2	0	2	0	0
1 saddle vase	2	2	0	2	0	0
1 candlestick each 71 and 72, 126/– pair	6	6	0	4	4	0
1 oval or moulu picture frame, each $6\frac{1}{4}$ inches by $7\frac{1}{2}$ 15/–, 5 inches by $6\frac{1}{2}$ 12/–, 13 inches by 11 34/–	2	19	0	2	19	0
A pair of metal bronzed dancing boy vases	2	12	6	1	1	0
2 or moulu Penelope frames $11\frac{1}{2}$ by $9\frac{1}{2}$ inches	2	10	0	2	10	0

N.B. The prices in the first columns of these two pages are those at which they have been for many years, and as these pieces in general are very old and mostly damaged 'tis thought necessary to reduce them to the prices stated in the last columns.

APPENDIX V **NUMBERED ORNAMENTS**

Number	Date	
11	1780	Essence vase, blue john (pair, Duncan McAllister, £12 12s. 0d.)
55	1780	Candle vase, white marble (pair, Duncan McAllister, £4 14s. 6d.)
	1782	Vase, marble (6 pairs, Richard Bentley's workshop, ungilt, £9 9s. 0d.)
59	1780	Vase, white marble pedestal (pair, Earl of Chesterfield, £14 14s. 0d.)
67	1782	Vase, small, candlestick (2 or 3, warehouse, with 68, £6 11s. 3d.)
68	1782	Vase, small, candlestick (warehouse)
71	1775	Vases (pair, Earl of Craven)
74		Girandole, triton (Pattern Book 1) (Plate 210.2)
75	1782	Vase, stone, two-handled (warehouse, £5 5s. 0d.)
76	1782	Vase, stone, two-handled (warehouse, £4 4s. 0d.)
86	1782	Vase, candlestick, old round step foot (warehouse, £3 13s. 6d.)
108	1780	Venus essence vase, white marble (Earl of Chesterfield, £15 15s. 0d.)
125		Candle branches (Pattern Book 1) (Plate 312.1)
212	1782	Vase, marble (pair, Richard Bentley's workshop, ungilt, £2 14s. 0d.)
238		Wing-figured candle vase (Pattern Book 1) (Plate 370)
295	1782	Vase, marble (pair, toy room, £11 11s. 0d.)
308		Clock case, wing-figured (Pattern Book 1) (Plate 143)
349	1780	Vase, small, white marble pedestal (Earl of Chesterfield, £4 14s. 6d.)
		Vase, white marble, round pedestal (Pattern Book 1) (Plate 257)
399		King's vase (Pattern Book 1) (Plate 341)
419		Candle branch (Pattern Book 1) (Plate 210.1)
516		Vase, marble (Pattern Book 5) (Plate 311)
520		Clock case, marble, round pedestal (Pattern Book 1) (Plate 149)
755		Triton candlestick (Pattern Book 1) (Plate 139)
767		Minerva clock case (Pattern Book 1) (Plate 165)
834	1780	Essence vase, white marble (Sir Joshua Reynolds, in error, 280/– each)
859	1782	Vase, blue john (Richard Bentley's workshop, ungilt, £2 3s. 0d.)
		Vase, candle (Pattern Book 1) (Plate 275)
860		Vase, white marble (Pattern Book 1) (Plate 297)
863		Vase, candle (Pattern Book 1) (Plate 290)
1013		Vase, white marble (Pattern Book 1) (Plate 309.2)
1080		Frame (Pattern Book 1) (Plate 226)
1108		Frame (Pattern Book 1) (Plate 226)
1109		Frame (Pattern Book 1) (Plate 226)
1110		Frame (Pattern Book 1) (Plate 226)
1111		Frame (Pattern Book 1) (Plate 226)
1112		Frame (Pattern Book 1) (Plate 226)
1237		Vase, medallion (Pattern Book 1) (Plate 307)
1241		Vase, satyr mask handle (Pattern Book 1) (Plate 294)
1514		Candlestick, column (Pattern Book 1) (Plate 127)
1625		Plate warmer, triangular (Pattern Book 1) (Plate 126)
1663		Frame (Pattern Book 1) (Plate 226)
1664		ditto (Plate 226)
1665		ditto (Plate 227.3)
1668		ditto (Plate 227.2)
1691		ditto (Plate 226)
1695		ditto (Plate 227.1)

APPENDIX VI **INDENTURE OF EDWARD PARDOE**

The indenture reproduced here (P.1 Box, C.L.B.) is a typical example of the contracts which were signed between Boulton and Fothergill and their employees in the toy business. The terms of employment, however, varied. Pardoe was to be paid by the week, provided he worked the stipulated hours, at rates of eleven shillings during the first year, twelve shillings during the second and fourteen shillings during the third. Joseph Burton, another chaser, who was also engaged in 1768, was to be paid piece rates for those jobs for which there was an agreed price but otherwise fourteen shillings a week in the first year, fifteen in the second and sixteen in the third. His indenture (B.6 Box, C.L.B.), was in all other respects the same as Pardoe's.

The Indenture

Articles of agreement indented made concluded and agreed upon this thirty first day of August in the eighth year of the reign of our Sovereign Lord George the third of Great Britain and so forth and in the year of our Lord one thousand seven hundred and sixty eight between Edward Pardoe of Birmingham in the County of Warwick chaser of the one part and Matthew Boulton and John Fothergill of Handsworth in the County of Stafford toymakers of the other part – First the said Edward Pardoe in consideration of the covenants herein after mentioned and on the part and behalf of the said Matthew Boulton and John Fothergill to be performed in pursuance thereof doth for himselfe covenant promise and agree to and with the said Matthew Boulton and John Fothergill their and each of their heirs executors administrators and assigns in manner and form following, (viz) that he the said Edward Pardoe from time to time during the space of three years from the day of the date hereof at and in such meet or reasonable shop or other place or places as they the said Matthew Boulton and John Fothergill shall provide and appoint or cause to be provided and appointed to or for that purpose shall and will work and labor for and with them the said Matthew Boulton and John Fothergill according to the best of his ability skill and judgement in the art trade or mystery of chaseing, or any other branch of their trade or manufactory of toymaking which they the said Matthew Boulton and John Fothergill shall from time to time during the aforesaid term of three years think fitt to employ him.
That he the said Edward Pardoe during all the said term neither shall nor will directly or indirectly work for or with any person or persons whatsoever without the licence or consent of them the said Matthew Boulton and John Fothergill first thereunto had and obtained in writing under each of their hands and seales that he the said Edward Pardoe during the said term of three years in and concerning all such his labor shall and will be true and faithfull and shall and will endeavour in all things as much as he lawfully may or can for the benefitt and profitt of them the said Matthew Boulton and John Fothergill, and that he shall not at any time or times during the said term either in an unreasonable manner or at unusual times neglect or absent himselfe from any such work or labor nor lend embezel or willfully spoile or otherways dispose of any tools utensils implements goods or chattels of them the said Matthew Boulton and John Fothergill their executors or assigns without their and each of their licence and consent, and also that he the said Edward Pardoe neither shall nor will directly or

indirectly to any person or persons whatsoever divulge discover or disclose any secret art or mystry whatsoever relating to the trades manufactories or business of them the said Matthew Boulton and John Fothergill at any time or times during the said term. And the said Matthew Boulton and John Fothergill for themselves their heirs executors and administrators jointly and separately doth hereby covenant promise and agree to and with the said Edward Pardoe in manner and form following, (viz) that they the said Matthew Boulton and John Fothergill for and during the aforesaid term of three years (provided the said Edward Pardoe shall so long live and be able to work as aforesaid) shall and will find and procure work or employment for the said Edward Pardoe in the art trade or manufactory aforesaid and likewise find and provide for him the materials and tools of all sorts that are necessary in the several kinds of work which they the said Matthew Boulton and John Fothergill shall think fitt to employ him, and also that they the said Matthew Boulton and John Fothergill shall and will pay or cause to be paid unto the said Edward Pardoe from time to time during the said term of three years, (viz) for the first year eleven shillings per week for the second year twelve shillings per week for the third and last year fourteen shillings provide he works the customary hours each day which are from six o'clock in the morning untill seven in the evening in the summer and from seven in the morning untill eight in the evening in the winter season allowing half an hour for breakfast and an hour for dinner and in case he neglects to work such accustomary hours as aforesaid then a proportionable part of his wages shall be deducted for such laps of time according to the before mentioned rates, and for the true and full preformance of all and every the said covenants and agreements herein before mentioned either of the said parties bind themselves to the other firmly by these presents. In witness whereof the said parties to these presents interchaingable have sett their hands and seals the day and year first above written.

Signed sealed and delivered
being first duly stamped
in the presence of us } Edward Pardoe

John Taylor
James Hammond

Matthew Boulton
John Fothergill

BIBLIOGRAPHY

Manuscript sources

This book is based chiefly on the extensive collection of manuscripts relating to Matthew Boulton and his businesses, described as the Matthew Boulton Papers and now in the Birmingham City Archives in the Central Library, Birmingham.

The following description of these records is based on their arrangement up to December 1998. Since that time, as a result of the work of the Archives of Soho Project, some rearrangement has taken place, and at the end of the project, in March 2003, new references will be introduced for the whole archive. Full cross-references from the old system to the new will be available, and are already available for the numbering sequence at present in use by the library.

A very large proportion of the papers consists of letters. Correspondence received by Matthew Boulton and by Boulton and Fothergill, memoranda, etc., are filed in boxes, many of which are devoted to particular correspondents, for example John Fothergill, John Hodges, James Keir, Mrs Montagu and the Wyatt family. The letters of less prolific correspondents are filed in alphabetical boxes.

Copies of outgoing letters from 1757 onwards are preserved in bound books, which are identified, under the categorisation devised when they were in the Assay Office Library, by letters of the alphabet. Although there is a continuous series of books up to 1798, they are not complete. Some of the books contain copies of letters by Boulton personally, some were written from Soho (1771–82) and others from the warehouse in Birmingham (1772–4, 1776–9). Among the Birmingham books there is a foreign letters book (1780–1) containing letters to foreign correspondents. There are gaps in the records of each office. These books of outgoing letters are also identified by a number sequence but are well cross-referenced with the old categorisation.

Among the other manuscripts are:

(1) Many of Boulton's personal papers, including some early accounts, his diaries for 1766–73, 1775, 1781, 1794–6 and 1798–1800, and a series of his notebooks, which he compiled at various dates from 1751.
(2) Memoranda relating to the businesses, brief summaries of the stock position, the capital of the partners, etc: many of these, including Boulton's comments on his partnership with Fothergill, are filed in the Fothergill box.
(3) Certain unbound cash accounts relating to sales and expenditure at the Soho Manufactory and at the warehouse.
(4) Several bound books of account. These include, for the Soho business, ledgers (1776–92), journals (1776–92), a cash debtor book, i.e. a record of cash received for goods sold, rents, etc. (1772–82), a day book, i.e. a record of goods dispatched to customers (1779–81) and a petty cash book (1763–6); and, for the Birmingham warehouse, cash and petty cash books (1762–5, 1767–75). Unfortunately many of the books of account are missing, and it is generally not possible to trace an order from its first record in a day book through the internal journals and into the ledgers. There are no clients' ledgers.
(5) A bound inventory of stock, which was compiled in 1782 on the dissolution of the

partnership of Boulton and Fothergill, following John Fothergill's death on 19th June. Extracts from this Inventory are reproduced in Appendix IV.
(6) Pattern books, which contain a large assortment of sketches of silverware, silver plate and ormolu ornaments. These appear to have been a record of objects produced at Soho, although it is possible that some of the drawings were of designs that were not executed. There are nine books, starting in the late 1760s and going through to the 1850s. Seven of them depict silver and plate, largely in number sequence, and represent an extraordinary survey of taste over some eighty years. The eighth book contains nineteenth-century tracings, and the ninth contains patterns of sword hilts and jewellery. Most of the drawings are numbered, the numbers often coinciding with numbers used in correspondence and other documents. The books were obviously used by factory hands as books of working reference. Books 1, 5 and 7 contain drawings of ormolu ornaments. Nearly all are in Book 1. Unfortunately the early drawings, including nearly all the ormolu ornaments, are not in number sequence, having almost all been cut and remounted in the nineteenth century. A note pasted in the first book explains that this was probably done by Elkington and Co., and that the eight books of plate etc. were bought by William Ryland, the works manager of Elkington, 'on behalf of the firm at the sale when the Soho Factory was broken up [i.e. in the 1850s]. Mr Ryland refused to buy the dyes saying that they were useless to anyone without these books which were all that he required'. Plate 124 shows a typical rearranged page in the first pattern book with the drawings cut and remounted. There are only three uncut sheets illustrating ormolu ornaments – Volume 1, p. 156 (Plate 122), Volume 5, p. 33 (Plate 123) and Volume 7, a loose sheet illustrating only one vase (Plate 232). These last two are misplaced in the later volumes in which they now reside. The uncut pages, with their ornaments in numerical sequence, demonstrate the historical loss as a result of the mutilation of the first book. It is no longer possible to deduce from the once numbered drawings, which have been cut from their original pages, the sequence of their design and manufacture.

When Fothergill died in 1782, Boulton dissolved the partnership. He arranged for the Inventory in (5) above to be taken and on 24th June a new firm, Matthew Boulton & Co. was established, with a new set of books. Entries continued to be made in the books of Boulton and Fothergill until 1792 as the business of the partnership was run off. The business of Matthew Boulton & Co. was carried on at the same two sites and the records are extensive, including much of the correspondence mentioned above, ledgers (1782–1816), journals (1785–1816), cash debtor books (1782–1816), and cash creditor books (1782–9, 1792–1811). These records have very little in them relevant to the ormolu business.

There are also large collections of manuscripts in the Central Library, Birmingham, relating to Boulton and Watt and to James Watt, and to Boulton's later businesses, including the mint. There are isolated references in these to the earlier businesses.

There are many references to Boulton and his ambitions for ormolu and vases in Josiah Wedgwood's correspondence with his partner Thomas Bentley, which survives in the Wedgwood Museum, Barlaston, and is temporarily in the care of Keele University, Staffordshire. I have used the typescript copies of this correspondence in the Wedgwood Museum. Other manuscripts in the Wedgwood Mosley Collection, also temporarily at Keele, include correspondence from Boulton and Fothergill and from Boulton himself.

The archives at Great Tew include the 'Register Book', a record of some of the visitors to Soho, extracts of which are reproduced in Appendix II.

The sale catalogues reproduced in Appendix III survive in the archives of

Christie's, whose store of past catalogues has been a source of much information.

I have consulted manuscripts in local reference libraries or in other collections wherever appropriate. References to these collections can be found in the notes.

Books, papers and articles

This list omits some of the books that may have helped Matthew Boulton in his quest for designs or his researches into manufacturing techniques. Details of these are given in the appropriate notes to Chapters 3 and 4. It also omits primary but ephemeral records such as newspapers and sale catalogues. These too are detailed in the notes. Several books and articles are included for the sake of completeness, even though they have been superseded by subsequent publications. This applies to most of my own articles.

Accademia Ercolense, *Le Antichità di Ercolano Esposte* (Naples, 1757–92).

Adam, Robert, *Ruins of the Palace of the Emperor Diocletian at Spalatro in Dalmatia* (London, 1764).

Adam, Robert and James, *The Works in Architecture* (London, 1778–1822).

Adams E. B., *The Dwight and Lucille Beeson Wedgwood Collection at the Birmingham Museum of Art* (Alabama, 1992).

Archer, Michael, 'Elegance for the Mantelpiece', *Country Life*, 13th June 1963.

Art Institute of Chicago, *Seventh Wedgwood International Seminar* (1962).

Ashton, T. S., *An Economic History of England: the 18th Century* (London, 1955).

Baillie, G. H., *Watchmakers and Clockmakers of the World* (third edition, London, 1951).

Baker, Malcolm, 'Patrick Robertson's Tea-Urn and the late Eighteenth-Century Edinburgh Silver Trade', *Connoisseur*, August 1973.

Baker, Malcolm, 'A Rage for Exhibitions' (1995) (see Young, *The Genius of Wedgwood*).

Baker, Malcolm, and Richardson, Brenda, *A Grand Design: the Art of the Victoria and Albert Museum* (London, 1997).

Barrier, Janine, 'The Franco-Italian Album and its Significance' (1996) (see Snodin (ed.), *Sir William Chambers*).

Barrier, Janine, 'Chambers in France and Italy' (1996) (see Harris and Snodin, *Sir William Chambers*).

Beard, Geoffrey, *Georgian Craftsmen* (London, 1966).

Beard, Geoffrey, and Gilbert, Christopher, *Dictionary of English Furniture Makers 1660–1840* (Haywards Heath, 1986).

Bellaigue, Geoffrey de, Harris, John, and Millar, Oliver, *Buckingham Palace* (London, 1968).

Bellaigue, Geoffrey de, *The James A. de Rothschild Collection at Waddesdon Manor: Furniture Clocks and Gilt Bronzes* (London, 1974).

Berg, Maxine, *The Age of Manufactures: Industry, Innovation and Work in Britain 1700–1820* (London, 1985).

Birmingham City Museum and Art Gallery, *The Lunar Society* (catalogue of exhibition, Birmingham, 1966).

Bolton, A. T., *The Architecture of Robert and James Adam 1758–94* (London, 1922).

Boynton, Lindsay, 'An Ince and Mayhew Correspondence', *Furniture History*, Vol. II (1966).

Boynton, Lindsay, 'Italian Craft in an English Cabinet', *Country Life*, 29th September 1966.

Britten, F. J., *Old Clocks and Watches and their Makers* (third edition, London, 1911).

Bury, Shirley, 'Assay Silver at Birmingham', *Country Life*, 13th and 20th June 1968.

Camden, William, *Britannia* (1586, second edition, (ed.) William Gibson, 1722).
Carpenter, T. H., *Art and Myth in Ancient Greece* (London, 1991).
Caylus, Comte de, *Recueil d'Antiquités Égyptiennes, Étrusques, Grecques et Romains* (Paris, 1761–7).
Chambers, William, *A Treatise on Civil Architecture* (London, 1759, third edition 1791).
Charleston R. J. (ed.), *English Porcelain 1745–80* (London, 1965).
Clifford, Timothy, 'John Bacon and the Manufacturers', *Apollo*, October 1985.
Clifford, Timothy, 'The Plaster Shops of the Rococo and Neo-Classical Era in Britain', *Journal of the History of Collections*, Vol. 4, no. 1 (1992).
Clifford, Timothy, 'Anglomania: Catherine's Patronage of British Decorative Arts', *British Art Journal*, Vol. II, no. 2 (2001).
Coleridge, Anthony, 'Pierre Langlois, his Œuvre and Some Recent Discoveries', *Gazette des Beaux Arts*, September 1967.
Coleridge, Anthony, *Chippendale Furniture* (London, 1968).
Coltman, Viccy, 'Sir William Hamilton's Vase Publications 1766–76', *Journal of Design History*, Vol. 14, no. 1 (2001).
Colvin, H. M., *Biographical Dictionary of English Architects 1600–1840* (third edition, New Haven and London, 1995).
Connell, Brian, *Portrait of a Whig Peer* (London, 1957).
Cook, Cyril, 'James Gwin and his Designs on Battersea Enamels', *Apollo*, August 1952.
Court, W. H. B., *The Rise of the Midlands Industries 1600–1838* (London, 1938).
Corbeiller, Clare le, 'James Cox: a Biographical Review', *Burlington Magazine*, June 1970.
Craven, Maxwell, *John Whitehurst of Derby, Clockmaker and Scientist 1713–88* (Ashbourne, 1996).
Cross, Anthony, *By the Banks of the Neva* (Cambridge, 1997).
Cule, J. E., 'Finance and Industry in the Eighteenth Century: the Firm of Boulton and Watt', *Economics Journal*, Vol. IV (1940).
Cule, J. E., *The Financial History of Matthew Boulton 1759–1800* (unpublished thesis for the Degree of Master of Commerce, Birmingham University, October 1935).
Cust, Lionel, *History of the Society of Dilettanti* (London, 1914).
Defoe, Daniel, *A Plan of the English Commerce* (London, 1728).
Delieb, Eric, *The Great Silver Manufactory* (London, 1971).
Dickinson, H. W., *Matthew Boulton* (Cambridge, 1937).
Diderot, M. (ed.), *Encyclopédie ou Dictionnaire Raisonné des Sciences, des Arts et des Métiers* (Paris, 1751–7).
Edwards, Ralph, *The Shorter Dictionary of Furniture* (London, 1964).
Edwards, Ralph, and Jourdain, Margaret, *Georgian Cabinet-Makers* (London, 1955).
Edwards, Ralph, 'Patrons of Taste and Sensibility', *Apollo*, December 1965.
Eriksen, Svend, 'Lalive de Jully's Furniture "à la grecque"', *Burlington Magazine*, August 1961.
Eriksen, Svend, *The James A. de Rothschild Collection at Waddesdon Manor: Sèvres Porcelain* (London, 1968).
Eriksen, Svend, and Watson, F. J. B., 'The Athénienne and the Revival of the Classical Tripod', *Burlington Magazine*, March 1963.
Eriksen, Svend, *Early Neo-Classicism in France* (London, 1974).
Farrar, Lady (ed.), *Letters of Josiah Wedgwood 1762–80* (London, 1903–6, reprinted Barlaston, 1973).
Ferber, J. J., *Versuch einer Oryctographie von Derbyshire in England* (Mittau, 1776, (trans.) J. Pinkerton, London 1808).
Ferguson, James, *Select Mechanical Exercises* (London, 1775).

Fergusson, Frances, 'Wyatt Silver', *Burlington Magazine*, December 1974.
Finer, Ann, and Savage, George, *Selected Letters of Josiah Wedgwood* (London, 1965).
Fitzmaurice, Lord Edmund, *Life of William, Earl of Shelburne afterwards First Marquess of Lansdowne* (second edition, London, 1912).
Fleming, John, *Robert Adam and his Circle in Edinburgh and Rome* (London, 1962).
Ford, Trevor D., 'Blue John Fluorspar', *Proceedings of the Yorkshire Geological Society*, Vol. 30, Part I (1955).
Ford, Trevor D., *Derbyshire Blue John* (Ashbourne, 2000).
Ford, Trevor D., 'Blue John Fluospar', *Geology Today*, Vol. 10, no. 5, September–October 1994.
Gibbon, Edward (ed.), *Decline and Fall of the Roman Empire* (London, 1898).
Gilbert, Christopher, *Furniture at Temple Newsam and Lotherton Hall*, Vol. II (Leeds, 1978).
Gilbert, Christopher, and Murdoch, Tessa, *John Channon and Brass-Inlaid Furniture* (New Haven and London, 1993).
Gill, Conrad, and Briggs, Asa, *History of Birmingham* (London, 1952).
Glanville, Philippa, *Silver in England* (London, 1987).
Goodison, Nicholas, 'Matthew Boulton's Geographical Clock', *Connoisseur*, December 1967.
Goodison, Nicholas, 'Matthew Boulton's Ormolu Door Furniture', *Burlington Magazine*, November 1969.
Goodison, Nicholas, 'Matthew Boulton and the King's Clock Case', *Connoisseur*, June 1970.
Goodison, Nicholas, 'The Door Furniture at Ely House', *Bulletin of the Irish Georgian Society*, Vol. XIII, nos. 2–3, April–September 1970.
Goodison, Nicholas, 'Matthew Boulton's Ornamental Ormolu', *Discovering Antiques*, no. 48 (1971).
Goodison, Nicholas, 'The King's Vases', *Furniture History*, Vol. VIII (1972).
Goodison, Nicholas, 'Mr Stuart's Tripod', *Burlington Magazine*, October 1972.
Goodison, Nicholas, 'Matthew Boulton's Allegorical Clock Cases', *Connoisseur*, February 1973.
Goodison, Nicholas, *Ormolu: the Work of Matthew Boulton* (London, 1974).
Goodison, Nicholas, 'An Offering to Diana', *Furniture History*, Vol. X (1974).
Goodison, Nicholas, 'The Victoria and Albert Museum's Collection of Metal-Work Pattern Books', *Furniture History*, Vol. XI (1975).
Goodison, Nicholas, 'Matthew Boulton's Bacchanalian Vase', *Connoisseur*, July 1977.
Goodison, Nicholas, 'Narcissus in Ormolu', *Burlington Magazine*, August 1980.
Goodison, Nicholas, 'Urania Observed', *Furniture History*, Vol. XXI (1985).
Goodison, Nicholas, 'Matthew Boulton's Sidereal Clock', *Apollo*, July 1988.
Goodison, Nicholas, 'Matthew Boulton's Minerva', *Burlington Magazine*, June 1996.
Goodison, Nicholas, 'William Chambers's Furniture Designs', *Furniture History*, Vol. XXVI (1990).
Gori, A. F., *Museum Florentinum*, Vols. I–III (Florence, 1731–4).
Gray, J. M., *James and William Tassie* (Edinburgh, 1894).
Grimwade, Arthur, *London Goldsmiths 1697–1837: Their Marks and Lives* (revised edition, London 1990).
Gunnis, Rupert, *Dictionary of British Sculptors 1660–1851* (London, 1953).
Hamilton, Henry, *The English Brass and Copper Industries to 1800* (London, 1926).
d'Hancarville, Baron, *Collection of Etruscan, Greek, and Roman Antiquities from the Cabinet of the Honourable William Hamilton, His Britannick Majesty's Envoy Extraordinary at the Court of Naples* (Naples, 1766–7).

Hardy, John, and Hayward, Helena, 'Kedleston Hall, Derbyshire, II', *Country Life*, 2nd February 1978.
Harris, Eileen, *The Furniture of Robert Adam* (London 1963).
Harris, Eileen, *The Genius of Robert Adam: his Interiors* (New Haven and London, 2001).
Harris, John, 'Early Neo-Classical Furniture', *Furniture History*, Vol. II (1966).
Harris, John, *Sir William Chambers* (London, 1970).
Harris, John, *Catalogue of British Drawings for Architecture, Decoration, Sculpture and Landscape Gardening 1550–1900* (New Jersey, 1971).
Harris, John, and Snodin, Michael (eds.), *Sir William Chambers, Architect to George III* (New Haven and London, 1996).
Harris, John, 'Newly Acquired Designs by James Stuart in the British Architectural Library, Drawings Collection', *Architectural History*, Vol. 22 (1979).
Harris, John, Snodin, Michael, and Astley, Stephen, 'The Drawings of Sir William Chambers and the V & A Collection' (1996) (see M. Snodin, *Sir William Chambers*).
Harris, Leslie, *Robert Adam and Kedleston* (London, 1987).
Haskell, Francis, and Nicholas Penny, *Taste and the Antique* (New Haven and London, 1981).
Haskell, Francis, 'Adventurer and Art Historian', *Country Life*, 2nd April 1987.
Havard, Henry, *Dictionnaire de l'Ameublement et de la Décoration* (Paris, 1887–90).
Hawkes Smith, W., *Birmingham and its Vicinity, as a Manufacturing and Commercial District* (Birmingham, 1836).
Hayward, Helena, 'The Drawings of John Linnell in the Victoria and Albert Museum', *Furniture History*, Vol. V (1969).
Hayward, Helena, and Kirkham, Pat, *William and John Linnell* (London, 1980).
Hayward, John, *Huguenot Silver in England 1688–1727* (London, 1959).
Hayward, John, 'English Brass-Inlaid Furniture', *Victoria and Albert Museum Bulletin*, Vol. I, no.1 (January 1965).
Hayward, John, 'The Channon Family of Exeter and London', *Victoria and Albert Museum Bulletin*, Vol. II, no. 2 (April 1966).
Hayward, John, 'Christopher Fuhrlogh, an Anglo-Swedish Cabinet-Maker', *Burlington Magazine*, November 1969.
Headley-Whitney Museum, *The Works of Matthew Boulton from the Collection of Mr James C. Codell Jr.* (Lexington, 1990).
Henderson, Ebenezer, *Life of James Ferguson* (Edinburgh, 1867).
Hermitage Rooms, *Treasures of Catherine the Great* (see Piotrovsky).
Holloway, James, *James Tassie 1735–1799* (Edinburgh, 1986).
Honour, Hugh, 'Bronze Statuettes by Giacomo and Giovanni Zoffoli', *Connoisseur*, Vol. 148 (1961).
Honour, Hugh, *Neo-Classicism* (London, 1968).
Hopkins, Eric, 'Boulton Before Watt: the Earlier Career Reconsidered', *Midland History*, Vol. IX (1984).
Hopkins, Eric, *Birmingham: the First Manufacturing Town in the World 1760–1840* (London, 1989).
Hotspur Ltd., 'Golden Jubilee Exhibition 1924–1974' (1974).
Hughes, Peter, *The Wallace Collection Catalogue of Furniture* (London, 1996).
Hugues, P. F., see Baron d'Hancarville.
Hunt, J., 'Bombelles in Britain, the Diary Kept by a French Diplomat During a Visit to Midland England from August 4th to September 10th 1784', *Romsley and Hunnington History Society*, September 2000.
Hussey, Christopher, 'Syon House, Middlesex', *Country Life*, 1st December 1950.

Hussey, Christopher, *English Country Houses, Mid Georgian 1760–1800* (revised edition, London, 1963).

Hutton, Charles, *The Works of John Whitehurst* (London, 1792).

Hutton, William, *An History of Birmingham to the End of the Year 1780* (Birmingham, 1781, and sixth edition, 1835).

Ince, William, and Mayhew, John, *The Universal System of Household Furniture* (London, 1762).

Irwin, David, 'Neo-Classical Design: Industry Plunders Antiquity', *Apollo*, October 1972.

Jenkins, Ian, '"Contemporary Minds": Sir William Hamilton's Affair with Antiquity' (1996) (see Jenkins and Sloan, *Vases and Volcanoes*).

Jenkins, Ian, and Sloan, Kim (ed.), *Vases and Volcanoes: Sir William Hamilton and his Collection* (London, 1996).

Jourdain, Margaret, 'Matthew Boulton: an Artist in Ormolu', *Country Life Annual*, 1950.

Jourdain, Margaret, *English Decoration and Furniture of the Later XVIIIth Century* (London, 1922).

Kelly, Alison, *Decorative Wedgwood in Architecture and Furniture* (London, 1965).

Kelly, Alison, *The Book of English Fireplaces* (London, 1968).

Kelly, Alison, *Mrs Coade's Stone* (Upton-upon-Severn, 1990).

Kirkham, P. A., 'The Careers of William and John Linnell', *Furniture History*, Vol. III (1967).

Koutchoumov, A., *Pavlovsk: Le Palais et le Parc* (Leningrad, 1976).

Lane, Joan, 'Thomas Blockley of Birmingham: "One of the first locksmiths in the kingdom"', *Apollo*, May 1991.

Langford, J. A. (ed.), *A Century of Birmingham Life: or, a Chronicle of Local Events from 1741 to 1841* (Birmingham and London, 1868).

Leland, John, *Itinerary* (1538, (ed.) Thomas Hearne, 1711).

Lennox-Boyd, Edward, (ed.), *Masterpieces of English Furniture: the Gerstenfeld Collection* (London, 1998).

Lever, Jill, *Architects' Designs for Furniture* (London, 1982).

Lewis, W. S., Hunting-Smith, Warren, and Lam, George L., *Horace Walpole's Correspondence with Horace Mann* (New Haven and London, 1967).

Llanover, Lady (ed.), *Autobiography and Correspondence of Mary Granville, Mrs Delaney* (second series, London, 1862).

Lloyd, Samuel, *The Lloyds of Birmingham* (Birmingham, 1907).

McKendrick, N., 'Josiah Wedgwood', *Economic History Review*, second series, Vol. XII, no. 3 (1960).

McKendrick, N., Brewer, J., and Plumb, J. H., *The Birth of a Consumer Society* (London, 1982).

Macht, Carol, *Classical Wedgwood Designs* (New York, 1957).

Macquoid, P., and Edwards, R., *The Dictionary of English Furniture* (second edition, London, 1954).

Mallet, J. V. G., 'Two Documented Chelsea Gold-Anchor Vases', *Victoria and Albert Museum Bulletin*, Vol. I, no. 1 (1965).

Mallett, *The Age of Matthew Boulton* (London, 2000).

Mankowitz, Wolf, *Wedgwood* (second edition, London, 1966).

Mantoux, Paul, *The Industrial Revolution in the Eighteenth Century* (revised edition, London, 1964).

Mare, M. L., and Quarrell, W. H., *Lichtenberg's Visits to England as Described in his Letters and Diaries* (Oxford, 1938).

Marillier, H. C., 'Christie's 1766 to 1925' (London, 1926).

Mayhew and Ince, see Ince and Mayhew.
Meteyard, Eliza, *Wedgwood and his Works* (London, 1873).
Meteyard, Eliza, *Memorials of Wedgwood* (London, 1874).
Meteyard, Eliza, *The Life of Josiah Wedgwood* (London, 1865–6).
Meteyard, Eliza, *The Wedgwood Handbook* (London, 1875).
Meteyard, Eliza, *Choice Examples of Wedgwood Art* (London, 1879).
Metropolitan Museum of Art, New York, *Bronzes, Other Metalwork and Sculpture in the Irwin Untermyer Collection* (New York, 1962, being the fifth volume of the Catalogue of the Untermyer Collection).
Millburn, J. R., 'James Ferguson's Lecture Tour of the English Midlands in 1771', *Annals of Science*, 42 (1985).
Montagu, Jennifer, 'A Renaissance Work Copied by Wedgwood', *Journal of the Warburg and Courtauld Institutes*, Vol. XVII, nos. 3–4 (1954).
Montfauçon, Bernard de, *L'Antiquité Expliquée et Representée en Figures* (Paris, 1719).
Morgan, Kenneth (ed.), *An American Quaker in the British Isles. The Travel Journals of Jabez Maud Fisher, 1775–9* (Oxford, 1992).
Mulliner, H. H., *The Decorative Arts in England* (London, 1924).
Norman, Geraldine, *The Hermitage* (London, 1997).
O'Connor, Cynthia, 'The Charlemont House Medal Cabinet', *Irish Arts Review*, I (1989).
Oman, Charles, *English Silversmiths' Work* (London, 1965).
Ottomeyer, Hans, Pröschel, Peter, and Augarde, J.-D., *Vergoldete Bronzen* (Munich, 1986).
Owsley, David, and Rieder, William, *The Glass Drawing Room from Northumberland House* (London, 1974).
Pagani, Catherine, 'The Clocks of James Cox: Chinoiserie and the Clock Trade with China in the Eighteenth Century', *Apollo*, January 1995.
Page, William (ed.), *Victorian History of the County of Warwick* (London, 1908).
Patte, Pierre, *Cours d'Architecture* (Paris, 1777).
Piotrovsky, Mikhail, and others, *Treasures of Catherine the Great* (London, 2000).
Piranesi, Giovanni Battista, *Le Antichità Romane* (Rome, 1756).
Piranesi, Giovanni Battista, *Diverse Manieri d'adornare i cammini ed ogni altre parte degli edifizi desunte dall' architettura Egizia, Etrusca, e Greca* (Rome, 1769).
Potts, J. D., *Platt of Rotherham, Mason-Architects 1700–1810* (Sheffield, 1959).
Prosser, R. B., *Birmingham Inventors and Inventions* (Birmingham, 1881).
Pyne, J. B., *Buckingham House* (London, 1819).
Quickenden, Kenneth, *Boulton and Fothergill Silver* (unpublished thesis for PhD., Westfield College, London, 1989).
Quickenden, Kenneth, 'Boulton and Fothergill Silver: Business Plans and Miscalculations', *Art History*, Vol. 3, no. 3 (September 1980).
Quickenden, Kenneth, 'Boulton and Fothergill Silver: an Épergne Designed by James Wyatt', *Burlington Magazine*, June 1986.
Quickenden, Kenneth, '"Lyon-Faced Candlesticks" and Candelabra', *Silver Society Journal*, Autumn 1999.
Rackham, Bernard, 'Vases, or the Status of Pottery in Europe', *Society of Antiquaries Occasional Paper I*, 28th October 1943.
Rackham, Bernard, *Catalogue of English Porcelain, Earthenware, Enamels and Glass* (Schreiber Collection, London, 1924).
Ransome-Wallis, Rosemary, *Matthew Boulton and the Toymakers: Silver from the Birmingham Assay Office* (London, 1982).
Raspe, R. E., *A Descriptive Catalogue of a General Collection of Ancient and Modern Engraved Gems, Cameos as well as Intaglios, taken from the most celebrated Cabinets in*

Europe, and cast in Coloured Pastes, White Enamel, and Sulphur, by James Tassie, Modeller ... (London, 1791).
Rees, Abraham (ed.), *Cyclopaedia: or, an Universal Dictionary of Arts and Sciences* (London, 1788).
Reilly, Robin, and Savage, George, *The Portrait Medallion* (London, 1973).
Reilly, Robin, *Wedgwood* (London, 1989).
Reilly, Robin, *Josiah Wedgwood 1730–1795* (London, 1992).
Reilly, Robin, *Wedgwood Jasper* (London, 1994).
Reinach, Salomon, *Répertoire de la Statuaire Grecque et Romaine* (Paris, 1897).
Reynolds, Sir Joshua, *Discources on Painting and the Fine Arts* (London, 1837).
Richardson, George, *Iconology, or a Collection of Emblematical Figures* (London, 1779).
Rieder, William, 'More on Pierre Langlois', *Connoisseur*, September 1974.
Ripa, Cesare, *Iconologia* (Venice, 1645, first edition, Rome, 1593).
Roberts, Hugh, 'Sir William Chambers and Furniture' (1996) (see Harris and Snodin, *Sir William Chambers*).
Roberts, Jane, 'Sir William Chambers and George III' (1996) (see Harris and Snodin, *Sir William Chambers*).
Robinson, Eric, 'Matthew Boulton, Patron of the Arts', *Annals of Science*, Vol. IX, no. 4 (December 1953).
Robinson, Eric, 'Birmingham Capitalists and Russian Workers', *History Today*, October 1956.
Robinson, Eric, 'The International Exchange of Men and Machines 1750–1800', *Business History*, Vol. I, no. 1 (1958).
Robinson, Eric, 'Boulton and Fothergill 1762–82 and the Birmingham Export of Hardware', *University of Birmingham Historical Journal*, Vol. VII, no. 1 (1959).
Robinson, Eric, 'Eighteenth Century Commerce and Fashion: Matthew Boulton's Marketing Techniques', *Economic History Review*, 2nd series, Vol. XVI, no. 1 (1963).
Robinson, Eric, 'Matthew Boulton and Josiah Wedgwood, Apostles of Fashion', *Business History*, Vol. XXVIII, no. 3 (July 1986).
Robinson, Eric, and Thompson, Keith R., 'Matthew Boulton's Mechanical Paintings', *Burlington Magazine*, August 1970.
Roll, Eric, *An Early Experiment in Industrial Organisation, Being a History of the Firm of Boulton and Watt 1775–1805* (London, 1930).
Rowe, Robert, *Adam Silver* (London, 1965).
Sargentson, Carolyn, *Merchants and Luxury Markets* (London, 1996).
Sayer, Robert, *The Compleat Drawing Book* (third edition, London, 1762).
Schofield, R. E., *The Lunar Society of Birmingham* (Oxford, 1963).
Schroder, Timothy, *The National Trust Book of English Domestic Silver 1500–1900* (London, 1986).
Seaby, W. A., 'A Letter Book of Boulton and Fothergill 1773', *Apollo*, September 1951.
Seaby, W. A., and Hetherington, R. J., 'The Matthew Boulton Pattern Books', *Apollo*, February and March 1950.
Sketchley and Adams, *Tradesman's True Guide; or an Universal Directory, for the Towns of Birmingham, Wolverhampton, etc.* (1770).
Smiles, Samuel, *Lives of Boulton and Watt* (London, 1865).
Smith, Anthony D., 'The Suffering Hero: Belisarius and Oedipus in Late 18th Century French and British Art', *Royal Society of Arts Journal*, September 1989.
Smith, H. C., *Buckingham Palace* (London, 1931).
Smith, John P., *James Tassie 1735–99* (London, 1995).
Smith, Roger, 'James Cox (*c.*1723–1800): a Revised Biography', *Burlington Magazine*, June 2000.
Snodin, Michael, 'Matthew Boulton's Sheffield Plate Catalogues', *Apollo*, July 1987.

Snodin, Michael (ed.), *Sir William Chambers* (London, 1996).
Soane, Sir John, *Lectures on Architecture* ((ed.) A. T. Bolton, London, 1929).
Stalker, John, and Parker, George, *A Treatise of Japanning and Varnishing* (Oxford, 1688).
Stosch, Philippe, *Pierres Antiques Gravées* (Amsterdam, 1724).
Stuart, James, and Revett, Nicholas, *The Antiquities of Athens* (London, 1762–1816).
Swinney, M., *The New Birmingham Directory* (Birmingham, 1773).
Tassie, James, *A Catalogue of Impressions in Sulphur of Antique and Modern Gems* (London, 1775).
Taylor, E. G. R., *Mathematical Practitioners of Hanoverian England* (Cambridge, 1966).
Thornton, Peter, and Hardy, John, 'The Spencer Furniture at Althorp, Section II', *Apollo*, June 1968.
Thornton, Peter, and Rieder, William, 'Pierre Langlois, Ébéniste', *Connoisseur*, December 1971 and February 1972.
Timmins, S. (ed.), *The Resources, Products and Industrial History of Birmingham and the Midland Hardware District* (London, 1866).
Tomlin, Maurice, 'The Inventory at Osterley Park', *Furniture History*, Vol. XXII (1986).
Verlet, Pierre, 'The Wallace Collection and the Study of French Eighteenth-Century Bronzes d'Ameublement', *Burlington Magazine*, June 1950.
Verlet, Pierre, *French Royal Furniture* (London, 1963).
Verlet, Pierre, *Les Bronzes Dorés Français du XVIIIe Siècle* (Paris, 1987).
Visconti, C. L., *I Monumenti de Museo Torlonia* (Rome, 1885).
Watkin, David, *Athenian Stuart* (London, 1982).
Watney, Bernard, and Charleston, Robert, 'Petitions for Patents Concerning Porcelain, Glass and Enamels, with Special Reference to Birmingham "The Great Toyshop of Europe"', *English Ceramic Circle Transactions*, Vol. VI (1966).
Watson, F. J. B., *Catalogue of Furniture in the Wallace Collection* (London, 1956).
Wedgwood and Bentley, *A Catalogue of Cameos, Intaglios, Medals, and Bas-Reliefs; with a general account of Vases and other Ornaments, after the antique, made by Wedgwood and Bentley; and sold at their rooms in Great Newport Street, London* (London, 1773, second edition with 'Busts and Small Statues' added to the title in 1774, later editions 1775, 1777, etc.).
Westwood, Arthur, *The Assay Office at Birmingham* (Birmingham, 1936).
White, W. D., 'The Whitehurst Family', Supplement to *Derbyshire Miscellany* (the Bulletin of the Local History Section of the Derbyshire Archaeological and Natural History Society), March 1958.
Wilcox, William (ed.), *Papers of Benjamin Franklin* (New Haven and London, 1974).
Williams, J. D., *Audley End: the Restoration of 1762–97* (Chelmsford, 1966).
Wilson, Eva, *8000 Years of Ornament* (London, 1994).
Wittkower, R., *Gian Lorenzo Bernini* (London, 1956).
Young, Hilary, 'Sir William Chambers and John Yenn: Designs for Silver', *Burlington Magazine*, January 1986.
Young, Hilary (ed.), *The Genius of Wedgwood* (London, 1995).
Young, Hilary, 'Silver, Ormolu and Ceramics' (1996) (see Harris and Snodin, *Sir William Chambers*).
Young, W. A., *Old English Pattern Books of the Metal Trades* (London, 1913).

Index